Tom Boyle
Please return

MIPS R4000 USER'S MANUAL

Joseph Heinrich

PTR Prentice Hall
Upper Saddle River, NJ 07458

Library of Congress Cataloging-in-Publication Data

HEINRICH, JOE.
MIPS R4000 user's manual / Joseph Heinrich.
p. cm.
Includes index.
ISBN 0-13-105925-4
1. MIPS R4000 (Microprocessor) I. Title.
QA76.8.M523H45 1993 93-15966
004.165—dc20 CIP

Prentice-Hall, Inc.
A Pearson Education Company
Upper Saddle River, NJ 07458

MIPS Technologies, Inc.
2011 North Shoreline
Mountain View, CA 94039

Printed in the United States of America
10 9 8 7 6 5 4 3 2

ISBN 0-13-105925-4

Prentice-Hall International (UK) Limited, London
Prentice-Hall of Australia Pty. Limited, Sydney
Prentice-Hall Canada Inc., Toronto
Prentice-Hall Hispanoamericana, S.A., Mexico
Prentice-Hall of India Private Limited, New Delhi
Prentice-Hall of Japan, Inc., Tokyo
Pearson Education Asia Pte. Ltd., Singapore
Editoria Prentice-Hall do Brasil, Ltda., Rio De Janeiro

Acknowledgments

First of all, special thanks go to **Duk Chun** for his patient help in supplying and verifying the content of this manual; that this manual is technically correct is, in a very large part, directly attributable to him.

Thanks also to the following people for supplying portions of this book: **Shabbir Latif**, for, among other things, the exception handler flow charts, the description of the output buffer edge-control logic, and the interrupts; once again, **Duk Chun**, for his paper on R4000 processor synchronization support; **Paul Ries**, for confirming the accuracy of sections describing the memory management and the caches; **John Mashey**, for verifying the R4000 processor actually *does* employ the 64-bit architecture; **Dave Ditzel**, for raising the issue in the first place; and **Mike Gupta**, for substantiating various aspects of the errata. Finally, thanks to **Ed Reidenbach** for supplying a large portion of the parity and ECC sections of this manual, and **Michael Ngo** for checking their accuracy.

Thanks also to the following folks for their technical assistance: **Andy Keane**, **Keith Garrett**, **Viggy Mokkarala**, **Charles Price**, **Ali Moayedian**, **George Hsieh**, **Peter Fu**, **Stephen Przybylski**, **Michael Woodacre**, and **Earl Killian**. Also to be thanked are the people at *fvn@world.std.com*: **Bill Tuthill**, **Barry Shein**, **Bob Devine**, and **Alan Marr**, for helping place RISC in a pecuniary perspective. Also, thanks to the following people at the *mystery_train@swim2birds* news group: *toma*, *dan_sears*, *jharris@garnet*, *tut@cairo* (again), and *elvis@dalkey(mateo_b)*. Their night-for-day netversations, fueled by caffeine, concerning the viability of the cyberpsykinetic compute-core model helped form an important basis of this book.

On the editorial front, thanks once again to **Ms. Robin Cowan**, of the *Consortium of Editorial Arts* for her labors in editing this manual. Thanks to **Evelyn Spire** for slaving over that bottomless black well we refer to as an "Index." Thanks also, once again, to **Karen Gettman**, and **Lisa Iarkowski** at Prentice-Hall for their help.

On the artistic side, thanks to **Jeanne Simonian**, of the Creative department here at Silicon Graphics, for the book cover design; and thanks to **Pam Flanders** for providing MarCom tactical support.

Have we missed anyone? If so, here is where we apologize for doing so.

Joe Heinrich
April 1, 1993
Mt. View, California

Preface

This book describes the MIPS R4000 and R4400 family of RISC microprocessors (also referred to in this book as *processor*). An overview of the chapters and appendices in this book is given below.

Overview of the Contents

Chapter 1 is a discussion (including the historical context) of RISC development in general, and the R4000 microprocessor in particular.

Chapter 2 is an overview of the CPU instruction set.

Chapter 3 describes the operation of the R4000 instruction execution pipeline, including the basic operation of the pipeline and interruptions that are caused by interlocks and exceptions.

Chapter 4 describes the memory management system including address mapping and address spaces, virtual memory, the translation lookaside buffer (TLB), and the System Control Processor (CP0).

Chapter 5 describes the exception processing resources of R4000 processor. It includes an overview of the CPU exception handling process and describes the format and use of each CPU exception handling register.

Chapter 6 describes the Floating-Point Unit (FPU), a coprocessor for the CPU that extends the CPU instruction set to perform floating-point arithmetic operations. This chapter lists the FPU registers and instructions.

Chapter 7 describes the FPU exception processing.

Chapter 8 describes the signals that pass between the R4000 processor and other components in a system. The signals discussed include the System interface, the Clock/Control interface, the Secondary Cache interface, the Interrupt interface, the Initialization interface, and the JTAG interface.

Chapter 9 describes in more detail the Initialization interface, which includes the boot modes for the processor, as well as system resets.

Chapter 10 describes the clocks used in the R4000 processor, as well as the processor status reporting mechanism.

Chapter 11 discusses cache memory, including the operation of the primary and secondary caches, and cache coherency in a multiprocessor system.

Chapter 12 describes the System interface, which allows the processor access to external resources such as memory and input/output (I/O). It also allows an external agent access to the internal resources of the processor, such as the secondary cache.

Chapter 13 describes the Secondary Cache interface, including read and write cycle timing. This chapter also discusses the interface buses and signals.

Chapter 14 describes the Joint Test Action Group (JTAG) interface. The JTAG boundary scan mechanism tests the interconnections between the R4000 processor, the printed circuit board to which it is mounted, and other components on the board.

Chapter 15 describes the single nonmaskable processor interrupt, along with the six hardware and two software processor interrupts.

Chapter 16 describes the error checking and correcting (ECC) mechanisms of the R4000 processor.

Appendix A describes the R4000 CPU instructions, in both 32- and 64-bit modes. The instruction list is given in alphabetical order.

Appendix B describes the R4000 FPU instructions, listed alphabetically.

Appendix C describes sub-block ordering, a nonsequential method of retrieving data.

Appendix D describes the output buffer and the Δi/Δt control mechanism.

Appendix E describes the passive components that make up the phase-locked loop (PLL).

Appendix F describes Coprocessor 0 hazards.

A Note on Style

A brief note on some of the stylistic conventions used in this book: bits, fields, and registers of interest from a software perspective are italicized (such as *Config* register); signal names of more importance from a hardware point of view are rendered in bold (such as **Reset***).

A range of bits uses a colon as a separator; for instance, **(15:0)** represents the 16-bit range that runs from bit 0, inclusive, through bit 15. (In some places an ellipsis may used in place of the colon for visibility: **(15...0)**.)

For More Information

Some of the information contained in this manual may be volatile. For updates, please contact any of the semiconductor partners listed on the back cover of this book, and ask for the Errata.

Preface

1 Introduction

2

CPU Instruction Set Summary

3

The CPU Pipeline

4

Memory Management

5

CPU Exception Processing

6
Floating-Point Unit

7 Floating-Point Exceptions

8 R4000 Processor Signal Descriptions

9 Initialization Interface

10 Clock Interface

11
Cache Organization, Operation, and Coherency

12
System Interface

13 Secondary Cache Interface

14
JTAG Interface

15
R4000 Processor Interrupts

16
Error Checking and Correcting

A
CPU Instruction Set Details

B
FPU Instruction Set Details

C
Subblock Ordering

D
Output Buffer Δi/Δt Control Mechanism

E
PLL Passive Components

F
R4000 Coprocessor 0 Hazards

Introduction

1

Historically, the evolution of computer architectures has been dominated by families of increasingly complex central processors. Under market pressures to preserve existing software, complex instruction set computer (CISC) architectures evolved by the accretion of microcode and increasingly intricate instruction sets. This intricacy in architecture was itself driven by the need to support high-level languages and operating systems, as advances in semiconductor technology made it possible to fabricate integrated circuits of greater and greater complexity. And at that time it seemed self-evident to designers that architectures should continue to become more and more complex as technological advances made such VLSI designs possible.

In recent years, however, reduced instruction set computer (RISC) architectures are implementing a different model for the interaction between hardware, firmware, and software. RISC concepts emerged from a statistical analysis of the way in which software actually uses processor resources: dynamic measurement of system kernels and object modules generated by optimizing compilers showed that the simplest instructions were used most often—even in the code for CISC machines. Correspondingly, complex instructions often went unused because their single way of performing a complex operation rarely matched the precise needs of a high-level language.

RISC architecture eliminates microcode routines and turns low-level control of the machine over to software. The RISC approach is not new, but its application has become more prevalent in recent years, due to the increasing use of high-level languages, the development of compilers that are able to optimize at the microcode level, and dramatic advances in semiconductor memory and packaging. It is now feasible to replace relatively slow microcode ROM with faster RAM that is organized as an instruction cache. Machine control resides in this instruction cache that is, in effect, customized on-the-fly: the instruction stream generated by system- and compiler-generated code provides a precise fit between the requirements of high-level software and the low-level capabilities of the hardware.

Reducing or simplifying the instruction set was not the primary goal of RISC architecture; it is a pleasant side effect of techniques used to gain the highest performance possible from available technology. Thus, the term *reduced instruction set computers* is a bit misleading; it is the push for performance that really drives and shapes RISC designs.

1.1 Benefits of RISC Design

Some benefits that result from RISC design techniques are not directly attributable to the drive to increase performance, but are a result of the basic reduction in complexity—a simpler design allows both chip-area resources and human resources to be applied to features that enhance performance. Some of these benefits are described below.

Shorter Design Cycle

The architectures of RISC processors can be implemented more quickly than their CISC counterparts: it is easier to fabricate and debug a streamlined, simplified architecture with no microcode than a complex architecture that uses microcode. CISC processors have such a long design cycle that they may not be completely debugged by the time they are technologically obsolete. The shorter time required to design and implement RISC processors allows them to make use of the best available technologies.

Effective Utilization of Chip Area

The simplicity of RISC processors also frees scarce chip geography for performance-critical resources such as larger register files, translation lookaside buffers (TLBs), coprocessors, and fast multiply and divide units. Such resources help RISC processors obtain an even greater performance edge.

User (Programmer) Benefits

Simplicity in architecture also helps the user by providing a uniform instruction set that is easier to use. This allows a closer correlation between the instruction count and the cycle count, making it easier to measure code optimization activities.

Advanced Semiconductor Technologies

Each new VLSI technology is introduced with tight limits on the number of transistors that fit on each chip. Since the simplicity of a RISC processor allows it to be implemented in fewer transistors than its CISC counterpart, the first computers capable of exploiting these new VLSI technologies have been using and will continue to use RISC architecture.

Optimizing Compilers

RISC architecture is designed so that the compilers, not assembly languages, have the optimal working environment. RISC philosophy assumes that high-level language programming is used, which contradicts the older CISC philosophy that assumes assembly language programming is of primary importance.

The trend toward high-level language instructions has led to the development of more efficient compilers to convert high-level language instructions to machine code. Primary measures of compiler efficiency are the compactness of its generated code and the shortness of its execution time.

During the development of more efficient compilers, analysis of instruction streams revealed that the greatest amount of time was spent executing simple instructions and performing load and store operations, while the more complex instructions were used less frequently. It was also learned that compilers produce code that is often a narrow subset of the processor instruction set architecture (ISA). A compiler works more efficiently with instructions that perform simple, well-defined operations and generate minimal side-effects. Compilers do not use complex instructions and features; the more complex, powerful instructions are either too difficult for the compiler to employ or those instructions do not precisely fit high-level language requirements.

Thus, a natural match exists between RISC architectures and efficient, optimizing compilers. This match makes it easier for compilers to generate the most effective sequences of machine instructions to accomplish tasks defined by the high-level language.

MIPS RISCompiler Language Suite

Some compiler products are derived from disparate sources and consequently do not fit together very well. Instead of treating each language's compiler as a separate entity, the MIPS RISCompiler™ language suite shares common elements across the entire family of compilers. In this way the language suite offers both tight integration and broad language coverage.

The MIPS language suite supports:

- industry-standard front ends for six languages (C, FORTRAN, Pascal, Ada, PLI, COBOL)
- a common intermediate language, offering an efficient way to add language front ends over time
- all of the back end optimization and code generation
- the same object format and calling conventions
- mixed-language programs
- debugging of programs written in all languages, including mixtures

This language suite approach yields high-quality compilers for all languages, since common elements make up the majority of each of the language products. In addition, this approach provides the ability to develop and execute multi-language programs, promoting flexibility in development, avoiding the necessity of recoding proven program segments, and protecting the user's software investment. The common back-end also exports optimizing and code-generating improvements immediately throughout the language suite, thereby reducing maintenance.

1.2 Compatibility

The R4000 processor provides complete application software compatibility with the MIPS R2000, R3000, and R6000 processors. Although the MIPS processor architecture has evolved in response to a compromise between software and hardware resources in the computer system, the R4000 processor implements the MIPS ISA for user-mode programs. This guarantees that user programs conforming to the ISA execute on any MIPS hardware implementation.

1.3 Processor General Features

This section briefly describes the programming model, the memory management unit (MMU), and the caches in the R4000 processor. A more detailed description is given in succeeding sections.

- **Full 32-bit and 64-bit Operations.** The R4000 processor contains 32 general purpose 64-bit registers. (When operating as a 32-bit processor, the general purpose registers are 32-bits wide.) All instructions are 32 bits wide.
- **Efficient Pipeline.** The superpipeline design of the processor results in an execution rate approaching one instruction per cycle. Pipeline stalls and exceptional events are handled precisely and efficiently.
- **MMU.** The R4000 processor uses an on-chip TLB that provides rapid virtual-to-physical address translation.
- **Cache Control.** The R4000 primary instruction and data caches reside on-chip, and can each hold 8 Kbytes. In the R4400 processor, the primary caches can each hold 16 Kbytes. Architecturally, each primary cache can be increased to hold up to 32 Kbytes. An off-chip secondary cache (R4000SC and R4000MC processors only) can hold from 128 Kbytes to 4 Mbytes. All processor cache control logic, including the secondary cache control logic, is on-chip.
- **Floating-Point Unit.** The FPU is located on-chip and implements the ANSI/IEEE standard 754-1985.

1.4 R4000 Processor Configurations

The R4000 processor† is packaged in three different configurations. All processors are implemented in sub-1-micron CMOS technology.

- **R4000PC** is designed for cost-sensitive systems such as inexpensive desktop systems and high-end embedded controllers. It is packaged in a 179-pin PGA, and does not support a secondary cache.
- **R4000SC** is designed for high-performance uniprocessor systems. It is packaged in a 447-pin LGA/PGA and includes integrated control for large secondary caches built from standard SRAMs.
- **R4000MC** is designed for large cache-coherent multiprocessor systems. It is packaged in a 447-pin LGA/PGA and, in addition to the features of R4000SC, includes support for a wide variety of bus designs and cache-coherency mechanisms.

Table 1-1 lists the features in each of the three configurations (**X** indicates the feature is present). R4400 processor enhancements are described in the section following.

1.5 R4400 Processor Enhancements

In addition to the features contained in the R4000 processor, the R4400 processor has the following enhancements:

- fully functional Status pins (described in Chapter 10)
- Master/Checker mode (described in Chapter 16)
- larger primary caches (described in Processor General Features, in this chapter)
- uncached store buffer (described in Chapter 3)
- divide-by-6 and divide-by-8 modes (described in Chapter 10)
- cache error bit, *EW*, added to the *CacheErr* register (described in Chapter 5).

† Features of the R4400 processor that differ from the R4000 processor are noted throughout this book; for instance, R4400 processor enhancements are listed in the next section. Otherwise, references to the R4000 processor may be taken to include the R4400 processor.

Table 1-1 R4000 Features

Feature	R4000PC	R4000SC	R4000MC
Primary Cache States			
Valid	X	X	X
Shared			X
Clean Exclusive		X	X
Dirty Exclusive	X	X	X
Secondary Cache Interface		X	X
Secondary Cache States			
Valid	X	X	X
Shared			X
Dirty Shared			X
Clean Exclusive		X	X
Dirty Exclusive	X	X	X
Multiprocessing			X
Cache Coherency Attributes			
Uncached	X	X	X
Noncoherent	X	X	X
Sharable			X
Update			X
Exclusive			X
Packages			
PGA (179-pin)	X		
LGA (447-pin)		X	X
PGA (447-pin)		X	X

1.6 R4000 Processor

This section describes the following:

- the 64-bit architecture of the R4000 processor
- the superpipeline design of the CPU instruction pipeline (described in detail in Chapter 3)
- an overview of the System interface (described in detail in Chapter 12)
- an overview of the CPU registers (detailed in Chapters 4 and 5) and CPU instruction set (detailed in Chapter 2 and Appendix A)
- data formats and byte ordering
- the System Control Coprocessor, CP0, and the floating-point unit, CP1
- caches and memory, including a description of primary and secondary caches, the memory management unit (MMU), the translation lookaside buffer (TLB), and the Secondary Cache interface (described in more detail in Chapters 4 and 11). The Secondary Cache interface is detailed in Chapter 13.

64-bit Architecture

The natural mode of operation for the R4000 processor is as a 64-bit microprocessor; however, 32-bit applications maintain compatibility even when the processor operates as a 64-bit processor.

The R4000 processor provides the following:

- 64-bit on-chip floating-point unit (FPU)
- 64-bit integer arithmetic logic unit (ALU)
- 64-bit integer registers
- 64-bit virtual address space
- 64-bit system bus

Figure 1-1 is a block diagram of the R4000 processor internals.

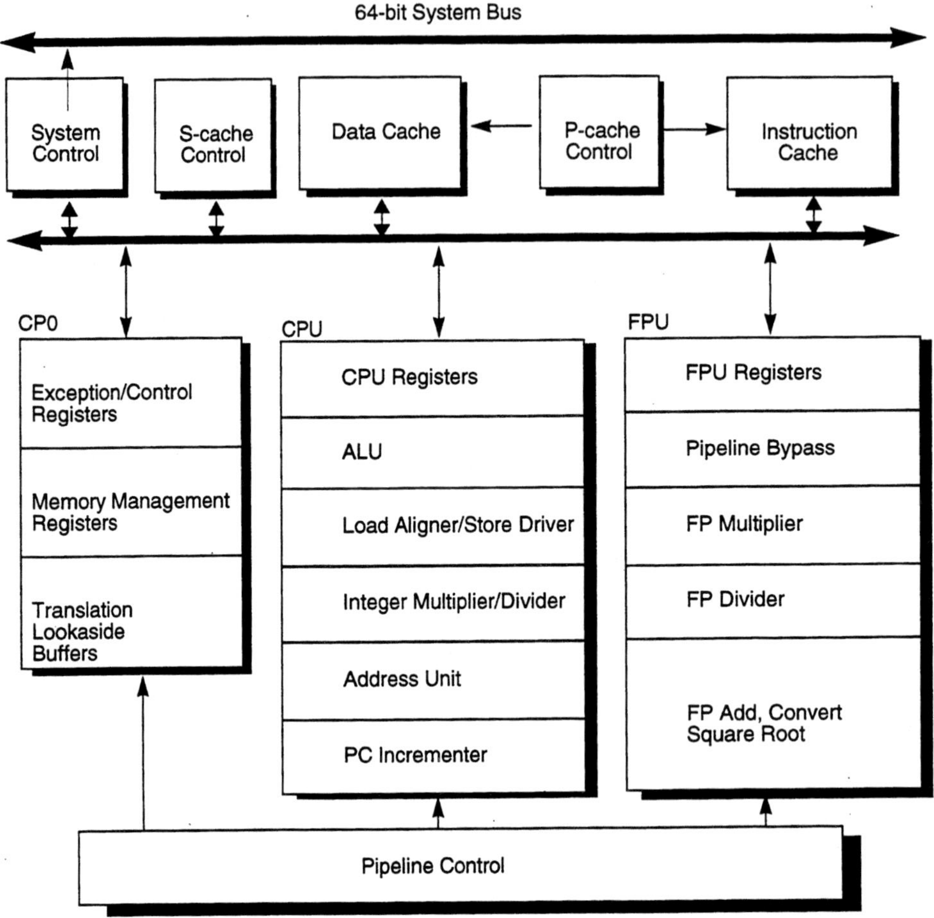

Figure 1-1 R4000 Processor Internal Block Diagram

Superpipeline Architecture

The R4000 processor exploits instruction parallelism by using an eight-stage superpipeline which places no restrictions on the instruction issued. Under normal circumstances, two instructions are issued each cycle.

The internal pipeline of the R4000 processor operates at twice the frequency of the master clock, as discussed in Chapter 3. The processor achieves high throughput by pipelining cache accesses, shortening register access times, implementing virtual-indexed primary caches, and allowing the latency of functional units to span more than one pipeline clock cycles.

System Interface

The R4000 processor supports a 64-bit System interface that can construct uniprocessor systems with a direct DRAM interface—with or without a secondary cache—or cache-coherent multiprocessor systems. The System interface includes:

- a 64-bit multiplexed address and data bus
- 8 check bits
- a 9-bit parity-protected command bus
- 8 handshake signals

The interface is capable of transferring data between the processor and memory at a peak rate of 400 Mbytes/second, when running at 50 MHz.

CPU Register Overview

The central processing unit (CPU) provides the following registers:

- 32 general purpose registers
- a Program Counter (*PC*) register
- 2 registers that hold the results of integer multiply and divide operations (*HI* and *LO*).

Floating-point unit (FPU) registers are described in Chapter 6.

CPU registers can be either 32 bits or 64 bits wide, depending on the R4000 processor mode of operation.

Figure 1-2 shows the CPU registers.

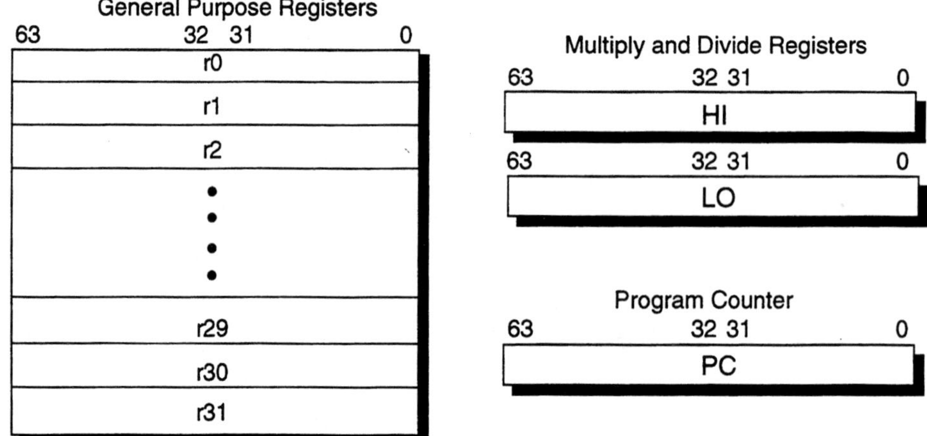

Figure 1-2 CPU Registers

Two of the CPU general purpose registers have assigned functions:

- *r0* is hardwired to a value of zero, and can be used as the target register for any instruction whose result is to be discarded. *r0* can also be used as a source when a zero value is needed.
- *r31* is the link register used by Jump and Link instructions. It should not be used by other instructions.

The CPU has three special purpose registers:

- *PC* — Program Counter register
- *HI* — Multiply and Divide register higher result
- *LO* — Multiply and Divide register lower result

The two Multiply and Divide registers (*HI, LO*) store:

- the product of integer multiply operations, or
- the quotient (in *LO*) and remainder (in *HI*) of integer divide operations

The R4000 processor has no *Program Status Word* (PSW) register as such; this is covered by the *Status* and *Cause* registers incorporated within the System Control Coprocessor (CP0). CP0 registers are described later in this chapter.

CPU Instruction Set Overview

Each CPU instruction is 32 bits long. As shown in Figure 1-3, there are three instruction formats:

- immediate (I-type)
- jump (J-type)
- register (R-type)

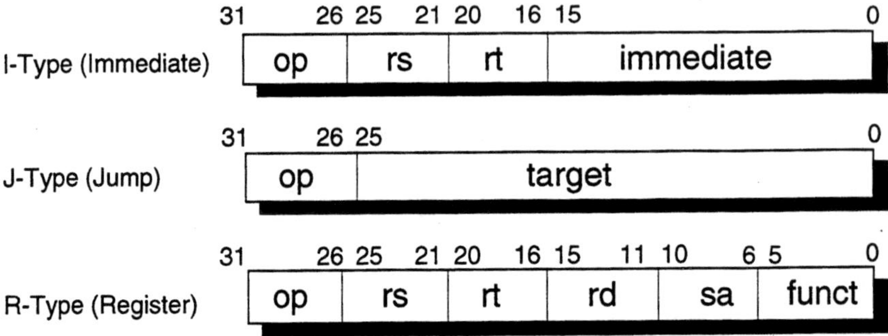

Figure 1-3 CPU Instruction Formats

Each format contains a number of different instructions, which are described further in this chapter. Fields of the instruction formats are described in Chapter 2.

Instruction decoding is greatly simplified by limiting the number of formats to these three. This limitation means that the more complicated (and less frequently used) operations and addressing modes can be synthesized by the compiler, using sequences of these same simple instructions.

The instruction set can be further divided into the following groupings:

- **Load and Store** instructions move data between memory and general registers. They are all immediate (I-type) instructions, since the only addressing mode supported is base register plus 16-bit, signed immediate offset.
- **Computational** instructions perform arithmetic, logical, shift, multiply, and divide operations on values in registers. They include.register (R-type, in which both the operands and the result are stored in registers) and immediate (I-type, in which one operand is a 16-bit immediate value) formats.
- **Jump and Branch** instructions change the control flow of a program. Jumps are always made to a paged, absolute address formed by combining a 26-bit target address with the high-order bits of the Program Counter (J-type format) or register address (R-type format). Branches have 16-bit offsets relative to the program counter (I-type). Jump And Link instructions save their return address in register 31.
- **Coprocessor** instructions perform operations in the coprocessors. Coprocessor load and store instructions are I-type.
- **Coprocessor 0** (system coprocessor) instructions perform operations on CP0 registers to control the memory management and exception handling facilities of the processor. These are listed in Table 1-18.
- **Special** instructions perform system calls and breakpoint operations. These instructions are always R-type.
- **Exception** instructions cause a branch to the general exception-handling vector based upon the result of a comparison. These instructions occur in both R-type (both the operands and the result are registers) and I-type (one operand is a 16-bit immediate value) formats.

Chapter 2 provides a more detailed summary and Appendix A gives a complete description of each instruction.

Tables 1-2 through 1-17 list CPU instructions common to MIPS R-Series processors, along with those instructions that are extensions to the instruction set architecture. The extensions result in code space reductions, multiprocessor support, and improved performance in operating system kernel code sequences—for instance, in situations where run-time bounds-checking is frequently performed. Table 1-18 lists CP0 instructions.

Table 1-2 CPU Instruction Set: Load and Store Instructions

OpCode	Description
LB	Load Byte
LBU	Load Byte Unsigned
LH	Load Halfword
LHU	Load Halfword Unsigned
LW	Load Word
LWL	Load Word Left
LWR	Load Word Right
SB	Store Byte
SH	Store Halfword
SW	Store Word
SWL	Store Word Left
SWR	Store Word Right

Table 1-3 CPU Instruction Set: Arithmetic Instructions (ALU Immediate)

OpCode	Description
ADDI	Add Immediate
ADDIU	Add Immediate Unsigned
SLTI	Set on Less Than Immediate
SLTIU	Set on Less Than Immediate Unsigned
ANDI	AND Immediate
ORI	OR Immediate
XORI	Exclusive OR Immediate
LUI	Load Upper Immediate

Table 1-4 CPU Instruction Set: Arithmetic (3-Operand, R-Type)

OpCode	Description
ADD	Add
ADDU	Add Unsigned
SUB	Subtract
SUBU	Subtract Unsigned
SLT	Set on Less Than
SLTU	Set on Less Than Unsigned
AND	AND
OR	OR
XOR	Exclusive OR
NOR	NOR

Table 1-5 CPU Instruction Set: Multiply and Divide Instructions

OpCode	Description
MULT	Multiply
MULTU	Multiply Unsigned
DIV	Divide
DIVU	Divide Unsigned
MFHI	Move From HI
MTHI	Move To HI
MFLO	Move From LO
MTLO	Move To LO

Table 1-6 CPU Instruction Set: Jump and Branch Instructions

OpCode	Description
J	Jump
JAL	Jump And Link
JR	Jump Register
JALR	Jump And Link Register
BEQ	Branch on Equal
BNE	Branch on Not Equal
BLEZ	Branch on Less Than or Equal to Zero
BGTZ	Branch on Greater Than Zero
BLTZ	Branch on Less Than Zero
BGEZ	Branch on Greater Than or Equal to Zero
BLTZAL	Branch on Less Than Zero And Link
BGEZAL	Branch on Greater Than or Equal to Zero And Link

Table 1-7 CPU Instruction Set: Shift Instructions

OpCode	Description
SLL	Shift Left Logical
SRL	Shift Right Logical
SRA	Shift Right Arithmetic
SLLV	Shift Left Logical Variable
SRLV	Shift Right Logical Variable
SRAV	Shift Right Arithmetic Variable

Table 1-8 CPU Instruction Set: Coprocessor Instructions

OpCode	Description
LWCz	Load Word to Coprocessor z
SWCz	Store Word from Coprocessor z
MTCz	Move To Coprocessor z
MFCz	Move From Coprocessor z
CTCz	Move Control to Coprocessor z
CFCz	Move Control From Coprocessor z
COPz	Coprocessor Operation z
BCzT	Branch on Coprocessor z True
BCzF	Branch on Coprocessor z False

Table 1-9 CPU Instruction Set: Special Instructions

OpCode	Description
SYSCALL	System Call
BREAK	Break

Table 1-10 Extensions to the ISA: Load and Store Instructions

OpCode	Description
LD	Load Doubleword
LDL	Load Doubleword Left
LDR	Load Doubleword Right
LL	Load Linked
LLD	Load Linked Doubleword
LWU	Load Word Unsigned
SC	Store Conditional
SCD	Store Conditional Doubleword
SD	Store Doubleword
SDL	Store Doubleword Left
SDR	Store Doubleword Right
SYNC	Sync

Table 1-11 Extensions to the ISA: Arithmetic Instructions (ALU Immediate)

OpCode	Description
DADDI	Doubleword Add Immediate
DADDIU	Doubleword Add Immediate Unsigned

Table 1-12 Extensions to the ISA: Multiply and Divide Instructions

OpCode	Description
DMULT	Doubleword Multiply
DMULTU	Doubleword Multiply Unsigned
DDIV	Doubleword Divide
DDIVU	Doubleword Divide Unsigned

Table 1-13 Extensions to the ISA: Branch Instructions

OpCode	Description
BEQL	Branch on Equal Likely
BNEL	Branch on Not Equal Likely
BLEZL	Branch on Less Than or Equal to Zero Likely
BGTZL	Branch on Greater Than Zero Likely
BLTZL	Branch on Less Than Zero Likely
BGEZL	Branch on Greater Than or Equal to Zero Likely
BLTZALL	Branch on Less Than Zero And Link Likely
BGEZALL	Branch on Greater Than or Equal to Zero And Link Likely
BCzTL	Branch on Coprocessor z True Likely
BCzFL	Branch on Coprocessor z False Likely

Table 1-14 Extensions to the ISA: Arithmetic Instructions (3-operand, R-type)

OpCode	Description
DADD	Doubleword Add
DADDU	Doubleword Add Unsigned
DSUB	Doubleword Subtract
DSUBU	Doubleword Subtract Unsigned

Table 1-15 Extensions to the ISA: Shift Instructions

OpCode	Description
DSLL	Doubleword Shift Left Logical
DSRL	Doubleword Shift Right Logical
DSRA	Doubleword Shift Right Arithmetic
DSLLV	Doubleword Shift Left Logical Variable
DSRLV	Doubleword Shift Right Logical Variable
DSRAV	Doubleword Shift Right Arithmetic Variable
DSLL32	Doubleword Shift Left Logical + 32
DSRL32	Doubleword Shift Right Logical + 32
DSRA32	Doubleword Shift Right Arithmetic + 32

Table 1-16 Extensions to the ISA: Exception Instructions

OpCode	Description
TGE	Trap if Greater Than or Equal
TGEU	Trap if Greater Than or Equal Unsigned
TLT	Trap if Less Than
TLTU	Trap if Less Than Unsigned
TEQ	Trap if Equal
TNE	Trap if Not Equal
TGEI	Trap if Greater Than or Equal Immediate
TGEIU	Trap if Greater Than or Equal Immediate Unsigned
TLTI	Trap if Less Than Immediate
TLTIU	Trap if Less Than Immediate Unsigned
TEQI	Trap if Equal Immediate
TNEI	Trap if Not Equal Immediate

Table 1-17 Extensions to the ISA: Coprocessor Instructions

OpCode	Description
DMFCz	Doubleword Move From Coprocessor z
DMTCz	Doubleword Move To Coprocessor z
LDCz	Load Double Coprocessor z
SDCz	Store Double Coprocessor z

Table 1-18 CP0 Instructions

OpCode	Description
DMFC0	Doubleword Move From CP0
DMTC0	Doubleword Move To CP0
MTC0	Move to CP0
MFC0	Move from CP0
TLBR	Read Indexed TLB Entry
TLBWI	Write Indexed TLB Entry
TLBWR	Write Random TLB Entry
TLBP	Probe TLB for Matching Entry
CACHE	Cache Operation
ERET	Exception Return

Data Formats and Addressing

The R4000 processor uses four data formats: a 64-bit doubleword, a 32-bit word, a 16-bit halfword, and an 8-bit byte. Byte ordering within each of the larger data formats—halfword, word, doubleword—can be configured in either big-endian or little-endian order. Endianness refers to the location of byte 0 within the multi-byte data structure. Figures 1-4 and 1-5 show the ordering of bytes within words and the ordering of words within multiple-word structures for the big-endian and little-endian conventions.

When the R4000 processor is configured as a big-endian system, byte 0 is the most-significant (leftmost) byte, thereby providing compatibility with MC 68000® and IBM 370® conventions. Figure 1-4 shows this configuration.

Bit #

Higher Address ↑ Lower Address	Word Address	31 … 24	23 … 16	15 … 8	7 … 0
	12	12	13	14	15
	8	8	9	10	11
	4	4	5	6	7
	0	0	1	2	3

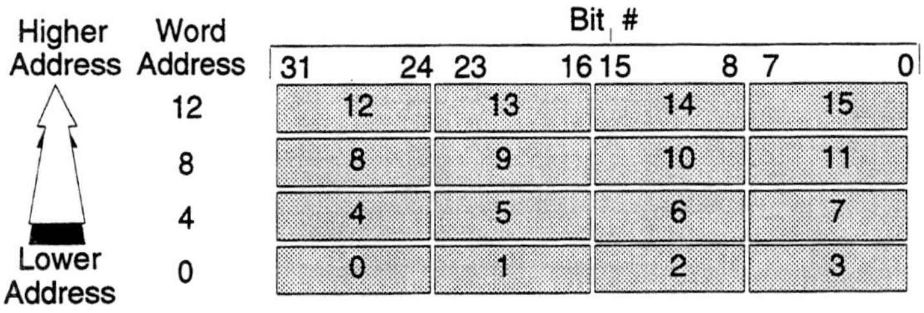

Figure 1-4 Big-Endian Byte Ordering

When configured as a little-endian system, byte 0 is always the least-significant (rightmost) byte, which is compatible with iAPX® x86 and DEC VAX® conventions. Figure 1-5 shows this configuration.

Bit #

Higher Address ↑ Lower Address	Word Address	31 … 24	23 … 16	15 … 8	7 … 0
	12	15	14	13	12
	8	11	10	9	8
	4	7	6	5	4
	0	3	2	1	0

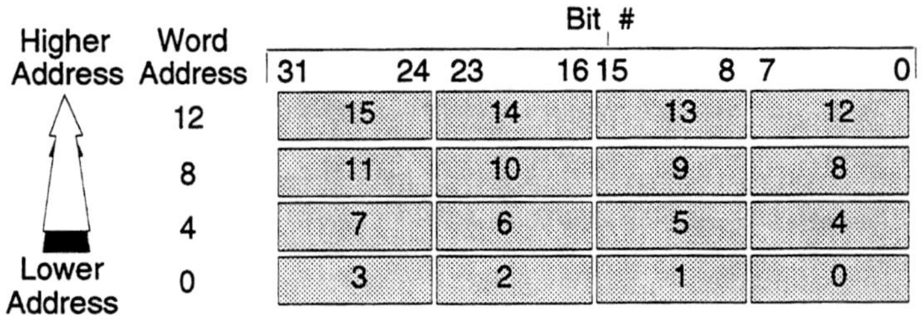

Figure 1-5 Little-Endian Byte Ordering

In this text, bit 0 is always the least-significant (rightmost) bit; thus, bit designations are always little-endian (although no instructions explicitly designate bit positions within words).

Figures 1-6 and 1-7 show little-endian and big-endian byte ordering in doublewords.

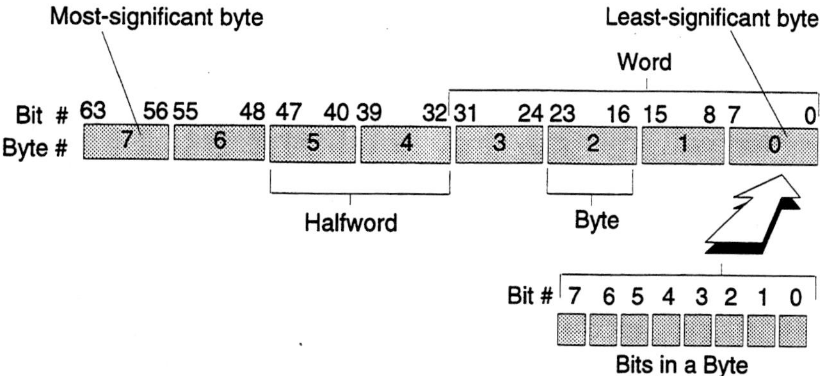

Figure 1-6 Little-Endian Data in a Doubleword

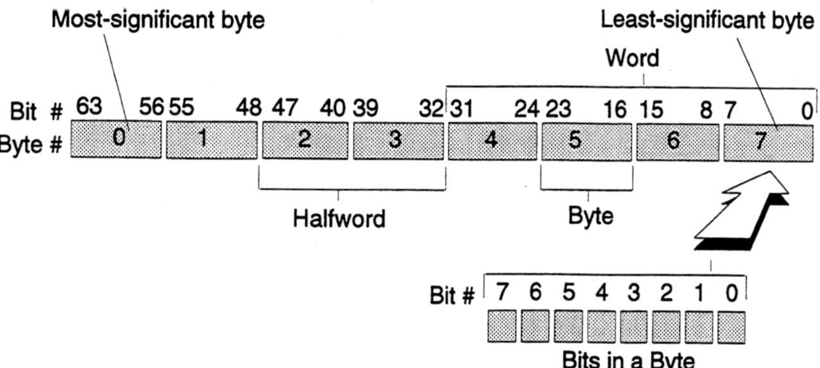

Figure 1-7 Big-Endian Data in a Doubleword

The CPU uses byte addressing for halfword, word, and doubleword accesses with the following alignment constraints:

- Halfword accesses must be aligned on an even byte boundary (0, 2, 4...).
- Word accesses must be aligned on a byte boundary divisible by four (0, 4, 8...).
- Doubleword accesses must be aligned on a byte boundary divisible by eight (0, 8, 16...).

The following special instructions load and store words that are not aligned on 4-byte (word) or 8-word (doubleword) boundaries:

LWL	**LWR**	**SWL**	**SWR**
LDL	**LDR**	**SDL**	**SDR**

These instructions are used in pairs to provide addressing of misaligned words. Addressing misaligned data incurs one additional instruction cycle over that required for addressing aligned data.

Figures 1-8 and 1-9 show the access of a misaligned word that has byte address 3.

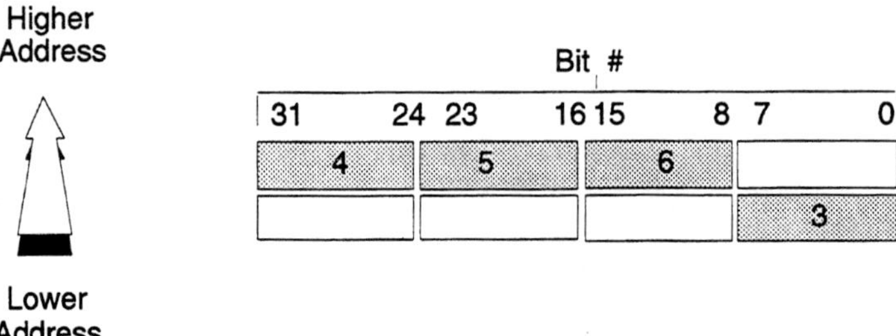

Figure 1-8 Big-Endian Misaligned Word Addressing

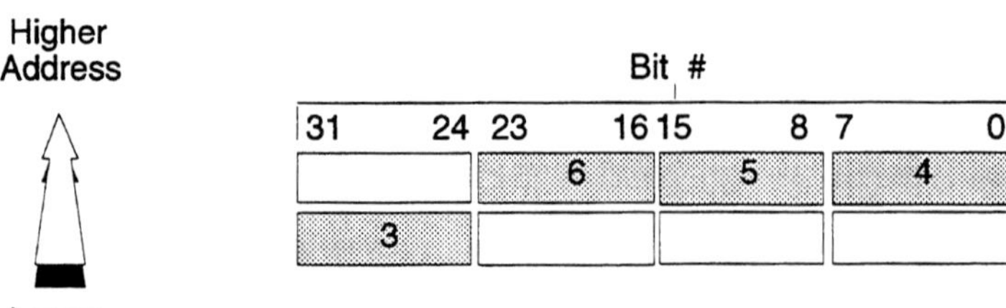

Figure 1-9 Little-Endian Misaligned Word Addressing

Coprocessors (CP0-CP3)

The MIPS ISA defines four coprocessors (designated CP0 through CP3):

- Coprocessor 0 (**CP0**) is incorporated on the CPU chip and supports the virtual memory system and exception handling CP0 is also referred to as the *System Control Coprocessor.*
- Coprocessor 1 (**CP1**) is reserved for the on-chip, floating-point coprocessor, the FPU.
- Coprocessor 2 (**CP2**) is reserved for future definition by MIPS.
- Coprocessor 3 (**CP3**) provides extensions to the MIPS ISA.

CP0 and CP1 are described in the sections that follow.

System Control Coprocessor, CP0

CP0 translates virtual addresses into physical addresses and manages exceptions and transitions between kernel, supervisor, and user states. CP0 also controls the cache subsystem, as well as providing diagnostic control and error recovery facilities.

The CP0 registers shown in Figure 1-10 and described in Table 1-19 manipulate the memory management and exception handling capabilities of the CPU.

Register Name	Reg. #	Register Name	Reg. #
Index	0	*Config*	16
Random	1	*LLAddr*	17
EntryLo0	2	*WatchLo*	18
EntryLo1	3	*WatchHi*	19
Context	4	*XContext*	20
PageMask	5		21
Wired	6		22
	7		23
BadVAddr	8		24
Count	9		25
EntryHi	10	*ECC*	26
Compare	11	*CacheErr*	27
SR	12	*TagLo*	28
Cause	13	*TagHi*	29
EPC	14	*ErrorEPC*	30
PRId	15		31

Exception Processing — *Memory Management* — *Reserved*

Figure 1-10 R4000 CP0 Registers

Table 1-19 System Control Coprocessor (CP0) Register Definitions

Number	Register	Description
0	Index	Programmable pointer into TLB array
1	Random	Pseudorandom pointer into TLB array *(read only)*
2	EntryLo0	Low half of TLB entry for even virtual address (VPN)
3	EntryLo1	Low half of TLB entry for odd virtual address (VPN)
4	Context	Pointer to kernel virtual page table entry (PTE) in 32-bit addressing mode
5	PageMask	TLB Page Mask
6	Wired	Number of wired TLB entries
7	—	Reserved
8	BadVAddr	Bad virtual address
9	Count	Timer Count
10	EntryHi	High half of TLB entry
11	Compare	Timer Compare
12	SR	Status register
13	Cause	Cause of last exception
14	EPC	Exception Program Counter
15	PRId	Processor Revision Identifier
16	Config	Configuration register
17	LLAddr	Load Linked Address
18	WatchLo	Memory reference trap address low bits
19	WatchHi	Memory reference trap address high bits
20	XContext	Pointer to kernel virtual PTE table in 64-bit addressing mode
21–25	—	Reserved
26	ECC	Secondary-cache error checking and correcting (ECC) and Primary parity
27	CacheErr	Cache Error and Status register
28	TagLo	Cache Tag register
29	TagHi	Cache Tag register
30	ErrorEPC	Error Exception Program Counter
31	—	Reserved

Floating-Point Unit (FPU), CP1

The MIPS floating-point unit (FPU) is designated CP1; the FPU extends the CPU instruction set to perform arithmetic operations on floating-point values. The FPU, with associated system software, fully conforms to the requirements of ANSI/IEEE Standard 754–1985, *IEEE Standard for Binary Floating-Point Arithmetic*.

The FPU features include:

- **Full 64-bit Operation**. The FPU can contain either 16 or 32 64-bit registers to hold single-precision or double-precision values. The FPU also includes a 32-bit *Status/Control* register that provides access to all IEEE-Standard exception handling capabilities.
- **Load and Store Instruction Set**. Like the CPU, the FPU uses a load- and store-based instruction set. Floating-point operations are started in a single cycle and their execution overlaps other fixed-point or floating-point operations.
- **Tightly-coupled Coprocessor Interface**. The FPU is on the CPU chip, and appears to the programmer as a simple extension of the CPU (accessed as CP1). Together, the CPU and FPU form a tightly-coupled unit with a seamless integration of floating-point and fixed-point instruction sets. Since each unit receives and executes instructions in parallel, some floating-point instructions can execute at the same rate (two instructions per cycle) as fixed-point instructions.

Memory Management System (MMU)

The R4000 processor has a 36-bit physical addressing range of 64 Gbytes. However, since it is rare for systems to implement a physical memory space this large, the CPU provides a logical expansion of memory space by translating addresses composed in the large virtual address space into available physical memory addresses. The R4000 processor supports the following two addressing modes:

- 32-bit mode, in which the virtual address space is divided into 2 Gbytes per user process and 2 Gbytes for the kernel.
- 64-bit mode, in which the virtual address is expanded to 1 Tbyte (2^{40} bytes) of user virtual address space.

A detailed description of these address spaces is given in Chapter 4.

The Translation Lookaside Buffer (TLB)

Virtual memory mapping is assisted by a translation lookaside buffer, which caches virtual-to-physical address translations. This fully-associative, on-chip TLB contains 48 entries, each of which maps a pair of variable-sized pages ranging from 4 Kbytes to 16 Mbytes, in multiples of four.

Instruction TLB

The R4000 processor has a two-entry instruction TLB (ITLB) which assists in instruction address translation. The ITLB is completely invisible to software and exists only to increase performance.

Joint TLB

An address translation value is tagged with the most-significant bits of its virtual address (the number of these bits depends upon the size of the page) and a per-process identifier. If there is no matching entry in the TLB, an exception is taken and software refills the on-chip TLB from a page table resident in memory; this TLB is referred to as the joint TLB (JTLB) because it contains both data and instructions jointly. The JTLB entry to be rewritten is selected at random.

Operating Modes

The R4000 processor has three operating modes:

- User mode
- Supervisor mode
- Kernel mode

The manner in which memory addresses are translated or *mapped* depends on the operating mode of the CPU; this is described in Chapter 4.

Cache Memory Hierarchy

To achieve a high performance in uniprocessor and multiprocessor systems, the R4000 processor supports a two-level cache memory hierarchy that increases memory access bandwidth and reduces the latency of load and store instructions. This hierarchy consists of on-chip instruction and data caches, together with an optional external secondary cache that varies in size from 128 Kbytes to 4 Mbytes.

The secondary cache is assumed to consist of one bank of industry-standard static RAM (SRAM) with output enables, arranged as a quadword (128-bit) data array, with a 25-bit-wide tag array. Check fields are added to both data and tag arrays to improve data integrity.

The secondary cache can be configured as a joint cache, or split into separate instruction and data caches. The maximum secondary cache size is 4 Mbytes; the minimum secondary cache size is 128 Kbytes for a joint cache, or 256 Kbytes total for split instruction/data caches. The secondary cache is direct mapped, and is addressed with the lower part of the physical address.

Primary and secondary caches are described in more detail in Chapter 11.

Primary Caches

The R4000 processor incorporates separate on-chip primary instruction and data caches to fill the high-performance pipeline. Each cache has its own 64-bit data path, and each can be accessed in parallel.

The R4000 processor primary caches hold from 8 Kbytes to 32 Kbytes; the R4400 processor primary caches are fixed at 16 Kbytes.

Cache accesses can occur up to twice each cycle. This provides the integer and floating-point units with an aggregate bandwidth of 1.6 Gbytes per second at a MasterClock frequency of 50 MHz.

Secondary Cache Interface

The R4000SC (secondary cache) and R4000MC (multiprocessor) versions of the processor allow connection to an optional secondary cache. These processors provide all of the secondary cache control circuitry, including error checking and correcting (ECC) protection, on chip.

The Secondary Cache interface includes:

- a 128-bit data bus
- a 25-bit tag bus
- an 18-bit address bus
- SRAM control signals

The 128-bit-wide data bus is designed to minimize cache miss penalties, and allow the use of standard low-cost SRAM in secondary cache.

CPU Instruction Set Summary

2

This chapter is an overview of the central processing unit (CPU) instruction set; refer to Appendix A for detailed descriptions of individual CPU instructions.

An overview of the floating-point unit (FPU) instruction set is in Chapter 6; refer to Appendix B for detailed descriptions of individual FPU instructions.

2.1 CPU Instruction Formats

Each CPU instruction consists of a single 32-bit word, aligned on a word boundary. There are three instruction formats—immediate (I-type), jump (J-type), and register (R-type)—as shown in Figure 2-1. The use of a small number of instruction formats simplifies instruction decoding, allowing the compiler to synthesize more complicated (and less frequently used) operations and addressing modes from these three formats as needed.

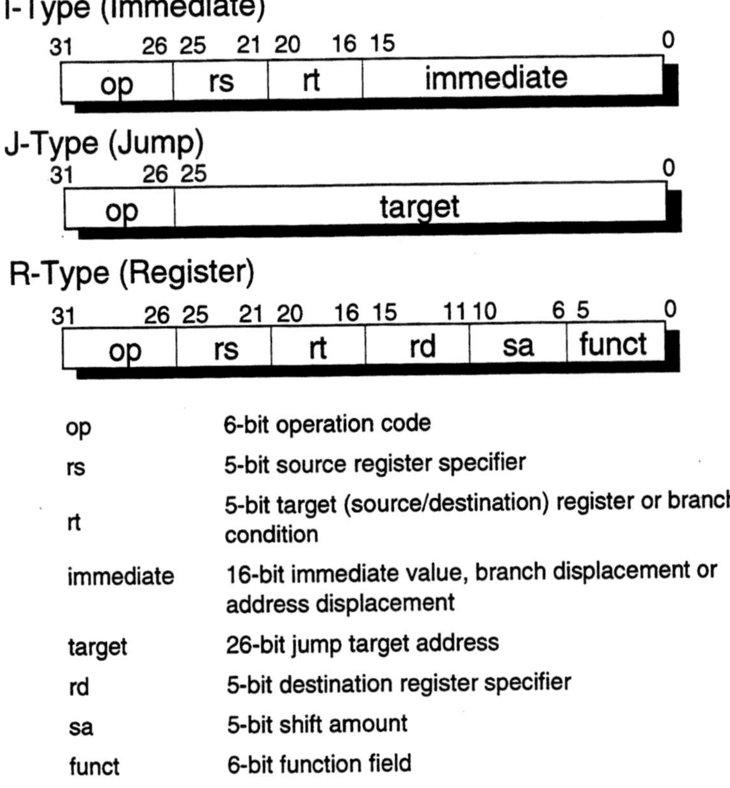

Figure 2-1 CPU Instruction Formats

In the MIPS architecture, coprocessor instructions are implementation-dependent; see Appendix A for details of individual Coprocessor 0 instructions.

Load and Store Instructions

Load and store are immediate (I-type) instructions that move data between memory and the general registers. The only addressing mode that load and store instructions directly support is *base register plus 16-bit signed immediate offset*.

Scheduling a Load Delay Slot

A load instruction that does not allow its result to be used by the instruction immediately following is called a *delayed load instruction*. The instruction slot immediately following this delayed load instruction is referred to as the *load delay slot*.

In the R4000 processor, the instruction immediately following a load instruction can use the contents of the loaded register, however in such cases hardware interlocks insert additional real cycles. Consequently, scheduling load delay slots can be desirable, both for performance and R-Series processor compatibility. However, the scheduling of load delay slots is not absolutely required.

Defining Access Types

Access type indicates the size of an R4000 processor data item to be loaded or stored, set by the load or store instruction opcode. Access types are defined in Appendix A.

Regardless of access type or byte ordering (endianness), the address given specifies the low-order byte in the addressed field. For a big-endian configuration, the low-order byte is the most-significant byte; for a little-endian configuration, the low-order byte is the least-significant byte.†

The access type, together with the three low-order bits of the address, define the bytes accessed within the addressed doubleword (shown in Table 2-1). Only the combinations shown in Table 2-1 are permissible; other combinations cause address error exceptions. See Appendix A for individual descriptions of CPU load and store instructions.

† Data formats are described in Chapter 1.

Table 2-1 Byte Access within a Doubleword

Access Type Mnemonic (*Value*)	Low Order Address Bits			Bytes Accessed															
				Big endian (63----------31----------0) Byte								Little endian (63----------31----------0) Byte							
	2	1	0																
Doubleword (7)	0	0	0	0	1	2	3	4	5	6	7	7	6	5	4	3	2	1	0
Septibyte (6)	0	0	0	0	1	2	3	4	5	6			6	5	4	3	2	1	0
	0	0	1		1	2	3	4	5	6	7	7	6	5	4	3	2	1	
Sextibyte (5)	0	0	0	0	1	2	3	4	5					5	4	3	2	1	0
	0	1	0			2	3	4	5	6	7	7	6	5	4	3	2		
Quintibyte (4)	0	0	0	0	1	2	3	4							4	3	2	1	0
	0	1	1				3	4	5	6	7	7	6	5	4	3			
Word (3)	0	0	0	0	1	2	3									3	2	1	0
	1	0	0					4	5	6	7	7	6	5	4				
Triplebyte (2)	0	0	0	0	1	2											2	1	0
	0	0	1		1	2	3									3	2	1	
	1	0	0					4	5	6			6	5	4				
	1	0	1						5	6	7	7	6	5					
Halfword (1)	0	0	0	0	1													1	0
	0	1	0			2	3									3	2		
	1	0	0					4	5					5	4				
	1	1	0							6	7	7	6						
Byte (0)	0	0	0	0															0
	0	0	1		1													1	
	0	1	0			2											2		
	0	1	1				3									3			
	1	0	0					4							4				
	1	0	1						5					5					
	1	1	0							6			6						
	1	1	1								7	7							

Computational Instructions

Computational instructions can be either in register (R-type) format, in which both operands are registers, or in immediate (I-type) format, in which one operand is a 16-bit immediate.

Computational instructions perform the following operations on register values:

- arithmetic
- logical
- shift
- multiply
- divide

These operations fit in the following four categories of computational instructions:

- ALU Immediate instructions
- three-Operand Register-Type instructions
- shift instructions
- multiply and divide instructions

64-bit Operations

When operating in 64-bit mode, 32-bit operands must be sign extended. The result of operations that use incorrect sign-extended 32-bit values is unpredictable.

Cycle Timing for Multiply and Divide Instructions

MFHI and MFLO instructions (described in Appendix A) are interlocked so that any attempt to read them before prior instructions complete delays the execution of these instructions until the prior instructions finish.

Table 2-2 gives the number of processor cycles (PCycles) required to resolve an interlock or stall between various multiply or divide instructions, and a subsequent MFHI or MFLO instruction.

Table 2-2 Multiply/Divide Instruction Cycle Timing

Instruction	PCycles Required
MULT	10
MULTU	10
DIV	69
DIVU	69
DMULT	20
DMULTU	20
DDIV	133
DDIVU	133

For more information about computational instructions, refer to the individual instruction as described in Appendix A.

Jump and Branch Instructions

Jump and branch instructions change the control flow of a program. All jump and branch instructions occur with a delay of one instruction: that is, the instruction immediately following the jump or branch (this is known as the instruction in the *delay slot*) always executes while the target instruction is being fetched from storage.†

Overview of Jump Instructions

Subroutine calls in high-level languages are usually implemented with Jump or Jump and Link instructions, both of which are J-type instructions. In J-type format, the 26-bit target address shifts left 2 bits and combines with the high-order 4 bits of the current program counter to form an absolute address.

Returns, dispatches, and large cross-page jumps are usually implemented with the Jump Register or Jump and Link Register instructions. Both are R-type instructions that take the 32-bit or 64-bit byte address contained in one of the general purpose registers.

For more information about jump instructions, refer to the individual instruction as described in Appendix A.

Overview of Branch Instructions

All branch instruction target addresses are computed by adding the address of the instruction in the delay slot to the 16-bit *offset* (shifts left 2 bits and is sign-extended to 32 bits). All branches occur with a delay of one instruction.

If a conditional branch is not taken, the instruction in the delay slot is nullified.

For more information about branch instructions, refer to the individual instruction as described in Appendix A.

† Taken branches have a 3 cycle penalty in this implementation. See Chapter 3 for more information.

Special Instructions

Special instructions allow the software to initiate traps; they are always R-type. For more information about special instructions, refer to the individual instruction as described in Appendix A.

Exception Instructions

Exception instructions are extensions to the MIPS ISA. For more information about exception instructions, refer to the individual instruction as described in Appendix A.

Coprocessor Instructions

Coprocessor instructions perform operations in their respective coprocessors. Coprocessor loads and stores are I-type, and coprocessor computational instructions have coprocessor-dependent formats.

Individual coprocessor instructions are described in Appendices A (for CP0) and B (for the FPU, CP1).

CP0 instructions perform operations specifically on the System Control Coprocessor registers to manipulate the memory management and exception handling facilities of the processor. Appendix A details CP0 instructions.

The CPU Pipeline

3

This chapter describes the basic operation of the CPU pipeline, which includes descriptions of the delay instructions (instructions that follow a branch or load instruction in the pipeline), interruptions to the pipeline flow caused by interlocks and exceptions, and R4400 implementation of an uncached store buffer.

The FPU pipeline is described in Chapter 6.

3.1 CPU Pipeline Operation

The CPU has an eight-stage instruction pipeline; each stage takes one PCycle (one cycle of PClock, which runs at twice the frequency of MasterClock). Thus, the execution of each instruction takes at least eight PCycles (four MasterClock cycles). An instruction can take longer—for example, if the required data is not in the cache, the data must be retrieved from main memory.

Once the pipeline has been filled, eight instructions are executed simultaneously. Figure 3-1 shows the eight stages of the instruction pipeline; the next section describes the pipeline stages.

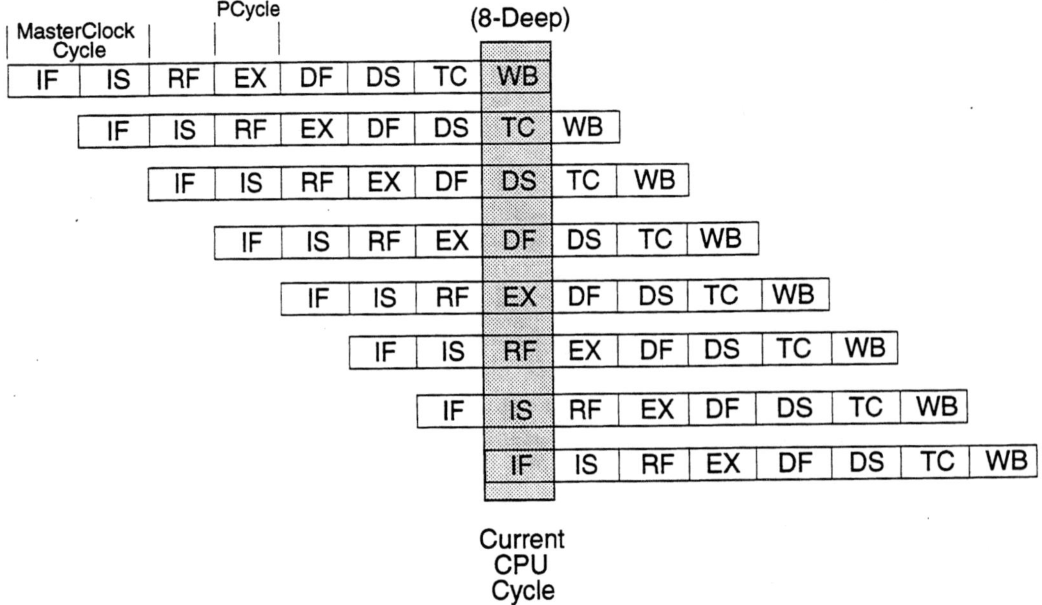

Figure 3-1 Instruction Pipeline Stages

3.2 CPU Pipeline Stages

This section describes each of the eight pipeline stages:

- IF - Instruction Fetch, First Half
- IS - Instruction Fetch, Second Half
- RF - Register Fetch
- EX - Execution
- DF - Data Fetch, First Half
- DS - Data Fetch, Second Half
- TC - Tag Check
- WB - Write Back

IF - Instruction Fetch, First Half

During the IF stage, the following occurs:

- Branch logic selects an instruction address and the instruction cache fetch begins.
- The instruction translation lookaside buffer (ITLB) begins the virtual-to-physical address translation.

IS - Instruction Fetch, Second Half

During the IS stage, the instruction cache fetch and the virtual-to-physical address translation are completed.

RF - Register Fetch

During the RF stage, the following occurs:

- The instruction decoder (IDEC) decodes the instruction and checks for interlock conditions.
- The instruction cache tag is checked against the page frame number obtained from the ITLB.
- Any required operands are fetched from the register file.

EX - Execution

During the EX stage, one of the following occurs:

- The arithmetic logic unit (ALU) performs the arithmetic or logical operation for register-to-register instructions.
- The ALU calculates the data virtual address for load and store instructions.
- The ALU determines whether the branch condition is true and calculates the virtual branch target address for branch instructions.

DF - Data Fetch, First Half

During the DF stage, one of the following occurs:

- The data cache fetch and the data virtual-to-physical translation begins for load and store instructions.
- The branch instruction address translation and translation lookaside buffer (TLB)† update begins for branch instructions.
- No operations are performed during the DF, DS, and TC stages for register-to-register instructions.

DS - Data Fetch, Second Half

During the DS stage, one of the following occurs:

- The data cache fetch and data virtual-to-physical translation are completed for load and store instructions. The Shifter aligns data to its word or doubleword boundary.
- The branch instruction address translation and TLB update are completed for branch instructions.

TC - Tag Check

For load and store instructions, the cache performs the tag check during the TC stage. The physical address from the TLB is checked against the cache tag to determine if there is a hit or a miss.

† The TLB is described in Chapter 4.

WB - Write Back

For register-to-register instructions, the instruction result is written back to the register file during the WB stage. Branch instructions perform no operation during this stage.

Figure 3-2 shows the activities occurring during each ALU pipeline stage, for load, store, and branch instructions.

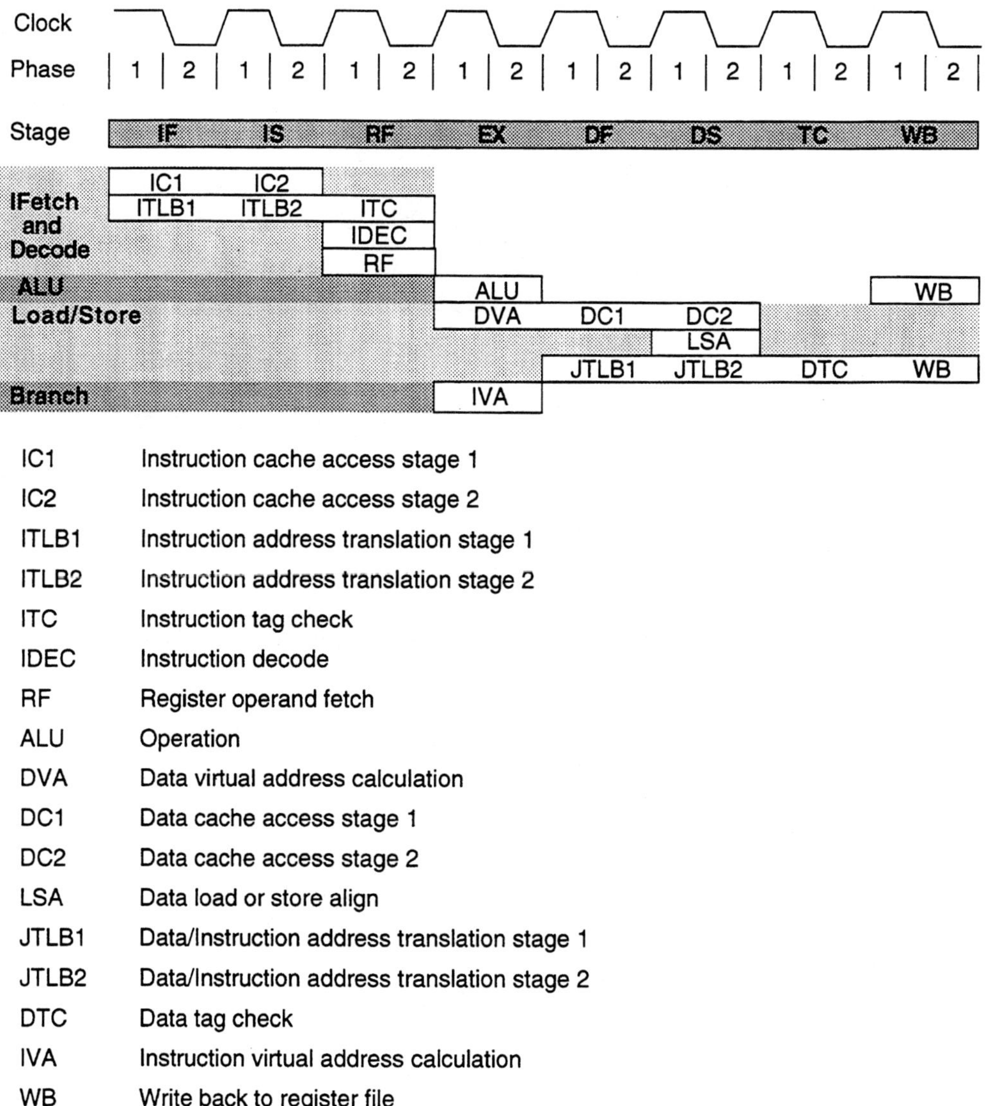

Figure 3-2 CPU Pipeline Activities

3.3 Branch Delay

The CPU pipeline has a branch delay of three cycles and a load delay of two cycles. The three-cycle branch delay is a result of the branch comparison logic operating during the EX pipeline stage of the branch, producing an instruction address that is available in the IF stage, four instructions later.

Figure 3-3 illustrates the branch delay.

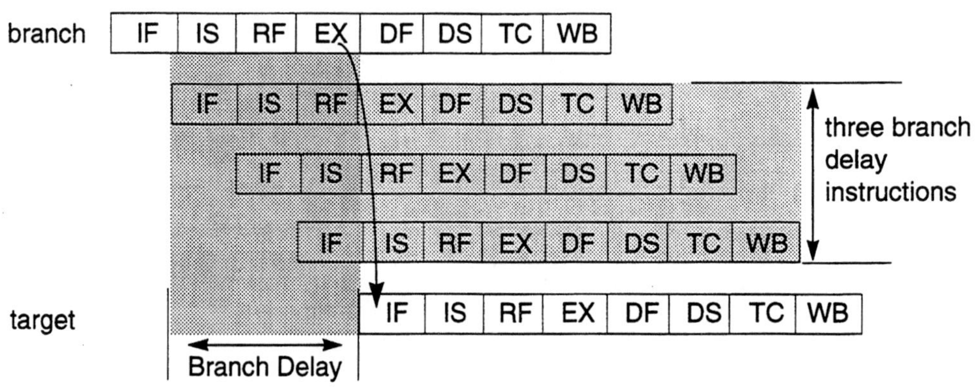

Figure 3-3 CPU Pipeline Branch Delay

3.4 Load Delay

The completion of a load at the end of the DS pipeline stage produces an operand that is available for the EX pipeline stage of the third subsequent instruction.

Figure 3-4 shows the load delay of two pipeline stages.

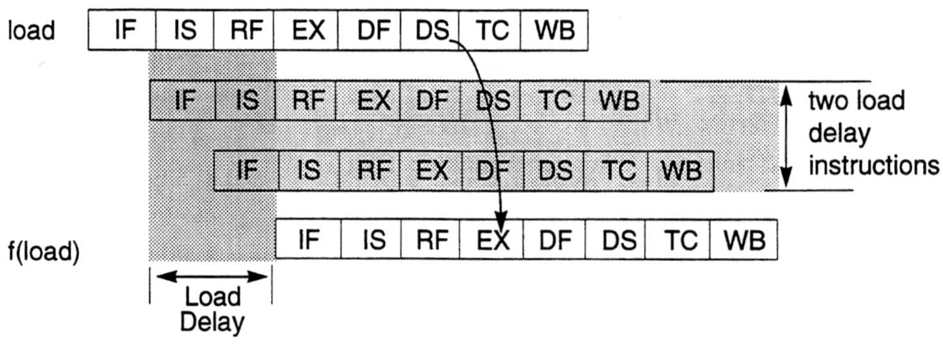

Figure 3-4 CPU Pipeline Load Delay

3.5 Interlock and Exception Handling

Smooth pipeline flow is interrupted when cache misses or exceptions occur, or when data dependencies are detected. Interruptions handled using hardware, such as cache misses, are referred to as *interlocks*, while those that are handled using software are called exceptions.

As shown in Figure 3-5, all interlock and exception conditions are collectively referred to as faults.

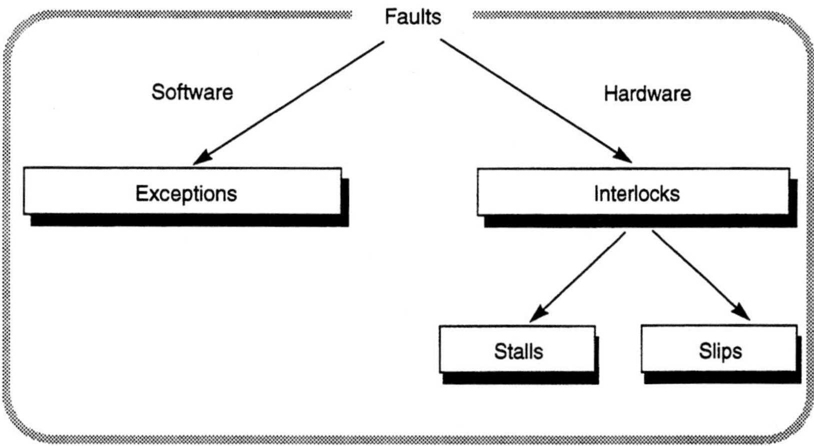

Figure 3-5 Interlocks, Exceptions, and Faults

There are two types of interlocks:

- stalls, which are resolved by halting the pipeline
- slips, which require one part of the pipeline to advance while another part of the pipeline is held static

At each cycle, exception and interlock conditions are checked for all active instructions.

Because each exception or interlock condition corresponds to a particular pipeline stage, a condition can be traced back to the particular instruction in the exception/interlock stage, as shown in Figure 3-6. For instance, an Illegal Instruction (II) exception is raised in the execution (EX) stage.

Tables 3-1 and 3-2 describe the pipeline interlocks and exceptions listed in Figure 3-6.

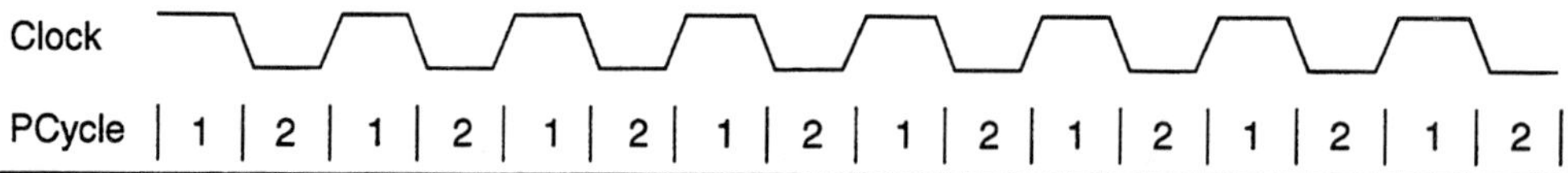

Clock

PCycle | 1 | 2 | 1 | 2 | 1 | 2 | 1 | 2 | 1 | 2 | 1 | 2 | 1 | 2 | 1 | 2 |

State	Pipeline Stage							
	IF	IS	RF	EX	DF	DS	TC	WB
Stall*		ITM	ICM		CPBE		DCM	
					SXT		WA	
					STI			
*MP stalls can occur at any stage; they are not associated with any instruction or pipe stage								
	IF	IS	RF	EX	DF	DS	TC	WB
Slip			LDI					
			MultB					
			DivB					
			MDOne					
			ShSlip					
			FCBsy					
	IF	IS	RF	EX	DF	DS	TC	WB
Exceptions			ITLB	Intr		OVF	DTLB	DBE
				IBE		FPE	TLBMod	Watch
				IVACoh		ExTrap		DVACoh
				II				DECCErr
				BP				NMI
				SC				Reset
				CUn				
				IECCErr				

Figure 3-6 Correspondence of Pipeline Stage to Interlock Condition

Table 3-1 Pipeline Exceptions

Exception	Description
ITLB	Instruction Translation or Address Exception
Intr	External Interrupt
IBE	IBus Error
IVACoh	IVA Coherent
II	Illegal Instruction
BP	Breakpoint
SC	System Call
CUn	Coprocessor Unusable
IECCErr	Instruction ECC Error
OVF	Integer Overflow
FPE	FP Interrupt
ExTrap	EX Stage Traps
DTLB	Data Translation or Address Exception
TLBMod	TLB Modified
DBE	Data Bus Error
Watch	Memory Reference Address Compare
DVACoh	DVA Coherent
DECCErr	Data ECC Error
NMI	Non-maskable Interrupt
Reset	Reset

Table 3-2 Pipeline Interlocks

Interlock	Description
ITM	Instruction TLB Miss
ICM	Instruction Cache Miss
CPBE	Coprocessor Possible Exception
SXT	Integer Sign Extend
STI	Store Interlock
DCM	Data Cache Miss
WA	Watch Address Exception
LDI	Load Interlock
MultB	Multiply Unit Busy
DivB	Divide Unit Busy
MDOne	Mult/Div One Cycle Slip
ShSlip	Var Shift or Shift > 32 bits
FCBsy	FP Busy

Exception Conditions

When an exception condition occurs, the relevant instruction and all those that follow it in the pipeline are cancelled. Accordingly, any stall conditions and any later exception conditions that may have referenced this instruction are inhibited; there is no benefit in servicing stalls for a cancelled instruction.

After instruction cancellation, a new instruction stream begins, starting execution at a predefined exception vector. System Control Coprocessor registers are loaded with information that identifies the type of exception and auxiliary information such as the virtual address at which translation exceptions occur.

Stall Conditions

Often, a stall condition is only detected after parts of the pipeline have advanced using incorrect data; this is called a *pipeline overrun*. When a stall condition is detected, all eight instructions—each different stage of the pipeline—are frozen at once. In this stalled state, no pipeline stages can advance until the interlock condition is resolved.

Once the interlock is removed, the restart sequence begins two cycles before the pipeline resumes execution. The restart sequence reverses the pipeline overrun by inserting the correct information into the pipeline.

Slip Conditions

When a slip condition is detected, pipeline stages that must advance to resolve the dependency continue to be retired (completed), while dependent stages are held until the required data is available.

External Stalls

External stall is another class of interlocks. An external stall originates outside the processor and is not referenced to a particular pipeline stage. This interlock is not affected by exceptions.

Interlock and Exception Timing

To prevent interlock and exception handling from adversely affecting the processor cycle time, the R4000 processor uses both logic and circuit pipeline techniques to reduce critical timing paths. Interlock and exception handling have the following effects on the pipeline:

- In some cases, the processor pipeline must be backed up (reversed and started over again from a prior stage) to recover from interlocks.
- In some cases, interlocks are serviced for instructions that will be aborted, due to an exception.

These two cases are discussed below.

Backing Up the Pipeline

An example of pipeline back-up occurs in a data cache miss, in which the late detection of the miss causes a subsequent instruction to compute an incorrect result.

When this occurs, not only must the cache miss be serviced but the EX stage of the dependent instruction must be re-executed before the pipeline can be restarted. Figure 3-7 illustrates this procedure; a minus (–) after the pipeline stage descriptor (for instance, EX–) indicates the operation produced an incorrect result, while a plus (+) indicates the successful re-execution of that operation.

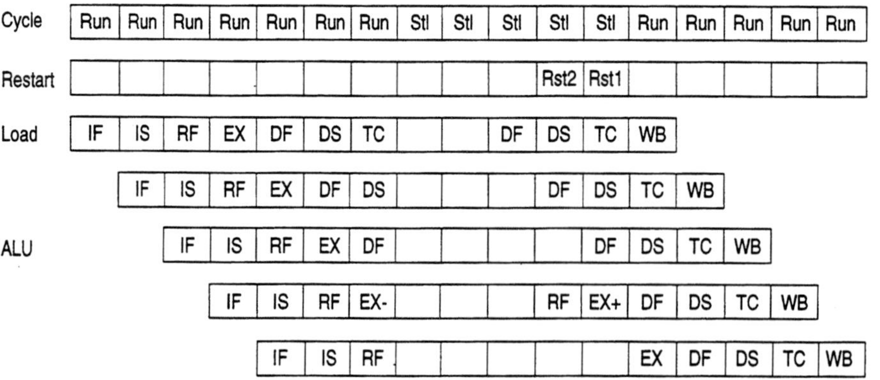

Figure 3-7 Pipeline Overrun

Aborting an Instruction Subsequent to an Interlock

The interaction between an integer overflow and an instruction cache miss is an example of an interlock being serviced for an instruction that is subsequently aborted.

In this case, pipelining the overflow exception handling into the DF stage allows an instruction cache miss to occur on the next immediate instruction. Figure 3-8 illustrates this; aborted instructions are indicated with an asterisk (*).

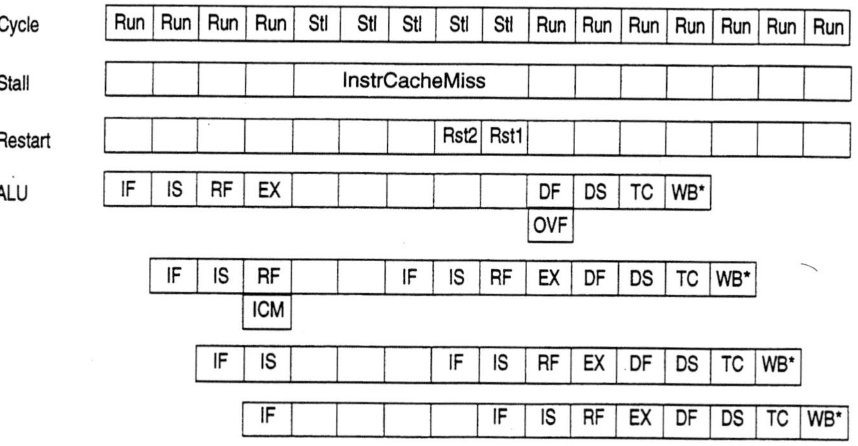

Figure 3-8 Instruction Cache Miss

Even though the line brought in by the instruction cache could have been replaced by a line of the exception handler, no performance loss occurs, since the instruction cache miss would have been serviced anyway, after returning from the exception handler. Handling of the exception is done in this fashion because the frequency of an exception occurring is, by definition, relatively low.

Pipelining the Exception Handling

Pipelining of interlock and exception handling is done by pipelining the logical resolution of possible fault conditions with the buffering and distributing of the pipeline control signals.

In particular, a half clock period is provided for buffering and distributing the *run* control signal; during this time the logic evaluation to produce run for the next cycle begins. Figure 3-9 shows this process for a sequence of loads.

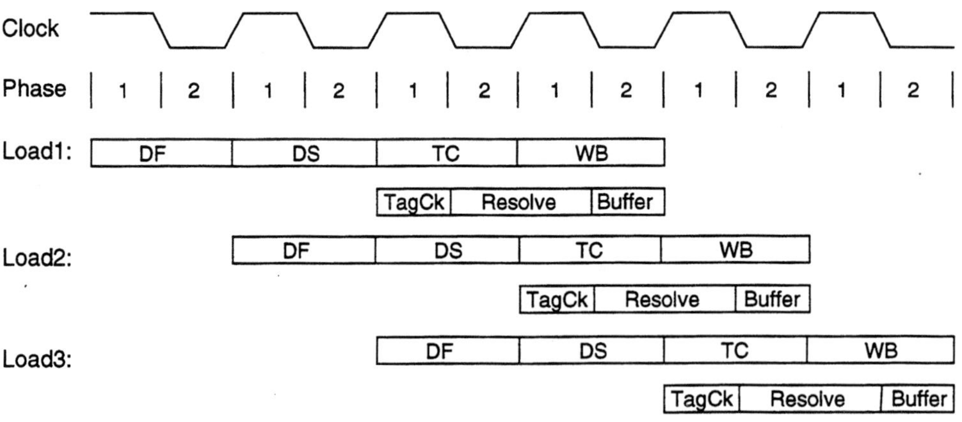

Figure 3-9 Pipelining of Interlock and Exception Handling

The decision whether or not to advance the pipeline is derived from these three rules:

- All possible fault-causing events, such as cache misses, translation exceptions, load interlocks, etc., must be individually evaluated.
- The fault to be serviced is selected, based on a predefined priority as determined by the pipeline stage of the asserted faults.
- Pipeline advance control signals are buffered and distributed.

Figure 3-10 illustrates this process.

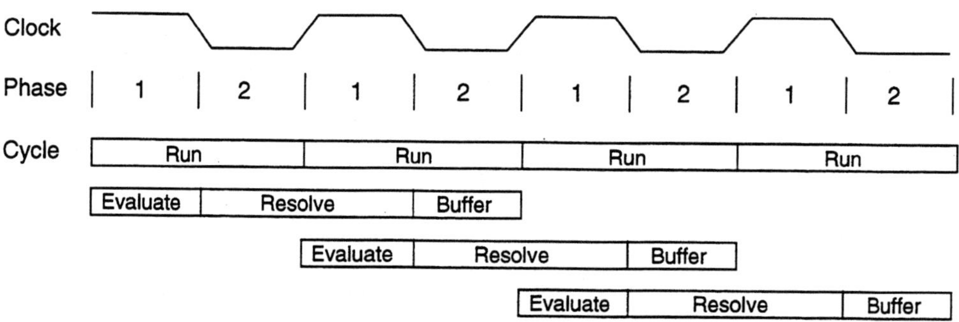

Figure 3-10 Pipeline Advance Decision

Special Cases

In some instances, the pipeline control state machine is bypassed. This occurs due to performance considerations or to correctness considerations, which are described in the following sections.

Performance Considerations

A performance consideration occurs when there is a cache load miss. By bypassing the pipeline state machine, it is possible to eliminate up to two cycles of load miss latency. Two techniques, *address acceleration* and *address prediction*, increase performance.

Address Acceleration

Address acceleration bypasses a potential cache miss address. It is relatively straightforward to perform this bypass since sending the cache miss address to the secondary cache has no negative impact even if a subsequent exception nullifies the effect of this cache access. Power is wasted when the miss is inhibited by some fault, but this is a minor effect.

Address Prediction

Another technique used to reduce miss latency is the automatic increment and transmission of instruction miss addresses following an instruction cache miss. This form of latency reduction is called *address prediction*: the subsequent instruction miss address is predicted to be a simple increment of the previous miss address. Figure 3-11 shows a cache miss in which the cache miss address is changed based on the detection of the miss.

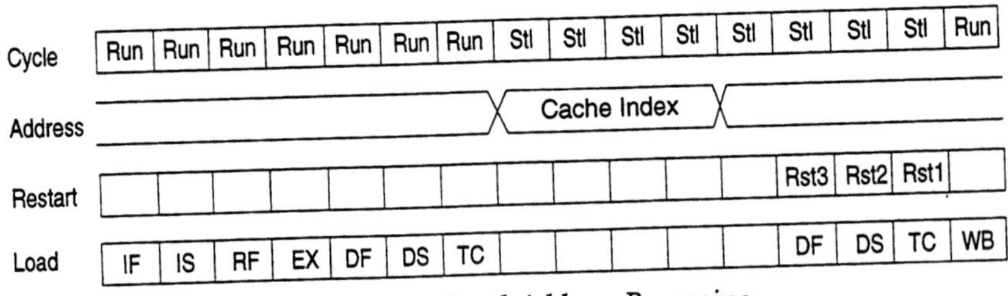

Figure 3-11 Load Address Bypassing

Correctness Considerations

An example in which bypassing is necessary to guarantee correctness is a cache write.

3.6 R4400 Processor Uncached Store Buffer

The R4400 processor contains an uncached store buffer to improve the performance of uncached stores over that available from an R4000 processor. When an uncached store reaches the write-back (WB) stage in the CPU pipeline, the CPU must stall until the store is sent off-chip. In the R4400 processor, a single-entry buffer stores this uncached WB-stage data on the chip without stalling the pipeline.

If a second uncached store reaches the WB stage in the R4400 processor before the first uncached store has been moved off-chip, the CPU stalls until the store buffer completes the first uncached store. To avoid this stall, the compiler can insert seven instruction cycles between the two uncached stores, as shown in Figure 3-12. A single instruction that requires seven cycles to complete could be used in place of the seven No Operation (NOP) instructions.

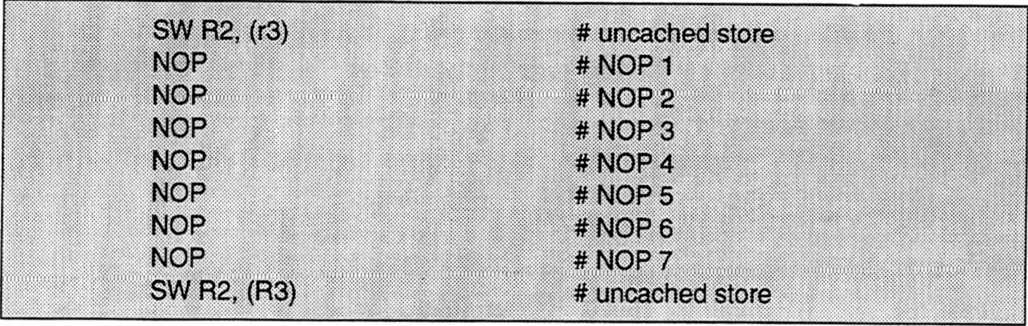

```
SW R2, (r3)        # uncached store
NOP                # NOP 1
NOP                # NOP 2
NOP                # NOP 3
NOP                # NOP 4
NOP                # NOP 5
NOP                # NOP 6
NOP                # NOP 7
SW R2, (R3)        # uncached store
```

Figure 3-12 Pipeline Sequence for Back-to-Back Uncached Stores

If the two uncached stores execute within a loop, the two killed instructions which are part of the loop branch latency are included in the count of seven interpolated cycles. Figure 3-13 shows the four NOP instructions that need to be scheduled in this case.

```
Loop:   SW R2, (R3)            # uncached store
        NOP
        NOP
        NOP
        B Loop                 # branch to loop
        NOP
        killed                 # branch latency
        killed                 # branch latency
```

Figure 3-13 Back-to-Back Uncached Stores in a Loop

The timing requirements of the System interface govern the latency between uncached stores; back-to-back stores can be sent across the interface at a maximum rate of one store for every four external cycles. If the R4400 processor is programmed to run in divide-by-2 mode (for more information about divided clock, see the description of SClock in Chapter 10), an uncached store can occur every eight pipeline cycles. If a larger clock divisor is used, more pipeline cycles are required for each store.

Memory Management

4

The MIPS R4000 processor provides a full-featured memory management unit (MMU) which uses an on-chip translation lookaside buffer (TLB) to translate virtual addresses into physical addresses.

This chapter describes the processor virtual and physical address spaces, the virtual-to-physical address translation, the operation of the TLB in making these translations, and those System Control Coprocessor (CP0) registers that provide the software interface to the TLB.

4.1 Translation Lookaside Buffer (TLB)

Mapped virtual addresses are translated into physical addresses using an on-chip TLB.† The TLB is a fully associative memory that holds 48 entries, which provide mapping to 48 odd/even page pairs (96 pages). When address mapping is indicated, each TLB entry is checked simultaneously for a match with the virtual address that is extended with an ASID stored in the *EntryHi* register.

The address mapped to a page ranges in size from 4 Kbytes to 16 Mbytes, in multiples of 4—that is, 4K, 16K, 64K, 256K, 1M, 4M, 16M.

Hits and Misses

If there is a virtual address match, or hit, in the TLB, the physical page number is extracted from the TLB and concatenated with the offset to form the physical address (see Figure 4-1).

If no match occurs (TLB miss), an exception is taken and software refills the TLB from the page table resident in memory. Software can write over a selected TLB entry or use a hardware mechanism to write into a random entry.

Multiple Matches

If more than one entry in the TLB matches the virtual address being translated, the operation is undefined and the TLB can be disabled. The TLB-Shutdown *(TS)* bit in the *Status* register is set to 1 if the TLB is disabled.

† There are virtual-to-physical address translations that occur outside of the TLB. For example, addresses in *the kseg0* and *kseg1* spaces are unmapped translations. In these spaces the physical address is derived by subtracting the base address of the space from the virtual address.

4.2 Address Spaces

This section describes the virtual and physical address spaces and the manner in which virtual addresses are converted or "translated" into physical addresses in the TLB.

Virtual Address Space

The processor virtual address can be either 32 or 64 bits wide,† depending on whether the processor is operating in 32-bit or 64-bit mode.

- In 32-bit mode, addresses are 32 bits wide. The maximum user process size is 2 gigabytes (2^{31}).
- In 64-bit mode, addresses are 64 bits wide. The maximum user process size is 1 terabyte (2^{40}).

Figure 4-1 shows the translation of a virtual address into a physical address.

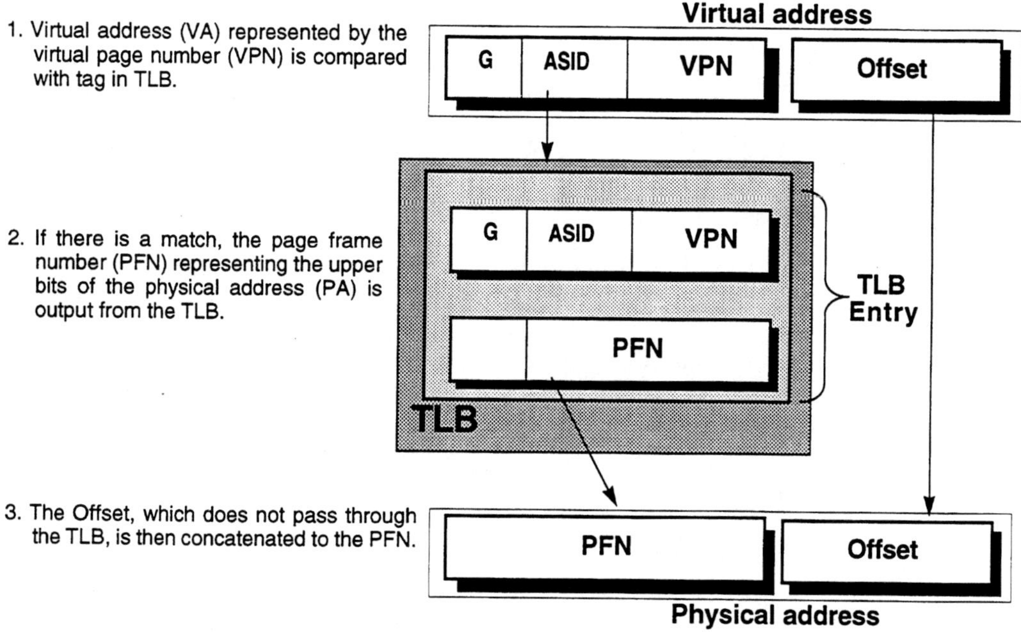

1. Virtual address (VA) represented by the virtual page number (VPN) is compared with tag in TLB.
2. If there is a match, the page frame number (PFN) representing the upper bits of the physical address (PA) is output from the TLB.
3. The Offset, which does not pass through the TLB, is then concatenated to the PFN.
Virtual address
G
ASID
VPN
Offset
G
ASID
VPN
PFN
TLB
TLB Entry
PFN
Offset
Physical address

Figure 4-1 Overview of a Virtual-to-Physical Address Translation

† Figure 4-8 shows the 32-bit and 64-bit versions of the processor TLB entry.

As shown in Figures 4-2 and 4-3, the virtual address is extended with an 8-bit address space identifier (ASID), which reduces the frequency of TLB flushing when switching contexts. This 8-bit ASID is in the CP0 *EntryHi* register, described later in this chapter. The *Global* bit (*G*) is in the *EntryLo0* and *EntryLo1* registers, described later in this chapter.

Physical Address Space

Using a 36-bit address, the processor physical address space encompasses 64 gigabytes. The section following describes the translation of a virtual address to a physical address.

Virtual-to-Physical Address Translation

Converting a virtual address to a physical address begins by comparing the virtual address from the processor with the virtual address in the TLB; there is a match when the virtual page number (VPN) of the address is the same as the VPN field of the entry, and either:

- the Global (*G*) bit of the TLB entry is set, or
- the ASID field of the virtual address is the same as the ASID field of the TLB entry.

This match is referred to as a *TLB hit*. If there is no match, a TLB Miss exception is taken by the processor and software is allowed to refill the TLB from a page table of virtual/physical addresses in memory.

If there is a virtual address match in the TLB, the physical address is output from the TLB and concatenated with the *Offset*, which represents an address within the page frame space. The *Offset* does not pass through the TLB.

Virtual-to-physical translation is described in greater detail throughout the remainder of this chapter; Figure 4-20 is a flow diagram of the process shown at the end of this chapter.

The next two sections describe the 32-bit and 64-bit address translations.

32-bit Mode Address Translation

Figure 4-2 shows the virtual-to-physical-address translation of a 32-bit mode address.

- The top portion of Figure 4-2 shows a virtual address with a 12-bit, or 4-Kbyte, page size, labelled *Offset*. The remaining 20 bits of the address represent the VPN, and index the 1M-entry page table.
- The bottom portion of Figure 4-2 shows a virtual address with a 24-bit, or 16-Mbyte, page size, labelled *Offset*. The remaining 8 bits of the address represent the VPN, and index the 256-entry page table.

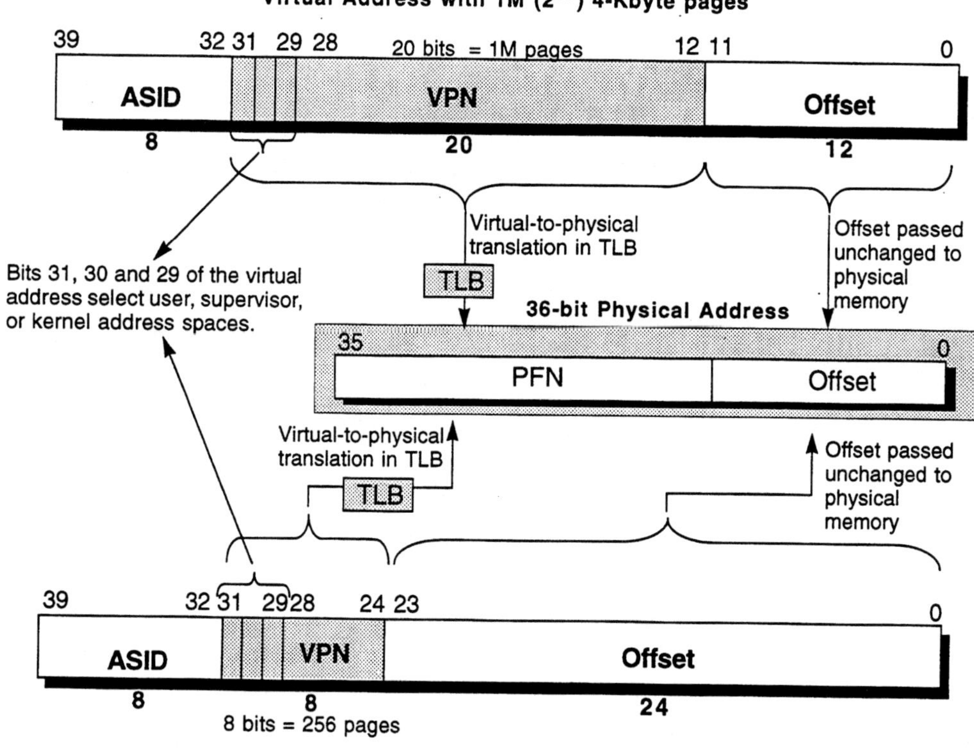

Figure 4-2 32-bit Mode Virtual Address Translation

64-bit Mode Address Translation

Figure 4-3 shows the virtual-to-physical-address translation of a 64-bit mode address. This figure illustrates the two extremes in the range of possible page sizes: a 4-Kbyte page (12 bits) and a 16-Mbyte page (24 bits).

- The top portion of Figure 4-3 shows a virtual address with a 12-bit, or 4-Kbyte, page size, labelled *Offset*. The remaining 28 bits of the address represent the VPN, and index the 256M-entry page table.
- The bottom portion of Figure 4-3 shows a virtual address with a 24-bit, or 16-Mbyte, page size, labelled *Offset*. The remaining 16 bits of the address represent the VPN, and index the 64K-entry page table.

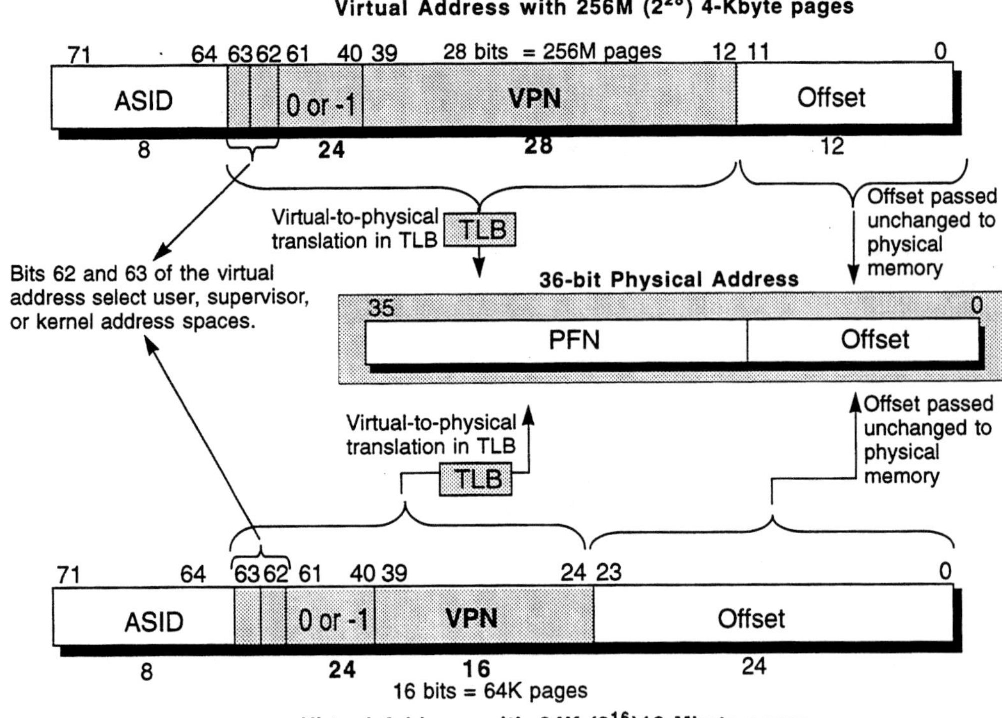

Figure 4-3 64-bit Mode Virtual Address Translation

Operating Modes

The processor has three operating modes that function in both 32- and 64-bit operations:

- User mode
- Supervisor mode
- Kernel mode

These modes are described in the next three sections.

User Mode Operations

In User mode, a single, uniform virtual address space—labelled User segment—is available; its size is:

- 2 Gbytes (2^{31} bytes) in 32-bit mode (*useg*)
- 1 Tbyte (2^{40} bytes) in 64-bit mode (*xuseg*)

Figure 4-4 shows User mode virtual address space.

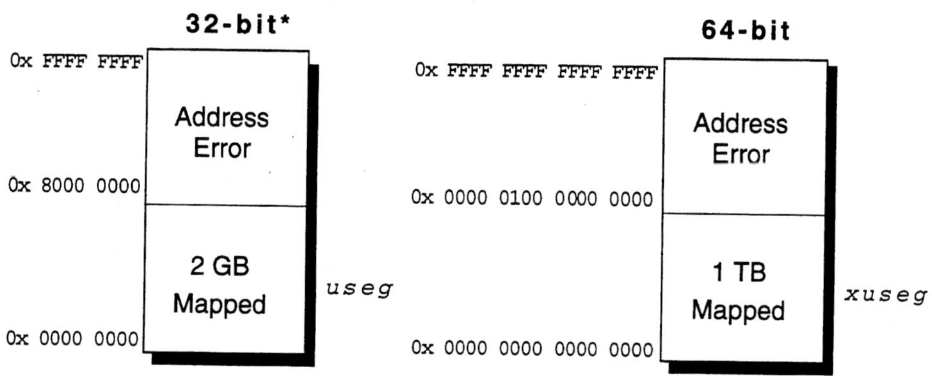

Figure 4-4 User Mode Virtual Address Space

*In 32-bit mode, bit 31 is sign-extended through bits 63:32. Failure results in an Address Error exception.

The User segment starts at address 0 and the current active user process resides in either *useg* (in 32-bit mode) or *xuseg* (in 64-bit mode). The TLB identically maps all references to *useg*/*xuseg* from all modes, and controls cache accessibility.†

The processor operates in User mode when the *Status* register contains the following bit-values:

- *KSU* bits = 10_2
- *EXL* = 0
- *ERL* = 0

In conjunction with these bits, the *UX* bit in the *Status* register selects between 32- or 64-bit User mode addressing as follows:

- when *UX* = 0, 32-bit *useg* space is selected
- when *UX* = 1, 64-bit *xuseg* space is selected

Table 4-1 lists the characteristics of the two user mode segments, *useg* and *xuseg*.

Table 4-1 32-bit and 64-bit User Mode Segments

Address Bit Values	Status Register Bit Values				Segment Name	Address Range	Segment Size
	KSU	EXL	ERL	UX			
32-bit A(31) = 0	10_2	0	0	0	*useg*	0x0000 0000 through 0x7FFF FFFF	2 Gbyte (2^{31} bytes)
64-bit A(63:40) = 0	10_2	0	0	1	*xuseg*	0x0000 0000 0000 0000 through 0x0000 00FF FFFF FFFF	1 Tbyte (2^{40} bytes)

† The cached (C) field in a TLB entry determines whether the reference is cached; see Figure 4-8.

32-bit User Mode (*useg*)

In User mode, when *UX* = 0 in the *Status* register, User mode addressing is compatible with the 32-bit addressing model shown in Figure 4-4, and a 2-Gbyte user address space is available, labelled *useg*.

All valid User mode virtual addresses have their most-significant bit cleared to 0; any attempt to reference an address with the most-significant bit set while in User mode causes an Address Error exception.

In 32-bit User mode addressing, the TLB refill exception vector is used for TLB misses.

The system maps all references to *useg* through the TLB, and bit settings within the TLB entry for the page determine the cacheability of a reference.

64-bit User Mode (*xuseg*)

In User mode, when *UX* =1 in the *Status* register, User mode addressing is extended to the 64-bit model shown in Figure 4-4. In 64-bit User mode, the processor provides a single, uniform address space of 2^{40} bytes, labelled *xuseg*.

All valid User mode virtual addresses have bits 63:40 equal to 0; an attempt to reference an address with bits 63:40 not equal to 0 causes an Address Error exception.

The extended addressing TLB refill exception vector is used for TLB misses.

Supervisor Mode Operations

Supervisor mode is designed for layered operating systems in which a true kernel runs in R4000 Kernel mode, and the rest of the operating system runs in Supervisor mode.

The processor operates in Supervisor mode when the *Status* register contains the following bit-values:

- *KSU* = 01_2
- *EXL* = 0
- *ERL* = 0

In conjunction with these bits, the *SX* bit in the *Status* register selects between 32- or 64-bit Supervisor mode addressing:

- when *SX* = 0, 32-bit supervisor space is selected
- when *SX* = 1, 64-bit supervisor space is selected

Figure 4-5 shows Supervisor mode address mapping. Table 4-2 lists the characteristics of the supervisor mode segments; descriptions of the address spaces follow.

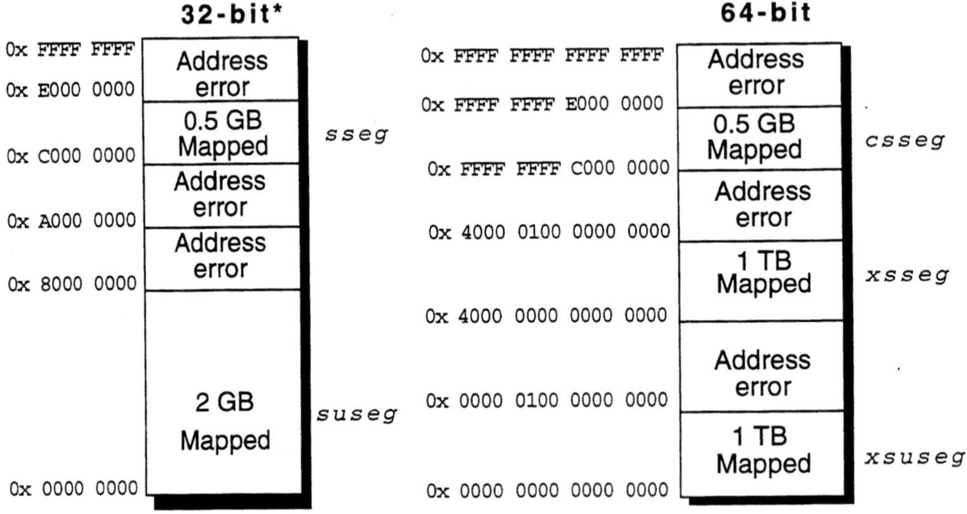

Figure 4-5 Supervisor Mode Address Space

*In 32-bit mode, bit 31 is sign-extended through bits 63:32. Failure results in an Address Error exception.

Table 4-2 32-bit and 64-bit Supervisor Mode Segments

Address Bit Values	Status Register Bit Values				Segment Name	Address Range	Segment Size
	KSU	EXL	ERL	SX			
32-bit A(31) = 0	01_2	0	0	0	*suseg*	0x0000 0000 through 0x7FFF FFFF	2 Gbytes (2^{31} bytes)
32-bit A(31:29) = 110_2	01_2	0	0	0	*ssseg*	0xC000 0000 through 0xDFFF FFFF	512 Mbytes (2^{29} bytes)
64-bit A(63:62) = 00_2	01_2	0	0	1	*xsuseg*	0x0000 0000 0000 0000 through 0x0000 00FF FFFF FFFF	1 Tbyte (2^{40} bytes)
64-bit A(63:62) = 01_2	01_2	0	0	1	*xsseg*	0x4000 0000 0000 0000 through 0x4000 00FF FFFF FFFF	1 Tbyte (2^{40} bytes)
64-bit A(63:62) = 11_2	01_2	0	0	1	*csseg*	0xFFFF FFFF C000 0000 through 0xFFFF FFFF DFFF FFFF	512 Mbytes (2^{29} bytes)

32-bit Supervisor Mode, User Space (*suseg*)

In Supervisor mode, when *SX* = 0 in the *Status* register and the most-significant bit of the 32-bit virtual address is set to 0, the *suseg* virtual address space is selected; it covers the full 2^{31} bytes (2 Gbytes) of the current user address space. The virtual address is extended with the contents of the 8-bit ASID field to form a unique virtual address.

This mapped space starts at virtual address 0x0000 0000 and runs through 0x7FFF FFFF.

32-bit Supervisor Mode, Supervisor Space (*sseg*)

In Supervisor mode, when *SX* = 0 in the *Status* register and the three most-significant bits of the 32-bit virtual address are 110_2, the *sseg* virtual address space is selected; it covers 2^{29}-bytes (512 Mbytes) of the current supervisor address space. The virtual address is extended with the contents of the 8-bit ASID field to form a unique virtual address.

This mapped space begins at virtual address 0xC000 0000 and runs through 0xDFFF FFFF.

64-bit Supervisor Mode, User Space (*xsuseg*)

In Supervisor mode, when *SX* = 1 in the *Status* register and bits 63:62 of the virtual address are set to 00_2, the *xsuseg* virtual address space is selected; it covers the full 2^{40} bytes (1 Tbyte) of the current user address space. The virtual address is extended with the contents of the 8-bit ASID field to form a unique virtual address.

This mapped space starts at virtual address 0x0000 0000 0000 0000 and runs through 0x0000 00FF FFFF FFFF.

64-bit Supervisor Mode, Current Supervisor Space (*xsseg*)

In Supervisor mode, when *SX* = 1 in the *Status* register and bits 63:62 of the virtual address are set to 01_2, the *xsseg* current supervisor virtual address space is selected. The virtual address is extended with the contents of the 8-bit ASID field to form a unique virtual address.

This mapped space begins at virtual address 0x4000 0000 0000 0000 and runs through 0x4000 00FF FFFF FFFF.

64-bit Supervisor Mode, Separate Supervisor Space (*csseg*)

In Supervisor mode, when *SX* = 1 in the *Status* register and bits 63:62 of the virtual address are set to 11_2, the *csseg* separate supervisor virtual address space is selected. Addressing of the *csseg* is compatible with addressing *sseg* in 32-bit mode. The virtual address is extended with the contents of the 8-bit ASID field to form a unique virtual address.

This mapped space begins at virtual address 0xFFFF FFFF C000 0000 and runs through 0xFFFF FFFF DFFF FFFF.

Kernel Mode Operations

The processor operates in Kernel mode when the *Status* register contains one of the following values:

- *KSU* = 00_2
- *EXL* = 1
- *ERL* = 1

In conjunction with these bits, the *KX* bit in the *Status* register selects between 32- or 64-bit Kernel mode addressing:

- when *KX* = 0, 32-bit kernel space is selected
- when *KX* = 1, 64-bit kernel space is selected

The processor enters Kernel mode whenever an exception is detected and it remains in Kernel mode until an Exception Return (ERET) instruction is executed. The ERET instruction restores the processor to the mode existing prior to the exception.

Kernel mode virtual address space is divided into regions differentiated by the high-order bits of the virtual address, as shown in Figure 4-6. Table 4-3 lists the characteristics of the 32-bit kernel mode segments, and Table 4-4 lists the characteristics of the 64-bit kernel mode segments

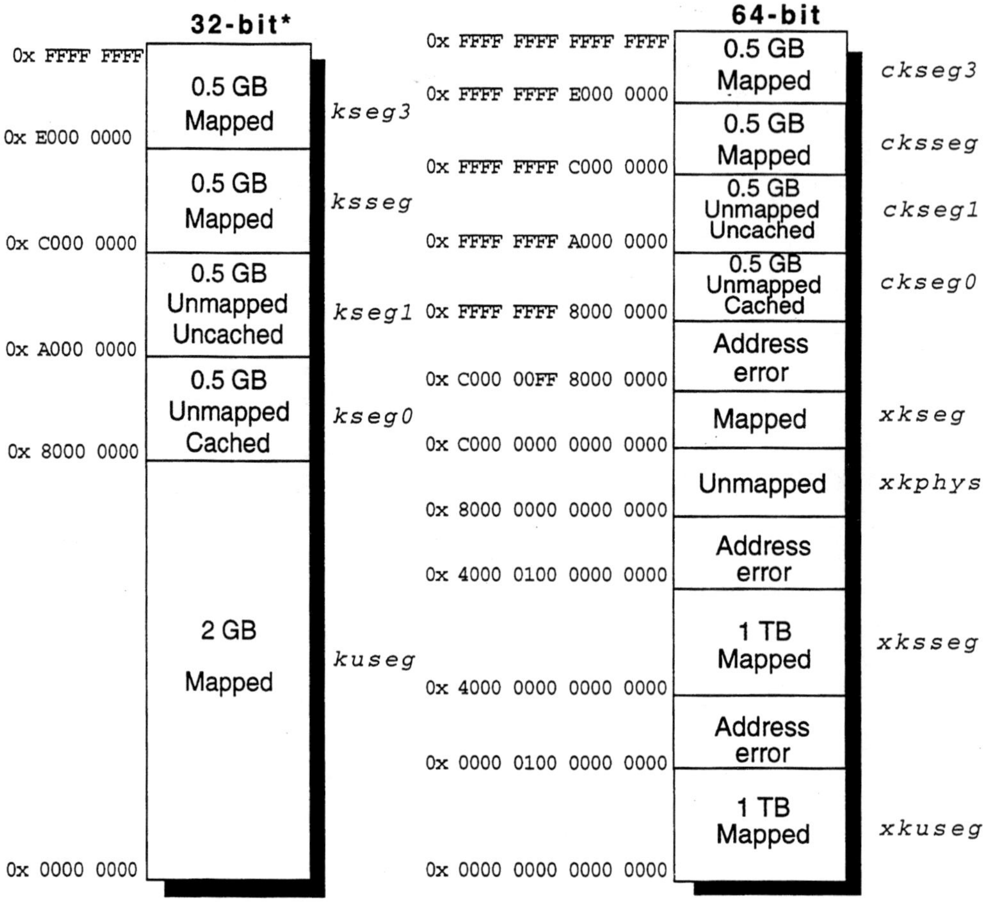

Figure 4-6 Kernel Mode Address Space

*In 32-bit mode, bit 31 is sign-extended through bits 63:32. Failure results in an Address Error exception.

Table 4-3 32-bit Kernel Mode Segments

Address Bit Values	Status Register Is One Of These Values: KSU	EXL	ERL	KX	Segment Name	Address Range	Segment Size
A(31) = 0	KSU = 00_2 *or* EXL = 1 *or* ERL =1			0	*kuseg*	0x0000 0000 through 0x7FFF FFFF	2 Gbytes (2^{31} bytes)
A(31:29) = 100_2				0	*kseg0*	0x8000 0000 through 0x9FFF FFFF	512Mbytes (2^{29} bytes)
A(31:29) = 101_2				0	*kseg1*	0xA000 0000 through 0xBFFF FFFF	512Mbytes (2^{29} bytes)
A(31:29) = 110_2				0	*ksseg*	0xC000 0000 through 0xDFFF FFFF	512Mbytes (2^{29} bytes)
A(31:29) = 111_2				0	*kseg3*	0xE000 0000 through 0xFFFF FFFF	512Mbytes (2^{29} bytes)

32-bit Kernel Mode, User Space (*kuseg*)

In Kernel mode, when *KX* = 0 in the *Status* register, and the most-significant bit of the virtual address, A31, is cleared, the 32-bit *kuseg* virtual address space is selected; it covers the full 2^{31} bytes (2 Gbytes) of the current user address space. The virtual address is extended with the contents of the 8-bit ASID field to form a unique virtual address.

32-bit Kernel Mode, Kernel Space 0 (*kseg0*)

In Kernel mode, when *KX* = 0 in the *Status* register and the most-significant three bits of the virtual address are 100_2, 32-bit *kseg0* virtual address space is selected; it is the current 2^{29}-byte (512-Mbyte) kernel physical space.

References to *kseg0* are not mapped through the TLB; the physical address selected is defined by subtracting 0x8000 0000 from the virtual address.

The *K0* field of the *Config* register, described in this chapter, controls cacheability and coherency.

32-bit Kernel Mode, Kernel Space 1 (*kseg1*)

In Kernel mode, when *KX* = 0 in the *Status* register and the most-significant three bits of the 32-bit virtual address are 101_2, 32-bit *kseg1* virtual address space is selected; it is the current 2^{29}-byte (512-Mbyte) kernel physical space.

References to *kseg1* are not mapped through the TLB; the physical address selected is defined by subtracting 0xA000 0000 from the virtual address.

Caches are disabled for accesses to these addresses, and physical memory (or memory-mapped I/O device registers) are accessed directly.

32-bit Kernel Mode, Supervisor Space (*ksseg*)

In Kernel mode, when *KX* = 0 in the *Status* register and the most-significant three bits of the 32-bit virtual address are 110_2, the *ksseg* virtual address space is selected; it is the current 2^{29}-byte (512-Mbyte) supervisor virtual space. The virtual address is extended with the contents of the 8-bit ASID field to form a unique virtual address.

32-bit Kernel Mode, Kernel Space 3 (*kseg3*)

In Kernel mode, when *KX* = 0 in the *Status* register and the most-significant three bits of the 32-bit virtual address are 111_2, the *kseg3* virtual address space is selected; it is the current 2^{29}-byte (512-Mbyte) kernel virtual space. The virtual address is extended with the contents of the 8-bit ASID field to form a unique virtual address.

Table 4-4 64-bit Kernel Mode Segments

Address Bit Values	Status Register Is One Of These Values (KSU, EXL, ERL)	KX	Segment Name	Address Range	Segment Size
A(63:62) = 00_2	KSU = 00_2 *or* EXL = 1 *or* ERL =1	1	*xksuseg*	0x0000 0000 0000 0000 through 0x0000 00FF FFFF FFFF	1 Tbyte (2^{40} bytes)
A(63:62) = 01_2		1	*xksseg*	0x4000 0000 0000 0000 through 0x4000 00FF FFFF FFFF	1 Tbyte (2^{40} bytes)
A(63:62) = 10_2		1	*xkphys*	0x8000 0000 0000 0000 through 0xBFFF FFFF FFFF FFFF	8 2^{36}-byte spaces
A(63:62) = 11_2		1	*xkseg*	0xC000 0000 0000 0000 through 0xC000 00FF 7FFF FFFF	2^{44} bytes
A(63:62) = 11_2 A(61:31) = -1		1	*ckseg0*	0xFFFF FFFF 8000 0000 through 0xFFFF FFFF 9FFF FFFF	512Mbytes (2^{29} bytes)
A(63:62) = 11_2 A(61:31) = -1		1	*ckseg1*	0xFFFF FFFF A000 0000 through 0xFFFF FFFF BFFF FFFF	512Mbytes (2^{29} bytes)
A(63:62) = 11_2 A(61:31) = -1		1	*cksseg*	0xFFFF FFFF C000 0000 through 0xFFFF FFFF DFFF FFFF	512Mbytes (2^{29} bytes)
A(63:62) = 11_2 A(61:31) = -1		1	*ckseg3*	0xFFFF FFFF E000 0000 through 0xFFFF FFFF FFFF FFFF	512Mbytes (2^{29} bytes)

64-bit Kernel Mode, User Space (*xkuseg*)

In Kernel mode, when *KX* = 1 in the *Status* register and bits 63:62 of the 64-bit virtual address are 00_2, the *xkuseg* virtual address space is selected; it covers the current user address space. The virtual address is extended with the contents of the 8-bit ASID field to form a unique virtual address.

As a special feature for the ECC handler, if the *ERL* bit of the *Status* register is set, the user address region becomes a 2^{31}-byte unmapped, uncached space. This allows the ECC exception code to operate uncached using *r0* as a base register.

64-bit Kernel Mode, Current Supervisor Space (*xksseg*)

In Kernel mode, when *KX* = 1 in the *Status* register and bits 63:62 of the 64-bit virtual address are 01_2, the *xksseg* virtual address space is selected; it is the current supervisor virtual space. The virtual address is extended with the contents of the 8-bit ASID field to form a unique virtual address.

64-bit Kernel Mode, Physical Spaces (*xkphys*)

In Kernel mode, when *KX* = 1 in the *Status* register and bits 63:62 of the 64-bit virtual address are 10_2, the *xkphys* virtual address space is selected; it is a set of eight 2^{36}-byte kernel physical spaces. Accesses with address bits 58:36 not equal to 0 cause an address error.

References to this space are not mapped; the physical address selected is taken from bits 35:0 of the virtual address. Bits 61:59 of the virtual address specify the cacheability and coherency attributes, as shown in Table 4-5.

Table 4-5 Cacheability and Coherency Attributes

Value (61:59)	Cacheability and Coherency Attributes	Starting Address
0	Reserved	0x8000 0000 0000 0000
1	Reserved	0x8800 0000 0000 0000
2	Uncached	0x9000 0000 0000 0000
3	Cacheable, noncoherent	0x9800 0000 0000 0000
4	Cacheable, coherent exclusive	0xA000 0000 0000 0000
5	Cacheable, coherent exclusive on write	0xA800 0000 0000 0000
6	Cacheable, coherent update on write	0xB000 0000 0000 0000
7	Reserved	0xB800 0000 0000 0000

64-bit Kernel Mode, Kernel Space (*xkseg*)

In Kernel mode, when *KX* = 1 in the *Status* register and bits 63:62 of the 64-bit virtual address are 11_2, the address space selected is one of the following:

- kernel virtual space, *xkseg*, the current supervisor virtual space; the virtual address is extended with the contents of the 8-bit ASID field to form a unique virtual address
- one of the four 32-bit kernel compatibility spaces, as described in the next section.

64-bit Kernel Mode, Compatibility Spaces (*ckseg1:0, cksseg, ckseg3*)

In Kernel mode, when *KX* = 1 in the *Status* register, bits 63:62 of the 64-bit virtual address are 11_2, and bits 61:31 of the virtual address equal –1, the lower two bytes of address, as shown in Figure 4-6, select one of the following 512-Mbyte compatibility spaces.

- *ckseg0*. This 64-bit virtual address space is an unmapped region, compatible with the 32-bit address model *kseg0*. The *K0* field of the *Config* register, described in this chapter, controls cacheability and coherency.
- *ckseg1*. This 64-bit virtual address space is an unmapped and uncached region, compatible with the 32-bit address model *kseg1*.
- *cksseg*. This 64-bit virtual address space is the current supervisor virtual space, compatible with the 32-bit address model *ksseg*.
- *ckseg3*. This 64-bit virtual address space is kernel virtual space, compatible with the 32-bit address model *kseg3*.

4.3 System Control Coprocessor

The System Control Coprocessor (CP0) is implemented as an integral part of the CPU, and supports memory management, address translation, exception handling, and other privileged operations. CP0 contains the registers shown in Figure 4-7 plus a 48-entry TLB. The sections that follow describe how the processor uses each of the memory management-related registers.

Each CP0 register has a unique number that identifies it; this number is referred to as the *register number*. For instance, the *Page Mask* register is register number 5.

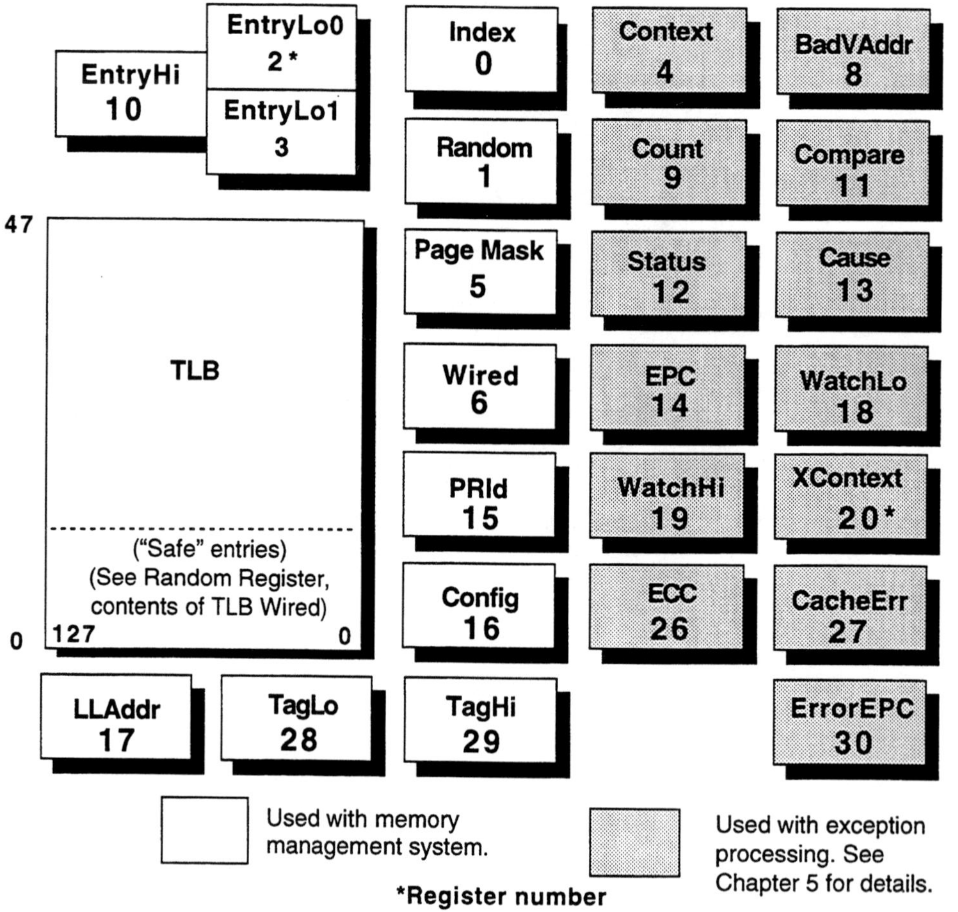

Figure 4-7 CP0 Registers and the TLB

Format of a TLB Entry

Figure 4-8 shows the TLB entry formats for both 32- and 64-bit modes. Each field of an entry has a corresponding field in the *EntryHi, EntryLo0, EntryLo1,* or *PageMask* registers, as shown in Figures 4-9 and 4-10; for example the *Mask* field of the TLB entry is also held in the *PageMask* register.

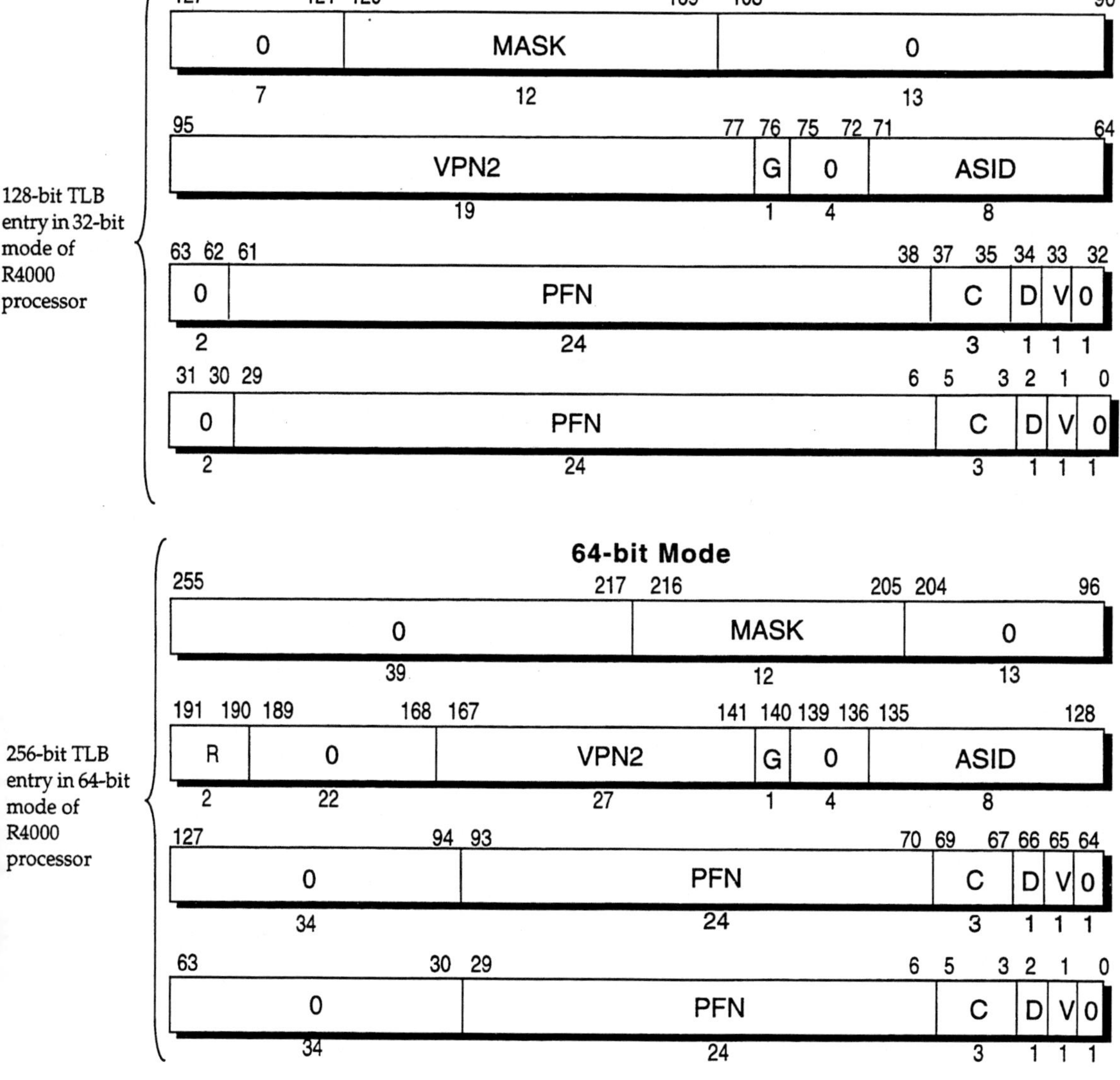

Figure 4-8 Format of a TLB Entry

The format of the *EntryHi, EntryLo0, EntryLo1,* and *PageMask* registers are nearly the same as the TLB entry. The one exception is the *Global* field (G bit), which is used in the TLB, but is reserved in the *EntryHi* register. Figures 4-9 and 4-10 describe the TLB entry fields shown in Figure 4-8.

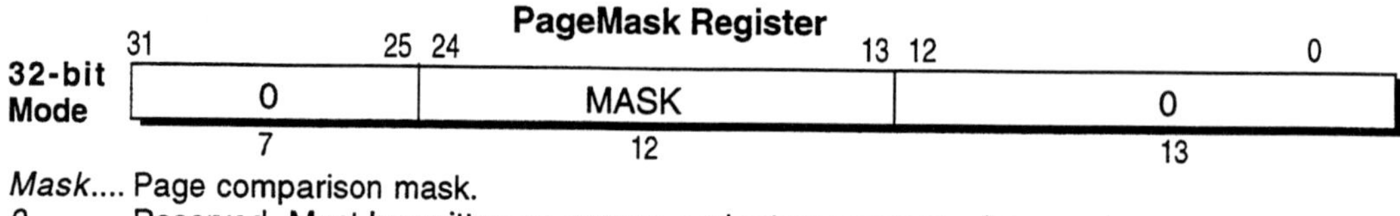

Mask.... Page comparison mask.
0 .... Reserved. Must be written as zeroes, and returns zeroes when read.

EntryHi Register

32-bit Mode

Bits	31–13	12–8	7–0
Field	VPN2	0	ASID
Width	19	5	8

64-bit Mode

Bits	63–62	61–40	39–13	12–8	7–0
Field	R	FILL	VPN2	0	ASID
Width	2	22	27	5	8

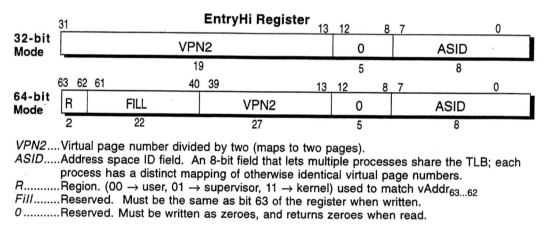

VPN2....Virtual page number divided by two (maps to two pages).
ASID.....Address space ID field. An 8-bit field that lets multiple processes share the TLB; each process has a distinct mapping of otherwise identical virtual page numbers.
R...........Region. (00 → user, 01 → supervisor, 11 → kernel) used to match $vAddr_{63...62}$
Fill........Reserved. Must be the same as bit 63 of the register when written.
0 ....Reserved. Must be written as zeroes, and returns zeroes when read.

Figure 4-9 Fields of the PageMask and EntryHi Registers

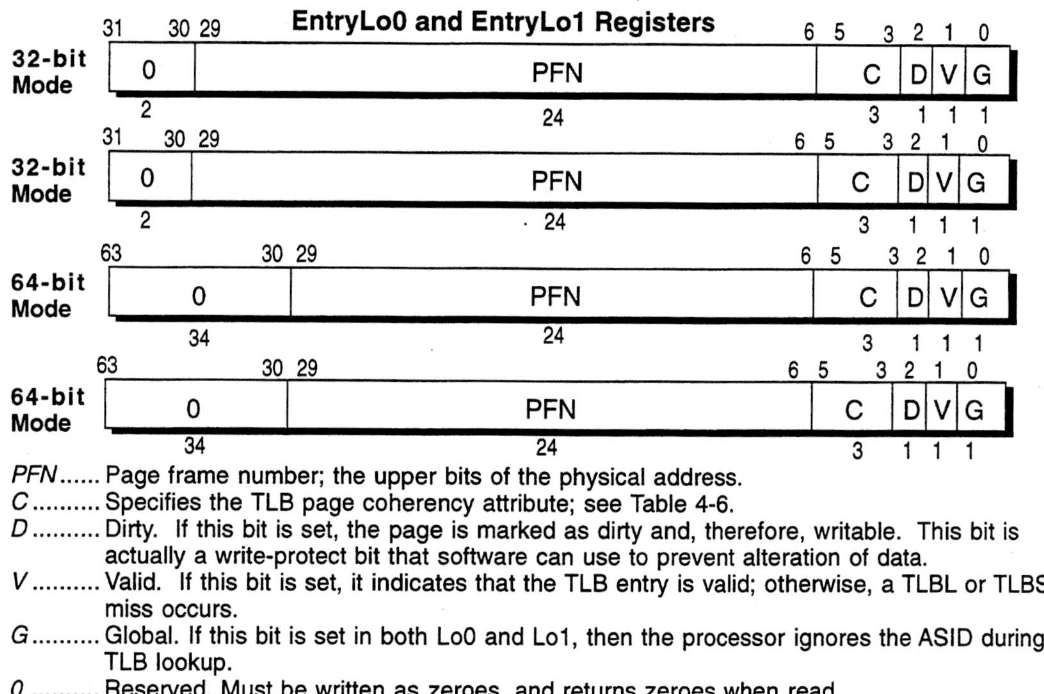

PFN...... Page frame number; the upper bits of the physical address.
C.......... Specifies the TLB page coherency attribute; see Table 4-6.
D.......... Dirty. If this bit is set, the page is marked as dirty and, therefore, writable. This bit is actually a write-protect bit that software can use to prevent alteration of data.
V.......... Valid. If this bit is set, it indicates that the TLB entry is valid; otherwise, a TLBL or TLBS miss occurs.
G.......... Global. If this bit is set in both Lo0 and Lo1, then the processor ignores the ASID during TLB lookup.
0 .... Reserved. Must be written as zeroes, and returns zeroes when read.

Figure 4-10 Fields of the EntryLo0 and EntryLo1 Registers

The TLB page coherency attribute (C) bits specify whether references to the page should be cached; if cached, the algorithm selects between several coherency attributes. Table 4-6 shows the coherency attributes selected by the *C* bits.

Table 4-6 TLB Page Coherency (C) Bit Values

C(5:3) Value	Page Coherency Attribute
0	Reserved
1	Reserved
2	Uncached
3	Cacheable noncoherent (noncoherent)
4	Cacheable coherent exclusive (exclusive)
5	Cacheable coherent exclusive on write (sharable)
6	Cacheable coherent update on write (update)
7	Reserved

CP0 Registers

The following sections describe the CP0 registers, shown in Figure 4-7, that are assigned specifically as a software interface with memory management (each register is followed by its register number in parentheses).

- *Index* register (CP0 register number 0)
- *Random* register (1)
- *EntryLo0* (2) and *EntryLo1* (3) registers
- *PageMask* register (5)
- *Wired* register (6)
- *EntryHi* register (10)
- *PRId* register (15)
- *Config* register (16)
- *LLAddr* register (17)
- *TagLo* (28) and *TagHi* (29) registers

Index Register (0)

The *Index* register is a 32-bit, read/write register containing six bits to index an entry in the TLB. The high-order bit of the register shows the success or failure of a TLB Probe (TLBP) instruction.

The *Index* register also specifies the TLB entry affected by TLB Read (TLBR) or TLB Write Index (TLBWI) instructions.

Figure 4-11 shows the format of the *Index* register; Table 4-7 describes the *Index* register fields.

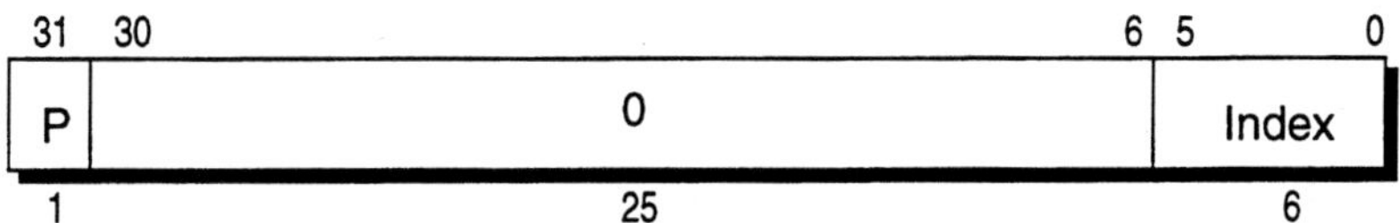

Figure 4-11 Index Register

Table 4-7 Index Register Field Descriptions

Field	Description
P	Probe failure. Set to 1 when the previous TLBProbe (TLBP) instruction was unsuccessful.
Index	Index to the TLB entry affected by the TLBRead and TLBWrite instructions
0	Reserved. Must be written as zeroes, and returns zeroes when read.

Random Register (1)

The *Random* register is a read-only register of which six bits index an entry in the TLB. This register decrements as each instruction executes, and its values range between an upper and a lower bound, as follows:

- A lower bound is set by the number of TLB entries reserved for exclusive use by the operating system (the contents of the *Wired* register).
- An upper bound is set by the total number of TLB entries (47 maximum).

The *Random* register specifies the entry in the TLB that is affected by the TLB Write Random instruction. The register does not need to be read for this purpose; however, the register is readable to verify proper operation of the processor.

To simplify testing, the *Random* register is set to the value of the upper bound upon system reset. This register is also set to the upper bound when the *Wired* register is written.

Figure 4-12 shows the format of the *Random* register; Table 4-8 describes the *Random* register fields.

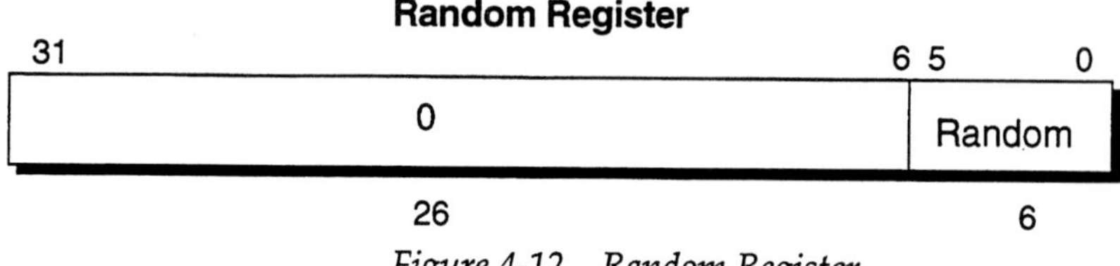

Figure 4-12 Random Register

Table 4-8 Random Register Field Descriptions

Field	Description
Random	TLB Random index
0	Reserved. Must be written as zeroes, and returns zeroes when read.

EntryLo0 (2), and EntryLo1 (3) Registers

The *EntryLo* register consists of two registers that have identical formats:

- *EntryLo0* is used for even virtual pages.
- *EntryLo1* is used for odd virtual pages.

The *EntryLo0* and *EntryLo1* registers are read/write registers. They hold the physical page frame number (PFN) of the TLB entry for even and odd pages, respectively, when performing TLB read and write operations. Figure 4-9 shows the format of these registers.

PageMask Register (5)

The *PageMask* register is a read/write register used for reading from or writing to the TLB; it holds a comparison mask that sets the variable page size for each TLB entry, as shown in Table 4-9.

TLB read and write operations use this register as either a source or a destination; when virtual addresses are presented for translation into physical address, the corresponding bits in the TLB identify which virtual address bits among bits 24:13 are used in the comparison. When the *Mask* field is not one of the values shown in Table 4-9, the operation of the TLB is undefined.

Table 4-9 Mask Field Values for Page Sizes

Page Size	Bit											
	24	23	22	21	20	19	18	17	16	15	14	13
4 Kbytes	0	0	0	0	0	0	0	0	0	0	0	0
16 Kbytes	0	0	0	0	0	0	0	0	0	0	1	1
64 Kbytes	0	0	0	0	0	0	0	0	1	1	1	1
256 Kbytes	0	0	0	0	0	0	1	1	1	1	1	1
1 Mbyte	0	0	0	0	1	1	1	1	1	1	1	1
4 Mbytes	0	0	1	1	1	1	1	1	1	1	1	1
16 Mbytes	1	1	1	1	1	1	1	1	1	1	1	1

Wired Register (6)

The *Wired* register is a read/write register that specifies the boundary between the *wired* and *random* entries of the TLB as shown in Figure 4-13. Wired entries are fixed, nonreplaceable entries, which cannot be overwritten by a TLB write operation. Random entries can be overwritten.

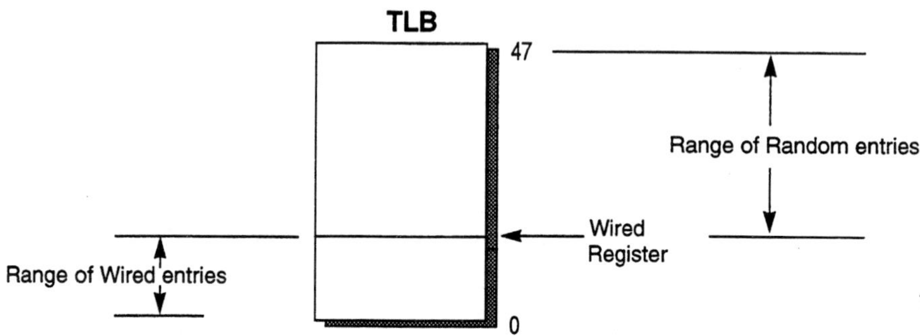

Figure 4-13 Wired Register Boundary

The *Wired* register is set to 0 upon system reset. Writing this register also sets the *Random* register to the value of its upper bound (see *Random* register, above). Figure 4-14 shows the format of the *Wired* register; Table 4-10 describes the register fields.

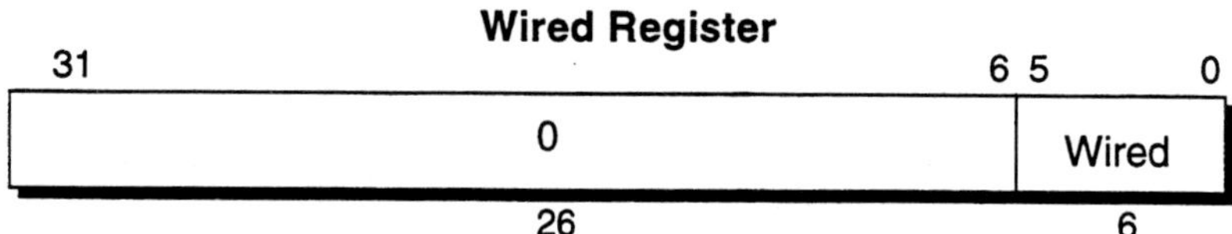

Figure 4-14 Wired Register

Table 4-10 Wired Register Field Descriptions

Field	Description
Wired	TLB Wired boundary
0	Reserved. Must be written as zeroes, and returns zeroes when read.

EntryHi Register (CP0 Register 10)

The *EntryHi* register holds the high-order bits of a TLB entry for TLB read and write operations.

The *EntryHi* register is accessed by the TLB Probe, TLB Write Random, TLB Write Indexed, and TLB Read Indexed instructions.

Figure 4-9 shows the format of this register.

When either a TLB refill, TLB invalid, or TLB modified exception occurs, the *EntryHi* register is loaded with the virtual page number (VPN2) and the ASID of the virtual address that did not have a matching TLB entry. (See Chapter 5 for more information about these exceptions.)

Processor Revision Identifier (PRId) Register (15)

The 32-bit, read-only *Processor Revision Identifier* (*PRId*) register contains information identifying the implementation and revision level of the CPU and CP0. Figure 4-15 shows the format of the *PRId* register; Table 4-11 describes the *PRId* register fields.

PRId Register

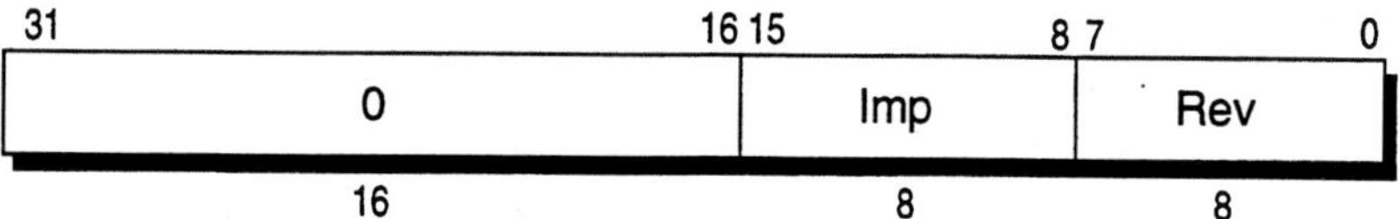

Figure 4-15 Processor Revision Identifier Register Format

Table 4-11 PRId Register Fields

Field	Description
Imp	Implementation number
Rev	Revision number
0	Reserved. Must be written as zeroes, and returns zeroes when read.

The low-order byte (bits 7:0) of the *PRId* register is interpreted as a revision number, and the high-order byte (bits 15:8) is interpreted as an implementation number. The implementation number of the R4000 processor is 0x04. The content of the high-order halfword (bits 31:16) of the register are reserved.

The revision number is stored as a value in the form *y.x*, where *y* is a major revision number in bits 7:4 and *x* is a minor revision number in bits 3:0.

The revision number can distinguish some chip revisions, however there is no guarantee that changes to the chip will necessarily be reflected in the *PRId* register, or that changes to the revision number necessarily reflect real chip changes. For this reason, these values are not listed and software should not rely on the revision number in the *PRId* register to characterize the chip.

Config Register (16)

The *Config* register specifies various configuration options selected on R4000 processors; Table 4-12 lists these options.

Some configuration options, as defined by *Config* bits 31:6, are set by the hardware during reset and are included in the *Config* register as read-only status bits for the software to access. Other configuration options are read/write (as indicated by *Config* register bits 5:0) and controlled by software; on reset these fields are undefined.

Certain configurations have restrictions. The *Config* register should be initialized by software before caches are used. Caches should be written back to memory before line sizes are changed, and caches should be reinitialized after any change is made.

Figure 4-16 shows the format of the *Config* register; Table 4-12 describes the *Config* register fields.

Config Register

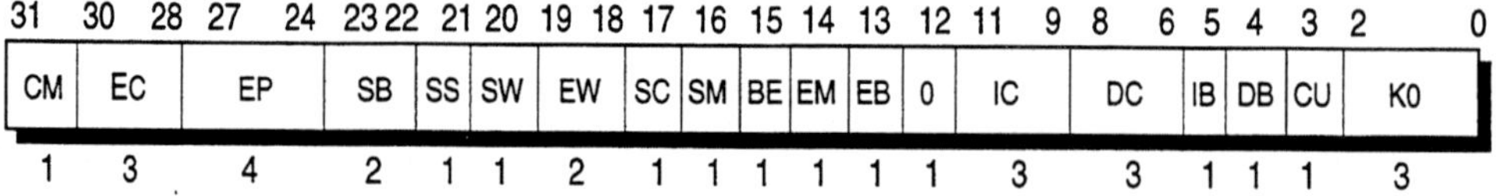

Figure 4-16 Config Register Format

Table 4-12 Config Register Fields

Field	Description
CM	Master-Checker Mode (1 → Master/Checker Mode is enabled). This bit is automatically 0 on a Soft Reset.
EC	System clock ratio: 0 → processor clock frequency divided by 2 1 → processor clock frequency divided by 3 2 → processor clock frequency divided by 4 3 → processor clock frequency divided by 6 (R4400 processor only) 4 → processor clock frequency divided by 8 (R4400 processor only)
EP	Transmit data pattern (pattern for write-back data): 0 → D Doubleword every cycle 1 → DDx 2 Doublewords every 3 cycles 2 → DDxx 2 Doublewords every 4 cycles 3 → DxDx 2 Doublewords every 4 cycles 4 → DDxxx 2 Doublewords every 5 cycles 5 → DDxxxx 2 Doublewords every 6 cycles 6 → DxxDxx 2 Doublewords every 6 cycles 7 → DDxxxxx 2 Doublewords every 7 cycles 8 → DxxxDxxx 2 Doublewords every 8 cycles
SB	Secondary Cache line size: 0 → 4 words 1 → 8 words 2 → 16 words 3 → 32 words
SS	Split Secondary Cache Mode 0 → instruction and data mixed in secondary cache (joint cache) 1 → instruction and data separated by SCAddr(17)
SW	Secondary Cache port width 0 → 128-bit data path to S-cache 1 → Reserved
EW	System Port width 0 → 64-bit 1 → Reserved
SC	Secondary Cache present 0 → S-cache present 1 → no S-cache present

Table 4-12 (cont.) Config Register Fields

Field Name	Description
SM	Dirty Shared coherency state 0 → Dirty Shared coherency state is enabled 1 → Dirty Shared state is disabled
BE	BigEndianMem 0 → kernel and memory are little endian 1 → kernel and memory are big endian
EM	ECC mode enable 0 → ECC mode enabled 1 → parity mode enabled
EB	Block ordering 0 → sequential 1 → sub-block
0	Reserved. Must be written as zeroes, returns zeroes when read.
IC	Primary I-cache Size (I-cache size = 2^{12+IC} bytes). In the R4000 processor, this is set to 8 Kbytes; in the R4400 processor, this is set to 16 Kbytes.
DC	Primary D-cache Size (D-cache size = 2^{12+DC} bytes). In the R4000 processor, this is set to 8 Kbytes, in the R4400 processor, this is set to 16 Kbytes.
IB	Primary I-cache line size 0 → 16 bytes 1 → 32 bytes
DB	Primary D-cache line size 0 → 16 bytes 1 → 32 bytes
CU	Update on Store Conditional 0 → Store Conditional uses coherency algorithm specified by TLB 1 → SC uses cacheable coherent update on write
K0	*kseg0* coherency algorithm (see *EntryLo0* and *EntryLo1* registers)

Load Linked Address (LLAddr) Register (17)

The read/write *Load Linked Address* (*LLAddr*) register contains the physical address read by the most recent Load Linked instruction.

This register is for diagnostic purposes only, and serves no function during normal operation.

Figure 4-17 shows the format of the *LLAddr* register; *PAddr* represents bits of the physical address, PA(35:4).

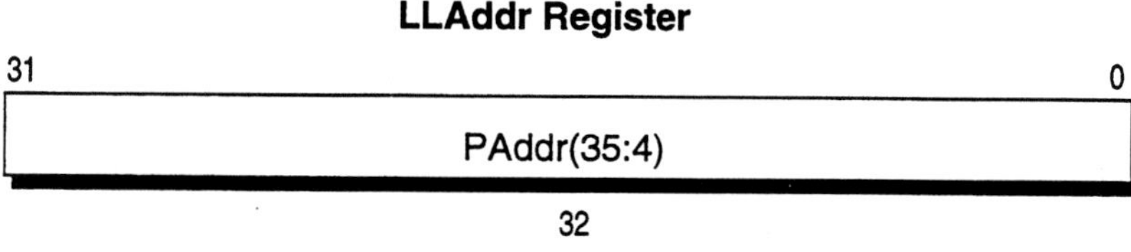

Figure 4-17 LLAddr Register Format

Cache Tag Registers [TagLo (28) and TagHi (29)]

The *TagLo* and *TagHi* registers are 32-bit read/write registers that hold either the primary cache tag and parity, or the secondary cache tag and ECC during cache initialization, cache diagnostics, or cache error processing. The *Tag* registers are written by the CACHE and MTC0 instructions.

The *P* and *ECC* fields of these registers are ignored on Index Store Tag operations. Parity and ECC are computed by the store operation.

Figure 4-18 shows the format of these registers for primary cache operations. Figure 4-19 shows the format of these registers for secondary cache operations.

Table 4-13 lists the field definitions of the *TagLo* and *TagHi* registers.

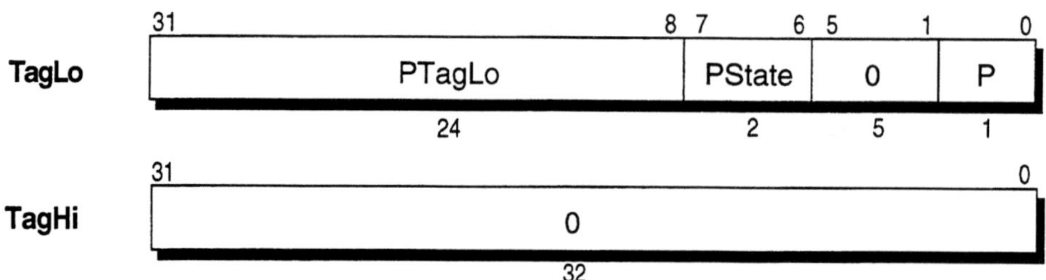

Figure 4-18 TagLo and TagHi Register (P-cache) Formats

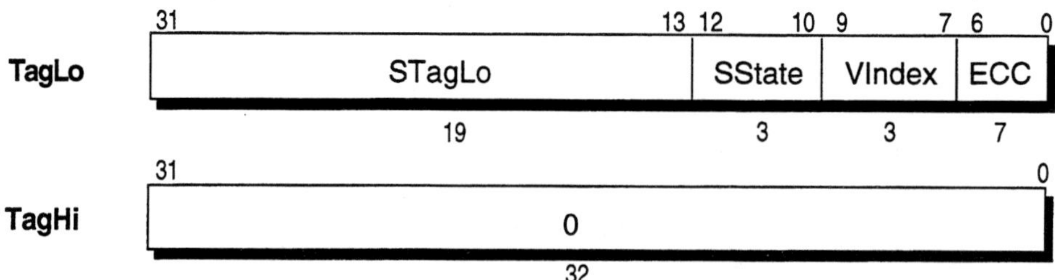

Figure 4-19 TagLo and TagHi Register (S-cache) Formats

Table 4-13 Cache Tag Register Fields

Field	Description
PTagLo	Specifies the physical address bits 35:12
PState	Specifies the primary cache state
P	Specifies the primary tag even parity bit
STagLo	Specifies the physical address bits 35:17
SState	Specifies the secondary cache state
VIndex	Specifies the virtual index of the associated Primary cache line, vAddr(14:12)
ECC	ECC for the *STag, SState,* and *VIndex* fields
0	Reserved. Must be written as zeroes; returns zeroes when read

Virtual-to-Physical Address Translation Process

During virtual-to-physical address translation, the CPU compares the 8-bit ASID (if the Global bit, *G*, is not set) of the virtual address to the ASID of the TLB entry to see if there is a match. One of the following comparisons are also made:

- In 32-bit mode, the highest 7-to-19 bits (depending upon the page size) of the virtual address are compared to the contents of the TLB virtual page number.
- In 64-bit mode, the highest 15-to-27 bits (depending upon the page size) of the virtual address are compared to the contents of the TLB virtual page number.

If a TLB entry matches, the physical address and access control bits (*C*, *D*, and *V*) are retrieved from the matching TLB entry. While the *V* bit of the entry must be set for a valid translation to take place, it is not involved in the determination of a matching TLB entry.

Figure 4-20 illustrates the TLB address translation process.

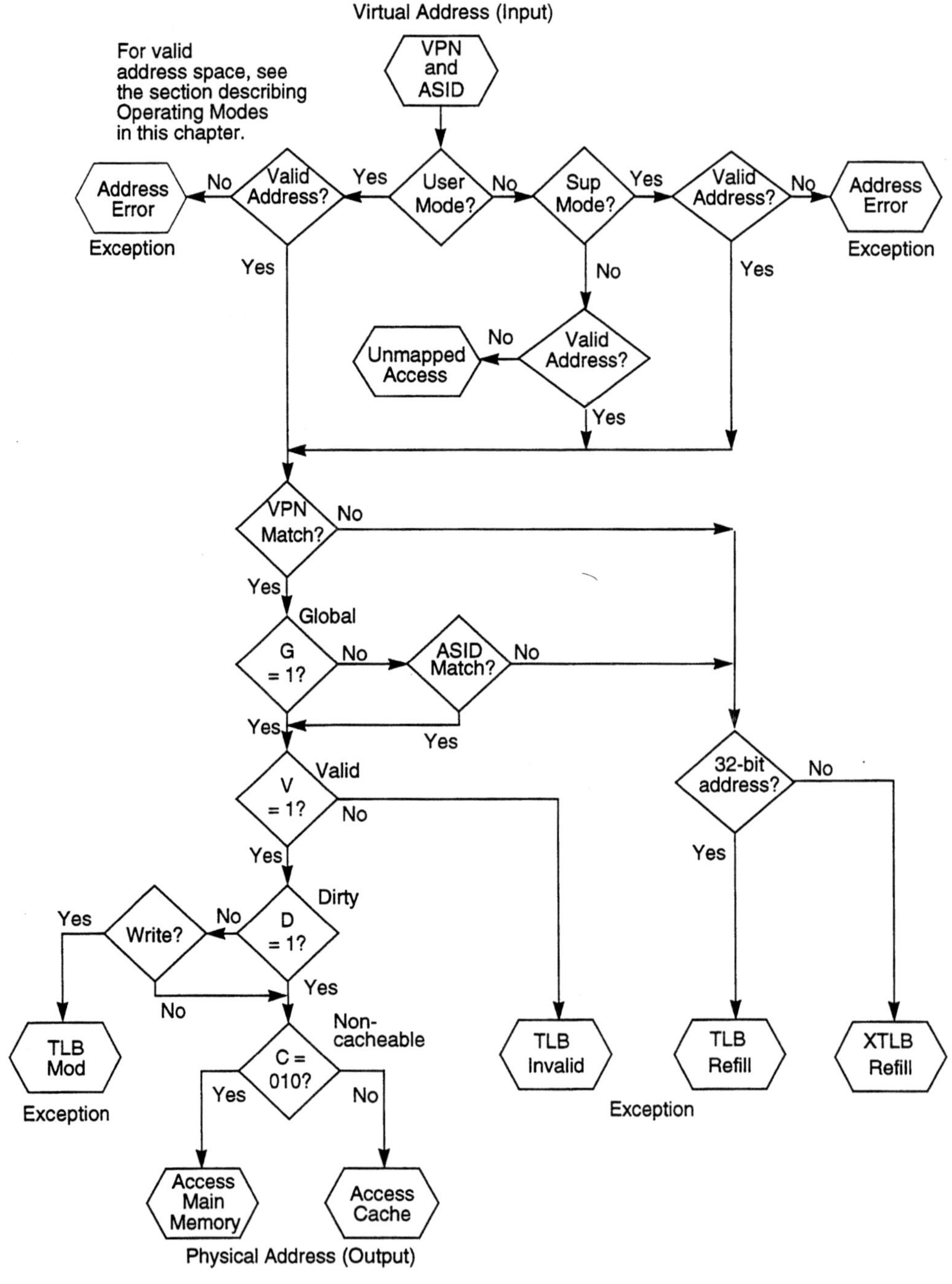

Figure 4-20 TLB Address Translation

TLB Misses

If there is no TLB entry that matches the virtual address, a TLB miss exception occurs.† If the access control bits (*D* and *V*) indicate that the access is not valid, a TLB modification or TLB invalid exception occurs. If the C bits equal 010_2, the physical address that is retrieved accesses main memory, bypassing the cache.

TLB Instructions

Table 4-14 lists the instructions that the CPU provides for working with the TLB. See Appendix A for a detailed description of these instructions.

Table 4-14 TLB Instructions

Op Code	Description of Instruction
TLBP	Translation Lookaside Buffer Probe
TLBR	Translation Lookaside Buffer Read
TLBWI	Translation Lookaside Buffer Write Index
TLBWR	Translation Lookaside Buffer Write Random

† TLB miss exceptions are described in Chapter 5.

CPU Exception Processing

5

This chapter describes the CPU exception processing, including an explanation of exception processing, followed by the format and use of each CPU exception register.

The chapter concludes with a description of each exception's cause, together with the manner in which the CPU processes and services these exceptions. For information about Floating-Point Unit exceptions, see Chapter 7.

5.1 How Exception Processing Works

The processor receives exceptions from a number of sources, including translation lookaside buffer (TLB) misses, arithmetic overflows, I/O interrupts, and system calls. When the CPU detects one of these exceptions, the normal sequence of instruction execution is suspended and the processor enters Kernel mode (see Chapter 4 for a description of system operating modes).

The processor then disables interrupts and forces execution of a software exception processor (called a *handler*) located at a fixed address. The handler saves the context of the processor, including the contents of the program counter, the current operating mode (User or Supervisor), and the status of the interrupts (enabled or disabled). This context is saved so it can be restored when the exception has been serviced.

When an exception occurs, the CPU loads the *Exception Program Counter* (*EPC*) register with a location where execution can restart after the exception has been serviced. The restart location in the *EPC* register is the address of the instruction that caused the exception or, if the instruction was executing in a branch delay slot, the address of the branch instruction immediately preceding the delay slot.

The registers described later in the chapter assist in this exception processing by retaining address, cause and status information.

For a description of the exception handling process, see the description of the individual exception contained in this chapter, or the flowcharts at the end of this chapter.

5.2 Exception Processing Registers

This section describes the CP0 registers that are used in exception processing. Table 5-1 lists these registers, along with their number—each register has a unique identification number that is referred to as its *register number*. For instance, the *ECC* register is register number 26. The remaining CP0 registers are used in memory management, as described in Chapter 4.

Software examines the CP0 registers during exception processing to determine the cause of the exception and the state of the CPU at the time the exception occurred. The registers in Table 5-1 are used in exception processing, and are described in the sections that follow.

Table 5-1 CP0 Exception Processing Registers

Register Name	Reg. No.
Context	4
BadVAddr (Bad Virtual Address)	8
Count	9
Compare register	11
Status	12
Cause	13
EPC (Exception Program Counter)	14
WatchLo (Memory Reference Trap Address Low)	18
WatchHi (Memory Reference Trap Address High)	19
XContext	20
ECC	26
CacheErr (Cache Error and Status)	27
ErrorEPC (Error Exception Program Counter)	30

Context Register (4)

The *Context* register is a read/write register containing the pointer to an entry in the page table entry (PTE) array; this array is an operating system data structure that stores virtual-to-physical address translations. When there is a TLB miss, the CPU loads the TLB with the missing translation from the PTE array. Normally, the operating system uses the *Context* register to address the current page map which resides in the kernel-mapped segment, *kseg3*. The *Context* register duplicates some of the information provided in the *BadVAddr* register, but the information is arranged in a form that is more useful for a software TLB exception handler. Figure 5-1 shows the format of the *Context* register; Table 5-2 describes the *Context* register fields.

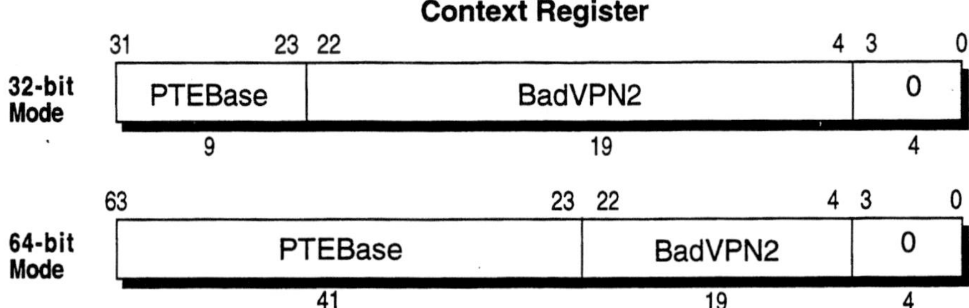

Figure 5-1 Context Register Format

Table 5-2 Context Register Fields

Field	Description
BadVPN2	This field is written by hardware on a miss. It contains the virtual page number (VPN) of the most recent virtual address that did not have a valid translation.
PTEBase	This field is a read/write field for use by the operating system. It is normally written with a value that allows the operating system to use the *Context* register as a pointer into the current PTE array in memory.

The 19-bit *BadVPN2* field contains bits 31:13 of the virtual address that caused the TLB miss; bit 12 is excluded because a single TLB entry maps to an even-odd page pair. For a 4-Kbyte page size, this format can directly address the pair-table of 8-byte PTEs. For other page and PTE sizes, shifting and masking this value produces the appropriate address.

Bad Virtual Address Register (BadVAddr) (8)

The Bad Virtual Address register (*BadVAddr*) is a read-only register that displays the most recent virtual address that caused one of the following exceptions: TLB Invalid, TLB Modified, TLB Refill, Virtual Coherency Data Access, or Virtual Coherency Instruction Fetch.

The processor does not write to the *BadVAddr* register when the *EXL* bit in the *Status* register is set to a 1.

Figure 5-2 shows the format of the *BadVAddr* register.

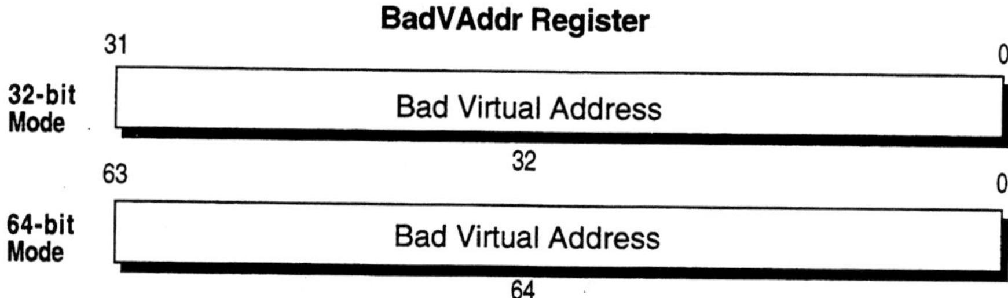

Figure 5-2 BadVAddr Register Format

Note: The *BadVAddr* register does not save any information for bus errors, since bus errors are not addressing errors.

Count Register (9)

The *Count* register acts as a timer, incrementing at a constant rate—half the maximum instruction issue rate—whether or not an instruction is executed, retired, or any forward progress is made through the pipeline.

This register can be read or written. It can be written for diagnostic purposes or system initialization; for example, to synchronize processors.

Figure 5-3 shows the format of the *Count* register.

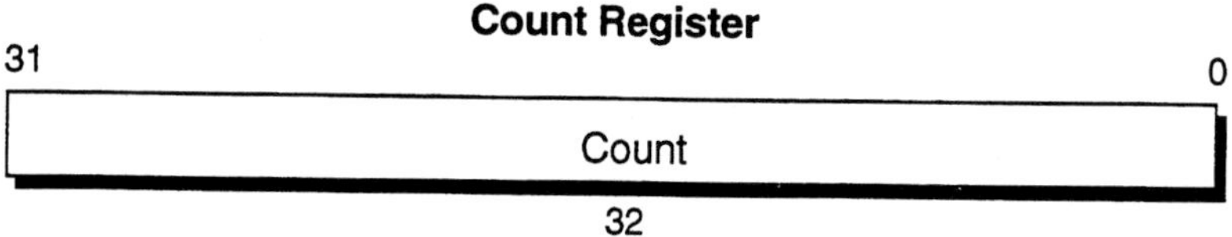

Figure 5-3 Count Register Format

Compare Register (11)

The *Compare* register acts as a timer (see also the *Count* register); it maintains a stable value that does not change on its own.

When the value of the *Count* register equals the value of the *Compare* register, interrupt bit *IP(7)* in the *Cause* register is set. This causes an interrupt as soon as the interrupt is enabled.

Writing a value to the *Compare* register, as a side effect, clears the timer interrupt.

For diagnostic purposes, the *Compare* register is a read/write register. In normal use however, the *Compare* register is write-only. Figure 5-4 shows the format of the *Compare* register.

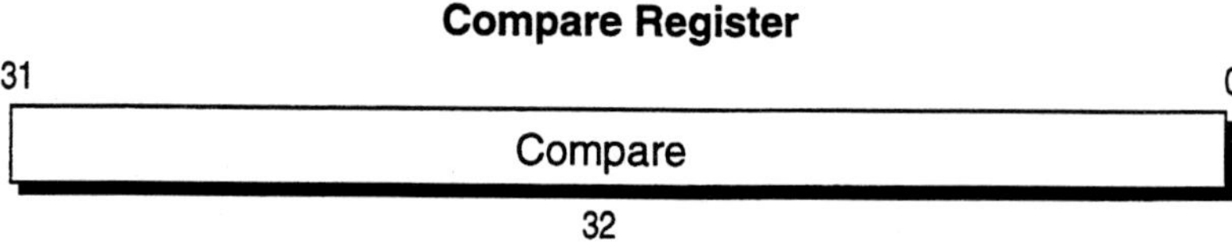

Figure 5-4 Compare Register Format

Status Register (12)

The *Status* register (SR) is a read/write register that contains the operating mode, interrupt enabling, and the diagnostic states of the processor. The following list describes the more important *Status* register fields; Figures 5-5 and 5-6 show the format of the entire register, including descriptions of the fields. Some of the important fields include:

- The 8-bit *Interrupt Mask* (*IM*) field controls the enabling of eight interrupt conditions. Interrupts must be enabled before they can be asserted, and the corresponding bits are set in both the *Interrupt Mask* field of the *Status* register and the *Interrupt Pending* field of the *Cause* register. For more information, refer to the *Interrupt Pending* (*IP*) field of the *Cause* register.
- The 4-bit *Coprocessor Usability* (*CU*) field controls the usability of 4 possible coprocessors. Regardless of the *CU0* bit setting, CP0 is always usable in Kernel mode.
- The 9-bit *Diagnostic Status* (*DS*) field is used for self-testing, and checks the cache and virtual memory system.
- The *Reverse-Endian (RE)* bit, bit 25, reverses the endianness of the machine. The processor can be configured as either little-endian or big-endian at system reset; reverse-endian selection is used in Kernel and Supervisor modes, and in the User mode when the *RE* bit is 0. Setting the *RE* bit to 1 inverts the User mode endianness.

Status Register Format

Figure 5-5 shows the format of the *Status* register. Table 5-3 describes the *Status* register fields. Figure 5-6 and Table 5-4 provide additional information on the *Diagnostic Status* (*DS*) field. All bits in the *DS* field except *TS* are readable and writable.

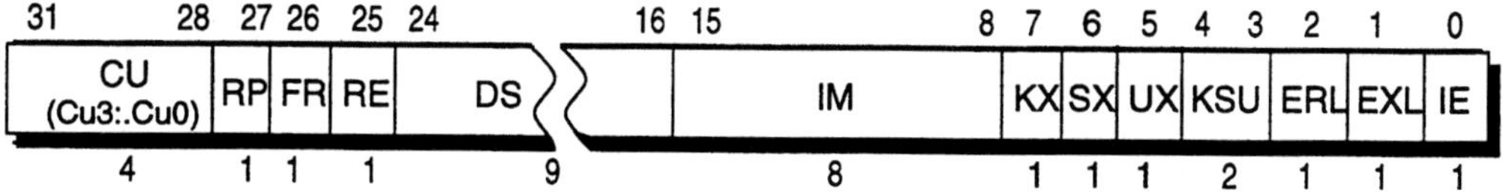

Figure 5-5 Status Register

Table 5-3 Status Register Fields

Field	Description
CU	Controls the usability of each of the four coprocessor unit numbers. CP0 is always usable when in Kernel mode, regardless of the setting of the CU_0 bit. 1 → usable 0 → unusable
RP	Enables reduced-power operation by reducing the internal clock frequency. The clock divisor is programmable at boot time. 0 → full speed 1→ reduced clock
FR	Enables additional floating-point registers 0 → 16 registers 1 → 32 registers
RE	*Reverse-Endian* bit, valid in User mode.
DS	*Diagnostic Status* field (see Figure 5-6).
IM	*Interrupt Mask*: controls the enabling of each of the external, internal, and software interrupts. An interrupt is taken if interrupts are enabled, and the corresponding bits are set in both the *Interrupt Mask* field of the *Status* register and the *Interrupt Pending* field of the *Cause* register. 0 → disabled 1→ enabled
KX	Enables 64-bit addressing in Kernel mode. The extended-addressing TLB refill exception is used for TLB misses on kernel addresses. 0 → 32–bit 1 → 64–bit
SX	Enables 64-bit addressing and operations in Supervisor mode. The extended-addressing TLB refill exception is used for TLB misses on supervisor addresses. 0 → 32–bit 1 → 64–bit

Table 5-3 (cont.) Status Register Fields

Field	Description
UX	Enables 64-bit addressing and operations in User mode. The extended-addressing TLB refill exception is used for TLB misses on user addresses. 0 → 32–bit 1 → 64–bit
KSU	Mode bits 10_2 → User 01_2 → Supervisor 00_2 → Kernel
ERL	Error Level 0 → normal 1 → error
EXL	Exception Level 0 → normal 1 → exception
IE	Interrupt Enable 0 → disable interrupts 1 → enables interrupts

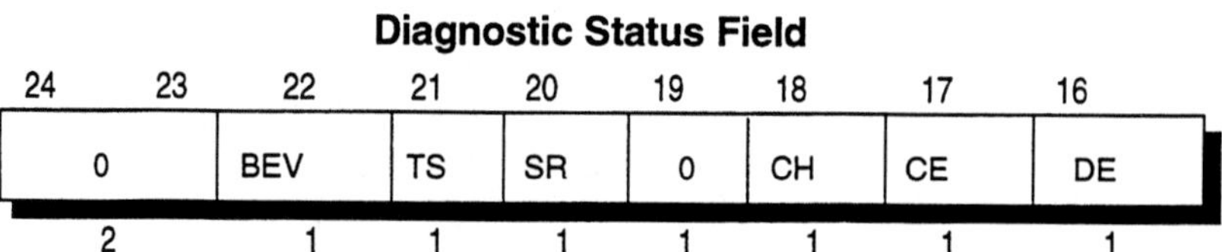

Figure 5-6 Status Register DS Field

Table 5-4 Status Register Diagnostic Status Bits

Bit	Description
BEV	Controls the location of TLB refill and general exception vectors. 0 → normal 1→ bootstrap
TS	1→ Indicates TLB shutdown has occurred (read-only).
SR	1→ Indicates a soft reset or NMI has occurred.
CH	Hit (tag match and valid state) or miss indication for last CACHE Hit Invalidate, Hit Write Back Invalidate, Hit Write Back, Hit Set Virtual, or Create Dirty Exclusive for a secondary cache. 0 → miss 1 → hit
CE	Contents of the ECC register set or modify the check bits of the caches when CE = 1; see description of the *ECC* register.
DE	Specifies that cache parity or ECC errors cannot cause exceptions. 0 → parity/ECC remain enabled 1 → disables parity/ECC
0	Reserved. Must be written as zeroes, and returns zeroes when read.

Status Register Modes and Access States

Fields of the *Status* register set the modes and access states described in the sections that follow.

Interrupt Enable: Interrupts are enabled when all of the following conditions are true:

- *IE* = 1
- *EXL* = 0
- *ERL* = 0

If these conditions are met, the settings of the *IM* bits identify the interrupt.

Operating Modes: The following CPU *Status* register bit settings are required for User, Kernel, and Supervisor modes (see Chapter 4 for more information about operating modes).

- The processor is in User mode when *KSU* = 10_2, *EXL* = 0, and *ERL* = 0.
- The processor is in Supervisor mode when *KSU* = 01_2, *EXL* = 0, and *ERL* = 0.
- The processor is in Kernel mode when *KSU* = 00_2, or *EXL* = 1, or *ERL* = 1.

32- and 64-bit Modes: The following CPU *Status* register bit settings select 32- or 64-bit operation for User, Kernel, and Supervisor operating modes. Enabling 64-bit operation permits the execution of 64-bit opcodes and translation of 64-bit addresses. 64-bit operation for User, Kernel and Supervisor modes can be set independently.

- 64-bit addressing for Kernel mode is enabled when *KX* = 1. 64-bit operations are always valid in Kernel mode.
- 64-bit addressing and operations are enabled for Supervisor mode when *SX* = 1.
- 64-bit addressing and operations are enabled for User mode when *UX* = 1.

Kernel Address Space Accesses: Access to the kernel address space is allowed when the processor is in Kernel mode.

Supervisor Address Space Accesses: Access to the supervisor address space is allowed when the processor is in Kernel or Supervisor mode, as described above in the section titled, Operating Modes: The following

CPU Status register bit settings are required for User, Kernel, and Supervisor modes (see Chapter 4 for more information about operating modes)..

User Address Space Accesses: Access to the user address space is allowed in any of the three operating modes.

Status Register Reset

The contents of the *Status* register are undefined at reset, except for the following bits in the *Diagnostic Status* field:

- *TS* = 0
- *ERL* and *BEV* = 1

The *SR* bit distinguishes between Reset and Soft Reset (Nonmaskable Interrupt [NMI]).

Cause Register (13)

The 32-bit read/write *Cause* register describes the cause of the most recent exception.

Figure 5-7 shows the fields of this register; Table 5-5 describes the *Cause* register fields. A 5-bit exception code (*ExcCode*) indicates one of the causes, as listed in Table 5-6.

All bits in the *Cause* register, with the exception of the *IP(1:0)* bits, are read-only; *IP(1:0)* are used for software interrupts.

Table 5-5 Cause Register Fields

Field	Description
BD	Indicates whether the last exception taken occurred in a branch delay slot. 1 → delay slot 0 → normal
CE	Coprocessor unit number referenced when a Coprocessor Unusable exception is taken.
IP	Indicates an interrupt is pending. 1 → interrupt pending 0 → no interrupt
ExcCode	Exception code field (see Table 5-6)
0	Reserved. Must be written as zeroes, and returns zeroes when read.

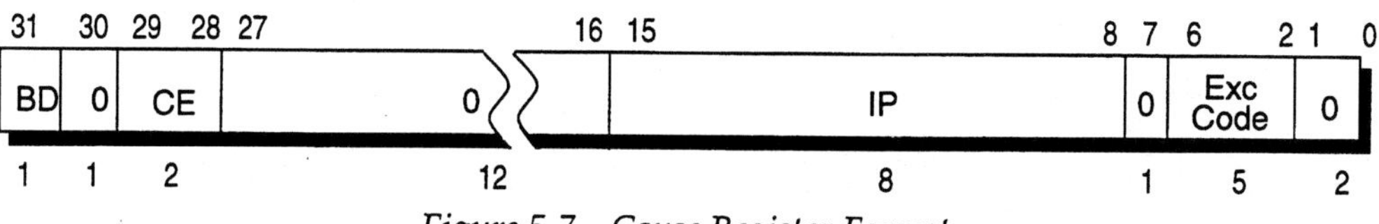

Figure 5-7 Cause Register Format

Table 5-6 Cause Register ExcCode Field

Exception Code Value	Mnemonic	Description
0	Int	Interrupt
1	Mod	TLB modification exception
2	TLBL	TLB exception (load or instruction fetch)
3	TLBS	TLB exception (store)
4	AdEL	Address error exception (load or instruction fetch)
5	AdES	Address error exception (store)
6	IBE	Bus error exception (instruction fetch)
7	DBE	Bus error exception (data reference: load or store)
8	Sys	Syscall exception
9	Bp	Breakpoint exception
10	RI	Reserved instruction exception
11	CpU	Coprocessor Unusable exception
12	Ov	Arithmetic Overflow exception
13	Tr	Trap exception
14	VCEI	Virtual Coherency Exception instruction
15	FPE	Floating-Point exception
16–22	–	Reserved
23	WATCH	Reference to *WatchHi*/*WatchLo* address
24–30	–	Reserved
31	VCED	Virtual Coherency Exception data

Exception Program Counter (EPC) Register (14)

The Exception Program Counter (*EPC*) is a read/write register that contains the address at which processing resumes after an exception has been serviced.

For synchronous exceptions, the *EPC* register contains either:

- the virtual address of the instruction that was the direct cause of the exception, or
- the virtual address of the immediately preceding branch or jump instruction (when the instruction is in a branch delay slot, and the *Branch Delay* bit in the *Cause* register is set).

The processor does not write to the *EPC* register when the *EXL* bit in the *Status* register is set to a 1.

Table 5-8 shows the format of the *EPC* register.

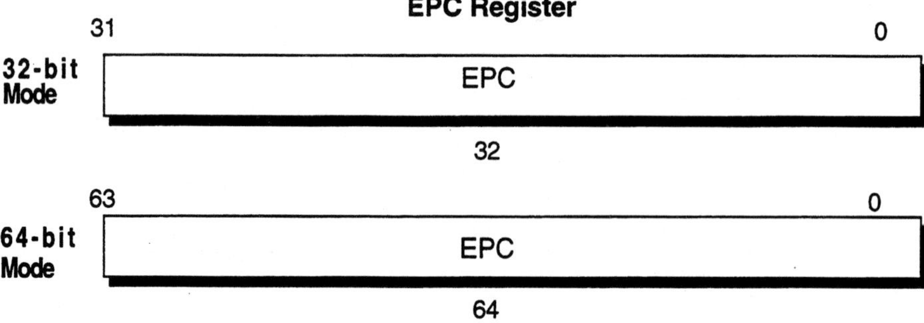

Figure 5-8 EPC Register Format

WatchLo (18) and WatchHi (19) Registers

R4000 processors provide a debugging feature to detect references to a selected physical address; load and store operations to the location specified by the *WatchLo* and *WatchHi* registers cause a Watch exception (described later in this chapter).

Figure 5-9 shows the format of the *WatchLo* and *WatchHi* registers; Table 5-7 describes the *WatchLo* and *WatchHi* register fields.

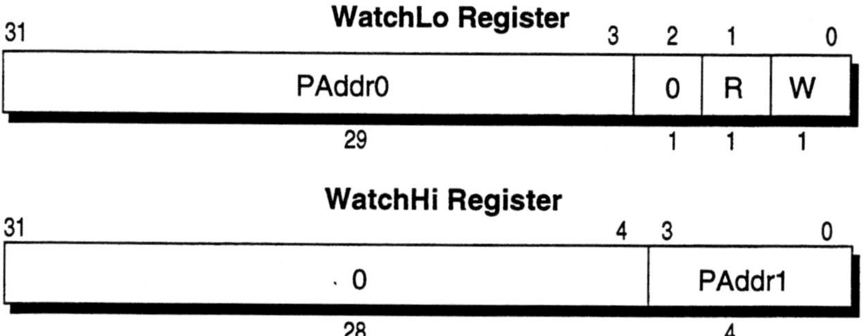

Figure 5-9 WatchLo and WatchHi Register Formats

Table 5-7 WatchHi and WatchLo Register Fields

Field	Description
PAddr1	Bits 35:32 of the physical address
PAddr0	Bits 31:3 of the physical address
R	Trap on load references if set to 1
W	Trap on store references if set to 1
0	Reserved. Must be written as zeroes, and returns zeroes when read.

XContext Register (20)

The read/write *XContext* register contains a pointer to an entry in the page table entry (PTE) array, an operating system data structure that stores virtual-to-physical address translations. When there is a TLB miss, the operating system software loads the TLB with the missing translation from the PTE array. The *XContext* register duplicates some of the information provided in the *BadVAddr* register, and puts it in a form useful for a software TLB exception handler. The *XContext* register is for use with the XTLB refill handler, which loads TLB entries for references to a 64-bit address space, and is included solely for operating system use. The operating system sets the PTE base field in the register, as needed. Normally, the operating system uses the *Context* register to address the current page map, which resides in the kernel-mapped segment *kseg3*. Figure 5-10 shows the format of the *XContext* register; Table 5-8 describes the *XContext* register fields.

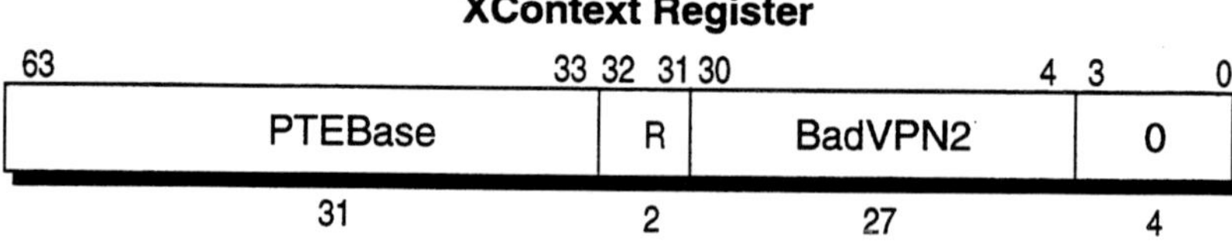

Figure 5-10 XContext Register Format

The 27-bit *BadVPN2* field has bits 39:13 of the virtual address that caused the TLB miss; bit 12 is excluded because a single TLB entry maps to an even-odd page pair. For a 4-Kbyte page size, this format may be used directly to address the pair-table of 8-byte PTEs. For other page and PTE sizes, shifting and masking this value produces the appropriate address.

Table 5-8 XContext Register Fields

Field	Description
BadVPN2	The *Bad Virtual Page Number/2* field is written by hardware on a miss. It contains the VPN of the most recent invalidly translated virtual address.
R	The *Region* field contains bits 63:62 of the virtual address. 00_2 = user 01_2 = supervisor 11_2 = kernel.
PTEBase	The *Page Table Entry Base* read/write field is normally written with a value that allows the operating system to use the *Context* register as a pointer into the current PTE array in memory.

Error Checking and Correcting (ECC) Register (26)

The 8-bit *Error Checking and Correcting* (*ECC*) register reads or writes either secondary-cache data ECC bits or primary-cache data parity bits for cache initialization, cache diagnostics, or cache error processing. (Tag ECC and parity are loaded from and stored to the *TagLo* register.)

The *ECC* register is loaded by the Index Load Tag CACHE operation. Content of the ECC register is:

- written into the primary data cache on store instructions (instead of the computed parity) when the *CE* bit of the *Status* register is set
- substituted for the computed instruction parity for the CACHE operation Fill
- XORed into the secondary cache computed ECC for the following primary data cache CACHE operations: Index Write Back Invalidate, Hit Write Back, and Hit Write Back Invalidate.

Figure 5-11 shows the format of the *ECC* register; Table 5-9 describes the register fields.

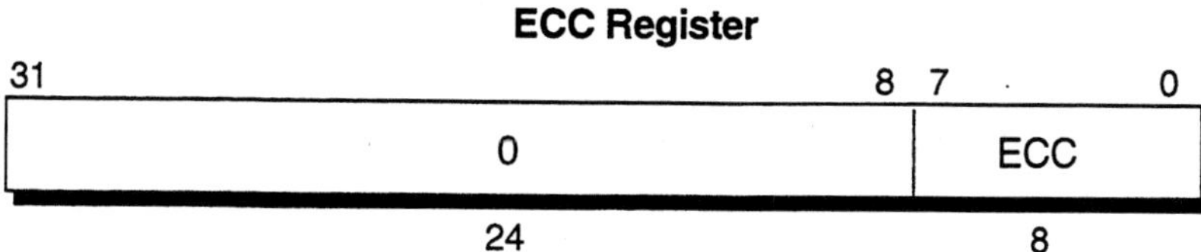

Figure 5-11 ECC Register Format

Table 5-9 ECC Register Fields

Field	Description
ECC	An 8-bit field specifying the ECC bits read from or written to a secondary cache, or the even byte parity bits to be read from or written to a primary cache.
0	Reserved. Must be written as zeroes, and returns zeroes when read.

Cache Error (CacheErr) Register (27)

The 32-bit read-only *CacheErr* register processes ECC errors in the secondary cache and parity errors in the primary cache. Parity errors cannot be corrected.

All single- and double-bit ECC errors in the secondary cache tag and data are detected; single-bit errors in the cache tag are automatically corrected. Single-bit ECC errors in the secondary cache data are not automatically corrected.

The *CacheErr* register holds cache index and status bits that indicate the source and nature of the error; it is loaded when a Cache Error exception is asserted.

Figure 5-12 shows the format of the *CacheErr* register and Table 5-10 describes the *CacheErr* register fields.

CacheErr Register

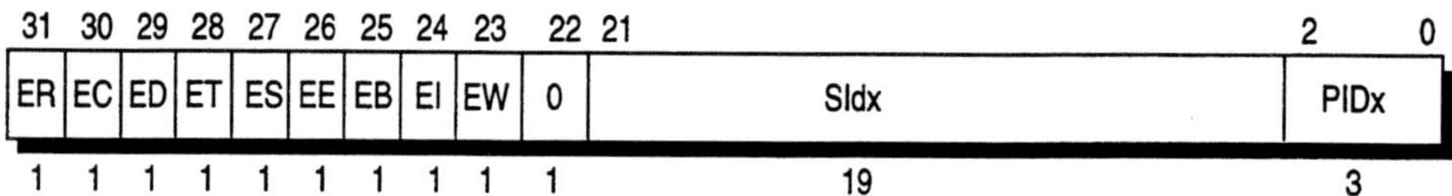

Figure 5-12 CacheErr Register Format

Table 5-10 CacheErr Register Fields

Field	Description
ER	Type of reference 0 → instruction 1 → data
EC	Cache level of the error 0 → primary 1 → secondary
ED	Indicates if a data field error occurred 0 → no error 1 → error
ET	Indicates if a tag field error occurred 0 → no error 1 → error

Table 5-10 (cont.) CacheErr Register Fields

Field	Description
ES	Indicates the error occurred while accessing primary or secondary cache in response to an external request. 0 → internal reference 1 → external reference
EE	This bit is set if the error occurred on the SysAD bus.
EB	This bit is set if a data error occurred in addition to the instruction error (indicated by the remainder of the bits). If so, this requires flushing the data cache after fixing the instruction error.
EI	This bit is set on a secondary data cache ECC error while refilling the primary cache on a store miss. The ECC handler must first do an Index Store Tag to invalidate the incorrect data from the primary data cache.
EW	This bit is only available on the R4400 processor. It is set on an multiprocessor cache error when the *CacheErr* register is already holding the values of a previous cache error. This bit could be set by the processor from the time the *CacheErr* register is loaded due to an error until the time that an ERET instruction is executed. Once the *EW* bit is set, it can only be cleared by a reset. The following errors set the *EW* bit: • Secondary cache tag errors arising from an external request (multibit errors only) • Secondary cache data errors arising from an external update • Primary cache tag errors arising from an external request • any external request, including intervention and snoop
SIdx	Bits pAddr(21:3) of the reference that encountered the error (which is not necessarily the same as the address of the doubleword in error, but is sufficient to locate that doubleword in the secondary cache).
PIdx	Bits vAddr(14:12) of the doubleword in error (used with *SIdx* to construct a virtual index for the primary caches).
0	Reserved. Must be written as zeroes, and returns zeroes when read.

Error Exception Program Counter (Error EPC) Register (30)

The *ErrorEPC* register is similar to the *EPC* register, except that *ErrorEPC* is used on ECC and parity error exceptions. It is also used to store the program counter (PC) on Reset, Soft Reset, and nonmaskable interrupt (NMI) exceptions.

The read/write *ErrorEPC* register contains the virtual address at which instruction processing can resume after servicing an error. This address can be:

- the virtual address of the instruction that caused the exception
- the virtual address of the immediately preceding branch or jump instruction, when this address is in a branch delay slot.

There is no branch delay slot indication for the *ErrorEPC* register.

Figure 5-13 shows the format of the *ErrorEPC* register.

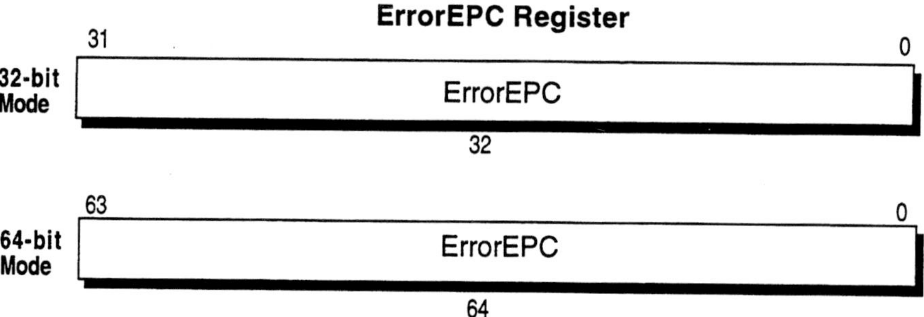

Figure 5-13 ErrorEPC Register Format

5.3 Processor Exceptions

This section describes the processor exceptions—it describes the cause of each exception, its processing by the hardware, and servicing by a handler (software). The types of exception, with exception processing operations, are described in the next section.

Exception Types

This section gives sample exception handler operations for the following exception types:

- reset
- soft reset
- nonmaskable interrupt (NMI)
- cache error
- remaining processor exceptions

When the *EXL* bit in the *Status* register is 0, either User or Supervisor operating mode is specified by the *KSU* bits in the *Status* register. When the *EXL* bit is a 1, the processor is in Kernel mode.

When the processor takes an exception, the *EXL* bit is set to 1, which means the system is in Kernel mode. After saving the appropriate state, the exception handler typically resets the *EXL* bit back to 0. When restoring the state and restarting, the handler sets the *EXL* bit back to 1.

Returning from an exception, also resets the *EXL* bit to 0 (see the ERET instruction in Appendix A).

In the following sections, sample hardware processes for various exceptions are shown, together with the servicing required by the handler (software).

Reset Exception Process

Figure 5-14 shows the Reset exception process.

```
T: undefined
   Random ← TLBENTRIES–1
   Wired ← 0
   Config <- CM || EC || EP || SB || SS || SW || EW || SC || SM || BE || EM || EB || 0 || 001
           || 001 || undefined⁶
   ErrorEPC ← PC
   SR ← SR31:23 || 1 || 0 || 0 || SR19:3 || 1 || SR1:0
   PC ← 0xBFC0 0000
```

Figure 5-14 Reset Exception Processing

Cache Error Exception Process

Figure 5-15 shows the Cache Error exception process.

```
T: ErrorEPC ← PC
   CacheErr ← ER || EC || ED || ET || ES || EE || EB || EI || 0² || SIdx || PIdx
   SR ← SR31:3 || 1 ||SR1:0
   if SR22 = 1 then
      PC ← 0xBFC0 0200 + 0x100
   else
      PC ← 0xA000 0000 + 0x100
   endif
```

Figure 5-15 Cache Error Exception Processing

Soft Reset and NMI Exception Process

Figure 5-16 shows the Soft Reset and NMI exception process.

```
T: ErrorEPC ← PC
   SR ← SR31:23 || 1 || 0 || 1 || SR19:3 || 1 || SR1:0
   PC ← 0xBFC0 0000
```

Figure 5-16 Soft Reset and NMI Exception Processing

General Exception Process

Figure 5-17 shows the process used for exceptions other than Reset, Soft Reset, NMI, and Cache Error.

```
T: Cause ← BD || 0 || CE || 0^12 || Cause15:8 || 0 || ExcCode || 0^2
   if SR1 = 0 then
      EPC ← PC
   endif
   SR ← SR31:2 || 1 || SR0
   if SR22 = 1 then
      PC ← 0xBFC0 0200 + vector
   else
      PC ← 0x8000 0000 + vector
   endif
```

Figure 5-17 General Exception Processing (Except Reset, Soft Reset, NMI, and Cache Error)

Exception Vector Locations

The Reset, Soft Reset, and NMI exceptions are always vectored to:

- location 0xBFC0 0000 in 32-bit mode
- location 0xFFFF FFFF BFC0 0000 in 64-bit mode

Addresses for all other exceptions are a combination of a *vector offset* and a *base address*. The base address is determined by the *BEV* bit of the *Status* register, as shown in Table 5-11. Table 5-12 shows the vector offset that is added to the base address to create the exception address.

Table 5-11 Exception Vector Base Addresses

BEV	**R4000 Processor Vector Base**	
	32-bit mode	**64-bit mode**
0	0x8000 0000	0xFFFF FFFF 8000 0000
1	0x BFC0 0200	0xFFFF FFFF BFC0 0200

Table 5-12 Exception Vector Offsets

Exception	**R4000 Processor Vector Offset**
TLB refill, EXL = 0	0x000
XTLB refill, EXL = 0 (X = 64-bit TLB)	0x080
Cache Error	0x100
Others	0x180

When *BEV* = 0, the vector base for the Cache Error exception changes from *kseg0* (0x8000 0000 in 32-bit mode, 0xFFFF FFFF 8000 0000 in 64-bit mode) to *kseg1* (0xA000 0000 in 32-bit mode, 0xFFFF FFFF A000 0000 in 64-bit mode). This indicates the caches are initialized and the vector can be cached.

When *BEV* = 1, the vector base for the Cache Error exception is 0xBFC0 0200 in 32-bit mode and 0xFFFF FFFF BFC0 0200 in 64-bit mode. This is an uncached and unmapped space, allowing the exception to bypass the cache and TLB.

Priority of Exceptions

The remainder of this chapter describes exceptions in the order of their priority shown in Table 5-13 with (certain of the exceptions, such as the TLB exceptions and Instruction/Data exceptions, grouped together for convenience). While more than one exception can occur for a single instruction, only the exception with the highest priority is reported.

Table 5-13 Exception Priority Order

Exception
Reset *(highest priority)*
Soft Reset
Nonmaskable Interrupt (NMI)
Address error — Instruction fetch
TLB refill — Instruction fetch
TLB invalid — Instruction fetch
Cache error — Instruction fetch
Virtual Coherency — Instruction fetch
Bus error — Instruction fetch
Integer overflow, Trap, System Call, Breakpoint, Reserved Instruction, Coprocessor Unusable, or Floating-Point Exception
Address error — Data access
TLB refill — Data access
TLB invalid — Data access
TLB modified — Data write
Cache error — Data access
Watch
Virtual Coherency — Data access
Bus error — Data access
Interrupt *(lowest priority)*

Generally speaking, the exceptions described in the following sections are handled ("processed") by hardware; these exceptions are then serviced by software.

Reset Exception

Cause

The Reset exception occurs when the **ColdReset***[†] signal is asserted and then deasserted. This exception is not maskable.

Processing

The CPU provides a special interrupt vector for this exception:

- location 0xBFC0 0000 in 32-bit mode
- location 0xFFFF FFFF BFC0 0000 in 64-bit mode

The Reset vector resides in unmapped and uncached CPU address space, so the hardware need not initialize the TLB or the cache to process this exception. It also means the processor can fetch and execute instructions while the caches and virtual memory are in an undefined state.

The contents of all registers in the CPU are undefined when this exception occurs, except for the following register fields:

- In the *Status* register, *SR* and *TS* are cleared to 0, and *ERL* and *BEV* are set to 1. All other bits are undefined.
- The *Random* register is initialized to the value of its upper bound.
- The *Wired* register is initialized to 0.

Reset exception processing is shown in Figure 5-14.

Servicing

The Reset exception is serviced by:

- initializing all processor registers, coprocessor registers, caches, and the memory system
- performing diagnostic tests
- bootstrapping the operating system

† In the following sections—indeed, throughout this book—a signal followed by an asterisk, such as **Reset***, is low active.

Soft Reset Exception

Cause

The Soft Reset exception occurs in response to the **Reset*** input signal, and execution begins at the Reset vector when **Reset*** is deasserted. This exception is not maskable.

Processing

The Reset exception vector is used for this exception, located within unmapped and uncached address space so that the cache and TLB need not be initialized to process this exception. When a Soft Reset occurs, the *SR* bit of the *Status* register is set to distinguish this exception from a Reset exception.

The primary purpose of the Soft Reset exception is to reinitialize the processor after a fatal error such as a Master/Checker mismatch. Unlike an NMI, all cache and bus state machines are reset by this exception. Like Reset, it can be used on the processor in any state; the caches, TLB, and normal exception vectors need not be properly initialized.

When this exception occurs, the contents of all registers are preserved except for:

- *ErrorEPC* register, which contains the restart PC
- *ERL* bit of the *Status* register, which is set to 1
- *SR* bit of the *Status* register, which is set to 1
- *BEV* bit of the *Status* register, which is set to 1

Because the Soft Reset can abort cache and bus operations, cache and memory state is undefined when this exception occurs.

Soft reset exception processing is shown in Figure 5-16.

Servicing

The Soft Reset exception is serviced by saving the current processor state for diagnostic purposes, and reinitializing for the Reset exception.

Nonmaskable Interrupt (NMI) Exception

Cause

The Nonmaskable Interrupt (NMI) exception occurs in response to the falling edge of the NMI pin, or an external write to the **Int*[6]** bit of the *Interrupt* register.

Unlike all other interrupts, this interrupt is not maskable; it occurs regardless of the settings of the *EXL*, *ERL*, and the *IE* bits in the *Status* register.

Processing

The Reset exception vector is used for this exception. This vector is located within unmapped and uncached address space so that the cache and TLB need not be initialized to process an NMI interrupt. When an NMI exception occurs, the *SR* bit of the *Status* register is set to differentiate this exception from a Reset exception.

Because an NMI can occur in the midst of another exception, it is not normally possible to continue program execution after servicing an NMI.

Unlike Reset and Soft Reset, but like other exceptions, NMI is taken only at instruction boundaries. The state of the caches and memory system are preserved by this exception.

When this exception occurs, the contents of all registers are preserved except for:

- *ErrorEPC* register, which contains the restart PC
- *ERL* bit of the *Status* register, which is set to 1
- *SR* bit of the *Status* register, which is set to 1
- *BEV* bit of the *Status* register, which is set to 1

NMI exception processing is shown in Figure 5-16.

Servicing

The NMI exception is serviced by saving the current processor state for diagnostic purposes, and reinitializing the system for the Reset exception.

Address Error Exception

Cause

The Address Error exception occurs when an attempt is made to execute one of the following:

- load or store a doubleword that is not aligned on a doubleword boundary
- load, fetch, or store a word that is not aligned on a word boundary
- load or store a halfword that is not aligned on a halfword boundary
- reference the kernel address space from User or Supervisor mode
- reference the supervisor address space from User mode

This exception is not maskable.

Processing

The common exception vector is used for this exception. The *AdEL* or *AdES* code in the *Cause* register is set, indicating whether the instruction caused the exception with an instruction reference, load operation, or store operation shown by the *EPC* register and *BD* bit in the *Cause* register.

When this exception occurs, the *BadVAddr* register retains the virtual address that was not properly aligned or referenced protected address space. The contents of the *VPN* field of the *Context* and *EntryHi* registers are undefined, as are the contents of the *EntryLo* register.

The *EPC* register contains the address of the instruction that caused the exception, unless this instruction is in a branch delay slot. If it is in a branch delay slot, the *EPC* register contains the address of the preceding branch instruction and the *BD* bit of the *Cause* register is set as indication.

Address Error exception processing is shown in Figure 5-17.

Servicing

The process executing at the time is handed a UNIX SIGSEGV (segmentation violation) signal. This error is usually fatal to the process incurring the exception.

TLB Exceptions

Three types of TLB exceptions can occur:

- TLB Refill occurs when there is no TLB entry that matches an attempted reference to a mapped address space.
- TLB Invalid occurs when a virtual address reference matches a TLB entry that is marked invalid.
- TLB Modified occurs when a store operation virtual address reference to memory matches a TLB entry which is marked valid but is not dirty (the entry is not writable).

The following three sections describe these TLB exceptions.

TLB Refill Exception

Cause

The TLB refill exception occurs when there is no TLB entry to match a reference to a mapped address space. This exception is not maskable.

Processing

There are two special exception vectors for this exception; one for references to 32-bit address spaces, and one for references to 64-bit address spaces. The *UX, SX,* and *KX* bits of the *Status* register determine whether the user, supervisor or kernel address spaces referenced are 32-bit or 64-bit spaces. All references use these vectors when the *EXL* bit is set to 0 in the *Status* register. This exception sets the *TLBL* or *TLBS* code in the *ExcCode* field of the *Cause* register. This code indicates whether the instruction, as shown by the *EPC* register and the *BD* bit in the *Cause* register, caused the miss by an instruction reference, load operation, or store operation.

When this exception occurs, the *BadVAddr, Context, XContext* and *EntryHi* registers hold the virtual address that failed address translation. The *EntryHi* register also contains the ASID from which the translation fault occurred. The *Random* register normally contains a valid location in which to place the replacement TLB entry. The contents of the *EntryLo* register are undefined. The *EPC* register contains the address of the instruction that caused the exception, unless this instruction is in a branch delay slot, in which case the *EPC* register contains the address of the preceding branch instruction and the *BD* bit of the *Cause* register is set.

TLB Refill exception processing is shown in Figure 5-17.

Servicing

To service this exception, the contents of the *Context* or *XContext* register are used as a virtual address to fetch memory locations containing the physical page frame and access control bits for a pair of TLB entries. The two entries are placed into the *EntryLo0/EntryLo1* register; the *EntryHi* and *EntryLo* registers are written into the TLB.

It is possible that the virtual address used to obtain the physical address and access control information is on a page that is not resident in the TLB. This condition is processed by allowing a TLB refill exception in the TLB refill handler. This second exception goes to the common exception vector because the *EXL* bit of the *Status* register is set.

TLB Invalid Exception

Cause

The TLB invalid exception occurs when a virtual address reference matches a TLB entry that is marked invalid (TLB valid bit cleared). This exception is not maskable.

Processing

The common exception vector is used for this exception. The *TLBL* or *TLBS* code in the *ExcCode* field of the *Cause* register is set. This indicates whether the instruction, as shown by the *EPC* register and *BD* bit in the *Cause* register, caused the miss by an instruction reference, load operation, or store operation.

When this exception occurs, the *BadVAddr*, *Context*, *XContext* and *EntryHi* registers contain the virtual address that failed address translation. The *EntryHi* register also contains the ASID from which the translation fault occurred. The *Random* register normally contains a valid location in which to put the replacement TLB entry. The contents of the *EntryLo* register are undefined.

The *EPC* register contains the address of the instruction that caused the exception unless this instruction is in a branch delay slot, in which case the *EPC* register contains the address of the preceding branch instruction and the *BD* bit of the *Cause* register is set.

TLB Invalid exception processing is shown in Figure 5-17.

Servicing

A TLB entry is typically marked invalid when one of the following is true:

- a virtual address does not exist
- the virtual address exists, but is not in main memory (a page fault)
- a trap is desired on any reference to the page (for example, to maintain a reference bit)

After servicing the cause of a TLB Invalid exception, the TLB entry is located with TLBP (TLB Probe), and replaced by an entry with that entry's *Valid* bit set.

TLB Modified Exception

Cause

The TLB modified exception occurs when a store operation virtual address reference to memory matches a TLB entry that is marked valid but is not dirty and therefore is not writable. This exception is not maskable.

Processing

The common exception vector is used for this exception, and the *Mod* code in the *Cause* register is set.

When this exception occurs, the *BadVAddr, Context, XContext* and *EntryHi* registers contain the virtual address that failed address translation. The *EntryHi* register also contains the ASID from which the translation fault occurred. The contents of the *EntryLo* register are undefined.

The *EPC* register contains the address of the instruction that caused the exception unless that instruction is in a branch delay slot, in which case the *EPC* register contains the address of the preceding branch instruction and the *BD* bit of the *Cause* register is set.

TLB Modified exception processing is shown in Figure 5-17.

Servicing

The kernel uses the failed virtual address or virtual page number to identify the corresponding access control information. The page identified may or may not permit write accesses; if writes are not permitted, a write protection violation occurs.

If write accesses are permitted, the page frame is marked dirty/writable by the kernel in its own data structures. The TLBP instruction places the index of the TLB entry that must be altered into the *Index* register. The *EntryLo* register is loaded with a word containing the physical page frame and access control bits (with the *D* bit set), and the *EntryHi* and *EntryLo* registers are written into the TLB.

Cache Error Exception

Cause

The Cache Error exception occurs when either a secondary cache ECC error or primary cache parity error is detected. This exception is maskable by the *DE* bit of the *Status* register.

Processing

The processor sets the *ERL* bit in the *Status* register, saves the exception restart address in *ErrorEPC* register, and then transfers to a special vector in uncached space. If the BEV bit = 0, the vector is one of the following:

- 0xA000 0100 in 32-bit mode
- 0xFFFF FFFF A000 0100 in 64-bit mode

If the BEV bit = 1, the vector is one of the following:

- 0xBFC0 0300 in 32-bit mode
- 0xFFFF FFFF BFC0 0300 in 64-bit mode

No other registers are changed.

Cache Error exception processing is shown in Figure 5-15.

Servicing

All errors should be logged. To correct single-bit ECC errors in the secondary cache, the system uses the CACHE instruction. Execution then resumes through an ERET instruction.

To correct cache parity errors and non-single-bit ECC errors in unmodified cache blocks, the system uses the CACHE instruction to invalidate the cache block, overwrites the old data through a cache miss, and resumes execution with an ERET.

Other errors are not correctable and are likely to be fatal to the current process.

Virtual Coherency Exception

Cause

A Virtual Coherency exception occurs when one of the following conditions is true:

- a primary cache miss hits in the secondary cache
- bits 14:12 of the virtual address were not equal to the corresponding bits of the *PIdx* field of the secondary cache tag
- the cache algorithm for the page (from the C field in the TLB) specifies that the page is cached

This exception is not maskable.

Processing

The common exception vector is used for this exception.

The *VCEI* or *VCED* code in the *Cause* register is set for instruction and data cache misses respectively.

The *BadVAddr* register holds the virtual address that caused the exception.

Virtual Coherency exception processing is shown in Figure 5-17.

Servicing

The CACHE instruction determines the previous virtual index, removes the data from the primary caches at the previous virtual index, and writes the *PIdx* field of the secondary cache with a new virtual index. Once this process is complete, the program is continued.

Software can avoid the cost of this exception by using consistent virtual primary cache indexes to access the same physical data.

Bus Error Exception

Cause

A Bus Error exception is raised by board-level circuitry for events such as bus time-out, backplane bus parity errors, and invalid physical memory addresses or access types. This exception is not maskable.

A Bus Error exception occurs only when a cache miss refill, uncached reference, or unbuffered write occurs synchronously; a Bus Error exception resulting from a buffered write transaction must be reported using the general interrupt mechanism.

Processing

The common interrupt vector is used for a Bus Error exception. The *IBE* or *DBE* code in the *ExcCode* field of the *Cause* register is set, signifying whether the instruction (as indicated by the *EPC* register and *BD* bit in the *Cause* register) caused the exception by an instruction reference, load operation, or store operation.

The *EPC* register contains the address of the instruction that caused the exception, unless it is in a branch delay slot, in which case the *EPC* register contains the address of the preceding branch instruction and the *BD* bit of the *Cause* register is set. Bus Error processing is shown in Figure 5-17.

Servicing

The physical address at which the fault occurred can be computed from information available in the CP0 registers.

- If the *IBE* code in the *Cause* register is set (indicating an instruction fetch reference), the virtual address is contained in the *EPC* register.
- If the *DBE* code is set (indicating a load or store reference), the instruction that caused the exception is located at the virtual address contained in the *EPC* register (or 4+ the contents of the *EPC* register if the *BD* bit of the *Cause* register is set).

The virtual address of the load and store reference can then be obtained by interpreting the instruction. The physical address can be obtained by using the TLBP instruction and reading the *EntryLo* register to compute the physical page number.

The process executing at the time of this exception is handed a UNIX SIGBUS (bus error) signal, which is usually fatal.

Integer Overflow Exception

Cause

An Integer Overflow exception occurs when an ADD, ADDI, SUB, DADD, DADDI or DSUB† instruction results in a 2's complement overflow. This exception is not maskable.

Processing

The common exception vector is used for this exception, and the *OV* code in the *Cause* register is set.

The *EPC* register contains the address of the instruction that caused the exception unless the instruction is in a branch delay slot, in which case the *EPC* register contains the address of the preceding branch instruction and the *BD* bit of the *Cause* register is set.

Integer Overflow exception processing is shown in Figure 5-17.

Servicing

The process executing at the time of the exception is handed a UNIX SIGFPE/FPE_INTOVF_TRAP (floating-point exception/integer overflow) signal. This error is usually fatal to the current process.

† See Appendix A for a description of these instructions.

Trap Exception

Cause

The Trap exception occurs when a TGE, TGEU, TLT, TLTU, TEQ, TNE, TGEI, TGEUI, TLTI, TLTUI, TEQI, or TNEI† instruction results in a TRUE condition. This exception is not maskable.

Processing

The common exception vector is used for this exception, and the *Tr* code in the *Cause* register is set.

The *EPC* register contains the address of the instruction causing the exception unless the instruction is in a branch delay slot, in which case the *EPC* register contains the address of the preceding branch instruction and the *BD* bit of the *Cause* register is set.

Trap exception processing is shown in Figure 5-17.

Servicing

The process executing at the time of a Trap exception is handed a UNIX SIGFPE/FPE_INTOVF_TRAP (floating-point exception/integer overflow) signal. This error is usually fatal.

† See Appendix A for a description of these instructions.

System Call Exception

Cause

A System Call exception occurs during an attempt to execute the SYSCALL instruction. This exception is not maskable.

Processing

The common exception vector is used for this exception, and the *Sys* code in the *Cause* register is set.

The *EPC* register contains the address of the SYSCALL instruction unless it is in a branch delay slot, in which case the *EPC* register contains the address of the preceding branch instruction.

If the SYSCALL instruction is in a branch delay slot, the *BD* bit of the *Status* register is set; otherwise this bit is cleared.

System Call exception processing is shown in Figure 5-17.

Servicing

When this exception occurs, control is transferred to the applicable system routine.

To resume execution, the *EPC* register must be altered so that the SYSCALL instruction does not re-execute; this is accomplished by adding a value of 4 to the *EPC* register (*EPC* register + 4) before returning.

If a SYSCALL instruction is in a branch delay slot, a more complicated algorithm, beyond the scope of this description, may be required.

Breakpoint Exception

Cause

A Breakpoint exception occurs when an attempt is made to execute the BREAK instruction. This exception is not maskable.

Processing

The common exception vector is used for this exception, and the *BP* code in the *Cause* register is set.

The *EPC* register contains the address of the BREAK instruction unless it is in a branch delay slot, in which case the *EPC* register contains the address of the preceding branch instruction.

If the BREAK instruction is in a branch delay slot, the *BD* bit of the *Status* register is set, otherwise the bit is cleared.

Breakpoint exception processing is shown in Figure 5-17.

Servicing

When the Breakpoint exception occurs, control is transferred to the applicable system routine. Additional distinctions can be made by analyzing the unused bits of the BREAK instruction (bits 25:6), and loading the contents of the instruction whose address the *EPC* register contains. A value of 4 must be added to the contents of the *EPC* register (*EPC* register + 4) to locate the instruction if it resides in a branch delay slot.

To resume execution, the *EPC* register must be altered so that the BREAK instruction does not re-execute; this is accomplished by adding a value of 4 to the *EPC* register (*EPC* register + 4) before returning.

If a BREAK instruction is in a branch delay slot, interpretation of the branch instruction is required to resume execution.

Reserved Instruction Exception

Cause

The Reserved Instruction exception occurs when one of the following conditions occurs:

- an attempt is made to execute an instruction with an undefined major opcode (bits 31:26)
- an attempt is made to execute a SPECIAL instruction with an undefined minor opcode (bits 5:0)
- an attempt is made to execute a REGIMM instruction with an undefined minor opcode (bits 20:16)
- an attempt is made to execute 64-bit operations in 32-bit mode when in User or Supervisor modes

64-bit operations are always valid in Kernel mode regardless of the value of the *KX* bit in the *Status* register.

This exception is not maskable.

Reserved Instruction exception processing is shown in Figure 5-17.

Processing

The common exception vector is used for this exception, and the *RI* code in the *Cause* register is set.

The *EPC* register contains the address of the reserved instruction unless it is in a branch delay slot, in which case the *EPC* register contains the address of the preceding branch instruction.

Servicing

No instructions in the MIPS ISA are currently interpreted. The process executing at the time of this exception is handed a UNIX SIGILL/ILL_RESOP_FAULT (illegal instruction/reserved operand fault) signal. This error is usually fatal.

Coprocessor Unusable Exception

Cause

The Coprocessor Unusable exception occurs when an attempt is made to execute a coprocessor instruction for either:

- a corresponding coprocessor unit that has not been marked usable, or
- CP0 instructions, when the unit has not been marked usable and the process executes in User mode.

This exception is not maskable.

Processing

The common exception vector is used for this exception, and the *CPU* code in the *Cause* register is set. The contents of the *Coprocessor Usage Error* field of the coprocessor *Control* register indicate which of the four coprocessors was referenced. The *EPC* register contains the address of the unusable coprocessor instruction unless it is in a branch delay slot, in which case the *EPC* register contains the address of the preceding branch instruction.

Coprocessor Unusable exception processing is shown in Figure 5-17.

Servicing

The coprocessor unit to which an attempted reference was made is identified by the Coprocessor Usage Error field, which results in one of the following situations:

- If the process is entitled access to the coprocessor, the coprocessor is marked usable and the corresponding user state is restored to the coprocessor.
- If the process is entitled access to the coprocessor, but the coprocessor does not exist or has failed, interpretation of the coprocessor instruction is possible.
- If the *BD* bit is set in the *Cause* register, the branch instruction must be interpreted; then the coprocessor instruction can be emulated and execution resumed with the *EPC* register advanced past the coprocessor instruction.
- If the process is not entitled access to the coprocessor, the process executing at the time is handed a UNIX SIGILL/ ILL_PRIVIN_FAULT (illegal instruction/privileged instruction fault) signal. This error is usually fatal.

Floating-Point Exception

Cause

The Floating-Point exception is used by the floating-point coprocessor. This exception is not maskable.

Processing

The common exception vector is used for this exception, and the *FPE* code in the *Cause* register is set.

The contents of the *Floating-Point Control/Status* register indicate the cause of this exception.

Floating-Point exception processing is shown in Figure 5-17.

Servicing

This exception is cleared by clearing the appropriate bit in the *Floating-Point Control/Status* register.

For an unimplemented instruction exception, the kernel should emulate the instruction; for other exceptions, the kernel should pass the exception to the user program that caused the exception.

Watch Exception

Cause

A Watch exception occurs when a load or store instruction references the physical address specified in the *WatchLo*/*WatchHi* System Control Coprocessor (CP0) registers. The *WatchLo* register specifies whether a load or store initiated this exception.

The CACHE instruction never causes a Watch exception.

The Watch exception is postponed if the *EXL* bit is set in the *Status* register, and Watch is only maskable by setting the *EXL* bit in the *Status* register.

Processing

The common exception vector is used for this exception, and the *Watch* code in the *Cause* register is set.

Watch exception processing is shown in Figure 5-17.

Servicing

The Watch exception is a debugging aid; typically the exception handler transfers control to a debugger, allowing the user to examine the situation.

To continue, the Watch exception must be disabled to execute the faulting instruction. The Watch exception must then be reenabled. The faulting instruction can be executed either by interpretation or by setting breakpoints.

Interrupt Exception

Cause

The Interrupt exception occurs when one of the eight interrupt conditions is asserted. The significance of these interrupts is dependent upon the specific system implementation.

Each of the eight interrupts can be masked by clearing the corresponding bit in the *Int-Mask* field of the *Status* register, and all of the eight interrupts can be masked at once by clearing the *IE* bit of the *Status* register.

Processing

The common exception vector is used for this exception, and the *Int* code in the *Cause* register is set.

The *IP* field of the *Cause* register indicates current interrupt requests. It is possible that more than one of the bits can be simultaneously set (or even *no* bits may be set) if the interrupt is asserted and then deasserted before this register is read.

Interrupt exception processing is shown in Figure 5-17.

Servicing

If the interrupt is caused by one of the two software-generated exceptions (*SW1* or *SW0*), the interrupt condition is cleared by setting the corresponding *Cause* register bit to 0.

If the interrupt is hardware-generated, the interrupt condition is cleared by correcting the condition causing the interrupt pin to be asserted.

5.4 Exception Handling and Servicing Flowcharts

The remainder of this chapter contains flowcharts for the following exceptions and guidelines for their handlers:

- general exceptions and their exception handler
- TLB/XTLB miss exception and their exception handler
- cache error exception and its handler
- reset, soft reset and NMI exceptions, and a guideline to their handler.

Generally speaking, the exceptions are handled by hardware (HW); the exceptions are then serviced by software (SW).

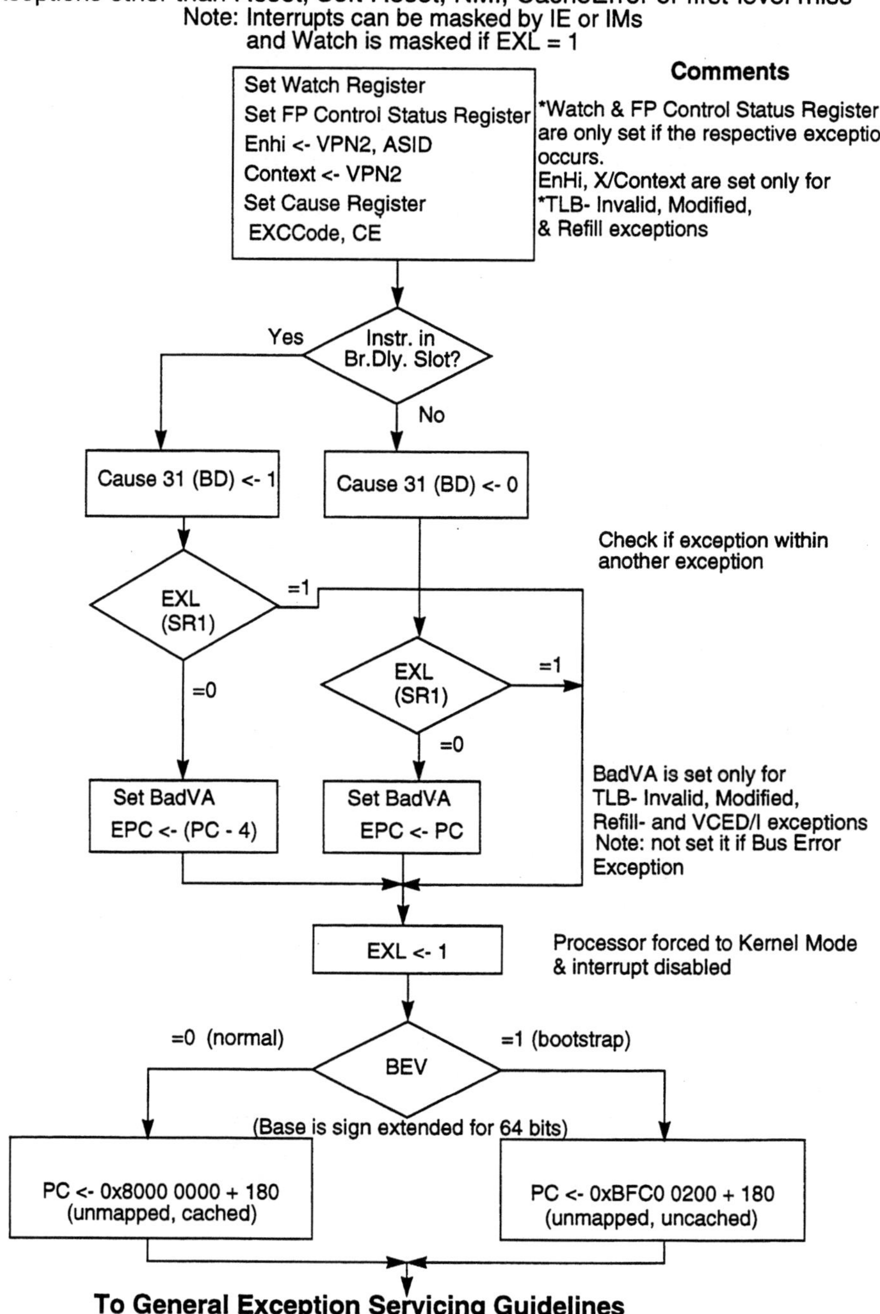
Exceptions other than Reset, Soft Reset, NMI, CacheError or first-level miss
Note: Interrupts can be masked by IE or IMs
and Watch is masked if EXL = 1
Comments
Set Watch Register
Set FP Control Status Register
Enhi <- VPN2, ASID
Context <- VPN2
Set Cause Register
EXCCode, CE
*Watch & FP Control Status Register are only set if the respective exception occurs.
EnHi, X/Context are set only for
*TLB- Invalid, Modified,
& Refill exceptions
Yes
Instr. in Br.Dly. Slot?
No
Cause 31 (BD) <- 1
Cause 31 (BD) <- 0
Check if exception within another exception
EXL (SR1)
=1
EXL (SR1)
=1
=0
=0
Set BadVA
EPC <- (PC - 4)
Set BadVA
EPC <- PC
BadVA is set only for
TLB- Invalid, Modified,
Refill- and VCED/I exceptions
Note: not set it if Bus Error Exception
EXL <- 1
Processor forced to Kernel Mode & interrupt disabled
=0 (normal)
BEV
=1 (bootstrap)
(Base is sign extended for 64 bits)
PC <- 0x8000 0000 + 180
(unmapped, cached)
PC <- 0xBFC0 0200 + 180
(unmapped, uncached)
To General Exception Servicing Guidelines

Figure 5-18 General Exception Handler (HW)

Comments

MFC0 -
X/Context
EPC
Status
Cause

* Unmapped vector so TLBMod, TLBInv, TLB Refill exceptions not possible
* EXL=1 so Watch, Interrupt exceptions disabled
* OS/System to avoid all other exceptions
* Only CacheError, Reset, Soft Reset, NMI exceptions possible.

MTC0 -
(Set Status Bits:)
KSU<- 00
EXL <- 0
& IE=1

(optional - only to enable Interrupts while keeping Kernel Mode)

Check CAUSE REG. & Jump to appropriate Service Code

* After EXL=0, all exceptions allowed. (except interrupt if masked by IE or IM and CacheError if masked by DE)

Status bit 21(TS)

=1 → Reset the processor

=0 ↓

Optional: Check only if 2nd-level TLB miss

Service Code

EXL = 1

MTC0 -
EPC
STATUS

ERET

* ERET is not allowed in the branch delay slot of another Jump Instruction
* Processor does not execute the instruction which is in the ERET's branch delay slot
* PC <- EPC; EXL <- 0
* LLbit <- 0

Figure 5-19 General Exception Servicing Guidelines (SW)

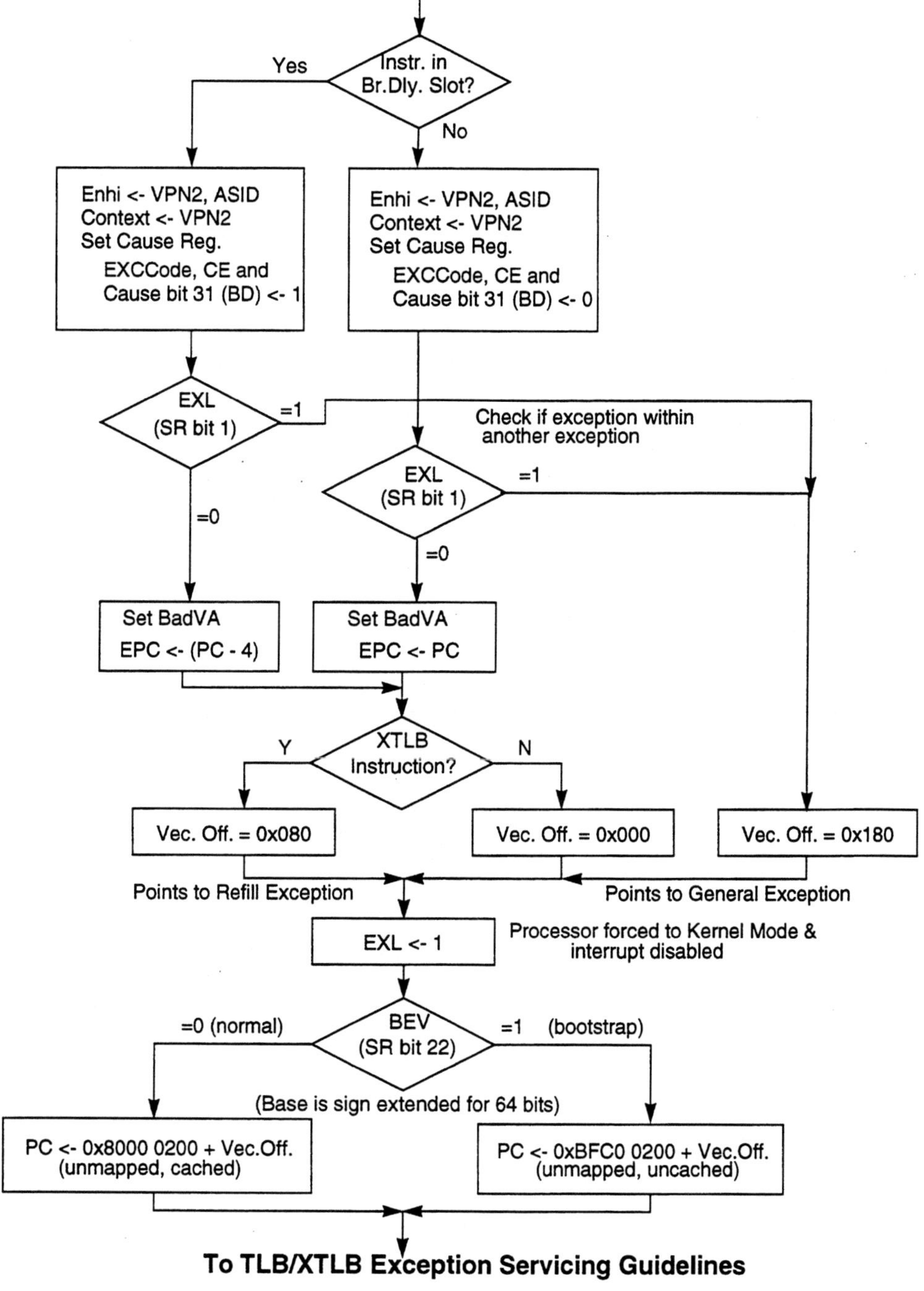
Yes
Instr. in
Br.Dly. Slot?
No
Enhi <- VPN2, ASID
Context <- VPN2
Set Cause Reg.
EXCCode, CE and
Cause bit 31 (BD) <- 1
Enhi <- VPN2, ASID
Context <- VPN2
Set Cause Reg.
EXCCode, CE and
Cause bit 31 (BD) <- 0
EXL
(SR bit 1)
=1
Check if exception within
another exception
EXL
(SR bit 1)
=1
=0
=0
Set BadVA
EPC <- (PC - 4)
Set BadVA
EPC <- PC
Y
XTLB
Instruction?
N
Vec. Off. = 0x080
Vec. Off. = 0x000
Vec. Off. = 0x180
Points to Refill Exception
Points to General Exception
EXL <- 1
Processor forced to Kernel Mode &
interrupt disabled
=0 (normal)
BEV
(SR bit 22)
=1 (bootstrap)
(Base is sign extended for 64 bits)
PC <- 0x8000 0200 + Vec.Off.
(unmapped, cached)
PC <- 0xBFC0 0200 + Vec.Off.
(unmapped, uncached)
To TLB/XTLB Exception Servicing Guidelines

Figure 5-20 TLB/XTLB Miss Exception Handler (HW)

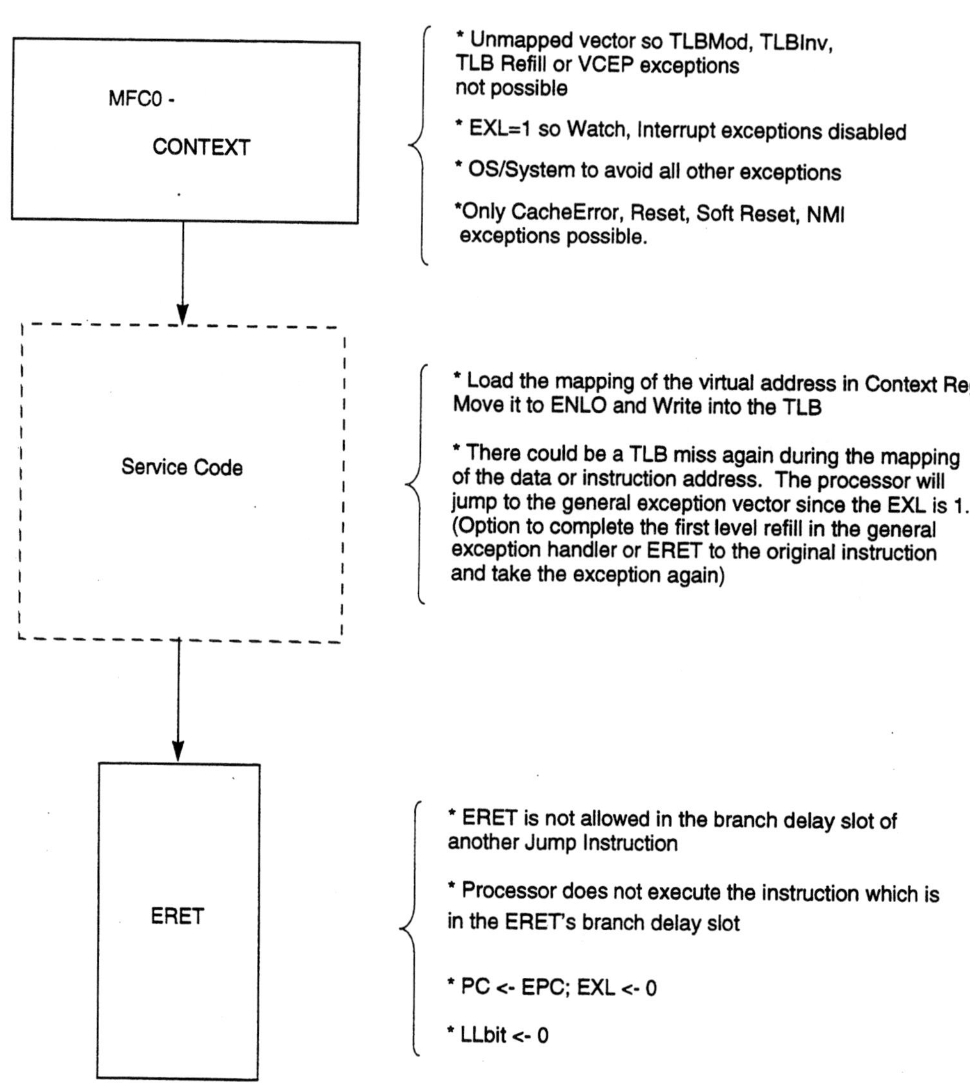

Comments
MFC0 -
CONTEXT
* Unmapped vector so TLBMod, TLBInv, TLB Refill or VCEP exceptions not possible
* EXL=1 so Watch, Interrupt exceptions disabled
* OS/System to avoid all other exceptions
*Only CacheError, Reset, Soft Reset, NMI exceptions possible.
Service Code
* Load the mapping of the virtual address in Context Reg. Move it to ENLO and Write into the TLB
* There could be a TLB miss again during the mapping of the data or instruction address. The processor will jump to the general exception vector since the EXL is 1. (Option to complete the first level refill in the general exception handler or ERET to the original instruction and take the exception again)
ERET
* ERET is not allowed in the branch delay slot of another Jump Instruction
* Processor does not execute the instruction which is in the ERET's branch delay slot
* PC <- EPC; EXL <- 0
* LLbit <- 0

Figure 5-21 TLB/XTLB Exception Servicing Guidelines (SW)

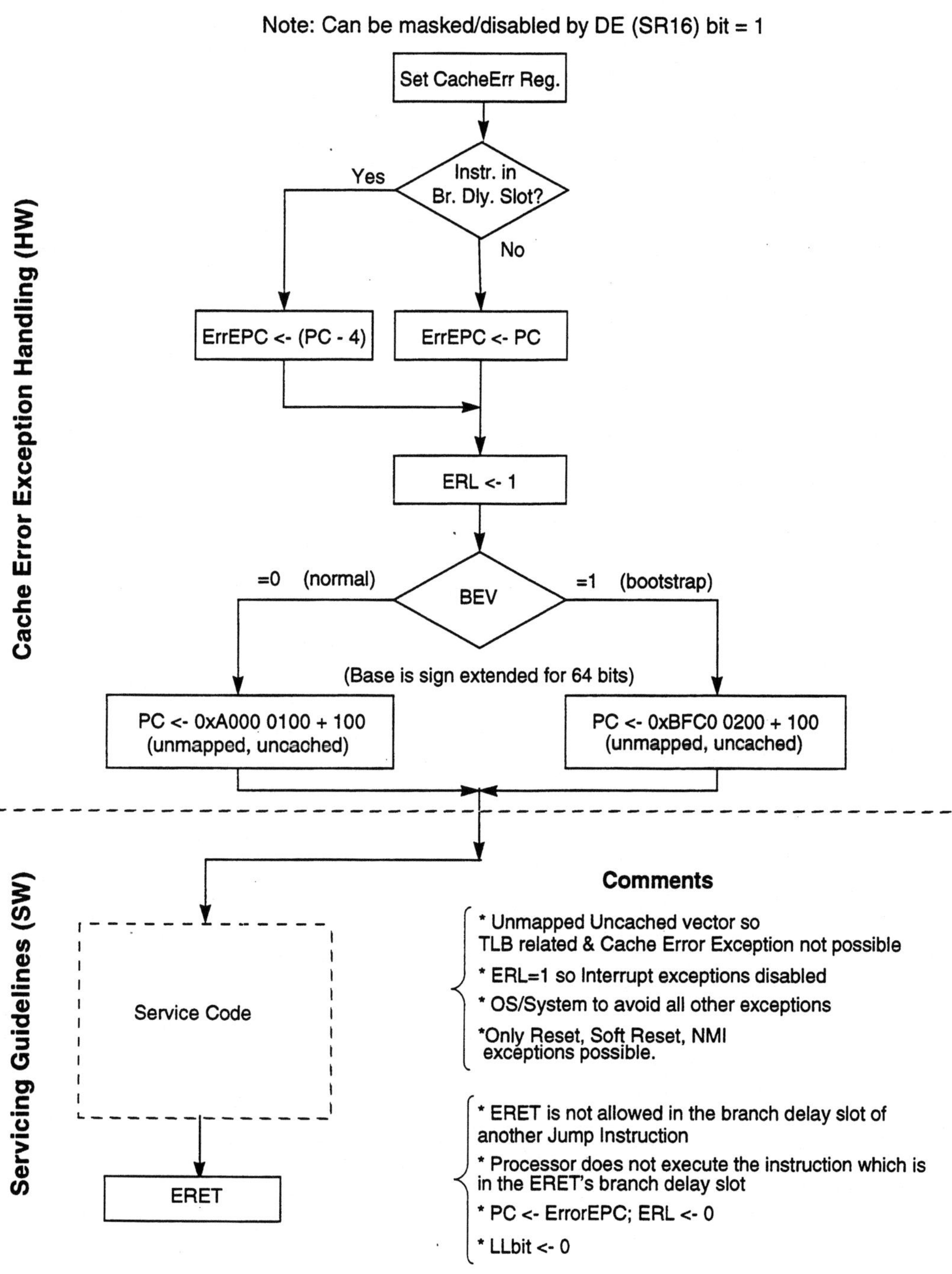
Note: Can be masked/disabled by DE (SR16) bit = 1
Cache Error Exception Handling (HW)
Set CacheErr Reg.
Instr. in Br. Dly. Slot?
Yes
No
ErrEPC <- (PC - 4)
ErrEPC <- PC
ERL <- 1
BEV
=0 (normal)
=1 (bootstrap)
(Base is sign extended for 64 bits)
PC <- 0xA000 0100 + 100 (unmapped, uncached)
PC <- 0xBFC0 0200 + 100 (unmapped, uncached)
Servicing Guidelines (SW)
Service Code
ERET
Comments
* Unmapped Uncached vector so TLB related & Cache Error Exception not possible
* ERL=1 so Interrupt exceptions disabled
* OS/System to avoid all other exceptions
*Only Reset, Soft Reset, NMI exceptions possible.
* ERET is not allowed in the branch delay slot of another Jump Instruction
* Processor does not execute the instruction which is in the ERET's branch delay slot
* PC <- ErrorEPC; ERL <- 0
* LLbit <- 0

Figure 5-22 Cache Error Exception Handling (HW) and Servicing Guidelines (SW)

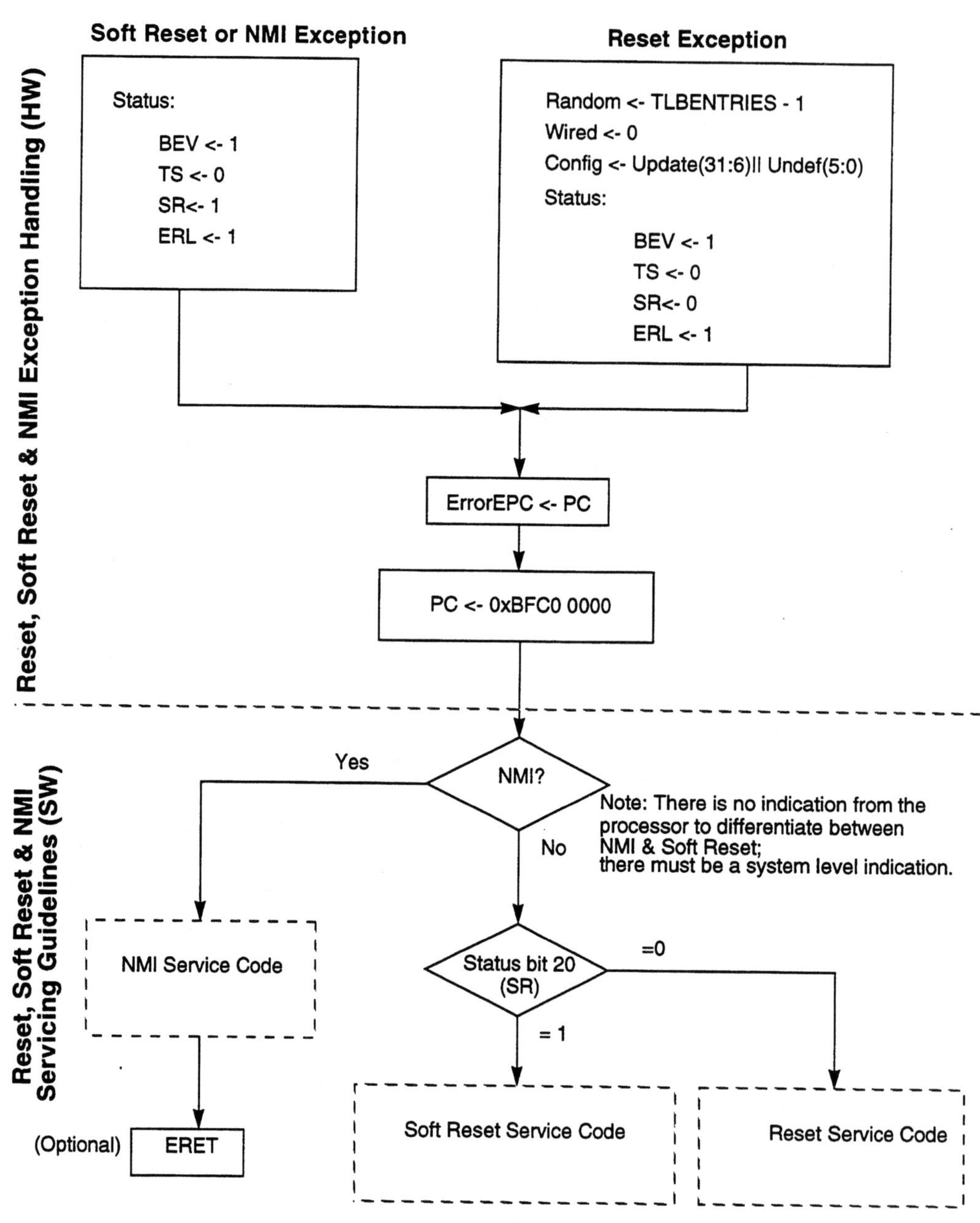

Figure 5-23 Reset, Soft Reset & NMI Exception Handling (HW) and Servicing Guidelines (SW)

Floating-Point Unit

6

This chapter describes the MIPS floating-point unit (FPU) features, including the programming model, instruction set and formats, and the pipeline.

The FPU, with associated system software, fully conforms to the requirements of ANSI/IEEE Standard 754–1985, *IEEE Standard for Binary Floating-Point Arithmetic*. In addition, the MIPS architecture fully supports the recommendations of the standard and precise exceptions.

6.1 Overview

The FPU operates as a coprocessor for the CPU (it is assigned coprocessor label *CP1*), and extends the CPU instruction set to perform arithmetic operations on floating-point values.

Figure 6-1 illustrates the functional organization of the FPU.

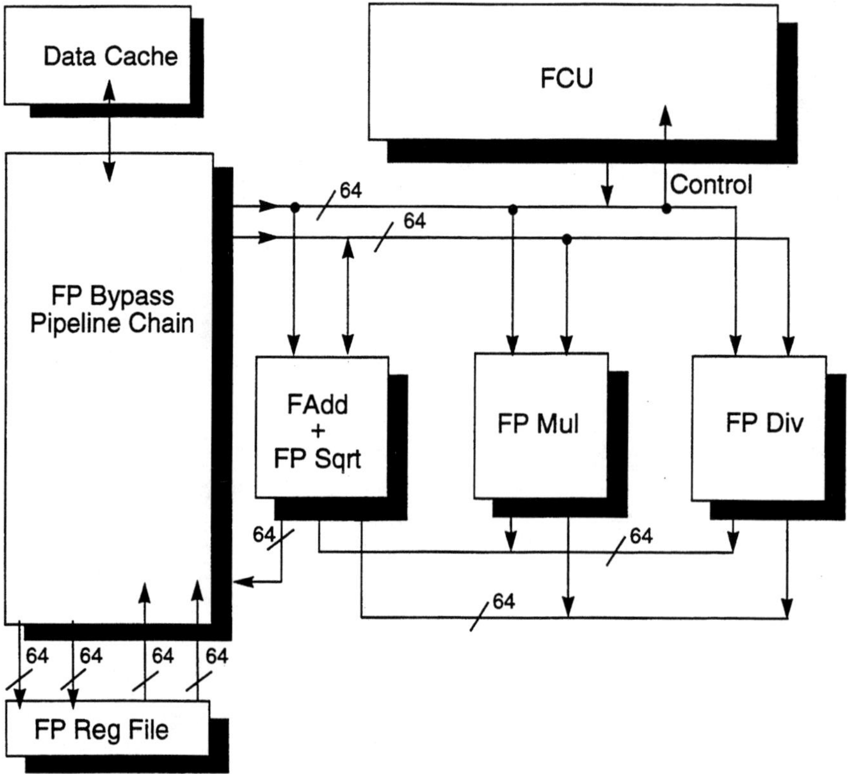

Figure 6-1 FPU Functional Block Diagram

6.2 FPU Features

This section briefly describes the operating model, the load/store instruction set, and the coprocessor interface in the FPU. A more detailed description is given in the sections that follow.

- **Full 64-bit Operation**. When the *FR* bit in the CPU *Status* register equals 0, the FPU is in 32-bit mode and contains thirty-two 32-bit registers that hold single- or, when used in pairs, double-precision values. When the *FR* bit in the CPU *Status* register equals 1, the FPU is in 64-bit mode and the registers are expanded to 64 bits wide. Each register can hold single- or double-precision values. The FPU also includes a 32-bit *Control/Status* register that provides access to all IEEE-Standard exception handling capabilities.
- **Load and Store Instruction Set**. Like the CPU, the FPU uses a load- and store-oriented instruction set, with single-cycle load and store operations. Floating-point operations are started in a single cycle and their execution overlaps other fixed-point or floating-point operations.
- **Tightly Coupled Coprocessor Interface**. The FPU resides on-chip to form a tightly coupled unit with a seamless integration of floating-point and fixed-point instruction sets. Since each unit receives and executes instructions in parallel, some floating-point instructions can execute at the same single-cycle-per-instruction rate as fixed-point instructions.

6.3 FPU Programming Model

This section describes the set of FPU registers and their data organization. The FPU registers include *Floating-Point General Purpose* registers *(FGRs)* and two control registers: *Control/Status* and *Implementation/Revision*.

Floating-Point General Registers (FGRs)

The FPU has a set of *Floating-Point General Purpose* registers *(FGRs)* that can be accessed in the following ways:

- As 32 general purpose registers (32 FGRs), each of which is 32 bits wide when the *FR* bit in the CPU *Status* register equals 0; or as 32 general purpose registers (32 FGRs), each of which is 64-bits wide when *FR* equals 1. The CPU accesses these registers through move, load, and store instructions.
- As 16 floating-point registers (see the next section for a description of FPRs), each of which is 64-bits wide, when the *FR* bit in the CPU *Status* register equals 0. The FPRs hold values in either single- or double-precision floating-point format. Each FPR corresponds to adjacently numbered FGRs as shown in Figure 6-2.
- As 32 floating-point registers (see the next section for a description of FPRs), each of which is 64-bits wide, when the *FR* bit in the CPU *Status* register equals 1. The FPRs hold values in either single- or double-precision floating-point format. Each FPR corresponds to an FGR as shown in Figure 6-2.

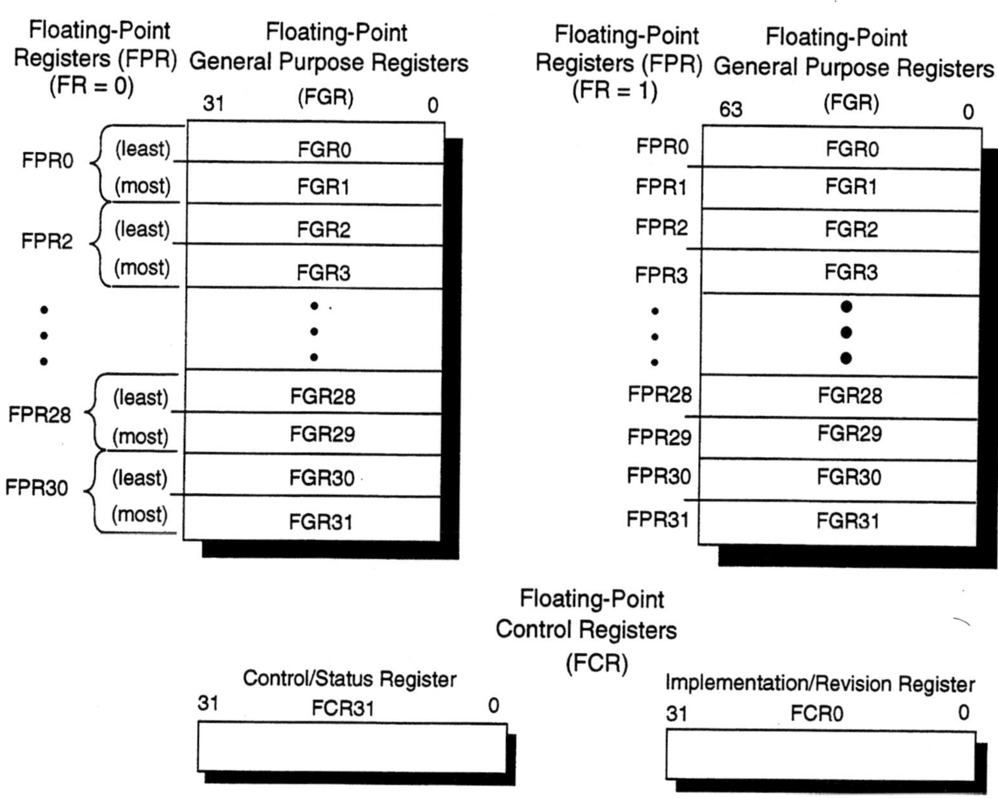

Figure 6-2 FPU Registers

Floating-Point Registers

The FPU provides:

- 16 *Floating-Point* registers (*FPR*s) when the *FR* bit in the *Status* register equals 0, or
- 32 *Floating-Point* registers (*FPR*s) when the *FR* bit in the *Status* register equals 1.

These 64-bit registers hold floating-point values during floating-point operations and are physically formed from the *General Purpose* registers (*FGRs*). When the *FR* bit in the *Status* register equals 1, the *FPR* references a single 64-bit *FGR*.

The *FPR*s hold values in either single- or double-precision floating-point format. If the *FR* bit equals 0, only even numbers (the *least* register, as shown in Figure 6-2) can be used to address *FPR*s. When the *FR* bit is set to a 1, all *FPR* register numbers are valid.

If the *FR* bit equals 0 during a double-precision floating-point operation, the general registers are accessed in double pairs. Thus, in a double-precision operation, selecting *Floating-Point Register 0* (*FPR0*) actually addresses adjacent *Floating-Point General Purpose* registers *FGR0* and *FGR1*.

Floating-Point Control Registers

The FPU has 32 control registers (*FCR*s) that can only be accessed by move operations. The *FCR*s are described below:

- The *Implementation/Revision* register *(FCR0)* holds revision information about the FPU.
- The *Control/Status* register *(FCR31)* controls and monitors exceptions, holds the result of compare operations, and establishes rounding modes.
- *FCR1* to *FCR30* are reserved.

Table 6-1 lists the assignments of the *FCR*s.

Table 6-1 Floating-Point Control Register Assignments

FCR Number	Use
FCR0	Coprocessor implementation and revision register
FCR1 to FCR30	Reserved
FCR31	Rounding mode, cause, trap enables, and flags

Implementation and Revision Register, (FCR0)

The read-only *Implementation and Revision* register (*FCR0*) specifies the implementation and revision number of the FPU. This information can determine the coprocessor revision and performance level, and can also be used by diagnostic software.

Figure 6-3 shows the layout of the register; Table 6-2 describes the *Implementation and Revision* register (*FCR0*) fields.

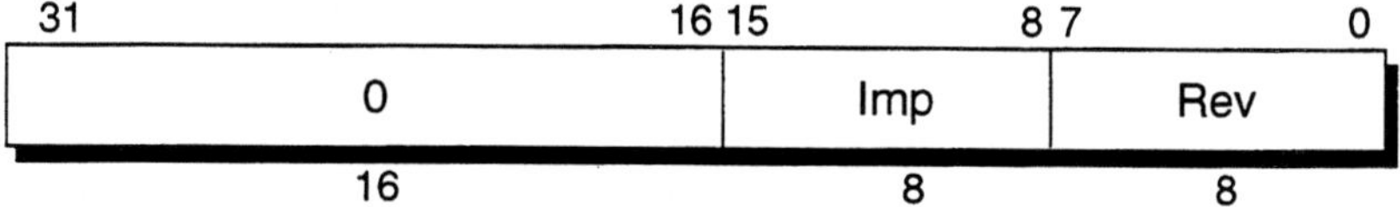

Figure 6-3 Implementation/Revision Register

Table 6-2 FCR0 Fields

Field	Description
Imp	Implementation number (0x05)
Rev	Revision number in the form of *y.x*
0	Reserved. Must be written as zeroes, and returns zeroes when read.

The revision number is a value of the form *y.x*, where:

- *y* is a major revision number held in bits 7:4.
- *x* is a minor revision number held in bits 3:0.

The revision number distinguishes some chip revisions; however, MIPS does not guarantee that changes to its chips are necessarily reflected by the revision number, or that changes to the revision number necessarily reflect real chip changes. For this reason revision number values are not listed, and software should not rely on the revision number to characterize the chip.

Control/Status Register (FCR31)

The *Control/Status* register *(FCR31)* contains control and status information that can be accessed by instructions in either Kernel or User mode. *FCR31* also controls the arithmetic rounding mode and enables User mode traps, as well as identifying any exceptions that may have occurred in the most recently executed instruction, along with any exceptions that may have occurred without being trapped.

Figure 6-4 shows the format of the *Control/Status* register, and Table 6-3 describes the *Control/Status* register fields. Figure 6-5 shows the *Control/Status* register *Cause, Flag,* and *Enable* fields.

Control/Status Register (FCR31)

Bits	31–25	24	23	22–18	17–12	11–7	6–2	1–0
Field	0	FS	C	0	Cause E V Z O U I	Enables V Z O U I	Flags V Z O U I	RM
Width	7	1	1	5	6	5	5	2

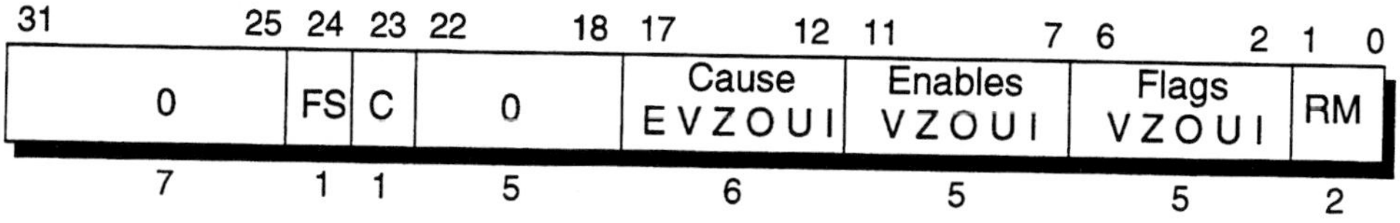

Figure 6-4 FP Control/Status Register Bit Assignments

Table 6-3 Control/Status Register Fields

Field	Description
FS	When set, denormalized results are flushed to 0 instead of causing an unimplemented operation exception.
C	Condition bit. See description of *Control/Status* register *Condition* bit.
Cause	Cause bits. See Figure 6-5 and the description of *Control/Status* register *Cause, Flag,* and *Enable* bits.
Enables	Enable bits. See Figure 6-5 and the description of *Control/Status* register *Cause, Flag,* and *Enable* bits.
Flags	Flag bits. See Figure 6-5 and the description of *Control/Status* register *Cause, Flag,* and *Enable* bits.
RM	Rounding mode bits. See Table 6-4 and the description of *Control/Status* register *Rounding Mode Control* bits.

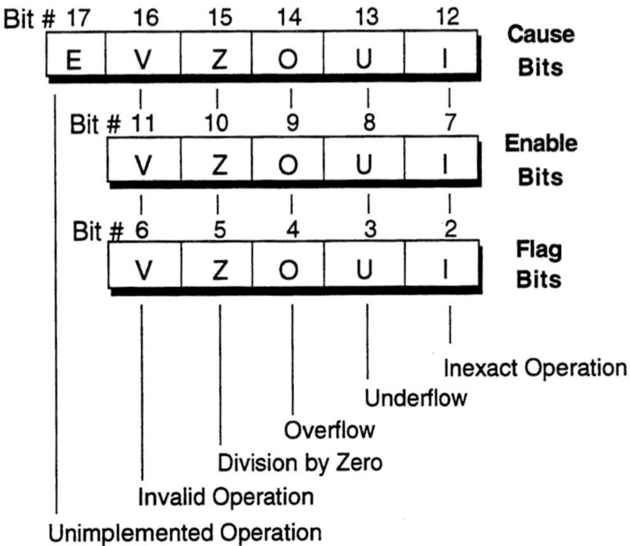

Figure 6-5 Control/Status Register Cause, Flag, and Enable Fields

Accessing the Control/Status Register

When the *Control / Status* register is read by a Move Control From Coprocessor 1 (CFC1) instruction, all unfinished instructions in the pipeline are completed before the contents of the register are moved to the main processor. If a floating-point exception occurs as the pipeline empties, the FP exception is taken and the CFC1 instruction is re-executed after the exception is serviced.

The bits in the *Control/Status* register can be set or cleared by writing to the register using a Move Control To Coprocessor 1 (CTC1) instruction. *FCR31* must only be written to when the FPU is not actively executing floating-point operations; this can be ensured by reading the contents of the register to empty the pipeline.

IEEE Standard 754

IEEE Standard 754 specifies that floating-point operations detect certain exceptional cases, raise flags, and can invoke an exception handler when an exception occurs. These features are implemented in the MIPS architecture with the *Cause*, *Enable*, and *Flag* fields of the *Control/Status* register. The *Flag* bits implement IEEE 754 exception status flags, and the *Cause* and *Enable* bits implement exception handling.

Control/Status Register FS Bit

When the *FS* bit is set, denormalized results are flushed to 0 instead of causing an unimplemented operation exception.

Control/Status Register Condition Bit

When a floating-point Compare operation takes place, the result is stored at bit 23, the *Condition* bit, to save or restore the state of the condition line. The C bit is set to 1 if the condition is true; the bit is cleared to 0 if the condition is false. Bit 23 is affected only by compare and Move Control To FPU instructions.

Control/Status Register Cause, Flag, and Enable Fields

Figure 6-5 illustrates the *Cause*, *Flag*, and *Enable* fields of the *Control/Status* register.

Cause Bits

Bits 17:12 in the *Control/Status* register contain *Cause* bits, as shown in Figure 6-5, which reflect the results of the most recently executed instruction. The *Cause* bits are a logical extension of the CP0 *Cause* register; they identify the exceptions raised by the last floating-point operation and raise an interrupt or exception if the corresponding enable bit is set. If more than one exception occurs on a single instruction, each appropriate bit is set.

The *Cause* bits are written by each floating-point operation (but not by load, store, or move operations). The Unimplemented Operation (*E*) bit is set to a 1 if software emulation is required, otherwise it remains 0. The other bits are set to 0 or 1 to indicate the occurrence or non-occurrence (respectively) of an IEEE 754 exception.

When a floating-point exception is taken, no results are stored, and the only states affected are the *Cause* and *Flag* bits. Exceptions caused by an immediately previous floating-point operation can be determined by reading the *Cause* field.

Enable Bits

A floating-point exception is generated any time a *Cause* bit and the corresponding *Enable* bit are set. A floating-point operation that sets an enabled *Cause* bit forces an immediate exception, as does setting both *Cause* and *Enable* bits with CTC1.

There is no enable for Unimplemented Operation (*E*). Setting Unimplemented Operation always generates a floating-point exception.

Before returning from a floating-point exception, or doing a CTC1, software must first clear the enabled *Cause* bits to prevent a repeat of the interrupt. Thus, User mode programs can never observe enabled *Cause* bits set; if this information is required in a User mode handler, it must be passed somewhere other than the *Status* register.

For a floating-point operation that sets only unenabled *Cause* bits, no exception occurs and the default result defined by IEEE 754 is stored. In this case, the exceptions that were caused by the immediately previous floating-point operation can be determined by reading the *Cause* field.

Flag Bits

The appropriate *Flag* bits are set by the operation when a User mode exception handler is invoked. This is not implemented in hardware; floating-point exception software is responsible for setting these bits before invoking a user handler.

The *Flag* bits are cumulative and indicate that an exception was raised by an operation that was executed since they were explicitly reset. *Flag* bits are set to 1 if an IEEE 754 exception is raised, otherwise they remain unchanged. The *Flag* bits are never cleared as a side effect of floating-point operations; however, they can be set or cleared by writing a new value into the *Status* register, using a Move To Coprocessor Control instruction.

Control/Status Register Rounding Mode Control Bits

Bits 1 and 0 in the *Control/Status* register constitute the *Rounding Mode* (*RM*) field.

As shown in Table 6-4, these bits specify the rounding mode that the FPU uses for all floating-point operations.

Table 6-4 Rounding Mode Bit Decoding

Rounding Mode RM(1:0)	Mnemonic	Description
0	RN	Round result to nearest representable value; round to value with least-significant bit 0 when the two nearest representable values are equally near.
1	RZ	Round toward 0: round to value closest to and not greater in magnitude than the infinitely precise result.
2	RP	Round toward +∞: round to value closest to and not less than the infinitely precise result.
3	RM	Round toward – ∞: round to value closest to and not greater than the infinitely precise result.

6.4 Floating-Point Formats

The FPU performs both 32-bit (single-precision) and 64-bit (double-precision) IEEE standard floating-point operations. The 32-bit single-precision format has a 24-bit signed-magnitude fraction field (*f+s*) and an 8-bit exponent (*e*), as shown in Figure 6-6.

Figure 6-6 Single-Precision Floating-Point Format

The 64-bit double-precision format has a 53-bit signed-magnitude fraction field (*f+s*) and an 11-bit exponent, as shown in Figure 6-7.

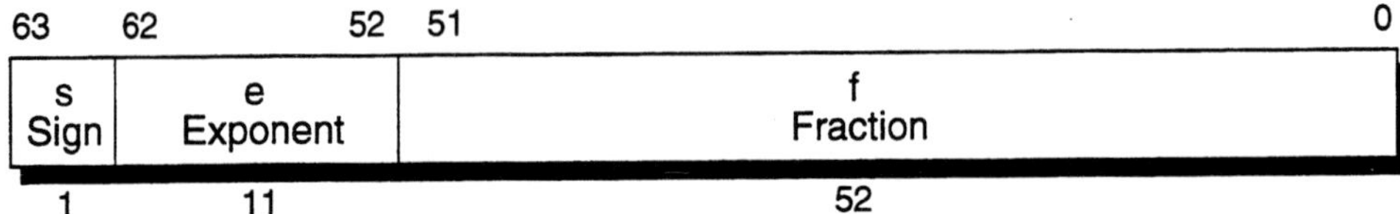

Figure 6-7 Double-Precision Floating-Point Format

As shown in the above figures, numbers in floating-point format are composed of three fields:

- sign field, s
- biased exponent, $e = E + bias$
- fraction, $f = .b_1b_2....b_{p-1}$

The range of the unbiased exponent *E* includes every integer between the two values E_{min} and E_{max} inclusive, together with two other reserved values:

- E_{min} -1 (to encode ±0 and denormalized numbers)
- E_{max} +1 (to encode $\pm\infty$ and NaNs [Not a Number])

For single- and double-precision formats, each representable nonzero numerical value has just one encoding.

For single- and double-precision formats, the value of a number, *v*, is determined by the equations shown in Table 6-5.

Table 6-5 Equations for Calculating Values in Single and Double-Precision Floating-Point Format

No.	Equation
(1)	if $E = E_{max}+1$ and $f \neq 0$, then v is NaN, regardless of s
(2)	if $E = E_{max}+1$ and $f = 0$, then $v = (-1)^s \infty$
(3)	if $E_{min} \leq E \leq E_{max}$, then $v = (-1)^s 2^E (1.f)$
(4)	if $E = E_{min}-1$ and $f \neq 0$, then $v = (-1)^s 2^{Emin} (0.f)$
(5)	if $E = E_{min}-1$ and $f = 0$, then $v = (-1)^s 0$

For all floating-point formats, if *v* is NaN, the most-significant bit of *f* determines whether the value is a signaling or quiet NaN: *v* is a signaling NaN if the most-significant bit of *f* is set, otherwise, *v* is a quiet NaN.

Table 6-6 defines the values for the format parameters; minimum and maximum floating-point values are given in Table 6-7.

Table 6-6 Floating-Point Format Parameter Values

Parameter	Format	
	Single	Double
f	24	53
E_{max}	+127	+1023
E_{min}	–126	–1022
Exponent *bias*	+127	+1023
Exponent width in bits	8	11
Integer bit	hidden	hidden
Fraction width in bits	24	53
Format width in bits	32	64

Table 6-7 Minimum and Maximum Floating-Point Values

Type	Value
Float Minimum	1.40129846e–45
Float Minimum Norm	1.17549435e–38
Float Maximum	3.40282347e+38
Double Minimum	4.9406564584124654e–324
Double Minimum Norm	2.2250738585072014e–308
Double Maximum	1.7976931348623157e+308

6.5 Binary Fixed-Point Format

Binary fixed-point values are held in 2's complement format. Unsigned fixed-point values are not directly provided by the floating-point instruction set. Figure 6-8 illustrates binary fixed-point format; Table 6-8 lists the binary fixed-point format fields.

Figure 6-8 Binary Fixed-Point Format

Field assignments of the binary fixed-point format are:

Table 6-8 Binary Fixed-Point Format Fields

Field	Description
sign	sign bit
integer	integer value

6.6 Floating-Point Instruction Set Overview

All FPU instructions are 32 bits long, aligned on a word boundary. They can be divided into the following groups:

- **Load, Store, and Move** instructions move data between memory, the main processor, and the *FPU General Purpose* registers.
- **Conversion** instructions perform conversion operations between the various data formats.
- **Computational** instructions perform arithmetic operations on floating-point values in the FPU registers.
- **Compare** instructions perform comparisons of the contents of registers and set a conditional bit based on the results.
- **Branch on FPU Condition** instructions perform a branch to the specified target if the specified coprocessor condition is met.

Table 6-9 lists the instruction set of the FPU. A complete description of each instruction is provided in Appendix B.

In the instruction formats shown in Tables 6-9 through 6-12, the *fmt* appended to the instruction opcode specifies the data format: *s* specifies single-precision binary floating-point, *d* specifies double-precision binary floating-point, and *w* specifies binary fixed-point.

Table 6-9 FPU Instruction Summary: Load, Move and Store Instructions

OpCode	Description
LWC1	Load Word to FPU
SWC1	Store Word from FPU
LDC1	Load Doubleword to FPU
SDC1	Store Doubleword From FPU
MTC1	Move Word To FPU
MFC1	Move Word From FPU
CTC1	Move Control Word To FPU
CFC1	Move Control Word From FPU
DMTC1	Doubleword Move To FPU
DMFC1	Doubleword Move From FPU

Table 6-10 FPU Instruction Summary: Conversion Instructions

OpCode	Description
CVT.S.fmt	Floating-point Convert to Single FP
CVT.D.fmt	Floating-point Convert to Double FP
CVT.W.fmt	Floating-point Convert to Single Fixed Point
ROUND.w.fmt	Floating-point Round
TRUNC.w.fmt	Floating-point Truncate
CEIL.w.fmt	Floating-point Ceiling
FLOOR.w.fmt	Floating-point Floor

Table 6-11 FPU Instruction Summary: Computational Instructions

OpCode	Description
ADD.fmt	Floating-point Add
SUB.fmt	Floating-point Subtract
MUL.fmt	Floating-point Multiply
DIV.fmt	Floating-point Divide
ABS.fmt	Floating-point Absolute Value
MOV.fmt	Floating-point Move
NEG.fmt	Floating-point Negate
SQRT.fmt	Floating-point Square Root

Table 6-12 FPU Instruction Summary: Compare and Branch Instructions

OpCode	Description
C.cond.fmt	Floating-point Compare
BC1T	Branch on FPU True
BC1F	Branch on FPU False
BC1TL	Branch on FPU True Likely
BC1FL	Branch on FPU False Likely

Floating-Point Load, Store, and Move Instructions

This section discusses the manner in which the FPU uses the load, store and move instructions listed in Table 6-9; Appendix B provides a detailed description of each instruction.

Transfers Between FPU and Memory

All data movement between the FPU and memory is accomplished by using one of the following instructions:

- Load Word To Coprocessor 1 (LWC1) or Store Word To Coprocessor 1 (SWC1) instructions, which reference a single 32-bit word of the FPU general registers
- Load Doubleword (LDC1) or Store Doubleword (SDC1) instructions, which reference a 64-bit doubleword.

These load and store operations are unformatted; no format conversions are performed and therefore no floating-point exceptions can occur due to these operations.

Transfers Between FPU and CPU

Data can also be moved directly between the FPU and the CPU by using one of the following instructions:

- Move To Coprocessor 1 (MTC1)
- Move From Coprocessor 1 (MFC1)
- Doubleword Move To Coprocessor 1 (DMTC1)
- Doubleword Move From Coprocessor 1 (DMFC1)

Like the floating-point load and store operations, these operations perform no format conversions and never cause floating-point exceptions.

Load Delay and Hardware Interlocks

The instruction immediately following a load can use the contents of the loaded register. In such cases the hardware interlocks, requiring additional real cycles; for this reason, scheduling load delay slots is desirable, although it is not required for functional code.

Data Alignment

All coprocessor loads and stores reference the following aligned data items:

- For word loads and stores, the access type is always WORD, and the low-order 2 bits of the address must always be 0.
- For doubleword loads and stores, the access type is always DOUBLEWORD, and the low-order 3 bits of the address must always be 0.

Endianness

Regardless of byte-numbering order (endianness) of the data, the address specifies the byte that has the smallest byte address in the addressed field. For a big-endian system, it is the leftmost byte; for a little-endian system, it is the rightmost byte.

Floating-Point Conversion Instructions

Conversion instructions perform conversions between the various data formats such as single- or double-precision, fixed- or floating-point formats. Table 6-10 lists conversion instructions; Appendix B gives a detailed description of each instruction.

Floating-Point Computational Instructions

Computational instructions perform arithmetic operations on floating-point values, in registers. Table 6-11 lists the computational instructions and Appendix B provides a detailed description of each instruction. There are two categories of computational instructions:

- 3-Operand Register-Type instructions, which perform floating-point addition, subtraction, multiplication, division, and square root operations
- 2-Operand Register-Type instructions, which perform floating-point absolute value, move, and negate operations.

Branch on FPU Condition Instructions

Table 6-12 lists the Branch on FPU (coprocessor unit 1) condition instructions that can test the result of the FPU compare (C.cond) instructions. Appendix B gives a detailed description of each instruction.

Floating-Point Compare Operations

The floating-point compare (C.fmt.cond) instructions interpret the contents of two FPU registers (*fs, ft*) in the specified format (*fmt*) and arithmetically compare them. A result is determined based on the comparison and conditions (*cond*) specified in the instruction.

Table 6-12 lists the compare instructions; Appendix B gives a detailed description of each instruction. Table 6-13 lists the mnemonics for the compare instruction conditions.

Table 6-13 Mnemonics and Definitions of Compare Instruction Conditions

Mnemonic	Definition	Mnemonic	Definition
F	False	**T**	True
UN	Unordered	**OR**	Ordered
EQ	Equal	**NEQ**	Not Equal
UEQ	Unordered or Equal	**OLG**	Ordered or Less Than or Greater Than
OLT	Ordered Less Than	**UGE**	Unordered or Greater Than or Equal
ULT	Unordered or Less Than	**OGE**	Ordered Greater Than
OLE	Ordered Less Than or Equal	**UGT**	Unordered or Greater Than
ULE	Unordered or Less Than or Equal	**OGT**	Ordered Greater Than
SF	Signaling False	**ST**	Signaling True
NGLE	Not Greater Than or Less Than or Equal	**GLE**	Greater Than, or Less Than or Equal
SEQ	Signaling Equal	**SNE**	Signaling Not Equal
NGL	Not Greater Than or Less Than	**GL**	Greater Than or Less Than
LT	Less Than	**NLT**	Not Less Than
NGE	Not Greater Than or Equal	**GE**	Greater Than or Equal
LE	Less Than or Equal	**NLE**	Not Less Than or Equal
NGT	Not Greater Than	**GT**	Greater Than

6.7 FPU Instruction Pipeline Overview

The FPU provides an instruction pipeline that parallels the CPU instruction pipeline. It shares the same eight-stage pipeline architecture with the CPU (see Chapter 3).

Instruction Execution

Figure 6-9 illustrates the 8-instruction overlap in the FPU pipeline.

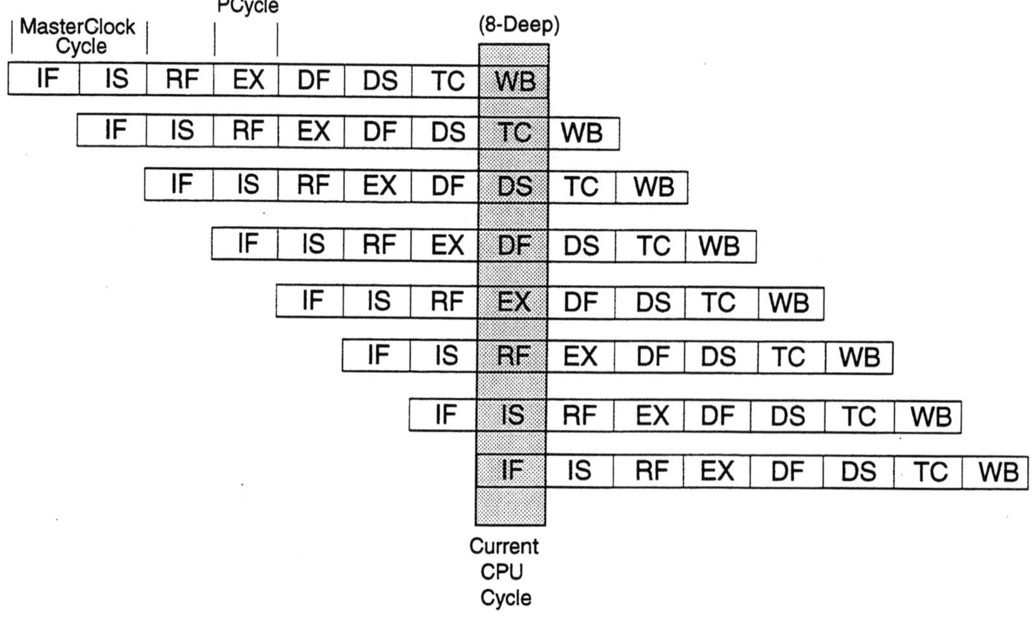

Figure 6-9 FPU Instruction Pipeline

Figure 6-9 assumes that one instruction is completed every PCycle. Most FPU instructions, however, require more than one cycle in the EX stage. This means the FPU must stall the pipeline if an instruction execution cannot proceed because of register or resource conflicts.

Figure 6-10 illustrates the effect of a three-cycle stall on the FPU pipeline.

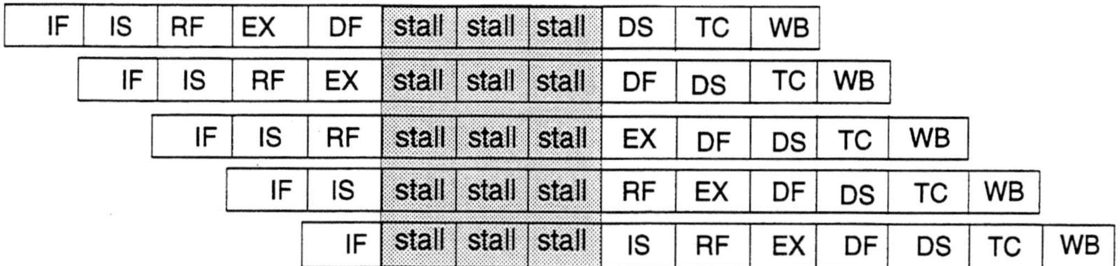

Figure 6-10 FPU Pipeline Stall

To lessen the performance impact that results from stalling the instruction pipeline, the FPU allows instructions to overlap so that instruction execution can proceed as long as there are no resource conflicts, data dependencies, or exception conditions. The following sections describe the timing and overlapping of FPU instructions.

Instruction Execution Cycle Time

Unlike the CPU, which executes almost all instructions in a single cycle, more time may be required to execute FPU instructions.

Table 6-14 gives the minimum latency, in processor pipeline cycles, of each floating-point operation for the currently implemented configurations. These latency calculations assume the result of the operation is immediately used in a succeeding operation.

Table 6-14 Floating-Point Operation Latencies

Operation	Pipeline Cycles			Operation	Pipeline Cycles		
	Single	Double	Word		Single	Double	Word
ADD.fmt	4	4	(b)	**CVT.W.fmt**	4	4	(b)
SUB.fmt	4	4	(b)	**C.fmt.cond**	3(a)	3(a)	(b)
MUL.fmt	7	8	(b)	**BC1T**	(c)	1	(c)
DIV.fmt	23	36	(b)	**BC1F**	(c)	1	(c)
SQRT.fmt	54	112	(b)	**BC1TL**	(c)	1	(c)
ABS.fmt	2	2	(b)	**BC1FL**	(c)	1	(c)
MOV.fmt	1	1	(b)	**LWC1**	(c)	3	(c)
NEG.fmt	2	2	(b)	**SWC1**	(c)	1	(c)
ROUND.W.fmt	4	4	(b)	**LDC1**	(c)	3	(c)
TRUNC.W.fmt	4	4	(b)	**SDC1**	(c)	1	(c)
CEIL.W.fmt	4	4	(b)	**MTC1**	(c)	3(a)	(c)
FLOOR.W.fmt	4	4	(b)	**MFC1**	(c)	3	(c)
CVT.S.fmt	(b)	4	6	**CTC1**	(c)	3(a)	(c)
CVT.D.fmt	2	(b)	5	**CFC1**	(c)	2	(c)

(a)........ Software *must* schedule operations so that an FPU register that is the target of a floating-point load or move is not read until at least two instructions later. Software *must* also schedule a floating-point branch instruction two or more instructions after a floating-point compare instruction.
(b)........ These operations are illegal.
(c)........ These operations are undefined.

Scheduling FPU Instructions

The floating-point architecture permits the overlapping of floating-point load, store, and move instructions with some of the other processor operations.

To permit this, the FPU coprocessor implements three separate operation (op) units:

- divider
- multiplier
- adder (for remaining operations)

The multiplier and divider can overlap adder operations; however, they use the adder on their final cycles, which imposes some limitations.

The multiplier can begin a new double-precision multiplication every four cycles, and a new single-precision multiplication every three cycles. The adder generally begins a new operation one cycle before the previous cycle completes; therefore, a floating-point addition or subtraction can start every three cycles.

The FPU coprocessor pipeline is fully bypassed and interlocked.

FPU Pipeline Overlapping

Each of the three op units is controlled by an FPU resource scheduler, which issues instructions under constraints described in the following section. Table 6-15 lists the pipe stages used in each of the op units (although not all stages are used by each unit).

Table 6-15 FPU Operational Unit Pipe Stages

Stage	Description
A	FPU Adder Mantissa Add stage
E	FPU Adder Exception Test stage
EX	CPU EX stage
M	FPU Multiplier 1st stage
N	FPU Multiplier 2nd stage
R	FPU Adder Result Round stage
S	FPU Adder Operand Shift stage
U	FPU Unpack stage

Instruction Scheduling Constraints

The FPU resource scheduler is kept from issuing instructions to the FPU op units (adder, multiplier, and divider) by the limitations in their micro-architectures. If any of the following constraints are violated, the op unit assumes the outstanding instruction in its pipe is discarded, and then continues operation on the most recently issued instruction.

FPU Divider Constraints

The FPU divider can handle only one non-overlapped division instruction in its pipe at any one time.

FPU Multiplier Constraints

The FPU multiplier allows up to two pipelined MUL.[S,D] instructions to be processed as long as the following constraints are met:

- Two idle cycles are required after a MUL.S instruction (as shown in Figure 6-11).
- Three idle cycles are required after MUL.D instruction (as shown in Figure 6-12).

These figures are not meant to imply that back-to-back multiplications are allowed. Rather, as shown in Figure 6-11, instructions **I2** and **I3** are illegal and **I5, I6, I7,** and **I8** are successive stages of **I4,** referenced to **I1.**

Figure 6-12 is similar, in that **I6, I7,** and **I8** are successive stages of **I5.**

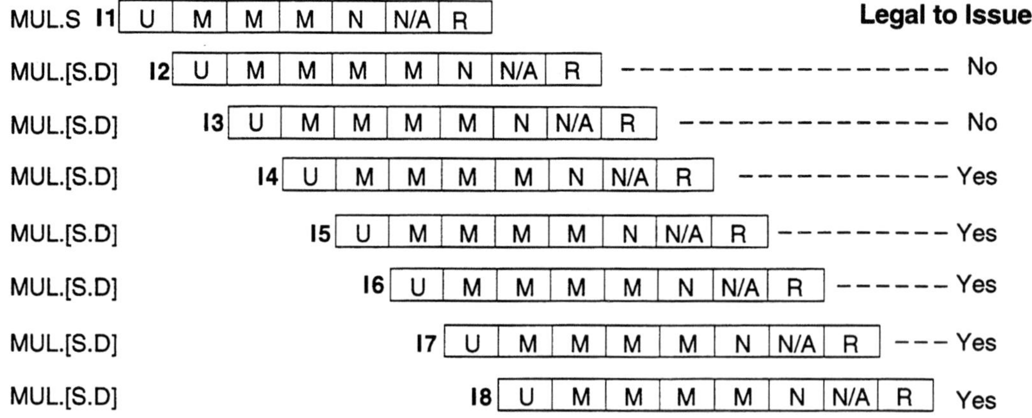

Figure 6-11 MUL.S Instruction Scheduling in the FPU Multiplier

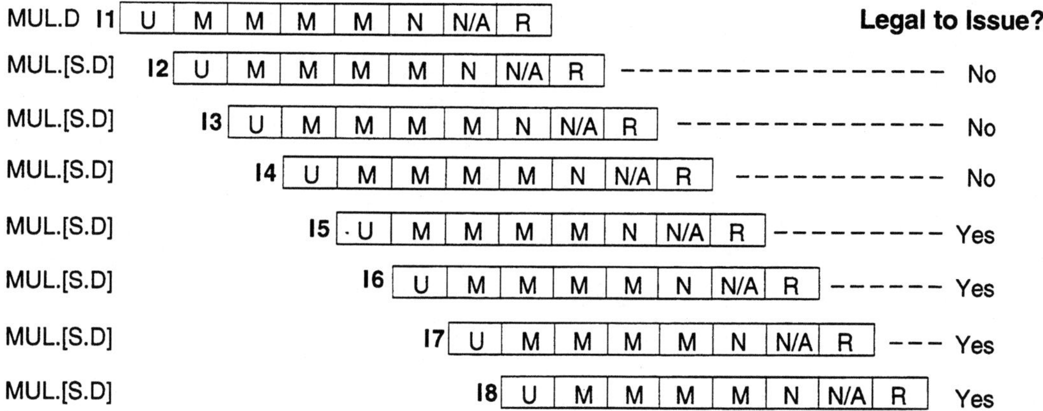

Figure 6-12 MUL.D Instruction Scheduling in the FPU Multiplier

FPU Adder Constraints

Following are the constraints that must be met in the FPU adder op unit.

Cycle Overlap. The adder op unit must allow a clock cycle overlap between each newly issued instruction and the instruction being completed, as shown in Figure 6-13.

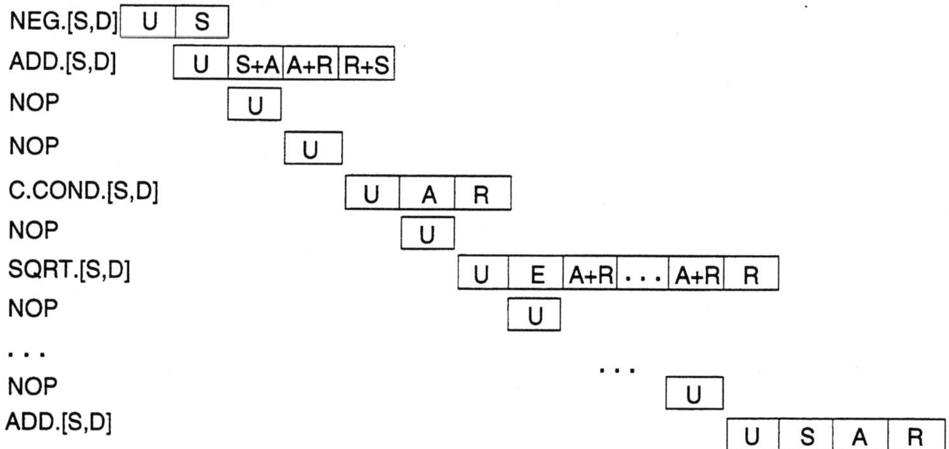

Figure 6-13 Instruction Cycle Overlap in FPU Adder

Resource Conflict. The adder must allow the cleanup stages (A, R) of a multiplication instruction to be pipelined with the execution of an ADD.[S,D], SUB.[S,D], or C.COND.[S,D] instruction, as long as no two instructions simultaneously attempt to use the same A and R pipe stages. For instance, Figure 6-14 shows a resource conflict between the mantissa add (A, stage 7) of instructions 1, 5, and 6. This figure also shows the resource conflict between result round (R), stage 8, of instructions 1, 5, and 6. The multiplication cleanup cycles (A, R) can neither overlap nor pipeline with any other instruction currently in the adder pipe.

Figures 6-14 through 6-17 show these constraints.

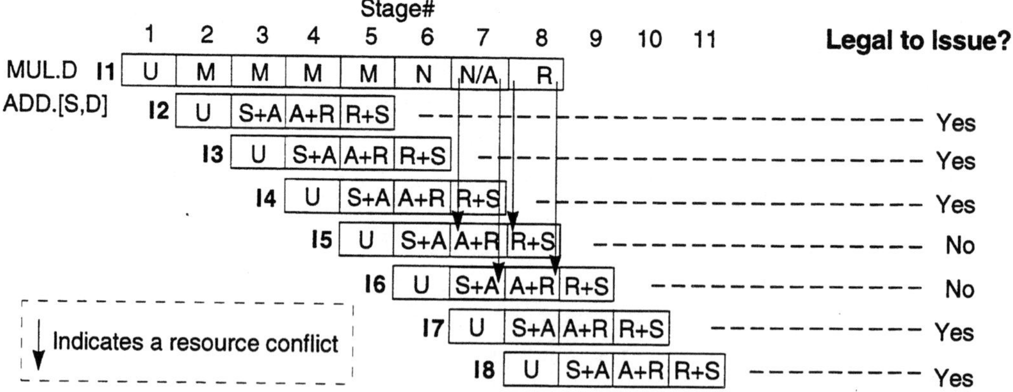

Figure 6-14 MUL.D and ADD.[S,D] Cycle Conflict in FPU Adder

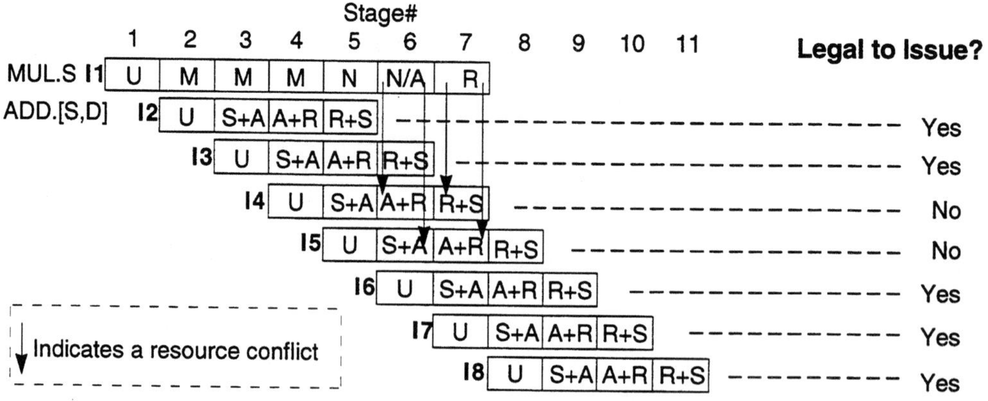

Figure 6-15 MUL.S and ADD.[S,D] Cycle Conflict in FPU Adder

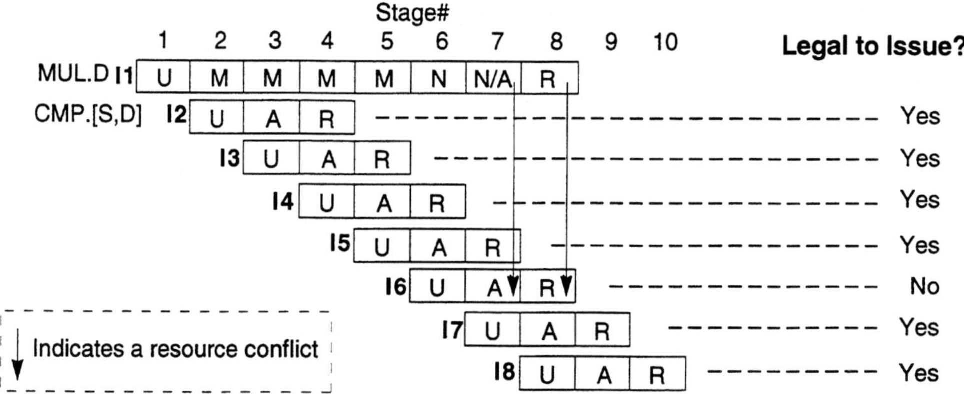

Figure 6-16 MUL.D and CMP.[S,D] Cleanup Cycle Conflict in FPU Adder

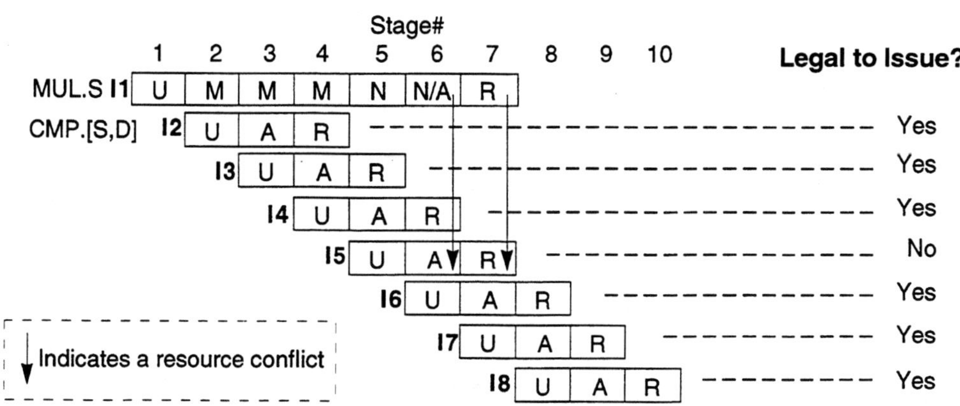

Figure 6-17 MUL.S and CMP.[S,D] Cleanup Cycle Conflict in FPU Adder

Prep and Cleanup Cycle Overlap. The adder does not allow the preparation (U stage) and cleanup cycles (N, A, R) of a division instruction to be pipelined with any other instruction; however, the adder does allow the last cycle of preparation or cleanup to be overlapped one clock by the following instruction's U stage (the CPU EX cycle). Figure 6-18 shows this process.

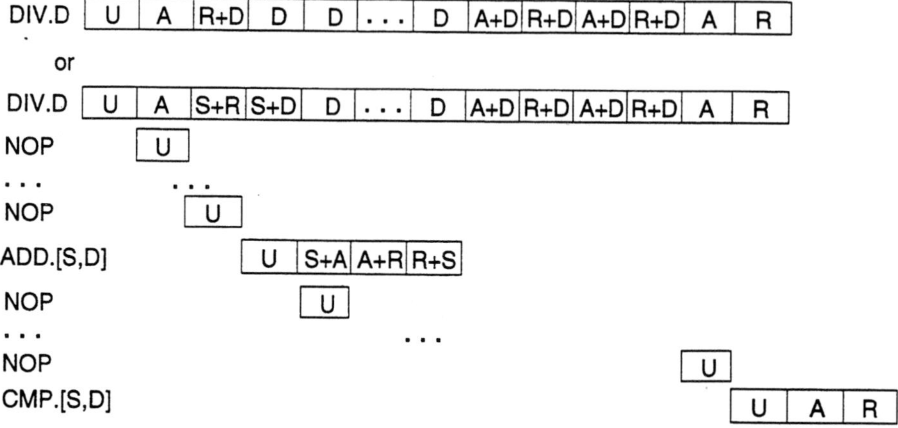

Figure 6-18 Adder Prep and Cleanup Cycle Overlap

Instruction Latency, Repeat Rate, and Pipeline Stage Sequences

Table 6-16 lists the latency and repeat rate between instructions, together with the sequence of pipeline stages for each instruction. For example, the latency of the ADD.[S,D] is 4, which means it takes four processor cycles to complete. The Repeat Rate column indicates how soon an instruction can be repeated; for example, an ADD.[S,D] can be repeated after the conclusion of the third pipeline stage.

Table 6-16 Latency, Repeat Rate, and Pipe Stages of FPU Instructions

Instruction Type	Latency	Repeat Rate	Pipeline Stage Sequence
MOV.[S,D]	1	1	EX
ADD.[S,D]	4	3	U→ S+A→ A+R→ R+S
SUB.[S,D]	4	3	U→ S+A→ A+R→ R+S
C.COND.[S,D]	3	2	U→ A→ R
NEG.[S,D]	2	1	U→ S
ABS.[S,D]	2	1	U→ S
CVT.S.W	6	5	U→ A→ R→ S→ A→ R
CVT.D.W	5	4	U→ S→ A→ R→ S
CVT.S.L	7	6	U→ A→ R→ S→ S→ A→ R
CVT.D.L	4	3	U→ A→ R→ S
CVT.D.S	2	1	U→ S
CVT.S.D	4	3	U→ S→ A→ R
CVT.W.[S,D] *or* ROUND.W.[S,D] *or* TRUNC.W.[S,D] *or* CEIL.W.[S,D] *or* FLOOR.W.[S,D]	4	3	U→ S→ A→ R
MUL.S	7	3	U→ E/M→ M→ M→ N→ N/A→ R
MUL.D	8	4	U→ E/M→ M→ M→ M→ N→ N/A→ R
DIV.S	23	22	U→ S+A→ S+R→ S→ D...D→ D/A→ D/R→ D/A→ D/R→A→R
DIV.D	36	35	U→ A→ R→ D...D→ D/A→ D/R→ D/A → D/R→ A→ R
SQRT.S	2–54	2–53	U→ E→ A+R→...→ A+R→ A→ R
SQRT.D	2–112	2–111	U→ E→ A+R→...→ A+R→ A→ R

Resource Scheduling Rules

The FPU Resource Scheduler issues instructions while adhering to the rules described below. These scheduling rules optimize op unit executions; if the rules are not followed, the hardware interlocks to guarantee correct operation.

DIV.[S,D] can start only when all of the following conditions are met in the RF stage:

- The *divider* is idle.
- The *adder* is either idle, or in its second-to-last execution cycle.
- The *multiplier* is either idle, or in its first execution cycle.

Idle means an operation unit—adder, multiplier, or divider—is either not processing any instruction, or is currently in its last execution cycle completing an instruction.

MUL.[S,D] can start only when all of the following conditions are met in the RF stage.

- The *multiplier* is one of the following:
  - idle
  - within the third execution cycle (EX+2) if the most recent instruction in the multiplier pipe is MUL.S
  - within the fourth execution cycle (EX+3) if the most recent instruction in the multiplier pipe is MUL.D.
- The *adder* is one of the following:
  - idle
  - not processing the first execution cycle (EX) of a conversion from long integer to short floating-point, CVT.S.L
  - not within the first three preparation cycles (EX…EX+2) of a DIV.S
  - not in the second preparation cycle (EX+1) of a DIV.D
  - not processing a square root instruction.

- The *divider* is one of the following:
  - idle
  - not executing within the last 15 cycles of a DIV.[S,D]
  - not in the second execution cycle (EX+1) of a DIV.D
  - not in the first three execution cycles (EX...EX+2) of a DIV.S.

SQRT.[S,D] can start when the following conditions are met in the RF stage.

- The *adder* is either:
  - idle
  - in its second-to-last execution cycle.
- The *multiplier* and *divider* must be idle.

CVT.fmt instructions can only start when all of the following conditions are met in the RF stage.

- The *adder* is either:
  - idle
  - in its second-to-last execution cycle.
- The *multiplier* is idle, or in one of the following states:
  - If the instruction is an CVT.S.L, CVT.S.W or CVT.D.W, the multiplier must be idle.
  - If the instruction is an CVT.D.L, CVT.S.D, CVT.W.[S,D], CEIL.W.[S,D], FLOOR.W.[S,D], ROUND.W.[S,D], or TRUNC.W.[S,D], the multiplier must not be executing beyond the first cycle (EX) of a MUL.S or the second cycle (EX+1) of a MUL.D. If two multiplication instructions have already been initiated in the multiplier, none of these convert instructions are allowed to start.
  - If the instruction is a CVT.D.S, the multiplier must not be executing the second-to-last execution cycle of either the first or second MUL.[S,D] in the multiplier pipe.
- The *divider* is idle, or not executing the first three (EX...EX+2) cycles nor the last 15 cycles of a DIV.[S,D].

ADD.[S,D] or **SUB.[S,D]** can start only when all of the following conditions are met in the RF stage.

- The *adder* is either:
  - idle
  - in its second-to-last execution cycle.
- The *multiplier* is either:
  - idle
  - among two possible MUL.[S,D] instructions, and is not executing within the fourth or fifth execution cycle from the last.
- The *divider* is either:
  - idle
  - not executing within the first 3 cycles (EX...EX+2) nor the last 15 cycles of a DIV.[S,D].

NEG.[S,D] or **ABS.[S,D]** can start only when all of the following conditions are met in the RF stage.

- The *adder* is either:
  - idle
  - in its second-to-last execution cycle.
- The *multiplier* is either:
  - idle
  - not executing the second-to-last execution cycle.
- The *divider* is either:
  - idle
  - not executing the first 3 cycles (EX...EX+2) nor the last 15 cycles of a DIV.[S,D].

C.COND.[S,D] can start only when all of the following conditions are met in the RF stage.

- The *adder* is either:
  - idle
  - in its second-to-last execution cycle.
- The *multiplier* is either:
  - idle
  - not executing the fourth cycle from the last.
- The *divider* is either:
  - idle
  - not executing the first 3 (EX...EX+2) nor the last 15 cycles of a DIV.[S,D].

Floating-Point Exceptions

7

This chapter describes FPU floating-point exceptions, including FPU exception types, exception trap processing, exception flags, saving and restoring state when handling an exception, and trap handlers for IEEE Standard 754 exceptions.

A floating-point exception occurs whenever the FPU cannot handle either the operands or the results of a floating-point operation in its normal way. The FPU responds by generating an exception to initiate a software trap or by setting a status flag.

7.1 Exception Types

The FP *Control/Status* register described in Chapter 6 contains an *Enable* bit for each exception type; exception *Enable* bits determine whether an exception will cause the FPU to initiate a trap or set a status flag.

- If a trap is taken, the FPU remains in the state found at the beginning of the operation and a software exception handling routine executes.
- If no trap is taken, an appropriate value is written into the FPU destination register and execution continues.

The FPU supports the five IEEE Standard 754 exceptions:

- Inexact (I)
- Underflow (U)
- Overflow (O)
- Division by Zero (Z)
- Invalid Operation (V)

Cause bits, *Enables*, and *Flag* bits (status flags) are used.

The FPU adds a sixth exception type, Unimplemented Operation (E), to use when the FPU cannot implement the standard MIPS floating-point architecture, including cases in which the FPU cannot determine the correct exception behavior. This exception indicates the use of a software implementation. The Unimplemented Operation exception has no *Enable* or *Flag* bit; whenever this exception occurs, an unimplemented exception trap is taken (if the FPU interrupt input to the CPU is enabled).

Figure 7-1 illustrates the *Control/Status* register bits that support exceptions.

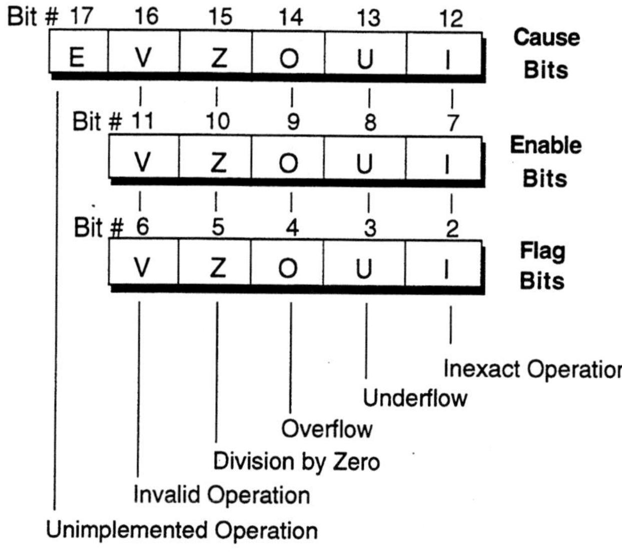

Figure 7-1 Control/Status Register Exception/Flag/Trap/Enable Bits

Each of the five IEEE Standard 754 exceptions (V, Z, O, U, I) is associated with a trap under user control, and is enabled by setting one of the five *Enable* bits. When an exception occurs, both the corresponding *Cause* and *Flag* bits are set. If the corresponding *Enable* bit is set, the FPU generates an interrupt to the CPU and the subsequent exception processing allows a trap to be taken.

7.2 Exception Trap Processing

When a floating-point exception trap is taken, the *Cause* register indicates the floating-point coprocessor is the cause of the exception trap. The Floating-Point Exception (FPE) code is used, and the *Cause* bits of the floating-point *Control/Status* register indicate the reason for the floating-point exception. These bits are, in effect, an extension of the system coprocessor *Cause* register.

7.3 Flags

A *Flag* bit is provided for each IEEE exception. This *Flag* bit is set to a 1 on the assertion of its corresponding exception, with no corresponding exception trap signaled.

The *Flag* bit is reset by writing a new value into the *Status* register; flags can be saved and restored by software either individually or as a group.

When no exception trap is signaled, floating-point coprocessor takes a default action, providing a substitute value for the exception-causing result of the floating-point operation. The particular default action taken depends upon the type of exception. Table 7-1 lists the default action taken by the FPU for each of the IEEE exceptions.

Table 7-1 Default FPU Exception Actions

Field	Description	Rounding Mode	Default action
I	Inexact exception	Any	Supply a rounded result
U	Underflow exception	Any	Supply a rounded result
O	Overflow exception	RN	Modify overflow values to ∞ with the sign of the intermediate result
		RZ	Modify overflow values to the format's largest finite number with the sign of the intermediate result
		RP	Modify negative overflows to the format's most negative finite number; modify positive overflows to + ∞
		RM	Modify positive overflows to the format's largest finite number; modify negative overflows to – ∞
Z	Division by zero	Any	Supply a properly signed ∞
V	Invalid operation	Any	Supply a quiet Not a Number (NaN)

The FPU detects the eight exception causes internally. When the FPU encounters one of these unusual situations, it causes either an IEEE exception or an Unimplemented Operation exception (E).

Table 7-2 lists the exception-causing situations and contrasts the behavior of the FPU with the requirements of the IEEE Standard 754.

Table 7-2 FPU Exception-Causing Conditions

FPA Internal Result	IEEE Standard 754	Trap Enable	Trap Disable	Notes
Inexact result	I	I	I	Loss of accuracy
Exponent overflow	O,I†	O,I	O,I	Normalized exponent > E_{max}
Division by zero	Z	Z	Z	Zero is (exponent = E_{min}-1, mantissa = 0)
Overflow on convert	V	V	E	Source out of integer range
Signaling NaN source	V	V	E	Quiet NaN source produces quiet NaN result
Invalid operation	V	V	E	0/0, etc.
Exponent underflow	U	E	E	Normalized exponent < E_{min}
Denormalized source	None	E	E	Exponent = E-1 and mantissa <> 0

† The IEEE Standard 754 specifies an inexact exception on overflow only if the overflow trap is disabled.

7.4 FPU Exceptions

The following sections describe the conditions that cause the FPU to generate each of its exceptions, and details the FPU response to each exception-causing condition.

Inexact Exception (I)

The FPU generates the Inexact exception if the rounded result of an operation is not exact or if it overflows. The FPU usually examines the operands of floating-point operations before execution actually begins, to determine (based on the exponent values of the operands) if the operation can *possibly* cause an exception. If there is a possibility of an instruction causing an exception trap, the FPU uses a coprocessor stall to execute the instruction.

It is impossible, however, for the FPU to predetermine if an instruction will produce an inexact result. If Inexact exception traps are enabled, the FPU uses the coprocessor stall mechanism to execute all floating-point operations that require more than one cycle. Since this mode of execution can impact performance, Inexact exception traps should be enabled only when necessary.

Trap Enabled Results: If Inexact exception traps are enabled, the result register is not modified and the source registers are preserved.

Trap Disabled Results: The rounded or overflowed result is delivered to the destination register if no other software trap occurs.

Invalid Operation Exception (V)

The Invalid Operation exception is signaled if one or both of the operands are invalid for an implemented operation. When the exception occurs without a trap, the MIPS ISA defines the result as a quiet Not a Number (NaN). The invalid operations are:

- Addition or subtraction: magnitude subtraction of infinities, such as: $(+\infty) + (-\infty)$ or $(-\infty) - (-\infty)$
- Multiplication: 0 times ∞, with any signs
- Division: 0/0, or ∞/∞, with any signs
- Conversion of a floating-point number to a fixed-point format when an overflow, operand value of infinity, or NaN precludes a faithful representation in that format
- Comparison of predicates involving < or > without ?, when the operands are unordered
- Any arithmetic operation on a signaling NaN. A move (MOV) operation is not considered to be an arithmetic operation, but absolute value (ABS) and negate (NEG) are considered to be arithmetic operations and cause this exception if one or both operands is a signaling NaN.
- Square root: $\sqrt{x}$, where x is less than zero

Software can simulate the Invalid Operation exception for other operations that are invalid for the given source operands. Examples of these operations include IEEE Standard 754-specified functions implemented in software, such as Remainder: x REM y, where y is 0 or x is infinite; conversion of a floating-point number to a decimal format whose value causes an overflow, is infinity, or is NaN; and transcendental functions, such as ln (–5) or cos–1(3). Refer to Appendix B for examples or for routines to handle these cases.

Trap Enabled Results: The original operand values are undisturbed.

Trap Disabled Results: The FPU always signals an Unimplemented exception because it does not create the NaN that the IEEE Standard 754 specifies should be returned under these circumstances.

Division-by-Zero Exception (Z)

The Division-by-Zero exception is signaled on an implemented divide operation if the divisor is zero and the dividend is a finite nonzero number. Software can simulate this exception for other operations that produce a signed infinity, such as ln(0), sec($\pi/2$), csc(0), or 0^{-1}.

Trap Enabled Results: The result register is not modified, and the source registers are preserved.

Trap Disabled Results: The result, when no trap occurs, is a correctly signed infinity.

Overflow Exception (O)

The Overflow exception is signaled when the magnitude of the rounded floating-point result, with an unbounded exponent range, is larger than the largest finite number of the destination format. (This exception also sets the Inexact exception and *Flag* bits.)

Trap Enabled Results: The result register is not modified, and the source registers are preserved.

Trap Disabled Results: The result, when no trap occurs, is determined by the rounding mode and the sign of the intermediate result (as listed in Table 7-1).

Underflow Exception (U)

Two related events contribute to the Underflow exception:

- creation of a tiny nonzero result between $\pm 2^{Emin}$ which can cause some later exception because it is so tiny
- extraordinary loss of accuracy during the approximation of such tiny numbers by denormalized numbers.

IEEE Standard 754 allows a variety of ways to detect these events, but requires they be detected the same way for all operations.

Tininess can be detected by one of the following methods:

- after rounding (when a nonzero result, computed as though the exponent range were unbounded, would lie strictly between $\pm 2^{Emin}$)
- before rounding (when a nonzero result, computed as though the exponent range and the precision were unbounded, would lie strictly between $\pm 2^{Emin}$).

The MIPS architecture requires that tininess be detected after rounding.

Loss of accuracy can be detected by one of the following methods:

- denormalization loss (when the delivered result differs from what would have been computed if the exponent range were unbounded)
- inexact result (when the delivered result differs from what would have been computed if the exponent range and precision were both unbounded).

The MIPS architecture requires that loss of accuracy be detected as an inexact result.

Trap Enabled Results: When an underflow trap is enabled, underflow is signaled when tininess is detected regardless of loss of accuracy. If underflow traps are enabled, the result register is not modified, and the source registers are preserved.

Trap Disabled Results: When an underflow trap is not enabled, underflow is signaled (using the underflow flag) only when both tininess and loss of accuracy have been detected. The delivered result might be 0, denormalized, or $\pm 2^{Emin}$.

Unimplemented Instruction Exception (E)

Any attempt to execute an instruction with an operation code or format code that has been reserved for future definition sets the *Unimplemented* bit in the *Cause* field in the FPU *Control/Status* register and traps. The operand and destination registers remain undisturbed and the instruction is emulated in software. Any of the IEEE Standard 754 exceptions can arise from the emulated operation, and these exceptions in turn are simulated.

The Unimplemented Instruction exception can also be signaled when unusual operands or result conditions are detected that the implemented hardware cannot handle properly. These include:

- Denormalized operand
- Not a Number operand
- Denormalized result
- Underflow
- Reserved opcodes
- Unimplemented formats
- Operations which are invalid for their format (for instance, CVT.S.S)

NOTE: Denormalized and NaN operands are only trapped if the instruction is a convert or computational operation. Moves do not trap if their operands are either denormalized or NaNs.

The use of this exception for such conditions is optional; most of these conditions are newly developed and are not expected to be widely used in early implementations. Loopholes are provided in the architecture so that these conditions can be implemented with assistance provided by software, maintaining full compatibility with the IEEE Standard 754.

Trap Enabled Results: The original operand values are undisturbed.

Trap Disabled Results: This trap cannot be disabled.

7.5 Saving and Restoring State

Sixteen doubleword coprocessor load or store operations save or restore the coprocessor floating-point register state in memory. The remainder of control and status information can be saved or restored through Move To/From Coprocessor Control Register instructions, and saving and restoring the processor registers. Normally, the *Control / Status* register is saved first and restored last.

When the coprocessor *Control/Status* register (*FCR31*) is read, and the coprocessor is executing one or more floating-point instructions, the instruction(s) in progress are either completed or reported as exceptions. The architecture requires that no more than one of these pending instructions can cause an exception. If the pending instruction cannot be completed, this instruction is placed in the *Exception* register, if present. Information indicating the type of exception is placed in the *Control/Status* register. When state is restored, state information in the status word indicates that exceptions are pending.

Writing a zero value to the *Cause* field of *Control/Status* register clears all pending exceptions, permitting normal processing to restart after the floating-point register state is restored.

The *Cause* field of the *Control/Status* register holds the results of only one instruction; the FPU examines source operands before an operation is initiated to determine if this instruction can possibly cause an exception. If an exception is possible, the FPU executes the instruction in stall mode to ensure that no more than one instruction (that might cause an exception) is executed at a time.

7.6 Trap Handlers for IEEE Standard 754 Exceptions

The IEEE Standard 754 strongly recommends that users be allowed to specify a trap handler for any of the five standard exceptions that can compute; the trap handler can either compute or specify a substitute result to be placed in the destination register of the operation.

By retrieving an instruction using the processor *Exception Program Counter (EPC)* register, the trap handler determines:

- exceptions occurring during the operation
- the operation being performed
- the destination format

On Overflow or Underflow exceptions (except for conversions), and on Inexact exceptions, the trap handler gains access to the correctly rounded result by examining source registers and simulating the operation in software.

On Overflow or Underflow exceptions encountered on floating-point conversions, and on Invalid Operation and Divide-by-Zero exceptions, the trap handler gains access to the operand values by examining the source registers of the instruction.

The IEEE Standard 754 recommends that, if enabled, the overflow and underflow traps take precedence over a separate inexact trap. This prioritization is accomplished in software; hardware sets the bits for both the Inexact exception and the Overflow or Underflow exception.

R4000 Processor Signal Descriptions

8

This chapter describes the signals used by and in conjunction with the R4000 processor. The signals include the System interface, the Clock/Control interface, the Secondary Cache interface, the Interrupt interface, the Joint Test Action Group (JTAG) interface, and the Initialization interface.

Signals are listed in bold, and low active signals have a trailing asterisk—for instance, the low-active Read Ready signal is **RdRdy***. The signal description also tells if the signal is an input (the processor receives it) or output (the processor sends it out).

Figure 8-1 illustrates the functional groupings of the processor signals.

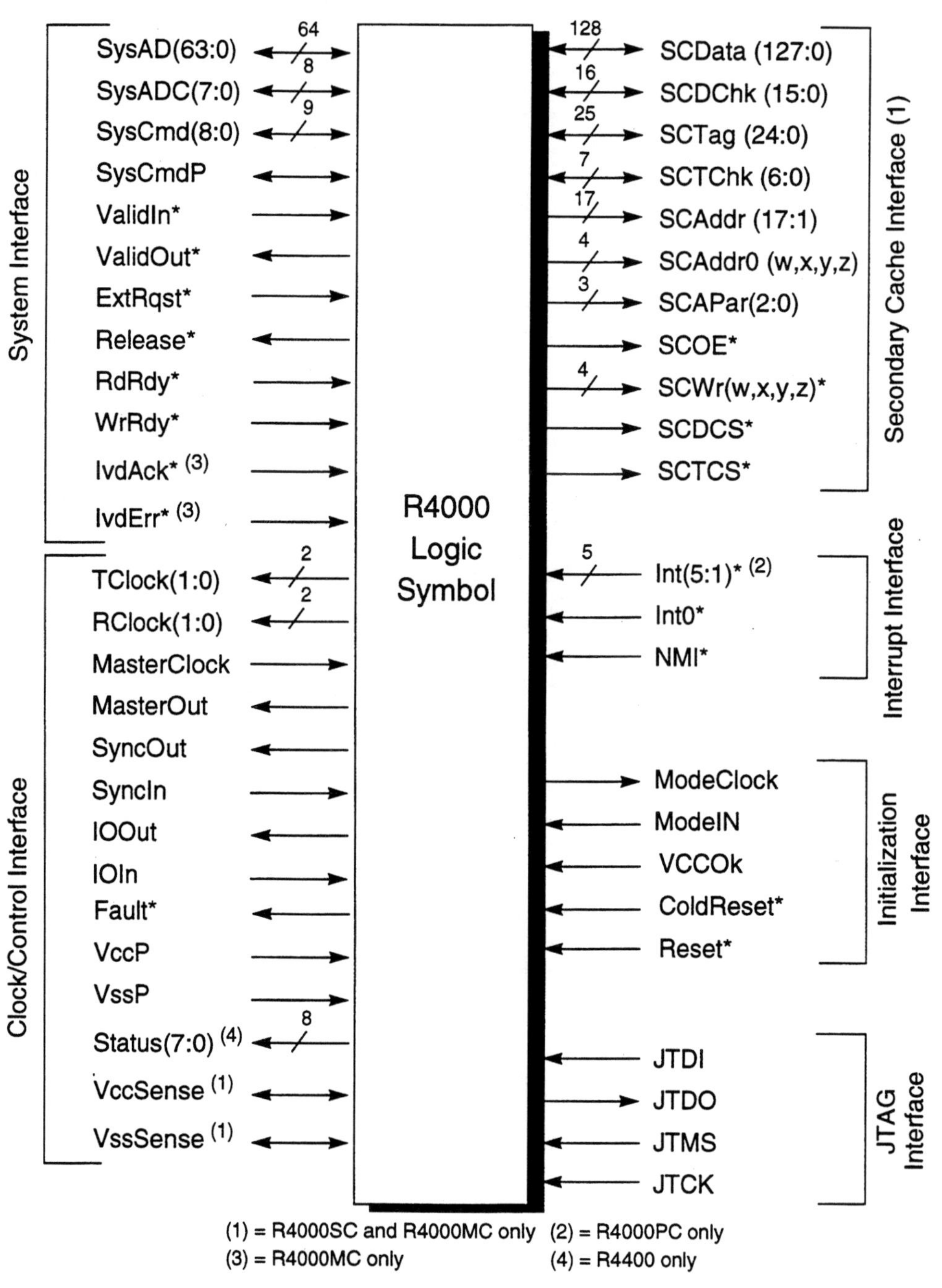

Figure 8-1 R4000 Processor Signals

8.1 System Interface Signals

System interface signals provide the connection between the R4000 processor and the other components in the system. **IvdAck*** and **IvdErr*** signals are applicable only on R4000MC; on the R4000SC they must be tied to Vcc. The remaining signals are available on all three of the package configurations.

Table 8-1 lists the system interface signals.

Table 8-1 System Interface Signals

Name	Definition	Direction	Description
ExtRqst*	External request	Input	An external agent asserts **ExtRqst*** to request use of the System interface. The processor grants the request by asserting **Release***.
IvdAck*	Invalidate acknowledge	Input	An external agent asserts **IvdAck*** to signal successful completion of a processor invalidate or update request (R4000MC only; tie to Vcc on R4000SC).
IvdErr*	Invalidate error	Input	An external agent asserts **IvdErr*** to signal unsuccessful completion of a processor invalidate or update request (R4000MC only; tie to Vcc on R4000SC).
Release*	Release interface	Output	In response to the assertion of **ExtRqst***, the processor asserts **Release***, signalling to the requesting device that the System interface is available.
RdRdy*	Read ready	Input	The external agent asserts **RdRdy*** to indicate that it can accept processor read, invalidate, or update requests in both secondary-cache and no-secondary-cache mode; or can accept a read followed by write request, a read followed by a potential update request, or a read followed by a potential update followed by a write request in secondary cache mode.
SysAD(63:0)	System address/ data bus	Input/ Output	A 64-bit address and data bus for communication between the processor and an external agent.

Table 8-1 (cont.) System Interface Signals

Name	Definition	Direction	Description
SysADC(7:0)	System address/ data check bus	Input/Output	An 8-bit bus containing check bits for the SysAD bus.
SysCmd(8:0)	System command/ data identifier	Input/Output	A 9-bit bus for command and data identifier transmission between the processor and an external agent.
SysCmdP	System command/ data identifier bus parity	Input/Output	A single, even-parity bit for the SysCmd bus.
ValidIn*	Valid input	Input	The external agent asserts **ValidIn*** when it is driving a valid address or data on the SysAD bus and a valid command or data identifier on the SysCmd bus.
ValidOut*	Valid output	Output	The processor asserts **ValidOut*** when it is driving a valid address or data on the SysAD bus and a valid command or data identifier on the SysCmd bus.
WrRdy*	Write ready	Input	An external agent asserts **WrRdy*** when it can accept a processor write request.

8.2 Clock/Control Interface Signals

The Clock/Control interface signals make up the interface for clocking and maintenance. Table 8-2 lists the Clock/Control interface signals.

Table 8-2 Clock/Control Interface Signals

Name	Definition	Direction	Description
IOOut	I/O output	Output	Output slew rate control feedback loop output. Must be connected to **IOIn** through a delay loop that models the I/O path from the processor to an external agent.
IOIn	I/O input	Input	Output slew rate control feedback loop input (see **IOOut**).
MasterClock	Master clock	Input	Master clock input that establishes the processor operating frequency.
MasterOut	Master clock out	Output	Master clock output aligned with **MasterClock**.
RClock(1:0)	Receive clocks	Output	Two identical receive clocks that establish the System interface frequency.
SyncOut	Synchronization clock out	Output	Synchronization clock output. Must be connected to **SyncIn** through an interconnect that models the interconnect between **MasterOut**, **TClock**, **RClock**, and the external agent.
SyncIn	Synchronization clock in	Input	Synchronization clock input.
TClock(1:0)	Transmit clocks	Output	Two identical transmit clocks that establish the System interface frequency.
Fault*	Fault	Output	The processor asserts **Fault*** to indicate a mismatch output of boundary comparators, and indication of System interface input parity or ECC errors.

Table 8-2 (cont.) Clock/Control Interface Signals

Name	Definition	Direction	Description
Status(7:0)	Status	Output	An 8-bit bus that indicates the current operational status of the processor. R4400 only.
VccP	Quiet Vcc for PLL	Input	Quiet Vcc for the internal phase locked loop.
VccSense	Vcc sense	Input/ Output	A special pin used only in component testing and characterization, **VccSense** provides a separate, direct connection from the on-chip Vcc node to a package pin, without connecting to the in-package power planes. Test fixtures treat **VccSense** as an analog output pin; the voltage at this pin directly exhibits the behavior of the on-chip Vcc. Thus, characterization engineers can easily observe the effects of Δi/Δt noise, transmission line reflections, etc. **VccSense** should be connected to Vcc in functional system designs.
VssP	Quiet Vss for PLL	Input	Quiet Vss for the internal phase locked loop.
VssSense	Vss sense	Input/ Output	**VssSense** provides a separate, direct connection from the on-chip Vss node to a package pin without having to connect to the in-package ground planes. **VssSense** should be connected to Vss in functional system designs.

8.3 Secondary Cache Interface Signals

Secondary Cache interface signals constitute the interface between the R4000 processor and secondary cache. These signals are available only on the R4000MC and R4000SC. Table 8-3 lists the Secondary Cache interface signals.

Table 8-3 Secondary Cache Interface Signals

Name	Definition	Direction	Description
SCAddr(17:1)	Secondary cache address bus	Output	The 18-bit address bus for the secondary cache. Bit 0 has four output lines, (**SCAddr0W:Z**), to provide additional drive current.
SCAddr0W	Secondary cache address LSB	Output	
SCAddr0X	Secondary cache address LSB	Output	
SCAddr0Y	Secondary cache address LSB	Output	
SCAddr0Z	Secondary cache address LSB	Output	
SCAPar(2:0)	Secondary cache address parity bus	Output	A 3-bit bus that carries the parity of the SCAddr bus and the cache control line **SCWr***. The individual bit definitions are:
SCAPar2	Secondary cache address parity bus	Output	Even parity for **SCAddr(17:12)** and **SCWr***
SCAPar1	Secondary cache address parity bus	Output	Even parity for **SCAddr(11:6)** and **SCDCS***
SCAPar0	Secondary cache address parity bus	Output	Even parity for **SCAddr(5:0)** and **SCTCS***
SCData(127:0)	Secondary cache data bus	Input/Output	A 128-bit bus used to read or write cache data from and to the secondary cache data RAM.

Table 8-3 (cont.) Secondary Cache Interface Signals

Name	Definition	Direction	Description
SCDChk(15:0)	Secondary cache data ECC bus	Input/Output	A 16-bit bus that carries two 8-bit ECC fields that cover the 128 bits of SCData from/to secondary cache. **SCDChk(15:8)** corresponds to **SCData(127:64)** and **SCDChk(7:0)** corresponds to **SCData(63:0)**.
SCDCS*	Secondary cache data chip select	Output	Chip select enable signal for the secondary cache data RAM.
SCOE*	Secondary cache output enable	Output	Output enable for the secondary cache data and tag RAM.
SCTag(24:0)	Secondary cache tag bus	Input/Output	A 25-bit bus used to read or write cache tags from and to the secondary cache.
SCTChk(6:0)	Secondary cache tag ECC bus	Input/Output	A 7-bit bus that carries an ECC field covering the SCTag from and to the secondary cache.
SCTCS*	Secondary cache tag chip select	Output	Chip select enable signal for the secondary cache tag RAM.
SCWrW*	Secondary cache write enable	Output	Write enable for the secondary cache data and tag RAM.
SCWrX*	Secondary cache write enable	Output	Write enable for the secondary cache data and tag RAM.
SCWrY*	Secondary cache write enable	Output	Write enable for the secondary cache data and tag RAM.
SCWrZ*	Secondary cache write enable	Output	Write enable for the secondary cache data and tag RAM.

8.4 Interrupt Interface Signals

The Interrupt interface signals make up the interface used by external agents to interrupt the R4000 processor. **Int*(5:1)** are available only on the R4000PC; **Int*(0)** and **NMI*** are available on all three configurations. Table 8-4 lists the Interrupt interface signals.

Table 8-4 Interrupt Interface Signals

Name	Definition	Direction	Description
Int*(5:1)	Interrupt	Input	Five of six general processor interrupts, bit-wise ORed with bits 5:1 of the interrupt register. R4000PC only.
Int*(0)	Interrupt	Input	One of six general processor interrupts, bit-wise ORed with bit 0 of the interrupt register.
NMI*	Nonmaskable interrupt	Input	Nonmaskable interrupt, ORed with bit 6 of the interrupt register.

8.5 JTAG Interface Signals

The JTAG interface signals make up the interface that provides the JTAG boundary scan mechanism. Table 8-5 lists the JTAG interface signals.

Table 8-5 JTAG Interface Signals

Name	Definition	Direction	Description
JTDI	JTAG data in	Input	Data is serially scanned in through this pin.
JTCK	TAG clock input	Input	The processor outputs a serial clock on **JTCK**. On the rising edge of **JTCK**, both **JTDI** and **JTMS** are sampled.
JTDO	JTAG data out	Output	Data is serially scanned out through this pin.
JTMS	JTAG command	Input	JTAG command signal, indicating the incoming serial data is command data.

8.6 Initialization Interface Signals

The Initialization interface signals make up the interface by which an external agent initializes the processor operating parameters. These signals are available on each of the three processor configurations. Table 8-6 lists the Initialization interface signals.

Table 8-6 Initialization Interface Signals

Name	Definition	Direction	Description
ColdReset*	Cold reset	Input	This signal must be asserted for a power on reset or a cold reset. The clocks **SClock**, **TClock**, and **RClock** begin to cycle and are synchronized with the deasserted edge of **ColdReset***. **ColdReset*** must be deasserted synchronously with **MasterOut**.
ModeClock	Boot mode clock	Output	Serial boot-mode data clock output; runs at the system clock frequency divided by 256: (**MasterClock**/256).
ModeIn	Boot mode data in	Input	Serial boot-mode data input.
Reset*	Reset	Input	This signal must be asserted for any reset sequence. It can be asserted synchronously or asynchronously for a cold reset, or synchronously to initiate a warm reset. **Reset*** must be deasserted synchronously with **MasterOut**.
VCCOk	Vcc is OK	Input	When asserted, this signal indicates to the processor that the +5 volt power supply has been above 4.75 volts for more than 100 milliseconds and will remain stable. The assertion of **VCCOk** initiates the initialization sequence.

8.7 Signal Summary

Table 8-7 R4000SC/MC Processor Signal Summary

Description	Name	I/O	Asserted State	3-State
Secondary cache data bus	SCData(127:0)	I/O	High	Yes
Secondary cache data ECC bus	SCDChk(15:0)	I/O	High	Yes
Secondary cache tag bus	SCTag(24:0)	I/O	High	Yes
Secondary cache tag ECC bus	SCTChk(6:0)	I/O	High	Yes
Secondary cache address bus	SCAddr(17:1)	O	High	No
Secondary cache address LSB	SCAddr0Z	O	High	No
Secondary cache address LSB	SCAddr0Y	O	High	No
Secondary cache address LSB	SCAddr0X	O	High	No
Secondary cache address LSB	SCAddr0W	O	High	No
Secondary cache address parity bus	SCAPar(2:0)	O	High	No
Secondary cache output enable	SCOE*	O	Low	No
Secondary cache write enable	SCWrZ*	O	Low	No
Secondary cache write enable	SCWrY*	O	Low	No
Secondary cache write enable	SCWrX*	O	Low	No
Secondary cache write enable	SCWrW*	O	Low	No
Secondary cache data chip select	SCDCS*	O	Low	No
Secondary cache tag chip select	SCTCS*	O	Low	No
System address/data bus	SysAD(63:0)	I/O	High	Yes
System address/data check bus	SysADC(7:0)	I/O	High	Yes
System command/data identifier bus	SysCmd(8:0)	I/O	High	Yes
System command/data identifier bus parity	SysCmdP	I/O	High	Yes
Valid input	ValidIn*	I	Low	No
Valid output	ValidOut*	O	Low	No
External request	ExtRqst*	I	Low	No
Release interface	Release*	O	Low	No
Read ready	RdRdy*	I	Low	No
Write ready	WrRdy*	I	Low	No
Invalidate acknowledge	IvdAck*	I	Low	No
Invalidate error	IvdErr*	I	Low	No

Table 8-7 (cont.) R4000SC/MC Processor Signal Summary

Description	Name	I/O	Asserted State	3-State
Interrupt	Int*(0)	I	Low	No
Nonmaskable interrupt	NMI*	I	Low	No
Boot mode data in	ModeIn	I	High	No
Boot mode clock	ModeClock	O	High	No
JTAG data in	JTDI	I	High	No
JTAG data out	JTDO	O	High	No
JTAG command	JTMS	I	High	No
JTAG clock input	JTCK	I	High	No
Transmit clocks	TClock(1:0)	O	High	No
Receive clocks	RClock(1:0)	O	High	No
Master clock	MasterClock	I	High	No
Master clock out	MasterOut	O	High	No
Synchronization clock out	SyncOut	O	High	No
Synchronization clock in	SyncIn	I	High	No
I/O output	IOOut	O	High	No
I/O input	IOIn	I	High	No
Vcc is OK	VCCOk	I	High	No
Cold reset	ColdReset*	I	Low	No
Reset	Reset*	I	Low	No
Fault	Fault*	O	Low	No
Quiet Vcc for PLL	VccP	I	High	No
Quiet Vss for PLL	VssP	I	High	No
Status	Status(7:0)	O	High	No
Vcc sense	VccSense	I/O	N/A	No
Vss sense	VssSense	I/O	N/A	No

Table 8-8 R4000PC Processor Signal Summary

Description	Name	I/O	Asserted State	3-State
System address/data bus	SysAD(63:0)	I/O	High	Yes
System address/data check bus	SysADC(7:0)	I/O	High	Yes
System command/data identifier bus	SysCmd(8:0)	I/O	High	Yes
System command/data identifier bus parity	SysCmdP	I/O	High	Yes
Valid input	ValidIn*	I	Low	No
Valid output	ValidOut*	O	Low	No
External request	ExtRqst*	I	Low	No
Release interface	Release*	O	Low	No
Read ready	RdRdy*	I	Low	No
Write ready	WrRdy*	I	Low	No
Interrupts	Int*(5:1)	I	Low	No
Interrupt	Int*(0)	I	Low	No
Nonmaskable interrupt	NMI*	I	Low	No
Boot mode data in	ModeIn	I	High	No
Boot mode clock	ModeClock	O	High	No
JTAG data in	JTDI	I	High	No
JTAG data out	JTDO	O	High	No
JTAG command	JTMS	I	High	No
JTAG clock input	JTCK	I	High	No
Transmit clocks	TClock(1:0)	O	High	No
Receive clocks	RClock(1:0)	O	High	No
Master clock	MasterClock	I	High	No
Master clock out	MasterOut	O	High	No
Synchronization clock out	SyncOut	O	High	No
Synchronization clock in	SyncIn	I	High	No
I/O output	IOOut	O	High	No
I/O input	IOIn	I	High	No
Vcc is OK	VCCOk	I	High	No

Table 8-8 (cont.) R4000PC Processor Signal Summary

Description	Name	I/O	Asserted State	3-State
Cold reset	ColdReset*	I	Low	No
Reset	Reset*	I	Low	No
Fault	Fault*	O	Low	No
Quiet Vcc for PLL	VccP	I	High	No
Quiet Vss for PLL	VssP	I	High	No

Initialization Interface

9

This chapter describes the R4000 Initialization interface. This includes the reset signal description and types, initialization sequence, with signals and timing dependencies, and boot modes, which are set at initialization time.

Signal names are listed in bold letters—for instance the signal **VCCOk** indicates +5 voltage is stable. Low-active signals are indicated by a trailing asterisk, such as **ColdReset***, the power-on/cold reset signal.

9.1 Functional Overview

The R4000 processor has the following three types of resets; they use the **VCCOk, ColdReset***, and **Reset*** input signals.

- **Power-on reset**: starts when the power supply is turned on and completely reinitializes the internal state machine of the processor without saving any state information.
- **Cold reset**: restarts all clocks, but the power supply remains stable. A cold reset completely reinitializes the internal state machine of the processor without saving any state information.
- **Warm reset**: restarts processor, but does not affect clocks. A warm reset preserves the processor internal state.

The operation of each type of reset is described in sections that follow. Refer to Figures 9-1, 9-2, and 9-3 later in this chapter for timing diagrams of the power-on, cold, and warm resets.

The Initialization interface is a serial interface that operates at the frequency of the **MasterClock** divided by 256: (**MasterClock**/256). This low-frequency operation allows the initialization information to be stored in a low-cost EPROM.

9.2 Reset Signal Description

This section describes the three reset signals, **VCCOk, ColdReset***, and **Reset***.

VCCOk: When asserted†, **VCCOk** indicates to the processor that the +5 volt power supply (Vcc) has been above 4.75 volts for more than 100 milliseconds (ms) and is expected to remain stable. The assertion of **VCCOk** initiates the reading of the boot-time mode control serial stream (described in Initialization Sequence, in this chapter).

ColdReset*: The **ColdReset*** signal must be asserted (low) for either a power-on reset or a cold reset. The clocks **SClock, TClock,** and **RClock** begin to cycle and are synchronized with the deasserted edge (high) of **ColdReset***. **ColdReset*** must be deasserted synchronously with **MasterClock.**

Reset*: the **Reset*** signal must be asserted for any reset sequence. It can be asserted synchronously or asynchronously for a cold reset, or synchronously to initiate a warm reset. **Reset*** must be deasserted synchronously with **MasterClock.**

ModeIn: Serial boot mode data in.

ModeClock: Serial boot mode data out, at the **MasterClock** frequency divided by 256 (**MasterClock**/256).

---

† *Asserted* means the signal is true, or in its valid state. For example, the low-active **Reset*** signal is said to be asserted when it is in a low (true) state; the high-active **VCCOk** signal is true when it is asserted high.

Power-on Reset

The sequence for a power-on reset is listed below.

1. Power-on reset applies a stable Vcc of at least 4.75 volts from the +5 volt power supply to the processor. It also supplies a stable, continuous system clock at the processor operational frequency.
2. After at least 100 ms of stable Vcc and **MasterClock**, the **VCCOk** signal is asserted to the processor. The assertion of **VCCOk** initializes the processor operating parameters. After the mode bits have been read in, the processor allows its internal phase locked loops to lock, stabilizing the processor internal clock, **PClock**, the **SyncOut-SyncIn** clock path (described in Chapter 10), and the master clock output, **MasterOut**.
3. **ColdReset*** is asserted for at least 64K (2^{16}) **MasterClock** cycles after the assertion of **VCCOk**. Once the processor reads the boot-time mode control serial data stream, **ColdReset*** can be deasserted. **ColdReset*** must be deasserted synchronously with **MasterClock**.
4. The deasserted edge of **ColdReset*** synchronizes the edges of **SClock**, **TClock**, and **RClock** (to all processors, if in a multiprocessor system).
5. After **ColdReset*** is deasserted synchronously and **SClock**, **TClock**, and **RClock** have stabilized, **Reset*** is deasserted to allow the processor to begin running. (**Reset*** must be held asserted for at least 64 **MasterClock** cycles after the deassertion of **ColdReset***.) **Reset*** must be deasserted synchronously with **MasterClock**.

NOTE: **ColdReset*** must be asserted when **VCCOk** asserts. The behavior of the processor is undefined if **VCCOk** asserts while **ColdReset*** is deasserted.

Cold Reset

A cold reset can begin anytime after the processor has read the initialization data stream, causing the processor to start with the Reset exception.

A cold reset requires the same sequence as a power-on reset except that the power is presumed to be stable before the assertion of the reset inputs and the deassertion of **VCCOk**.

To begin the reset sequence, **VCCOk** must be deasserted for a minimum of 100 ms before reassertion.

Warm Reset

To execute a warm reset, the **Reset*** input is asserted synchronously with **MasterClock**. It is then held asserted for at least 64 **MasterClock** cycles before being deasserted synchronously with **MasterClock**. The processor internal clocks, **PClock** and **SClock**, and the System interface clocks, **TClock** and **RClock**, are not affected by a warm reset. The boot-time mode control serial data stream is not read by the processor on a warm reset. A warm reset forces the processor to start with a Soft Reset exception.

The master clock output, **MasterOut**, generates any reset-related signals for the processor that must be synchronous with **MasterClock**.

After a power-on reset, cold reset, or warm reset, all processor internal state machines are reset, and the processor begins execution at the reset vector. All processor internal states are preserved during a warm reset, although the precise state of the caches depends on whether or not a cache miss sequence has been interrupted by resetting the processor state machines.

9.3 Initialization Sequence

The boot-mode initialization sequence begins immediately after **VCCOk** is asserted. As the processor reads the serial stream of 256 bits through the **ModeIn** pin, the boot-mode bits initialize all fundamental processor modes (the signals used are described in Chapter 8).

The initialization sequence is listed below.

1. The system deasserts the **VCCOk** signal. The **ModeClock** output ais held asserted.
2. The processor synchronizes the **ModeClock** output at the time **VCCOk** is asserted. The first rising edge of **ModeClock** occurs 256 **MasterClock** cycles after **VCCOk** is asserted.
3. Each bit of the initialization stream is presented at the **ModeIn** pin after each rising edge of the **ModeClock**. The processor samples 256 initialization bits from the **ModeIn** input.

Figures 9-1, 9-2, and 9-3 on the next three pages show the timing diagrams for the power-on, warm, and cold resets.

Power-on Reset (POR)

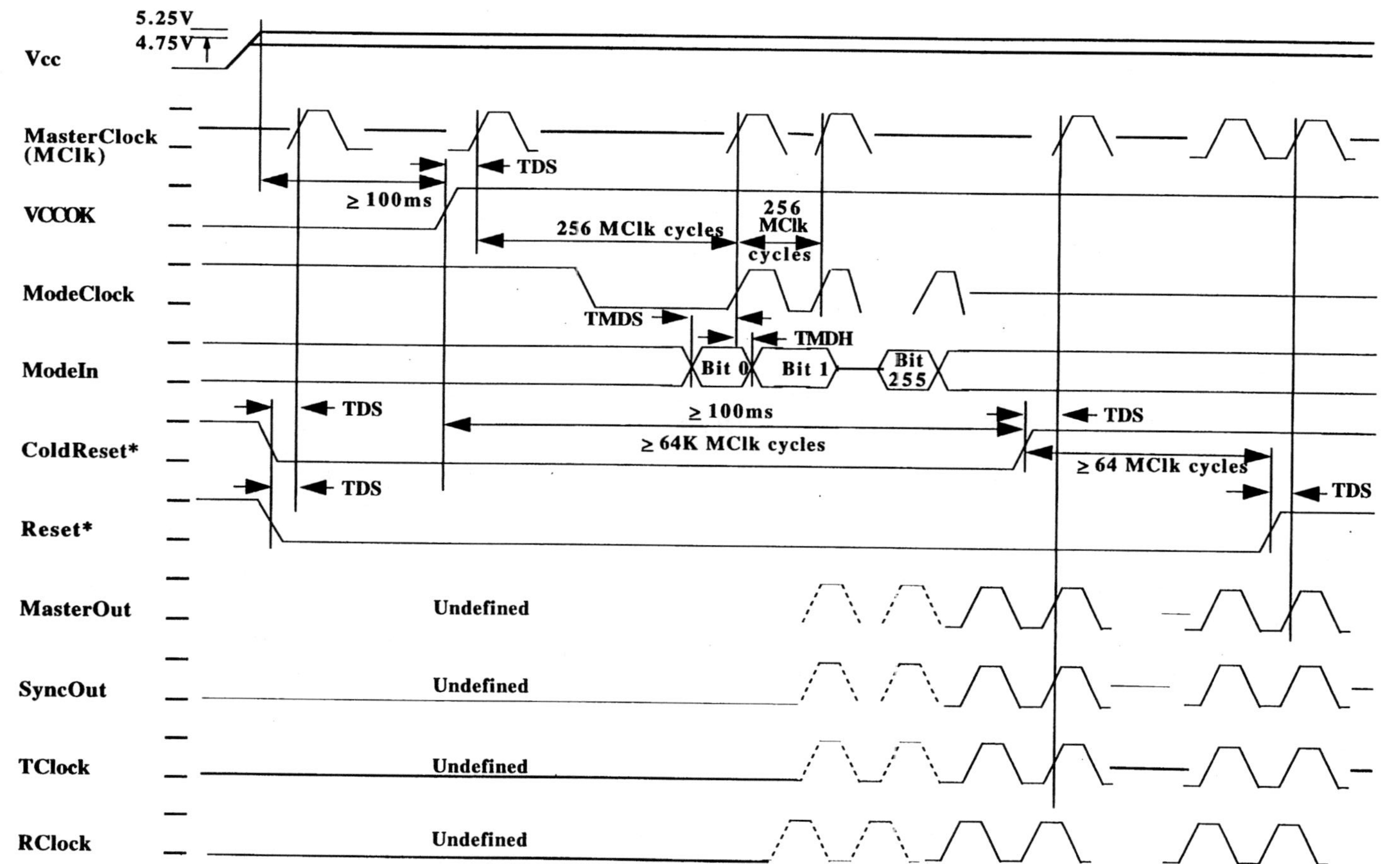

Figure 9-1 Power-on Reset

Cold Reset

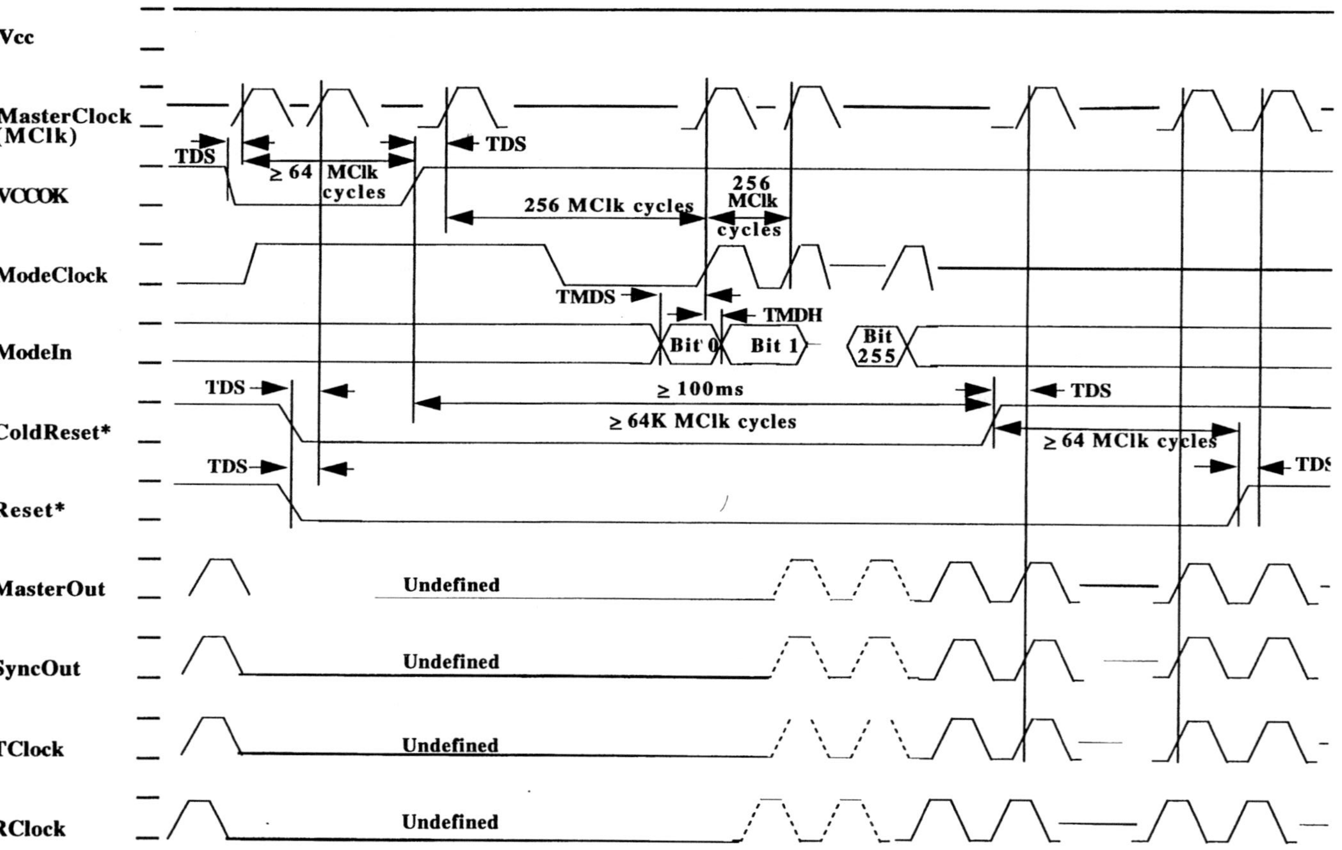

Figure 9-2 Cold Reset

Warm Reset

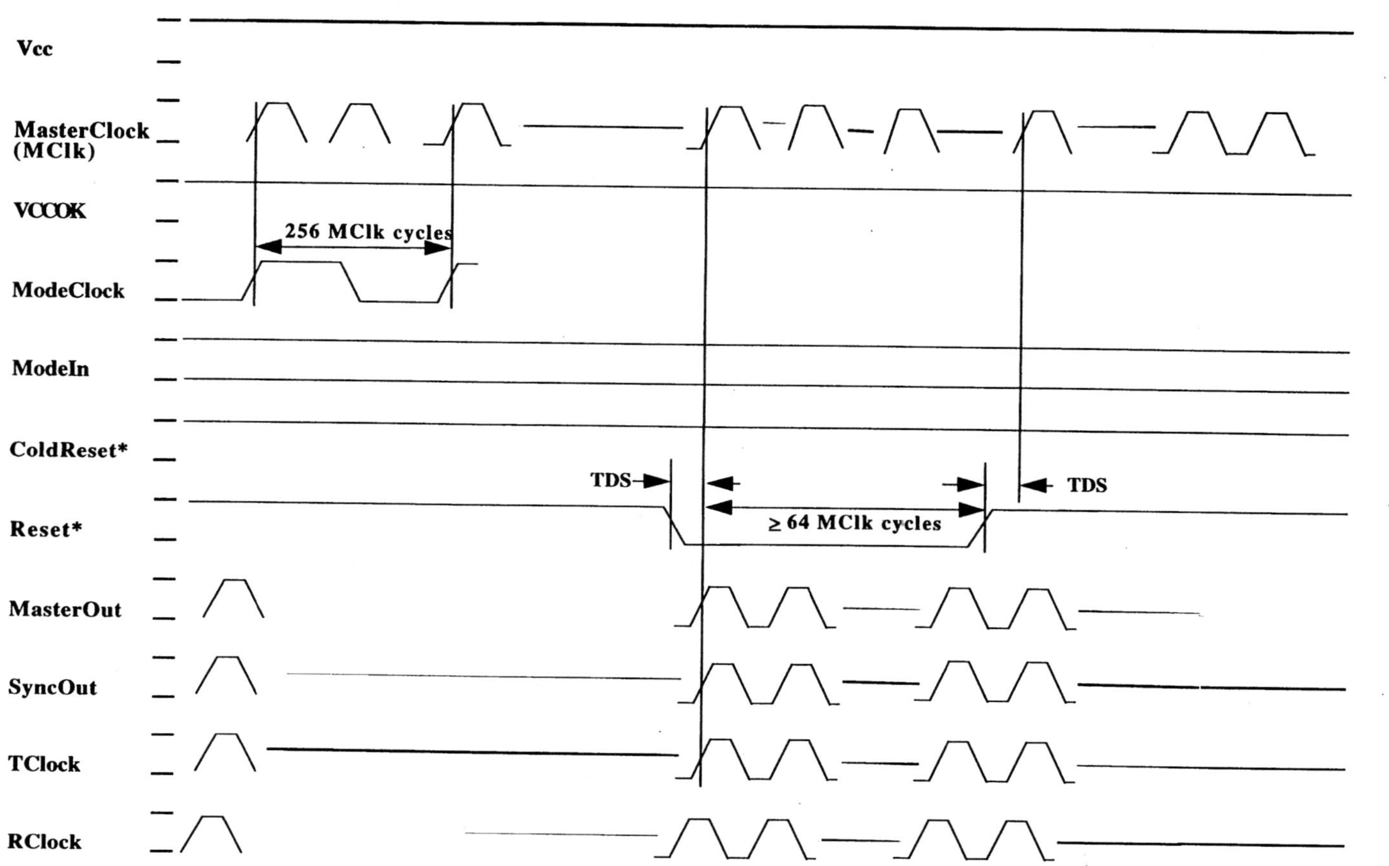

Figure 9-3 Warm Reset

9.4 Boot-Mode Settings

Table 9-1 lists the processor boot-mode settings. The following rules apply to the boot-mode settings listed in this table:

- Bit 0 of the stream is presented to the processor when **VCCOk** is first asserted.
- Selecting a reserved value results in undefined processor behavior.
- Bits 65 to 255 are reserved bits.
- Zeros must be scanned in for all reserved bits.

Table 9-1 Boot-Mode Settings

Serial Bit	Value	Mode Setting
0	**BlkOrder:** Secondary Cache Mode block read response ordering	
	0	Sequential ordering
	1	Subblock ordering
1	**EIBParMode:** Specifies nature of System interface check bus	
	0	Single error correcting, double error detecting (SECDED) error checking and correcting mode
	1	Byte parity
2	**EndBIt:** Specifies byte ordering	
	0	Little-endian ordering
	1	Big-endian ordering
3	**DShMdDis:** Dirty shared mode; enables the transition to dirty shared state on a successful processor update	
	0	Dirty shared mode enabled
	1	Dirty shared mode disabled
4	**NoSCMode:** Specifies presence of secondary cache	
	0	Secondary cache present
	1	No secondary cache present
5:6	**SysPort:** System Interface port width, bit 6 most significant	
	0	64 bits
	1-3	Reserved
7	**SC64BitMd:** Secondary cache interface port width	
	0	128 bits
	1	Reserved
8	**EISpltMd:** Specifies secondary cache organization	
	0	Secondary cache unified
	1	Reserved

Table 9-1 (cont.) Boot-Mode Settings

Serial Bit	Value	Mode Setting
9:10	**SCBlkSz:** Secondary cache line length, bit 10 most significant	
	0	4 words
	1	8 words
	2	16 words
	3	32 words
11:14	**XmitDatPat:** System interface data rate, bit 14 most significant	
	0	D
	1	DDx
	2	DDxx
	3	DxDx
	4	DDxxx
	5	DDxxxx
	6	DxxDxx
	7	DDxxxxxx
	8	DxxxDxxx
	9-15	Reserved
15:17	**SysCkRatio:** PClock to SClock divisor, frequency relationship between SClock, RClock, and TClock and PClock, bit 17 most significant	
	0	Divide by 2
	1	Divide by 3
	2	Divide by 4
	3	Divide by 6 (R4400 processor only)
	4	Divide by 8 (R4400 processor only)
	5-7	Reserved
18	**SIMasterMd:** Master/Checker Mode (see mode bit 42); used in R4400 only.	
19	**TimIntDis:** Timer Interrupt enable allows timer interrupts, otherwise the interrupt used by the timer becomes a general purpose interrupt	
	0	Timer Interrupt enabled
	1	Timer Interrupt disabled
20	**PotUpdDis:** Potential update enable allows potential updates to be issued. Otherwise, only compulsory updates are issued	
	0	Potential updates enabled
	1	Potential updates disabled
21:24	**TWrSUp:** Secondary cache write deassertion delay, T_{WrSup} in PCycles, bit 24 most significant	
	0-2	Undefined
	3-15	Number of PClock cycles: Min 3, Max 15

Table 9-1 (cont.) Boot-Mode Settings

<table>
<tr><th>Serial Bit</th><th colspan="2">Value</th><th>Mode Setting</th></tr>
<tr><td rowspan="3">25:26</td><td colspan="3">TWr2Dly: Secondary cache write assertion delay 2, T_{Wr2Dly} in PCycles, bit 26 most significant</td></tr>
<tr><td colspan="2">0</td><td>Undefined</td></tr>
<tr><td colspan="2">1-3</td><td>Number of PClock cycles: Min 1, Max 3</td></tr>
<tr><td rowspan="3">27:28</td><td colspan="3">TWr1Dly: Secondary cache write assertion delay 1, T_{Wr1Dly} in PCycles, bit 28 most significant</td></tr>
<tr><td colspan="2">0</td><td>Undefined</td></tr>
<tr><td colspan="2">1-3</td><td>Number of PClock cycles; Min 1, Max 3</td></tr>
<tr><td rowspan="3">29</td><td colspan="3">TWrRc: Secondary cache write recovery time, T_{WrRc} in PCycles, either 0 or 1 cycle</td></tr>
<tr><td colspan="2">0</td><td>0 cycle</td></tr>
<tr><td colspan="2">1</td><td>1 cycle</td></tr>
<tr><td rowspan="3">30:32</td><td colspan="3">TDis: Secondary cache disable time, T_{Dis} in PCycles, bit 32 most significant</td></tr>
<tr><td colspan="2">0-1</td><td>Undefined</td></tr>
<tr><td colspan="2">2-7</td><td>Number of PClock cycles: Min 2, Max 7</td></tr>
<tr><td rowspan="3">33:36</td><td colspan="3">TRd2Cyc: Secondary cache read cycle time 2, T_{RdCyc2} in PCycles, bit 36 most significant</td></tr>
<tr><td colspan="2">0-2</td><td>Undefined</td></tr>
<tr><td colspan="2">3-15</td><td>Number of PClock cycles: Min 3, Max 15</td></tr>
<tr><td rowspan="3">37:40</td><td colspan="3">TRd1Cyc: Secondary cache read cycle time 1, T_{RdCyc1} in PCycles, bit 40 most significant</td></tr>
<tr><td colspan="2">0-3</td><td>Undefined</td></tr>
<tr><td colspan="2">4-15</td><td>Number of PClock cycles: Min 4, Max 15</td></tr>
<tr><td>41</td><td colspan="2">0</td><td>Reserved</td></tr>
<tr><td rowspan="6">42</td><td colspan="3">SCMasterMd: selects the type of Master/Checker mode (also see description of mode bit 18). Used in R4400 only.</td></tr>
<tr><th>SCMasterMd (Bit 42)</th><th>SIMasterMd (Bit 18)</th><th>Mode</th></tr>
<tr><td>0</td><td>0</td><td>Complete Master
(required for single-chip operation)</td></tr>
<tr><td>1</td><td>1</td><td>Complete Listener
(paired with Complete Master)</td></tr>
<tr><td>1</td><td>0</td><td>System Interface Master
(SIMaster)</td></tr>
<tr><td>0</td><td>1</td><td>Secondary Cache Master
(SCMaster, paired with SIMaster)</td></tr>
<tr><td>43:45</td><td colspan="2">0</td><td>Reserved</td></tr>
</table>

Table 9-1 (cont.) Boot-Mode Settings

Serial Bit	Value	Mode Setting
46	**Pkg179:** R4000 Processor Package type	
	0	Large (447 pin)
	1	Small (179 pin)
47:49	**CycDivisor:** This mode determines the clock divisor for the reduced power mode. When the *RP* bit in the *Status* register is set to 1, the pipeline clock is divided by one of the following values. Bit 49 is the most significant.	
	0	Divide by 2
	1	Divide by 4
	2	Divide by 8
	3	Divide by 16
	4-7	Reserved
50:52	**Drv0_50, Drv0_75, Drv1_00:** Drive the outputs out in *n* x **MasterClock** period. Bit 52 is the most significant. Combinations not defined below are reserved.	
	1	Drive at 0.50 x **MasterClock** period
	2	Drive at 0.75 x **MasterClock** period
	4	Drive at 1.00 x **MasterClock** period
53:56	**InitP:** Initial values for the state bits that determine the pull-down $\Delta i/\Delta t$ and switching speed of the output buffers. Bit 53 is the most significant.	
	0	Fastest pull-down rate
	1-14	Intermediate pull-down rates
	15	Slowest pull-down rate
57:60	**InitN:** Initial values for the state bits that determine the pull-up $\Delta i/\Delta t$ and switching speed of the output buffers. Bit 57 is the most significant.	
	0	Slowest pull-up rate
	1-14	Intermediate pull-up rates
	15	Fastest pull-up rate
61	**EnblDPLLR:** Enables the negative feedback loop that determines the $\Delta i/\Delta t$ and switching speed of the output buffers during ColdReset.	
	0	Disable $\Delta i/\Delta t$ mechanism
	1	Enable $\Delta i/\Delta t$ mechanism
62	**EnblDPLL:** Enables the negative feedback loop that determines the $\Delta i/\Delta t$ and switching speed of the output buffers during ColdReset and during normal operation.	
	0	Disable $\Delta i/\Delta t$ control mechanism
	1	Enable $\Delta i/\Delta t$ control mechanism

Table 9-1 (cont.) Boot-Mode Settings

Serial Bit	Value	Mode Setting
63	**DsblPLL:** Disables the phase-locked loops (PLLs) that match **MasterClock** and produce **RClock, TClock, SClock,** and the internal clocks.	
	0	Enable PLLs
	1	Disable PLLs
64	**SRTristate:** Controls when output-only pins are tristated	
	0	Only when **ColdReset*** is asserted
	1	When **Reset*** or **ColdReset*** are asserted
65:255	Reserved. Scan in zeros.	

Clock Interface

10

This chapter describes the clock signals ("clocks") used in the R4000 processor and the processor status reporting mechanism.

The subject matter includes basic system clocks, system timing parameters, connecting clocks to a phase-locked system, connecting clocks to a system without phase locking, and processor status outputs.

10.1 Signal Terminology

The following terminology is used in this chapter (and book) when describing signals:

- *Rising edge* indicates a low-to-high transition.
- *Falling edge* indicates a high-to-low transition.
- *Clock-to-Q delay* is the amount of time it takes for a signal to move from the input of a device (*clock*) to the output of the device (*Q*).

Figures 10-1 and 10-2 illustrate these terms.

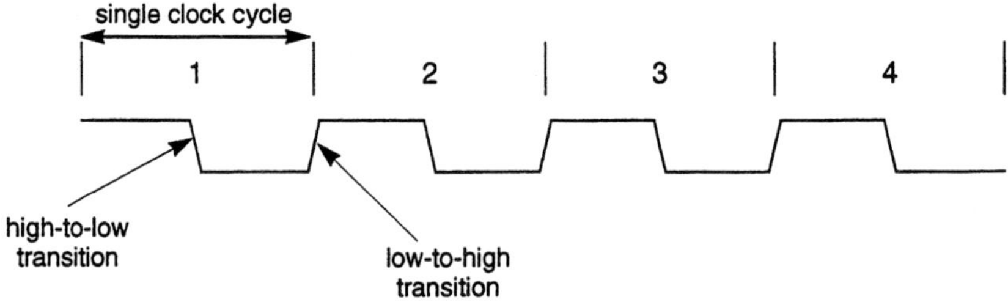

Figure 10-1 Signal Transitions

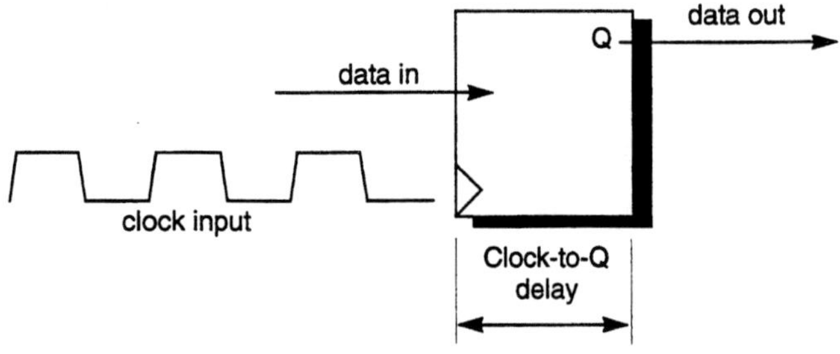

Figure 10-2 Clock-to-Q Delay

10.2 Basic System Clocks

The various clock signals used in the R4000 processor are described below, starting with **MasterClock**, upon which the processor bases all internal and external clocking.

MasterClock

The processor bases all internal and external clocking on the single **MasterClock** input signal. The processor generates the clock output signal, **MasterOut**, at the same frequency as **MasterClock** and aligns **MasterOut** with **MasterClock**, if **SyncIn** is connected to **SyncOut**.

MasterOut

The processor generates the clock output signal, **MasterOut**, at the same frequency as **MasterClock** and aligns **MasterOut** with **MasterClock**, if **SyncIn** is connected to **SyncOut**. **MasterOut** clocks external logic, such as the reset logic.

SyncIn/SyncOut

The processor generates **SyncOut** at the same frequency as **MasterClock** and aligns **SyncIn** with **MasterClock**.

SyncOut must be connected to **SyncIn** either directly, or through an external buffer. The processor can compensate for both output driver and input buffer delays (and, when necessary, delay caused by an external buffer) when aligning **SyncIn** with **MasterClock**. Figure 10-7 gives an illustration of **SyncOut** connected to **SyncIn** through an external buffer.

PClock

The processor generates an internal clock, **PClock**, at twice the frequency of **MasterClock** and precisely aligns every other rising edge of **PClock** with the rising edge of **MasterClock**.

All internal registers and latches use **PClock**.

SClock

The R4000 processor divides **PClock** by 2, 3, or 4 (as programmed at boot-mode initialization) to generate the internal clock signal, **SClock**. The R4400 processor divides **PClock** by 2, 3, 4, 6 or 8 (as programmed at boot-mode initialization) to generate **SClock**. The processor uses **SClock** to sample data at the system interface and to clock data into the processor system interface output registers.

The first rising edge of **SClock**, after **ColdReset*** is deasserted, is aligned with the first rising edge of **MasterClock**.

TClock

TClock (transmit clock) clocks the output registers of an external agent,[†] and can be a global system clock for any other logic in the external agent.

TClock is identical to **SClock**. The edges of **TClock** align precisely with the edges of **SClock** and **TClock** can also be aligned with **MasterClock**, when **SyncIn** is connected to **SyncOut**.

RClock

The external agent uses **RClock** (receive clock) to clock its input registers. The processor generates **RClock** at the same frequency as **SClock**, although **RClock** leads **TClock** and **SClock** by 25 percent of **SClock** cycle time.

Figure 10-3 shows the clocks for a **PClock-to-SClock** division by 2; Figure 10-4 shows the clocks for a **PClock-to-SClock** division by 4.

† *External agent* is defined in Chapter 12.

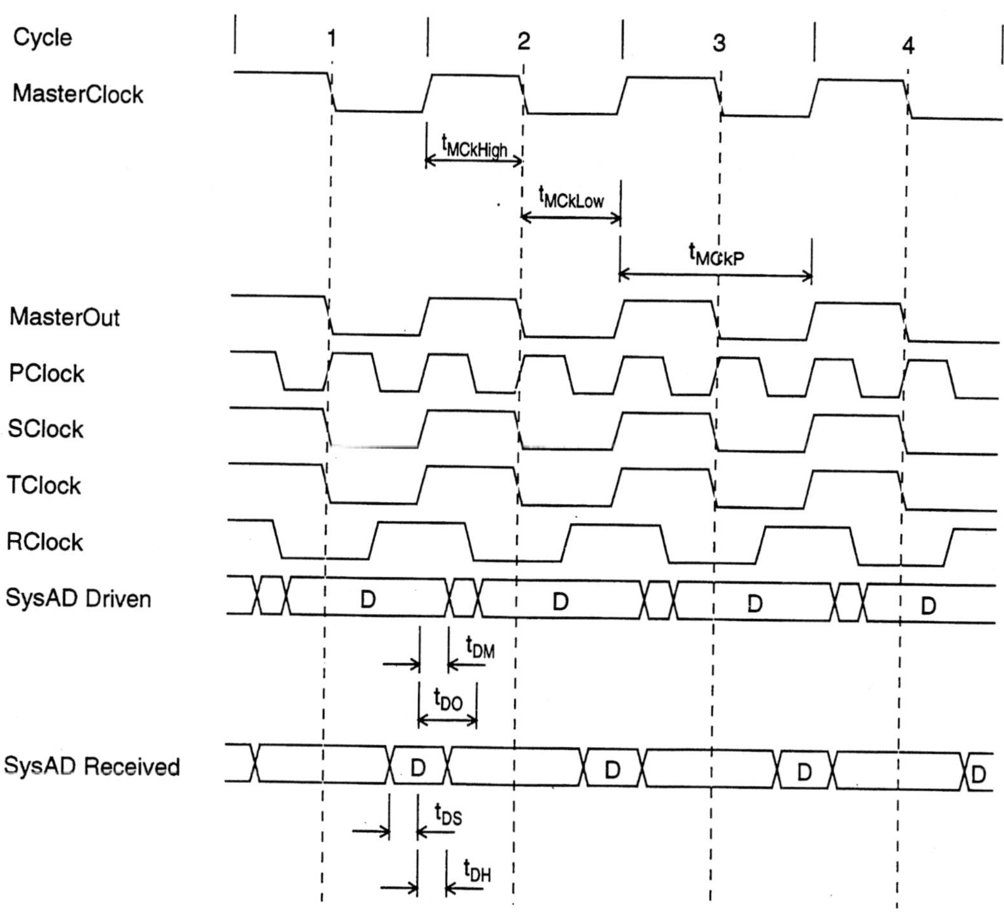

Figure 10-3 Processor Clocks, PClock-*to*-SClock *Division by 2*

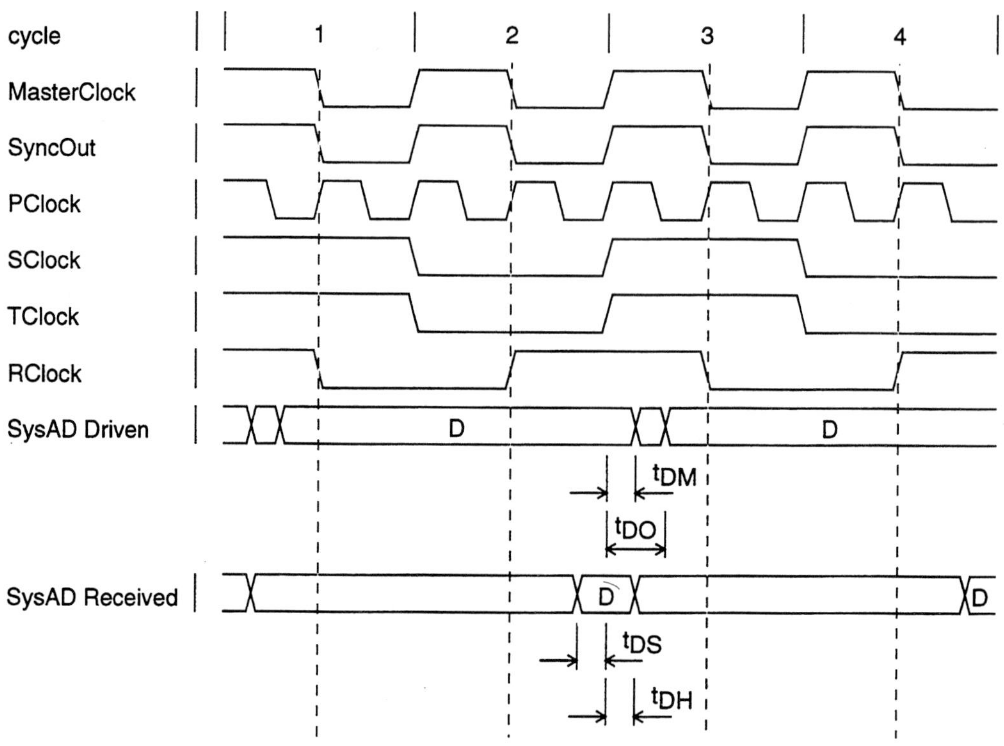

Figure 10-4 Processor Clocks, PClock-*to*-SClock *Division by 4*

10.3 System Timing Parameters

As shown in Figures 10-3 and 10-4, data provided to the processor must be stable a minimum of t_{DS} nanoseconds (ns) before the rising edge of **SClock** and be held valid for a minimum of t_{DH} ns after the rising edge of **SClock**.

Alignment to SClock

Processor data becomes stable a minimum of t_{DM} ns and a maximum of t_{DO} ns after the rising edge of **SClock**. This drive-time is the sum of the maximum delay through the processor output drivers together with the maximum clock-to-Q delay of the processor output registers.

Alignment to MasterClock

Certain processor inputs (specifically **VCCOk**, **ColdReset***, and **Reset***) are sampled based on **MasterClock**, while others (specifically, **Status(7:0)**) are output based on **MasterClock**. The same setup, hold, and drive-off parameters, t_{DS}, t_{DH}, t_{DM}, and t_{DO}, shown in Figures 10-3 and 10-4, apply to these inputs and outputs, but they are measured by **MasterClock** instead of **SClock**.

Phase-Locked Loop (PLL)

The processor aligns **SyncOut**, **PClock**, **SClock**, **TClock**, and **RClock** with internal phase-locked loop (PLL) circuits that generate aligned clocks based on **SyncOut/SyncIn**. By their nature, PLL circuits are only capable of generating aligned clocks for **MasterClock** frequencies within a limited range.

Clocks generated using PLL circuits contain some inherent inaccuracy, or *jitter*; a clock aligned with **MasterClock** by the PLL can lead or trail **MasterClock** by as much as the related maximum jitter allowed by the individual vendor.

10.4 Connecting Clocks to a Phase-Locked System

When the processor is used in a phase-locked system, the external agent must phase lock its operation to a common **MasterClock**. In such a system, the delivery of data and data sampling have common characteristics, even if the components have different delay values. For example, *transmission time* (the amount of time a signal takes to move from one component to another along a trace on the board) between any two components A and B of a phase-locked system can be calculated from the following equation:

Transmission Time = (**SClock** period) – (t_{DO} for A) – (t_{DS} for B) –
(Clock Jitter for A Max) – (Clock Jitter for B Max)

Figure 10-5 shows a block-level diagram of a phase-locked system using the R4000 processor.

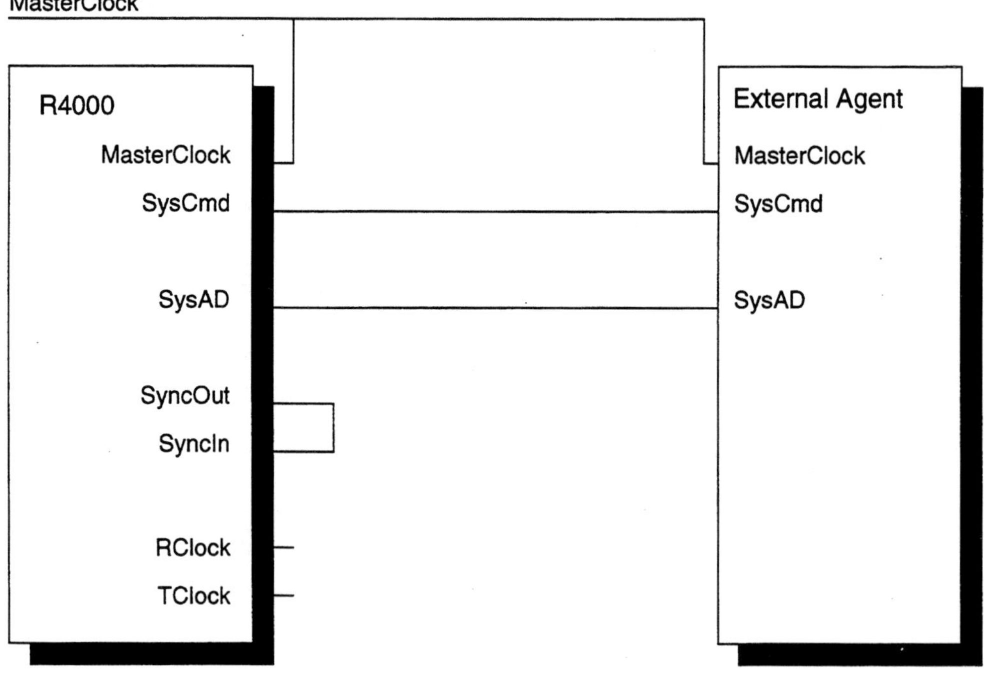

Figure 10-5 R4000 Processor Phase-Locked System

10.5 Connecting Clocks to a System without Phase Locking

When the R4000 processor is used in a system in which the external agent cannot lock its phase to a common **MasterClock**, the output clocks **RClock** and **TClock** can clock the remainder of the system. Two clocking methodologies are described in this section: connecting to a gate-array device or connecting to discrete CMOS logic devices.

Connecting to a Gate-Array Device

When connecting to a gate-array device, both **RClock** and **TClock** are used within the gate-array. The gate array internally buffers **RClock** and uses this buffered version to clock registers that sample processor outputs.

These sampling registers should be immediately followed by staging registers clocked by an internally buffered version of **TClock**. This buffered version of **TClock** should be the global system clock for the logic inside the gate array and the clock for all registers that drive processor inputs. Figure 10-6 is a block diagram of this circuit.

Staging registers place a constraint on the sum of the clock-to-Q delay of the sample registers and the setup time of the synchronizing registers inside the gate arrays, as shown in the following equation:

Clock-to-Q Delay + Setup of Synch Register ≤ 0.25 (**RClock** period)
– (Maximum Clock Jitter for **RClock**)
– (Maximum Delay Mismatch for Internal Clock
Buffers on **RClock** and **TClock**)

Figure 10-6 is a block diagram of a system without phase lock, using the R4000 processor with an external agent implemented as a gate array.

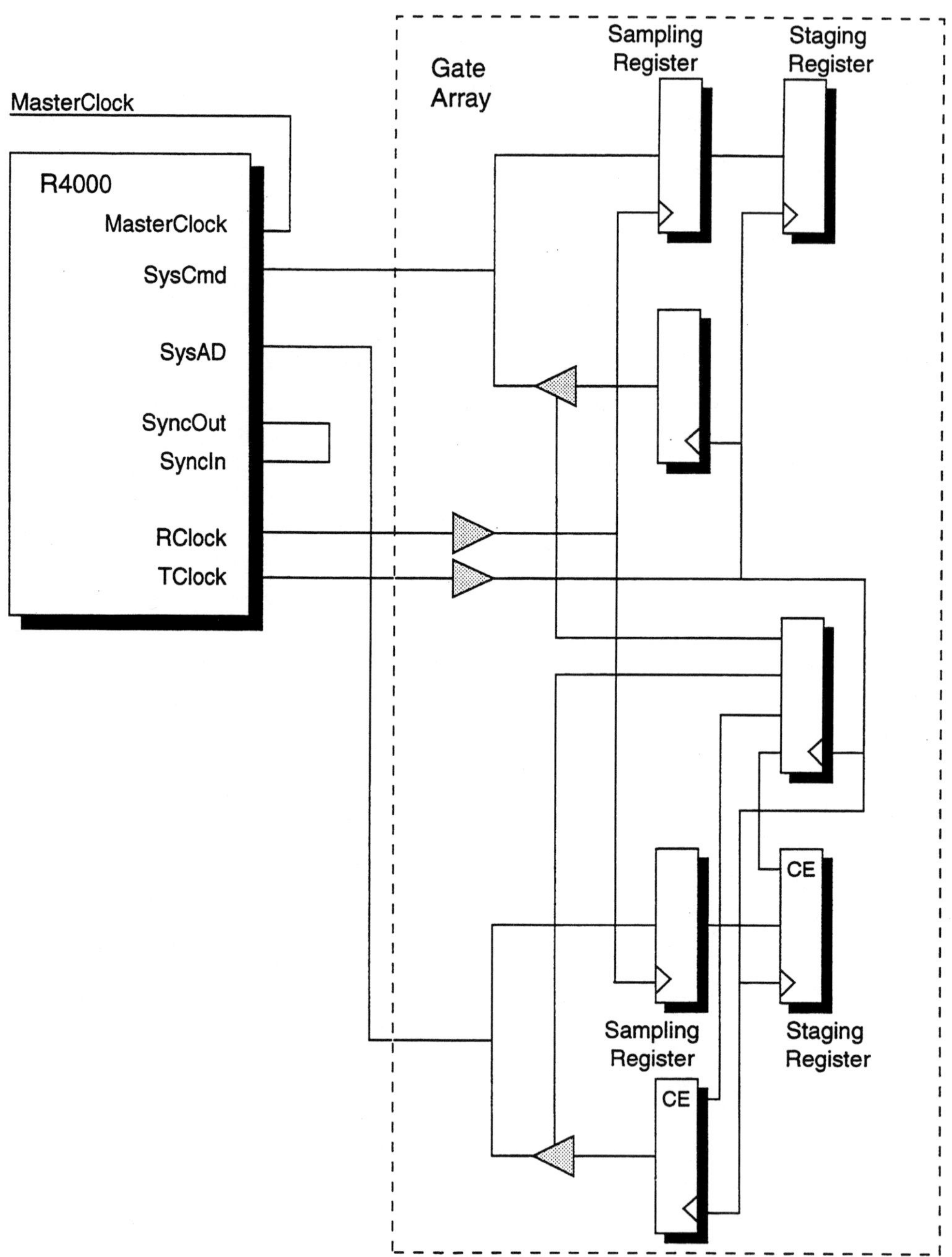

Figure 10-6 Gate-Array System without Phase Lock, using the R4000 Processor

In a system without phase lock, the transmission time for a signal *from* the processor *to* an external agent composed of gate arrays can be calculated from the following equation:

Transmission Time = (75 percent of **TClock** period) – (t_{DO} for R4000)
+ (Minimum External Clock Buffer Delay)
– (External Sample Register Setup Time)
– (Maximum Clock Jitter for R4000 Internal Clocks)
– (Maximum Clock Jitter for **RClock**)

The transmission time for a signal *from* an external agent composed of gate arrays *to* the processor in a system without phase lock can be calculated from the following equation:

Transmission Time = (**TClock** period) – (t_{DS} for R4000)
– (Maximum External Clock Buffer Delay)
– (Maximum External Output Register Clock-to-Q Delay)
– (Maximum Clock Jitter for **TClock**)
– (Maximum Clock Jitter for R4000 Internal Clocks)

Connecting to a CMOS Logic System

The processor uses matched delay clock buffers to generate aligned clocks to external CMOS logic. A matched delay clock buffer is inserted in the **SyncOut/SyncIn** alignment path of the processor, skewing **SyncOut**, **MasterOut**, **RClock**, and **TClock** to lead **MasterClock** by the buffer delay amount, while leaving **PClock** aligned with **MasterClock**.

The remaining matched delay clock buffers are available to generate a buffered version of **TClock** aligned with **MasterClock**. Alignment error of this buffered **TClock** is the sum of the maximum delay mismatch of the matched delay clock buffers, and the maximum clock jitter of **TClock.**

As the global system clock for the discrete logic that forms the external agent, the buffered version of **TClock** clocks registers that sample processor outputs, as well as clocking the registers that drive the processor inputs.

The transmission time for a signal from the processor to an external agent composed of discrete CMOS logic devices can be calculated from the following equation:

Transmission Time = (**TClock** period) – (t_{DO} for R4000)

– (External Sample Register Setup Time)

– (Maximum External Clock Buffer Delay Mismatch)

– (Maximum Clock Jitter for R4000 Internal Clocks)

– (Maximum Clock Jitter for **TClock**)

Figure 10-7 is a block diagram of a system without phase lock, employing the R4000 processor and an external agent composed of both a gate array and discrete CMOS logic devices.

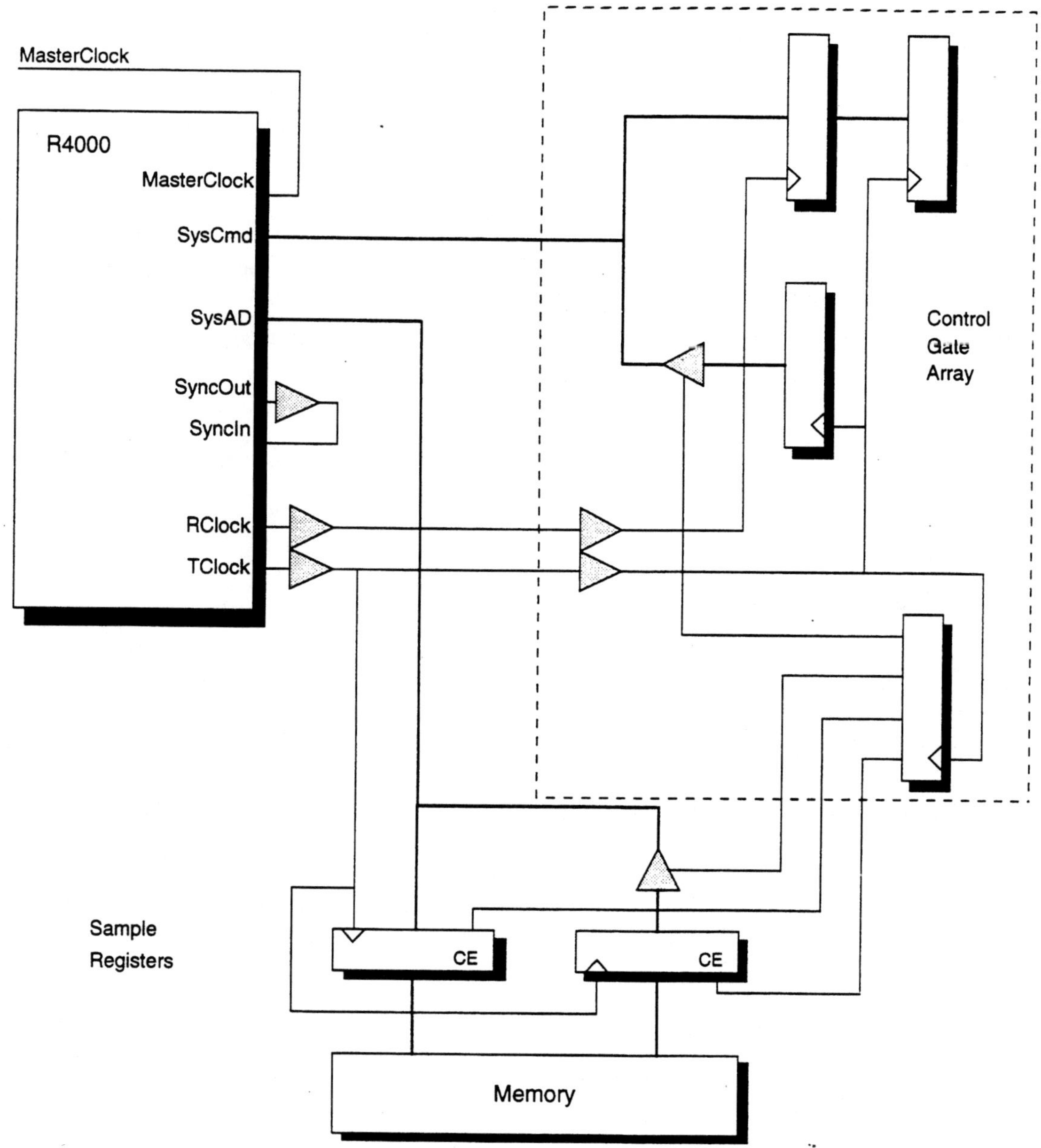

Figure 10-7 Gate Array and CMOS System without Phase Lock, using the R4000 Processor

The transmission time for a signal from an external agent composed of discrete CMOS logic devices can be calculated from the following equation:

Transmission Time = (**TClock** period) – (t_{DS} for R4000)

– (Maximum External Output Register Clock-to-Q Delay)

– (Maximum External Clock Buffer Delay Mismatch)

– (Maximum Clock Jitter for R4000 Internal Clocks)

– (Maximum Clock Jitter for **TClock**)

In this clocking methodology, the hold time of data driven from the processor to an external sampling register is a critical parameter. To guarantee hold time, the minimum output delay of the processor, t_{DM}, must be greater than the sum of:

minimum hold time for the external sampling register

+ maximum clock jitter for R4000 internal clocks

+ maximum clock jitter for **TClock**

+ maximum delay mismatch of the external clock buffers

10.6 Processor Status Outputs

The R4400 processor provides eight status outputs†, **Status(7:0)**, aligned with each rising edge of **MasterClock**. At time T (the present PCycle) these status outputs indicate whether the machine was running or stalled during the previous T-2 and T-3 PCycles, as follows:

- If the machine was stalled during the T-2 or T-3 PCycles, the status outputs indicate the type of stall which occurred (listed in Table 10-1).
- If the machine was running during the T-3 or T-2 PCycles, the status outputs describe the type of instruction which occupied the WriteBack pipeline stage during the T-2 or T-3 PCycles, and which was successfully completed (listed in Table 10-1).
- The status outputs also indicate if an instruction in the T-2 or T-3 PCycle was killed, and if so, states the cause (listed in Table 10-1.

The **Status(7:0)** bits are treated as two fields, as follows:

- The **Status(7:4)** field indicates the internal state of the processor during PCycle T-3.
- The **Status(3:0)** bits indicate the internal state of the processor during the PCycle T-2.

† The pins are present, but nonfunctional, on the R4000 processor.

Table 10-1 shows the encoding of processor internal state for **Status(7:4)** or **Status(3:0)**. The 4-bit value, 0x0 to 0xF, encodes the instruction occupying the WriteBack pipeline stage during a given **PCycle** (see Chapter 3 for a description of pipeline stages).

Table 10-1 Encoding of R4400 Processor Internal State by Status(7:4) *or* Status(3:0)

Status(7:4) or Status(3:0)	Cycle	Processor Internal State
0	Run cycle	Other integer instruction (not load/store/conditional branch. Includes ERET and Jump instructions.)
1	Run cycle	Load
2	Run cycle	Untaken conditional branch
3	Run cycle	Taken conditional branch
4	Run cycle	Store
5	Reserved	
6	Stall cycle	MP stall
7	Run cycle	Integer instruction killed by slip
8	Stall cycle	Other stall type
9	Stall cycle	Primary instruction cache stall
a	Stall cycle	Primary data cache stall
b	Stall cycle	Secondary cache stall
c	Run cycle	Other floating-point instruction (not load, store, or conditional branch)
d	Run cycle	Instruction killed by branch, jump, or ERET
e	Run cycle	Instruction killed by exception
f	Run cycle	Floating-point instruction killed by slip

Cache Organization, Operation, and Coherency

11

This chapter describes in detail the cache memory: its place in the R4000 memory organization, individual operations of the primary and secondary caches, cache interactions, and an example of a cache coherency request cycle. The chapter concludes with a description of R4000 processor synchronization in a multiprocessor environment.

This chapter uses the following terminology:

- The primary cache may also be referred to as the P-cache.
- The secondary cache may also be referred to as the S-cache.
- The primary data cache may also be referred to as the D-cache.
- The primary instruction cache may also be referred to as the I-cache.

These terms are used interchangeably throughout this book.

11.1 Memory Organization

Figure 11-1 shows the R4000 system memory hierarchy. In the logical memory hierarchy, caches lie between the CPU and main memory. They are designed to make the speedup of memory accesses transparent to the user. Each functional block in Figure 11-1 has the capacity to hold more data than the block above it. For instance, physical main memory has a larger capacity than the secondary cache. At the same time, each functional block takes longer to access than any block above it. For instance, it takes longer to access data in main memory than in the CPU on-chip registers.

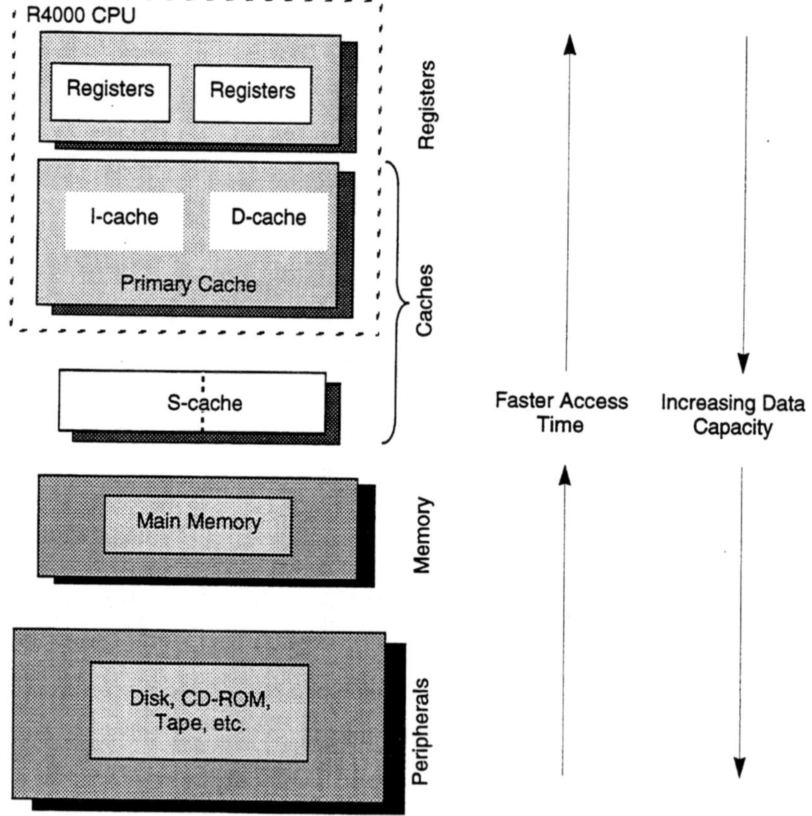

Figure 11-1 Logical Hierarchy of Memory

The R4000 processor has two on-chip primary caches: one holds instructions (the instruction cache), the other holds data (the data cache). Off-chip, the R4000 processor supports a secondary cache on the R4000SC and MC models.

11.2 Overview of Cache Operations

As described earlier, caches provide fast temporary data storage, and they make the speedup of memory accesses transparent to the user. In general, the processor accesses cache-resident instructions or data through the following procedure:

1. The processor, through the on-chip cache controller, attempts to access the next instruction or data in the primary cache.
2. The cache controller checks to see if this instruction or data is present in the primary cache.
    - If the instruction/data is present, the processor retrieves it. This is called a primary-cache *hit*.
    - If the instruction/data is not present in the primary cache, the cache controller must retrieve it from the secondary cache or memory. This is called a primary-cache *miss*.
3. If a primary-cache miss occurs, the cache controller checks to see if the instruction/data is in the secondary cache.
    - If the instruction/data is present in the secondary cache, it is retrieved and written into the primary cache.
    - If the instruction/data is not present in the secondary cache, it is retrieved as a cache line (a block whose size set in the *Config* register; see the section titled Variable-Length Cache Lines in this chapter for available cache line lengths) from memory and is written into both the secondary cache and the appropriate primary cache.
4. The processor retrieves the instruction/data from the primary cache and operation continues.

It is possible for the same data to be in three places simultaneously: main memory, secondary cache, and primary cache. This data is kept consistent through the use of write back methodology; that is, modified data is not written back to memory until the cache line is replaced.

11.3 R4000 Cache Description

As Figure 11-1 shows, the R4000 contains separate primary instruction and data caches. Figure 11-1 also shows that the R4000 supports a secondary cache that can be split into separate portions, one portion containing data and the other portion containing instructions, or it can be a joint cache, holding combined instructions and data.

This section describes the organization of on-chip primary caches and the optional off-chip secondary cache. Table 11-1 lists the cache and cache coherency support for the three R4000 models.

Table 11-1 R4000 Cache and Coherency Support

R4000 Model	Support Primary Cache?	Support Secondary Cache?	Support Cache Coherency?
R4000PC	Yes	No	No
R4000SC	Yes	Yes	No
R4000MC	Yes	Yes	Yes

Figure 11-2 provides block diagrams of the three R4000 models:

- R4000PC, which supports only the primary cache
- R4000SC and R4000MC, which support both primary and secondary caches

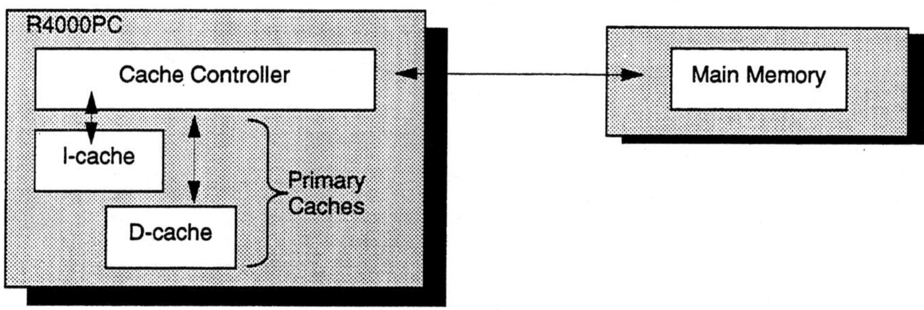

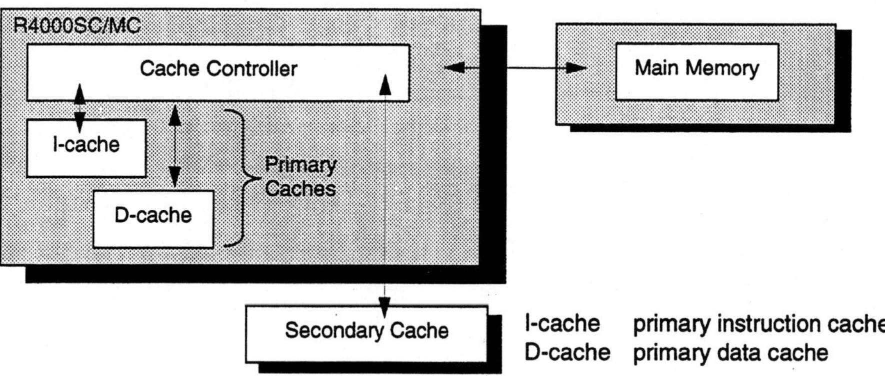

Figure 11-2 Cache Support in the R4000PC, R4000SC, and R4000MC

Secondary Cache Size

Table 11-2 lists the range of secondary cache sizes. The secondary cache is user-configurable at boot time through the boot-mode bits (see Chapter 9); it can be a joint cache, containing both data and instructions in a single cache, or split into separate data and instruction caches.

Table 11-2 Secondary Cache Sizes

Cache	Minimum Size	Maximum Size
Secondary Joint Cache	128 Kbytes	4 Mbytes
Secondary Split I-Cache	128 Kbytes	2 Mbytes
Secondary Split D-Cache	128 Kbytes	2 Mbytes

Variable-Length Cache Lines

A *cache line* is the smallest unit of information that can be fetched from the cache, and that is represented by a single tag.† A primary cache line can be either 4 or 8 words in length; a secondary cache line can be either 4, 8, 16, or 32 words in length. Primary cache line length is set in the *Config* register; see Chapter 4 for more information. Secondary cache line length is set at boot time through the boot-mode bits, as described in Chapter 9.

Upon a cache miss in both primary and secondary caches, the missing secondary cache line is loaded first from memory into the secondary cache, whereupon the appropriate subset of the secondary cache line is loaded into the primary cache.

The primary cache line length can never be longer than that of the secondary cache; it must always be less than or equal to the secondary cache line length. This means the secondary cache cannot have a 4-word line length while the primary cache has an 8-word line length.

Cache Organization and Accessibility

This section describes the organization of the primary and secondary caches, including the manner in which they are mapped, the addressing (either virtual or physical) used to index the cache, and composition of the cache lines. The primary instruction and data caches are indexed with a virtual address (VA), while the secondary cache is indexed with a physical address (PA).

† Primary and secondary cache tags are described in the following sections.

Organization of the Primary Instruction Cache (I-Cache)

Each line of primary I-cache data (although it is actually an instruction, it is referred to as data to distinguish it from its tag) has an associated 26-bit tag that contains a 24-bit physical address, a single valid bit, and a single parity bit. Byte parity is used on I-cache data.

The R4000 processor primary I-cache has the following characteristics:

- direct-mapped
- indexed with a virtual address
- checked with a physical tag
- organized with either a 4-word (16-byte) or 8-word (32-byte) cache line.

Figure 11-3 shows the format of an 8-word (32-byte) primary I-cache line.

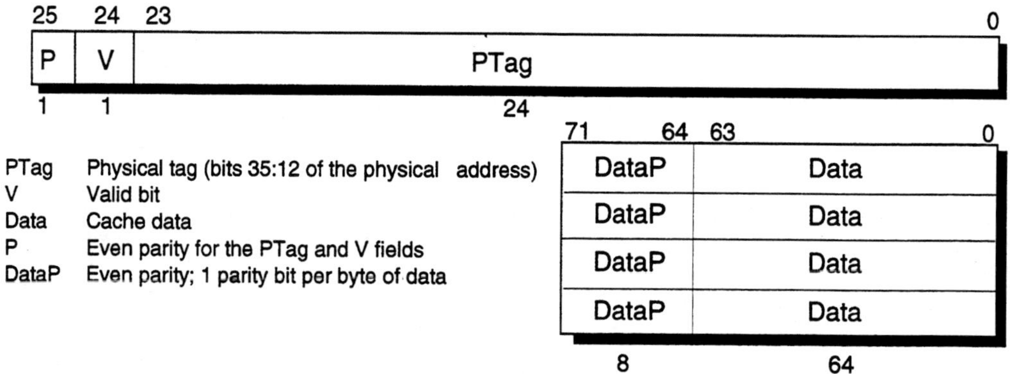

Figure 11-3 R4000 8-Word Primary I-Cache Line Format

Organization of the Primary Data Cache (D-Cache)

Each line of primary D-cache data has an associated 29-bit tag that contains a 24-bit physical address, 2-bit cache line state, a write-back bit, a parity bit for the physical address and cache state fields, and a parity bit for the write-back bit.

The R4000 processor primary D-cache has the following characteristics:

- write-back
- direct-mapped
- indexed with a virtual address
- checked with a physical tag
- organized with either a 4-word (16-byte) or 8-word (32-byte) cache line.

Figure 11-4 shows the format of a 8-word (32-byte) primary D-cache line.

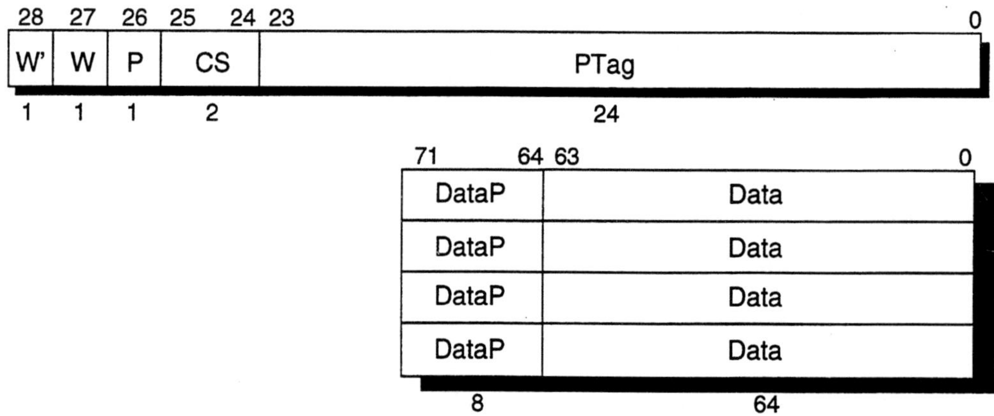

W' Even parity for the write-back bit
W Write-back bit (set if cache line has been written)
P Even parity for the PTag and CS fields
CS Primary cache state:
0 = Invalid in all R4000 configurations
1 = Shared (either Clean or Dirty) in R4000MC configuration only
2 = Clean Exclusive in R4000SC and MC configurations only
3 = Dirty Exclusive in all R4000 configurations
PTag Physical tag (bits 35:12 of the physical address)
DataP Even parity for the data
Data Cache data

Figure 11-4 R4000 8-Word Primary Data Cache Line Format

In all R4000 processors, the *W* (write-back) bit, not the cache state, indicates whether or not the primary cache contains modified data that must be written back to memory or to the secondary cache.

Accessing the Primary Caches

Figure 11-5 shows the virtual address (VA) index into the primary caches. Each instruction and data cache range in size from 8 Kbytes to 32 Kbytes; therefore, the number of virtual address bits used to index the cache depends on the cache size. For example, VA(12:4) accesses a 8-Kbyte page tag in a cache with a 4-word line (VA(12) addresses 8 Kbytes and VA(4) provides quadword resolution); similarly, VA(14:5) accesses an 8-word tag: VA(5) provides octalword access in a 32-Kbyte cache (VA(14) addresses 32 Kbytes).

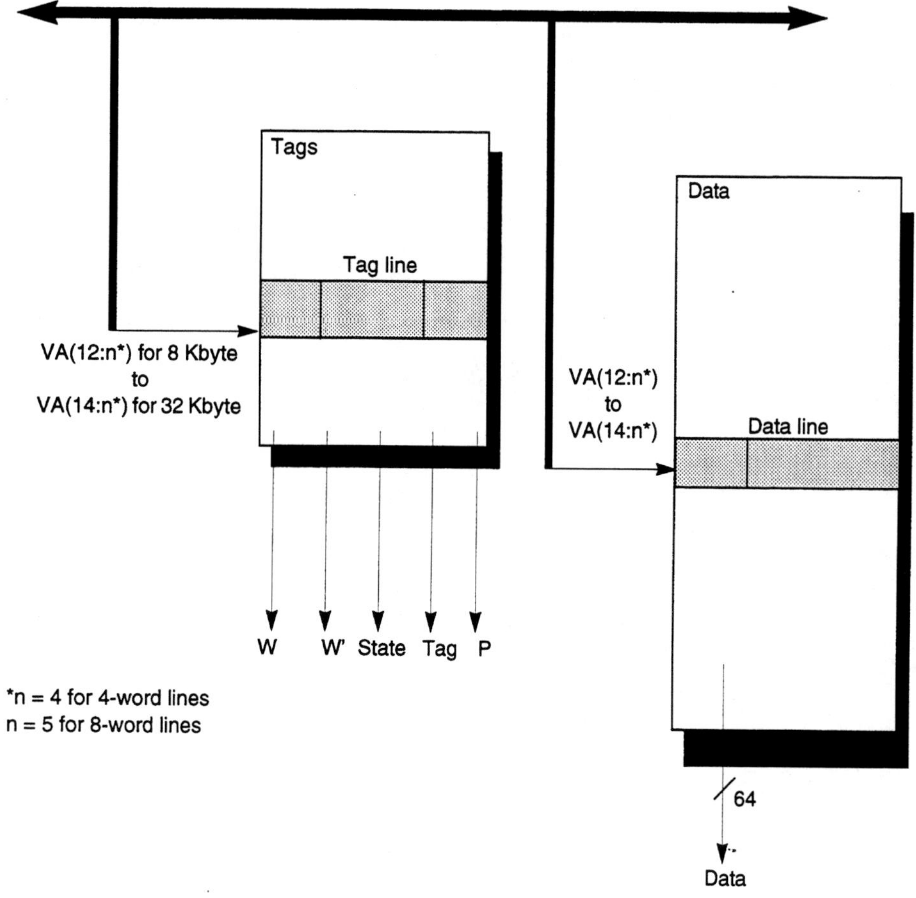

Figure 11-5 Primary Cache Data and Tag Organization

Organization of the Secondary Cache

Each secondary cache line has an associated 19-bit tag that contains bits 35:17 of the physical address, a 3-bit primary cache index, VA(14:12), and a 3-bit cache line state. These 25 bits are protected by a 7-bit ECC code.

The secondary cache is accessible to the processor and to the system interface; by setting the appropriate boot-mode bits, it can be configured at chip reset as a joint cache, or as separate I- and D-caches.

Figure 11-6 shows the format of the R4000 processor secondary-cache line. The size of the secondary cache line is set in the *SB* field of the *Config* register.

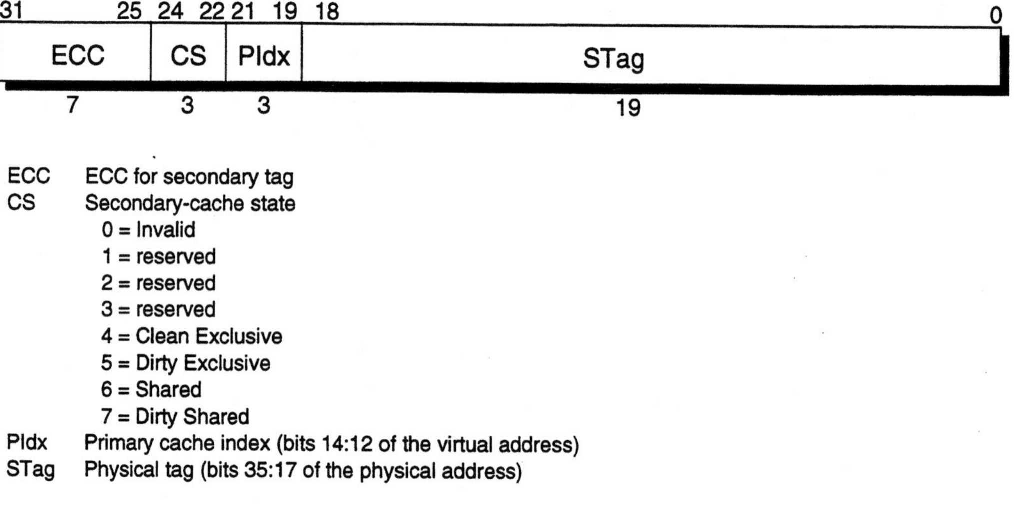

Figure 11-6 R4000 Secondary Cache Line Format

The R4000 processor secondary cache has the following characteristics:

- write-back
- direct-mapped
- indexed with a physical address
- checked with a physical tag
- organized with either a 4-word (16-byte), 8-word (32-byte), 16-word (64-byte), or 32-word (128-byte) cache line.

The secondary cache state (*CS*) bits indicate whether:

- the cache line data and tag are valid
- the data is *potentially* present in the caches of other processors (shared versus exclusive)
- the processor is responsible for updating main memory (clean versus dirty).

The *PIdx* field provides the processor with an index to the virtual address of primary cache lines that may contain data from the secondary cache line.

The *PIdx* field also detects a cache alias. Cache aliasing occurs when the physical address tag matches during a data reference to the secondary cache, but the *PIdx* field does not match in the virtual address. This indicates that the cache reference was made from a different virtual address than the one that created the secondary-cache line, and the processor signals a Virtual Coherency exception.

Accessing the Secondary Cache

Figure 11-7 shows the physical address (PA) index into the secondary cache. The secondary cache ranges in size from 128 Kbytes to 4 Mbytes, and the number of physical address bits used to index the cache depends upon the cache size. For instance, PA(16:4) accesses the tags in a 128-Kbyte secondary cache with 4-word lines; PA(21:5) accesses the tags in a 4-Mbyte secondary cache with 8-word lines.

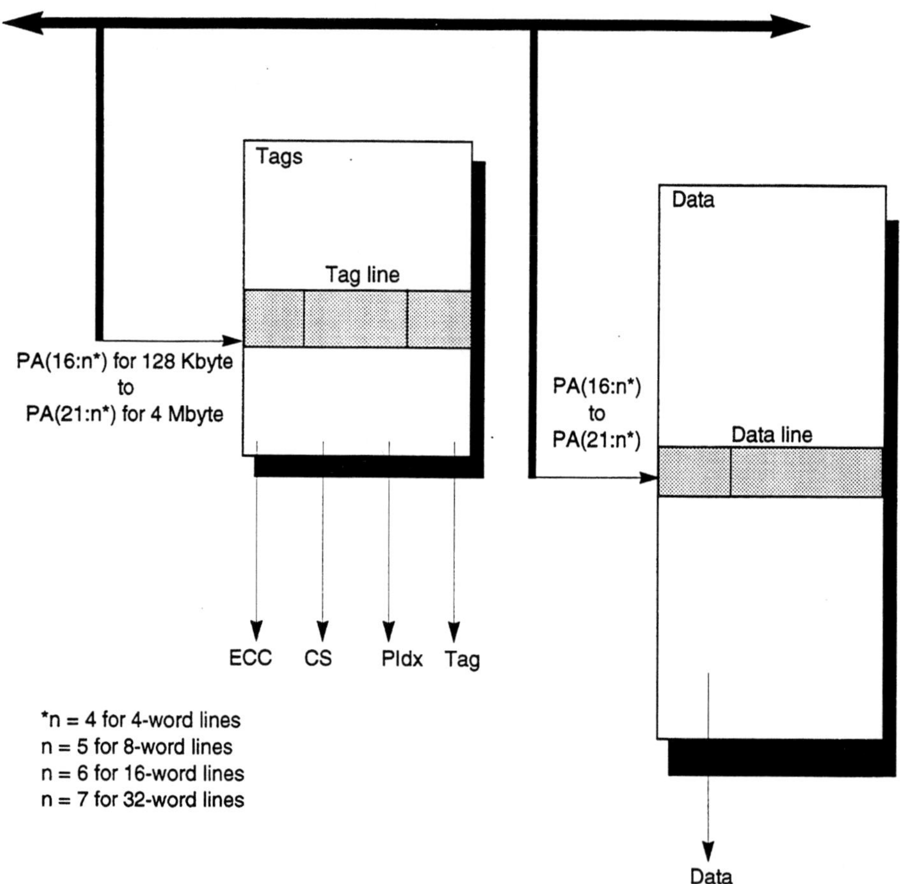

Figure 11-7 Secondary Cache Data and Tag Organization

11.4 Cache States

The four terms below are used to describe the *state* of a cache line:

- **Exclusive**: a cache line that is present in exactly one cache in the system is exclusive, and may be in one of the exclusive states.
- **Dirty**: a cache line that contains data that has changed since it was loaded from memory is dirty, and must be in one of the dirty or shared states.
- **Clean**: a cache line that contains data that has not changed since it was loaded from memory is clean, and may be in one of the clean states.
- **Shared**: a cache line that is present in more than one cache in the system.

Each primary and secondary cache line in the R4000 system is in one of the states described in Table 11-3. Table 11-3 also lists with the types of cache and the R4000 models in which the various states may be found.

Table 11-3 Cache States

Cache Line State	Description	Where the State is Used	Available on the Following R4000 Models
Invalid	A cache line that does not contain valid information must be marked invalid, and cannot be used. For example, a cache line is marked invalid if the same information, located in another cache, is modified. A cache line in any other state than invalid is assumed to contain valid information.	Primary or Secondary Cache	R4000PC R4000SC R4000MC
Shared	A cache line that is present in more than one cache in the system is shared.	Primary or Secondary Cache	R4000MC only
Dirty Shared	A dirty shared cache line contains valid information and can be present in another cache. This cache line is inconsistent with memory and is owned by the processor (see the section titled Cache Line Ownership in this chapter).	Secondary cache only	R4000MC only

Table 11-3 (cont.) Cache States

Cache Line State	Description	Where the State is Used	Available on the Following R4000 Models
Clean Exclusive	A clean exclusive cache line contains valid information and this cache line is not present in any other cache. The cache line is consistent with memory and is not owned by the processor (see the section titled Cache Line Ownership in this chapter).	Primary or Secondary Cache	R4000SC R4000MC
Dirty Exclusive	A dirty exclusive cache line contains valid information and is not present in any other cache. The cache line is inconsistent with memory and is owned by the processor (see the section titled Cache Line Ownership in this chapter).	Primary or Secondary Cache	R4000PC R4000SC R4000MC

Primary Cache States

Each primary data cache line is in one of the following states:

- invalid
- shared
- clean exclusive
- dirty exclusive

Each primary instruction cache line is in one of the following states:

- invalid
- valid

Secondary Cache States

Each secondary cache line is in one of the following states:

- invalid
- shared
- dirty shared
- clean exclusive
- dirty exclusive

Mapping States Between Caches

Secondary cache states correspond, or map, to primary cache states (this mapping is listed in Table 11-6, later on in this chapter). For example, the secondary cache shared and dirty shared states map to the primary cache shared state.

Therefore, when the primary cache line is filled from the secondary cache, the state of the secondary cache line is also mapped into the primary cache; in the case described above, the shared or dirty shared secondary state is mapped to the shared primary cache state.

As shown in Figure 11-8, a primary cache line in the R4000PC model can be in either an invalid or dirty exclusive state. In the R4000SC model, a primary cache line can be in the invalid, clean exclusive, or dirty exclusive state. In the R4000MC model, the primary cache line can be invalid, clean exclusive, dirty exclusive, or shared.

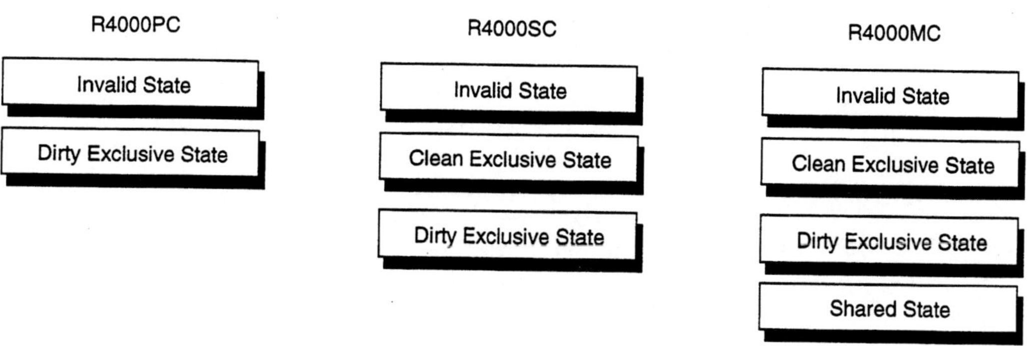

Figure 11-8 Primary Cache States Available to Each Type of Processor

11.5 Cache Line Ownership

A processor becomes the owner of a cache line after it writes to that cache line (that is, by entering the dirty exclusive or dirty shared state), and is responsible for providing the contents of that line on a read request. There can only be one owner for each cache line.

The ownership of a cache line is set and maintained through the rules described below.

- A processor assumes ownership of the cache line if the state of the secondary cache line is dirty shared or dirty exclusive.
- A processor that owns a cache line is responsible for writing the cache line back to memory if the line is replaced during the execution of a Write-back or Write-back Invalidate cache instruction. For *read responses* to a processor *coherent read request* (both of these terms are defined in Chapter 12) in which the data is returned in the dirty shared or dirty exclusive state, the cache state is set when the last word of read response data is returned. Therefore, the processor assumes ownership of the cache line when the last word of response data is returned.
- For processor coherent write requests, the state of the cache line changes to invalid if the cache line is replaced, or to either clean exclusive or shared if the cache line is retained (provided the cache line was written back to memory). In either case, the cache state transition occurs when the last word of write data is transmitted to the external agent. Therefore, the processor gives up ownership of the cache line when the last word of write data is transmitted to the external agent (Chapter 12 defines *external agent*).
- Memory always owns clean cache lines.
- The processor gives up ownership of a cache line when the state of the cache line changes to invalid, shared, or clean exclusive.

11.6 Cache Write Policy

The R4000 processor manages its primary and secondary caches by using a *write-back* policy; that is, it stores write data into the caches, instead of writing it directly to memory.† Some time later this data is independently written into memory. In the R4000 implementation, a modified cache line is not written back to memory until the cache line is replaced either in the course of satisfying a cache miss, or during the execution of a Write-back CACHE instruction.

If a primary cache line is in either the dirty exclusive or shared state and that cache line has been modified (the *W* bit is set), the processor writes this cache line back to memory (or the secondary cache, if it is present) when the line is replaced, either in the course of satisfying a cache miss or during the execution of a Write-back or Write-back Invalidate CACHE instruction.

If a secondary cache line is in either the dirty exclusive or dirty shared state, the processor writes this cache line back to memory when the line is replaced, either in the course of satisfying a cache miss or during the execution of a Write-back CACHE instruction.

Many systems, in particular multiprocessor systems, or systems employing I/O devices that are capable of DMA, require the system to behave as if the caches are always consistent both with memory and with each other. Schemes for maintaining consistency between more than one cache, or between caches and memory, are defined by the system cache coherency protocols (see the section titled Cache Coherency Overview later in this chapter). In the R4000 system, when the content of a cache line is inconsistent with memory, it is classified as dirty and is written back to memory according to the rules of the cache write-back policy.

When the processor writes a cache line back to memory, it does not ordinarily retain a copy of the cache line, and the state of the cache line is changed to invalid. However, there are exceptions. For example, the processor retains a copy of the cache line if a cache line is written back by the Hit Write-back cache instruction. The processor changes the retained cache line state to either clean exclusive if the secondary cache state was dirty exclusive before the write, or shared if the secondary cache state was dirty shared before the write. The processor signals this line retention during a write by setting **SysCmd(2)** to a 1, as described in Chapter 12.

† An alternative to this is a *write-through* cache, in which information is written simultaneously to cache and memory.

11.7 Cache State Transition Diagrams

The following sections describe the cache state diagrams that illustrate the cache state transitions for both the primary and secondary caches. Figures 11-9 and 11-10 are state diagrams of the primary and secondary caches, respectively.

When an external agent supplies a cache line, the initial state of the cache line is specified by the external agent (see Chapter 12 for a definition of an external agent). Otherwise, the processor changes the state of the cache line during one of the following events:

- A store to a clean exclusive cache line causes the state to be changed to dirty exclusive in both the primary and secondary caches.
- A store to a shared cache line—that is a line marked shared in the primary cache and either shared or dirty shared in the secondary cache—causes the processor to issue either an invalidate request or an update request (depending on the coherency attribute in the TLB entry for the page containing the cache line). And update page attribute causes an update request to be issued; a sharable page attribute causes an invalidate request to be issued.
    - Upon successful completion of an invalidate, the processor completes the store and changes the state of the cache line to dirty exclusive in both the primary and secondary caches.
    - Upon successful completion of an update, the processor completes the store and changes the state of the cache line to shared in the primary cache and dirty shared in the secondary cache if dirty shared mode is enabled. Dirty shared mode is programmable through the boot-time mode control interface (see Chapter 9 for a description of boot mode bits). If dirty shared mode is not enabled, the state of the primary and secondary caches are left in a shared state, after successful completion of an update.
- A store to a dirty exclusive line remains in a dirty exclusive state.

These state diagrams do not cover the initial state of the system since the initial state is system dependent.

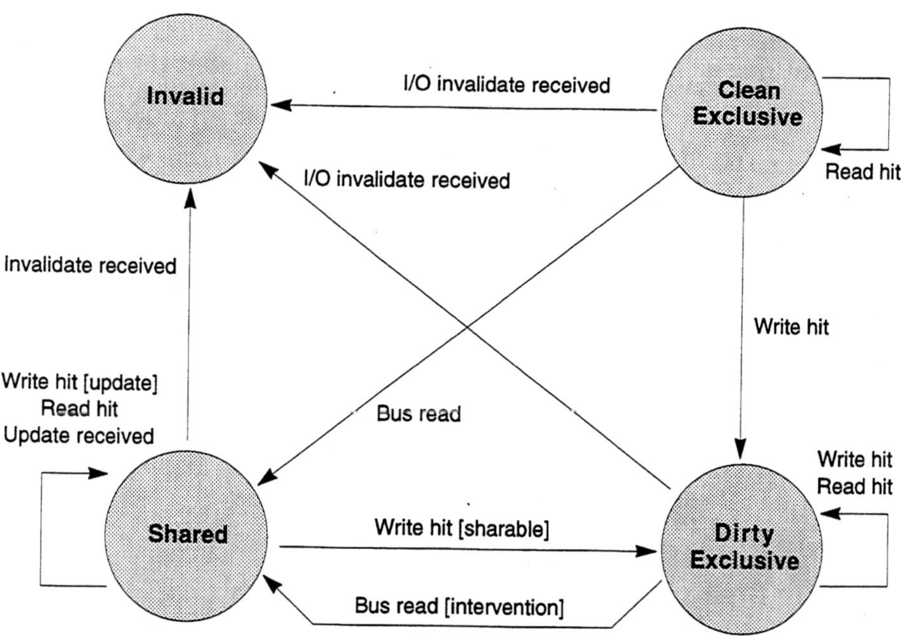

Figure 11-9 Primary Data Cache State Diagram

If the system is in no-secondary-cache mode, the cache state provided by the system is ignored, and the primary data cache state is set to dirty exclusive.

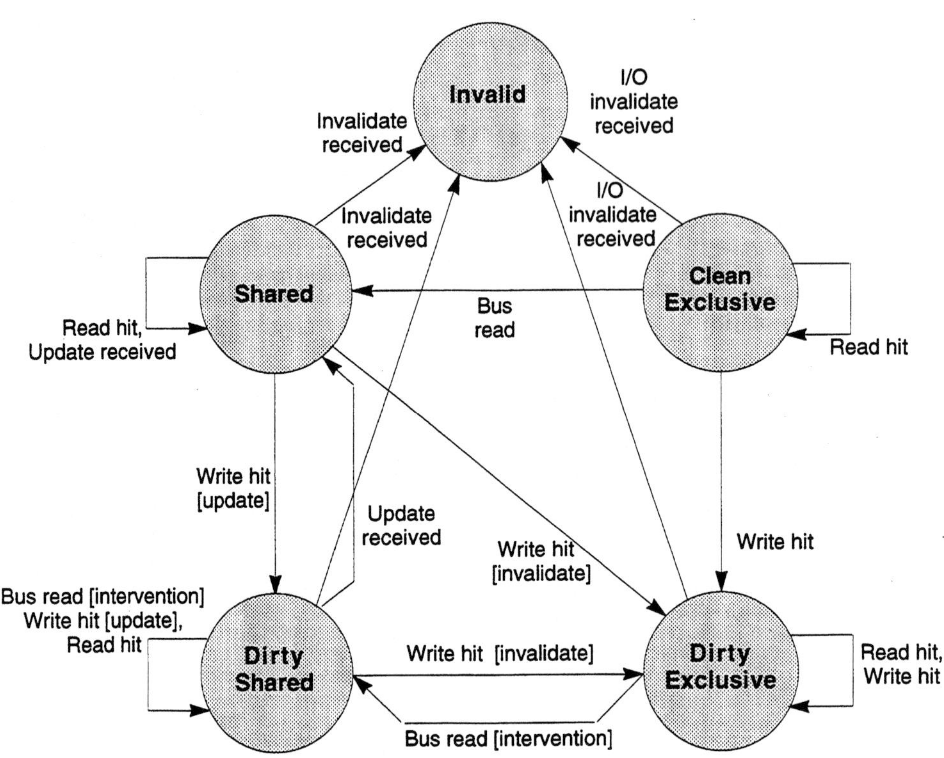

Figure 11-10 Secondary Cache State Diagram

The state of a secondary cache line is provided by the external agent and is set as follows:

Case 1. If the cache line is not present in another cache, it should be loaded in the clean exclusive state.

Case 2. If the cache line is retained by another cache and the state of the line in that cache remains shared or dirty shared, the line should be loaded in the shared state.

Case 3. If the cache line is retained by another cache and the cache relinquishes ownership to the processor making the read request, the line should be returned in the dirty shared state.

Case 4. If the cache line is retained by another cache and ownership is relinquished to memory, the line should be loaded in the shared state.

Case 5. If the cache line is relinquished by another cache and ownership is transferred to the processor making the read request, the line should be loaded in the dirty exclusive or dirty shared state.

For case 1, if the refill occurs on a store miss, the processor changes the cache line state to dirty exclusive. For each of the remaining cases listed above, the R4000 processor passes the state received from the external agent to the secondary cache.

The invalid state is never used for a refill. Software, however, should initialize the secondary cache to the invalid state after the system is powered up.

11.8 Cache Coherency Overview

Systems using more than one R4000MC processor must have a mechanism to maintain data consistency throughout a multi-cache, multiprocessor system. This mechanism is called a cache coherency protocol.

Cache Coherency Attributes

Cache coherency attributes are necessary to ensure the consistency of data throughout the multitude of caches that can be present in the multiprocessor environment.

Bits in the translation look-aside buffer (TLB) control coherency on a per-page basis. Specifically, the TLB contains 3 bits per entry that provide five possible coherency attributes; they are listed below and described more fully in the following sections.

- *uncached* (R4000PC, R4000SC, R4000MC)
- *noncoherent* (R4000PC, R4000SC, R4000MC)
- *sharable* (R4000MC only, with secondary cache)
- *update* (R4000MC only, with secondary cache)
- *exclusive* (R4000MC only, with secondary cache)

Only uncached or noncoherent attributes can be used by an R4000PC or an R4000SC processor.

Table 11-4 summarizes the behavior of the processor on load misses, store misses, and store hits to shared cache lines for each of the five coherency attributes listed above. The following sections describe in detail the five coherency attributes.

Table 11-4 Coherency Attributes and Processor Behavior

Attribute	Load Miss	Store Miss	Store Hit Shared
Uncached	Main memory read	Main memory write	NA
Noncoherent	Noncoherent read	Noncoherent read	Invalidate †
Exclusive	Coherent read exclusive	Coherent read exclusive	Invalidate †
Sharable	Coherent read	Coherent read exclusive	Invalidate
Update	Coherent read	Coherent read	Update

† These should not occur under normal circumstances.

Uncached

Lines within an *uncached* page are never in a cache. When a page has the uncached coherency attribute, the processor issues a doubleword, partial-doubleword, word, or partial-word read or write request directly to main memory (bypassing the cache) for any load or store to a location within that page.

Noncoherent

Lines with a *noncoherent* attribute can reside in a cache; a load or store miss causes the processor to issue a noncoherent block read request to a location within the cached page.

Sharable

Lines with a *sharable* attribute must be in a multiprocessor environment (using the R4000MC), since shared lines can be in more than one cache at a time. When the coherency attribute is *sharable,* the processor operates as follows:

- a coherent block read request is issued for a load miss to a location within the page, or
- a coherent block read request that requests exclusivity is issued for a store miss to a location within the page.

In most systems, coherent read requests require snoops or directory checks, and noncoherent read requests do not.† Cache lines within the page are managed with a *write invalidate* protocol; that is, the processor issues an invalidate request on a store hit to a shared cache line.

Update

Lines with an *update* coherency attribute must be in a multiprocessor environment and can reside in more than one cache at a time. When the coherency attribute is update, the processor issues a coherent block read request for a load or store miss to a location within the page. Cache lines within the page are managed with a *write update* protocol; that is, the processor issues an update request on a store hit to a shared cache line.

† A coherent read that requests exclusivity implies that the processor functions most efficiently if the requested cache line is returned to it in an exclusive state, but the processor still performs correctly if the cache line is returned in a shared state.

Exclusive

Lines with an *exclusive* coherency attribute must be in a multiprocessor environment. When the coherency attribute is exclusive, the processor issues a coherent block read request that requests exclusivity for a load or store miss to a location within the page.

Cache lines within the page are managed with a write invalidate protocol.

NOTE: Load Linked-Store Conditional instruction sequences must ensure that the link location is not in a page managed with the exclusive coherency attribute.

Cache Operation Modes

The R4000 processor supports the following two *cache modes*:

- secondary-cache mode (R4000MC and R4000SC models; for R4000MC all five cache coherency attributes described above are applicable, and for R4000SC only uncached and noncoherent coherency attributes are applicable)
- no-secondary-cache mode (only uncached and noncoherent coherency attributes are applicable).

Secondary-Cache Mode

In its *secondary-cache* mode, an R4000MC model provides a set of cache states and mechanisms that implement a variety of cache coherency protocols. In particular, the processor simultaneously supports both the write-invalidate and write-update protocols.

No-Secondary-Cache Mode

A processor in *no-secondary-cache* mode supports the uncached and noncoherent coherency attributes. These two attributes are described in the section titled Cache Coherency Attributes in this chapter.

Strong Ordering

Cache-coherent multiprocessor systems must obey ordering constraints on stores to shared data. A multiprocessor system that exhibits the same behavior as a uniprocessor system in a multiprogramming environment is said to be *strongly ordered.*

An Example of Strong Ordering

Given that locations X and Y have no particular relationship—that is, they are not in the same cache line—an example of strong ordering is as follows:

1. At time **T**, Processor A performs a store to location X and at the same time processor B performs a store to location Y.
2. At time **T+1**, Processor A does a load from location Y and at the same time processor B does a load from location X.

For the system to be considered strongly ordered, either processor A must load the new value of Y, or processor B must load the new value of X, or both processors A and B must load the new values of Y and X, respectively, under all conditions.

If processors A and B load old values of Y and X, respectively, under any conditions, the system is not strongly ordered.

Testing for Strong Ordering

Table 11-5 shows the algorithm for testing strong ordering.

Table 11-5 Algorithm for Testing Strong Ordering

Time	Processor A	Processor B
T	Store to location X	Store to location Y
T+1	Load from location Y	Load from location X

For this algorithm to succeed, stores must have a global ordering in time; that is, every processor in the system must agree that either the store to location X precedes the store to location Y, or vice versa. If this global ordering is enforced, the test algorithm for strong ordering succeeds.

Restarting the Processor

Strong ordering requires precise control of a processor restart. Specifically, after completion of a processor coherency request, the system must ensure the completion of any cache state changes before allowing a processor restart.

The following sections describe processor restarts in a strong-ordered system after a processor coherency request.

Restart after a Coherent Read Request

Unless a processor invalidate or update request is unacknowledged after a coherent read request, the processor restarts (if sequential ordering is enabled) after the last word in the block has been transmitted to the processor.

Any external requests that must be completed before the read request is finished must be issued to the processor before the read response is issued.

Restart after a Coherent Write Request

The processor restarts after the coherent write request is completed. That is, the processor restarts after the last doubleword of data associated with the write request has been transmitted to the external agent, *unless* a processor read request is pending,† or a processor invalidate or update request is unacknowledged.

Restart after an Invalidate or Update Request

Following an invalidate or update request, the processor restarts after the external agent asserts **IvdAck*** or **IvdErr***, *unless* a processor read request is pending or the processor is processing an external request when either **IvdAck*** or **IvdErr*** is asserted.

If either **IvdAck*** or **IvdErr*** is asserted during or after the first cycle that the external agent asserts **ExtRqst***, the processor accepts the external request and completes any cache state changes associated with the external request before restarting.

---

† That is, present but not yet executed.

If either **IvdAck*** or **IvdErr*** is asserted before, but not asserted during or after the first cycle that the external agent asserts **ExtRqst***, the processor restarts before beginning the external request.

External requests must be completed before a processor invalidate or update completes. They can be completed, provided the processor receives an asserted **ExtRqst*** by the external agent either before or during the same cycle **IvdAck*** or **IvdErr*** is asserted.

11.9 Maintaining Coherency on Loads and Stores

Cache coherency protocols maintain data consistency throughout a multiprocessor environment. Table 11-6 lists the coherency effects of load and store operations on primary and secondary cache states in a multiprocessor environment (using an R4000MC processor).

Table 11-6 R4000MC Data Cache Coherency States

Primary Cache States	Secondary Cache States	Action on Load	Action on Store
Invalid	Any	Miss	Miss
Shared	Shared Dirty Shared	None	Read secondary tag. If the coherency algorithm is Update on Write, then send update and set the secondary cache state to Dirty Shared. If the coherency algorithm is Invalidate on Write, then send invalidate and set the primary and secondary cache states to Dirty Exclusive.
	Dirty Exclusive	None	Set the primary cache state to Dirty Exclusive.
Clean Exclusive	Clean Exclusive	None	Set the primary and secondary cache states to Dirty Exclusive.
	Dirty Exclusive	None	Set the primary data cache state to Dirty Exclusive.
Dirty Exclusive†	Dirty Exclusive	None	None

† The dirty exclusive primary state allows the primary cache to be written without a secondary access.

11.10 Manipulation of the Cache by an External Agent

Just as the processor accesses caches, so too can an external agent examine and manipulate the state and content of the primary and secondary caches through the following transactions:

- invalidate
- update
- snoop
- intervention

These transactions are described in the following sections. Encodings of these request transactions are given in Chapter 12.

Invalidate

An invalidate request causes the processor to change the state of the specified cache line to invalid in both the primary and secondary caches.

Update

An update request causes the processor to write the specified data element into the specified cache line, and either change the state of the cache line to shared in both the primary and secondary caches, or leave the state of the cache line unchanged, depending on the nature of the update request. An external agent can issue updates to cache lines that are in either the exclusive or shared states without changing the state of the cache line (see the **SysCmd(3)** bit description in Chapter 12).

Snoop

A snoop request to the processor causes the processor to return the secondary cache state of the specified cache line.

At the same time, the processor atomically† sets the state of the specified cache line in both the primary and secondary caches according to the value of the **SysCmd(2:0)** bits, which define cache state change, and are supplied by the external agent.

† An atomic operation is one that cannot be split, or portions of it deferred. In this case, the processor sets the state of both secondary and primary caches in an indivisible action; it cannot set the state of one cache line, allow another process to interrupt, and then complete the first process by setting the state of the remaining cache line.

Intervention

An intervention request causes the processor to return the secondary cache state of the specified cache line and, under certain conditions related to the state of the cache line and the nature of the intervention request, the contents of the specified secondary cache line.

At the same time, the processor atomically sets the state of the specified cache line in both the primary and secondary caches according to the value of the **SysCmd(2:0)** bits which define cache state change, and are supplied by an external agent.

11.11 Coherency Conflicts

The R4000MC processor must handle competing coherency conflicts that arise from the processor and an external source. This section describes how coherency conflicts arise and how they are handled. A system model illustrates the implications of coherency conflicts in a multiprocessor environment; a coherent read request cycle is described at the end of this section.

Figure 11-11 shows the R4000MC processor issuing processor coherency requests and accepting external coherency requests.

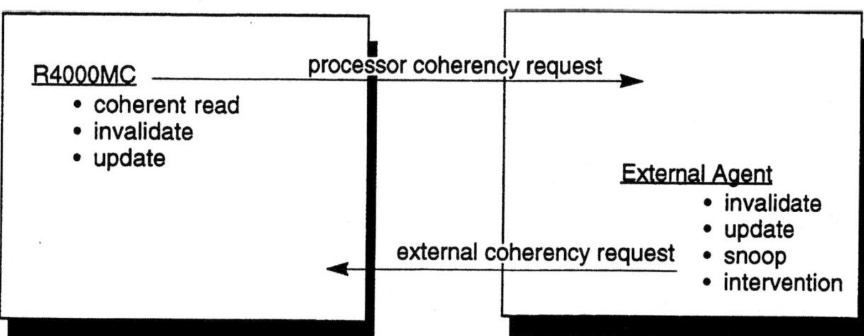

Figure 11-11 Coherency Requests: Processor and External

The R4000MC processor issues the following processor coherency requests:

- processor coherent read requests
- processor invalidate requests
- processor update requests

The R4000MC processor accepts the following external coherency requests:

- external invalidate requests
- external update requests
- external snoop requests
- external intervention requests

How Coherency Conflicts Arise

Because of the overlapped nature of the system interface, it is possible for an external coherency request to target the same cache physical address as a pending processor read request, an unacknowledged processor invalidate, or an update request. The processor does not contain the comparison mechanism necessary to detect such conflicts; instead, it uses the secondary cache as a point of reference to determine suitable coherency actions, and only checks the state of the secondary cache at specific times.

Processor Coherent Read Requests

When the processor wants to service either a store or load cache miss for a page that has a coherent page attribute in the TLB (meaning the data passed back and forth should follow a defined multiprocessor coherency scheme), a coherent read request is used.

Conflicting external coherency requests cannot affect the behavior of the processor for pending processor coherent read requests. The processor only issues read requests for a range of physical addresses not currently in the cache; consequently, an external coherency request that targets the same physical address range will not find this physical address range in the cache. In such a case, the processor simply discards any external coherency requests that conflict with a pending processor coherent read request.

Processor Invalidate or Update Requests

For processor invalidate or compulsory update requests, a *cancellation* mechanism indicates a conflict. For example, if an external coherency request is submitted while a processor invalidate or compulsory update request has been issued but not yet acknowledged, the conflict is resolved when the external agent cancels the processor invalidate or compulsory update.

Cancellation is accomplished by setting the cancellation bit in the command for the coherency request [**SysCmd(4)**]. The processor, upon receiving an external coherency request with the cancellation bit set, considers its invalidate or update request to be acknowledged and cancelled. The processor again accesses the secondary cache to determine whether to reissue the invalidate or update request, or to issue a read request.

An external agent can only assert the cancellation bit during an unacknowledged processor invalidate or unacknowledged compulsory update request. If an external coherency request is issued with the cancellation bit set, and there is no unacknowledged processor invalidate or update request pending, the behavior of the processor is undefined.

If an external coherency request is issued with the cancellation bit set when a processor update request remains potential—in other words, while a processor read request is currently pending—the behavior of the processor is undefined.

Processor potential update requests cannot be cancelled. Potential updates are always issued with processor read requests and become compulsory only after the response to the processor read request is returned in one of the shared states.

External Coherency Requests

If an external agent issues an external coherency request that conflicts with an unacknowledged processor invalidate or update request, without setting the cancellation bit, the system will operate in an undefined manner. In this case, the processor has no indication of the conflict and does not reevaluate the cache state to determine the correct action; it simply waits for an acknowledge to its invalidate or update request as it would for any invalidate or update request.

It is not possible for external coherency requests to conflict with processor write requests, since the processor does not accept external requests while a processor write request is in progress.

Tables 11-7 and 11-8 summarize the interactions between processor coherency requests and conflicting external coherency requests, organized by processor state. These two tables show the processor in one of the following states:

Idle: no processor transactions are pending.

Read Pending: a processor coherent read request has been issued, but the read response has not been received.

Potential Update Unacknowledged: a processor update request has been issued while a processor coherent read request is pending but not yet acknowledged. By definition, therefore, the response to the coherent read request has not been received.

Invalidate or Update Unacknowledged: a processor invalidate or update request has been issued but has not yet been acknowledged. By definition, no coherent read request is pending.

Table 11-7 Summary of Coherency Conflicts: Invalidate and Update

Processor State	Conflicting External Coherency Request			
	Invalidate	**Invalidate with Cancel**	**Update**	**Update with Cancel**
Idle	NA	Undefined	NA	Undefined
Read Pending	OK	Undefined	OK	Undefined
Potential Update Unacknowledged	OK	Undefined	OK	Undefined
Invalidate or Update Unacknowledged	OK†	OK	OK†	OK

† This can cause incorrect system operation and normally should not be allowed to occur.

Table 11-8 Summary of Coherency Conflicts: Intervention and Snoop

Processor State	Conflicting External Coherency Request			
	Intervention	**Intervention with Cancel**	**Snoop**	**Snoop with Cancel**
Idle	NA	Undefined	NA	Undefined
Read Pending	OK	Undefined	OK	Undefined
Potential Update Unacknowledged	OK	Undefined	OK	Undefined
Invalidate or Update Unacknowledged	OK†	OK	OK†	OK

† This can cause incorrect system operation and normally should not be allowed to occur.

System Implications of Coherency Conflicts

The constraints that the processor must place on the handling of coherency conflicts have certain implications on the design of a multiprocessor system using the R4000MC model. These constraints and their implications are described in this section.

System Model

To describe the implications of a coherency conflict, this section uses a system model that is snooping, split-read, and bus-based; I/O is not considered in this model.

The system model used in this example has the following components:

- Four processor subsystems, each consisting of an R4000MC processor, a secondary cache, and an external agent (shown in Figure 11-12). The external agent communicates with the R4000MC processor, accepting processor requests and issuing external requests. Likewise, the system bus issues and receives bus requests.
- A memory subsystem that communicates with main memory and the system bus.
- A system bus that has the following characteristics:
    - It is a multiple master, request-based, arbitrated bus. When an agent wishes to perform a transaction on the bus, it must request the bus and wait for global arbitration logic to assert a grant signal before assuming mastership of the bus. Once mastership has been granted, the agent can begin a transaction.
    - It supports read transactions, read exclusive transactions, write transactions, and invalidate transactions.
    - It is a split-read bus. This means bus operations can separate a read request from the return of its data.
    - It is a snooping bus. All agents connected to the bus must monitor all bus traffic to correctly maintain cache coherency.
- All of the TLB pages in the system have either a noncoherent or a sharable coherency attribute. (Noncoherent data is not allowed; noncoherent page attributes are used for instructions only.)
- The sharable coherency attribute allows data to be shared between the four caches in the system by using a write invalidate cache coherency protocol.
- The secondary cache states used are invalid, shared, clean exclusive, and dirty exclusive; the dirty shared secondary cache state is not allowed.

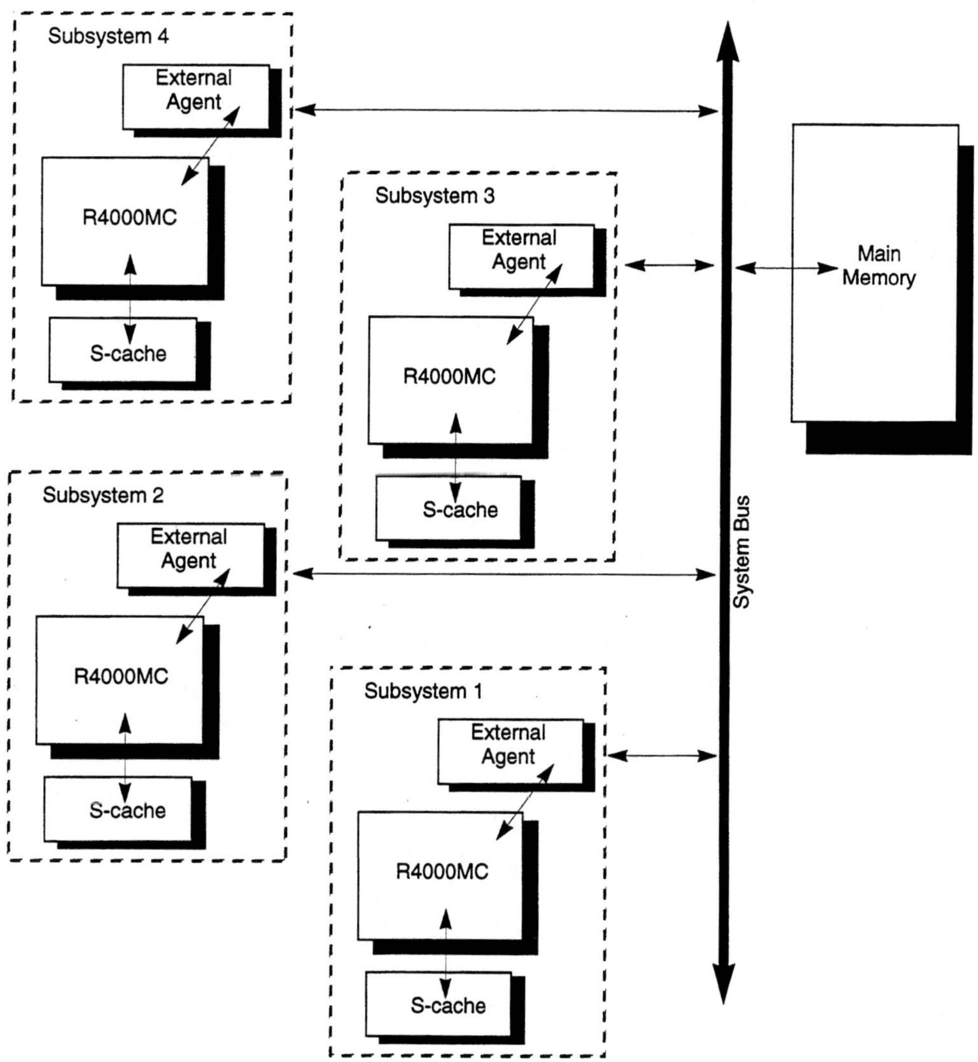

Figure 11-12 4-Processor System Illustrating Coherency Transactions

Given this system model, the following operations are described:

- loads and stores
- processor coherent read request and read response
- processor invalidate
- processor write

Load

A shown in Figure 11-12, when a processor misses in the primary and secondary caches on a load, the processor issues a read request. The subsystem external agent translates this to a read request on the bus. The returned data is loaded in either the clean exclusive or shared state, based on the shared indication returned with the read response data.†

Store

In this system model, when a processor misses in the primary and secondary caches on a store, it issues a read request with exclusivity; this is translated to a read exclusive on the bus and data is loaded in the dirty exclusive state.

When a processor hits in the cache on a store to shared data, it issues an invalidate request that must be forwarded to the system bus. Before the store can be completed and the state changed to dirty exclusive, the invalidate request must be acknowledged.

Processor Coherent Read Request and Read Response

In this system model, when one of the external agents observes a coherent read request on the system bus, it does not take immediate action. Instead, the external agent issues an intervention request to its processor during the read response. This is referred to as a *response complete* read protocol; that is, the read is complete after the read response has occurred.

At the end of the read response, each of the external agents in the system model indicate whether it was able to obtain the state of the cache line that is the target of the intervention; if successful, the external agent indicates either sharing or takeover. Takeover occurs when an external agent discovers that its processor has a dirty exclusive copy of the cache line that is the target of the read.

The read response is extended until all external agents have obtained the state of the cache line from their processors.

In this system model, the response from an external agent at the end of a read response depends on whether the read request was an ordinary read request or a read exclusive request. These are described in the following sections.

† The shared indication is the result of an intervention request to another processor, and is supplied by an external agent that is a part of the other three processor subsystems.

Ordinary Read Request

For an ordinary read request, an external agent indicates *shared* at the end of the read response if it finds that its processor has a copy of the requested cache line in the clean exclusive or shared state.

An external agent indicates both shared and takeover at the end of a read response if it finds that its processor has a copy of the requested cache line in the dirty exclusive state. Having indicated takeover, the external agent supplies the contents of the cache line (returned by the processor in response to the intervention request) over the bus to the read requester, and causes the processor to change the state of the cache line to shared. At the same time the cache line is supplied to the read requester, it is also written back to memory.

Read Exclusive Request

For a read exclusive request, an external agent never indicates shared at the end of the read response, regardless of the state the cache line is in. Instead, the cache line must be in one of the following states:

- If the current state of the cache line is clean exclusive or shared, the external agent changes the state of the cache line to invalid.
- If the current state of the cache line is dirty exclusive, the external agent indicates takeover but not shared. Having indicated takeover, the external agent supplies the contents of the cache line to the read requester, and the processor changes the state of the cache line to invalid. While the cache line is supplied to the read requester, it is also written back to memory.

Processor Invalidate

In this system model, an invalidate request is considered complete as soon as it appears on the system bus. When an external agent observes an invalidate request on the system bus, it reacts as if the invalidate has changed the state of all caches at that instant.

Processor Write

In this system model, an external agent takes no action in response to a write request on the bus.

Handling Coherency Conflicts

Coherency conflicts are examined and resolved based on the current state of the processor. Referring to Figure 11-12, the following conflicts and their resolutions are described in this section:

- coherent read conflicts
- coherent write conflicts
- invalidate conflicts

Coherent Read Conflicts

External coherency requests that conflict with pending processor coherent read requests can be issued to the processor without affecting processor behavior. In the system model shown in Figure 11-12, no conflict detection is performed by the external agent for processor coherent read requests; if an external intervention request or invalidate request is forwarded to the processor that is in conflict with a pending processor coherent read request, it does not affect the processor cache since the targeted cache line is, by definition, absent from the cache. The processor effectively discards the conflicting external intervention request, responding with an invalid indication for the targeted cache line. Similarly, the processor discards a conflicting external invalidate request since the targeted cache line is not present and therefore invalid.

For pending processor coherent read requests, conflict detection could be added to a system similar to the one shown in Figure 11-12. In such a case, when the external agent sees a read response on the bus that conflicts with a pending processor coherent read request, the external agent does not issue an intervention request to the processor. Rather, it simply reacts as if an intervention request has been completed and the cache line is not present in the processor cache.

Similarly, when an external agent sees an invalidate request on the bus that conflicts with a pending processor coherent read request, it does not forward the invalidate request to the processor since the targeted cache line is absent from the processor cache. This scheme for conflict detection on processor coherent read requests could reduce the number of external intervention and invalidate requests issued to the processor. However, since the intervention and invalidate requests that would otherwise be issued to the processor cannot result in any state modification within the processor (since the targeted cache line is not present in the cache), conflict detection for processor coherent read requests is not necessary.

Coherent Write Conflicts

As soon as a write request has been issued to the external agent, the external agent becomes responsible for the cache line. No conflicts are possible with a processor write request; however, the external agent must manage ownership of the cache line while it is waiting to acquire mastership of the system bus so that it can forward the write request. The external agent is responsible for the cache line from the time the issue cycle of the write request completes until the write request is forwarded to the system bus.

If the response to a coherent read request conflicts with a waiting processor write request, or with a processor write request that is transmitting data, the external agent detects the conflict and does not issue an intervention request to the processor. Instead, it reacts as if an intervention request has been completed and the line is in the dirty exclusive state. The external agent indicates takeover and supplies the read data to the read requester itself without disturbing the processor. After providing the read data to the read requester, the external agent must discard the write request if the read request was a read exclusive. In fact, the external agent can ignore the write request for either type of read, since processor-supplied read data is also written back to memory.

It is not possible for an invalidate request, or a write request that conflicts with a waiting processor write request, to appear on the system bus; before a processor write request can be issued, the state of the processor cache line must be set to dirty exclusive.

Invalidate Conflicts

From the time the processor issues an invalidate request until that request is acknowledged, any external coherency request issued to the processor that conflicts with the unacknowledged invalidate must include a cancellation.

In the model system shown in Figure 11-12, an acknowledge for the invalidate is sent to the processor as soon as the invalidate is forwarded to the system bus. Therefore, while the external agent is waiting to become a bus master to forward the invalidate request, the external agent must detect, by using comparators, any external coherency request that conflicts with the unacknowledged invalidate. If a conflict is detected, the external agent must not forward the invalidate request to the system bus; instead, it must rescind the invalidate request and submit the conflicting external request to the processor, with a cancellation for the invalidate request.

If the response to a coherent read request conflicts with a waiting unacknowledged processor invalidate request, the external agent detects this conflict and does not forward the processor invalidate request to the bus. Instead, it discards the processor invalidate request and issues to the processor an intervention request that includes a cancellation. The processor then reevaluates its cache state and either reissues the invalidate request or issues a coherent read request.

If an invalidate request appears on the bus while the external agent has a processor invalidate request waiting, and the external agent detects the conflict, the external agent does not forward the processor invalidate request. Instead, it discards the processor invalidate request and issues an external invalidate request that includes a cancellation to the processor. The processor then reevaluates its cache state and either reissues the invalidate request or issues a coherent read request.

It is not possible for a write request that conflicts with a waiting processor invalidate request to appear on the system bus. To issue an invalidate request, the state of the cache line must be shared with every cache in the system that contains the line.

Sample Cycle: Coherent Read Request

This section describes a multiprocessor system within which a coherent read request cycle[†] services a secondary cache load miss. The system has two processors, P_A and P_B, and two external agents linked to these processors, external agent A (E_A) and external agent B (E_B). The external agents connect the processors to a system bus. Each of the processors has its own secondary cache.

The sample cycle follows the steps below (these steps are also numbered in Figures 11-13, 11-14, and 11-15):

1. Processor B has a load miss within a sharable page.
2. Processor B issues a *coherent read request* (CRR) through E_B.
3. The CRR is placed on the bus.

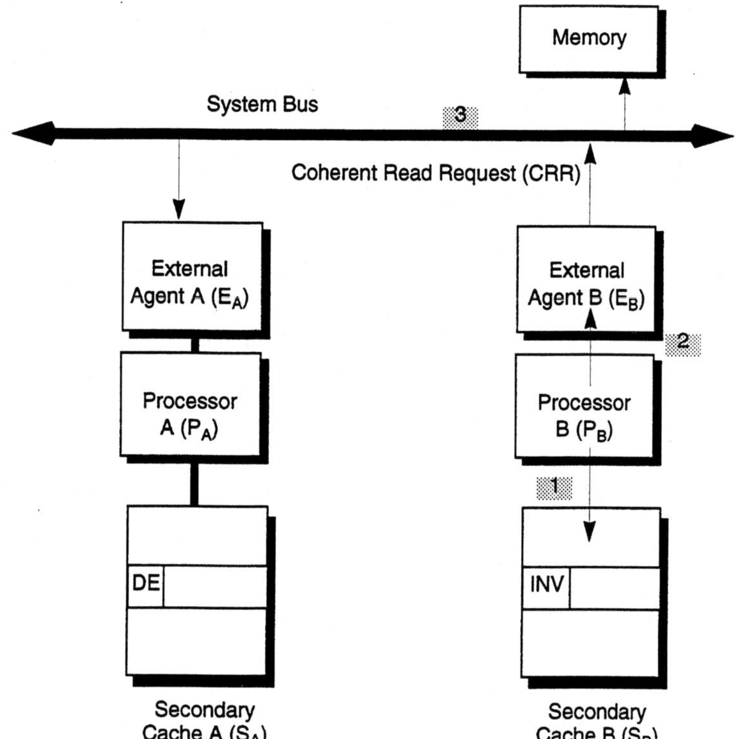

Figure 11-13 Cache Load Miss Cycle: Coherent Read Request

† Request Cycles are described in Chapter 12.

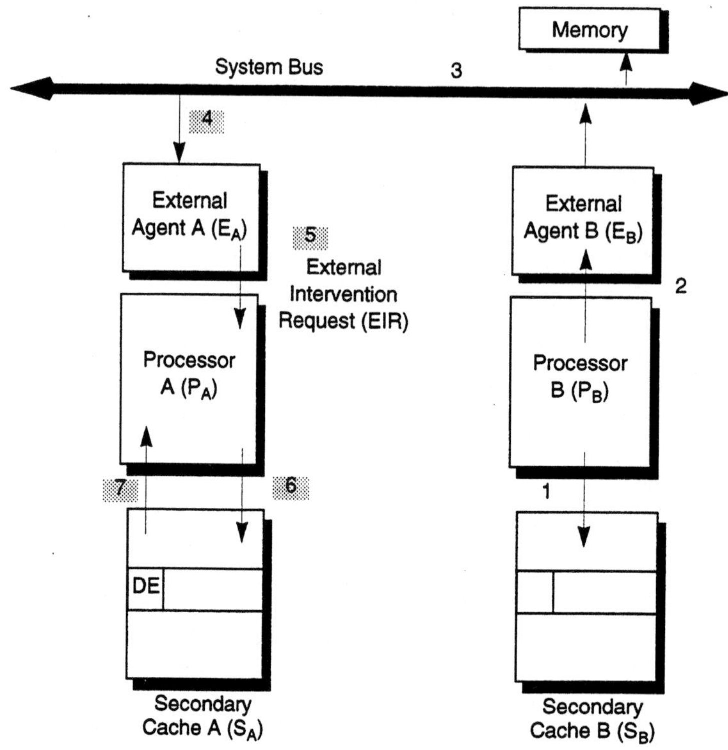

Figure 11-14 Cache Load Miss Cycle: External Intervention

4. As shown in Figure 11-14, external agent E_A reads the CRR from the bus.
5. To service this CRR, E_A issues an external intervention request (EIR) to processor A, P_A.
6. P_A receives the EIR and examines its secondary cache, S_A.
7. Depending on the type of intervention request—based on the state of the *SysCmd(3)* bit—one of the following actions is taken:
   - If the cache line in S_A is in the dirty exclusive state, the entire cache line is returned.
   - Otherwise, P_A just returns the state of the secondary cache line.

   In Figure 11-14 the retrieved data is in the dirty exclusive state (DE), servicing a load miss, when the state of cache line S_A goes from dirty exclusive to dirty shared (DS),† indicating P_A is owner of the line.

† Assuming DS mode is enabled.

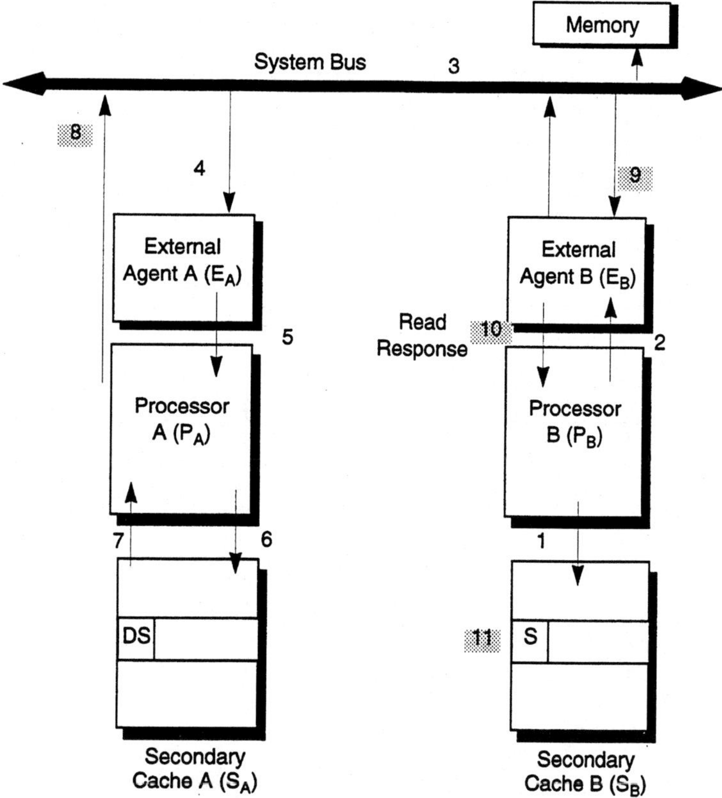

Figure 11-15 Cache Load Miss Cycle: Read Response

8. Figure 11-15 shows the cache state and cache data returned from P_A, through E_A to the bus.
9. This cache state and data are returned to E_B.
10. E_B issues a read response to P_B.
11. P_A remains owner of the cache line.

11.12 R4000 Processor Synchronization Support

In a multiprocessor system, it is essential that two or more processors working on a common task execute without corrupting each other's subtasks. Synchronization, an operation that guarantees an orderly access to shared memory, must be implemented for a properly functioning multiprocessor system. Two of the more widely used methods are discussed in this section: test-and-set, and counter.

Test-and-Set

Test-and-set uses a variable called the *semaphore,* which protects data from being simultaneously modified by more than one processor. In other words, a processor can lock out other processors from accessing shared data when the processor is in a *critical section,* a part of program in which no more than a fixed number of processors is allowed to execute. In the case of test-and-set, only one processor can enter the critical section.

Figure 11-16 illustrates a test-and-set synchronization procedure that uses a semaphore; when the semaphore is set to 0, the shared data is unlocked, and when the semaphore is set to 1, the shared data is locked.

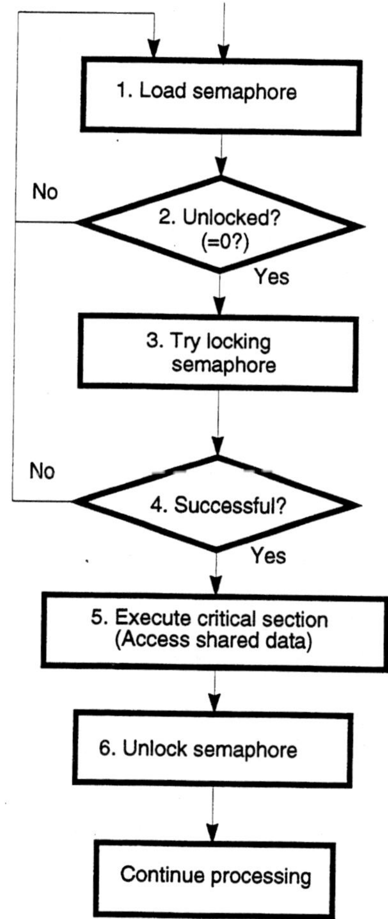

Figure 11-16 Synchronization with Test-and-Set

The processor begins by loading the semaphore and checking to see if it is unlocked (set to 0) in steps 1 and 2. If the semaphore is not 0, the processor loops back to step 1. If the semaphore is 0, indicating the shared data is not locked, the processor next tries to lock out any other access to the shared data (step 3). If not successful, the processor loops back to step 1, and reloads the semaphore.

If the processor is successful at setting the semaphore (step 4), it executes the critical section of code (step 5) and gains access to the shared data, completes its task, unlocks the semaphore (step 6), and continues processing.

Counter

Another common synchronization technique uses a *counter. A counter is* a designated memory location that can be incremented or decremented.

In the test-and-set method, only one processor at a time is permitted to enter the critical section. Using a counter, up to *N* processors are allowed to concurrently execute the critical section. All processors after the *N*th processor must wait until one of the *N* processors exits the critical section and a space becomes available.

The counter works by not allowing more than one processor to modify it at any given time. Conceptually, the counter can be viewed as a variable that counts the number of limited resources (for example, the number of processes, or software licenses, etc.). Figure 11-17 shows this process.

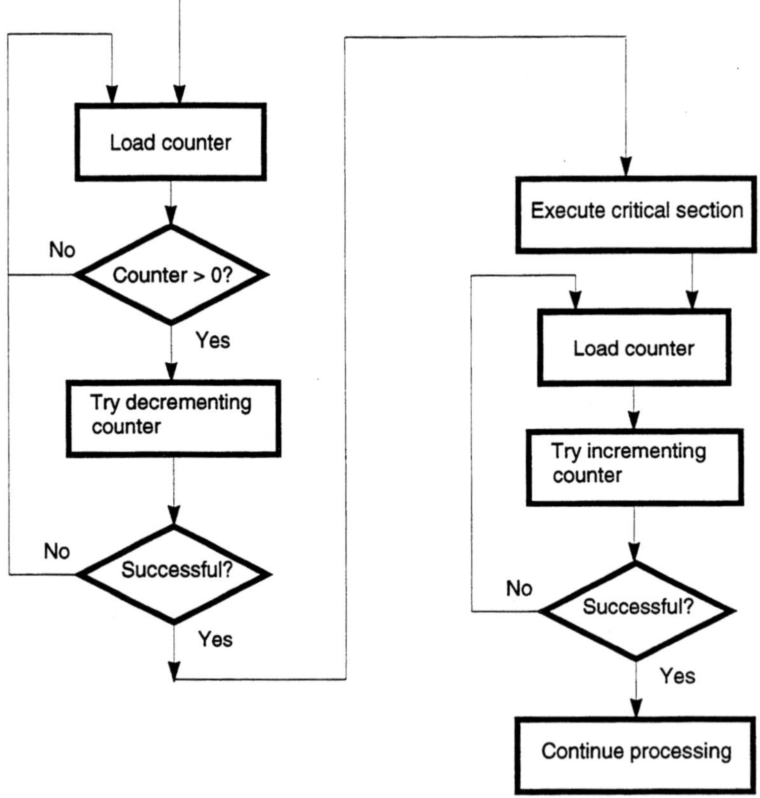

Figure 11-17 Synchronization Using a Counter

LL and SC

MIPS instructions *Load Linked* (LL) and *Store Conditional* (SC) provide support for processor synchronization. These two instructions work very much like their simpler counterparts, load and store. The LL instruction, in addition to doing a simple load, has the side effect of setting a bit called the *link bit*. This link bit forms a breakable link between the LL instruction and the subsequent SC instruction. The SC performs a simple store if the link bit is set when the store executes. If the link bit is not set, then the store fails to execute. The success or failure of the SC is indicated in the target register of the store.

The link is broken in the following circumstances:†

- if an external request changes the state of the line containing the lock variable (for example, an external invalidate or update request)
- upon completion of an ERET (return from exception) instruction.

The most important features of LL and SC are:

- They provide a mechanism for generating all of the common synchronization primitives including test-and-set, counters, sequencers, etc., with no additional overhead.
- When they operate, bus traffic is generated only if the state of the cache line changes; lock words stay in the cache until some other processor takes ownership of that cache line.

† The most obvious case where the link is broken occurs when an invalidate to the cache line is the subject of the load. In this case, some other processor has successfully completed a store to that line.

Examples Using LL and SC

Figure 11-18 shows how to implement test-and-set using LL and SC instructions.

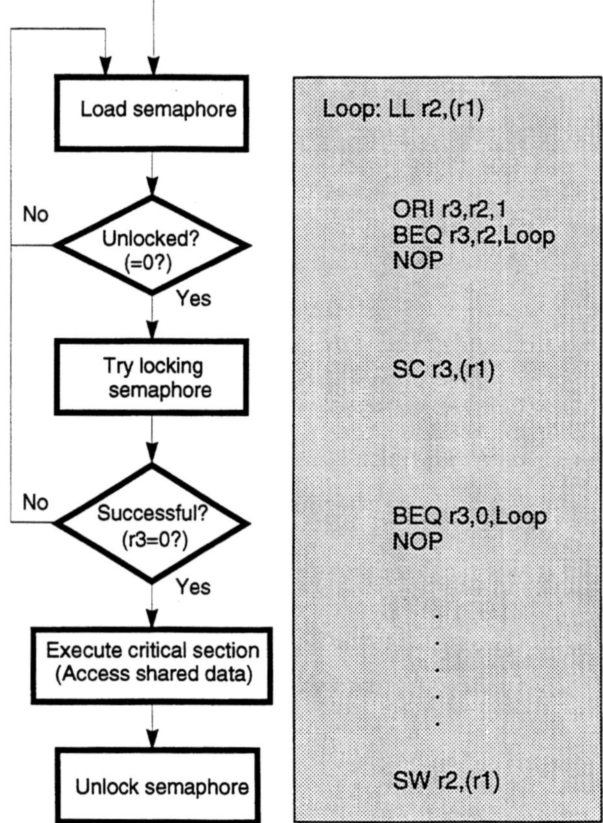

Figure 11-18 Test-and-Set using LL and SC

Figure 11-19 shows synchronization using a counter.

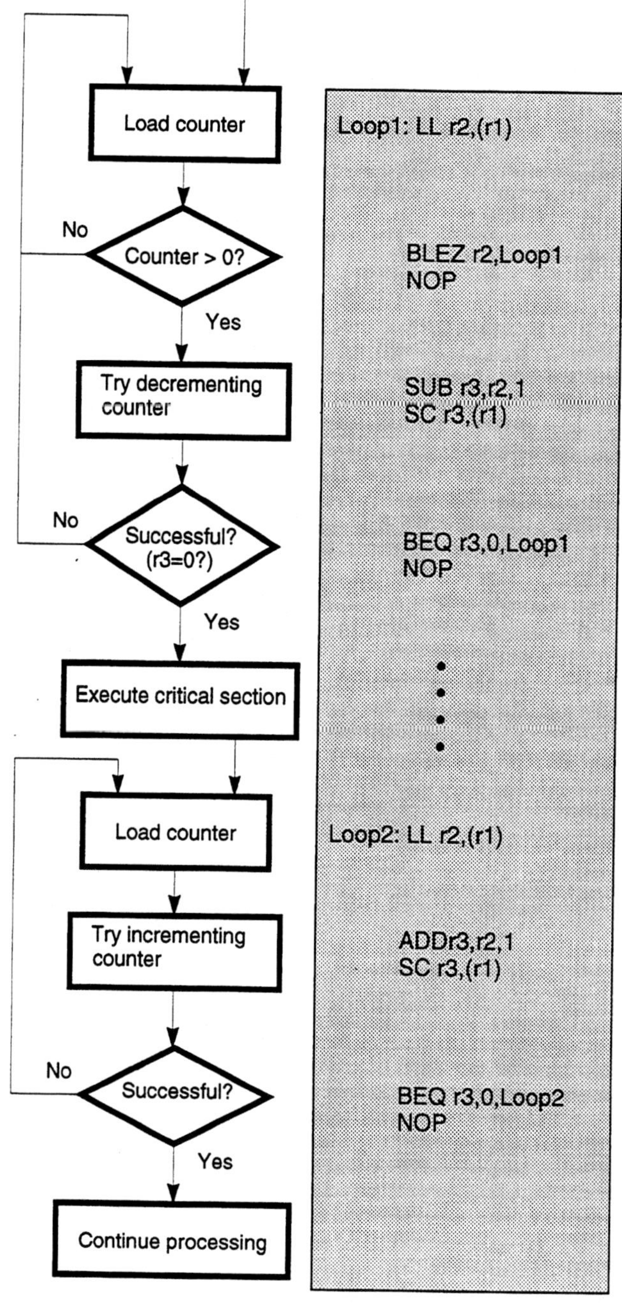

Figure 11-19 Counter Using LL and SC

System Interface

12

The System interface allows the processor to access external resources needed to satisfy cache misses and uncached operations, while permitting an external agent access to some of the processor internal resources.

In the R4000MC configuration, the System interface also provides the processor with mechanisms to maintain the cache coherency of shared data, while providing an external agent the mechanisms to maintain system-wide multiprocessor cache coherency.

This chapter describes the System interface from the point of view of both the processor and the external agent.

12.1 Terminology

The following terms are used in this chapter:

- An *external agent* is any logic device connected to the processor, over the System interface, that allows the processor to issue requests.
- A *system event* is an event that occurs within the processor and requires access to external system resources.
- *Sequence* refers to the precise series of requests that a processor generates to service a system event.
- *Protocol* refers to the cycle-by-cycle signal transitions that occur on the System interface pins to assert a processor or external request.
- *Syntax* refers to the precise definition of bit patterns on encoded buses, such as the command bus.

12.2 System Interface Description

The R4000 processor supports a 64-bit address/data interface that can construct systems ranging from a simple uniprocessor with main memory to a multiprocessor system with caches and complete cache coherency. The System interface consists of:

- 64-bit address and data bus, **SysAD**
- 8-bit SysAD check bus, **SysADC**
- 9-bit command bus, **SysCmd**
- eight handshake signals:
    - **RdRdy*, WrRdy***
    - **ExtRqst*, Release***
    - **ValidIn*, ValidOut***
    - **IvdAck*, IvdErr***

The processor uses the System interface to access external resources such as cache misses and uncached operations. In the case of R4000MC, the System interface also supports multiprocessor cache coherency.

Interface Buses

Figure 12-1 shows the primary communication paths for the System interface: a 64-bit address and data bus, **SysAD(63:0)**, and a 9-bit command bus, **SysCmd(8:0)**. These **SysAD** and the **SysCmd** buses are bidirectional; that is, they are driven by the processor to issue a processor request, and by the external agent to issue an external request (see Processor and External Requests, in this chapter, for more information).

A request through the System interface consists of:

- an address
- a System interface command that specifies the precise nature of the request
- a series of data elements if the request is for a write, read response, or update.

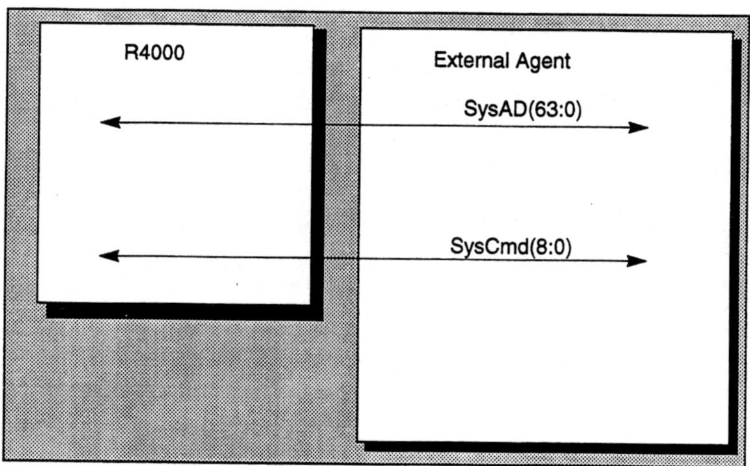

Figure 12-1 System Interface Buses

Address and Data Cycles

Cycles in which the **SysAD** bus contains a valid address are called *address cycles*. Cycles in which the **SysAD** bus contains valid data are called *data cycles*. Validity is determined by the state of the **ValidIn*** and **ValidOut*** signals (described in Interface Buses, in this chapter).

The **SysCmd** bus identifies the contents of the **SysAD** bus during any cycle in which it is valid. The most significant bit of the **SysCmd** bus is always used to indicate whether the current cycle is an address cycle or a data cycle.

- During address cycles [**SysCmd(8)** = 0], the remainder of the **SysCmd** bus, **SysCmd(7:0)**, contains a *System interface command* (the encoding of System interface commands is detailed in System Interface Commands and Data Identifiers, in this chapter).
- During data cycles [**SysCmd(8)** = 1], the remainder of the **SysCmd** bus, **SysCmd(7:0)**, contains a *data identifier* (the encoding of data identifiers is detailed in System Interface Commands and Data Identifiers, in this chapter).

Issue Cycles

There are two types of processor issue cycles:

- processor read, invalidate, and update request issue cycles
- processor write request issue cycles.

The processor samples the signal **RdRdy*** to determine the issue cycle for a processor read, invalidate, or update request; the processor samples the signal **WrRdy*** to determine the issue cycle of a processor write request.

As shown in Figure 12-2, **RdRdy*** must be asserted two cycles prior to the address cycle of the processor read/invalidate/update request to define the address cycle as the issue cycle.

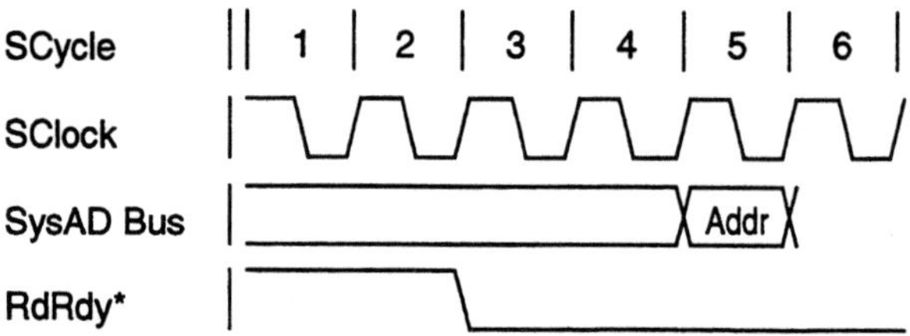

Figure 12-2 State of RdRdy Signal for Read, Invalidate, or Update Requests*

As shown in Figure 12-3, **WrRdy*** must be asserted two cycles prior to the first address cycle of the processor write request to define the address cycle as the issue cycle.

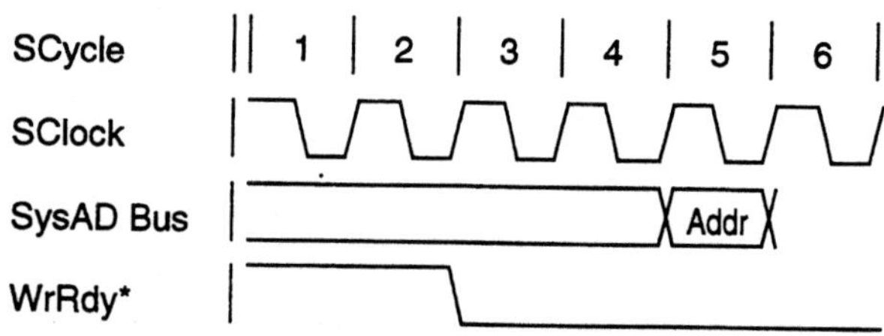

Figure 12-3 State of WrRdy Signal for Write Requests*

The processor repeats the address cycle for the request until the conditions for a valid issue cycle are met. After the issue cycle, if the processor request requires data to be sent, the data transmission begins. There is only one issue cycle for any processor request.

The processor accepts external requests, even while attempting to issue a processor request, by releasing the System interface to slave state in response to an assertion of **ExtRqst*** by the external agent.

Note that the rules governing the issue cycle of a processor request are strictly applied to determine the action the processor takes. The processor either:

- completes the issuance of the processor request in its entirety before the external request is accepted, or
- releases the System interface to slave state without completing the issuance of the processor request.

In the latter case, the processor issues the processor request (provided the processor request is still necessary) after the external request is complete. The rules governing an issue cycle again apply to the processor request.

Handshake Signals

The processor manages the flow of requests through the following eight control signals:

- **RdRdy***, **WrRdy*** are used by the external agent to indicate when it can accept a new read (**RdRdy***) or write (**WrRdy***) transaction.
- **ExtRqst***, **Release*** are used to transfer control of the **SysAD** and **SysCmd** buses. **ExtRqst*** is used by an external agent to indicate a need to control the interface. **Release*** is asserted by the processor when it transfers the mastership of the System interface to the external agent.
- The R4000 processor uses **ValidOut*** and the external agent uses **ValidIn*** to indicate valid command/data on the **SysCmd/SysAD** buses.
- **IvdAck***, **IvdErr*** are used in multiprocessor systems; they are asserted by the external agent to indicate the successful completion (**IvdAck***) or the unsuccessful completion (**IvdErr***) of a pending processor invalidate or update request.†

† When using the R4000SC processor, **IvdAck*** and **IvdErr*** must be connected to Vcc.

12.3 System Interface Protocols

Figure 12-4 shows the System interface operates from register to register. That is, processor outputs come directly from output registers and begin to change with the rising edge of **SClock.**†

Processor inputs are fed directly to input registers that latch these input signals with the rising edge of **SClock**. This allows the System interface to run at the highest possible clock frequency.

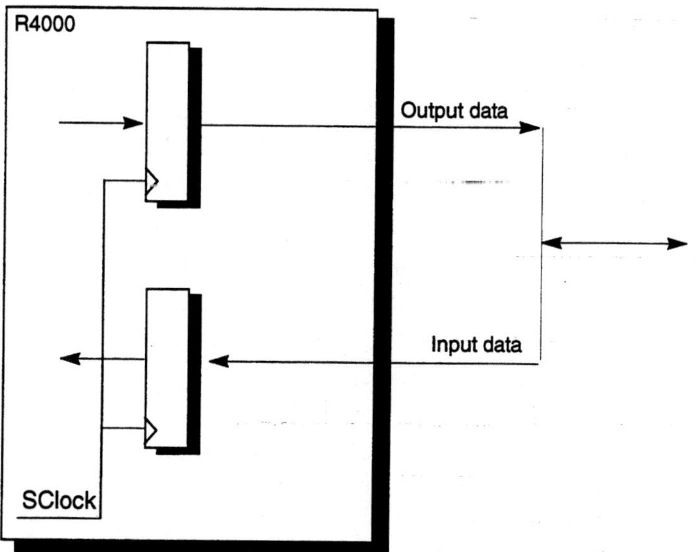

Figure 12-4 System Interface Register-to-Register Operation

Master and Slave States

When the R4000 processor is driving the **SysAD** and **SysCmd** buses, the System interface is in *master state.* When the external agent is driving the **SysAD** and **SysCmd** buses, the System interface is in *slave state.*

In master state, the processor asserts the signal **ValidOut*** whenever the **SysAD** and **SysCmd** buses are valid.

In slave state, the external agent asserts the signal **ValidIn*** whenever the **SysAD** and **SysCmd** buses are valid.

† **SClock** is an internal clock used by the processor to sample data at the System interface and to clock data into the processor System interface output registers; see Chapter 10 for more details.

Moving from Master to Slave State

The System interface remains in master state unless one of the following occurs:

- The external agent requests and is granted the System interface (external arbitration).
- The processor issues a read request or completes the issue of a cluster (uncompelled change to slave state).

External Arbitration

The System interface must be in slave state for the external agent to issue an external request through the System interface. The transition from master state to slave state is arbitrated by the processor using the System interface handshake signals **ExtRqst*** and **Release***. This transition is described by the following procedure:

1. An external agent signals that it wishes to issue an external request by asserting **ExtRqst***.
2. When the processor is ready to accept an external request, it releases the System interface from master to slave state by asserting **Release*** for one cycle.
3. The System interface returns to master state as soon as the issue of the external request is complete.

This process is described in External Arbitration Protocol, later in this chapter.

Uncompelled Change to Slave State

An *uncompelled* change to slave state is the transition of the System interface from master state to slave state, initiated by the processor when a processor read request is pending. **Release*** is asserted automatically after a read request or cluster (see Clusters, later in this chapter, for a definition of a cluster). An uncompelled change to slave state occurs either during or some number of cycles after the issue cycle of a read request, or either during or some number of cycles after the last cycle of the last request in a cluster.

The uncompelled release latency depends on the state of the cache, the presence or absence of a secondary cache, and the secondary cache parameters (see Release Latency, in this chapter). After an uncompelled change to slave state, the processor returns to master state at the end of the next external request. This can be a read response, or some other type of external request.

An external agent must note that the processor has performed an uncompelled change to slave state and begin driving the **SysAD** bus along with the **SysCmd** bus. As long as the System interface is in slave state, the external agent can begin an external request without arbitrating for the System interface; that is, without asserting **ExtRqst***.

After the external request, the System interface returns to master state.

Whenever a processor read request is pending, after the issue of a read request or after the issue of all of the requests in a cluster, the processor automatically switches the System interface to slave state, even though the external agent is not arbitrating to issue an external request. This transition to slave state allows the external agent to return read response data.

12.4 Processor and External Requests

There are two broad categories of requests: *processor requests* and *external requests*. These two categories are described in this section.

When a system event occurs, the processor issues either a single request or a series of requests—called *processor requests*—through the System interface, to access an external resource and service the event. For this to work, the processor System interface must be connected to an external agent that is compatible with the System interface protocol, and can coordinate access to system resources.

An external agent requesting access to processor caches or to a processor status register generates an *external request*. This access request passes through the System interface. System events and request cycles are shown in Figure 12-5.

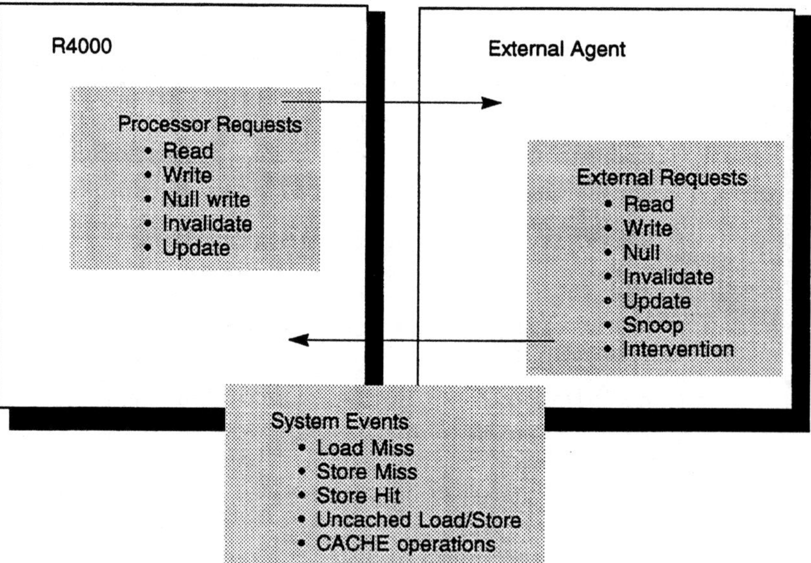

Figure 12-5 Requests and System Events

Rules for Processor Requests

The following rules apply to processor requests.

- After issuing a processor read request, either individually or as part of a cluster, the processor cannot issue a subsequent read request until it has received a read response.
- After issuing a processor update request, or after a potential update request becomes compulsory, the processor cannot issue a subsequent request until it has received an acknowledge for the update request.
- After the processor has issued a write request, the processor cannot issue a subsequent request until at least four cycles after the issue cycle of the write request. This means back-to-back write requests with a single data cycle are separated by two unused system cycles, as shown in Figure 12-6.

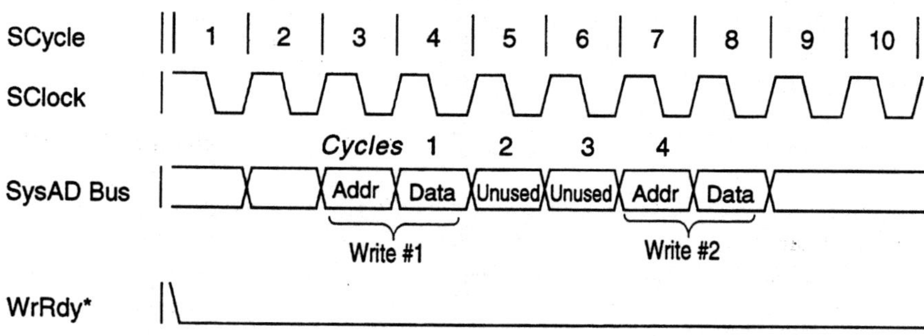

Figure 12-6 Back-to-Back Write Cycle Timing

Processor Requests

A processor request is a request or a series of requests, through the System interface, to access some external resource. As shown in Figure 12-7, processor requests include read, write, null write, invalidate, and update. This section also describes clusters.

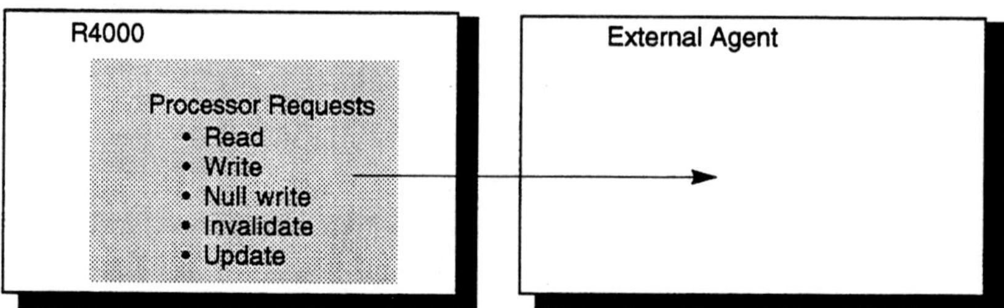

Figure 12-7 Processor Requests

Read request asks for a block, doubleword, partial doubleword, word, or partial word of data either from main memory or from another system resource.

Write request provides a block, doubleword, partial doubleword, word, or partial word of data to be written either to main memory or to another system resource.

Null write request indicates that an expected write has been cancelled as a result of an external request.

Invalidate request specifies a line in every other cache in the system that must be marked invalid.

Update request provides a block, doubleword, partial doubleword, word, or partial word of data that must be transferred to every other cache in the system.

Table 12-1 lists the processor requests that each type of R4000 can issue.

Table 12-1 Supported Processor Requests

Request	R4000PC	R4000SC	R4000MC
Processor Read	X	X	X
Processor Write	X	X	X
Processor Null Write		X	X
Processor Invalidate			X
Processor Update			X

Processor requests are managed by the processor in two distinct modes: *secondary-cache mode* and *no-secondary-cache mode* (see Chapter 11 for a description of these two modes), which are programmable through the boot-time mode control interface described in Chapter 9.

The permissible modes of operation are dependent on the following processor package configurations; if not programmed correctly, the behavior of the processor is undefined.

- An R4000PC must be programmed to run in no-secondary-cache mode.
- An R4000SC or R4000MC can be programmed to run in either secondary-cache or no-secondary-cache mode.

In no-secondary-cache mode, the processor issues requests in a strict sequential fashion; that is, the processor is only allowed to have one request pending at any time. For example, the processor issues a read request and waits for a read response before issuing any subsequent requests. The processor submits a write request only if there are no read requests pending.

The processor has the input signals **RdRdy*** and **WrRdy*** to allow an external agent to manage the flow of processor requests. **RdRdy*** controls the flow of processor read, invalidate, and update requests, while **WrRdy*** controls the flow of processor write requests. Processor null write requests must always be accepted and cannot be delayed by either **RdRdy*** or **WrRdy***. The processor request cycle sequence is shown in Figure 12-8.

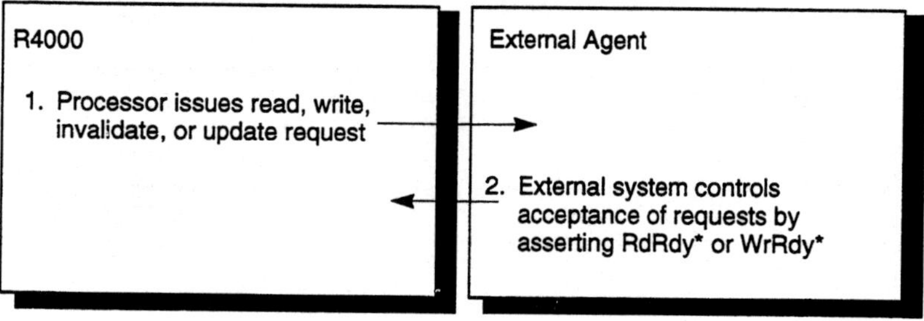

Figure 12-8 Processor Request

Processor Read Request

When a processor issues a read request, the external agent must access the specified resource and return the requested data. (Processor read requests are described in this section; external read requests are described in External Requests, later on in this chapter.)

A processor read request can be split from the external agent's return of the requested data; in other words, the external agent can initiate an unrelated external request before it returns the response data for a processor read. A processor read request is completed after the last word of response data has been received from the external agent.

Note that the data identifier (see System Interface Commands and Data Identifiers, in this chapter) associated with the response data can signal that the returned data is erroneous, causing the processor to take a bus error.

Processor read requests that have been issued, but for which data has not yet been returned, are said to be *pending*. A read remains pending until the requested read data is returned.

In secondary-cache mode, the external agent must be capable of accepting a processor read request followed by a potential update request any time all three of the following conditions are met:

- There is no processor read request pending.
- There is no unacknowledged processor update request.
- The signal **RdRdy*** has been asserted for two or more cycles.

In no-secondary-cache mode, the external agent must be capable of accepting a processor read request any time the following two conditions are met:

- There is no processor read request pending.
- The signal **RdRdy*** has been asserted for two or more cycles.

Processor Write Request

When a processor issues a write request, the specified resource is accessed and the data is written to it. (Processor write requests are described in this section; external write requests are described in External Requests, later on in this chapter.)

A processor write request is complete after the last word of data has been transmitted to the external agent.

In secondary-cache mode, the external agent must be capable of accepting a processor write request any time all three of the following conditions are met:

- There is no processor read request pending.
- There is no unacknowledged processor update request that is compulsory.
- The signal **WrRdy*** has been asserted for two or more cycles.

In no-secondary-cache mode, the external agent must be capable of accepting a processor write request any time the following two conditions are met:

- No processor read request is pending.
- The signal **WrRdy*** has been asserted for two or more cycles.

Processor Invalidate Request

An invalidate request notifies all processors that the specified cache line must be marked invalid in all caches in the system. Invalidate requests can only be used in a multiprocessing system.

When a processor issues an invalidate request, the specified resource is accessed and the line is marked invalid. (Processor invalidate requests are described in this section; external invalidate requests are described in External Requests, later on in this chapter.)

A processor invalidate request requires a completion acknowledge by either the invalidate acknowledge signal **IvdAck*** or the invalidate error signal **IvdErr***, unless the invalidate is canceled by the external agent. A processor invalidate request that has been submitted, but for which the processor has not yet received an acknowledge or a cancellation, is said to be *unacknowledged*. When the processor invalidate request fails (**IvdErr*** is asserted), the issuing processor takes a bus error on the store instruction that generated the failed request. Figure 12-10 shows a sample processor invalidate/update request cycle.

Invalidate cancellation is signaled to the processor during external invalidate, update, snoop, and intervention requests; **IvdErr*** signals a processor invalidate request has failed.

A completion acknowledge for processor invalidate requests is signaled through the System interface on dedicated pins, and this acknowledgment can occur in parallel with processor and external requests.

State changes in the external system are not instantaneously reflected in the caches of every processor, which means an external agent can discover that a processor request for an invalidate cannot be completed. For example, a processor store can hit on a shared cache line and issue an invalidate to the external agent. However, before the external agent can transmit the invalidate to the rest of the system another invalidate for the same cache line can be received by the external agent. If this occurs, the processor cache does not reflect the current state of the system and the processor invalidate must not be transmitted to the system; instead, the external agent must cancel the processor unacknowledged invalidate. Figure 12-9 shows this cancellation cycle.

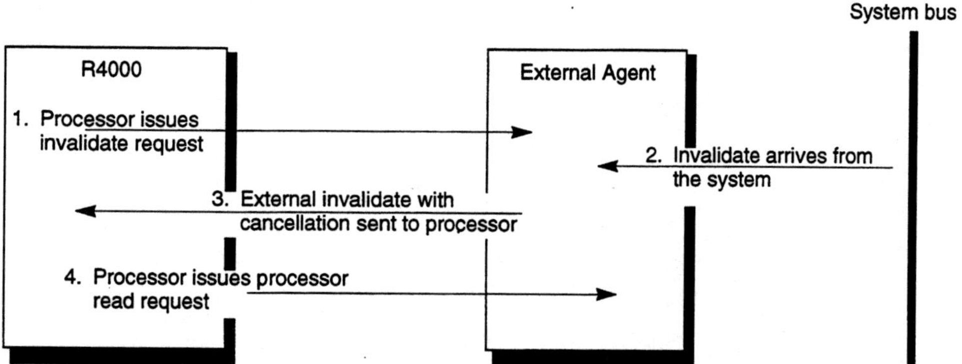

Figure 12-9 Cancelling an Invalidate Request

The steps shown in Figure 12-9 are described below:

1. The processor issues an invalidate on a store hit to a shared line in its cache.
2. An invalidate request, coming from the system bus, is received by the processor's external agent targeting the same cache line.
3. The external invalidate invalidates the cache line, and the processor invalidate request is cancelled.
4. The processor re-examines the state of the cache line and discovers the cache line which was target of the store is now invalid. The processor issues a processor read request to service the store miss.

Processor Update Request

An update request notifies all processors that a specified cache line in all caches throughout a multiprocessor system must be replaced with modified data. An update request can only be used in a multiprocessing system.

When a processor issues an update request, the specified resource is accessed and the line is updated. (Processor update requests are described in this section; external update requests are described in External Requests, later on in this chapter.)

A processor update request requires a completion acknowledge by either the invalidate acknowledge signal **IvdAck*** or the invalidate error signal **IvdErr*** (shown in Figure 12-10), unless the update is canceled by the external agent. A processor update request that has been submitted, but for which the processor has not yet received an acknowledge or a cancellation, is said to be *unacknowledged.* When the processor update request fails (**IvdErr*** is asserted), the issuing processor takes a bus error on the store instruction that generated the failed request. Figure 12-10 shows a sample processor invalidate/update request cycle.

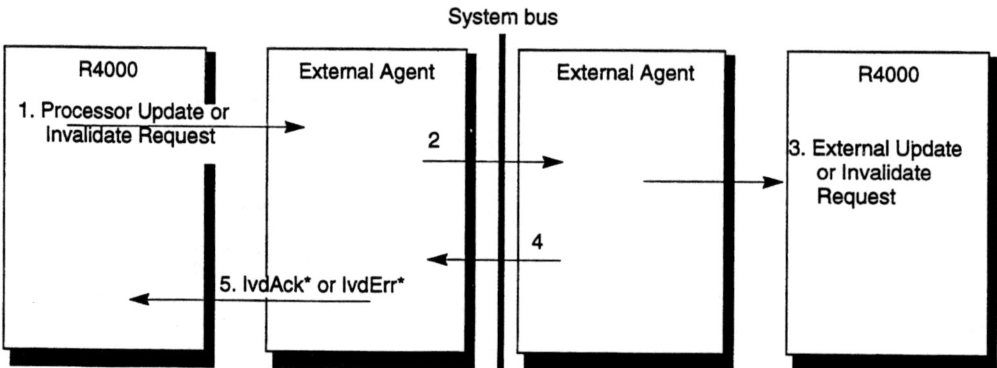

Figure 12-10 Processor Update/Invalidate Acknowledge Cycle

Update cancellation is signaled to the processor during external invalidate, update, snoop, and intervention requests; **IvdErr*** signals a processor update request has failed.

Since a completion acknowledge for processor update requests is signaled through the System interface on dedicated pins, this acknowledgment can occur in parallel with processor and external requests.

Clusters

A cluster consists of a single processor read request, followed by one or two additional processor requests that are issued while the initial read request is pending.

The processor supports three types of clusters:

- a processor read request, followed by a write request
- a processor read request, followed by potential update request
- a processor read request, followed by a potential update request, followed by a write request.

In secondary-cache mode, the processor issues individual requests (as in no-secondary-cache mode), or cluster requests. All requests in the cluster must be accepted before the response to the read request that began the cluster can be returned to the processor.

Potential update requests within a cluster can be disabled through the boot-time mode control interface.

Read With Write Forthcoming Request as Part of a Cluster

The processor signals that it is issuing a cluster containing a processor write request by issuing a *read-with-write-forthcoming* request, instead of starting the cluster with an ordinary read request. The read-with-write-forthcoming request is identified by a bit in the command for processor read requests.

The external agent must accept all requests that form the cluster before it can respond to the read request that began the cluster. The behavior of the processor is undefined if the external agent returns a response to a processor read request before accepting all of the requests of the cluster.

Potential Update as Part of a Cluster

Potential updates are identified by setting a bit in the processor update command. A processor potential update request is any update request that is issued while a processor read request is pending.

Once the processor issues a read request, a potential update request follows, regardless of the state of **RdRdy***. Potential update requests do not obey the **RdRdy*** flow control rules for issuance, but rather issue with a single address cycle regardless of the state of **RdRdy***.

A processor potential update request remains potential until the read response to the pending processor read request which began the cluster is received by the external agent.

- If the read response data is returned in one of the shared states—*shared* or *dirty shared*—the potential update becomes compulsory and is no longer potential. A compulsory update must receive an acknowledge either by the signal **IvdAck*** or **IvdErr***.
- If the read response data is returned in one of the exclusive states—*clean exclusive* or *dirty exclusive*—the potential update is nullified and the processor neither expects nor requires an acknowledge.

Write Request as Part of a Cluster

A write request that is part of a cluster obeys the **WrRdy*** timing rules for issuing, as shown earlier in Figure 12-3.

Null Write Request as Part of a Cluster

Since the processor accepts external requests between the issue of a read-with-write-forthcoming request that begins a cluster and the issue of the write request that completes a cluster, it is possible for an external request to eliminate the need for the write request in the cluster. For example, if the external agent issued an external invalidate request that targeted the cache line the processor was attempting to write back, the state of the cache line would be changed to invalid and the write back for the cache line would no longer be needed. In this event, the processor issues a processor null write request after completing the external request to complete the cluster.

Processor null write requests do not obey the **WrRdy*** flow control rules for issuance, rather they issue with a single address cycle regardless of the state of **WrRdy***. Any external request that changes the state of a cache line from dirty exclusive or dirty shared to clean exclusive, shared, or invalid obviates the need for a write back of that cache line.

External Requests

External requests include read, write, invalidate, update, snoop, intervention, and null requests, as shown in Figure 12-11. External invalidate, update, snoop and intervention requests, as a group, are referred to as *external coherence requests*. This section also includes a description of read response, a special case of an external request.

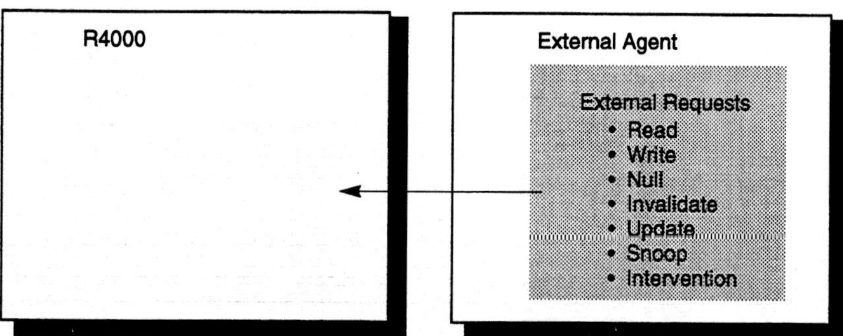

Figure 12-11 External Requests

Read request asks for a word of data from the processor's internal resource.

Write request provides a word of data to be written to the processor's internal resource.

Invalidate request specifies a cache line, in the primary and secondary caches of the processor, that must be marked invalid.

Update request provides a doubleword, partial doubleword, word, or partial word of data to be written to the processor's primary and secondary caches.

Snoop request checks the processor's secondary cache to see if a valid copy of a particular cache line exists. If a valid copy exists, the processor returns the state of the cache line at the specified physical address in the secondary cache, and can modify the state of the cache line.

Intervention request requires the processor to return the state of the secondary cache line at the specified physical address. Under certain conditions related to the state of the cache line and the nature of the intervention request, the contents of the primary and secondary cache line can be returned. The state of the line can also be modified by this request.

Null request requires no action by the processor; it provides a mechanism for the external agent to either return control of the secondary cache to the processor, or return the System interface to the master state without affecting the processor.

Table 12-2 lists the external requests that each type of R4000 can receive (an X indicates the request is supported on that model).

Table 12-2 Supported External Requests

Request Type	R4000PC	R4000SC	R4000MC
External Read	X	X	X
External Write	X	X	X
External Null (System interface)	X	X	X
External Null (Secondary Cache)		X	X
External Invalidate			X
External Update			X
External Snoop			X
External Intervention			X

The processor controls the flow of external requests through the arbitration signals **ExtRqst*** and **Release***, as shown in Figure 12-12. The external agent must acquire mastership of the System interface before it is allowed to issue an external request; the external agent arbitrates for mastership of the System interface by asserting **ExtRqst*** and then waiting for the processor to assert **Release*** for one cycle.

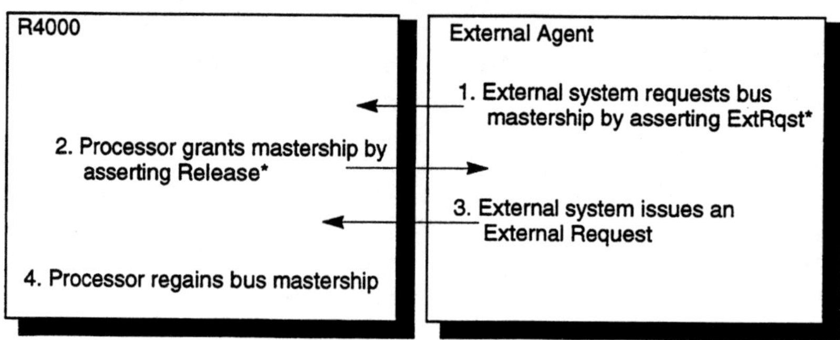

Figure 12-12 External Request

Mastership of the System interface always returns to the processor after an external request is issued. The processor does not accept a subsequent external request until it has completed the current request. The processor accepts external requests between the issue of a processor read request, or a processor read request followed by a potential update request and the issue of a processor write request within a cluster.

If there are no processor requests pending, the processor decides, based on its internal state, whether to accept the external request, or to issue a new processor request. The processor can issue a new processor request even if the external agent is requesting access to the System interface.

The external agent asserts **ExtRqst*** indicating that it wishes to begin an external request. The external agent then waits for the processor to signal that it is ready to accept this request by asserting **Release***. The processor signals that it is ready to accept an external request based on the criteria listed below.

- The processor completes any processor request or processor request cluster that is in progress.
- While waiting for the assertion of **RdRdy*** to issue a processor read request, the processor can accept an external request if the request is delivered to the processor one or more cycles before **RdRdy*** is asserted.
- While waiting for the assertion of **WrRdy*** to issue a processor write request, the processor can accept an external request provided the request is delivered to the processor one or more cycles before **WrRdy*** is asserted.
- If waiting for the response to a read request after the processor has made an uncompelled change to a slave state, the external agent can issue an external request before providing the read response data.

External Read Request

In contrast to a processor read request, data is returned directly in response to an external read request; no other requests can be issued until the processor returns the requested data. An external read request is complete after the processor returns the requested word of data.

The data identifier (see System Interface Commands and Data Identifiers in this chapter) associated with the response data can signal that the returned data is erroneous, causing the processor to take a bus error.

NOTE: The processor does not contain any resources that are readable by an external read request; in response to an external read request the processor returns undefined data and a data identifier with its *Erroneous Data* bit, **SysCmd(5)**, set.

External Write Request

When an external agent issues a write request, the specified resource is accessed and the data is written to it. An external write request is complete after the word of data has been transmitted to the processor.

The only processor resource available to an external write request is the *Interrupt* register.

External Invalidate Request

When an external agent issues an invalidate request, the specified resource is accessed and the line is marked invalid. An external invalidate request is considered to be complete after the request has been transmitted.

External Update Request

When an external agent issues an update request, the specified resource is accessed and the line is replaced. An external update request is considered complete after the request has been transmitted.

External Snoop Request

An external snoop request makes the processor inspect the secondary cache to see if the cache contains a valid version of the specified cache line. If the valid cache line is present, the processor reports the cache line state and can modify this state.

An external snoop request is complete after the processor returns the state of the specified cache line.

External Intervention Request

When an external agent issues an intervention request, the specified secondary cache line is inspected. Upon inspection, the cache line state is reported and/or modified. Under certain circumstances the specified cache line may also be retrieved. The external intervention request is complete after one of the following occurs:

- the processor returns the state of the specified cache line
- the processor returns the last word of data for the specified cache line.

Read Response

A *read response* returns data in response to a processor read request, as shown in Figure 12-13. While a read response is technically an external request, it has one characteristic that differentiates it from all other external requests—it does not perform System interface arbitration. For this reason, read responses are handled separately from all other external requests, and are simply called read responses.

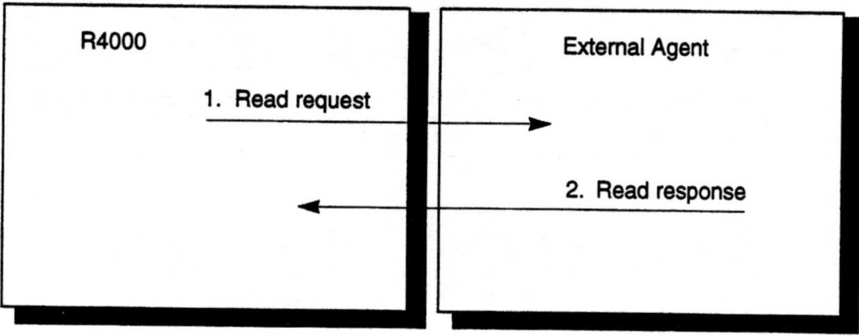

Figure 12-13 Read Response

12.5 Handling Requests

This section details the *sequence, protocol,* and *syntax* (See Terminology, in this chapter, for definitions of these terms) of both processor and external requests. The following system events are discussed:

- load miss in secondary-cache mode and no-secondary-cache mode
- store miss in secondary-cache mode and no-secondary-cache mode
- store hit
- uncached loads/stores
- CACHE operations
- load linked store conditional.

Load Miss

When a processor load misses in both the primary and secondary caches, before the processor can proceed it must obtain the cache line that contains the data element to be loaded from the external agent.

If the new cache line replaces a current dirty exclusive or dirty shared cache line, the current cache line must be written back before the new line can be loaded in the primary and secondary caches.

The processor examines the coherency attribute (cache coherency attributes are described in Chapter 11) in the TLB entry for the page that contains the requested cache line, and executes one of the following requests:

- If the coherency attribute is *exclusive,* the processor issues a coherent read request that also requests exclusivity.
- If the coherency attribute is *sharable* or *update,* the processor issues a coherent read request.
- If the coherency attribute is *noncoherent,* the processor issues a noncoherent read request.

Table 12-3 shows the actions taken on a load miss to primary and secondary caches.

Table 12-3 Load Miss to Primary and Secondary Caches

Page Attribute (Write-back policy)	Processor Configuration	State of Data Cache Line Being Replaced			
		No-Secondary-Cache Mode		Secondary-Cache Mode	
		Clean/Invalid	Dirty	Clean/Invalid	Dirty
Noncoherent	All R4000 models	NCR	NCR/W	NCR	NCR-W
Exclusive (read and write invalidate)	R4000SC R4000MC	N/A	N/A	R_{Ex}	R_{Ex}-W
Shareable (write invalidate)	R4000MC	N/A	N/A	R	R-W
Update (write update)	R4000MC	N/A	N/A	R	R-W

NCR.................. Processor noncoherent block read request

NCR/W .... Processor noncoherent block read request followed by processor block write request

NCR-W .... *Cluster*: Processor noncoherent block read request with write forthcoming followed by processor block write request

R........................ Processor coherent block read request

R-W .... *Cluster*: Processor coherent block read request with write forthcoming followed by processor block write request

R_{Ex} .... Processor coherent block read request with exclusivity

R_{Ex}-W................ *Cluster*: Processor coherent block read request with exclusivity and write forthcoming followed by processor block write request

Secondary-Cache Mode

In secondary-cache mode, if the current cache line does not have to be written back and the coherency attribute for the page that contains the requested cache line is not exclusive, the processor issues a coherent block read request for the cache line that contains the data element to be loaded.

If the current cache line needs to be written back and the coherency attribute for the requested cache line is sharable or update, the processor issues a cluster. The cluster consists of a coherent block read-with-write-forthcoming request for the cache line that contains the data element to be loaded, followed by a block write request for the current cache line.

If the current cache needs to be written back and the coherency attribute for the page containing the requested cache line is exclusive, the processor issues a cluster consisting of an exclusive read-with-write-forthcoming request, followed by a write request for the current cache line.

Table 12-3 lists these actions.

No-Secondary-Cache Mode

In no-secondary-cache mode, if the cache line must be written back on a load miss, the read request is issued and completed before the write request is handled. The processor takes the following steps:

1. The processor issues a noncoherent read request† for the cache line that contains the data element to be loaded.
2. The processor then waits for an external agent to provide the read response.

If the current cache line must be written back, the processor issues a write request to save the dirty cache line in memory.

† Only noncoherent and uncached attributes are supported in no-secondary-cache mode.

Store Miss

When a processor store misses in both the primary and secondary caches, the processor must obtain, from the external agent, the cache line that contains the target location of the store. The processor examines the coherency attribute in the TLB entry for the page (TLB page coherency attributes are listed in Chapter 4) that contains the requested cache line to see if the cache line is being maintained with either a write invalidate or a write update cache coherency protocol.

The processor then executes one of the following requests:

- If the coherency attribute is either *sharable* or *exclusive*, a write invalidate protocol is in effect, and a coherent block read that requests exclusivity is issued.
- If the coherency attribute is *update*, a write update protocol is in effect and a coherent block read request is issued.
- If the coherency attribute is *noncoherent*, a noncoherent block read request is issued.

Table 12-4 shows the actions taken on a store miss to primary and secondary caches.

Table 12-4 Store Miss to Primary and Secondary Caches

Page Attribute (Write-back policy)	Processor Configuration	State of Data Cache Line Being Replaced					
		No-Secondary-Cache Mode		Secondary-Cache Mode			
		Clean/Invalid	Dirty	Clean/Invalid		Dirty	
Noncoherent	All R4000 models	NCR	NCR/ W	NCR		NCR-W	
Exclusive (write invalidate)	R4000SC R4000MC	N/A	N/A	R_{Ex}		R_{Ex}-W	
Shareable (write invalidate)	R4000MC	N/A	N/A	R_{Ex}		R_{Ex}-W	
Update (write update)	R4000MC	N/A	N/A	Dis[1] R/U	En[2] R-PU	Dis[1] R-W/U	En[2] R-PU- W

NCR .... Processor noncoherent block read request

NCR/W .... Processor noncoherent block read request followed by processor block write request

NCR-W .... *Cluster*: Processor noncoherent block read request with write forthcoming followed by processor block write request

R_{Ex} .... Processor coherent block read request with exclusivity

R_{Ex}-W .... *Cluster*: Processor coherent block read request with exclusivity and write forthcoming followed by processor block write request

R/U .... Processor coherent block read request followed by processor update request (if read response data is shared or dirty shared)

R-PU .... *Cluster*: Processor coherent block read request followed by processor potential update request

R-PU-W .... *Cluster*: Processor coherent block read request followed by processor potential update request, followed by processor block write request

R-W/U .... *Cluster*: Processor coherent block read request with write forthcoming followed by processor block write request, followed by processor update request (if read response data is shared or dirty shared)

Dis[1] .... Potential update disable [**Modebit(20)**: **PotUpdDis** = 1]

En[2] .... Potential update enable [**Modebit(20)**: **PotUpdDis** = 0]

Secondary-Cache Mode

In secondary-cache mode, if the new cache line replaces a current cache line that is in either the dirty exclusive or dirty shared state, the current cache line must be written back before the new line can be loaded in the primary and secondary caches. The processor requests issued are a function of the page attributes listed below.

Noncoherent Page Attribute

If the current cache line must be written back, and the coherency attribute for the requested cache line is noncoherent, the processor issues a cluster consisting of a noncoherent block read-with-write-forthcoming request for the cache line that contains the store target location, followed by a block write request for the current cache line.

If the current cache line does not need to be written back and the coherency attribute for the page that contains the requested cache line is noncoherent, the processor issues a noncoherent block read request for the cache line that contains the store target location.

Sharable or Exclusive Page Attribute

If the current cache line must be written back and the coherency attribute for the page that contains the requested cache line is sharable or exclusive, the processor issues a cluster consisting of a coherent block read request with exclusivity and write forthcoming, followed by a processor block write request for the current cache line.

If the current cache line does not need to be written back and the coherency attribute for the page that contains the requested cache line is sharable or exclusive, the processor issues a coherent block read request that also requests exclusivity.

Update Page Attribute

If the current cache line must be written back and the coherency attribute for the page that contains the requested cache line is update, and potential updates are enabled, the processor issues a cluster consisting of a coherent block read-with-write-forthcoming request, followed by a potential update request, followed by a write request for the current cache line.

If the current cache line does not need to be written back, the coherency attribute for the page that contains the requested cache line is update, and potential updates are enabled, the processor issues a cluster consisting of a read request, followed by a potential update request.

In an update protocol, the cache line requested by a processor coherent read request can be returned in a shared state; the processor then has to issue an update request before it can complete a store instruction. A potential update issued with a read request in a cluster allows the external agent to anticipate the read response on the system bus. If the read response is in a shared state, the required update is quickly transmitted to the rest of the system. This provides the processor with the acknowledge and allows the processor to complete the store instruction as rapidly as possible.

Without the potential update request, the response data must be returned to the processor. If the line is returned in the shared or dirty shared state, the processor issues an update request, which must then be forwarded to the system bus before an acknowledge can be returned to the processor.

Note that potential updates behave as if they have not yet been issued by the processor. Potential updates are not subject to cancellation, and do not require an acknowledge. When a potential update is nullified, the processor behaves as if no update request was ever issued; when a potential update becomes compulsory, the processor behaves as if it had issued an update request at that instant.

Compulsory Update: If the processor issues a cluster that contains a potential update, and the response data for the read request is returned with an indication that it must be placed in the cache in either a shared or dirty shared state, the potential update then becomes compulsory. Once a potential update becomes compulsory, it is subject to cancellation, and the processor requires an acknowledge for the update request. The external agent must forward the update to the system, then signal the acknowledge to the processor when the update is complete. The processor will not complete the store until it has received an acknowledge for the update request.

Nullifying a Potential Update: If the processor issues a cluster that contains a potential update, and the response data for the read request is returned in either a clean exclusive or dirty exclusive state, the potential update is nullified. Once a potential update has been nullified, the external agent must discard the update. The processor does not wait for or expect an acknowledge to a potential update that has been nullified. It is not correct to assert either **IvdAck*** or **IvdErr*** in this situation.

If the read response data is returned in either the clean exclusive or dirty exclusive state, the processor cannot issue an update request. It is assumed that the external agent will take the appropriate action to change the state of the cache line to invalid in other caches.

An external request indicating processor update cancellation can be issued when a processor read is not pending or when compulsory update is unacknowledged. Processor state is undefined if a cancellation is signaled on an external coherence request to the processor when a processor read is pending, or there is no unacknowledged compulsory update.

No-Secondary-Cache Mode

The processor issues a read request for the cache line that contains the data element to be loaded, then awaits the external agent to provide read data in response to the read request. Then, if the current cache line must be written back, the processor issues a write request for the current cache line.

In no-secondary-cache mode, if the new cache line replaces a current cache line whose *Write back* (W) bit is set, the current cache line moves to an internal write buffer before the new cache line is loaded in the primary cache.

Store Hit

This section describes store hits in both secondary-cache and no-secondary-cache mode.

Secondary-Cache Mode

When the processor hits in the secondary cache, on a line that is marked either shared or dirty shared, the processor must issue an update or invalidate request and then wait to receive an acknowledge, before the store is complete. The processor checks the coherency attribute in the TLB for the page containing the cache line that is target of the store, to determine if the cache line is managed by either a write invalidate or write update cache coherency protocol.

- If the coherency attribute is sharable or exclusive, a write invalidate protocol is in effect, and the processor issues an invalidate request. The processor cannot complete the store until the external agent signals an acknowledge for this invalidate request.
- If the coherency attribute is update, a write update protocol is in effect, and the processor issues an update request. The processor cannot complete the store until the external agent signals an acknowledge for this update request.

No-Secondary-Cache Mode

In no-secondary-cache mode, all lines are set to the dirty exclusive state. This means store hits cause no bus transactions.

Uncached Loads or Stores

When the processor performs an uncached load, it issues a noncoherent doubleword, partial doubleword, word, or partial word read request. When the processor performs an uncached store, it issues a doubleword, partial doubleword, word, or partial word write request.

External requests have a higher priority than uncached stores. When using the uncached store buffer on an R4400 processor, it is possible for the external agent to receive cached and uncached stores out of program order, as the example below illustrates. Figure 12-14 shows a cached and uncached store instruction sequence:

```
SW  r2, (r3)                        # uncached store
SW  r4, (r5)                        # cached store
```

Figure 12-14   R4400 Processor Cached and Uncached Store Sequence

Referring to Figure 12-14, suppose an external intervention or snoop is issued to the R4400 processor while the uncached store is still in the store buffer (the uncached store data has not yet been stored off-chip). The cached store from Figure 12-14 has hit in the primary cache and is in the tag check (TC) stage of the pipeline (see Chapter 3 for a description of the pipeline stages). In this case, the external agent sees the state of the internal caches after the cached store but *before* the result of the uncached store is available off the chip. Figure 12-15 shows how a SYNC instruction can force the uncached store to occur before the cached store.

```
SW  r2, (r3)                        # uncached store
SYNC
SW  r4, (r5)                        # cached store
```

Figure 12-15   R4400 Processor Cached and Uncached Stores, Using SYNC

CACHE Operations

The processor provides a variety of CACHE operations to maintain the state and contents of the primary and secondary caches. During the execution of the CACHE operation instructions, the processor can issue either write requests or invalidate requests.

Load Linked Store Conditional Operation

Generally, the execution of a Load Linked Store Conditional instruction sequence is not visible at the System interface; that is, no special requests are generated due to the execution of this instruction sequence.

There is, however, one situation in which the execution of a Load Linked Store Conditional instruction sequence is visible, as indicated by the *link address retained* bit during a processor read request, as programmed by the **SysCmd(2)** bit. This situation occurs when the data location targeted by a Load Linked Store Conditional instruction sequence maps to the same cache line to which the instruction area containing the Load Linked Store Conditional code sequence is mapped. In this case, immediately after executing the Load Linked instruction, the cache line that contains the link location is replaced by the instruction line containing the code. The link address is kept in a register separate from the cache, and remains active as long as the *link* bit, set by the Load Linked instruction, is set.

The *link* bit, which is set by the load linked instruction, is cleared by a change of cache state for the line containing the link address, or by a Return From Exception.

In order for the Load Linked Store Conditional instruction sequence to work correctly, all coherency traffic targeting the link address must be visible to the processor, and the cache line containing the link location must remain in a shared state in every cache in the system. This guarantees that a Store Conditional executed by some other processor is visible to the processor as a coherence request, changing the state of the cache line containing the link location.

To accomplish this, a read request issued by the processor, causing the cache line containing the link location to be replaced. In the mean time, the *link address retained* bit is set, indicating the link address is being retained. This informs the external agent that, although the processor has replaced this cache line, the processor must still see any coherence traffic that targets this cache line.

Any snoop or intervention request that targets a cache line which is not present in the cache—but for which the snoop or intervention address matches the current link address while the link bit is set—returns an indication that the cache line is present in the cache in a shared state. This is consistent with the coherency model, since the processor never returns data, in response to an intervention request, for a cache line that is in the shared state. The shared response guarantees that the cache line containing the link location remains in a shared state in all other processor's caches, and therefore that any other processor attempting a store conditional to this link location must issue a coherence request in order to complete the store conditional.

For more information, refer to Chapter 11, or see the specific Load Linked and Store Conditional instructions described in Appendix A.

12.6 Processor and External Request Protocols

The following sections contain a cycle-by-cycle description of the bus arbitration protocols for each type of processor and external request. Table 12-5 lists the abbreviations and definitions for each of the buses that are used in the timing diagrams that follow.

Table 12-5 System Interface Requests

Scope	Abbreviation	Meaning
Global	Unsd	Unused
SysAD bus	Addr	Physical address
	Data<n>	Data element number n of a block of data
SysCmd bus	Cmd	An unspecified System interface command
	Read	A processor or external read request command
	RwWF	A processor read-with-write-forthcoming request command
	Write	A processor or external write request command
	Null	A processor null request command
	SINull	A System interface release external null request command
	SCNull	A secondary cache release external null request command
	Ivd	A processor or external invalidate request command
	Upd	A processor or external update request command
	Ivtn	An external intervention request command
	Snoop	An external snoop request command
	NData	A noncoherent data identifier for a data element other than the last data element
	NEOD	A noncoherent data identifier for the last data element
	CData	A coherent data identifier for a data element other than the last data element
	CEOD	A coherent data identifier for the last data element

Processor Request Protocols

Processor request protocols described in this section include:

- read
- write
- invalidate and update
- null write
- cluster

NOTE: In the timing diagrams, the two closely spaced, wavy vertical lines (such as those in SCycle 5, Figure 12-18) indicate one or more identical cycles.

Processor Read Request Protocol

The following sequence describes the protocol for a processor read request (the numbered steps below correspond to Figures 12-17 and 12-18).

1. **RdRdy*** is asserted low, indicating the external agent is ready to accept a read request.
2. With the System interface in master state, a processor read request is issued by driving a read command on the **SysCmd** bus and a read address on the **SysAD** bus.
3. At the same time, the processor asserts **ValidOut*** for one cycle, indicating valid data is present on the **SysCmd** and the **SysAD** buses.

   NOTE: Only one processor read request can be pending at a time.
4. The processor makes an uncompelled change to slave state either at the issue cycle of the read request, or sometime after the issue cycle of the read request by asserting the **Release*** signal for one cycle.

   NOTE: The external agent must not assert the signal **ExtRqst*** for the purposes of returning a read response, but rather must wait for the uncompelled change to slave state. The signal **ExtRqst*** can be asserted before or during a read response to perform an external request other than a read response.
5. The processor releases the **SysCmd** and the **SysAD** buses one SCycle after the assertion of **Release***.
6. The external agent drives the **SysCmd** and the **SysAD** buses within two cycles after the assertion of **Release***.

Once in slave state (starting at cycle 5 in Figure 12-17), the external agent can return the requested data through a read response. The read response can return the requested data or, if the requested data could not be successfully retrieved, an indication that the returned data is erroneous. If the returned data is erroneous, the processor takes a bus error exception.

Figure 12-17 illustrates a processor read request, coupled with an uncompelled change to slave state, that occurs as the read request is issued. Figure 12-18 illustrates a processor read request, and the subsequent uncompelled change to slave state, that occurs sometime after the read request is issued.

> **NOTE:** Timings for the **SysADC** and **SysCmdP** buses are the same as those of the **SysAD** and **SysCmd** buses, respectively.

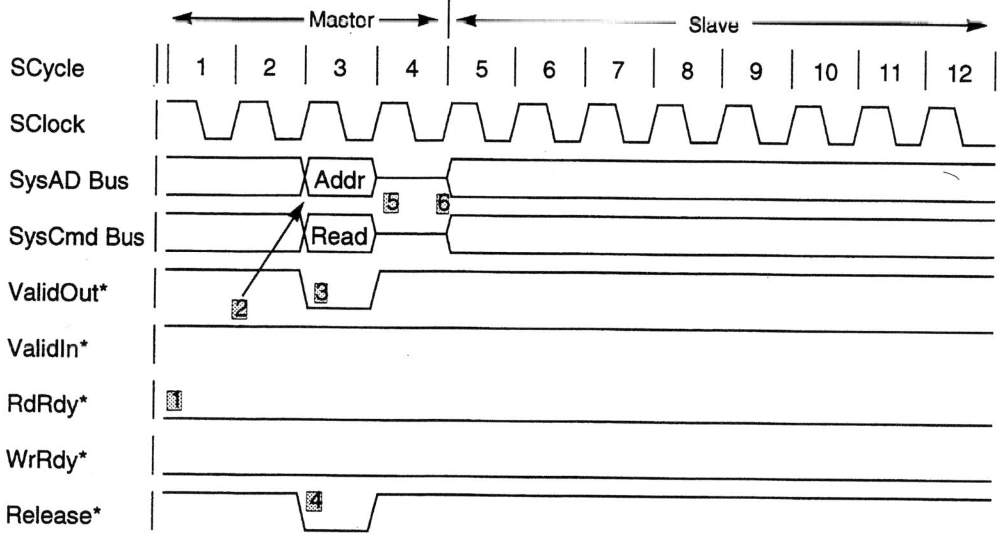

Figure 12-17 Processor Read Request Protocol

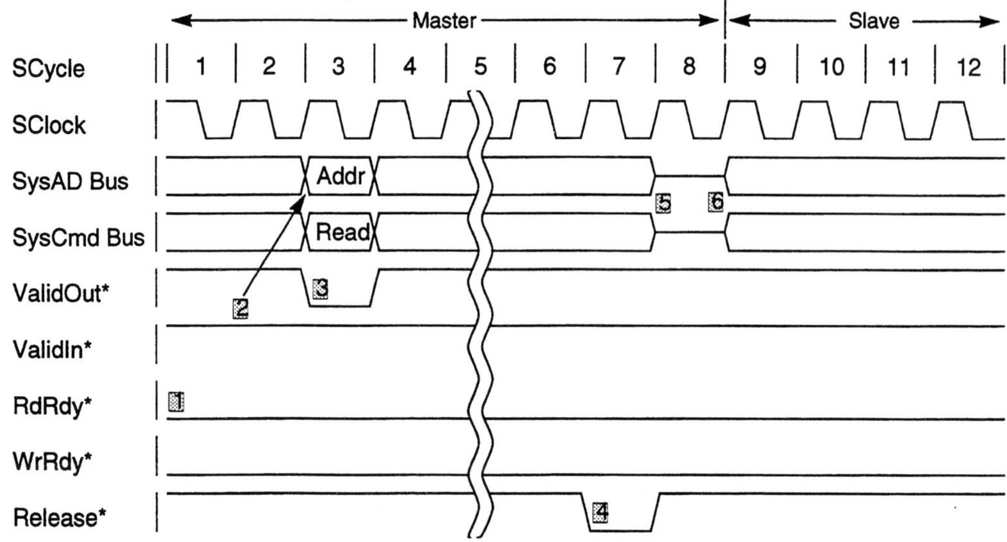

Figure 12-18 Processor Read Request Protocol, Change to Slave State Delayed

When the following three events occur—a read request is pending, **ExtRqst*** is asserted, and **Release*** is asserted for one cycle—it may be unclear if the assertion of **Release*** is in response to **ExtRqst***, or represents an uncompelled change to slave state. The only situation in which the assertion of **Release*** cannot be considered an uncompelled change to slave state is if the following three conditions exist simultaneously:

- the System interface is operating in secondary-cache mode
- the read request was a read-with-write-forthcoming request
- the expected write request has not been issued by the processor.

If these three conditions exist, the processor cannot accept the read response; rather, it accepts the external request. The write request must be accepted by the external agent before the read response can be issued.

In all other cases, the assertion of **Release*** indicates either an uncompelled change to slave state, or a response to the assertion of **ExtRqst***, whereupon the processor accepts either a read response, or any other external request. If any external request other than a read response is issued, the processor performs another uncompelled change to slave state after processing the external request.

Processor Write Request Protocol

Processor write requests are issued using one of two protocols.

- Doubleword, partial doubleword, word, or partial word writes use a word† write request protocol.
- Block writes use a block write request protocol.

Processor doubleword write requests are issued with the System interface in master state, as described below in the steps below; Figure 12-19 shows a processor noncoherent single word write request cycle.

1. A processor single word write request is issued by driving a write command on the **SysCmd** bus and a write address on the **SysAD** bus.
2. The processor asserts **ValidOut***.
3. The processor drives a data identifier on the **SysCmd** bus and data on the **SysAD** bus.
4. The data identifier associated with the data cycle must contain a last data cycle indication. At the end of the cycle, **ValidOut*** is deasserted.

   NOTE: Timings for the **SysADC** and **SysCmdP** buses are the same as those of the **SysAD** and **SysCmd** buses, respectively.

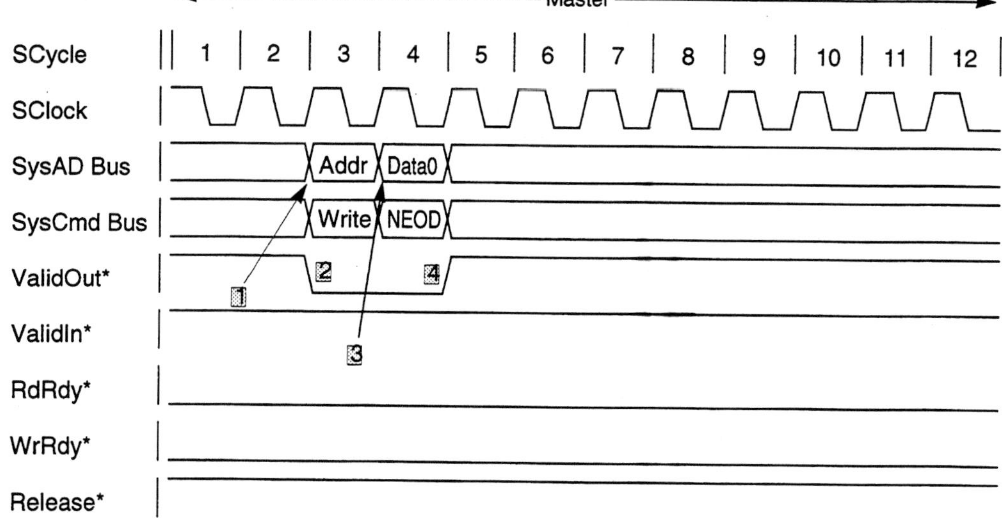

Figure 12-19 Processor Noncoherent Single Word Write Request Protocol

† Called *word* to distinguish it from *block* request protocol. Data transferred can actually be doubleword, partial doubleword, word, or partial word.

Processor block write requests are issued with the System interface in master state, as described below; a processor coherent block request for eight words of data is illustrated in Figures 12-20 and 12-21.

1. The processor issues a write command on the **SysCmd** bus and a write address on the **SysAD** bus.
2. The processor asserts **ValidOut***.
3. The processor drives a data identifier on the **SysCmd** bus and data on the **SysAD** bus.
4. The processor asserts **ValidOut*** for a number of cycles sufficient to transmit the block of data.
5. The data identifier associated with the last data cycle must contain a last data cycle indication.

   NOTE: As shown in Figure 12-21, however, the first data cycle does not have to immediately follow the address cycle.

Figures 12-20 and 12-21 illustrate a processor coherent block request for eight words of data.

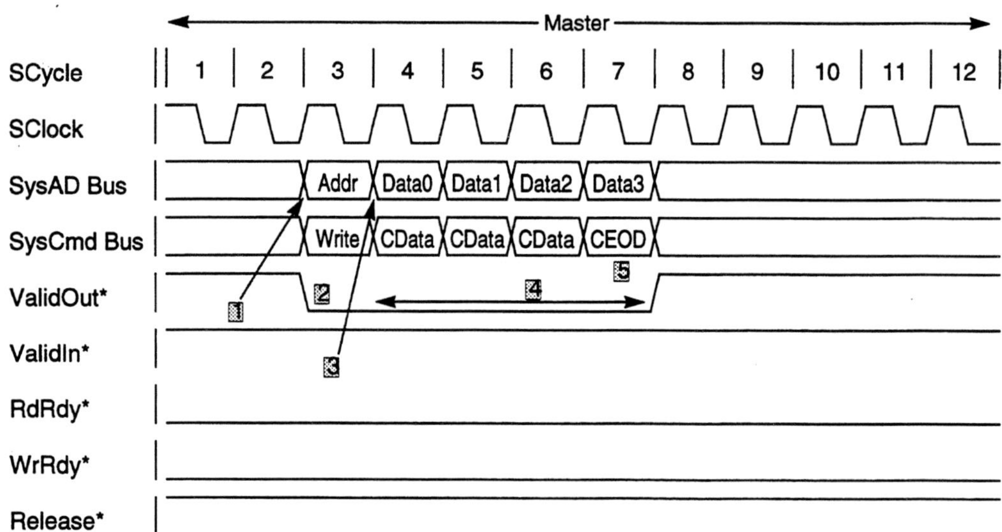

Figure 12-20 Processor Coherent Block Write Request Protocol

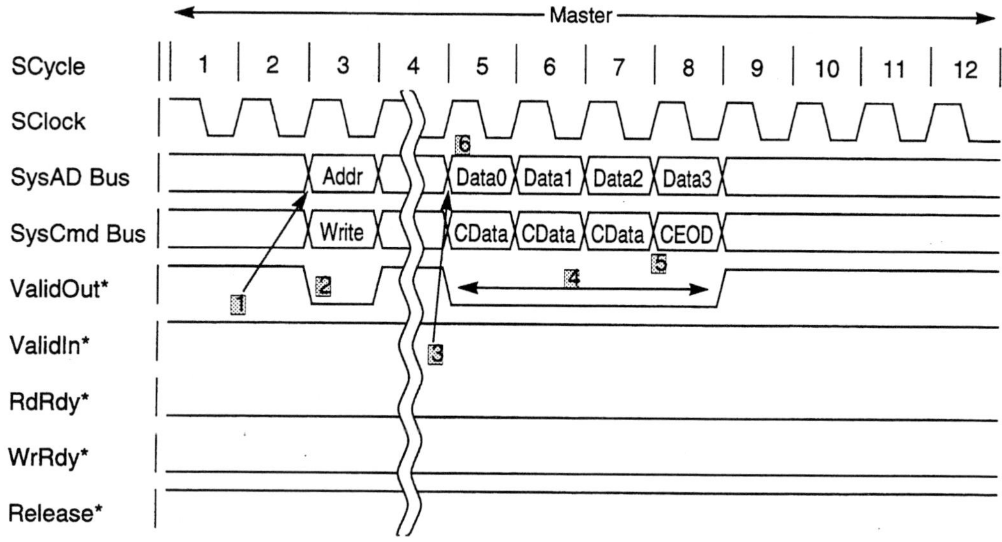

Figure 12-21 Processor Coherent Block Write Request Protocol (Delayed)

Processor Invalidate and Update Request Protocol

Processor invalidate request, or update request protocols, are the same as a coherent word write request except the command associated with the address cycle indicates that the request is either an invalidate or update. The single data cycle transfer is not used by an invalidate request.

Processor invalidate and update requests are acknowledged using the signals **IvdAck*** and **IvdErr***. The external agent drives either **IvdAck*** or **IvdErr*** for one cycle to signal the completion of the current processor update or invalidate request; **IvdAck*** occurs in parallel with requests on the **SysAD** and **SysCmd** buses. **IvdAck*** or **IvdErr*** can be driven at any time after a processor update or invalidate request is issued, provided the update request is compulsory.

Processor Null Write Request Protocol

A processor null write request is issued with the System interface in master state; the request consists of a single address cycle. The processor drives a null command on the **SysCmd** bus and asserts **ValidOut*** for one cycle. The **SysAD** bus is unused during the address cycle associated with a null write request, and processor null write requests cannot be controlled with either **RdRdy*** or **WrRdy*** signals. Figure 12-22 illustrates a processor null write request.

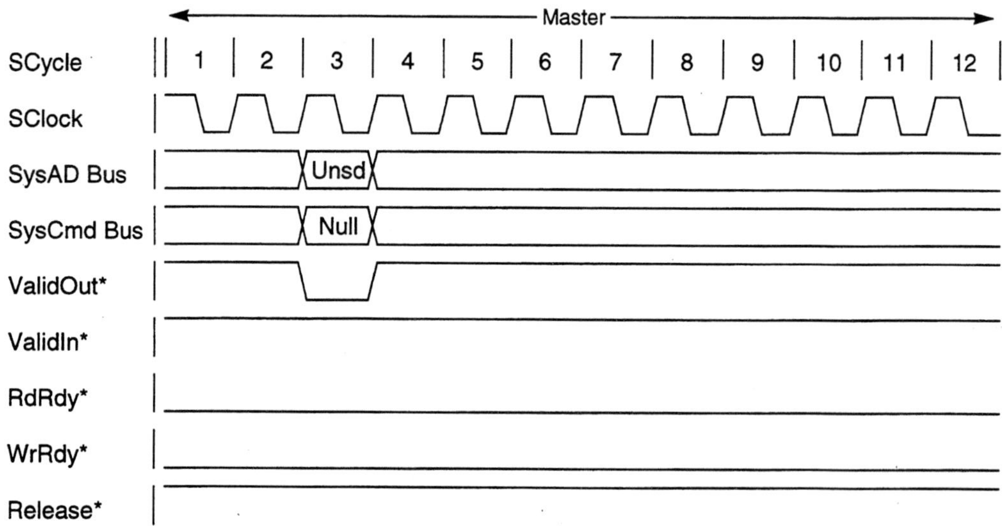

Figure 12-22 Processor Null Write Request Protocol

Processor Cluster Request Protocol

In secondary-cache mode, the processor can issue two types of requests: individual and cluster.

All of the requests that are part of a cluster must be accepted by the external agent before a response to the read request, that began the cluster, can be returned to the processor. A cluster consists of:

- a processor read with write forthcoming request followed by a write request
- a processor read request followed by a potential update request
- a processor read with write forthcoming request followed by a potential update request, followed by a write request.

Figure 12-23 illustrates a cluster consisting of a read with write forthcoming request, followed by a potential update request, followed by a coherent block write request for eight words of data (with minimum spacing between the requests that form the cluster), followed by an uncompelled change to slave state at the earliest opportunity.

> **NOTE:** Timings for the **SysADC** and **SysCmdP** buses are the same as those of the **SysAD** and **SysCmd** buses, respectively. There may be unused cycles between the requests that form a cluster.

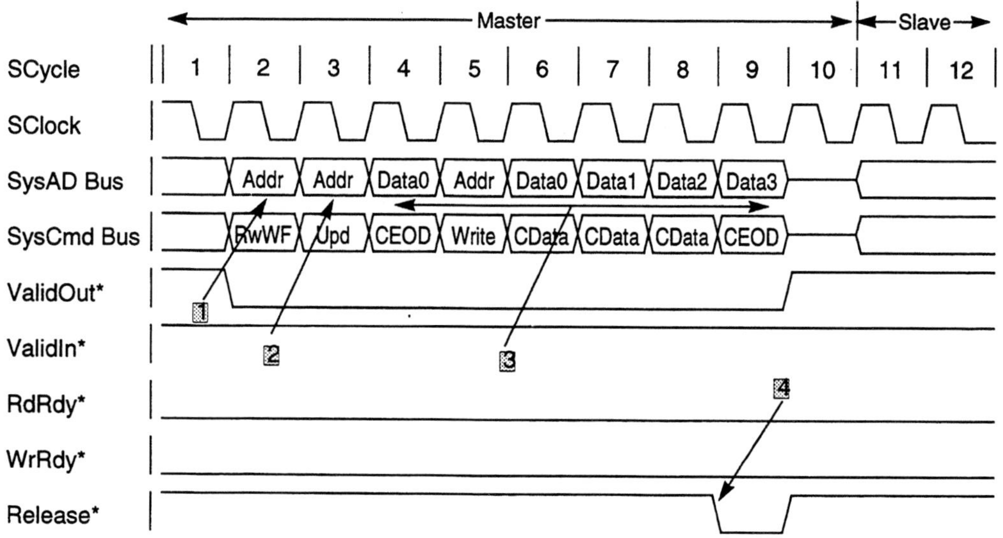

Figure 12-23 Processor Cluster Request Protocol

Processor Request and Cluster Flow Control

The external agent uses **RdRdy*** to control the flow of the following processes:

- processor read request
- processor invalidate request
- processor update request
- processor read request, followed by a potential update request within a cluster.

Figures 12-24 through 12-27 illustrate this flow control, as described in the steps below.

1. The processor samples the signal **RdRdy*** to determine if the external agent is capable of accepting a read, invalidate, update request, or a read request followed by a potential update request.
2. The signal **WrRdy*** controls the flow of a processor write request.
3. The processor does not complete the issue of a read, invalidate, update request, or a read request followed by a potential update request, until it issues an address cycle in response to the request for which the signal **RdRdy*** was asserted two cycles earlier.
4. The processor does not complete the issue of a write request until it issues an address cycle in response to the write request for which the signal **WrRdy*** was asserted two cycles earlier.

Figure 12-24 illustrates two processor write requests in which the issue of the second is delayed for the assertion of **WrRdy***.

Figure 12-25 illustrates a processor cluster in which the issue of the read and a potential update request are delayed for the assertion of **RdRdy***.

Figure 12-26 illustrates a processor cluster in which the issue of the write request is delayed for the assertion of **WrRdy***.

Figure 12-27 illustrates the issue of a processor write request delayed for the assertion of **WrRdy*** and the completion of an external invalidate request.

> **NOTE:** Timings for the **SysADC** and **SysCmdP** buses are the same as those of the **SysAD** and **SysCmd** buses, respectively.

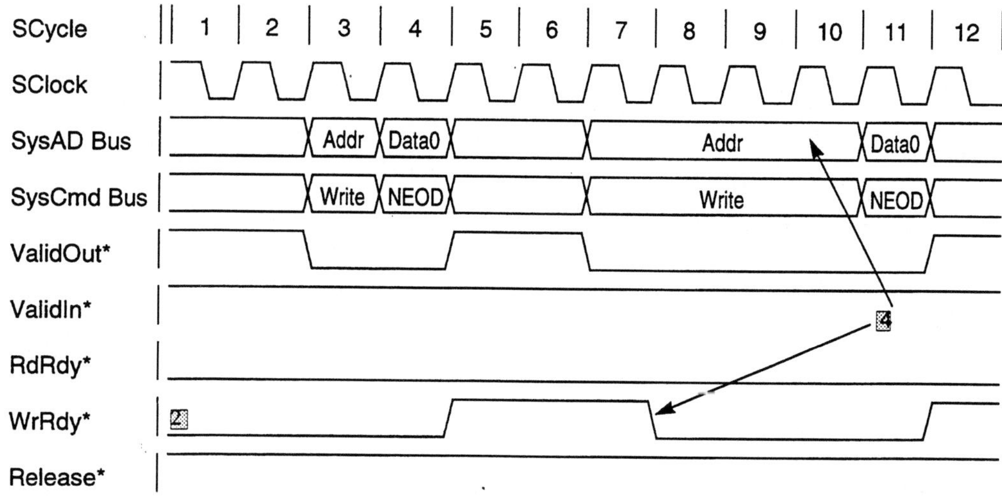

Figure 12-24 Two Processor Write Requests, Second Write Delayed for the Assertion of WrRdy*

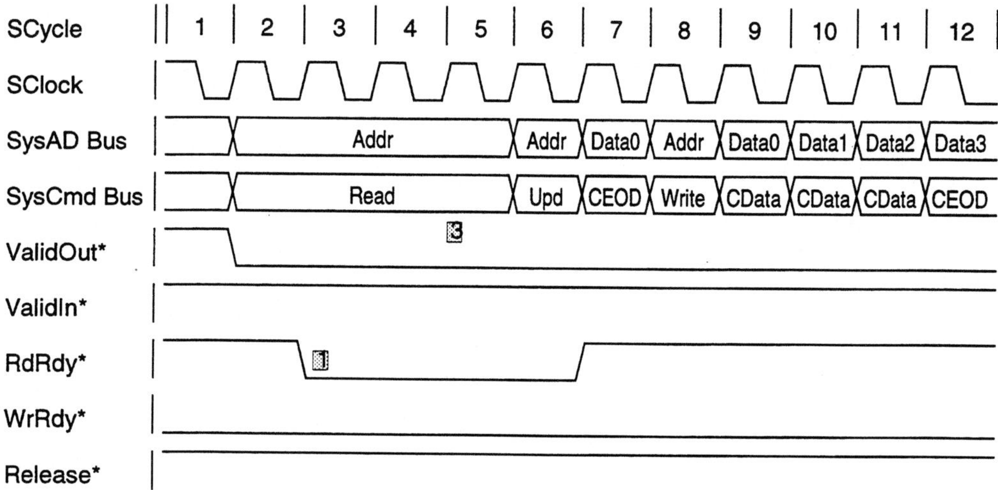

Figure 12-25 Processor Read Request within a Cluster Delayed for the Assertion of RdRdy*

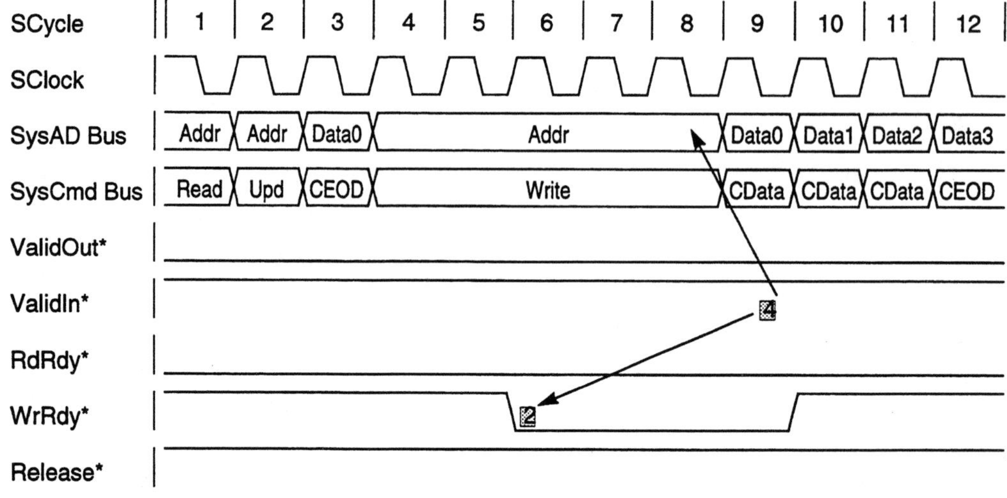

Figure 12-26 Processor Write Request within a Cluster Delayed for the Assertion of WrRdy*

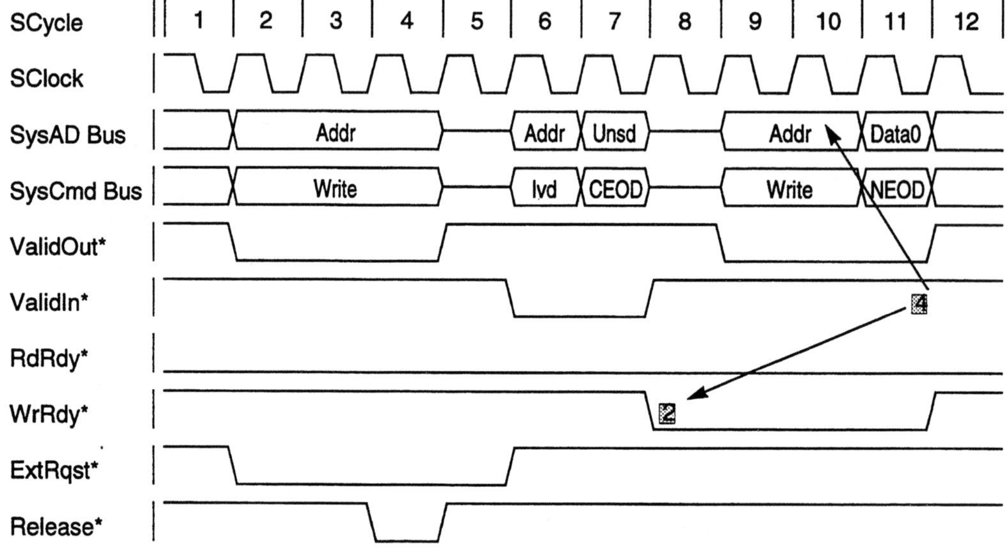

Figure 12-27 Processor Write Request Delayed for the Assertion of WrRdy* *and the Completion of an External Invalidate Request*

External Request Protocols

External requests can only be issued with the System interface in slave state. An external agent asserts **ExtRqst*** to arbitrate (see External Arbitration Protocol, below) for the System interface, then waits for the processor to release the System interface to slave state by asserting **Release*** before the external agent issues an external request. If the System interface is already in slave state—that is, the processor has previously performed an uncompelled change to slave state—the external agent can begin an external request immediately.

After issuing an external request, the external agent must return the System interface to master state. If the external agent does not have any additional external requests to perform, **ExtRqst*** must be deasserted two cycles after the cycle in which **Release*** was asserted. For a string of external requests, the **ExtRqst*** signal is asserted until the last request cycle, whereupon it is deasserted two cycles after the cycle in which **Release*** was asserted.

The processor continues to handle external requests as long as **ExtRqst*** is asserted; however, the processor cannot release the System interface to slave state for a subsequent external request until it has completed the current request. As long as **ExtRqst*** is asserted, the string of external requests is not interrupted by a processor request.

This section describes the following external request protocols:

- read
- null
- write
- invalidate and update
- intervention
- snoop
- read response

External Arbitration Protocol

System interface arbitration uses the signals **ExtRqst*** and **Release*** as described above. Figure 12-28 is a timing diagram of the arbitration protocol, in which slave and master states are shown.

The arbitration cycle consists of the following steps:

1. The external agent asserts **ExtRqst*** when it wishes to submit an external request.
2. The processor waits until it is ready to handle an external request, whereupon it asserts **Release*** for one cycle.
3. The processor sets the **SysAD** and **SysCmd** buses to tri-state.
4. The external agent must begin driving the **SysAD** bus and the **SysCmd** bus two cycles after the assertion of **Release***.
5. The external agent deasserts **ExtRqst*** two cycles after the assertion of **Release***, unless the external agent wishes to perform an additional external request.
6. The external agent sets the **SysAD** and the **SysCmd** buses to tri-state at the completion of an external request.

The processor can start issuing a processor request one cycle after the external agent sets the bus to tri-state.

> **NOTE:** Timings for the **SysADC** and **SysCmdP** buses are the same as those of the **SysAD** and **SysCmd** buses, respectively.

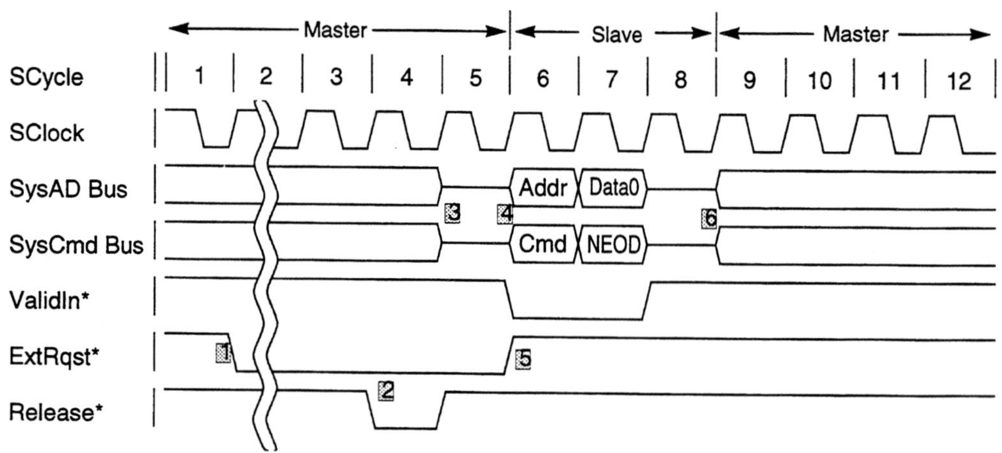

Figure 12-28 Arbitration Protocol for External Requests

External Read Request Protocol

External reads are requests for a word of data from a processor internal resource, such as a register. External read requests cannot be split; that is, no other request can occur between the external read request and its read response.

Figure 12-29 shows a timing diagram of an external read request, which consists of the following steps:

1. An external agent asserts **ExtRqst*** to arbitrate for the System interface.
2. The processor releases the System interface to slave state by asserting **Release*** for one cycle and then deasserting **Release***.
3. After **Release*** is deasserted, the **SysAD** and **SysCmd** buses are set to a tri-state for one cycle.
4. The external agent drives a read request command on the **SysCmd** bus and a read request address on the **SysAD** bus and asserts **ValidIn*** for one cycle.
5. After the address and command are sent, the external agent releases the **SysCmd** and **SysAD** buses by setting them to tri-state and allowing the processor to drive them. The processor, having accessed the data that is the target of the read, returns this data to the external agent. The processor accomplishes this by driving a data identifier on the **SysCmd** bus, the response data on the **SysAD** bus, and asserting **ValidOut*** for one cycle. The data identifier indicates that this is last-data-cycle response data.
6. The System interface is in master state. The processor continues driving the **SysCmd** and **SysAD** buses after the read response is returned.

   NOTE: Timings for the **SysADC** and **SysCmdP** buses are the same as those of the **SysAD** and **SysCmd** buses, respectively.

External read requests are only allowed to read a word of data from the processor. The processor response to external read requests for any data element other than a word is undefined.

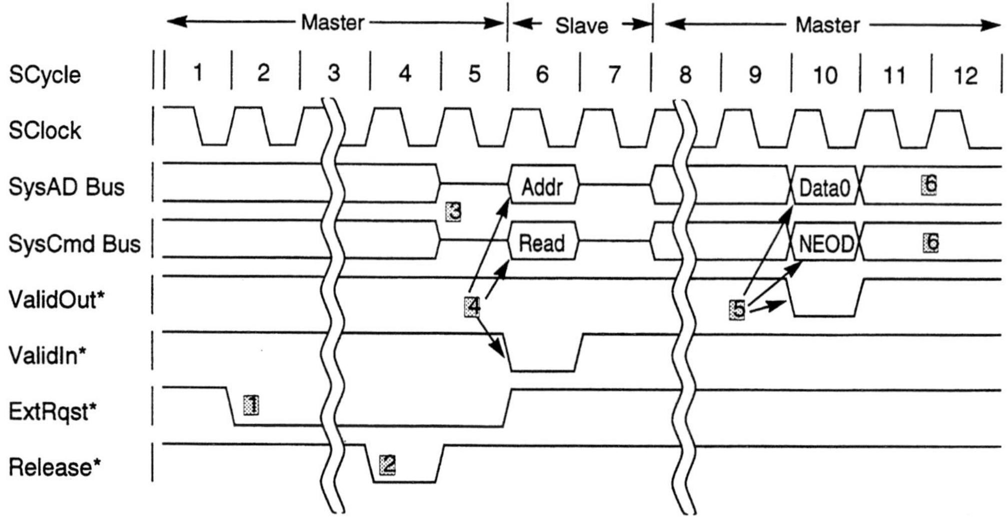

Figure 12-29 External Read Request, System Interface in Master State

NOTE: The processor does not contain any resources that are readable by an external read request; in response to an external read request the processor returns undefined data and a data identifier with its *Erroneous Data* bit, **SysCmd(5)**, set.

External Null Request Protocol

The processor supports two kinds of external null requests.

- A *secondary cache release external null request* returns ownership of the secondary cache to the processor while the System interface remains in slave state, until another external null request returns it to master state.
- A *System interface release external null request* returns the System interface to master state from slave state without otherwise affecting the processor.

Any time the processor releases the System interface to slave state to accept an external request, it also allows the external agent to use the secondary cache, in anticipation of a cache coherence request. When the external agent uses the **SysAD** bus for a transfer unrelated to the processor (for example, a DMA transfer), this ownership of the secondary cache prevents the processor from satisfying subsequent primary cache misses. To satisfy such a primary cache miss, the external agent issues a *secondary cache release external null request*, returning ownership of the secondary cache to the processor.

External null requests require no action from the processor other than to return the System interface to master state, or to regain ownership of the secondary cache.

Figures 12-30 and 12-31 show timing diagrams of the two external null request cycles, which consist of the following steps:

1. The external agent asserts **ExtRqst*** to arbitrate for the System interface.
2. The processor releases the System interface to slave state by asserting **Release***.
3. The external agent drives a secondary cache release external null request command on the **SysCmd** bus, and asserts **ValidIn*** for one cycle to return the secondary cache interface ownership to the processor.
4. The **SysAD** bus is unused (does not contain valid data) during the address cycle associated with an external null request.
5. After the address cycle is issued, the null request is complete.

For a *secondary cache release external null request*, the System interface remains in slave state.

For a *System interface release external null request*, the external agent releases the **SysCmd** and **SysAD** buses, and expects the System interface to return to master state.

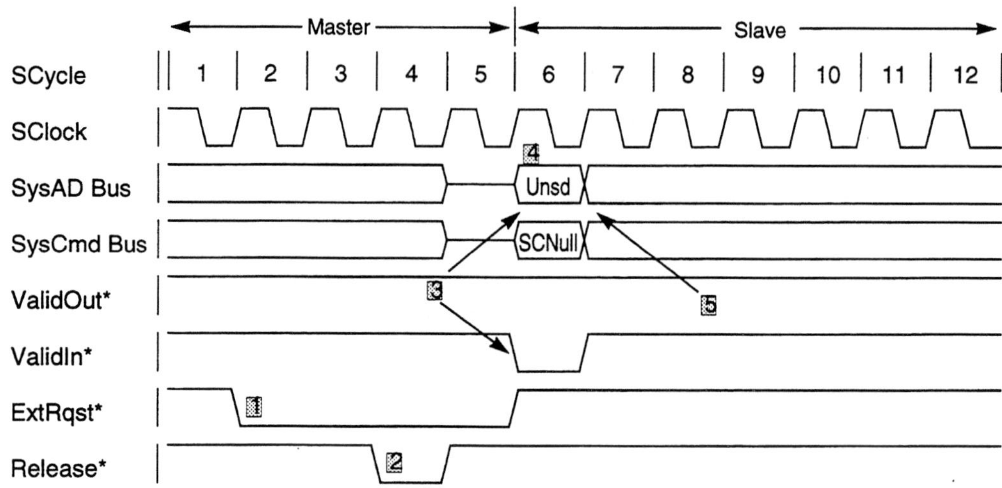

Figure 12-30 Secondary Cache Release External Null Request

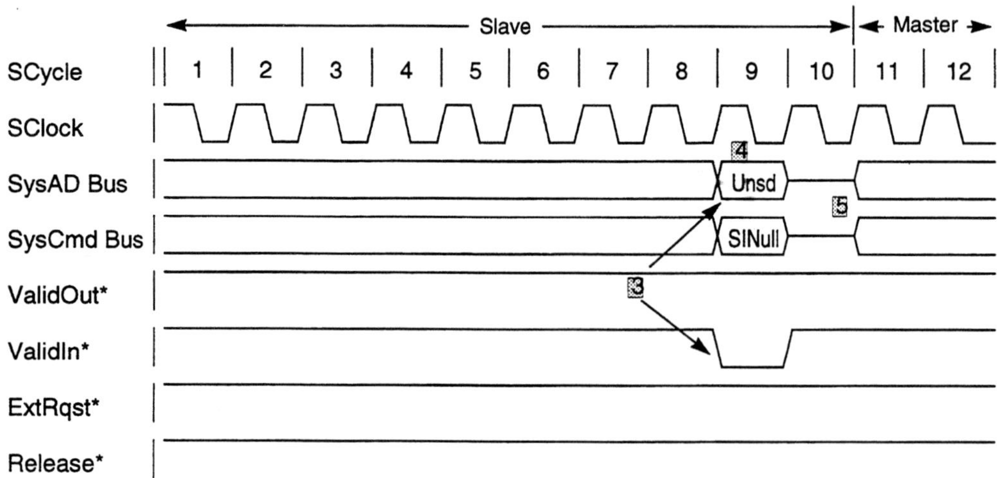

Figure 12-31 System Interface Release External Null Request

External Write Request Protocol

External write requests use a protocol identical to the processor single word write protocol except the **ValidIn*** signal is asserted instead of **ValidOut***. Figure 12-32 shows a timing diagram of an external write request, which consists of the following steps:

1. The external agent asserts **ExtRqst*** to arbitrate for the System interface.
2. The processor releases the System interface to slave state by asserting **Release***.
3. The external agent drives a write command on the **SysCmd** bus, a write address on the **SysAD** bus, and asserts **ValidIn***.
4. The external agent drives a data identifier on the **SysCmd** bus, data on the **SysAD** bus, and asserts **ValidIn***.
5. The data identifier associated with the data cycle must contain a coherent or noncoherent last data cycle indication.
6. After the data cycle is issued, the write request is complete and the external agent sets the **SysCmd** and **SysAD** buses to a tri-state, allowing the System interface to return to master state. Timings for the **SysADC** and **SysCmdP** buses are the same as those of the **SysAD** and **SysCmd** buses, respectively.

External write requests are only allowed to write a word of data to the processor. Processor behavior in response to an external write request for any data element other than a word is undefined.

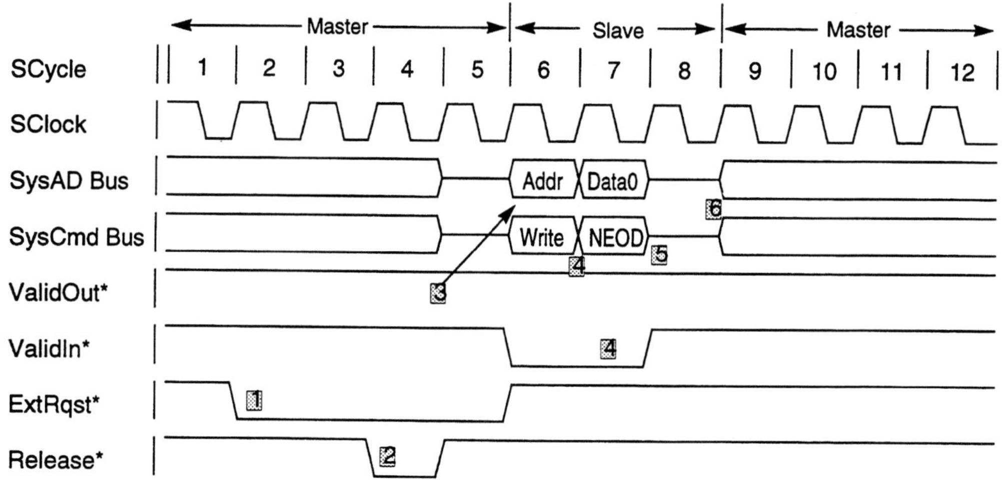

Figure 12-32 External Write Request, with System Interface initially a Bus Master

External Invalidate and Update Request Protocols

External invalidate and update request protocols are the same as the external write request protocol. The data element provided with an update or invalidate request can be a doubleword, partial doubleword, word, or partial word. The single data cycle transfer is not used (it does not contain valid data) for an invalidate request.

Figure 12-33 illustrates an external invalidate request following an uncompelled change to slave state.

> **NOTE:** Timings for the **SysADC** and **SysCmdP** buses are the same as those of the **SysAD** and **SysCmd** buses, respectively.

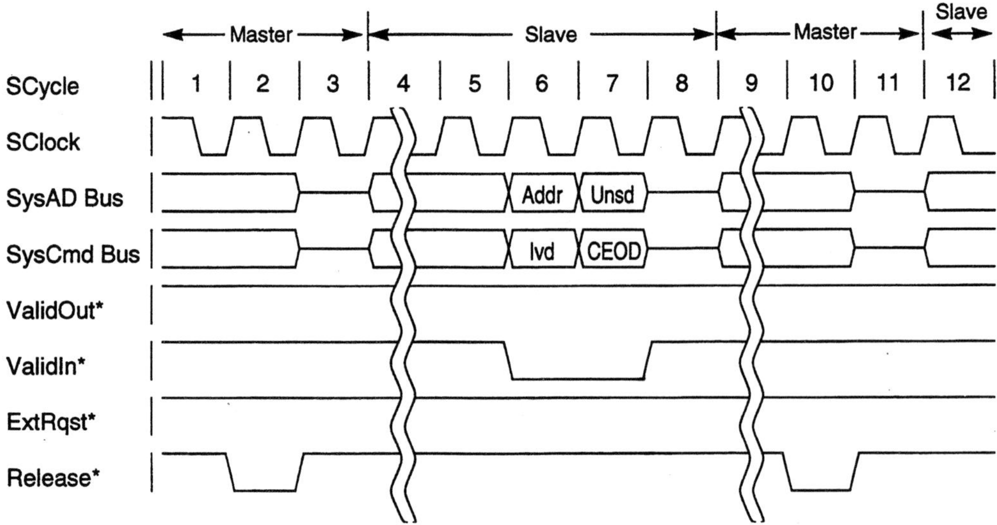

Figure 12-33 External Invalidate Request following an Uncompelled Change to Slave State

External Intervention Request Protocol

External intervention requests use a protocol similar to that of external read requests, except that a cache line size block of data can be returned along with an indication of the cache state for the cache line. The cache state indication depends upon the state of the cache line and the value of the *data return* bit in the intervention request command.†

The *data return* bit indicates either *return on dirty* or *return on exclusive*:

- If the *data return* bit indicates return on dirty, and the cache line that is target of the intervention request is in the dirty exclusive or dirty shared state, the contents of the cache line are returned in response to the intervention request.
- If the *data return* bit indicates return on exclusive, and the cache line that is the target of the intervention request is in the clean exclusive or dirty exclusive state, the contents of the cache line are returned in response to the intervention request.

If neither of the two cases above are true, the response to the intervention request does not include the *contents* of the cache line, but simply indicates the *state* of the cache line that is the target of the intervention request.

The case in which the processor returns a cache line state, but not cache line contents, is described in the following steps:

1. The external agent asserts **ExtRqst*** to arbitrate for the System interface.
2. The processor releases the System interface to slave state by asserting **Release***.
3. The external intervention request is driven onto the **SysCmd** bus and the address onto the **SysAD** bus. **ValidIn*** is asserted for one cycle.
4. The processor drives a coherent data identifier that indicates the state of the cache line on the **SysCmd** bus and asserts **ValidOut*** for one cycle.
5. The **SysAD** bus is not used during the data cycle.
6. The data identifier indicates a response data cycle that contains a last data cycle indication.

† If the cache line that is the target of the intervention request is not present in the cache—that is, the tag comparison for the cache line at the target cache address fails—the cache line that is the target of the intervention request is considered to be in the invalid state.

Figure 12-34 shows an external intervention request to a cache line found in the shared state, with the System interface initially in a master state. Figure 12-35 shows an external intervention request to a cache line found in the dirty exclusive state, with the System interface initially in a slave state.

> **NOTE:** Timings for the **SysADC** and **SysCmdP** buses are the same as those of the **SysAD** and **SysCmd** buses, respectively.

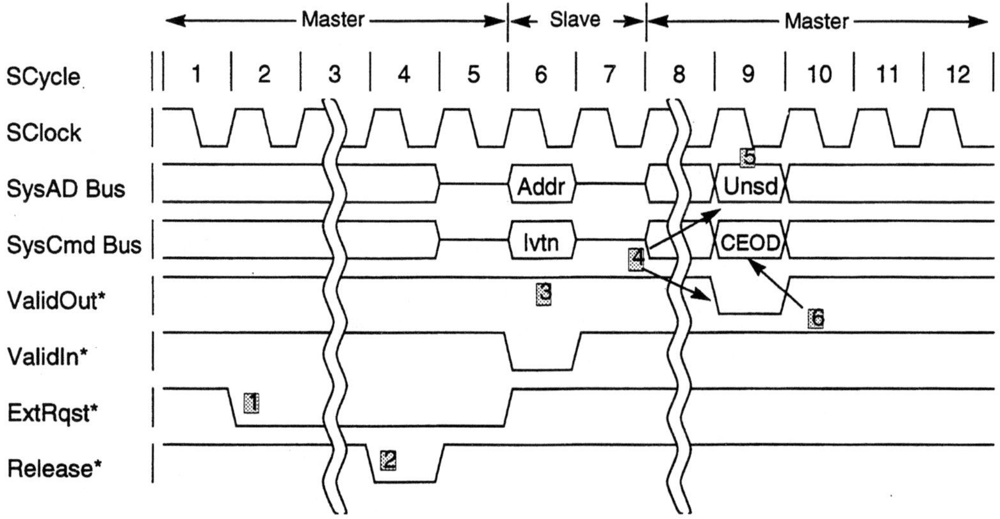

Figure 12-34 External Intervention Request, Shared Line, System Interface in Master State

The case in which the processor returns cache line contents is described in the steps below. In this example, the system is already in slave state.

1. The external intervention request is driven onto the **SysCmd** bus and the address onto the **SysAD** bus. **ValidIn*** is asserted for one cycle.
2. The processor drives data on the **SysAD** bus and a data identifier on the **SysCmd** bus. The processor asserts **ValidOut*** for each data cycle.
3. The data identifier associated with the last data cycle must contain a last data cycle indicator.

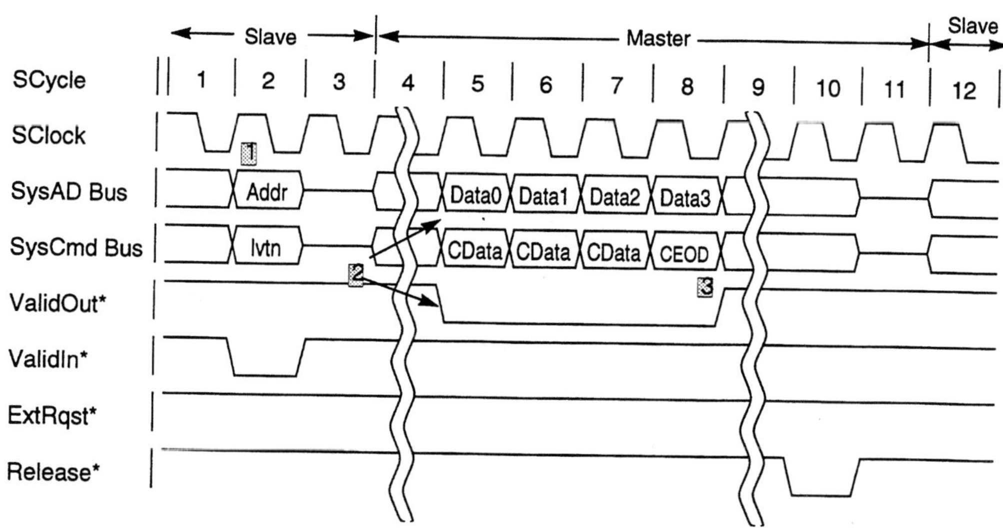

Figure 12-35 External Intervention Request, Dirty Exclusive Line, System Interface in Slave State

The processor returns the contents of a cache line, along with an indication of the cache state in which it was found, by issuing a sequence of data cycles sufficient to transmit the contents of the cache line, as shown in Figure 12-35. The data identifier transmitted with each data cycle indicates the cache state in which the cache line was found, together with an indication that this data is response data. The data identifier associated with the last data cycle contains a last data cycle indication.

If the contents of a cache line are returned in response to an intervention request, they are returned in subblock order starting with the doubleword at the address supplied with the intervention request. Note, however, that if the intervention address targets the doubleword at the beginning of the block, subblock ordering is equivalent to sequential ordering.

External Snoop Request Protocol

External snoop requests use a protocol identical to the external read request protocol, except that, instead of returning data, the processor responds with an indication of the current cache state for the targeted cache line. This protocol is described by the following steps:

1. The external agent asserts **ExtRqst*** to arbitrate for the System interface.
2. The processor releases the System interface to slave state by asserting **Release***.
3. The external snoop request is driven onto the **SysCmd** bus and the address onto the **SysAD** bus. **ValidIn*** is asserted for one cycle.
4. The processor drives a coherent data identifier on the **SysCmd** bus and asserts **ValidOut*** for one cycle.
5. The **SysAD** bus is unused during the snoop response.
6. The processor continues driving the **SysCmd** and **SysAD** buses after the snoop response is returned, to move the System interface back to master state.

Note that if the cache line that is the target of the snoop request is not present in the cache—that is, a tag comparison for the cache line at the target cache address fails—the cache line that is the target of the snoop request is considered to be in the invalid state.

Figure 12-36 shows an external snoop request submitted with the System interface in the master state. Figure 12-37 shows an external snoop request submitted with the System interface in slave state.

> **NOTE:** Timings for the **SysADC** and **SysCmdP** buses are the same as those of the **SysAD** and **SysCmd** buses, respectively.

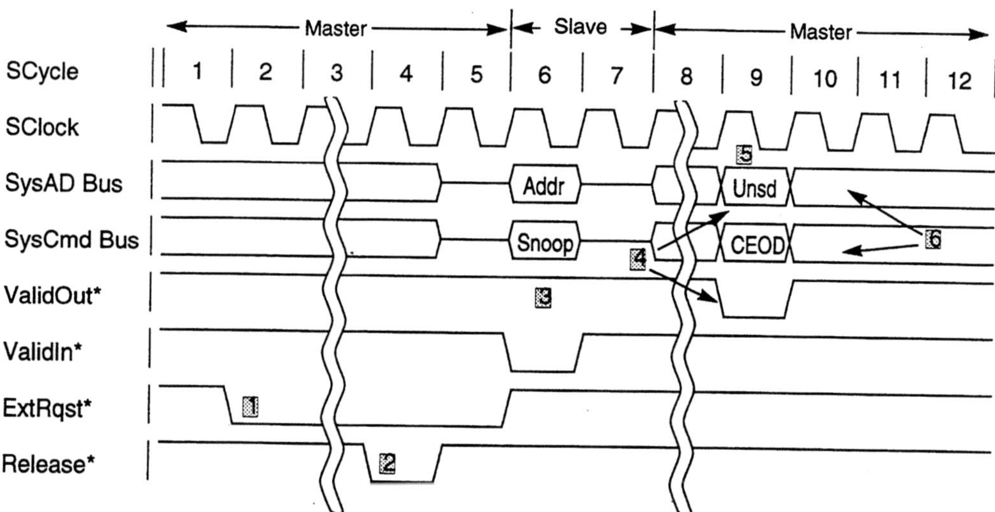

Figure 12-36 External Snoop Request, System Interface in Master State

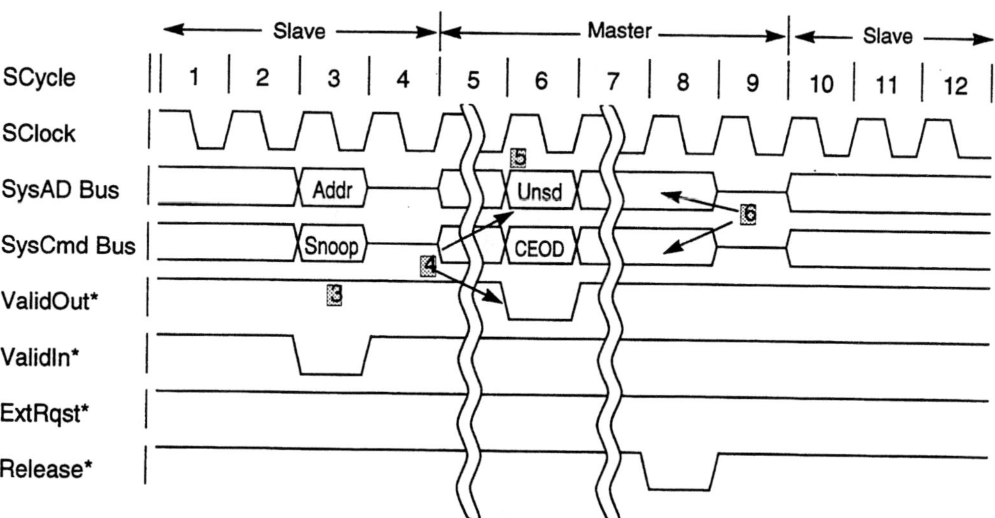

Figure 12-37 External Snoop Request, System Interface in Slave State

Read Response Protocol

An external agent must return data to the processor in response to a processor read request by using a read response protocol. A read response protocol consists of the following steps:

1. The external agent waits for the processor to perform an uncompelled change to slave state.
2. The processor returns the data through a single data cycle or a series of data cycles.
3. After the last data cycle is issued, the read response is complete and the external agent sets the **SysCmd** and **SysAD** buses to a tri-state.
4. The System interface returns to master state.

   NOTE: The processor always performs an uncompelled change to slave state after issuing a read request.
5. The data identifier for data cycles must indicate the fact that this data is *response data*.
6. The data identifier associated with the last data cycle must contain a *last data cycle* indication.

For read responses to coherent block read requests, each data identifier must include the cache state of the response data. The cache state provided with each data identifier must be the same and must be clean exclusive, dirty exclusive, shared, or dirty shared. The behavior of the processor is undefined if the cache state provided with the data identifiers changes during the transfer of the block of data, or if the cache state provided is invalid.

The data identifier associated with a data cycle can indicate that the data transmitted during that cycle is erroneous; however, an external agent must return a data block of the correct size regardless of the fact that the data may be in error. If a read response includes one or more erroneous data cycles, the processor then takes a bus error.

Read response data must only be delivered to the processor when a processor read request is pending. The behavior of the processor is undefined when a read response is presented to it and there is no processor read pending. Further, if the processor issues a read-with-write-forthcoming request, a processor write request or a processor null write request must be accepted before the read response can be returned. The behavior of the processor is undefined if the read response is returned before a processor write request is accepted.

Figure 12-38 illustrates a processor word read request followed by a word read response. Figure 12-39 illustrates a read response for a processor block read with the System interface already in slave state.

> **NOTE:** Timings for the **SysADC** and **SysCmdP** buses are the same as those of the **SysAD** and **SysCmd** buses, respectively.

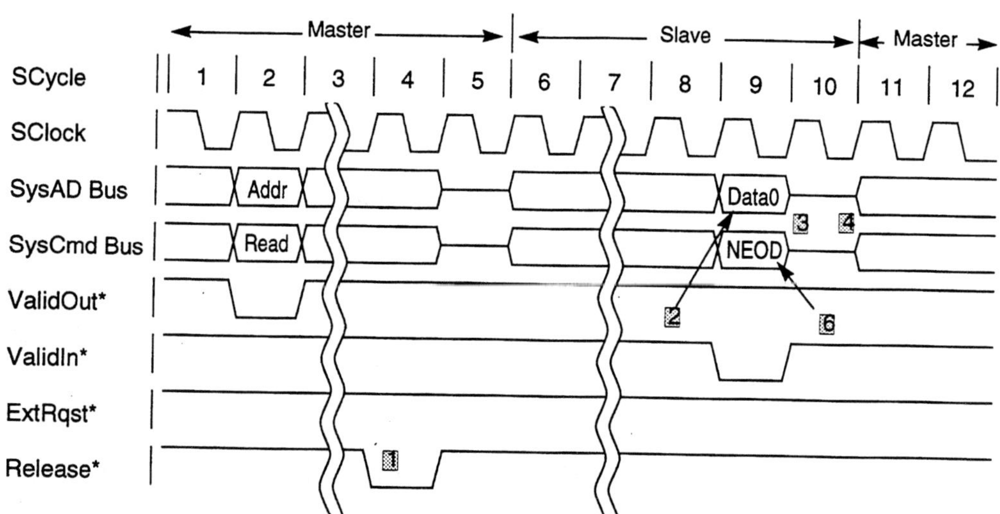

Figure 12-38 Processor Word Read Request, followed by a Word Read Response

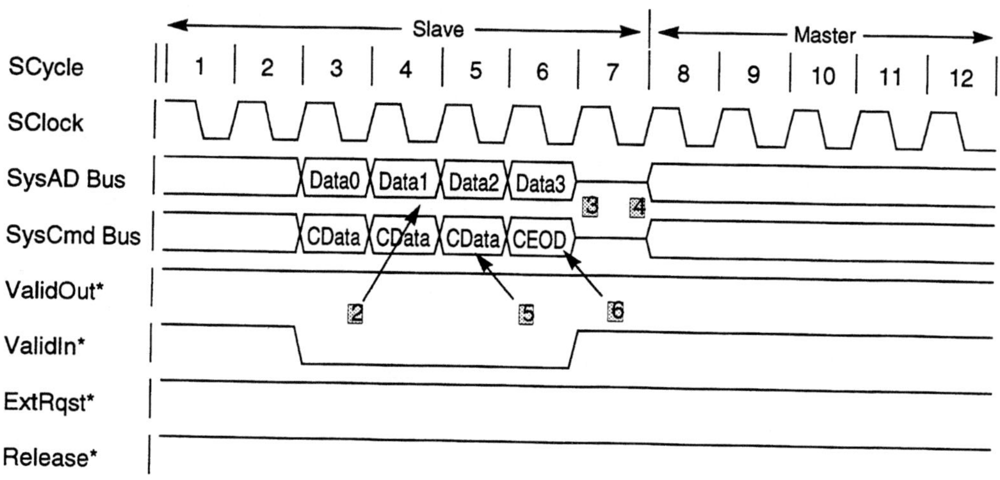

Figure 12-39 Block Read Response, System Interface already in Slave State

12.7 Data Rate Control

The System interface supports a maximum data rate of one doubleword per cycle. The data rate the processor can support is directly related to the secondary cache access time; if the access time is too long, the processor cannot transmit and accept data at the maximum rate.

The rate at which data is delivered to the processor can be determined by the external agent—for example, the external agent can drive data and assert **ValidIn*** every *n* cycles, instead of every cycle. An external agent can deliver data at any rate it chooses, but must not deliver data to the processor any faster than the processor is capable of receiving it.

The processor only accepts cycles as valid when **ValidIn*** is asserted and the **SysCmd** bus contains a data identifier; thereafter, the processor continues to accept data until it receives the data word tagged as the last one.

Data Transfer Patterns

A data pattern is a sequence of letters indicating the *data* and *unused* cycles that repeat to provide the appropriate data rate. For example, the data pattern **DDxx** specifies a repeatable data rate of two doublewords every four cycles, with the last two cycles unused. Table 12-6 lists the maximum processor data rate for each of the possible secondary cache write cycle times, and the most efficient data pattern for each data rate.

Table 12-6 Transmit Data Rates and Patterns

Maximum Data Rate	Data Pattern	Maximum Secondary Cache Access
1 Double/1 SClock Cycle	D	4 PCycles
2 Doubles/3 SClock Cycles	DDx	6 PCycles
1 Double/2 SClock Cycles	DDxx	8 PCycles
1 Double/2 SClock Cycles	DxDx	8 PCycles
2 Doubles/5 SClock Cycles	DDxxx	10 PCycles
1 Double/3 SClock Cycles	DDxxxx	12 PCycles
1 Double/3 SClock Cycles	DxxDxx	12 PCycles
1 Double/4 SClock Cycles	DDxxxxxx	16 PCycles
1 Double/4 SClock Cycles	DxxxDxxx	16 PCycles

In Tables 12-6 and 12-7, data patterns are specified using the letters **D** and **x**; **D** indicates a data cycle and **x** indicates an unused cycle. Figure 12-40 shows a read response in which data is provided to the processor at a rate of two doublewords every three cycles using the data pattern **DDx**.

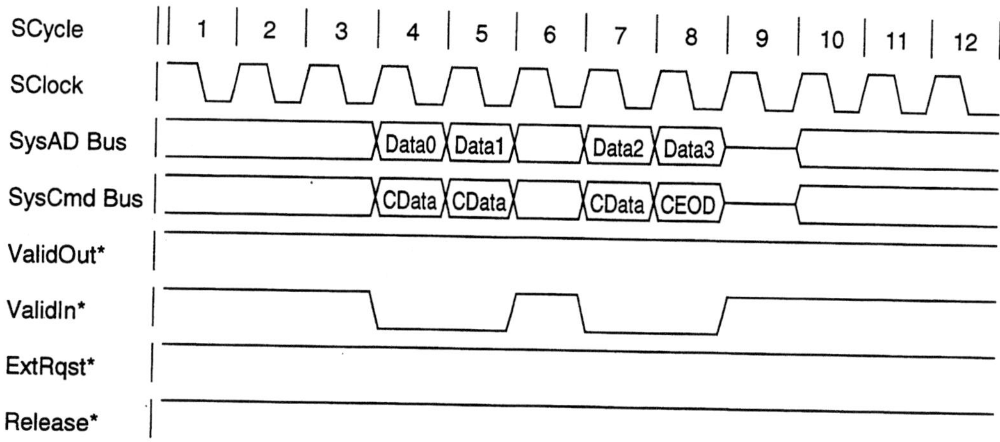

Figure 12-40 Read Response, Reduced Data Rate, System Interface in Slave State

Secondary Cache Transfers

The processor operates most efficiently if data is delivered in pairs of doublewords, since the secondary cache is organized as a 128-bit RAM array. The most efficient way of reducing the data rate is to deliver a pair of doublewords followed by some number of unused cycles, followed by another pair of doublewords. The secondary cache write cycle time should determine the rate at which this pattern is repeated. However, the processor accepts data in any pattern as long as the time between the transfer of any pair of odd-numbered doublewords is greater than, or equal to, the write cycle time of the secondary cache. Doublewords in the transfer pattern are numbered beginning at 0: the odd-numbered doublewords are the second, fourth, sixth, and so on.

Secondary Cache Write Cycle Time

Behavior of the processor is undefined if, based on the secondary cache write cycle time, data is delivered to the processor faster than the processor can handle it. Secondary cache write cycle time is defined as the sum of the parameters:

$$T_{Wr1Dly}, T_{WrSUp}, \text{ and } T_{WrRc}$$

These parameters are defined in Chapter 9, Table 9-1.

The rate at which the processor transmits data to an external agent is programmable at boot time through the boot-time mode control interface. The transmit data rate can be programmed to any of the data rates and data patterns listed in Table 12-6, as long as the programmed data rate does not exceed the maximum rate the processor can handle, based on the secondary cache write cycle time. The behavior of the processor is undefined if a programmed transmit data rate exceeds the maximum the processor can support.

Figure 12-41 shows a processor write request in which the processor transmit data rate is programmed as one doubleword every two cycles, using the data pattern **DDxx**.

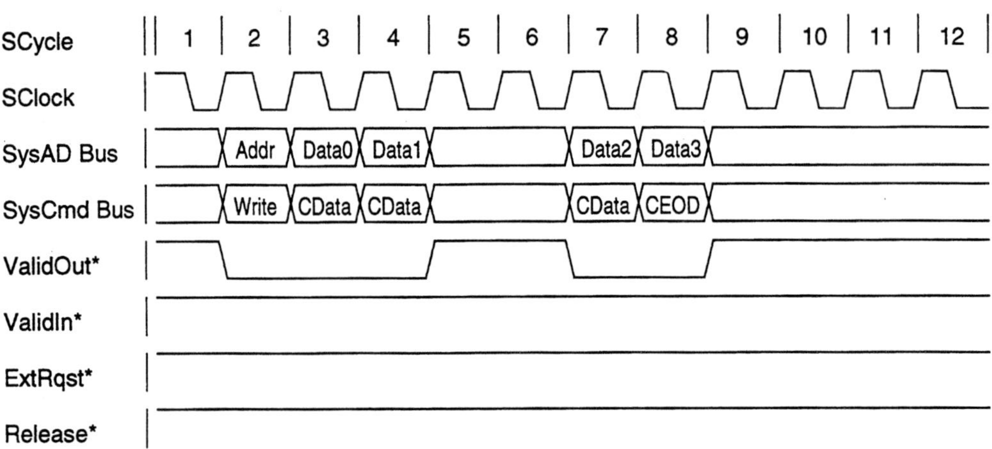

Figure 12-41 Processor Write Request, Transmit Data Rate Reduced

Table 12-7 shows the maximum transmit data rates for a given set of secondary cache parameters, based on a PClock-to-SClock divisor of 2. To find the maximum allowable secondary cache write cycle time and secondary cache access time, multiply the maximum secondary cache numbers for each pattern by:

(PClock_to_SClock_Divisor)/2

The minimum number for these parameters is always the minimum access time supported by processor.

Table 12-7 Maximum Transmit Data Rates

Secondary Cache Write Cycle Time	Maximum Data Rate	Best Data Pattern
1-4 PCycles	1 Double/1 SClock Cycle	D
5-6 PCycles	2 Doubles/3 SClock Cycles	DDx
7-8 PCycles	1 Double/2 SClock Cycles	DDxx
9-10 PCycles	2 Doubles/5 SClock Cycles	DDxxx
11-12 PCycles	1 Double/3 SClock Cycles	DDxxxx

Independent Transmissions on the SysAD Bus

In most applications, the **SysAD** bus is a point-to-point connection, running from the processor to a bidirectional registered transceiver residing in an external agent. For these applications, the **SysAD** bus has only two possible drivers, the processor or the external agent.

Certain applications may require connection of additional drivers and receivers to the **SysAD** bus, to allow transmissions over the **SysAD** bus that the processor is not involved in. These are called *independent transmissions*. To effect an independent transmission, the external agent must coordinate control of the **SysAD** bus by using arbitration handshake signals and external null requests.

An independent transmission on the **SysAD** bus follows this procedure:

1. The external agent requests mastership of the **SysAD** bus, to issue an external request.
2. The processor releases the System interface to slave state.
3. If the processor is being used with a secondary cache, the external agent issues a *secondary cache release external null request* to return ownership of the secondary cache to the processor.
4. The external agent then allows the independent transmission to take place on the **SysAD** bus, making sure that **ValidIn*** is not asserted while the transmission is occurring.
5. When the transmission is complete, the external agent must issue a *System interface release external null request* to return the System interface to master state.

System Interface Endianness

The endianness of the System interface is programmed at boot time through the boot-time mode control interface, and remains fixed until the next time the processor mode bits are read. Software cannot change the endianness of the System interface and the external system; software can set the reverse endian bit to reverse the interpretation of endianness inside the processor, but the endianness of the System interface remains unchanged.

12.8 System Interface Cycle Time

The processor specifies minimum and maximum cycle counts for various processor transactions and for the processor response time to external requests. Processor requests themselves are constrained by the System interface request protocol, and request cycle counts can be determined by examining the protocol. The following System interface interactions can vary within minimum and maximum cycle counts:

- spacing between requests within a cluster (*cluster request spacing*)
- waiting period for the processor to release the System interface to slave state in response to an external request (*release latency*)
- response time for an external request that requires a response (*external response latency*).

The remainder of this section describes and tabulates the minimum and maximum cycle counts for these System interface interactions.

Cluster Request Spacing

Processor internal activity determines the minimum and maximum number of unused cycles allowed between the requests within a cluster.

- The minimum number of unused cycles allowed between requests within a cluster is 0: in other words, the requests can be adjacent.
- The maximum number of unused cycles separating requests within a cluster varies depending on the requests that form the cluster.

Table 12-8 summarizes the minimum and maximum number of unused cycles allowed between requests within a cluster.

Table 12-8 Unused Cycles Separating Requests within a Cluster

From Processor Request	To Processor Request	Minimum Unused SClock Cycles	Maximum Unused SClock Cycles
Read	Update	0	2
Read	Write	0	2
Update	Write	0	2

Release Latency

Release latency is generally defined as the number of cycles the processor can wait to release the System interface to slave state for an external request. When no processor requests are in progress, internal activity—such as refilling the primary cache from the secondary cache—can cause the processor to wait some number of cycles before releasing the System interface. Release latency is therefore more specifically defined as the number of cycles that occur between the assertion of **ExtRqst*** and the assertion of **Release***.

There are three categories of release latency:

- Category 1: when the external request signal is asserted two cycles before the last cycle of a processor request, or two cycles before the last cycle of the last request in a cluster.
- Category 2: when the external request signal is not asserted during a processor request or cluster, or is asserted during the last cycle of a processor request or cluster.
- Category 3: when the processor makes an uncompelled change to slave state.

Table 12-9 summarizes the minimum and maximum release latencies for requests that fall into categories 1, 2, 3a and 3b. Note that the maximum and minimum cycle count values are subject to change.

Table 12-9 Release Latency for External Requests

Category	Minimum PCycles	Maximum PCycles
1	4	6
2	4	24
3a	0	See (3a), below
3b	0	See (3b), below

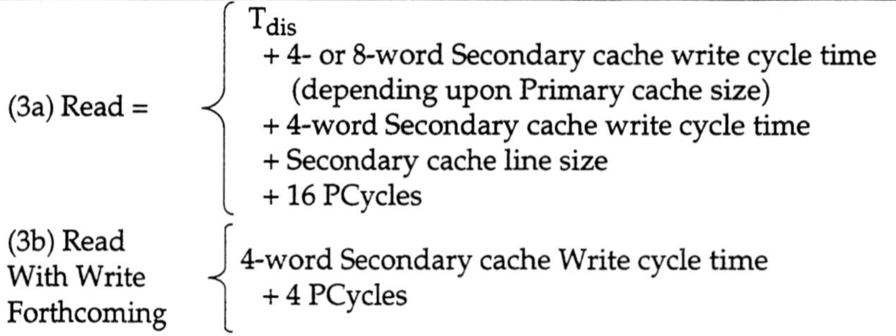

(3a) Read =
T_{dis}
+ 4- or 8-word Secondary cache write cycle time
(depending upon Primary cache size)
+ 4-word Secondary cache write cycle time
+ Secondary cache line size
+ 16 PCycles
(3b) Read With Write Forthcoming
4-word Secondary cache Write cycle time
+ 4 PCycles

External Request Response Latency

The number of cycles the processor takes to respond to an external intervention request, read request, or snoop request, are referred to as the *intervention response latency, external read response latency,* or *snoop response latency,* respectively.

The number of latency cycles is the number of unused cycles between the address cycle of the request and the first data cycle of the response. Intervention response latency and snoop response latency are a function of processor internal activity and secondary cache access time. Table 12-10 summarizes the minimum and maximum intervention response latency and snoop response latency. Note that the latency values are subject to change.

Table 12-10 Intervention Response and Snoop Response Latencies

Maximum Secondary Cache Access	Intervention Response Latency		Snoop Response Latency	
	Min	Max	Min	Max
1-4 PCycles	6	26	6	26
5-6 PCycles	8	28	8	28
7-8 PCycles	10	30	10	30
9-10 PCycles	12	32	12	32
11-12 PCycles	14	34	14	34

External read response latency is a function of processor internal activity. Minimum and maximum external read response latency is 4 PCycles.

12.9 System Interface Commands and Data Identifiers

System interface commands specify the nature and attributes of any System interface request; this specification is made during the address cycle for the request. System interface data identifiers specify the attributes of data transmitted during a System interface data cycle.

The following sections describe the syntax, that is, the bitwise encoding of System interface commands and data identifiers.

Reserved bits and reserved fields in the command or data identifier should be set to 1 for System interface commands and data identifiers associated with external requests. For System interface commands and data identifiers associated with processor requests, reserved bits and reserved fields in the command and data identifier are undefined.

Command and Data Identifier Syntax

System interface commands and data identifiers are encoded in 9 bits and are transmitted on the **SysCmd** bus from the processor to an external agent, or from an external agent to the processor, during address and data cycles. Bit 8 (the most-significant bit) of the **SysCmd** bus determines whether the current content of the **SysCmd** bus is a command or a data identifier and, therefore, whether the current cycle is an address cycle or a data cycle. For System interface commands, **SysCmd(8)** must be set to 0. For System interface data identifiers, **SysCmd(8)** must be set to 1.

System Interface Command Syntax

This section describes the **SysCmd** bus encoding for System interface commands. Figure 12-42 shows a common encoding used for all System interface commands.

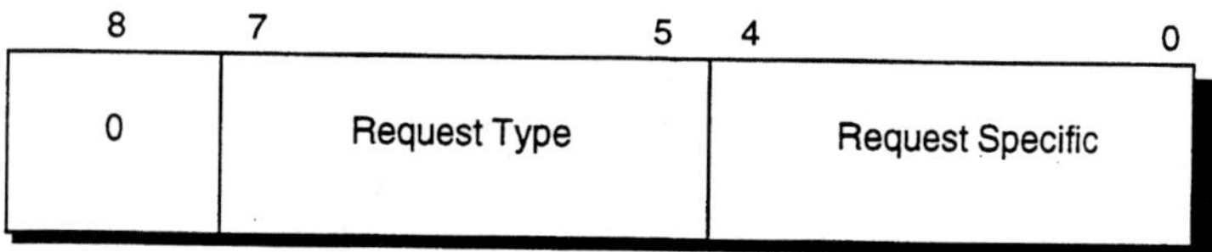

Figure 12-42 System Interface Command Syntax Bit Definition

SysCmd(8) must be set to 0 for all System interface commands.

SysCmd(7:5) specify the System interface request type which may be read, write, null, invalidate, update, intervention, or snoop; Table 12-11 lists the encoding of **SysCmd(7:5)**.

Table 12-11 shows the types of requests encoded by the **SysCmd(7:5)** bits.

Table 12-11 Encoding of SysCmd(7:5) *for System Interface Commands*

SysCmd(7:5)	Command
0	Read Request
1	Read-With-Write-Forthcoming Request
2	Write Request
3	Null Request
4	Invalidate Request
5	Update Request
6	Intervention Request
7	Snoop Request

SysCmd(4:0) are specific to each type of request and are defined in each of the following sections.

Read Requests

Figure 12-43 shows the format of a **SysCmd** read request.

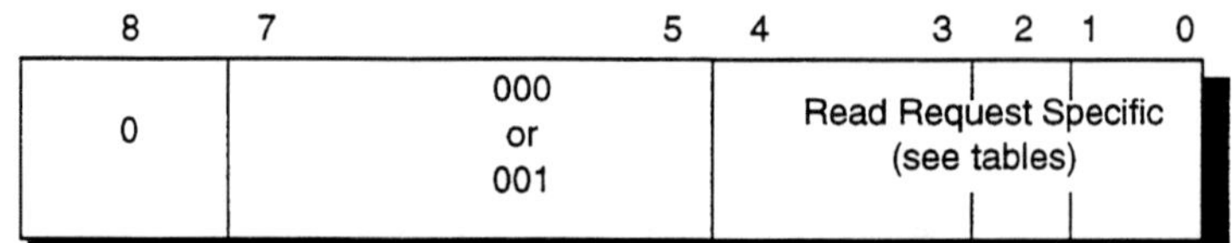

Figure 12-43 Read Request SysCmd *Bus Bit Definition*

Tables 12-12 through 12-14 list the encodings of **SysCmd(4:0)** for read requests.

Table 12-12 Encoding of SysCmd(4:3) *for Read Requests*

SysCmd(4:3)	Read Attributes
0	Coherent block read
1	Coherent block read, exclusivity requested
2	Noncoherent block read
3	Doubleword, partial doubleword, word, or partial word

Table 12-13 Encoding of SysCmd(2:0) *for Coherent and Noncoherent Block Read Request*

SysCmd(2)	Link Address Retained Indication
0	Link address not retained
1	Link address retained
SysCmd(1:0)	**Read Block Size**
0	4 words
1	8 words
2	16 words
3	32 words

Table 12-14 Doubleword, Word, or Partial-word Read Request Data Size Encoding of SysCmd(2:0)

SysCmd(2:0)	Read Data Size
0	1 byte valid (Byte)
1	2 bytes valid (Halfword)
2	3 bytes valid (Tribyte)
3	4 bytes valid (Word)
4	5 bytes valid (Quintibyte)
5	6 bytes valid (Sextibyte)
6	7 bytes valid (Septibyte)
7	8 bytes valid (Doubleword)

Write Requests

Figure 12-44 shows the format of a **SysCmd** write request.

Table 12-15 lists the write attributes encoded in bits **SysCmd(4:3)**. Table 12-16 lists the block write replacement attributes encoded in bits **SysCmd(2:0)**. Table 12-17 lists the write request bit encodings in **SysCmd(2:0)**.

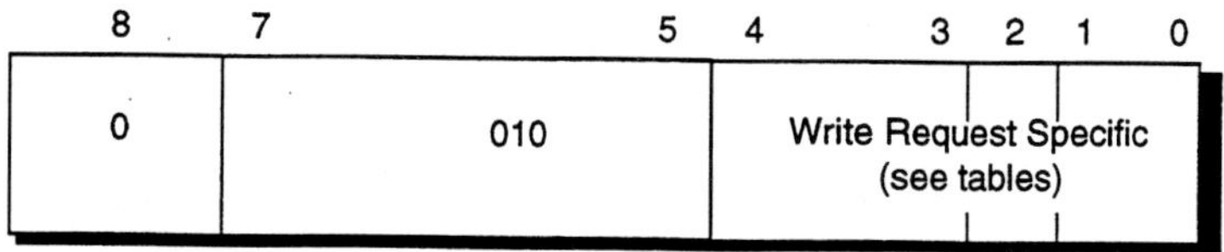

Figure 12-44 Write Request SysCmd *Bus Bit Definition*

Table 12-15 Write Request Encoding of SysCmd(4:3)

SysCmd(4:3)	Write Attributes
0	Reserved
1	Reserved
2	Block write
3	Doubleword, partial doubleword, word, or partial word

Table 12-16 Block Write Request Encoding of SysCmd(2:0)

SysCmd(2)	Cache Line Replacement Attributes
0	Cache line replaced
1	Cache line retained
SysCmd(1:0)	**Write Block Size**
0	4 words
1	8 words
2	16 words
3	32 words

Table 12-17 Doubleword, Word, or Partial-word Write Request Data Size Encoding of SysCmd(2:0)

SysCmd(2:0)	Write Data Size
0	1 byte valid (Byte)
1	2 bytes valid (Halfword)
2	3 bytes valid (Tribyte)
3	4 bytes valid (Word)
4	5 bytes valid (Quintibyte)
5	6 bytes valid (Sextibyte)
6	7 bytes valid (Septibyte)
7	8 bytes valid (Doubleword)

Null Requests

Figure 12-45 shows the format of a **SysCmd** null request.

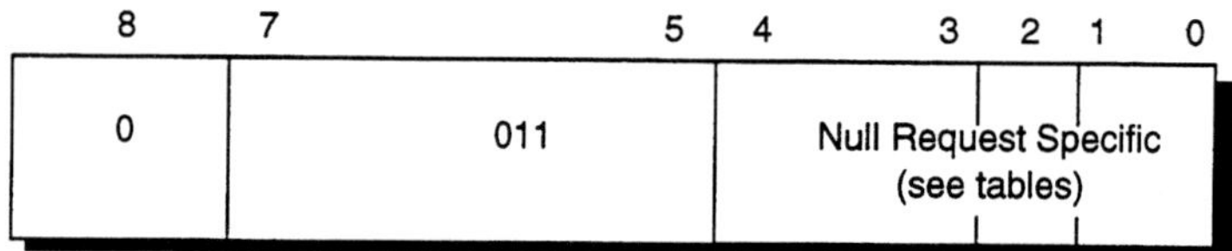

Figure 12-45 Null Request SysCmd *Bus Bit Definition*

Processor null write requests, System interface release external null requests, and secondary cache release external null requests all use the null request command. Table 12-18 lists the encodings of **SysCmd(4:3)** for processor null write requests. Table 12-19 lists the encodings of **SysCmd(4:3)** for external null requests.

SysCmd(2:0) are reserved for both instances of null requests.

Table 12-18 Processor Null Write Request Encoding of SysCmd(4:3)

SysCmd(4:3)	Null Write Attributes
0	Null write
1	Reserved
2	Reserved
3	Reserved

Table 12-19 External Null Request Encoding of SysCmd(4:3)

SysCmd(4:3)	Null Attributes
0	System Interface release
1	Secondary cache release
2	Reserved
3	Reserved

Invalidate Requests

Figure 12-46 shows the format for an invalidate request, and Table 12-20 lists the encodings of **SysCmd(4:0)** for an external invalidate request.

SysCmd(4:0) are reserved on a processor invalidate request.

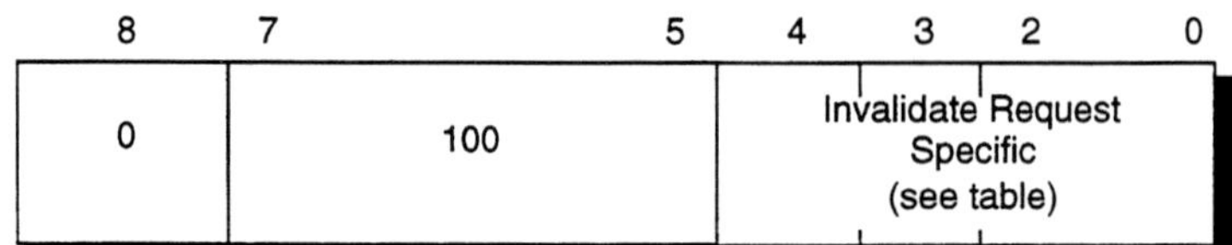

Figure 12-46 Invalidate Request SysCmd *Bus Bit Definition*

Table 12-20 Encoding of SysCmd(4:0) *for External Invalidate Requests*

SysCmd(4)	Processor Unacknowledged Invalidate Cancellation
0	Invalidate cancelled
1	No cancellation
SysCmd(3:0)	Reserved

Update Requests

Figure 12-47 shows the format for a **SysCmd** update request.

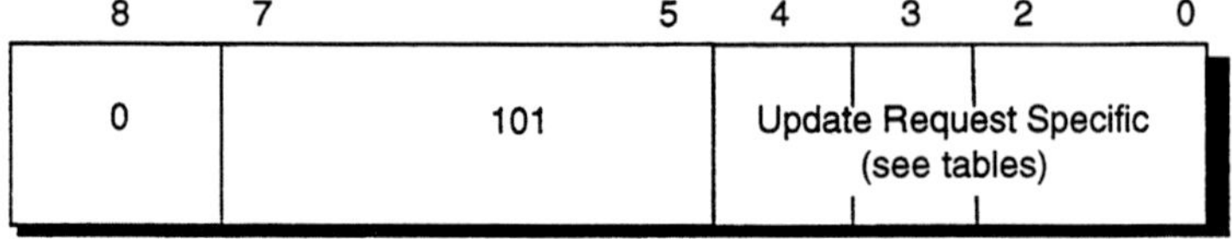

Figure 12-47 Update Request SysCmd *Bus Bit Definition*

Table 12-21 lists the encodings of **SysCmd(4:0)** for external update requests. Table 12-22 lists the encodings of **SysCmd(4:0)** for processor update requests. The remaining upper bits are the same for both processor and external update requests.

Table 12-21 Encoding of SysCmd(4:0) *for External Update Requests*

SysCmd(4)	Processor Unacknowledged Update Cancellation
0	Update cancelled
1	No cancellation
SysCmd(3)	**Update Cache State Change Attributes**
0	Cache state changed to shared
1	No change to cache state
SysCmd(2:0)	**Update Data Size**
0	1 byte valid (Byte)
1	2 bytes valid (Halfword)
2	3 bytes valid (Tribyte)
3	4 bytes valid (Word)
4	5 bytes valid (Quintibyte)
5	6 bytes valid (Sextibyte)
6	7 bytes valid (Septibyte)
7	8 bytes valid (Doubleword)

Table 12-22 Encoding of SysCmd(4:0) *for Processor Update Requests*

SysCmd(4)	Reserved
SysCmd(3)	**Update type**
0	Compulsory
1	Potential
SysCmd(2:0)	**Update Data Size**
0	1 byte valid (Byte)
1	2 bytes valid (Halfword)
2	3 bytes valid (Tribyte).
3	4 bytes valid (Word)
4	5 bytes valid (Quintibyte)
5	6 bytes valid (Sextibyte)
6	7 bytes valid (Septibyte)
7	8 bytes valid (Doubleword)

Intervention and Snoop Requests

Figure 12-48 shows the format of an intervention request; Figure 12-49 shows the format of a snoop request. Table 12-23 lists the encodings of **SysCmd(4:0)** for intervention requests; Table 12-24 lists the encodings **SysCmd(4:0)** for snoop requests.

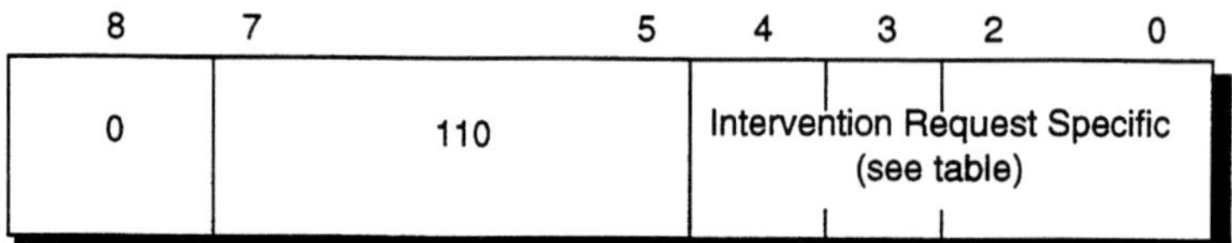

Figure 12-48 Intervention Request SysCmd *Bus Bit Definition*

Table 12-23 Encodings of SysCmd(4:0) *for Intervention Requests*

SysCmd(4)	Processor Unacknowledged Update Cancellation
0	Update cancelled
1	No cancellation
SysCmd(3)	**Response to Dirty or Exclusive State**
0	Return cache line data if in the dirty exclusive or dirty shared state
1	Return cache line data if in the clean exclusive or dirty exclusive state
SysCmd(2:0)	**Cache State Change Function**
0	No change to cache state
1	If cache state is clean exclusive, change to shared; otherwise no change to cache state
2	If cache state is clean exclusive or shared, change to invalid; otherwise no change to cache state
3	If cache state is clean exclusive, change to shared; if cache state is dirty exclusive, change to dirty shared; otherwise make no change to cache state
4	If cache state is clean exclusive, dirty exclusive, or dirty shared, change to shared; otherwise make no change to cache state
5	Change to invalid regardless of current cache state
6	Reserved
7	Reserved

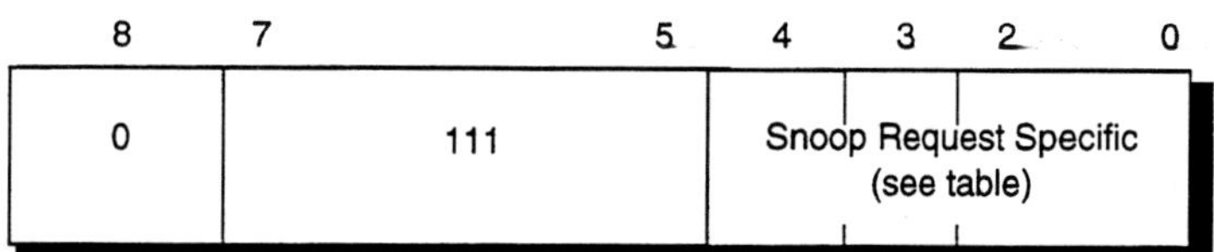

Figure 12-49 Snoop Request SysCmd *Bus Bit Definition*

Table 12-24 Encodings of SysCmd(4:0) *for Snoop Requests*

SysCmd(4)	**Processor Unacknowledged Update Cancellation**
0	Update cancelled
1	No cancellation
SysCmd(3)	Reserved
SysCmd(2:0)	**Cache State Change Function**
0	No change to cache state
1	If cache state is clean exclusive, change to shared state; otherwise make no change to cache state
2	If cache state is clean exclusive or shared, change to invalid state; otherwise make no change to cache state
3	If cache state is clean exclusive, change to shared; if cache state is dirty exclusive, change to dirty shared; otherwise make no change to cache state
4	If cache state is clean exclusive, dirty exclusive, or dirty shared, change to shared; otherwise make no change to cache state
5	Change to invalid regardless of current cache state
6	Reserved
7	Reserved

System Interface Data Identifier Syntax

This section defines the encoding of the **SysCmd** bus for System interface data identifiers. Figure 12-50 shows a common encoding used for all System interface data identifiers.

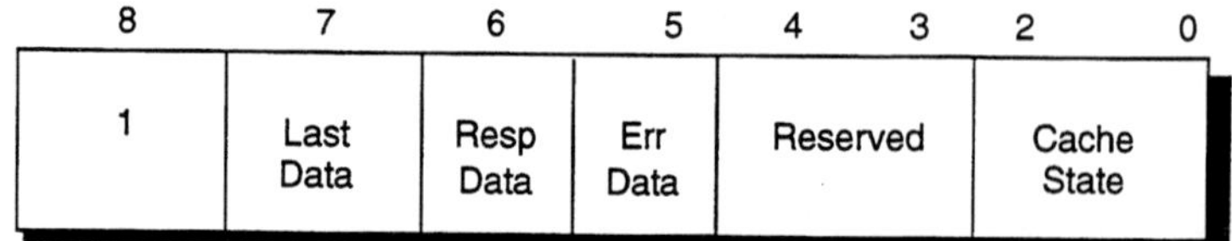

Figure 12-50 Data Identifier SysCmd *Bus Bit Definition*

SysCmd(8) must be set to 1 for all System interface data identifiers.

System interface data identifiers have two formats, one for coherent data and another for noncoherent data.

Coherent Data

Coherent data is defined as follows:

- data that is returned in response to a processor coherent block read request
- data that is returned in response to an external intervention request.

Noncoherent Data

Noncoherent data is defined as follows:

- data that is associated with processor block write requests and processor doubleword, partial doubleword, word, or partial word write requests
- data that is returned in response to a processor noncoherent block read request or a processor doubleword, partial doubleword, word, or partial word read request
- data that is associated with external update requests
- data that is associated with external write requests
- data that is returned in response to an external read request
- data that is associated with processor update requests.

Data Identifier Bit Definitions

SysCmd(7) marks the last data element and **SysCmd(6)** indicates whether or not the data is response data, for both processor and external coherent and noncoherent data identifiers. Response data is data returned in response to a read request or an intervention request.

SysCmd(5) indicates whether or not the data element is error free. Erroneous data contains an uncorrectable error and is returned to the processor, forcing a bus error. The processor delivers data with the good data bit deasserted if a primary parity error is detected for a transmitted data item. If the system is in ECC mode, a secondary cache data ECC error is detected by comparing the values transmitted on the **SysAD** and **SysADC**.

SysCmd(4) indicates to the processor whether to check the data and check bits for this data element, for both coherent and noncoherent external data identifiers.

SysCmd(3) is reserved for external data identifiers.

SysCmd(4:3) are reserved for both coherent and noncoherent processor data identifiers.

SysCmd(2:0) indicate the data cache state to load the cache line, in response to processor coherent read requests for coherent data identifiers. **SysCmd(2:0)** also indicate the cache state for response data to an external intervention request, or for the data cycle issued in response to an external snoop request. **SysCmd(2:0)** are reserved for noncoherent data identifiers.

Table 12-25 lists the encodings of **SysCmd(7:3)** for processor data identifiers. Table 12-26 lists the encodings of **SysCmd(7:3)** for external data identifiers. Table 12-27 lists the encodings of **SysCmd(2:0)** for coherent data identifiers.

Table 12-25 Processor Data Identifier Encoding of SysCmd(7:3)

SysCmd(7)	Last Data Element Indication
0	Last data element
1	Not the last data element
SysCmd(6)	**Response Data Indication**
0	Data is response data
1	Data is not response data
SysCmd(5)	**Good Data Indication**
0	Data is error free
1	Data is erroneous
SysCmd(4:3)	Reserved

Table 12-26 External Data Identifier Encoding of SysCmd(7:3)

SysCmd(7)	Last Data Element Indication
0	Last data element
1	Not the last data element
SysCmd(6)	**Response Data Indication**
0	Data is response data
1	Data is not response data
SysCmd(5)	**Good Data Indication**
0	Data is error free
1	Data is erroneous
SysCmd(4)	**Data Checking Enable**
0	Check the data and check bits
1	Do not check the data and check bits
SysCmd(3)	Reserved

Table 12-27 Coherent Data Identifiers Encoding of SysCmd(2:0)

SysCmd(2:0)	Cache State
0	Invalid
1	Reserved
2	Reserved
3	Reserved
4	Clean Exclusive
5	Dirty Exclusive
6	Shared
7	Dirty Shared

12.10 System Interface Addresses

System interface addresses are full 36-bit physical addresses presented on the least-significant 36 bits (bits 35 through 0) of the **SysAD** bus during address cycles; the remaining bits of the **SysAD** bus are unused during address cycles.

Addressing Conventions

Addresses associated with doubleword, partial doubleword, word, or partial word transactions and update requests, are aligned for the size of the data element. The system uses the following address conventions:

- Addresses associated with block requests are aligned to double-word boundaries; that is, the low-order 3 bits of address are 0.
- Doubleword requests set the low-order 3 bits of address to 0.
- Word requests set the low-order 2 bits of address to 0.
- Halfword requests set the low-order bit of address to 0.
- Byte, tribyte, quintibyte, sextibyte, and septibyte requests use the byte address.

Sequential and Subblock Ordering

The order in which data is returned in response to a processor block read request can be programmed to sequential ordering or subblock ordering, using the boot-time mode control interface. Appendix C has more information about subblock ordering. Either sequential or subblock ordering may be enabled, as follows:

- If sequential ordering is enabled on a block read request, the processor delivers the address of the doubleword at the start of the block. An external agent must return the block of data sequentially from the beginning of the block.
- If subblock ordering is enabled, the processor delivers the address of the requested doubleword within the block. An external agent must return the block of data using subblock ordering, starting with the addressed doubleword.

NOTE: Only R4000SC and R4000MC configurations (using a secondary cache) can be programmed to use sequential ordering.

For block write requests, the processor always delivers the address of the doubleword at the beginning of the block; the processor delivers data beginning with the doubleword at the beginning of the block and progresses sequentially through the doublewords that form the block.

During data cycles, the valid byte lines depend upon the position of the data with respect to the aligned doubleword (this may be a byte, halfword, tribyte, quadbyte/word, quintibyte, sextibyte, septibyte, or an octalbyte/doubleword). For example, in little-endian mode, on a byte request where the address modulo 8 is 0, **SysAD(7:0)** are valid during the data cycles.

12.11 Processor Internal Address Map

External reads and writes provide access to processor internal resources that may be of interest to an external agent. The processor decodes bits **SysAD(6:4)** of the address associated with an external read or write request to determine which processor internal resource is the target. However, the processor does not contain any resources that are *readable* through an external read request. Therefore, in response to an external read request the processor returns undefined data and a data identifier with its *Erroneous Data* bit, **SysCmd(5)**, set. The *Interrupt* register is the only processor internal resource available for *write* access by an external request. The *Interrupt* register is accessed by an external write request with an address of 000_2 on bits 6:4 of the **SysAD** bus.

Secondary Cache Interface

13

The R4000SC and R4000MC versions of the R4000 processor contain interface signals for an optional external secondary cache. This interface consists of:

- a 128-bit data bus
- a 25-bit tag bus
- an 18-bit address bus
- various static random access memory (SRAM) control signals.

The 128-bit-wide data bus minimizes the primary cache miss penalty, and allows the use of standard low-cost SRAMs in the design of the secondary cache.

The remainder of the System interface signals are described in Chapter 8.

13.1 Data Transfer Rates

The interface to the secondary cache maximizes service of primary cache misses. The Secondary Cache interface, **SCData(127:0)**, supports a data rate that is close to the processor-to-primary-cache bandwidth during normal operation. To ensure that this bandwidth is maintained, each data, tag, and check pin must be connected to a single SRAM device.

The **SCAddr** bus, together with the **SCOE***, **SCDCS***, and **SCTCS*** signals, drives a large number of SRAM devices; because of this, one level of external buffering between the processor and the cache array is used.

13.2 Duplicating Signals

The buffered control signals control the speed of the Secondary Cache interface. Critical control signals are duplicated by design to minimize this limitation: the **SCWR*** signal and **SCAddr(0)** have four versions so that external buffers are not needed to drive them. When an 8-word (256-bit) primary cache line is used, these signals can be controlled quickly, reducing the time of back-to-back transfers.

Each duplicated control signal can drive up to 11 SRAMs; therefore, a total of 44 SRAM packages can be used in the cache array. This allows a cache design using 16-Kbyte-by-64-bit, 64-Kbyte-by-4-bit, or 256-Kbyte-by-4-bit standard SRAM.†

The benefit of duplicating **SCAddr(0)** is greater in systems that use fast sequential static cache RAM and an 8-word primary cache line. If **SCAddr(0)** is attached to the SRAM address bit that affects column decode only, the read cycle time should approximate the output enable time of the RAM. For fast static RAM, this cycle time should be half of the nominal read cycle time.

† Other cache designs within this constraint are also acceptable. For example, a smaller cache design can use 22 8-Kbyte-by-8-bit static RAMs; this design presents less load on the address pins and control signals, and reduces the overall parts count.

13.3 Accessing a Split Secondary Cache

When the secondary cache is split into separate instruction and data portions, assertion of the high-order **SCAddr** bit, **SCAddr(17),** enables the instruction half of the cache.

It is possible to design a cache that supports both joint and split instruction/data configurations of less than the maximum cache size; in doing so, **SCAddr(12:0)** must address the cache in all configurations. **SCAddr(17)** must support the split instruction/data configuration, and any of **SCAddr(16:14)** bits can be omitted, because of the fixed width of the physical tag array.

13.4 SCDChk Bus

The secondary cache data check bus, **SCDChk**, is divided into two fields to cover the upper and lower 64 bits of **SCData**. This form is required by the 64-bit width of internal data paths.

13.5 SCTAG Bus

The secondary cache tag bus, **SCTag**, is divided into three fields, as shown in Figure 13-1. The *CS* field indicates the cache state: invalid, clean exclusive, dirty exclusive, shared, or dirty shared. The *PIdx* field is an index to the virtual address of primary cache lines that can contain data from the secondary cache. Bits 18:0 contain the upper physical address.

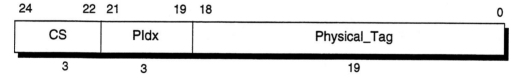

Figure 13-1 SCTag Fields

The **SCDCS*** and **SCTCS*** signals disable reads or writes of either the data array or tag array when the opposite array is being accessed. These signals are useful for saving power on snoop and invalidate requests since access to the data array is not necessary. These signals also write data from the primary data cache to the secondary cache.

13.6 Operation of the Secondary Cache Interface

The secondary cache can be configured for various clock rates and static RAM speeds. All configurable parameters are specified in multiples of **PClock**, which runs at twice the frequency of the external system clock, **MasterClock**.

During boot time, secondary cache timing parameters are programmed through the boot-time mode bits, as described in Chapter 9. Table 13-1 lists the secondary cache timing parameters. The following sections describe secondary cache read and write cycles.

Table 13-1 Secondary Cache Timing Parameters

Symbol	Number of Cycles
t_{Rd1Cyc}	4-15 PCycles
t_{Rd2Cyc}	3-15 PCycles
t_{Dis}	2-7 PCycles
t_{Wr1Dly}	1-3 PCycles
t_{Wr2Dly}	1-3 PCycles
t_{WrRC}	0-1 PCycles
t_{WrSUp}	3-15 PCycles

Read Cycles

There are two basic read cycles: 4-word read and 8-word read.

Each secondary cache read cycle begins by driving an address out on the address pins. The output enable signal **SCOE*** is asserted at the same time.

This section describes both 4-word and 8-word read cycles, including timing diagrams.

4-Word Read Cycle

The 4-word read cycle has two user-accessible timing parameters:

t_{Rd1Cyc} read sequence cycle time, which specifies the time from the assertion of the **SCAddr** bus to the sampling of the **SCData** bus

t_{Dis} cache output disable time, which specifies the time from the end of a read cycle to the start of the next write cycle

Figure 13-2 illustrates the 4-word read cycle, including the two user-accessible timing parameters.

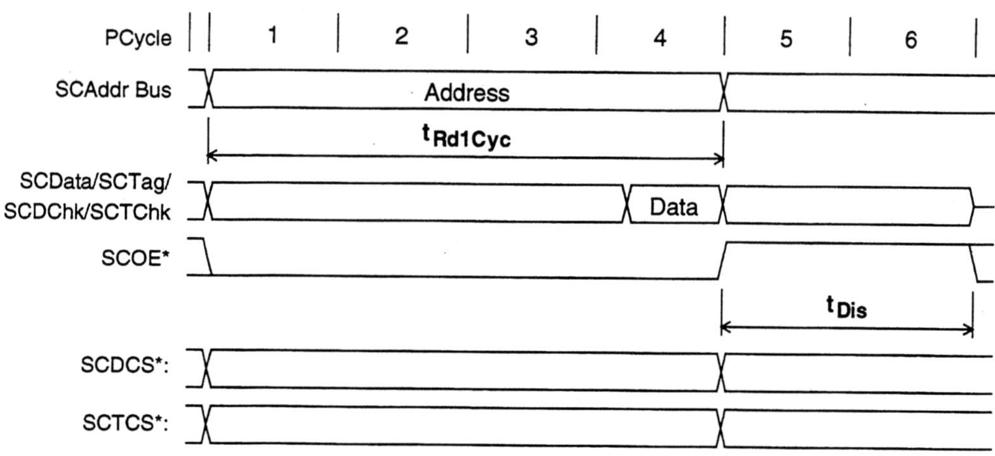

Figure 13-2 Timing Diagram of a 4-Word Read Cycle

8-Word Read Cycle

The 8-word read cycle has an additional user-accessible parameter beyond that of the 4-word read cycle described above: t_{Rd2Cyc}, the time from the first sample point to the second sample point.

In an 8-word read cycle, the low-order address bit, **SCAddr(0)**, changes at the same time as the first read sample point.

Figure 13-3 illustrates the 8-word read cycle, including the three user-accessible timing parameters.

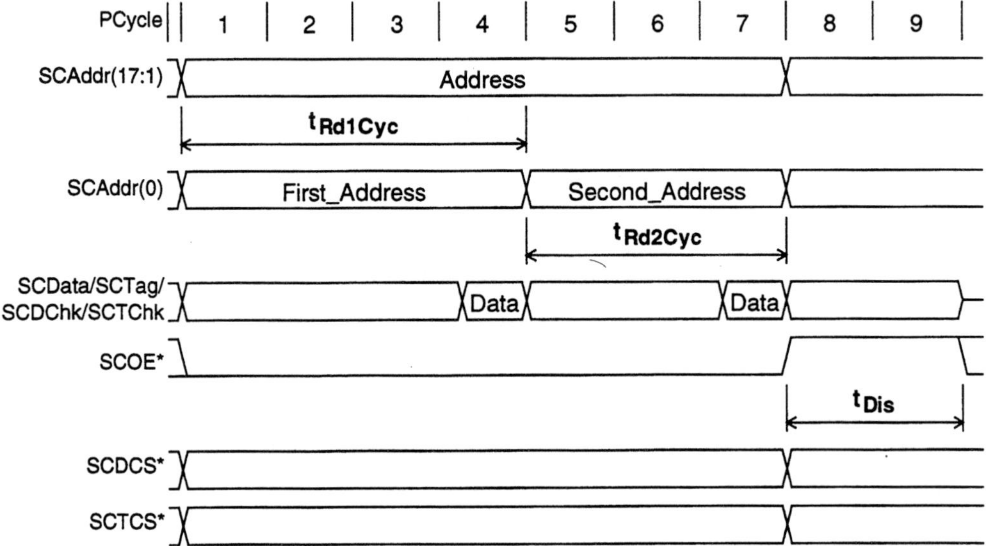

Figure 13-3 Timing Diagram of an 8-Word Read Cycle

Notes on a Secondary Cache Read Cycle

All read cycles can be aborted by changing the address; a new cycle begins with the edge on which the address is changed. Additionally, the period t_{Dis} after a read cycle can be interrupted any time by the start of a new read cycle. If a read cycle is aborted by a write cycle, **SCOE*** must be deasserted for the t_{Dis} period before the write cycle can begin.

Read cycles can also be extended indefinitely. There is no requirement to change the address at the end of a read cycle.

Write Cycles

There are two basic write cycles: a 4-word write cycle and an 8-word write cycle. The secondary cache write cycle begins with the assertion of an address onto the address pins.

This section describes both 4-word and 8-word write cycles, including timing diagrams.

4-Word Write Cycle

A 4-word write cycle has three timing parameters:

t_{Wr1Dly}	delay from the assertion of the address to the assertion of **SCWR***
t_{WrSUp}	delay from assertion of the second data doubleword to the deassertion of **SCWR***
t_{WrRc}	delay from the deassertion of **SCWR*** to the beginning of the next cycle

The timing parameter t_{WrRc} is 0 for most cache designs. Note that the upper data doubleword and the lower data doubleword are normally driven one cycle apart; this reduces the peak current consumption in the output drivers.

Figure 13-4 illustrates the 4-word write cycle. Either the upper or lower data doubleword can be driven first.

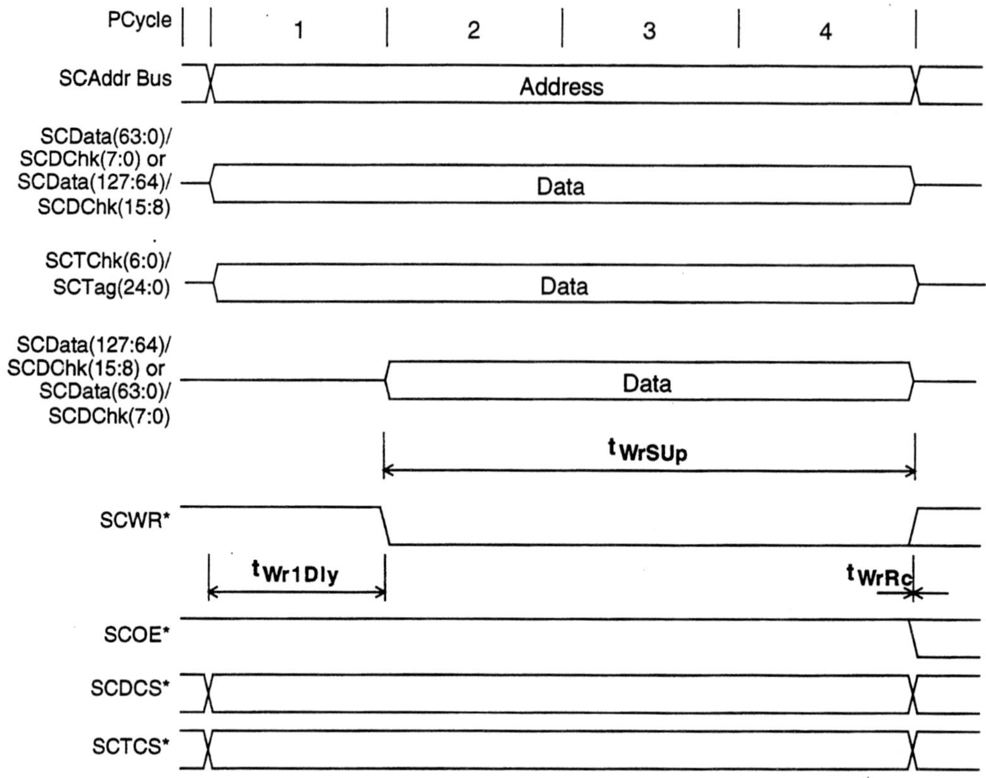

Figure 13-4 Timing Diagram of a 4-Word Write Cycle

8-Word Write Cycle

An 8-word write cycle has one additional parameter beyond those used by the 4-word write cycle: t_{Wr2Dly}. This is the time period that begins when the low-order address bit **SCAddr(0)** changes and ends when **SCWR*** is asserted for the second time. The lower half of **SCData** is driven on the same edge as the change in **SCAddr(0)**.

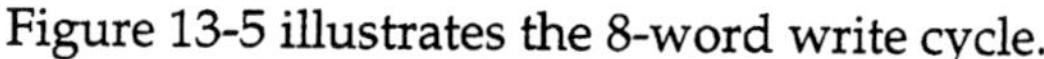

Figure 13-5 illustrates the 8-word write cycle.

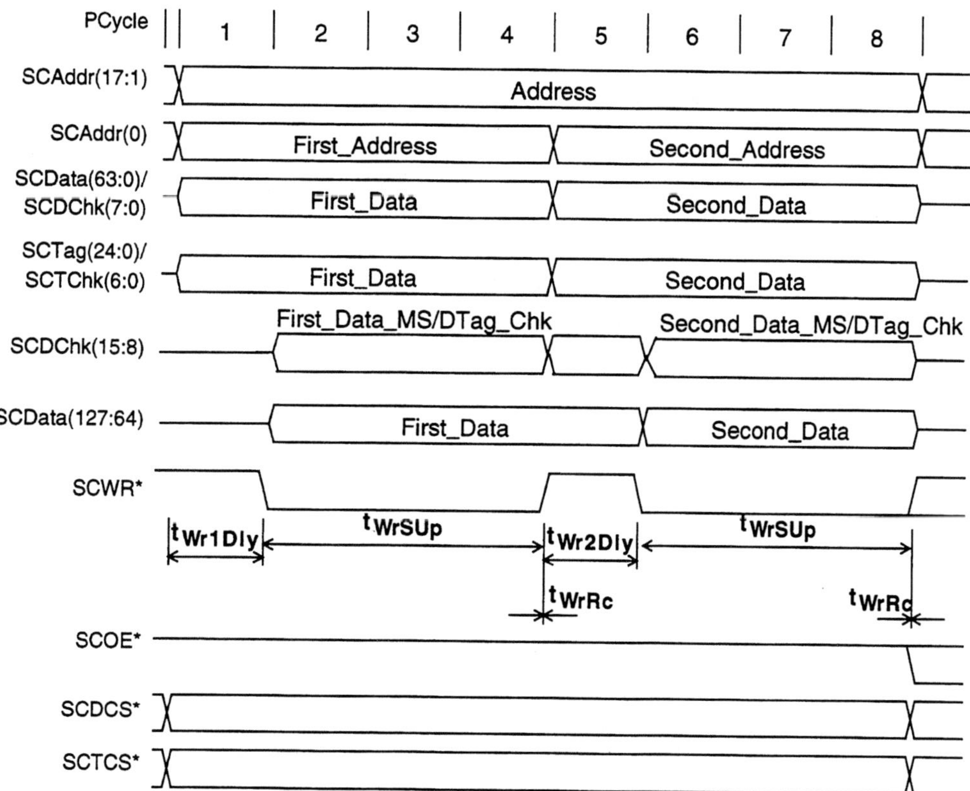

Figure 13-5 Timing Diagram of an 8-Word Write Cycle

Notes on a Secondary Cache Write Cycle

When receiving data from the System interface, the first data doubleword can arrive several cycles before the second data doubleword. In this case, the cache state machine enters a wait-state that extends **SCWR*** until t_{WrSUp} period after the second data item is transmitted.

JTAG Interface

14

The R4000 processor provides a boundary-scan interface that is compatible with Joint Test Action Group (JTAG) specifications, using the industry-standard JTAG protocol.

This chapter describes that interface, including descriptions of boundary scanning, the pins and signals used by the interface, and the Test Access Port (TAP).

14.1 What Boundary Scanning Is

With the evolution of ever-denser integrated circuits (ICs), surface-mounted devices, double-sided component mounting on printed-circuit boards (PCBs), and buried vias, in-circuit tests that depend upon making physical contact with internal board and chip connections have become more and more difficult to use. The greater complexity of ICs has also meant that tests to fully exercise these chips have become much larger and more difficult to write.

One solution to this difficulty has been the development of *boundary-scan* circuits. A boundary-scan circuit is a series of shift register cells placed between each pin and the internal circuitry of the IC to which the pin is connected, as shown in Figure 14-1. Normally, these boundary-scan cells are bypassed; when the IC enters test mode, however, the scan cells can be directed by the test program to pass data along the shift register path and perform various diagnostic tests. To accomplish this, the tests use the four signals described in the next section: **JTDI**, **JTDO**, **JTMS**, and **JTCK**.

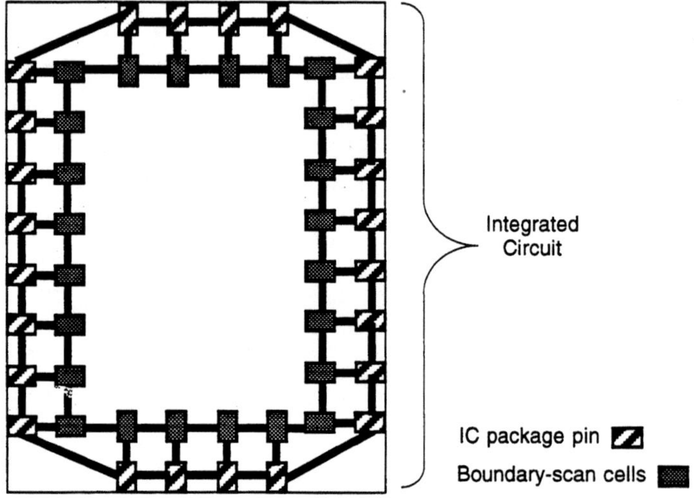

Figure 14-1 JTAG Boundary-scan Cells

14.2 Signal Summary

The JTAG interface signals are listed below and shown in Figure 14-2.

JTDI	JTAG serial data in
JTDO	JTAG serial data out
JTMS	JTAG test mode select
JTCK	JTAG serial clock input

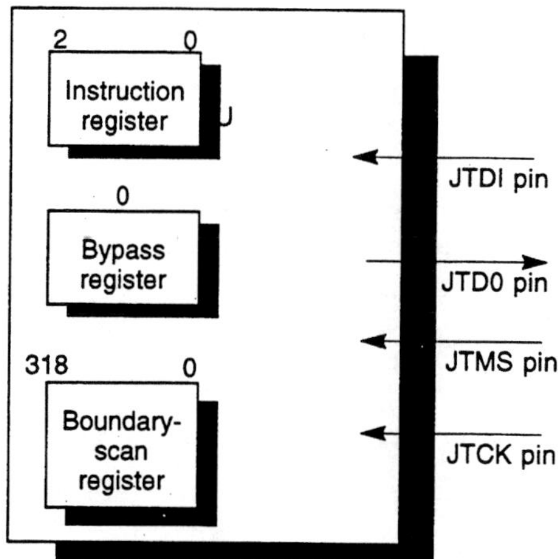

Figure 14-2 JTAG Interface Signals and Registers

The JTAG boundary-scan mechanism (referred to in this chapter as *JTAG mechanism*) allows testing of the connections between the processor, the printed circuit board to which it is attached, and the other components on the circuit board.

In addition, the JTAG mechanism provides rudimentary capability for low-speed logical testing of the secondary cache RAM. The JTAG mechanism does not provide any capability for testing the processor itself.

14.3 JTAG Controller and Registers

The processor contains the following JTAG controller and registers:

- *Instruction* register
- *Boundary-scan* register
- *Bypass* register
- Test Access Port (TAP) controller

The processor executes the standard JTAG EXTEST operation associated with External Test functionality testing.

Instruction Register

The JTAG *Instruction* register includes three shift register-based cells; this register is used to select the test to be performed and/or the test data register to be accessed. As listed in Table 14-1, this encoding selects either the *Boundary-scan* register or the *Bypass* register.

Table 14-1 JTAG Instruction Register Bit Encoding

MSB..... LSB	Data Register
0 0 0	Boundary-scan register (external test only)
x x 1	Bypass register
x 1 x	Bypass register
1 x x	Bypass register

The *Instruction* register has two stages:

- shift register
- parallel output latch

Figure 14-3 shows the format of the *Instruction* register.

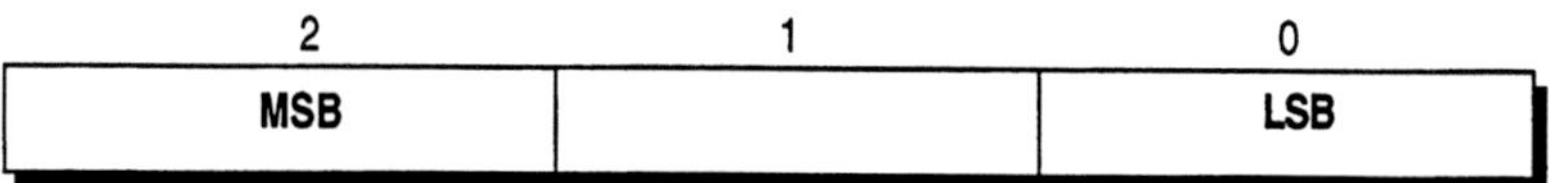

Figure 14-3 Instruction Register

Bypass Register

The *Bypass* register is 1 bit wide. When the TAP controller is in the Shift-DR (Bypass) state, the data on the **JTDI** pin is shifted into the *Bypass* register, and the *Bypass* register output shifts to the **JTDO** output pin.

In essence, the *Bypass* register is a short-circuit which allows bypassing of board-level devices, in the serial boundary-scan chain, which are not required for a specific test. The logical location of the *Bypass* register in the boundary-scan chain is shown in Figure 14-4. Use of the *Bypass* register speeds up access to boundary-scan registers in those ICs that remain active in the board-level test datapath.

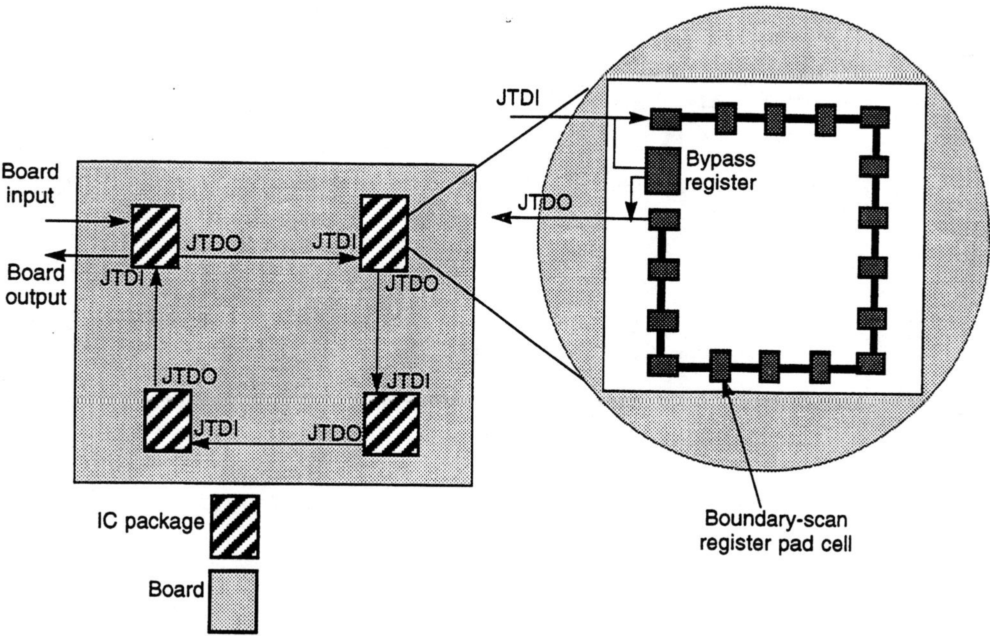

Figure 14-4 Bypass Register Operation

Boundary-Scan Register

The *Boundary-scan* register is a single, 319-bit-wide, shift register-based path containing cells connected to all input and output pads on the R4000 processor. Figure 14-5 shows the three most-significant bits of the *Boundary-scan* register; these three bits control the output enables on the various bidirectional buses.

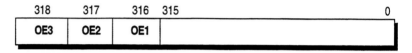

Figure 14-5 Output Enable Bits of the Boundary-scan Register

The most-significant bit, **OE3** (bit 318), is the JTAG output enable bit for the **SysAD, SysADC, SysCmd,** and **SysCmdP** buses. Output is enabled when this bit is set to 1.

OE2 (bit 317) is the JTAG output enable for the **SCData** and **SCDChk** buses. Output is enabled when this bit is set to 1.

OE1 (bit 316) is the JTAG output enable for the **SCTag** and **SCTChk** buses.

The remaining 316 bits correspond to 316 signal pads of the processor. Output is enabled when this bit is set to 1.

At the end of this chapter, Table 14-2 lists the scan order of these 316 scan bits, starting from **JTDI** and ending with **JTDO**.

Test Access Port (TAP)

The Test Access Port (TAP) consists of the four signal pins: **JTDI, JTDO, JTMS,** and **JTCK**. Serial test data and instructions are communicated over these four signal pins, along with control of the test to be executed.

As Figure 14-6 shows, data is serially scanned into one of the three registers (*Instruction* register, *Bypass* register, or the *Boundary-scan* register) from the **JTDI** pin, or it is scanned from one of these three registers onto the **JTDO** pin.

The **JTDI** input feeds the least-significant bit (LSB) of the selected register, whereas the most-significant bit (MSB) of the selected register appears on the **JTDO** output.

The **JTMS** input controls the state transitions of the main TAP controller state machine.

The **JTCK** input is a dedicated test clock that allows serial JTAG data to be shifted synchronously, independent of any chip-specific or system clocks.

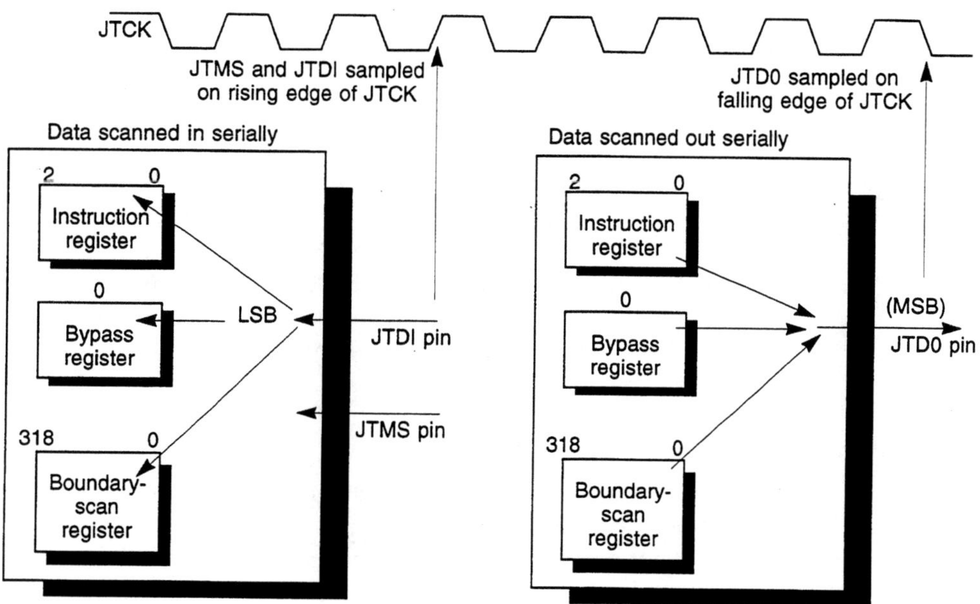

Figure 14-6 JTAG Test Access Port

Data on the **JTDI** and **JTMS** pins is sampled on the rising edge of the **JTCK** input clock signal. Data on the **JTDO** pin changes on the falling edge of the **JTCK** clock signal.

TAP Controller

The processor implements the 16-state TAP controller as defined in the IEEE JTAG specification.

Controller Reset

The TAP controller state machine can be put into Reset state by one of the following:

- deassertion of the **VCCOk** input resets the TAP controller
- keeping the **JTMS** input signal asserted through five consecutive rising edges of **JTCK** input sends the TAP controller state machine into its Reset state.

In either case, keeping **JTMS** asserted maintains the Reset state.

Controller States

The TAP controller has four states: Reset, Capture, Shift, and Update. They can reflect either instructions (as in the Shift-IR state) or data (as in the Capture-DR state).

- When the TAP controller is in the Reset state, the value 0x7 is loaded into the parallel output latch, selecting the *Bypass* register as default. The three most significant bits of the *Boundary-scan* register are cleared to 0, disabling the outputs.
- When the TAP controller is in the Capture-IR state, the value 0x4 is loaded into the shift register stage.
- When the TAP controller is in the Capture-DR (Boundary-scan) state, the data currently on the processor input and I/O pins is latched into the *Boundary-scan* register. In this state, the *Boundary-scan* register bits corresponding to output pins are arbitrary and cannot be checked during the scan out process.
- When the TAP controller is in the Shift-IR state, data is loaded serially into the shift register stage of the *Instruction* register from the **JTDI** input pin, and the MSB of the *Instruction* register's shift register stage is shifted onto the **JTDO** pin.

- When the TAP controller is in the Shift-DR (Boundary-scan) state, data is serially shifted into the *Boundary-scan* register from the **JTDI** pin, and the contents of the *Boundary-scan* register are serially shifted onto the **JTDO** pin.
- When the TAP controller is in the Update-IR state, the current data in the shift register stage is loaded into the parallel output latch.
- When the TAP controller is in the Update-DR (Boundary-scan) state, data in the *Boundary-scan* register is latched into the register parallel output latch. Bits corresponding to output pins, and those I/O pins whose outputs are enabled (by the three MSBs of the *Boundary-scan* register), are loaded onto the processor pins.

Table 14-2 shows the boundary scan order of the processor signals.

Table 14-2 JTAG Scan Order of R4000 Processor Pins

Pin # Signal Name	Pin # Signal Name	Pin # Signal Name	Pin # Signal Name
1. SCDChk(13)	2. SysADC(1)	3. SCDChk(1)	4. SysADC(5)
5. SCDChk(5)	6. Status(0)	7. Status(1)	8. Status(2)
9. Status(3)	10. IvdErr*	11. Status(4)	12. IvdAck*
13. Status(5)	14. Status(6)	15. Status(7)	16. SCDChk(7)
17. SysADC(7)	18. SCDChk(3)	19. SysADC(3)	20. SCDChk(15)
21. VCCOk	22. SCTag(16)	23. SCDChk(11)	24. SCData(63)
25. SysAD(63)	26. SCData(31)	27. SysAD(31)	28. SCData(127)
29. SCTag(17)	30. SCData(95)	31. SCData(62)	32. SysAD(62)
33. SCData(30)	34. SysAD(30)	35. SCData(126)	36. SCTag(18)
37. SCData(94)	38. RClock(1:0) (share the same JTAG bit)	39. SCTag(19)	40. SCData(61)
41. SysAD(61)	42. SCData(29)	43. SysAD(29)	44. SCData(125)
45. Reset*	46. SCTag(20)	47. SCData(93)	48. SCData(60)
49. SysAD(60)	50. SCData(28)	51. SysAD(28)	52. SCData(124)
53. ColdReset*	54. SCTag(21)	55. SCData(92)	56. SCData(59)
57. SysAD(59)	58. SCData(27)	59. SysAD(27)	60. SCData(123)
61. IOIn	62. SCTag(22)	63. SCData(91)	64. SCData(58)
65. SysAD(58)	66. SCData(26)	67. SysAD(26)	68. SCData(122)
69. IOOut	70. SCTag(23)	71. SCData(90)	72. SCData(57)
73. SysAD(57)	74. SCData(25)	75. SysAD(25)	76. SCData(121)
77. GrpRun*	78. SCTag(24)	79. SCData(89)	80. SCData(56)
81. SysAD(56)	82. SCData(24)	83. SysAD(24)	84. SCData(120)
85. GrpStall*	86. SCTChk(0)	87. SCData(88)	88. SCDChk(6)
89. SysADC(6)	90. SCDChk(2)	91. SysADC(2)	92. SCDChk(14)
93. NMI*	94. SCTChk(1)	95. SCDChk(10)	96. SCData(55)

Table 14-2 (cont.) JTAG Scan Order of R4000 Processor Pins

Pin # Signal Name	Pin # Signal Name	Pin # Signal Name	Pin # Signal Name
97. SysAD(55)	98. SCData(23)	99. SysAD(23)	100. SCData(119)
101. Release*	102. SCTChk(2)	103. SCData(87)	104. SCData(54)
105. SysAD(54)	106. SysAD(22)	107. ModeIn	108. SCData(22)
109. RdRdy*	110. SCData(118)	111. SCData(86)	112. SCData(53)
113. SysAD(53)	114. SCData(21)	115. SysAD(21)	116. SCData(117)
117. ExtRqst*	118. SCTChk(3)	119. SCData(85)	120. SCData(52)
121. SysAD(52)	122. SCData(20)	123. SysAD(20)	124. SCData(116)
125. ValidOut*	126. SCTChk(4)	127. SCData(84)	128. SCData(51)
129. SysAD(51)	130. SCData(19)	131. SysAD(19)	132. SCData(115)
133. ValidIn*	134. SCTChk(5)	135. SCData(83)	136. SCAddr0W,X (share the same JTAG bit)
137. SCAddr0Y,Z (share the same JTAG bit)	138. SCAddr(1)	139. SCData(50)	140. SysAD(50)
141. SCData(18)	142. SysAD(18)	143. SCData(114)	144. Int*(0)
145. SCTChk(6)	146. SCData(82)	147. SCData(49)	148. SysAD(49)
149. SCData(17)	150. SysAD(17)	151. SCData(113)	152. SCAddr(2)/Int*(1)
153. SCAddr(3)	154. SCData(81)	155. SCData(48)	156. SysAD(48)
157. SCData(16)	158. SysAD(16)	159. SCData(112)	160. SCAddr(4)/Int*(2)
161. SCAddr(5)	162. SCData(80)	163. SCAddr(6)	164. SCAddr(7)
165. SCAddr(8)	166. SCAddr(9)	167. SCAddr(10)	168. SCAddr(11)
169. SC64Addr	170. SCAddr(12)	171. SCAddr(13)	172. SCAddr(14)
173. SCAddr(15)	174. SCAddr(16)	175. SCAddr(17)	176. SCData(64)
177. SCAPar(0)	178. SCAPar(1)/Int*(3)	179. SCData(96)	180. SysAD(0)
181. SCData(0)	182. SysAD(32)	183. SCData(32)	184. SCData(65)
185. SCAPar(2)	186. SCOE*/Int*(4)	187. SCData(97)	188. SysAD(1)
189. SCData(1)	190. SysAD(33)	191. SCData(33)	192. SCData(66)
193. SCDCS*	194. SCTCS*/Int*(5)	195. SCData(98)	196. SysAD(2)
197. SCData(2)	198. SysAD(34)	199. SCData(34)	200. SCTag(0)
201. SCWrW,X* (share the same JTAG bit)	202. SCWrY,Z* (share the same JTAG bit)	203. SCData(67)	204. SCTag(1)
205. SysCmd(0)	206. SCData(99)	207. SysAD(3)	208. SCData(3)
209. SysAD(35)	210. SCData(35)	211. SCData(68)	212. SCTag(2)
213. SysCmd(1)	214. SCData(100)	215. SysAD(4)	216. SCData(4)
217. SysAD(36)	218. SCData(36)	219. SCData(69)	220. SCTag(3)
221. SysCmd(2)	222. SCData(101)	223. SysAD(5)	224. SCData(5)

Table 14-2 (cont.) JTAG Scan Order of R4000 Processor Pins

Pin # Signal Name	Pin # Signal Name	Pin # Signal Name	Pin # Signal Name
225. SysAD(37)	226. SCData(37)	227. SCData(70)	228. WrRdy*
229. ModeClock	230. SCData(102)	231. SysAD(6)	232. SCData(6)
233. SysAD(38)	234. SCData(38)	235. SCData(71)	236. SCTag(4)
237. SysCmd(3)	238. SCData(103)	239. SysAD(7)	240. SCData(7)
241. SysAD(39)	242. SCData(39)	243. SCDChk(8)	244. SCTag(5)
245. SysCmd(4)	246. SCDChk(12)	247. SysADC(0)	248. SCDChk(0)
249. SysADC(4)	250. SCDChk(4)	251. SCData(72)	252. SCTag(6)
253. SysCmd(5)	254. SCData(104)	255. SysAD(8)	256. SCData(8)
257. SysAD(40)	258. SCData(40)	259. SCData(73)	260. SCTag(7)
261. SysCmd(6)	262. SCData(105)	263. SysAD(9)	264. SCData(9)
265. SysAD(41)	266. SCData(41)	267. SCData(74)	268. SCTag(8)
269. SysCmd(7)	270. SCData(106)	271. SysAD(10)	272. SCData(10)
273. SysAD(42)	274. SCData(42)	275. SCData(75)	276. SCTag(9)
277. SysCmd(8)	278. SCData(107)	279. SysAD(11)	280. SCData(11)
281. SysAD(43)	282. SCData(43)	283. SCData(76)	284. SCTag(10)
285. SysCmdP	286. SCData(108)	287. SysAD(12)	288. SCData(12)
289. SysAD(44)	290. SCData(44)	291. SCData(77)	292. SCTag(11)
293. Fault*	294. SCData(109)	295. SysAD(13)	296. SCData(13)
297. SysAD(45)	298. SCData(45)	299. SCTag(12)	300. TClock(1:0) (share the same JTAG bit)
301. SCData(78)	302. SCTag(13)	303. SCData(110)	304. SysAD(14)
305. SCData(14)	306. SysAD(46)	307. SCData(46)	308. SCData(79)
309. SCTag(14)	310. SCData(111)	311. SysAD(15)	312. SCData(15)
313. SysAD(47)	314. SCData(47)	315. SCDChk(9)	316. SCTag(15)†

†See the section titled Boundary-Scan Register earlier in this chapter, for a description of the last three output enable bits, 319:317.

14.4 Implementation-Specific Details

This section describes details of JTAG boundary-scan operation that are specific to the processor.

- The **MasterClock**, **MasterOut**, **SyncIn**, and **SyncOut** signal pads do not support JTAG.
- The following pairs of output pads share a single JTAG bit:

  SCAddr0W *and* **SCAddr0X**
  SCAddr0Y *and* **SCAddr0Z**
  SCWrW* *and* **SCWrX***
  SCWrY* *and* **SCWrZ***
  TClock(0) *and* **TClock(1)**
  RClock(0) *and* **RClock(1)**

- All input pads data are first latched into a processor clock-based register in the pad cell before they are captured into the Boundary-scan register in the Capture-DR (Boundary-scan) state. When the phase-locked loop is disabled, the processor clock is half the frequency of **MasterClock**. Therefore, when the TAP controller is in the Capture-DR (Boundary-scan) state, the data setup required at the input pads is more than two **MasterClock** periods before the rising edge of the **JTCK**.
- The output enable controls generated from the three most-significant bits of the *Boundary-scan* register are latched into a Processor Clock-based register before they actually enable the data onto the pads. Therefore, the delay from the rising edge of **JTCK** in the Update-DR (Boundary-scan) state to data valid at the output pins of the chip is greater than two **MasterClock** periods.

R4000 Processor Interrupts

15

The R4000 processor supports the following interrupts: six hardware interrupts, one internal "timer interrupt," two software interrupts, and one nonmaskable interrupt. The processor takes an exception on any interrupt.

This chapter describes the six hardware and single nonmaskable interrupts. A description of the software and the timer interrupts can be found in Chapter 5. CPU exception processing is also described in Chapter 5.

Floating-point exception processing is described in Chapter 6.

15.1 Hardware Interrupts

The six CPU hardware interrupts can be caused by external write requests to the R4000SC, R4000MC, and R4000PC, or can be caused through dedicated interrupt pins. These pins are latched into an internal register by the rising edge of **SClock**. The R4000MC and R4000SC packages support a single interrupt pin, **Int*(0)**. The R4000PC package supports six interrupt pins, **Int*(5:0)**.

15.2 Nonmaskable Interrupt (NMI)

The nonmaskable interrupt is caused either by an external write request to the R4000 or by a dedicated pin in the R4000. This pin is latched into an internal register by the rising edge of **SClock**.

15.3 Asserting Interrupts

External writes to the CPU are directed to various internal resources, based on an internal address map of the processor. When **SysAD[6:4]** = 0, an external write to any address writes to an architecturally transparent register called the *Interrupt* register; this register is available for external write cycles, but not for external reads.

During a data cycle, **SysAD[22:16]** are the write enables for the seven individual *Interrupt* register bits and **SysAD[6:0]** are the values to be written into these bits. This allows any subset of the *Interrupt* register to be set or cleared with a single write request. Figure 15-1 shows the mechanics of an external write to the *Interrupt* register.

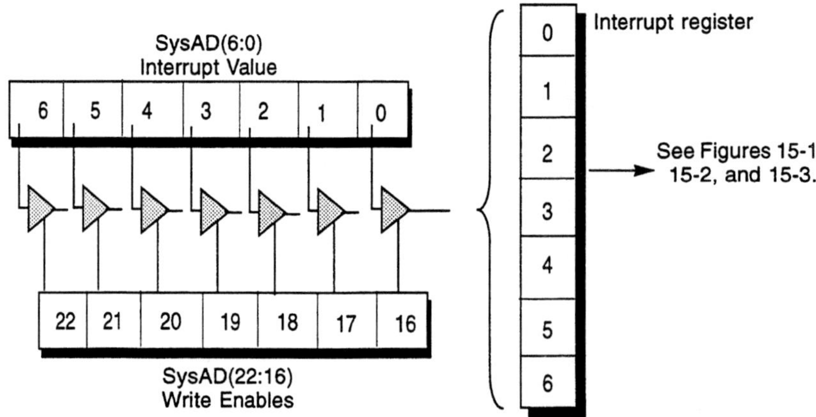

Figure 15-1 Interrupt Register Bits and Enables

Figure 15-2 shows how the R4000SC and R4000MC interrupts are readable through the *Cause* register.

- Bit 5 of the *Interrupt* register in the R4000SC and R4000MC is multiplexed with the **TimerInterrupt** signal and the result is directly readable as bit 15 of the *Cause* register.
- Bits 4:1 of the *Interrupt* register are directly readable as bits 14:11 of the *Cause* register.
- Bit 0 of the *Interrupt* register is latched into the internal register by the rising edge of **SClock**, then ORed with the **Int*(0)** pin, and the result is directly readable as bit 10 of the *Cause* register.

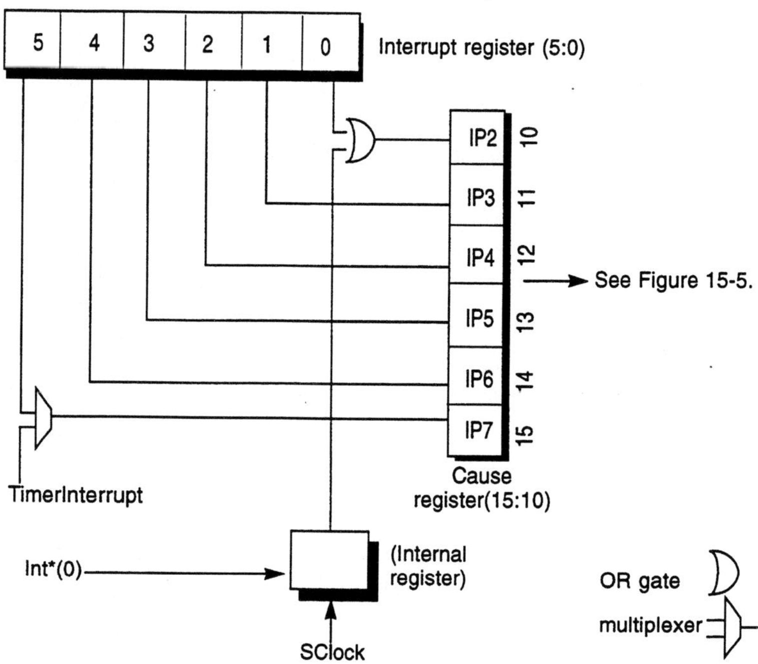

Figure 15-2 R4000SC/MC Interrupt Signals

Figure 15-3 shows how the R4000PC interrupts are readable through the *Cause* register. The interrupt bits, **Int*(5:0)**, are latched into the internal register by the rising edge of **SClock.**

- Bit 5 of the *Interrupt* register in the R4000PC is ORed with the **Int*(5)** pin and then multiplexed with the **TimerInterrupt** signal. This result is directly readable as bit 15 of the *Cause* register.
- Bits 4:0 of the *Interrupt* register are bit-wise ORed with the current value of the interrupt pins **Int*[4:0]** and the result is directly readable as bits 14:10 of the *Cause* register.

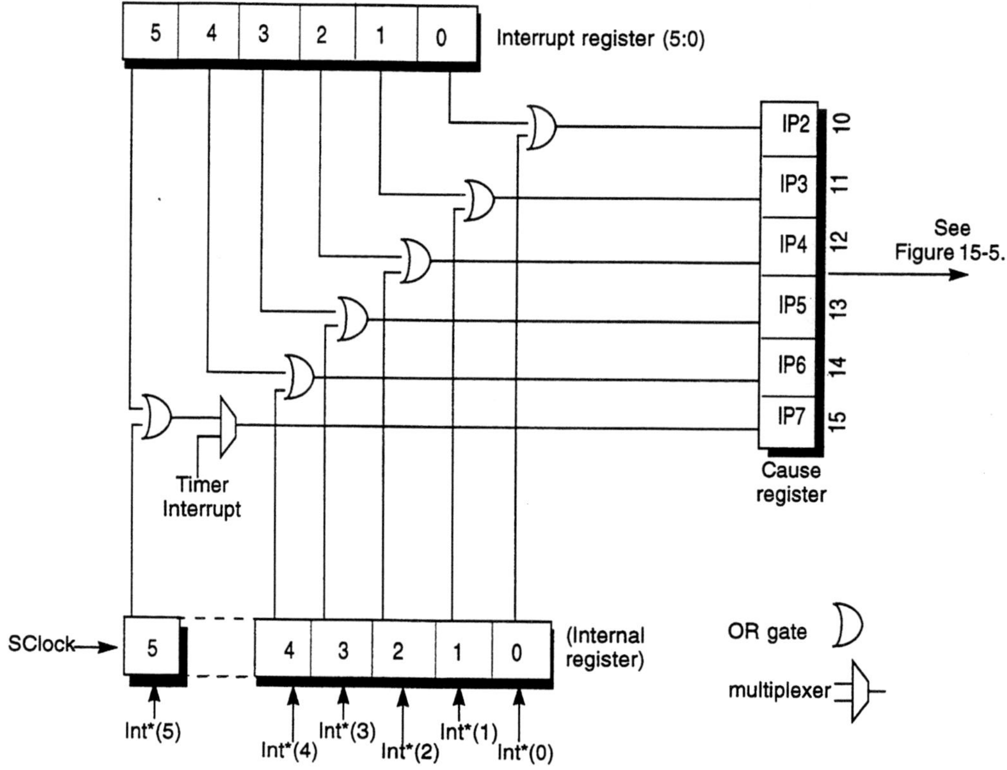

Figure 15-3 R4000PC Interrupt Signals

Figure 15-4 shows the internal derivation of the **NMI** signal, for all versions of the R4000 processor.

The **NMI*** pin is latched into an internal register by the rising edge of **SClock**. Bit 6 of the *Interrupt* register is then ORed with the inverted value of **NMI*** to form the nonmaskable interrupt.

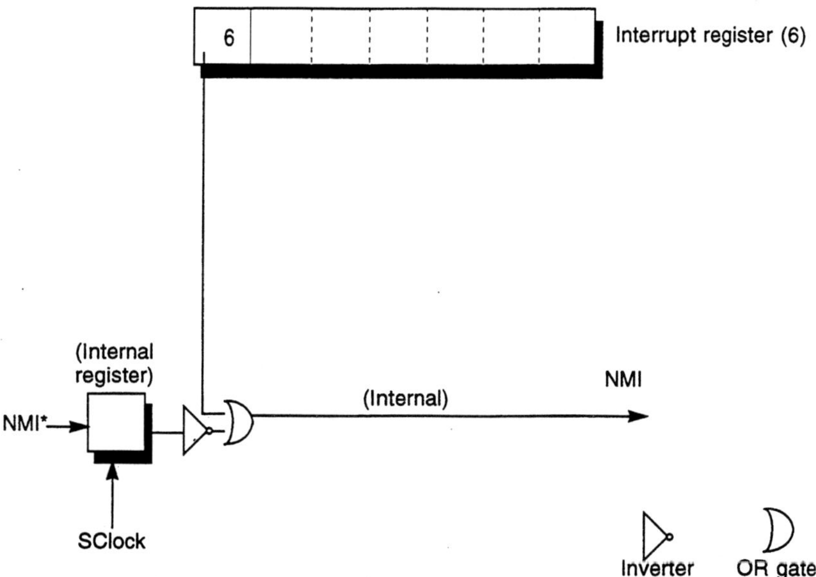

Figure 15-4 R4000 Nonmaskable Interrupt Signal

Figure 15-5 shows the masking of the R4000 interrupt signal.

- *Cause* register bits 15:8 (IP7-IP0) are AND-ORed with *Status* register interrupt mask bits 15:8 (IM7-IM0) to mask individual interrupts.
- *Status* register bit 0 is a global Interrupt Enable (IE). It is ANDed with the output of the AND-OR logic to produce the R4000 interrupt signal.

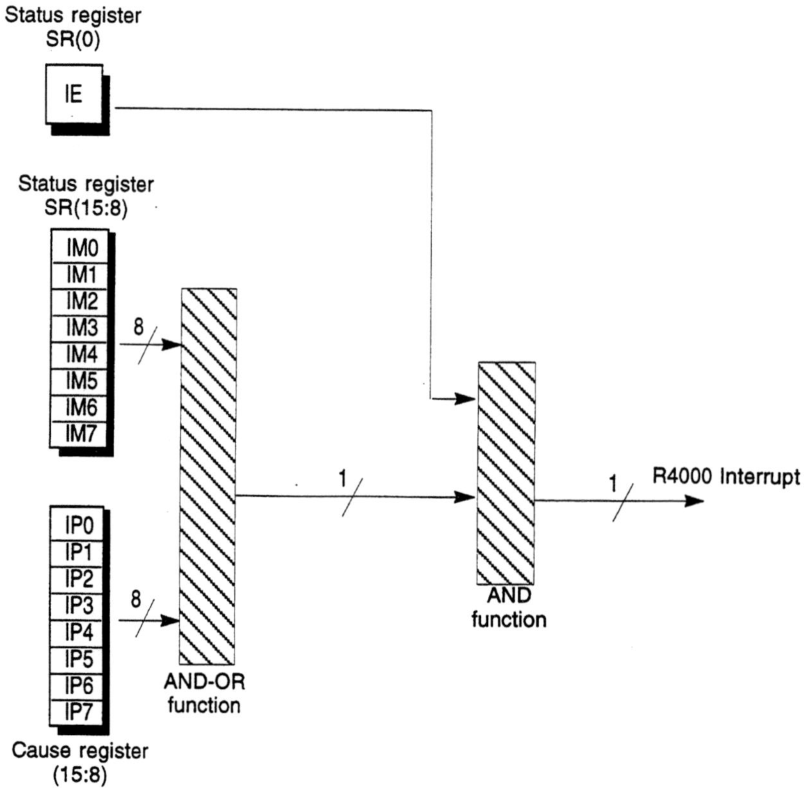

Figure 15-5 Masking of the R4000 Interrupt

Error Checking and Correcting

16

This chapter describes the Error Checking and Correcting (ECC) mechanism used in both the R4000 and R4400 processors.

This chapter also contains a description of the Master/Checker mode used in the R4400 processor.

16.1 Error Checking in the Processor

ECC code allows the processor to detect and sometimes correct errors made when moving data from one place to another.

Two major types of data errors can occur in data transmission:

- hard errors, which are permanent, arise from broken interconnects, internal shorts, or open leads
- soft errors, which are transient, are caused by system noise, power surges, and alpha particles.

Hard errors must be corrected by physical repair of the damaged equipment and restoration of data from backup. Soft errors can be corrected by using error checking and correcting codes.

Types of Error Checking

The processor uses two types of error checking: parity (error detection only), and single-bit error correction/double-bit error detection (SECDED).

Parity Error Detection

Parity is the simplest error detection scheme. By appending a bit to the end of an item of data—called a *parity bit*—single bit errors can be detected; however, these errors cannot be corrected.

There are two types of parity:

- **Odd Parity** adds 1 to any even number of 1s in the data, making the total number of 1s odd (including the parity bit).
- **Even Parity** adds 1 to any odd number of 1s in the data, making the total number of 1s even (including the parity bit).

Odd and even parity are shown in the example below:

Data(3:0)	Odd Parity Bit	Even Parity Bit
0 0 1 0	0	1

The example above shows a single bit in **Data(3:0)** with a value of 1; this bit is **Data(1)**.

- In even parity, the parity bit is set to 1. This makes 2 (an even number) the total number of bits with a value of 1.
- Odd parity makes the parity bit a 0 to keep the total number of 1-value bits an odd number—in the case shown above, the single bit **Data(1)**.

The example below shows odd and even parity bits for various data values:

Data(3:0)	Odd Parity Bit	Even Parity Bit
0 1 1 0	1	0
0 0 0 0	1	0
1 1 1 1	1	0
1 1 0 1	0	1

Parity allows single-bit error detection, but it does not indicate which bit is in error—for example, suppose an odd-parity value of 00011 arrives. The last bit is the parity bit, and since odd parity demands an odd number (1,3,5) of 1s, this data is in error: it has an even number of 1s. However it is impossible to tell *which* bit is in error. To resolve this problem, SECDED ECC was developed.

SECDED ECC Code

The ECC code chosen for processor secondary cache data and tag is single-bit error correction and double-bit error detection (SECDED) code.† SECDED ECC code is an improvement upon the parity scheme; not only does it detect single- and certain multi-bit errors, it corrects single-bit errors.

† The 64-bit data code is a modification of one of the 64-bit codes proposed by M. Y. Hsiao, to include the ability to detect 3- and 4-bit errors within a nibble. The 25-bit tag code was created using the patterns observed in the 64-bit data code.

Secondary Cache Data Bus SECDED Code

The SECDED code protecting secondary cache data bus has the properties listed below:

- It corrects single-bit errors.
- It detects double-bit errors.
- It detects 3- or 4-bit errors within a nibble.
- It provides 64 data bits protected by 8 check bits, and yields 8-bit syndromes (the *syndrome* is a generated value used to detect an error, and locate the position of the single bit in error).
- It is a minimal-length code; each parity tree used to generate the 8-bit syndrome has only 27 inputs, the minimum number possible.
- It provides byte Exclusive-ORs (XORs) of the data bits as part of the XOR trees used to build the parity generators. This allows selection of byte parity out of the XOR trees that generate or check the code.
- Single-bit errors are indicated either by syndromes that contain exactly three 1s, or by syndromes that contain exactly five 1s (in which bits 0-3 or bits 4-7 of the syndrome are all 1s).†
- Double-bit errors are indicated by syndromes that contain an even number of 1s.
- 3-bit errors within a nibble are indicated by syndromes that contain five 1s, in which bits 0-3 of the syndrome and bits 4-7 of the syndrome are not all 1s.
- 4-bit errors within a nibble are indicated by syndromes that contain four 1s. Because this is an even number of 1s, 4-bit errors within a nibble look like double-bit errors.

† This makes it possible to decode the syndrome to find which data bit is in error, using 4-input NAND gates, provided a pre-decode AND of bits 0-3 and bits 4-7 of the syndrome is available. For the check bits, a full 8-bit decode of the syndrome is required.

Secondary Cache Tag Bus SECDED Code

The SECDED ECC code protecting the secondary cache tag bus has the following properties:

- It corrects single-bit errors.
- It detects double-bit errors.
- It detects 3- or 4-bit errors within a nibble.
- It provides 25 data bits protected by 7 check bits, yielding 7-bit syndromes.
- It provides byte XORs of the data bits as part of the XOR trees used to build the parity generators. This allows selection of byte parity out of the XOR trees that generate or check the code.
- Single-bit errors are indicated by syndromes that contain exactly three 1s. This makes it possible to decode the syndrome to find which data bit is in error with 3-input NAND gates. For the check bits, a full 7-bit decode of the syndrome is required.
- Double-bit errors are indicated by syndromes that contain an even number of 1s.
- 3-bit errors within a nibble are indicated by syndromes that contain either five 1s or seven 1s.
- 4-bit errors within a nibble are indicated by syndromes that contain either four 1s or six 1s. Because these are even numbers of 1s, 4-bit errors within a nibble look like double-bit errors.

Error Checking Operation

The processor verifies data correctness by using either the parity or the SECDED code as it passes data from the System interface to the secondary cache, or it moves data from the secondary cache to the primary caches or to the System interface.

System Interface

The processor generates correct check bits for doubleword, word, or partial-word data transmitted to the System interface. As it checks for data correctness, the processor passes data check bits from the secondary cache, directly without changing the bits, to the System interface.

The processor does not check data received from the System interface for external updates and external writes. By setting the *NChck* bit in the data identifier, it is possible to prevent the processor from checking read response data from the System interface.

The processor does not check addresses received from the System interface, but does generate correct check bits for addresses transmitted to the System interface.

The processor does not contain a data corrector; instead, the processor takes a cache error exception when it detects an error based on data check bits. Software, in conjunction with an off-processor data corrector, is responsible for correcting the data when SECDED code is employed.

Secondary Cache Data Bus

The 16 check bits, **SCDChk(15:0)**, for the 128-bit secondary cache data bus are organized as 8 check bits for the upper 64 bits of data, and 8 check bits for the lower 64 bits of data.

System Interface and Secondary Cache Data Bus

The 8 check bits, **SysADC(7:0)**, for the System interface address and data bus provide even-byte parity, or are generated in accordance with a SECDED code that also detects any 3- or 4-bit error in a nibble. The 8 check bits for each half of the secondary cache data bus are always generated in accordance with the SECDED code.

Secondary Cache Tag Bus

The 7 check bits, **SCTChk(6:0)**, for the secondary cache tag bus are generated in accordance with the SECDED code, which also detects any 3- or 4-bit error in a nibble.

The processor generates check bits for the tag when it is written into the secondary cache and checks the tag whenever the secondary cache is accessed.

The processor contains a corrector for the secondary cache tag; the tag corrector is not in-line for processor accesses due to primary cache misses. The processor traps when a tag error is detected on a processor access due to a primary cache miss. Software, using the processor cache management primitives, is responsible for correcting the tag. When executing the cache management primitives, the processor uses the corrected tag to generate write back addresses and cache state.

For external accesses, the tag corrector is in-line; that is, the response to external accesses is based on the corrected tag. The processor still traps on tag errors detected during external accesses to allow software to repair the contents of the cache if possible.

System Interface Command Bus

In the R4000 processor, the System interface command bus has a single parity bit, **SysCmdP**, that provides even parity over the 9 bits of this bus. The **SysCmdP** parity bit is generated when the System interface is in master state, but it is not checked when the System interface is in slave state. In the R4400 processor, input parity is reported through the **Fault*** pin.

SECDED ECC Matrices for Data and Tag Buses

The check matrices for data and tags, specifying the distribution of data and check bits across nibbles, are shown in Figures 16-1 and 16-4.

The data bits in Figure 16-1 correspond to **SysAD(63:0)**, **SCData(127:64)**, or **SCData(63:0)**. The check bits in Figure 16-1 correspond to **SysADC(7:0)**, **SCDChk(15:8)**, or **SCDChk(7:0)**.

The check bits in Figure 16-4, shown later in this chapter, correspond to **SCTChk(6:0)** and the data bits in Figure 16-4 correspond to **SCTag(24:0)**.

The parity check matrices shown in these two figures generate the ECC code for a fixed-width data word; they can also locate the data bit in error. In Figure 16-1, the data word length is 64 bits; in Figure 16-4, the data word length is 25 bits.

ECC Check Bits

The R4000 processor provides the following check bits: 16 check bits, **SCDChk(15:0)**, are used for the secondary cache data bus; 7 check bits, **SCTChk(6:0)**, are used for the secondary cache tag bus; 8 check bits, **SysADC(7:0)**, are used for the System interface address and data bus; a single parity bit, **SysCmdP**, is used for the System interface command bus.

In the R4400 processor, the **Fault*** pin reports data parity or any ECC errors received from the System interface during an external update or an external write. The **Fault*** pin also reports errors among the address bits received from the System interface. In each case, the full 64-bit data and 8-bit ECC are significant. This checking is not affected by the state of the disable bit [**SysCmd(4)**] in the data identifier. No exceptions are generated for these checks.

Data ECC Generation

Each of the 64 data bits and 8 check bits has a unique 8-bit SECDED ECC check code; this check code is generated by taking the even parity of the ECC check code for a selected group of data bits. As Figure 16-1 shows, bit locations are numbered from right to left in ascending order, from data bit 0 (furthest right) to data bit 63 (furthest left). For example, data bit 0, in the far right column of Figure 16-1, has an 8-bit check value of 0001 0011_2 (0s are represented in this figure by periods, (.), because they are not used in the calculations).

Figure 16-1 also gives values for the 8 check bits, 7:0. For instance, the 8-bit SECDED ECC code for check bit 6 is in column 6, near the right hand edge of Figure 16-1.

Data bit 63 — Check bit 6 — Data bit 0

heck Bit			43		52											70		61	
ata Bit		6666 3210	55 98	5555 7654	55 32	5544 1098	4444 7654	4444 3210	3333 9876	3333 5432	3322 1098	2222 7654	2222 3210	1111 9876	1111 5432	11 10	9876	54	3210
MSB	27	1111	11..	11..	1...	1...	....	1111	1111	....	1...	1...	1...	1...	....	1.1.	.1..	1...	1...
	27	1111	1...	1...	1...	.1..	....	....	....	1111	.1..	.1..	.1..	.1..	1111	11..	11..	1.1.	.1..
CC	27	....	1...	11..	1.1.	..1.	1111	1111	....	....	..1.	..1.	..1.	..1.	1111	1...	1...	11..	..1.
ode	27	....	1.1.	.1..	11..	...1	1111	....	1111	1111	...1	...1	...1	...1	....	1...	11..	1...	...1
ts	27	1...	.1.1	..11	.1..	....	1...	1...	1...	1...	1111	1111	....	1111	1...	11..	...1	.1..	....
	27	.1..	11..	..1.	.1.1	1111	.1..	.1..	.1..	.1..	....	....	1111	1111	.1..	.1..	..11	.1..	....
	27	..1.	.1..	..11	11..	1111	..1.	..1.	..1.	..1.	1111	....	....	....	..1.	.1..	..1.	.1.1	1111
LSB	27	...1	.1..	...1	.1..	....	...1	...1	...1	...1	....	1111	1111	....	...1	.1.1	..11	11..	1111
umber of s in ndrome*		3333	5511	3333	5511	3333	3333	3333	3333	3333	3333	3333	3333	3333	3333	5511	3333	5511	3333

Figure 16-1 Check Matrix for Data ECC Code

NOTE: * This row indicates the number of 1s in the generated syndrome for each data bit in error.

As an example of this process, SECDED ECC for **Data(63:0)** = 0x0000 0000 0000 0001 is generated in the steps below.

1. Find any bits in **Data(63:0)** having a value of 1.

   To determine this, the 16-bit hexadecimal value of 0x0000 0000 0000 0001 must be expanded to its 64-bit binary equivalent before locating the data bit(s) with a value of 1. In this case, the only 1-value in 0x0000 0000 0000 0001 is in column 0.

2. Find the check bits in column 0.

   They are 0001 0011_2.

3. Take even parity of check bits 0001 0011_2.

	ECC	Parity (even)
MSB (7)	0	0
(6)	0	0
(5)	0	0
(4)	1	1
(3)	0	0
(2)	0	0
(1)	1	1
LSB (0)	1	1

4. This even parity value, 0001 0011_2, is sent out over the bus as ECC check bits, **ECC(7:0)**.

The following example uses data with several 1-value bits: **Data(63:0)** = 0x0000 0000 0000 0043.

1. Expand the data to its binary equivalent in order to generate the ECC check bits.

   0x0000 0000 0000 0043 has 1s in the last byte only. The last byte binary value is: 0x43 = $0100\ 0011_2$.

   ```
   column #    7654 3210
   0x0043 =    0100 0011₂
   ```

   Since only columns 0, 1, and 6 have 1s, they are the only columns that can generate the even parity bits.

2. Using Figure 16-1, generate even parity for the ECC check codes in columns 0, 1, and 6:

Column 0 ECC	Column 1 ECC	Column 6 ECC	Parity (even)
0	0	0	0
0	0	0	0
0	1	0	1
1	0	0	1
0	0	1	1
0	0	1	1
1	1	0	0
1	1	0	0

3. This parity value, $0011\ 1100_2$, is sent out over the **ECC(7:0)** check bus.

Detecting Data Transmission Errors

The following procedure detects data transmission errors.

1. System A transmits a 64-bit doubleword together with 8 bits of SECDED ECC (see Figure 16-2).

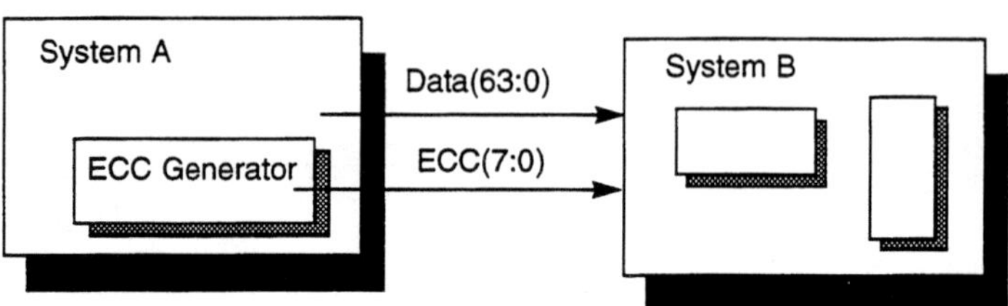

Figure 16-2 Detecting ECC Errors: Transmitting Data and ECC

2. System B receives the data doubleword, together with the byte of ECC check code.
3. To verify proper transmission of the 64-bit doubleword and 8-bit ECC check code, system B generates its own 8-bit ECC check code from the 64-bit doubleword of System A, as shown in Figure 16-3.
4. System B executes an Exclusive-OR (XOR) on the check bits of System A with its own newly-generated ECC check bits, (see Figure 16-3). The output of this XOR is called the *syndrome.*

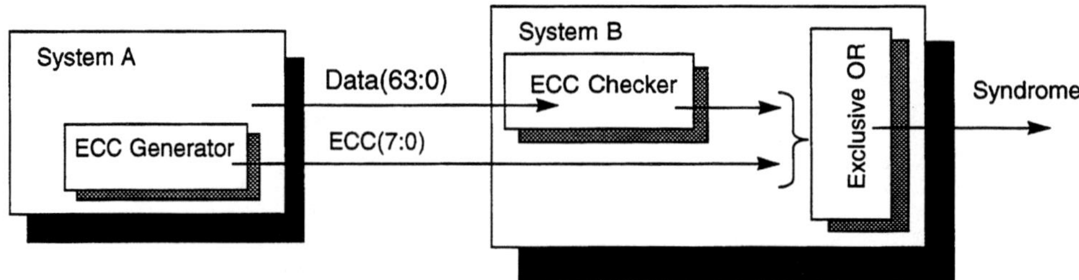

Figure 16-3 Detecting ECC Errors: Deriving the Syndrome

5. If the syndrome is $0000\ 0000_2$, the data System B received, together with the newly-generated ECC check bits from System B, are the same as the data and check bits from System A. If the syndrome is any other value than $0000\ 0000_2$, it is assumed either the received word or the received check bits are in error.

6. Using the data in Figure 16-1, it may be possible to correct either the data bit or check bit in error. Determine if the syndrome is in Figure 16-1 by counting the number on 1s in the syndrome.

    - If the syndrome contains either one, three, or five 1s, the syndrome is in Figure 16-1. Three or five 1s indicates that at least one data bit is in error. A single 1 indicates an ECC check bit is in error.
    - If the syndrome contains two 1s, a double-bit error has been detected, located in two consecutive bits of a nibble. This is not correctable.
    - If the syndrome contains four 1s, a 4-bit error has been detected, located in four consecutive bits of a nibble. This is not correctable.

    If the syndrome is identical to any of the syndromes in the Figure 16-1, the column number of that data or check bit indicates the location of the bit in error. The bit that is in error is corrected by inverting its state (a 1 is changed to 0; a 0 is changed to 1).

The following sections show how to use the check matrices in Figure 16-1 for detecting:

- single data bit error
- single data check bit error
- multiple data bit errors (2 consecutive bits in a nibble)
- multiple data bit errors (3 consecutive bits in a nibble)
- multiple data bit errors (4 consecutive bits in a nibble)

Single Data Bit ECC Error

The following procedure detects and corrects a single data bit ECC error.

1. System A transmits:

   Data(63:0) = 0x0000 0000 0000 0000

   and

   ECC(7:0) check code = $0000\ 0000_2$

2. System B receives the following incorrect data:

   Data(63:0) = 0x0000 0000 0000 0001

   and

   ECC(7:0) check code = $0000\ 0000_2$

3. System B regenerates ECC for the received data. The correct ECC check code for:

   Data(63:0) = 0x0000 0000 0000 0001

   is

   ECC(7:0) = $0001\ 0011_2$

4. A syndrome is generated by the XOR of the System A check bits, $0000\ 0000_2$, and the System B regenerated check bits, $0001\ 0011_2$. The resulting syndrome is $0001\ 0011_2$. Since the syndrome has three 1s, look for the column with three 1s in the parity check matrix table.
5. Searching the matrix (Figure 16-1) shows that the syndrome, $0001\ 0011_2$, corresponds to data bit 0. This means the state of received data bit 0 is incorrect.
6. To correct the error, the system inverts the state of the received data bit 0 from a value of 1 to 0.

Single Check Bit ECC Error

The following procedure detects and corrects a single check bit ECC error.

1. System A transmits:

   Data(63:0) = 0x0000 0000 0000 0000

   and

   ECC(7:0) check code = $0000\ 0000_2$

2. System B receives the following incorrect check code:

   Data(63:0) = 0x0000 0000 0000 0000

   and

   ECC(7:0) check code = $0000\ 0001_2$

3. System B regenerates the ECC for the received data. The correct ECC check code for:

   Data(63:0) = 0x0000 0000 0000 0000

   is

   ECC(7:0) = $0000\ 0000_2$

4. A syndrome is generated by the XOR of the System A check bits, $0000\ 0001_2$, and the System B regenerated check bits, $0000\ 0000_2$. The resulting syndrome is $0000\ 0001_2$.

   Since the syndrome has a single 1, it is contained in the check matrix. Figure 16-1 shows that the syndrome, $0000\ 0001_2$, corresponds to check bit 0. This indicates that the state of the received check bit 0 is incorrect. To correct the error, the system inverts the state of the received check bit 0 from a value of 1 to 0.

Double Data Bit ECC Errors

The following procedure detects double data bit ECC errors.

1. System A transmits:

   Data(63:0) = 0x0000 0000 0000 0000

   and

   ECC(7:0) check code = $0000\ 0000_2$.

2. System B receives the following incorrect data:

   Data(63:0) = 0x0000 0000 0000 0011

   and

   ECC(7:0) check code = $0000\ 0000_2$

3. System B regenerates the ECC for the received data. The correct ECC check code for:

   Data(63:0) = 0x0000 0000 0000 0011

   is

   ECC(7:0) = $0011\ 0000_2$

4. A syndrome is generated by the XOR of the System A check bits, $0000\ 0000_2$, and the System B regenerated check bits, $0011\ 0000_2$. The resulting syndrome is $0011\ 0000_2$.

   The syndrome of two 1s (or an even number of 1s) indicates that a double-bit error has been detected. Double-bit errors cannot be corrected.

Three Data Bit ECC Errors

The following procedure detects three data bit errors that occur within a nibble.

1. System A transmits:

   Data(63:0) = 0x0000 0000 0000 0000

   and

   ECC(7:0) check code = $0000\ 0000_2$

2. System B receives the following incorrect data:

   Data(63:0) = 0x0000 0000 0000 0111

   and

   ECC(7:0) check code = $0000\ 0000_2$

3. System B regenerates the ECC for the received data. The ECC check code for:

   Data(63:0) = 0x0000 0000 0000 0111

   is

   ECC(7:0) = $0111\ 0011_2$

4. A syndrome is generated by the XOR of the System A check bits, $0000\ 0000_2$, and the System B regenerated check bits, $0111\ 0011_2$. The resulting syndrome is $0111\ 0011_2$.

   The resulting syndrome has five 1s. Since no four of the 1s are contained in check bits (7:4) or check bits (3:0), three errors have occurred within a nibble. Triple-bit errors within a nibble cannot be corrected.

Four Data Bit ECC Errors

The following procedure detects four data bit errors that occur within a nibble.

1. System A transmits:

   Data(63:0) = 0x0000 0000 0000 0000

   and

   ECC(7:0) check code = $0000\ 0000_2$

2. System B receives the following incorrect data:

   Data(63:0) = 0x0000 0000 0000 1111

   and

   ECC(7:0) check code = $0000\ 0000_2$

3. System B regenerates the ECC for the received data. The ECC check code for:

   Data(63:0) = 0x0000 0000 0000 1111

   is

   ECC(7:0) = $1111\ 0000_2$

4. A syndrome is generated by the XOR of the System A check bits, $0000\ 0000_2$, and the System B regenerated check bits, $1111\ 0000_2$. The resulting syndrome is $1111\ 0000_2$.

   Since the resulting syndrome has four 1s (or an even number of 1s), this error is recognized as some variation of a double-bit error. A 4-bit error within a nibble cannot be corrected.

Tag ECC Generation

The 25-bit tag ECC check matrix is similar to the 64-bit data check matrix; the main difference is the number of check bits used and the manner in which the errors are decoded. Figure 16-4 shows the check matrix for the tag bits.

Check Bit	0	12	34	56				
Data Bit	222 432	22 10	11 98	11 76	1111 5432	11 1098	7654	3210
MSB 11	. 1 . .	1 . . .	1 . . .	. . . 1	1111	1 . . .	1 . . .	1 . . .
13	1 . . .	. 1 . .	. 1 . .	. . 1 .	1111	1111	. . . .	. 1 . .
ECC 10	. . 1 .	1 . . .	. . . 1	1 . . .	. . . .	1111	. 1 . .	. . 1 .
Code 10	. 1 . .	. 1 . .	. . 1 .	. 1 . .	1 . . .	. 1 . .	1111	. . . .
Bits 13	1 . . .	. . . 1	1 . . .	1 . . .	. 1 . .	. . . .	1111	1111
11	. . 1 .	. . 1 .	. 1 . .	. 1 . .	. . 1 .	. . 1 .	. . 1 .	1111
LSB 14	1111	11 . .	11 . .	11 . .	. . . 1	. . . 1	. . . 1	. . . 1
Number of 1s in syndrome*	3331	3311	3311	3311	3333	3333	3333	3333

Figure 16-4 Check Matrix for the Tag ECC Code

NOTE: * This row indicates the number of 1s in the generated syndrome for each data bit in error.

Summary of ECC Operations

ECC operations are summarized in Tables 16-1 through 16-4.

Table 16-1 Error Checking and Correcting Summary for Internal Transactions

Bus	Secondary Cache to Primary Cache	Primary Cache to Secondary Cache	Uncached Load	Uncached Store
Processor or Secondary Cache Data	Checked; Trap on Error	Primary Cache parity checked; Trap on Error	From System Interface	Not Checked
Secondary Cache Data Check Bits	Checked; Trap on Error	Generated	NA	NA
Secondary Cache Tag and Check Bits	Checked; not corrected in Secondary cache; Trap on error	NA	NA	NA
System Interface Address/Command and Check Bits: Transmit	NA	NA	Generated	Generated
System Interface Address/Command and Check Bits: Receive	NA	NA	Not Checked; reported to the **Fault*** pin	NA
System Interface Data	NA	NA	Checked Trap on error†	From Processor
System Interface Data Check Bits	NA	NA	Checked; Trap on Error†	Generated

† If error level (*ERL* bit of the *Status* register) is 1, the error is reported to the **Fault*** pin.

Table 16-2 Error Checking and Correcting Summary for Internal Transactions

Bus	Store to Shared Cache Line	Cache Instruction	Secondary Cache Load from System Interface	Secondary Cache Write to System Interface
Processor or Secondary Cache Data	NA	Check on cache writeback; Trap on Error	From System Interface unchanged	Checked; Trap on Error
Secondary Cache Data Check Bits	NA	Check on cache writeback; Trap on Error	From System Interface unchanged	Checked; Trap on Error
Secondary Cache Tag and Check Bits	Checked on read part of RMW†; correct Secondary cache tag; Trap on Error	Checked; corrected Secondary cache tag*; Trap on Error	Generated	Checked; not corrected; Trap on Error
System Interface Address, Command, and Check Bits: Transmit	Generated	Generated	Generated	Generated
System Interface Address, Command, and Check Bits: Receive	NA	NA	Not Checked	NA
System Interface Data	From Processor	From Primary or Secondary Cache	Checked; Trap on Error‡	From Secondary Cache
System Interface Data Check Bits	Generated	From Primary or Secondary Cache	Checked; Trap on Error‡	From Secondary Cache

† Read-Modify-Write cycle
‡ If error level (*ERL* bit of the *Status* register) is 1, the error is reported to the **Fault*** pin.
* Only if the current CACHE op needs to modify and write back the tag.

Table 16-3 Error Checking and Correcting Summary for External Transactions

Bus	Read Request	Write Request	Invalidate Request	Update Request
Processor or Secondary Cache Data	NA	NA	Not Checked	Checked on read part of RMW†; Trap on Error‡
Secondary Cache Data Check Bits	NA	NA	Not Checked	Checked on read part of RMW†; Trap on Error‡; Generation on write part of RMW if written
Secondary Cache Tag and Check Bits	NA	NA	Checked on read part of RMW†; Trap on Error‡; Generation on write part of RMW if written	Checked on read part of RMW†; Trap on Error; Generation on write part of RMW if written
System Interface Address, Command and Check Bits: Transmit	Generated	NA	NA	NA
System Interface Address, Command and Check Bits: Receive	Not Checked; reported to the **Fault*** pin	Not Checked; reported to the **Fault*** pin	Not Checked; reported to the **Fault*** pin	Not Checked; reported to the **Fault*** pin
System Interface Data	From Processor	Checked; Trap on Error	Not Checked	Not Checked; reported to the **Fault*** pin
System Interface Data Check Bits	Generated	Checked; Trap on Error	Not Checked	Not Checked; reported to the **Fault*** pin

† Read-Modify-Write cycle

‡ Only the pair of doublewords accessed on the read portion of RMW is checked.

Table 16-4 Error Checking and Correcting Summary for External Transactions

Bus	Intervention Request Data Returned	Intervention Request State Returned	Snoop Request
Processor or Secondary Cache Data	Checked; Trap on Error	Not Checked	Not Checked
Secondary Cache Data Check Bits	Checked; Trap on Error	Not Checked	Not Checked
Secondary Cache Tag and Check Bits	Checked and corrected on read part of RMW†; Trap on Error; Generation on write part of RMW if written.	Checked and corrected on read part of RMW†; Trap on Error; Generation on write part of RMW if written.	Checked and corrected on read part of RMW†; Trap on Error; Generation on write part of RMW if written.
System Interface Address, Command, and Check Bits: Transmit	Generated	Generated	Generated
System Interface Address, Command, and Check Bits: Receive	Not Checked; reported to the **Fault*** pin	Not Checked; reported to the **Fault*** pin	Not Checked; reported to the **Fault*** pin
System Interface Data	From Secondary Cache	NA	NA
System Interface Data Check Bits	From Secondary Cache	NA	NA

† Read-Modify-Write cycle

16.2 R4400 Master/Checker Mode

The R4400 processor supports four Master/Checker mode configurations, which are designated by boot-mode bit settings: Complete Master, Complete Listener, System Interface Master, and Secondary Cache Master. The boot-mode bits, **SIMasterMd** (mode bit 18) and **SCMasterMd** (mode bit 42), define Master/Checker configurations. Table 16-5 lists the configurations encoded by these bits.

Table 16-5 Boot-Mode Bit Encodings of Master/Checker Modes

SCMasterMd (Bit 42)	SIMasterMd (Bit 18)	Mode
0	0	Complete Master (required for single-chip operation)
1	1	Complete Listener (paired with Complete Master)
1	0	System Interface Master (SIMaster)
0	1	Secondary Cache Master (SCMaster, paired with SIMaster)

For a non-fault tolerant system, these bits must be set to 00_2. This is the *Complete Master* mode.

In a fault tolerant system, there are two possible configurations using the Master-Listener and Cross-Coupled modes described in Table 16-5. These are referred to as *lock-step configurations*, and are described later in this section.

Connecting a System in Lock Step

By operating in lock step, a system with more than one R4400 processor can be configured to improve data integrity. In such a configuration, output signals and I/O buses used during output are connected in parallel between the processors. One processor is defined at boot time as a bus driver, and the remaining processor(s) is defined as a bus monitor. Starting with the assertion of **Reset***, all microprocessors must be synchronous, and execute identical operations on a cycle-by-cycle basis. The processor(s) designated as bus monitor compares the outputs and buses at bus-cycle boundaries, and asserts the **Fault***† signal on any mismatch.

In a lock step operation, the following R4400 signal groups are connected in parallel:

- System interface
- Secondary Cache interface (R4400SC and R4400MC only)
- Interrupt interface

The following signals are not connected in parallel:

- Initialization interface, **ModeClock**, **ModeIn**, and **Reset*** signals
- JTAG interface signals, **JTDO** and **JTMS**
- all Clock/Control interface signals except **VssP** and **VccP**

The remaining processor signals can be connected either in parallel or independently.

† **Fault*** is a non-persistent signal which is synchronous with the System interface. **Fault*** signal timing is determined by the PClock-to-SClock divisor from boot-time mode bit settings.

Master-Listener Configuration

As shown in Figure 16-5, the Master-Listener lock step configuration pairs a Complete Master (mode bits 42 and 18 = 00_2) with a Complete Listener (mode bits 42 and 18 = 11_2). In this configuration, the Complete Listener has disabled output drivers; otherwise, the two R4400 processors operate identically, both receiving the same inputs. On all output cycles, the Complete Listener compares data on the output and I/O buses with expected data, and asserts the **Fault*** signal in the event of a miscomparison.

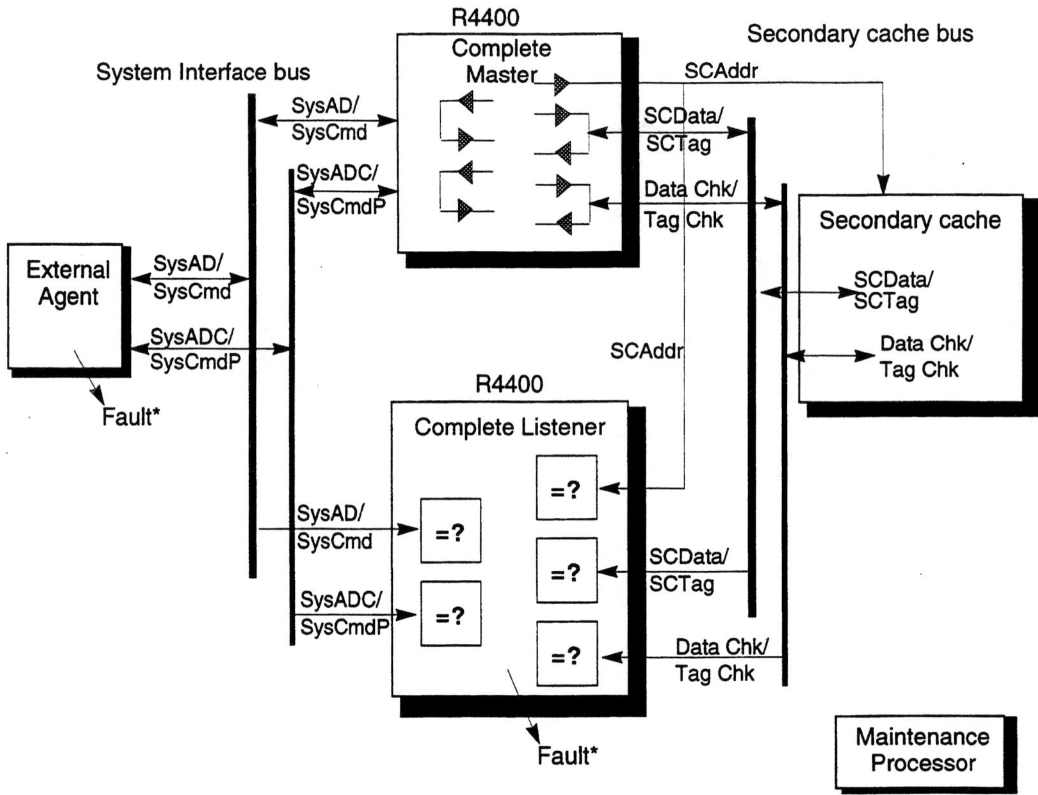

Figure 16-5 Master-Listener Configuration of Master/Checker Mode

Cross-Coupled Checking Configuration

In the Cross-Coupled Checking configuration, one of the R4400 processors drives the data bus pins and is labelled the System Interface Master (mode bits 42 and 18 = 10_2). The other R4400 processor drives the ECC or parity check pins on the same bus and is labelled the Secondary Cache Master (mode bits 42 and 18 = 01_2). This is shown in Figure 16-6.

Both processors monitor the buses and indicate a miscomparison by asserting their respective **Fault*** signals. The **Fault*** signal indicates error conditions not specifically covered by R4400 processor exceptions.†

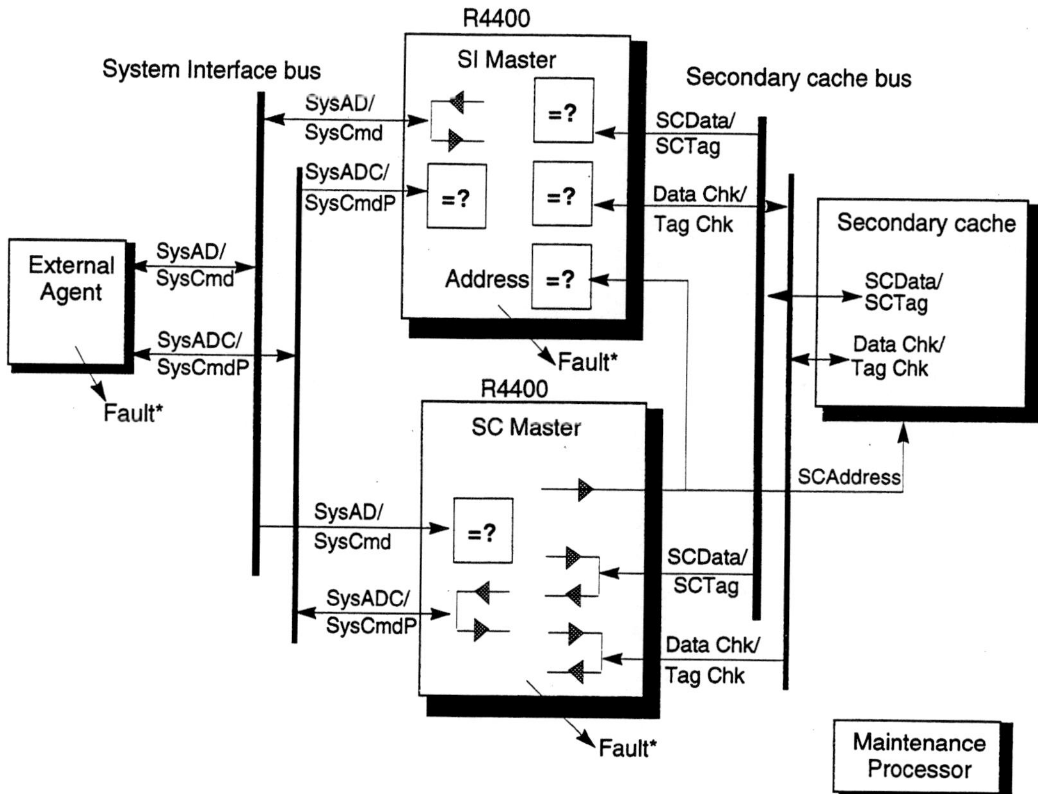

Figure 16-6 Cross-Coupled Configuration of Master/Checker Mode

† This includes such errors as an input parity error at **SysCmd**.

The signals that are connected in parallel and driven from the System Interface Master (*1* in Figure 16-6) include:

- **SysAD(63:0)**
- **SysCmd(8:0)**
- **SCAPar(2:0)**

Signals that are connected in parallel and driven from the Secondary Cache Master (2 in Figure 16-6) include:

- **SysADC(7:0)**
- **SysCmdP**
- **ValidOut***
- **Release***
- **SCAddr(17:1)**
- **SCAddr0(W:Z)**
- **SCOE***
- **SCWr(W:Z)***
- **SCData(127:0)**
- **SCDChk(15:0)**
- **SCTag(24:0)**
- **SCTChk(6:0)**
- **SCDCS***
- **SCTCS***

It should be noted that the fault detection mechanism associated with the **Fault*** pin does not cause any exceptions; the processor continues to run normally regardless of the state of the **Fault*** signal. It is up to external logic to handle an asserted **Fault*** signal.

Fault Detection

Fault detection of an output miscomparison occurs at the end of the bus cycle (the length of the cycle is programmed at boot-mode time; see Chapter 9). When the R4400 processor is in master state, outputs at the System interface are checked at the end of every System interface cycle. At the Secondary Cache interface, outputs are checked at the end of each read or write cycle.

SCAPar(2:0) transition and check times are delayed from the rest of the Secondary Cache interface by one **PClock**. **SCAPar(2:0)** transitions occur one **PClock** after **SCAddr** transitions, or when the R4400 is changing from a read cycle to a write cycle without an address change. **SCAPar(2:0)** signals do not follow the timing of **SCWr*** signals, which are set separately through the programming of the boot-time mode bits.

The R4400 processor has an internal fault detection latency of 4 PClocks (clock cycles are described in Chapter 10), whereupon **Fault*** is synchronized with the System interface. An output fault detected and propagated through the R4400 processor internal fault logic in a prior System interface cycle is reported in the current cycle.

In Complete Master mode, output fault reporting is disabled for the Secondary Cache interface, but enabled for the following System interface signals: **SysCmd, SysCmdP, SysAD, SysADC, ValidOut***, and **Release***.

Reset Operation

When the R4400 processor is a Complete Listener, SIMaster, or SCMaster, an assertion of **Reset*** after the initial boot sequence is significant.

If **Reset*** is asserted a second time and subsequently deasserted, the R4400 processor changes to Forced Complete Master mode and drives all outputs.

If **Reset*** is asserted and deasserted a third time, the R4400 processor returns to its prior mode, as programmed by the boot-mode bits.

On any subsequent assertion and deassertion of **Reset***, the processor alternates between the two modes described above: the mode determined by boot-time mode bits if the Master/Checker mode is Complete Listener, SIMaster, or SCMaster, or Forced Complete Master mode.

In Forced Complete Master mode, the **Fault*** pin reports all output faults, not just faults of the System interface as are reported in Complete Master mode.

Fault History

Two internal fault history bits, **Output Fault History** and **Input Fault History**, record output faults and certain input faults reported through the **Fault*** pin. These bits are cleared with each deassertion of **Reset***.

The two fault history bits are readable when **Reset*** is asserted, and the **Fault*** pin changes from reporting live faults to indicating which fault history bit was set when **Reset*** was deasserted in the previous cycle. The **ModeIn** pin acts as selector; if **ModeIn** = 0, **Fault*** indicates the inverted state of the **Output** fault history bit. If **ModeIn** = 1, **Fault*** indicates the inverted state of the **Input** fault history bit.

The fault history bits can be reset (cleared) while the R4400 processor is running by asserting 1 to the **ModeIn** pin. Consequently, **ModeIn** must be held to 0 to maintain the status of the fault history bits. Table 16-6 presents this information in tabular form.

Table 16-6 R4400 Fault History Bit Encoding

Boot/Reset Controls	ModeIn Pin	Fault History Bits	Fault* Pin	Master/Checker Mode
VccOk just asserted (goes from 0 to 1)	Used as boot-mode bits; scan data	N/A	N/A	N/A
Reset* just deasserted (goes from 0 to 1)	N/A	Cleared to 0	N/A	N/A
Reset* deasserted in normal operation	0	Set and latched, if fault occurs	Live faults are reported	N/A
Reset* deasserted in normal operation	1	Cleared	Live faults are reported	N/A
Reset* just asserted (goes from 1 to 0)	N/A	N/A	N/A	Changed, toggling between mode bits and Forced Complete Master
Reset* just asserted (R4400 is reset)	0	Output Fault History bit is connected to the **Fault*** pin	N/A	N/A
Reset just asserted (R4400 is reset)	1	Input Fault History bit is connected to **Fault*** pin	N/A	N/A

CPU Instruction Set Details

A

This appendix provides a detailed description of the operation of each R4000 instruction in both 32- and 64-bit modes. The instructions are listed in alphabetical order.

Exceptions that may occur due to the execution of each instruction are listed after the description of each instruction. Descriptions of the immediate cause and manner of handling exceptions are omitted from the instruction descriptions in this appendix.

Figures at the end of this appendix list the bit encoding for the constant fields of each instruction, and the bit encoding for each individual instruction is included with that instruction.

A.1 Instruction Classes

CPU instructions are divided into the following classes:

- **Load** and **Store** instructions move data between memory and general registers. They are all I-type instructions, since the only addressing mode supported is *base register + 16-bit immediate offset*.
- **Computational** instructions perform arithmetic, logical and shift operations on values in registers. They occur in both R-type (both operands are registers) and I-type (one operand is a 16-bit immediate) formats.
- **Jump** and **Branch** instructions change the control flow of a program. Jumps are always made to absolute 26-bit word addresses (J-type format), or register addresses (R-type), for returns and dispatches. Branches have 16-bit offsets relative to the program counter (I-type). **Jump and Link** instructions save their return address in register *31*.
- **Coprocessor** instructions perform operations in the coprocessors. Coprocessor loads and stores are I-type. Coprocessor computational instructions have coprocessor-dependent formats (see the FPU instructions in Appendix B). Coprocessor zero (CP0) instructions manipulate the memory management and exception handling facilities of the processor.
- **Special** instructions perform a variety of tasks, including movement of data between special and general registers, trap, and breakpoint. They are always R-type.

A.2 Instruction Formats

Every CPU instruction consists of a single word (32 bits) aligned on a word boundary and the major instruction formats are shown in Figure A-1.

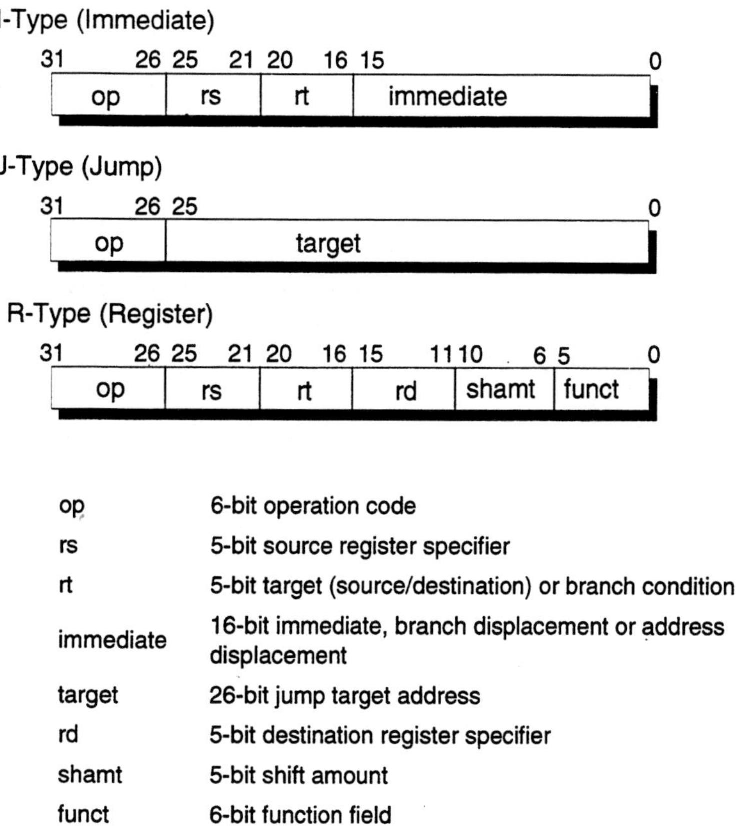

Figure A-1 CPU Instruction Formats

A.3 Instruction Notation Conventions

In this appendix, all variable subfields in an instruction format (such as *rs, rt, immediate,* etc.) are shown in lowercase names.

For the sake of clarity, we sometimes use an alias for a variable subfield in the formats of specific instructions. For example, we use *rs* = *base* in the format for load and store instructions. Such an alias is always lower case, since it refers to a variable subfield.

Figures with the actual bit encoding for all the mnemonics are located at the end of this Appendix, and the bit encoding also accompanies each instruction.

In the instruction descriptions that follow, the *Operation* section describes the operation performed by each instruction using a high-level language notation. The R4000 can operate as either a 32- or 64-bit microprocessor and the operation for both modes is included with the instruction description.

Special symbols used in the notation are described in Table A-1.

Table A-1 CPU Instruction Operation Notations

Symbol	Meaning
$\leftarrow$	Assignment.
||	Bit string concatenation.
x^y	Replication of bit value *x* into a *y*-bit string. Note: *x* is always a single-bit value.
$x_{y:z}$	Selection of bits *y* through *z* of bit string *x*. Little-endian bit notation is always used. If *y* is less than *z*, this expression is an empty (zero length) bit string.
+	2's complement or floating-point addition.
-	2's complement or floating-point subtraction.
*	2's complement or floating-point multiplication.
div	2's complement integer division.
mod	2's complement modulo.
/	Floating-point division.
<	2's complement less than comparison.
and	Bit-wise logical AND.
or	Bit-wise logical OR.
xor	Bit-wise logical XOR.
nor	Bit-wise logical NOR.
GPR[*x*]	General-Register x. The content of GPR[0] is always zero. Attempts to alter the content of GPR[0] have no effect.
CPR[*z*,*x*]	Coprocessor unit *z*, general register *x*.
CCR[*z*,*x*]	Coprocessor unit *z*, control register *x*.
COC[*z*]	Coprocessor unit *z* condition signal.
BigEndianMem	Big-endian mode as configured at reset (0 → Little, 1 → Big). Specifies the endianness of the memory interface (see LoadMemory and StoreMemory), and the endianness of Kernel and Supervisor mode execution.
ReverseEndian	Signal to reverse the endianness of load and store instructions. This feature is available in User mode only, and is effected by setting the *RE* bit of the *Status* register. Thus, ReverseEndian may be computed as (SR_{25} and User mode).
BigEndianCPU	The endianness for load and store instructions (0 → Little, 1 → Big). In User mode, this endianness may be reversed by setting SR_{25}. Thus, BigEndianCPU may be computed as BigEndianMem XOR ReverseEndian.
LLbit	Bit of state to specify synchronization instructions. Set by *LL*, cleared by *ERET* and *Invalidate* and read by *SC*.
T+*i*:	Indicates the time steps between operations. Each of the statements within a time step are defined to be executed in sequential order (as modified by conditional and loop constructs). Operations which are marked *T+i:* are executed at instruction cycle *i* relative to the start of execution of the instruction. Thus, an instruction which starts at time *j* executes operations marked T+*i:* at time *i* + *j*. The interpretation of the order of execution between two instructions or two operations which execute at the same time should be pessimistic; the order is not defined.

Instruction Notation Examples

The following examples illustrate the application of some of the instruction notation conventions:

Example #1:

GPR[rt] ← immediate || 0^{16}

Sixteen zero bits are concatenated with an immediate value (typically 16 bits), and the 32-bit string (with the lower 16 bits set to zero) is assigned to General-Purpose Register *rt*.

Example #2:

$(\text{immediate}_{15})^{16}$ || $\text{immediate}_{15...0}$

Bit 15 (the sign bit) of an immediate value is extended for 16 bit positions, and the result is concatenated with bits 15 through 0 of the immediate value to form a 32-bit sign extended value.

A.4 Load and Store Instructions

In the R4000 implementation, the instruction immediately following a load may use the loaded contents of the register. In such cases, the hardware *interlocks*, requiring additional real cycles, so scheduling load delay slots is still desirable, although not required for functional code.

Two special instructions are provided in the R4000 implementation of the MIPS ISA, Load Linked and Store Conditional. These instructions are used in carefully coded sequences to provide one of several synchronization primitives, including test-and-set, bit-level locks, semaphores, and sequencers/event counts.

In the load and store descriptions, the functions listed in Table A-2 are used to summarize the handling of virtual addresses and physical memory.

Table A-2 Load and Store Common Functions

Function	Meaning
AddressTranslation	Uses the TLB to find the physical address given the virtual address. The function fails and an exception is taken if the required translation is not present in the TLB.
LoadMemory	Uses the cache and main memory to find the contents of the word containing the specified physical address. The low-order two bits of the address and the *Access Type* field indicates which of each of the four bytes within the data word need to be returned. If the cache is enabled for this access, the entire word is returned and loaded into the cache.
StoreMemory	Uses the cache, write buffer, and main memory to store the word or part of word specified as data in the word containing the specified physical address. The low-order two bits of the address and the *Access Type* field indicates which of each of the four bytes within the data word should be stored.

As shown in Table A-3, the *Access Type* field indicates the size of the data item to be loaded or stored. Regardless of access type or byte-numbering order (endianness), the address specifies the byte which has the smallest byte address in the addressed field. For a big-endian machine, this is the leftmost byte and contains the sign for a 2's complement number; for a little-endian machine, this is the rightmost byte.

Table A-3 Access Type Specifications for Loads/Stores

Access Type Mnemonic	Value	Meaning
DOUBLEWORD	7	8 bytes (64 bits)
SEPTIBYTE	6	7 bytes (56 bits)
SEXTIBYTE	5	6 bytes (48 bits)
QUINTIBYTE	4	5 bytes (40 bits)
WORD	3	4 bytes (32 bits)
TRIPLEBYTE	2	3 bytes (24 bits)
HALFWORD	1	2 bytes (16 bits)
BYTE	0	1 byte (8 bits)

The bytes within the addressed doubleword which are used can be determined directly from the access type and the three low-order bits of the address.

A.5 Jump and Branch Instructions

All jump and branch instructions have an architectural delay of exactly one instruction. That is, the instruction immediately following a jump or branch (that is, occupying the delay slot) is always executed while the target instruction is being fetched from storage. A delay slot may not itself be occupied by a jump or branch instruction; however, this error is not detected and the results of such an operation are undefined.

If an exception or interrupt prevents the completion of a legal instruction during a delay slot, the hardware sets the *EPC* register to point at the jump or branch instruction that precedes it. When the code is restarted, both the jump or branch instructions and the instruction in the delay slot are reexecuted.

Because jump and branch instructions may be restarted after exceptions or interrupts, they must be restartable. Therefore, when a jump or branch instruction stores a return link value, register *31* (the register in which the link is stored) may not be used as a source register.

Since instructions must be word-aligned, a **Jump Register** or **Jump and Link Register** instruction must use a register whose two low-order bits are zero. If these low-order bits are not zero, an address exception will occur when the jump target instruction is subsequently fetched.

A.6 Coprocessor Instructions

Coprocessors are alternate execution units, which have register files separate from the CPU. The MIPS architecture provides four coprocessor units, or classes, and these coprocessors have two register spaces, each space containing thirty-two 32-bit registers.

- The first space, *coprocessor general* registers, may be directly loaded from memory and stored into memory, and their contents may be transferred between the coprocessor and processor.
- The second space, *coprocessor control* registers, may only have their contents transferred directly between the coprocessor and the processor. Coprocessor instructions may alter registers in either space.

A.7 System Control Coprocessor (CP0) Instructions

There are some special limitations imposed on operations involving CP0 that is incorporated within the CPU. Although load and store instructions to transfer data to/from coprocessors and to move control to/from coprocessor instructions are generally permitted by the MIPS architecture, CP0 is given a somewhat protected status since it has responsibility for exception handling and memory management. Therefore, the move to/from coprocessor instructions are the only valid mechanism for writing to and reading from the CP0 registers.

Several CP0 instructions are defined to directly read, write, and probe TLB entries and to modify the operating modes in preparation for returning to User mode or interrupt-enabled states.

ADD Add ADD

31 26	25 21	20 16	15 11	10 6	5 0
SPECIAL 000000	rs	rt	rd	0 00000	ADD 100000
6	5	5	5	5	6

Format:

ADD rd, rs, rt

Description:

The contents of general register *rs* and the contents of general register *rt* are added to form the result. The result is placed into general register *rd*. In 64-bit mode, the operands must be valid sign-extended, 32-bit values.

An overflow exception occurs if the carries out of bits 30 and 31 differ (2's complement overflow). The destination register *rd* is not modified when an integer overflow exception occurs.

Operation:

```
32    T:    GPR[rd] ←GPR[rs] + GPR[rt]

64    T:    temp ← GPR[rs] + GPR[rt]
            GPR[rd] ← (temp31)^32 || temp31...0
```

Exceptions:

Integer overflow exception

ADDI Add Immediate ADDI

31 — 26	25 — 21	20 — 16	15 — 0
ADDI 001000	rs	rt	immediate
6	5	5	16

Format:

ADDI rt, rs, immediate

Description:

The 16-bit *immediate* is sign-extended and added to the contents of general register *rs* to form the result. The result is placed into general register *rt*. In 64-bit mode, the operand must be valid sign-extended, 32-bit values.

An overflow exception occurs if carries out of bits 30 and 31 differ (2's complement overflow). The destination register *rt* is not modified when an integer overflow exception occurs.

Operation:

32	T:	$GPR[rt] \leftarrow GPR[rs] + (immediate_{15})^{16} \,\|\|\, immediate_{15...0}$
64	T:	$temp \leftarrow GPR[rs] + (immediate_{15})^{48} \,\|\|\, immediate_{15...0}$ $GPR[rt] \leftarrow (temp_{31})^{32} \,\|\|\, temp_{31...0}$

Exceptions:

Integer overflow exception

ADDIU Add Immediate Unsigned ADDIU

31 — 26	25 — 21	20 — 16	15 — 0
ADDIU 001001	rs	rt	immediate
6	5	5	16

Format:

ADDIU rt, rs, immediate

Description:

The 16-bit *immediate* is sign-extended and added to the contents of general register *rs* to form the result. The result is placed into general register *rt*. No integer overflow exception occurs under any circumstances. In 64-bit mode, the operand must be valid sign-extended, 32-bit values.

The only difference between this instruction and the ADDI instruction is that ADDIU never causes an overflow exception.

Operation:

32	T:	$GPR[rt] \leftarrow GPR[rs] + (immediate_{15})^{16} \,\|\, immediate_{15...0}$
64	T:	$temp \leftarrow GPR[rs] + (immediate_{15})^{48} \,\|\, immediate_{15...0}$ $GPR[rt] \leftarrow (temp_{31})^{32} \,\|\, temp_{31...0}$

Exceptions:

None

ADDU Add Unsigned ADDU

31–26	25–21	20–16	15–11	10–6	5–0
SPECIAL 000000	rs	rt	rd	0 00000	ADDU 100001
6	5	5	5	5	6

Format:

ADDU rd, rs, rt

Description:

The contents of general register *rs* and the contents of general register *rt* are added to form the result. The result is placed into general register *rd*. No overflow exception occurs under any circumstances. In 64-bit mode, the operands must be valid sign-extended, 32-bit values.

The only difference between this instruction and the ADD instruction is that ADDU never causes an overflow exception.

Operation:

32	T:	GPR[rd] ← GPR[rs] + GPR[rt]
64	T:	temp ← GPR[rs] + GPR[rt]
		GPR[rd] ← $(temp_{31})^{32}$ || $temp_{31...0}$

Exceptions:

None

AND   And   AND

31 – 26	25 – 21	20 – 16	15 – 11	10 – 6	5 – 0
SPECIAL 000000	rs	rt	rd	0 00000	AND 100100
6	5	5	5	5	6

Format:

AND rd, rs, rt

Description:

The contents of general register *rs* are combined with the contents of general register *rt* in a bit-wise logical AND operation. The result is placed into general register *rd*.

Operation:

32	T:	GPR[rd] ← GPR[rs] and GPR[rt]
64	T:	GPR[rd] ← GPR[rs] and GPR[rt]

Exceptions:

None

ANDI — And Immediate — ANDI

31 — 26	25 — 21	20 — 16	15 — 0
ANDI 001100	rs	rt	immediate
6	5	5	16

Format:

ANDI rt, rs, immediate

Description:

The 16-bit *immediate* is zero-extended and combined with the contents of general register *rs* in a bit-wise logical AND operation. The result is placed into general register *rt*.

Operation:

32	T:	GPR[rt] $\leftarrow 0^{16}$ || (immediate and GPR[rs]$_{15...0}$)
64	T:	GPR[rt] $\leftarrow 0^{48}$ || (immediate and GPR[rs]$_{15...0}$)

Exceptions:

None

BCzF Branch On Coprocessor z False BCzF

31 — 26	25 — 21	20 — 16	15 — 0
COPz 0 1 0 0 x x*	BC 0 1 0 0 0	BCF 0 0 0 0 0	offset
6	5	5	16

Format:

BCzF offset

Description:

A branch target address is computed from the sum of the address of the instruction in the delay slot and the 16-bit *offset*, shifted left two bits and sign-extended. If coprocessor z's condition signal (CpCond), as sampled during the previous instruction, is false, then the program branches to the target address with a delay of one instruction.

Because the condition line is sampled during the previous instruction, there must be at least one instruction between this instruction and a coprocessor instruction that changes the condition line.

Operation:

32	T–1:	condition ← not COC[z]
	T:	target ← $(offset_{15})^{14}$ || offset || 0^2

	T+1:	if condition then
		PC ← PC + target
		endif

64	T–1:	condition ← not COC[z]
	T:	target ← $(offset_{15})^{46}$ || offset || 0^2

	T+1:	if condition then
		PC ← PC + target
		endif

*See the table "Opcode Bit Encoding" on next page, or "CPU Instruction Opcode Bit Encoding" at the end of Appendix A.

BCzF Branch On Coprocessor z False (continued) BCzF

Exceptions:

Coprocessor unusable exception

Opcode Bit Encoding:

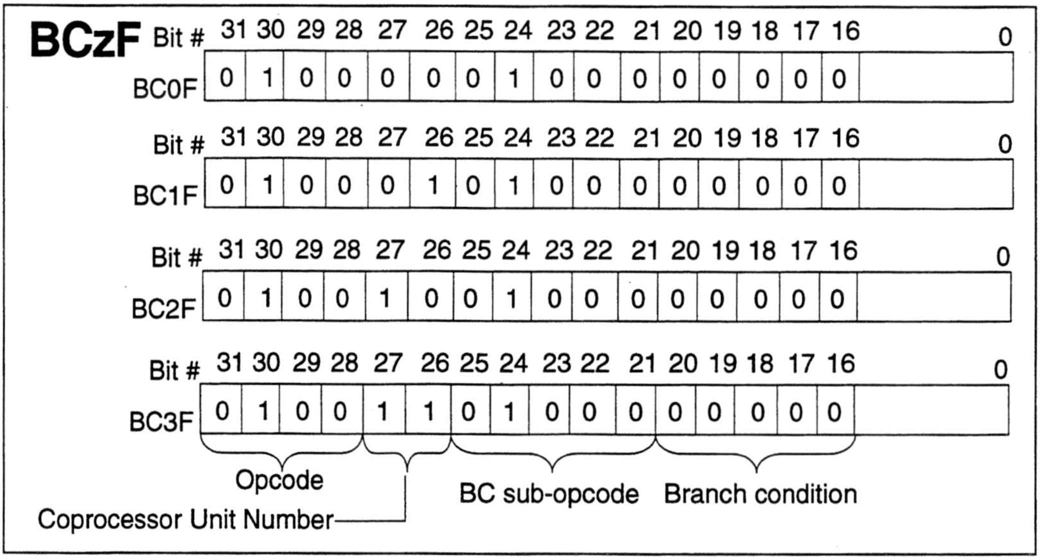
BCzF
Bit # 31 30 29 28 27 26 25 24 23 22 21 20 19 18 17 16 0
BC0F 0 1 0 0 0 0 0 1 0 0 0 0 0 0 0 0
Bit # 31 30 29 28 27 26 25 24 23 22 21 20 19 18 17 16 0
BC1F 0 1 0 0 0 1 0 1 0 0 0 0 0 0 0 0
Bit # 31 30 29 28 27 26 25 24 23 22 21 20 19 18 17 16 0
BC2F 0 1 0 0 1 0 0 1 0 0 0 0 0 0 0 0
Bit # 31 30 29 28 27 26 25 24 23 22 21 20 19 18 17 16 0
BC3F 0 1 0 0 1 1 0 1 0 0 0 0 0 0 0 0
Opcode
Coprocessor Unit Number
BC sub-opcode
Branch condition

BCzFL — Branch On Coprocessor z False Likely — BCzFL

31 — 26	25 — 21	20 — 16	15 — 0
COPz 0 1 0 0 x x*	BC 0 1 0 0 0	BCFL 0 0 0 1 0	offset
6	5	5	16

Format:

BCzFL offset

Description:

A branch target address is computed from the sum of the address of the instruction in the delay slot and the 16-bit *offset*, shifted left two bits and sign-extended. If the contents of coprocessor *z*'s condition line, as sampled during the previous instruction, is false, the target address is branched to with a delay of one instruction.

If the conditional branch is not taken, the instruction in the branch delay slot is nullified.

Because the condition line is sampled during the previous instruction, there must be at least one instruction between this instruction and a coprocessor instruction that changes the condition line.

*See the table "Opcode Bit Encoding" on next page, or "CPU Instruction Opcode Bit Encoding" at the end of Appendix A.

BCzFL Branch On Coprocessor z False Likely (continued) BCzFL

Operation:

```
32    T–1:  condition ← not  COC[z]
      T:    target ← (offset15)^14 || offset || 0^2
      T+1:  if condition then
                        PC ← PC + target
            else
                        NullifyCurrentInstruction
            endif
64    T–1:  condition ← not  COC[z]
      T:    target ← (offset15)^46 || offset || 0^2
      T+1:  if condition then
                        PC ← PC + target
            else
                        NullifyCurrentInstruction
            endif
```

Exceptions:

Coprocessor unusable exception

Opcode Bit Encoding:

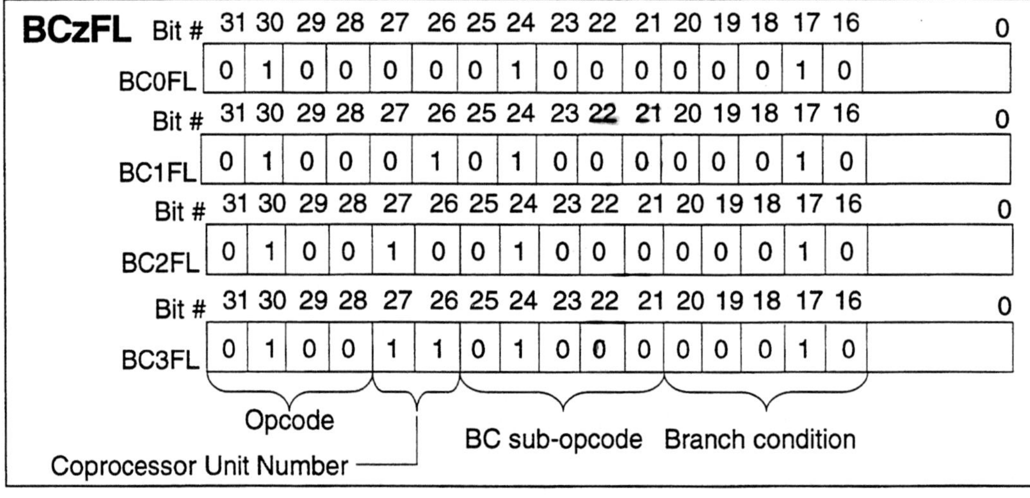

BCzFL Bit #	31	30	29	28	27	26	25	24	23	22	21	20	19	18	17	16	0
BC0FL	0	1	0	0	0	0	0	1	0	0	0	0	0	0	1	0	
BC1FL	0	1	0	0	0	1	0	1	0	0	0	0	0	0	1	0	
BC2FL	0	1	0	0	1	0	0	1	0	0	0	0	0	0	1	0	
BC3FL	0	1	0	0	1	1	0	1	0	0	0	0	0	0	1	0	

BCzT Branch On Coprocessor z True BCzT

31–26	25–21	20–16	15–0
COPz 0 1 0 0 x x*	BC 0 1 0 0 0	BCT 0 0 0 0 1	offset
6	5	5	16

Format:

BCzT offset

Description:

A branch target address is computed from the sum of the address of the instruction in the delay slot and the 16-bit *offset*, shifted left two bits and sign-extended. If the coprocessor *z*'s condition signal (CpCond) is true, then the program branches to the target address, with a delay of one instruction.

Because the condition line is sampled during the previous instruction, there must be at least one instruction between this instruction and a coprocessor instruction that changes the condition line.

Operation:

```
32   T–1:  condition ← COC[z]
     T:    target ← (offset_15)^14 || offset || 0^2
     T+1:  if condition then
                     PC ← PC + target
           endif
64   T–1:  condition ← COC[z]
     T:    target ← (offset_15)^46 || offset || 0^2
     T+1:  if condition then
                     PC ← PC + target
           endif
```

*See the table "Opcode Bit Encoding" on next page, or "CPU Instruction Opcode Bit Encoding" at the end of Appendix A.

BCzT Branch On Coprocessor z True (continued) BCzT

Exceptions:

Coprocessor unusable exception

Opcode Bit Encoding:

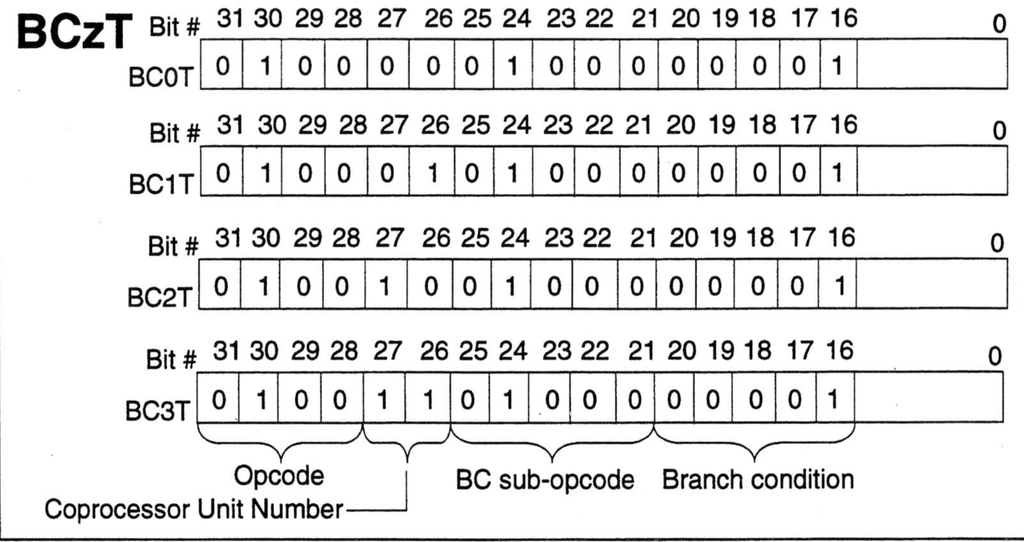

BCzTL — Branch On Coprocessor z True Likely — BCzTL

31–26	25–21	20–16	15–0
COPz 0100xx*	BC 01000	BCTL 00011	offset
6	5	5	16

Format:

BCzTL offset

Description:

A branch target address is computed from the sum of the address of the instruction in the delay slot and the 16-bit *offset*, shifted left two bits and sign-extended. If the contents of coprocessor *z*'s condition line, as sampled during the previous instruction, is true, the target address is branched to with a delay of one instruction.

If the conditional branch is not taken, the instruction in the branch delay slot is nullified.

Because the condition line is sampled during the previous instruction, there must be at least one instruction between this instruction and a coprocessor instruction that changes the condition line.

Operation:

```
32   T–1:  condition ← COC[z]
     T:    target ← (offset15)^14 || offset || 0^2
     T+1:  if condition then
                          PC ← PC + target
             else
                          NullifyCurrentInstruction
             endif
64   T–1:  condition ← COC[z]
     T:    target ← (offset15)^46 || offset || 0^2
     T+1:  if condition then
                          PC ← PC + target
             else
                          NullifyCurrentInstruction
             endif
```

*See the table "Opcode Bit Encoding" on next page, or "CPU Instruction Opcode Bit Encoding" at the end of Appendix A.

BCzTL Branch On Coprocessor z True Likely (continued) BCzTL

Exceptions:

Coprocessor unusable exception

Opcode Bit Encoding:

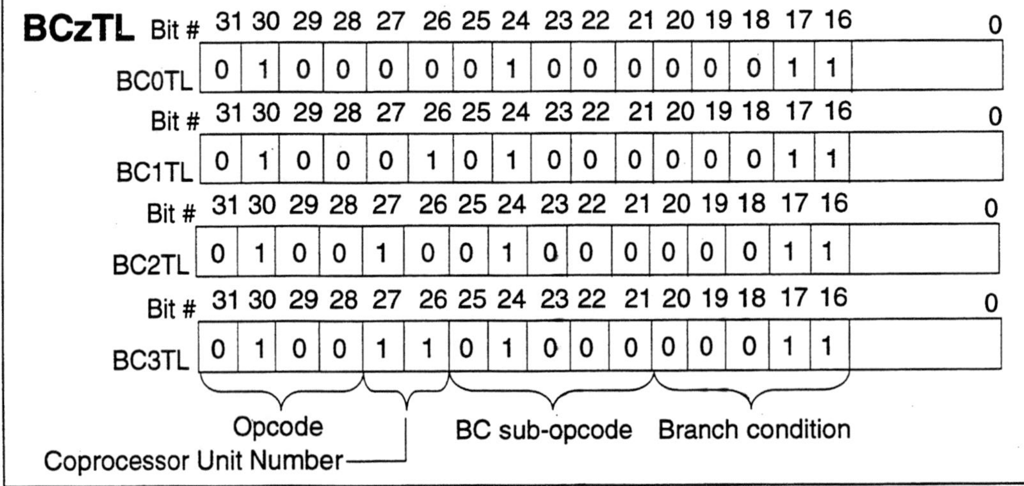

BEQ — Branch On Equal — BEQ

31–26	25–21	20–16	15–0
BEQ 000100	rs	rt	offset
6	5	5	16

Format:

BEQ rs, rt, offset

Description:

A branch target address is computed from the sum of the address of the instruction in the delay slot and the 16-bit *offset*, shifted left two bits and sign-extended. The contents of general register *rs* and the contents of general register *rt* are compared. If the two registers are equal, then the program branches to the target address, with a delay of one instruction.

Operation:

32	T:	target ← $(offset_{15})^{14}$ || offset || 0^2 condition ← (GPR[rs] = GPR[rt])

	T+1:	if condition then
		 PC ← PC + target
		 endif

64	T:	target ← $(offset_{15})^{46}$ || offset || 0^2 condition ← (GPR[rs] = GPR[rt])

	T+1:	if condition then
		 PC ← PC + target
		 endif

Exceptions:

None

BEQL Branch On Equal Likely BEQL

31 — 26	25 — 21	20 — 16	15 — 0
BEQL 010100	rs	rt	offset
6	5	5	16

Format:

BEQL rs, rt, offset

Description:

A branch target address is computed from the sum of the address of the instruction in the delay slot and the 16-bit offset, shifted left two bits and sign-extended. The contents of general register *rs* and the contents of general register *rt* are compared. If the two registers are equal, the target address is branched to, with a delay of one instruction. If the conditional branch is not taken, the instruction in the branch delay slot is nullified.

Operation:

```
32    T:    target ← (offset_15)^14 || offset || 0^2
            condition ← (GPR[rs] = GPR[rt])
      T+1:  if condition then
                        PC ← PC + target
            else
                  NullifyCurrentInstruction
            endif
64    T:    target ← (offset_15)^46 || offset || 0^2
            condition ← (GPR[rs] = GPR[rt])
      T+1:  if condition then
                  PC ← PC + target
            else
                  NullifyCurrentInstruction
            endif
```

Exceptions:

None

BGEZ — Branch On Greater Than Or Equal To Zero — BGEZ

31–26	25–21	20–16	15–0
REGIMM 000001	rs	BGEZ 00001	offset
6	5	5	16

Format:

BGEZ rs, offset

Description:

A branch target address is computed from the sum of the address of the instruction in the delay slot and the 16-bit *offset*, shifted left two bits and sign-extended. If the contents of general register *rs* have the sign bit cleared, then the program branches to the target address, with a delay of one instruction.

Operation:

```
32   T:    target ← (offset_15)^14 || offset || 0^2
           condition ← (GPR[rs]_31 = 0)
     T+1:  if condition then
                    PC ← PC + target
           endif
64   T:    target ← (offset_15)^46 || offset || 0^2
           condition ← (GPR[rs]_63 = 0)
     T+1:  if condition then
                    PC ← PC + target
           endif
```

Exceptions:

None

BGEZAL Branch On Greater Than Or Equal To Zero And Link BGEZAL

31 26	25 21	20 16	15 0
REGIMM 000001	rs	BGEZAL 10001	offset
6	5	5	16

Format:

BGEZAL rs, offset

Description:

A branch target address is computed from the sum of the address of the instruction in the delay slot and the 16-bit *offset*, shifted left two bits and sign-extended. Unconditionally, the address of the instruction after the delay slot is placed in the link register, *r31*. If the contents of general register *rs* have the sign bit cleared, then the program branches to the target address, with a delay of one instruction.

General register *rs* may not be general register *31*, because such an instruction is not restartable. An attempt to execute this instruction is not trapped, however.

Operation:

```
32    T:    target ← (offset_15)^14 || offset || 0^2
            condition ← (GPR[rs]_31 = 0)
            GPR[31] ← PC + 8
      T+1:  if condition then
                  PC ← PC + target
            endif
64    T:    target ← (offset_15)^46 || offset || 0^2
            condition ← (GPR[rs]_63 = 0)
            GPR[31] ← PC + 8
      T+1:  if condition then
                  PC ← PC + target
            endif
```

Exceptions:

None

BGEZALL Branch On Greater Than Or Equal To Zero And Link Likely BGEZALL

31 26	25 21	20 16	15 0
REGIMM 000001	rs	BGEZALL 10011	offset
6	5	5	16

Format:

BGEZALL rs, offset

Description:

A branch target address is computed from the sum of the address of the instruction in the delay slot and the 16-bit *offset*, shifted left two bits and sign-extended. Unconditionally, the address of the instruction after the delay slot is placed in the link register, *r31*. If the contents of general register *rs* have the sign bit cleared, then the program branches to the target address, with a delay of one instruction. General register *rs* may not be general register *31*, because such an instruction is not restartable. An attempt to execute this instruction is not trapped, however. If the conditional branch is not taken, the instruction in the branch delay slot is nullified.

Operation:

```
32    T:    target ← (offset15)^14 || offset || 0^2
            condition ← (GPR[rs]31 = 0)
            GPR[31] ← PC + 8
      T+1:  if condition then
                  PC ← PC + target
            else
                  NullifyCurrentInstruction
            endif
64    T:    target ← (offset15)^46 || offset || 0^2
            condition ← (GPR[rs]63 = 0)
            GPR[31] ← PC + 8
      T+1:  if condition then
                  PC ← PC + target
            else
                  NullifyCurrentInstruction
            endif
```

Exceptions:

None

BGEZL — Branch On Greater Than Or Equal To Zero Likely — BGEZL

31 26	25 21	20 16	15 0
REGIMM 000001	rs	BGEZL 00011	offset
6	5	5	16

Format:

BGEZL rs, offset

Description:

A branch target address is computed from the sum of the address of the instruction in the delay slot and the 16-bit *offset*, shifted left two bits and sign-extended. If the contents of general register *rs* have the sign bit cleared, then the program branches to the target address, with a delay of one instruction. If the conditional branch is not taken, the instruction in the branch delay slot is nullified.

Operation:

```
32   T:    target ← (offset15)^14 || offset || 0^2
           condition ← (GPR[rs]31 = 0)
     T+1:  if condition then
                PC ← PC + target
           else
                NullifyCurrentInstruction
           endif
64   T:    target ← (offset15)^46 || offset || 0^2
           condition ← (GPR[rs]63 = 0)
     T+1:  if condition then
                PC ← PC + target
           else
                NullifyCurrentInstruction
           endif
```

Exceptions:

None

BGTZ — Branch On Greater Than Zero — BGTZ

31–26	25–21	20–16	15–0
BGTZ 000111	rs	0 00000	offset
6	5	5	16

Format:

BGTZ rs, offset

Description:

A branch target address is computed from the sum of the address of the instruction in the delay slot and the 16-bit *offset*, shifted left two bits and sign-extended. The contents of general register *rs* are compared to zero. If the contents of general register *rs* have the sign bit cleared and are not equal to zero, then the program branches to the target address, with a delay of one instruction.

Operation:

```
32    T:     target ← (offset15)^14 || offset || 0^2
             condition ← (GPR[rs]31 = 0) and (GPR[rs] ≠ 0^32)
      T+1:   if condition then
                  PC ← PC + target
             endif
64    T:     target ← (offset15)^46 || offset || 0^2
             condition ← (GPR[rs]63 = 0) and (GPR[rs] ≠ 0^64)
      T+1:   if condition then
                  PC ← PC + target
             endif
```

Exceptions:

None

BGTZL — Branch On Greater Than Zero Likely — BGTZL

31–26	25–21	20–16	15–0
BGTZL 010111	rs	0 00000	offset
6	5	5	16

Format:

BGTZL rs, offset

Description:

A branch target address is computed from the sum of the address of the instruction in the delay slot and the 16-bit *offset*, shifted left two bits and sign-extended. The contents of general register *rs* are compared to zero. If the contents of general register *rs* have the sign bit cleared and are not equal to zero, then the program branches to the target address, with a delay of one instruction. If the conditional branch is not taken, the instruction in the branch delay slot is nullified.

Operation:

32	T:	target ← $(\text{offset}_{15})^{14}$ || offset || 0^2 condition ← $(\text{GPR[rs]}_{31} = 0)$ and $(\text{GPR[rs]} \neq 0^{32})$

	T+1:	if condition then
		    PC ← PC + target
		else
		    NullifyCurrentInstruction
		endif

64	T:	target ← $(\text{offset}_{15})^{46}$ || offset || 0^2 condition ← $(\text{GPR[rs]}_{63} = 0)$ and $(\text{GPR[rs]} \neq 0^{64})$

	T+1:	if condition then
		    PC ← PC + target
		else
		    NullifyCurrentInstruction
		endif

Exceptions:

None

BLEZ — Branch on Less Than Or Equal To Zero — BLEZ

31–26	25–21	20–16	15–0
BLEZ 000110	rs	0 00000	offset
6	5	5	16

Format:

BLEZ rs, offset

Description:

A branch target address is computed from the sum of the address of the instruction in the delay slot and the 16-bit *offset*, shifted left two bits and sign-extended. The contents of general register *rs* are compared to zero. If the contents of general register *rs* have the sign bit set, or are equal to zero, then the program branches to the target address, with a delay of one instruction.

Operation:

```
32   T:    target ← (offset15)^14 || offset || 0^2
           condition ← (GPR[rs]31 = 1) or (GPR[rs] = 0^32)
     T+1:  if condition then
                PC ← PC + target
           endif
64   T:    target ← (offset15)^46 || offset || 0^2
           condition ← (GPR[rs]63 = 1) and (GPR[rs] = 0^64)
     T+1:  if condition then
                PC ← PC + target
           endif
```

Exceptions:

None

BLEZL — Branch on Less Than Or Equal To Zero Likely — BLEZL

31–26	25–21	20–16	15–0
BLEZL 010110	rs	0 00000	offset
6	5	5	16

Format:

BLEZL rs, offset

Description:

A branch target address is computed from the sum of the address of the instruction in the delay slot and the 16-bit *offset*, shifted left two bits and sign-extended. The contents of general register *rs* is compared to zero. If the contents of general register *rs* have the sign bit set, or are equal to zero, then the program branches to the target address, with a delay of one instruction.

If the conditional branch is not taken, the instruction in the branch delay slot is nullified.

Operation:

```
32   T:    target ← (offset_15)^14 || offset || 0^2
           condition ← (GPR[rs]_31 = 1) and  (GPR[rs] = 0^32)
     T+1:  if condition then
                PC ← PC + target
           else
                NullifyCurrentInstruction
           endif
64   T:    target ← (offset_15)^46 || offset || 0^2
           condition ← (GPR[rs]_63 = 1) and  (GPR[rs] = 0^64)
     T+1:  if condition then
                PC ← PC + target
           else
                NullifyCurrentInstruction
           endif
```

Exceptions:

None

BLTZ Branch On Less Than Zero BLTZ

31 — 26	25 — 21	20 — 16	15 — 0
REGIMM 000001	rs	BLTZ 00000	offset
6	5	5	16

Format:

BLTZ rs, offset

Description:

A branch target address is computed from the sum of the address of the instruction in the delay slot and the 16-bit *offset*, shifted left two bits and sign-extended. If the contents of general register *rs* have the sign bit set, then the program branches to the target address, with a delay of one instruction.

Operation:

```
32    T:    target ← (offset_15)^14 || offset || 0^2
            condition ← (GPR[rs]_31 = 1)
      T+1:  if condition then
                  PC ← PC + target
            endif
64    T:    target ← (offset_15)^46 || offset || 0^2
            condition ← (GPR[rs]_63 = 1)
      T+1:  if condition then
                  PC ← PC + target
            endif
```

Exceptions:

None

BLTZAL — Branch On Less Than Zero And Link — BLTZAL

31–26	25–21	20–16	15–0
REGIMM 000001	rs	BLTZAL 10000	offset
6	5	5	16

Format:

BLTZAL rs, offset

Description:

A branch target address is computed from the sum of the address of the instruction in the delay slot and the 16-bit *offset*, shifted left two bits and sign-extended. Unconditionally, the address of the instruction after the delay slot is placed in the link register, *r31*. If the contents of general register *rs* have the sign bit set, then the program branches to the target address, with a delay of one instruction.

General register *rs* may not be general register *31*, because such an instruction is not restartable. An attempt to execute this instruction with register *31* specified as *rs* is not trapped, however.

Operation:

```
32   T:    target ← (offset_15)^14 || offset || 0^2
           condition ← (GPR[rs]_31 = 1)
           GPR[31] ← PC + 8
     T+1:  if condition then
                 PC ← PC + target
           endif
64   T:    target ← (offset_15)^46 || offset || 0^2
           condition ← (GPR[rs]_63 = 1)
           GPR[31] ← PC + 8
     T+1:  if condition then
                 PC ← PC + target
           endif
```

Exceptions:

None

BLTZALL Branch On Less Than Zero And Link Likely BLTZALL

31 — 26	25 — 21	20 — 16	15 — 0
REGIMM 000001	rs	BLTZALL 10010	offset
6	5	5	16

Format:

BLTZALL rs, offset

Description:

A branch target address is computed from the sum of the address of the instruction in the delay slot and the 16-bit *offset*, shifted left two bits and sign-extended. Unconditionally, the address of the instruction after the delay slot is placed in the link register, *r31*. If the contents of general register *rs* have the sign bit set, then the program branches to the target address, with a delay of one instruction.

General register *rs* may not be general register *31*, because such an instruction is not restartable. An attempt to execute this instruction with register *31* specified as *rs* is not trapped, however. If the conditional branch is not taken, the instruction in the branch delay slot is nullified.

Operation:

```
32    T:    target ← (offset15)^14 || offset || 0^2
            condition ← (GPR[rs]31 = 1)
            GPR[31] ← PC + 8
      T+1:  if condition then
                 PC ← PC + target
            else
                 NullifyCurrentInstruction
            endif
64    T:    target ← (offset15)^46 || offset || 0^2
            condition ← (GPR[rs]63 = 1)
            GPR[31] ← PC + 8
      T+1:  if condition then
                 PC ← PC + target
            else
                 NullifyCurrentInstruction
            endif
```

Exceptions:

None

BLTZL Branch On Less Than Zero Likely BLTZL

31 26	25 21	20 16	15 0
REGIMM 000001	rs	BLTZL 00010	offset
6	5	5	16

Format:

BLTZ rs, offset

Description:

A branch target address is computed from the sum of the address of the instruction in the delay slot and the 16-bit *offset*, shifted left two bits and sign-extended. If the contents of general register *rs* have the sign bit set, then the program branches to the target address, with a delay of one instruction. If the conditional branch is not taken, the instruction in the branch delay slot is nullified.

Operation:

```
32    T:     target ← (offset_15)^14 || offset || 0^2
             condition ← (GPR[rs]_31 = 1)
      T+1:   if condition then
                   PC ← PC + target
             else
                   NullifyCurrentInstruction
             endif
64    T:     target ← (offset_15)^46 || offset || 0^2
             condition ← (GPR[rs]_63 = 1)
      T+1:   if condition then
                   PC ← PC + target
             else
                   NullifyCurrentInstruction
             endif
```

Exceptions:

None

BNE — Branch On Not Equal — BNE

31–26	25–21	20–16	15–0
BNE 000101	rs	rt	offset
6	5	5	16

Format:

BNE rs, rt, offset

Description:

A branch target address is computed from the sum of the address of the instruction in the delay slot and the 16-bit *offset*, shifted left two bits and sign-extended. The contents of general register *rs* and the contents of general register *rt* are compared. If the two registers are not equal, then the program branches to the target address, with a delay of one instruction.

Operation:

```
32   T:     target ← (offset_15)^14 || offset || 0^2
            condition ← (GPR[rs] ≠ GPR[rt])
     T+1:   if condition then
                PC ← PC + target
            endif
64   T:     target ← (offset_15)^46 || offset || 0^2
            condition ← (GPR[rs] ≠ GPR[rt])
     T+1:   if condition then
                PC ← PC + target
            endif
```

Exceptions:

None

BNEL Branch On Not Equal Likely BNEL

31 — 26	25 — 21	20 — 16	15 — 0
BNEL 010101	rs	rt	offset
6	5	5	16

Format:

BNEL rs, rt, offset

Description:

A branch target address is computed from the sum of the address of the instruction in the delay slot and the 16-bit *offset*, shifted left two bits and sign-extended. The contents of general register *rs* and the contents of general register *rt* are compared. If the two registers are not equal, then the program branches to the target address, with a delay of one instruction.

If the conditional branch is not taken, the instruction in the branch delay slot is nullified.

Operation:

```
32   T:    target ← (offset15)^14 || offset || 0^2
           condition ← (GPR[rs] ≠ GPR[rt])
     T+1:  if condition then
                 PC ← PC + target
           else
                 NullifyCurrentInstruction
           endif
64   T:    target ← (offset15)^46 || offset || 0^2
           condition ← (GPR[rs] ≠ GPR[rt])
     T+1:  if condition then
                 PC ← PC + target
           else
                 NullifyCurrentInstruction
           endif
```

Exceptions:

None

BREAK Breakpoint BREAK

31 — 26	25 — 6	5 — 0
SPECIAL 000000	code	BREAK 001101
6	20	6

Format:

BREAK

Description:

A breakpoint trap occurs, immediately and unconditionally transferring control to the exception handler.

The code field is available for use as software parameters, but is retrieved by the exception handler only by loading the contents of the memory word containing the instruction.

Operation:

32, 64	T:	BreakpointException

Exceptions:

Breakpoint exception

CACHE Cache CACHE

31 — 26	25 — 21	20 — 16	15 — 0
CACHE 101111	base	op	offset
6	5	5	16

Format:

CACHE op, offset(base)

Description:

The 16-bit *offset* is sign-extended and added to the contents of general register *base* to form a virtual address. The virtual address is translated to a physical address using the TLB, and the 5-bit sub-opcode specifies a cache operation for that address.

If CP0 is not usable (User or Supervisor mode) the CP0 enable bit in the *Status* register is clear, and a coprocessor unusable exception is taken. The operation of this instruction on any operation/cache combination not listed below, or on a secondary cache when none is present, is undefined. The operation of this instruction on uncached addresses is also undefined.

The Index operation uses part of the virtual address to specify a cache block.

For a primary cache of $2^{CACHEBITS}$ bytes with $2^{LINEBITS}$ bytes per tag, $vAddr_{CACHEBITS ... LINEBITS}$ specifies the block.

For a secondary cache of $2^{CACHEBITS}$ bytes with $2^{LINEBITS}$ bytes per tag, $pAddr_{CACHEBITS ... LINEBITS}$ specifies the block.

Index Load Tag also uses $vAddr_{LINEBITS ... 3}$ to select the doubleword for reading ECC or parity. When the *CE* bit of the *Status* register is set, Hit WriteBack, Hit WriteBack Invalidate, Index WriteBack Invalidate, and Fill also use $vAddr_{LINEBITS ... 3}$ to select the doubleword that has its ECC or parity modified. This operation is performed unconditionally.

The Hit operation accesses the specified cache as normal data references, and performs the specified operation if the cache block contains valid data with the specified physical address (a hit). If the cache block is invalid or contains a different address (a miss), no operation is performed.

CACHE — Cache (continued) — CACHE

Write back from a primary cache goes to the secondary cache (if there is one), otherwise to memory. Write back from a secondary cache always goes to memory. A secondary write back always writes the most recent data; the data comes from the primary data cache, if present, and modified (the *W* bit is set). Otherwise the data comes from the specified secondary cache. The address to be written is specified by the cache tag and not the translated physical address.

TLB Refill and TLB Invalid exceptions can occur on any operation. For Index operations (where the physical address is used to index the cache but need not match the cache tag) unmapped addresses may be used to avoid TLB exceptions. This operation never causes TLB Modified or Virtual Coherency exceptions.

Bits 17...16 of the instruction specify the cache as follows:

Code	Name	Cache
0	I	primary instruction
1	D	primary data
2	SI	secondary instruction
3	SD	secondary data (or combined instruction/data)

CACHE — Cache (continued) — CACHE

Bits 20...18 (this value is listed under the **Code** column) of the instruction specify the operation as follows:

Code	Caches	Name	Operation
0	I, SI	Index Invalidate	Set the cache state of the cache block to Invalid.
0	D	Index WriteBack Invalidate	Examine the cache state and *W* bit of the primary data cache block at the Invalidate index specified by the virtual address. If the state is not Invalid and the *W* bit is set, then write back the block to the secondary cache (if present) or to memory (if no secondary cache). The address to write is taken from the primary cache tag. When a secondary cache is present, and the *CE* bit of the *Status* register is set, the content of the *ECC* register is XORed into the computed check bits during the write to the secondary cache for the addressed doubleword. Set cache state of primary cache block to Invalid.
0	SD	Index WriteBack Invalidate	Examine the cache state of the secondary data cache block at the index specified by the physical address. If the state is Dirty Exclusive or Dirty Shared, then write back the block to memory and set the cache state to Invalid. The address to write is taken from the secondary cache tag, which is not necessarily the physical address used to index the cache. Like all secondary write-backs, the operation writes any modified data (*W* bit set) from the primary data cache. Unlike Hit Write-back Invalidate the operation does not invalidate or clear the *W* bit in the primary D-cache. In all cases, the secondary cache block state is set to Invalid.
1	all	Index Load Tag	Read the tag for the cache block at the specified index and place it into the *TagLo* and *TagHi* CP0 registers, ignoring ECC and parity errors. Also load the data ECC or parity bits into the *ECC* register.
2	all	Index Store Tag	Write the tag for the cache block at the specified index from the *TagLo* and *TagHi* CP0 registers.

CACHE Cache (continued) CACHE

Code	Caches	Name	Operation
3	SD	Create Dirty Exclusive	This operation is used to avoid loading data needlessly from memory when writing new contents into an entire cache block. If the cache block is valid but does not contain the specified address (a valid miss) the secondary block is vacated. The data is written back to memory if dirty and all matching blocks in both primary caches are invalidated. As usual during a secondary write-back, if the primary data cache contains modified data (matching blocks with *W* bit set) that modified data is written to memory. If the cache block is valid and does contain the specified physical address (a hit), then the operation cleans up the primary caches to avoid any virtual alias problems: all blocks in both primary caches that match the secondary line are invalidated without write back. Note that the search for matching primary blocks uses the virtual index of the PIdx field of the secondary cache tag (the virtual index to the location last used) and not the virtual index of the virtual address used in the operation (the virtual index to the location now being used). If the secondary tag and address do not match (miss), or the tag and address do match (hit) and the block is in a shared state, send an invalidate for the specified address on the system interface. In all cases, set the cache block tag to the specified physical address, set the cache state to Dirty Exclusive, and set the virtual index field from the virtual address. The *CH* bit in the *Status* register is set or cleared to indicate a hit or miss.
3	D	Create Dirty Exclusive	This operation is used to avoid loading data needlessly from secondary cache or memory when writing new contents into an entire cache block. If the cache block does not contain the specified address, and the block is dirty, write it back to the secondary cache or memory. In all cases, set the cache block tag to the specified physical address, set the cache state to Dirty Exclusive.
4	I, D	Hit Invalidate	If the cache block contains the specified address, mark the cache block invalid.
4	SI, SD	Hit Invalidate	If the cache block contains the specified address, mark the cache block invalid and also invalidate all matching blocks, if present, in the primary caches (the PIdx field of the secondary tag is used to determine the locations in the primaries to search). The *CH* bit in the *Status* register is set or cleared to indicate a hit or miss.
5	D	HitWriteBack Invalidate	If the cache block contains the specified address, write back the data if it is dirty, and mark the cache block invalid. When a secondary cache is present and the *CE* bit of the *Status* register is set, contents of the *ECC* register is XORed into the computed check bits during the write to the secondary cache for the addressed doubleword.

CACHE — Cache (continued) — CACHE

Code	Caches	Name	Operation
5	SD	Hit WriteBack Invalidate	If the cache block contains the specified address, write back the data if it is dirty, and mark the secondary cache block and all matching blocks in both primary caches invalid. As usual with secondary write-backs, modified data in the primary data cache (matching block with the *W* bit set) is used during the write-back. The PIdx field of the secondary tag is used to determine the locations in the primaries to check for matching primary blocks. The *CH* bit in the *Status* register is set or cleared to indicate a hit or miss.
5	I	Fill	Fill the primary instruction cache block from secondary or memory. If the *CE* bit of the *Status* register is set, the contents of the *ECC* register is used instead of the computed parity bits for addressed doubleword when written to the instruction cache.
6	D	Hit WriteBack	If the cache block contains the specified address, and the *W* bit is set, write back the data to memory or the secondary cache, and clear the *W* bit. When a secondary cache is present, and the *CE* bit of the *Status* register is set, the contents of the *ECC* register is XORed into the computed check bits during the write to the secondary cache for the addressed doubleword.
6	SD	Hit WriteBack	If the cache block contains the specified address, and the cache state is Dirty Exclusive or Dirty Shared, write back the data to memory, and change the cache state to Clean Exclusive or Shared, respectively. The *CH* bit in the *Status* register is set or cleared to indicate a hit or miss. The write back looks in the primary data cache for modified data, but does *not* invalidate or clear the *W* bit in the primary data cache. This state, although perhaps not intuitive, is consistent since the primary block contains data that is at least as current as that in memory or secondary cache. A subsequent write-back of the primary line without further modification would be redundant, but not incorrect.
6	I	Hit WriteBack	If the cache block contains the specified address, write back the data unconditionally. When a secondary cache is present, and the *CE* bit of the *Status* register is set, the contents of the *ECC* register is XORed into the computed check bits during the write to the secondary cache for the addressed doubleword.

CACHE — Cache (continued) — CACHE

Code	Caches	Name	Operation
7	SI, SD	Hit Set Virtual	This operation is used to change the virtual index of secondary cache contents avoiding unnecessary memory operations. If the cache block contains the specified address, invalidate matching blocks in the primary caches at the index formed by concatenating PIdx in the secondary cache tag (not the virtual address of the operation) and $vAddr_{11...4}$, then set the virtual index field of the secondary cache tag from the specified virtual address. Modified data in the primary data cache is not preserved by the operation and should be explicitly written back before this operation. The *CH* bit in the *Status* register is set or cleared to indicate a hit or miss.

Operation:

32, 64	T:	$vAddr \leftarrow ((offset_{15})^{48} \parallel offset_{15...0}) + GPR[base]$
		(pAddr, uncached) ← AddressTranslation (vAddr, DATA)
		CacheOp (op, vAddr, pAddr)

Exceptions:

Coprocessor unusable exception

CFCz — Move Control From Coprocessor — CFCz

31 … 26	25 … 21	20 … 16	15 … 11	10 … 0
COPz 0 1 0 0 x x*	CF 0 0 0 1 0	rt	rd	0 0 0 0 0 0
6	5	5	5	11

Format:

CFCz rt, rd

Description:

The contents of coprocessor control register *rd* of coprocessor unit z are loaded into general register *rt*.

This instruction is not valid for CP0.

Operation:

32	T:	data ← CCR[z,rd]
	T+1:	GPR[rt] ← data
64	T:	data ← $(CCR[z,rd]_{31})^{32}$ || CCR[z,rd]
	T+1:	GPR[rt] ← data

Exceptions:

Coprocessor unusable exception

***Opcode Bit Encoding:**

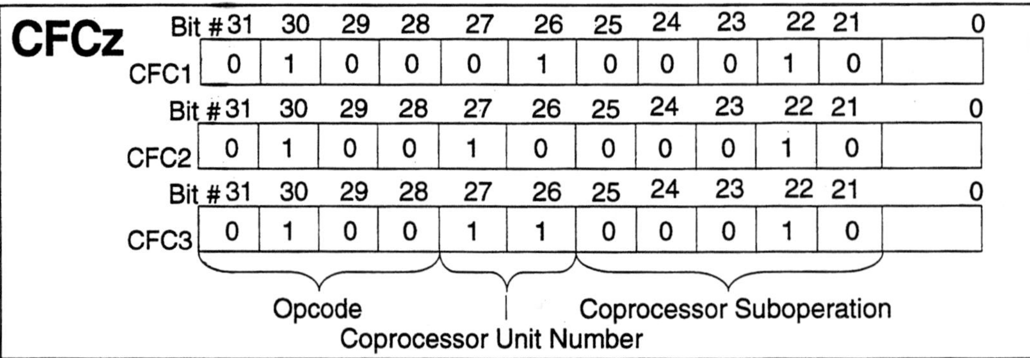

COPz Coprocessor Operation COPz

31 — 26	25	24 — 0
COPz 0 1 0 0 x x*	CO 1	cofun
6	1	25

Format:

COPz cofun

Description:

A coprocessor operation is performed. The operation may specify and reference internal coprocessor registers, and may change the state of the coprocessor condition line, but does not modify state within the processor or the cache/memory system. Details of coprocessor operations are contained in Appendix B.

Operation:

32, 64	T:	CoprocessorOperation (z, cofun)

Exceptions:

Coprocessor unusable exception
Coprocessor interrupt or Floating-Point Exception (R4000 CP1 only)

***Opcode Bit Encoding:**

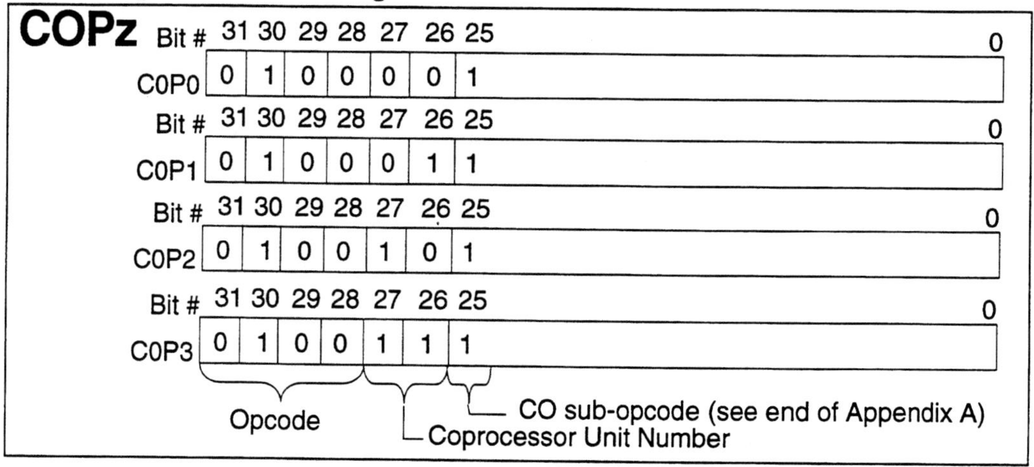

CTCz Move Control to Coprocessor CTCz

31 26	25 21	20 16	15 11	10 0
COPz 0 1 0 0 x x *	CT 0 0 1 1 0	rt	rd	0 000 0000 0000
6	5	5	5	11

Format:

CTCz rt, rd

Description:

The contents of general register *rt* are loaded into control register *rd* of coprocessor unit *z*.

This instruction is not valid for CP0.

Operation:

```
32,64    T:       data ← GPR[rt]
         T + 1:  CCR[z,rd] ← data
```

Exceptions:

Coprocessor unusable

*See "CPU Instruction Opcode Bit Encoding" at the end of Appendix A.

DADD Doubleword Add DADD

31–26	25–21	20–16	15–11	10–6	5–0
SPECIAL 000000	rs	rt	rd	0 00000	DADD 101100
6	5	5	5	5	6

Format:

DADD rd, rs, rt

Description:

The contents of general register *rs* and the contents of general register *rt* are added to form the result. The result is placed into general register *rd*.

An overflow exception occurs if the carries out of bits 62 and 63 differ (2's complement overflow). The destination register *rd* is not modified when an integer overflow exception occurs.

This operation is only defined for the R4000 operating in 64-bit mode. Execution of this instruction in 32-bit mode causes a reserved instruction exception.

Operation:

```
64    T:    GPR[rd] ←GPR[rs] + GPR[rt]
```

Exceptions:

Integer overflow exception
Reserved instruction exception (R4000 in 32-bit mode)

DADDI Doubleword Add Immediate DADDI

31 26	25 21	20 16	15 0
DADDI 011000	rs	rt	immediate
6	5	5	16

Format:

DADDI rt, rs, immediate

Description:

The 16-bit *immediate* is sign-extended and added to the contents of general register *rs* to form the result. The result is placed into general register *rt*.

An overflow exception occurs if carries out of bits 62 and 63 differ (2's complement overflow). The destination register *rt* is not modified when an integer overflow exception occurs.

This operation is only defined for the R4000 operating in 64-bit mode. Execution of this instruction in 32-bit mode causes a reserved instruction exception.

Operation:

64	T:	GPR [rt] ← GPR[rs] + $(\text{immediate}_{15})^{48}$ | | $\text{immediate}_{15...0}$

Exceptions:

Integer overflow exception
Reserved instruction exception (R4000 in 32-bit mode)

DADDIU — Doubleword Add Immediate Unsigned — DADDIU

31–26	25–21	20–16	15–0
DADDIU 011001	rs	rt	immediate
6	5	5	16

Format:

DADDIU rt, rs, immediate

Description:

The 16-bit *immediate* is sign-extended and added to the contents of general register *rs* to form the result. The result is placed into general register *rt*. No integer overflow exception occurs under any circumstances.

The only difference between this instruction and the DADDI instruction is that DADDIU never causes an overflow exception.

This operation is only defined for the R4000 operating in 64-bit mode. Execution of this instruction in 32-bit mode causes a reserved instruction exception.

Operation:

64	T:	$GPR[rt] \leftarrow GPR[rs] + (immediate_{15})^{48} \parallel immediate_{15...0}$

Exceptions:

Reserved instruction exception (R4000 in 32-bit mode)

DADDU Doubleword Add Unsigned DADDU

31 26	25 21	20 16	15 11	10 6	5 0
SPECIAL 000000	rs	rt	rd	0 00000	DADDU 101101
6	5	5	5	5	6

Format:

DADDU rd, rs, rt

Description:

The contents of general register *rs* and the contents of general register *rt* are added to form the result. The result is placed into general register *rd*.

No overflow exception occurs under any circumstances.

The only difference between this instruction and the DADD instruction is that DADDU never causes an overflow exception.

This operation is only defined for the R4000 operating in 64-bit mode. Execution of this instruction in 32-bit mode causes a reserved instruction exception.

Operation:

```
64    T:    GPR[rd] ←GPR[rs] + GPR[rt]
```

Exceptions:

Reserved instruction exception (R4000 in 32-bit mode)

DDIV Doubleword Divide DDIV

31–26	25–21	20–16	15–6	5–0
SPECIAL 000000	rs	rt	0 00 0000 0000	DDIV 011110
6	5	5	10	6

Format:

DDIV rs, rt

Description:

The contents of general register *rs* are divided by the contents of general register *rt*, treating both operands as 2's complement values. No overflow exception occurs under any circumstances, and the result of this operation is undefined when the divisor is zero.

This instruction is typically followed by additional instructions to check for a zero divisor and for overflow.

When the operation completes, the quotient word of the double result is loaded into special register *LO*, and the remainder word of the double result is loaded into special register *HI*.

If either of the two preceding instructions is MFHI or MFLO, the results of those instructions are undefined. Correct operation requires separating reads of *HI* or *LO* from writes by two or more instructions.

This operation is only defined for the R4000 operating in 64-bit mode. Execution of this instruction in 32-bit mode causes a reserved instruction exception.

Operation:

```
64   T–2:   LO    ← undefined
            HI    ← undefined
     T–1:   LO    ← undefined
            HI    ← undefined
     T:     LO    ← GPR[rs] div GPR[rt]
            HI    ← GPR[rs] mod GPR[rt]
```

Exceptions:

Reserved instruction exception (R4000 in 32-bit mode)

DDIVU Doubleword Divide Unsigned DDIVU

31 — 26	25 — 21	20 — 16	15 — 6	5 — 0
SPECIAL 000000	rs	rt	0 000000 0000	DDIVU 011111
6	5	5	10	6

Format:

DDIVU rs, rt

Description:

The contents of general register *rs* are divided by the contents of general register *rt*, treating both operands as unsigned values. No integer overflow exception occurs under any circumstances, and the result of this operation is undefined when the divisor is zero.

This instruction is typically followed by additional instructions to check for a zero divisor.

When the operation completes, the quotient word of the double result is loaded into special register *LO*, and the remainder word of the double result is loaded into special register *HI*.

If either of the two preceding instructions is MFHI or MFLO, the results of those instructions are undefined. Correct operation requires separating reads of *HI* or *LO* from writes by two or more instructions.

This operation is only defined for the R4000 operating in 64-bit mode. Execution of this instruction in 32-bit mode causes a reserved instruction exception.

Operation:

```
64   T–2:   LO    ← undefined
            HI    ← undefined
     T–1:   LO    ← undefined
            HI    ← undefined
     T:     LO    ← (0 || GPR[rs]) div (0 || GPR[rt])
            HI    ← (0 || GPR[rs]) mod  (0 || GPR[rt])
```

Exceptions:

Reserved instruction exception (R4000 in 32-bit mode)

DIV Divide DIV

31 26	25 21	20 16	15 6	5 0
SPECIAL 000000	rs	rt	0 00 0000 0000	DIV 011010
6	5	5	10	6

Format:

DIV rs, rt

Description:

The contents of general register *rs* are divided by the contents of general register *rt*, treating both operands as 2's complement values. No overflow exception occurs under any circumstances, and the result of this operation is undefined when the divisor is zero.

In 64-bit mode, the operands must be valid sign-extended, 32-bit values.

This instruction is typically followed by additional instructions to check for a zero divisor and for overflow.

When the operation completes, the quotient word of the double result is loaded into special register *LO*, and the remainder word of the double result is loaded into special register *HI*.

If either of the two preceding instructions is MFHI or MFLO, the results of those instructions are undefined. Correct operation requires separating reads of *HI* or *LO* from writes by two or more instructions.

DIV — Divide (continued) — DIV

Operation:

32	T–2:	LO	← undefined
		HI	← undefined
	T–1:	LO	← undefined
		HI	← undefined
	T:	LO	← GPR[rs] div GPR[rt]
		HI	← GPR[rs] mod GPR[rt]
64	T–2:	LO	← undefined
		HI	← undefined
	T–1:	LO	← undefined
		HI	← undefined
	T:	q	← $GPR[rs]_{31...0}$ div $GPR[rt]_{31...0}$
		r	← $GPR[rs]_{31...0}$ mod $GPR[rt]_{31...0}$
		LO	← $(q_{31})^{32} \mid\mid q_{31...0}$
		HI	← $(r_{31})^{32} \mid\mid r_{31...0}$

Exceptions:

None

DIVU Divide Unsigned DIVU

31 — 26	25 — 21	20 — 16	15 — 6	5 — 0
SPECIAL 000000	rs	rt	0 000000 0000	DIVU 011011
6	5	5	10	6

Format:

DIVU rs, rt

Description:

The contents of general register *rs* are divided by the contents of general register *rt*, treating both operands as unsigned values. No integer overflow exception occurs under any circumstances, and the result of this operation is undefined when the divisor is zero.

In 64-bit mode, the operands must be valid sign-extended, 32-bit values.

This instruction is typically followed by additional instructions to check for a zero divisor.

When the operation completes, the quotient word of the double result is loaded into special register *LO*, and the remainder word of the double result is loaded into special register *HI*.

If either of the two preceding instructions is MFHI or MFLO, the results of those instructions are undefined. Correct operation requires separating reads of *HI* or *LO* from writes by two or more instructions.

DIVU — Divide Unsigned (continued) — DIVU

Operation:

32	T–2:	LO	← undefined
		HI	← undefined
	T–1:	LO	← undefined
		HI	← undefined
	T:	LO	← (0 ‖ GPR[rs]) div (0 ‖ GPR[rt])
		HI	← (0 ‖ GPR[rs]) mod (0 ‖ GPR[rt])
64	T–2:	LO	← undefined
		HI	← undefined
	T–1:	LO	← undefined
		HI	← undefined
	T:	q	← (0 ‖ $GPR[rs]_{31...0}$) div (0 ‖ $GPR[rt]_{31...0}$)
		r	← (0 ‖ $GPR[rs]_{31...0}$) mod (0 ‖ $GPR[rt]_{31...0}$)
		LO	← $(q_{31})^{32}$ ‖ $q_{31...0}$
		HI	← $(r_{31})^{32}$ ‖ $r_{31...0}$

Exceptions:

None

DMFC0 Doubleword Move From System Control Coprocessor DMFC0

31 … 26	25 … 21	20 … 16	15 … 11	10 … 0
COP0 010000	DMF 00001	rt	rd	0 000 0000 0000
6	5	5	5	11

Format:

DMFC0 rt, rd

Description:

The contents of coprocessor register *rd* of the CP0 are loaded into general register *rt*.

This operation is defined for the R4000 operating in 64-bit mode and in 32-bit kernel mode. Execution of this instruction in 32-bit user or supervisor mode causes a reserved instruction exception. All 64-bits of the general register destination are written from the coprocessor register source. The operation of DMFC0 on a 32-bit coprocessor 0 register is undefined.

Operation:

```
64      T:     data ←CPR[0,rd]
        T+1:   GPR[rt] ← data
```

Exceptions:

Coprocessor unusable exception
Reserved instruction exception (R4000 in 32-bit user mode
R4000 in 32-bit supervisor mode)

DMTC0 Doubleword Move To System Control Coprocessor DMTC0

31 ... 26	25 ... 21	20 ... 16	15 ... 11	10 ... 0
COP0 010000	DMT 00101	rt	rd	0 000 0000 0000
6	5	5	5	11

Format:

DMTC0 rt, rd

Description:

The contents of general register *rt* are loaded into coprocessor register *rd* of the CP0.

This operation is defined for the R4000 operating in 64-bit mode or in 32-bit kernel mode. Execution of this instruction in 32-bit user or supervisor mode causes a reserved instruction exception.

All 64-bits of the coprocessor 0 register are written from the general register source. The operation of DMTC0 on a 32-bit coprocessor 0 register is undefined.

Because the state of the virtual address translation system may be altered by this instruction, the operation of load instructions, store instructions, and TLB operations immediately prior to and after this instruction are undefined.

Operation:

```
64      T:      data ← GPR[rt]
        T+1:    CPR[0,rd] ← data
```

Exceptions:

Coprocessor unusable exception (R4000 in 32-bit user mode
R4000 in 32-bit supervisor mode)

DMULT Doubleword Multiply DMULT

31–26	25–21	20–16	15–6	5–0
SPECIAL 000000	rs	rt	0 00 0000 0000	DMULT 011100
6	5	5	10	6

Format:

DMULT rs, rt

Description:

The contents of general registers *rs* and *rt* are multiplied, treating both operands as 2's complement values. No integer overflow exception occurs under any circumstances.

When the operation completes, the low-order word of the double result is loaded into special register *LO*, and the high-order word of the double result is loaded into special register *HI*.

If either of the two preceding instructions is MFHI or MFLO, the results of these instructions are undefined. Correct operation requires separating reads of *HI* or *LO* from writes by a minimum of two other instructions.

This operation is only defined for the R4000 operating in 64-bit mode. Execution of this instruction in 32-bit mode causes a reserved instruction exception.

Operation:

64	T–2:	LO	← undefined
		HI	← undefined
	T–1:	LO	← undefined
		HI	← undefined
	T:	t	← GPR[rs] * GPR[rt]
		LO	← $t_{63...0}$
		HI	← $t_{127...64}$

Exceptions:

Reserved instruction exception (R4000 in 32-bit mode)

DMULTU — Doubleword Multiply Unsigned — DMULTU

31–26	25–21	20–16	15–6	5–0
SPECIAL 000000	rs	rt	0 00 0000 0000	DMULTU 011101
6	5	5	10	6

Format:

DMULTU rs, rt

Description:

The contents of general register *rs* and the contents of general register *rt* are multiplied, treating both operands as unsigned values. No overflow exception occurs under any circumstances.

When the operation completes, the low-order word of the double result is loaded into special register *LO*, and the high-order word of the double result is loaded into special register *HI*.

If either of the two preceding instructions is MFHI or MFLO, the results of these instructions are undefined. Correct operation requires separating reads of *HI* or *LO* from writes by a minimum of two instructions.

This operation is only defined for the R4000 operating in 64-bit mode. Execution of this instruction in 32-bit mode causes a reserved instruction exception.

Operation:

```
64   T–2:  LO ← undefined
           HI ← undefined
     T–1:  LO ← undefined
           HI ← undefined
     T:    t ← (0 || GPR[rs]) * (0 || GPR[rt])
           LO ← t63...0
           HI ← t127...64
```

Exceptions:

Reserved instruction exception (R4000 in 32-bit mode)

DSLL Doubleword Shift Left Logical DSLL

31 26	25 21	20 16	15 11	10 6	5 0
SPECIAL 000000	0 00000	rt	rd	sa	DSLL 111000
6	5	5	5	5	6

Format:

DSLL rd, rt, sa

Description:

The contents of general register *rt* are shifted left by *sa* bits, inserting zeros into the low-order bits. The result is placed in register *rd.*

Operation:

64	T:	$s \leftarrow 0 \,\|\, sa$
		$GPR[rd] \leftarrow GPR[rt]_{(63-s)...0} \,\|\, 0^s$

Exceptions:

Reserved instruction exception (R4000 in 32-bit mode)

DSLLV — Doubleword Shift Left Logical Variable — DSLLV

31–26	25–21	20–16	15–11	10–6	5–0
SPECIAL 000000	rs	rt	rd	0 00000	DSLLV 010100
6	5	5	5	5	6

Format:

DSLLV rd, rt, rs

Description:

The contents of general register *rt* are shifted left by the number of bits specified by the low-order six bits contained in general register *rs*, inserting zeros into the low-order bits. The result is placed in register *rd*.

This operation is only defined for the R4000 operating in 64-bit mode. Execution of this instruction in 32-bit mode causes a reserved instruction exception.

Operation:

64	T:	$s \leftarrow GPR[rs]_{5...0}$
		$GPR[rd] \leftarrow GPR[rt]_{(63-s)...0} \parallel 0^s$

Exceptions:

Reserved instruction exception (R4000 in 32-bit mode)

DSLL32 Doubleword Shift Left Logical + 32 DSLL32

31 26	25 21	20 16	15 11	10 6	5 0
SPECIAL 000000	0 00000	rt	rd	sa	DSLL32 111100
6	5	5	5	5	6

Format:

DSLL32 rd, rt, sa

Description:

The contents of general register *rt* are shifted left by *32+sa* bits, inserting zeros into the low-order bits. The result is placed in register *rd*.

This operation is only defined for the R4000 operating in 64-bit mode. Execution of this instruction in 32-bit mode causes a reserved instruction exception.

Operation:

64	T:	$s \leftarrow 1 \parallel sa$
		$GPR[rd] \leftarrow GPR[rt]_{(63-s)...0} \parallel 0^s$

Exceptions:

Reserved instruction exception (R4000 in 32-bit mode)

DSRA — Doubleword Shift Right Arithmetic — DSRA

31 … 26	25 … 21	20 … 16	15 … 11	10 … 6	5 … 0
SPECIAL 000000	0 00000	rt	rd	sa	DSRA 111011
6	5	5	5	5	6

Format:

DSRA rd, rt, sa

Description:

The contents of general register *rt* are shifted right by *sa* bits, sign-extending the high-order bits. The result is placed in register *rd*.

This operation is only defined for the R4000 operating in 64-bit mode. Execution of this instruction in 32-bit mode causes a reserved instruction exception.

Operation:

64	T:	$s \leftarrow 0 \parallel sa$
		$GPR[rd] \leftarrow (GPR[rt]_{63})^{s} \parallel GPR[rt]_{63...s}$

Exceptions:

Reserved instruction exception (R4000 in 32-bit mode)

DSRAV Doubleword Shift Right Arithmetic Variable DSRAV

31 — 26	25 — 21	20 — 16	15 — 11	10 — 6	5 — 0
SPECIAL 000000	rs	rt	rd	0 00000	DSRAV 010111
6	5	5	5	5	6

Format:

DSRAV rd, rt, rs

Description:

The contents of general register *rt* are shifted right by the number of bits specified by the low-order six bits of general register *rs*, sign-extending the high-order bits. The result is placed in register *rd*.

This operation is only defined for the R4000 operating in 64-bit mode. Execution of this instruction in 32-bit mode causes a reserved instruction exception.

Operation:

64	T:	$s \leftarrow GPR[rs]_{5...0}$
		$GPR[rd] \leftarrow (GPR[rt]_{63})^{s} \parallel GPR[rt]_{63...s}$

Exceptions:

Reserved instruction exception (R4000 in 32-bit mode)

DSRA32 Doubleword Shift Right Arithmetic + 32 DSRA32

31 — 26	25 — 21	20 — 16	15 — 11	10 — 6	5 — 0
SPECIAL 000000	0 00000	rt	rd	sa	DSRA32 111111
6	5	5	5	5	6

Format:

DSRA32 rd, rt, sa

Description:

The contents of general register *rt* are shifted right by *32+sa* bits, sign-extending the high-order bits. The result is placed in register *rd*.

This operation is only defined for the R4000 operating in 64-bit mode. Execution of this instruction in 32-bit mode causes a reserved instruction exception.

Operation:

64	T:	$s \leftarrow 1 \parallel sa$
		$GPR[rd] \leftarrow (GPR[rt]_{63})^{s} \parallel GPR[rt]_{63...s}$

Exceptions:

Reserved instruction exception (R4000 in 32-bit mode)

DSRL — Doubleword Shift Right Logical — DSRL

31–26	25–21	20–16	15–11	10–6	5–0
SPECIAL 000000	0 00000	rt	rd	sa	DSRL 111010
6	5	5	5	5	6

Format:

DSRL rd, rt, sa

Description:

The contents of general register *rt* are shifted right by *sa* bits, inserting zeros into the high-order bits. The result is placed in register *rd*.

This operation is only defined for the R4000 operating in 64-bit mode. Execution of this instruction in 32-bit mode causes a reserved instruction exception.

Operation:

```
64    T:    s ← 0 || sa
            GPR[rd] ← 0^s || GPR[rt]63...s
```

Exceptions:

Reserved instruction exception (R4000 in 32-bit mode)

DSRLV — Doubleword Shift Right Logical Variable — DSRLV

31 … 26	25 … 21	20 … 16	15 … 11	10 … 6	5 … 0
SPECIAL 000000	rs	rt	rd	0 00000	DSRLV 010110
6	5	5	5	5	6

Format:

DSRLV rd, rt, rs

Description:

The contents of general register *rt* are shifted right by the number of bits specified by the low-order six bits of general register *rs*, inserting zeros into the high-order bits. The result is placed in register *rd*.

This operation is only defined for the R4000 operating in 64-bit mode. Execution of this instruction in 32-bit mode causes a reserved instruction exception.

Operation:

64	T:	$s \leftarrow GPR[rs]_{5...0}$
		$GPR[rd] \leftarrow 0^{s} \mid\mid GPR[rt]_{63...s}$

Exceptions:

Reserved instruction exception (R4000 in 32-bit mode)

DSRL32 Doubleword Shift Right Logical + 32 DSRL32

31–26	25–21	20–16	15–11	10–6	5–0
SPECIAL 000000	0 00000	rt	rd	sa	DSRL32 111110
6	5	5	5	5	6

Format:

DSRL32 rd, rt, sa

Description:

The contents of general register *rt* are shifted right by *32+sa* bits, inserting zeros into the high-order bits. The result is placed in register *rd.*

This operation is only defined for the R4000 operating in 64-bit mode. Execution of this instruction in 32-bit mode causes a reserved instruction exception.

Operation:

64	T:	$s \leftarrow 1 \parallel sa$
		$GPR[rd] \leftarrow 0^{s} \parallel GPR[rt]_{63...s}$

Exceptions:

Reserved instruction exception (R4000 in 32-bit mode)

DSUB Doubleword Subtract DSUB

31 … 26	25 … 21	20 … 16	15 … 11	10 … 6	5 … 0
SPECIAL 000000	rs	rt	rd	0 00000	DSUB 101110
6	5	5	5	5	6

Format:

DSUB rd, rs, rt

Description:

The contents of general register *rt* are subtracted from the contents of general register *rs* to form a result. The result is placed into general register *rd*.

The only difference between this instruction and the DSUBU instruction is that DSUBU never traps on overflow.

An integer overflow exception takes place if the carries out of bits 62 and 63 differ (2's complement overflow). The destination register *rd* is not modified when an integer overflow exception occurs.

This operation is only defined for the R4000 operating in 64-bit mode. Execution of this instruction in 32-bit mode causes a reserved instruction exception.

Operation:

```
64      T:    GPR[rd] ← GPR[rs] – GPR[rt]
```

Exceptions:

Integer overflow exception
Reserved instruction exception (R4000 in 32-bit mode)

DSUBU Doubleword Subtract Unsigned DSUBU

31–26	25–21	20–16	15–11	10–6	5–0
SPECIAL 000000	rs	rt	rd	0 00000	DSUBU 101111
6	5	5	5	5	6

Format:

DSUBU rd, rs, rt

Description:

The contents of general register *rt* are subtracted from the contents of general register *rs* to form a result. The result is placed into general register *rd*.

The only difference between this instruction and the DSUB instruction is that DSUBU never traps on overflow. No integer overflow exception occurs under any circumstances.

This operation is only defined for the R4000 operating in 64-bit mode. Execution of this instruction in 32-bit mode causes a reserved instruction exception.

Operation:

64	T:	GPR[rd] ← GPR[rs] – GPR[rt]

Exceptions:

Reserved instruction exception (R4000 in 32-bit mode)

ERET Exception Return ERET

31 ... 26	25	24 ... 6	5 ... 0
COP0 010000	CO 1	0 000 0000 0000 0000 0000	ERET 011000
6	1	19	6

Format:

ERET

Description:

ERET is the R4000 instruction for returning from an interrupt, exception, or error trap. Unlike a branch or jump instruction, ERET does not execute the next instruction.

ERET must not itself be placed in a branch delay slot.

If the processor is servicing an error trap ($SR_2 = 1$), then load the PC from the *ErrorEPC* and clear the *ERL* bit of the *Status* register (SR_2). Otherwise ($SR_2 = 0$), load the PC from the *EPC*, and clear the *EXL* bit of the *Status* register (SR_1).

An ERET executed between a LL and SC also causes the SC to fail.

Operation:

```
32, 64      T:  if SR2 = 1 then
                     PC ← ErrorEPC
                     SR ← SR31...3 || 0 || SR1...0
                else
                     PC ← EPC
                     SR ← SR31...2 || 0 || SR0
                endif
                LLbit ← 0
```

Exceptions:

Coprocessor unusable exception

J Jump J

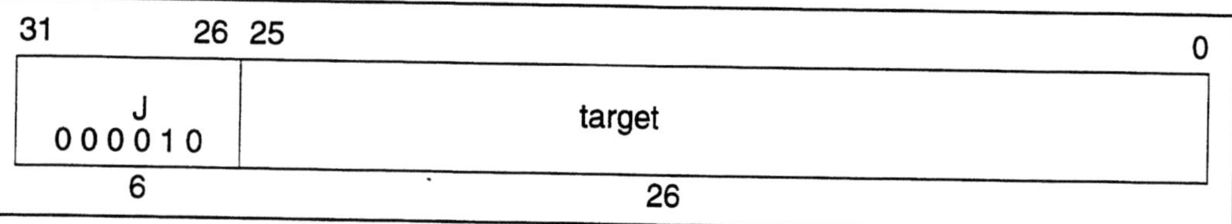

Format:

J target

Description:

The 26-bit target address is shifted left two bits and combined with the high-order bits of the address of the delay slot. The program unconditionally jumps to this calculated address with a delay of one instruction.

Operation:

32	T:	temp ← target
	T+1:	PC ← $PC_{31...28}$ ‖ temp ‖ 0^2
64	T:	temp ← target
	T+1:	PC ← $PC_{63...28}$ ‖ temp ‖ 0^2

Exceptions:

None

JAL — Jump And Link — JAL

31 … 26	25 … 0
JAL 000011	target
6	26

Format:

JAL target

Description:

The 26-bit target address is shifted left two bits and combined with the high-order bits of the address of the delay slot. The program unconditionally jumps to this calculated address with a delay of one instruction. The address of the instruction after the delay slot is placed in the link register, *r31*.

Operation:

32	T:	temp ← target
		GPR[31] ← PC + 8
	T+1:	PC ← $PC_{31...28}$ ‖ temp ‖ 0^2
64	T:	temp ← target
		GPR[31] ← PC + 8
	T+1:	PC ← $PC_{63...28}$ ‖ temp ‖ 0^2

Exceptions:

None

JALR Jump And Link Register JALR

31–26	25–21	20–16	15–11	10–6	5–0
SPECIAL 000000	rs	0 00000	rd	0 00000	JALR 001001
6	5	5	5	5	6

Format:

JALR rs
JALR rd, rs

Description:

The program unconditionally jumps to the address contained in general register *rs*, with a delay of one instruction. The address of the instruction after the delay slot is placed in general register *rd*. The default value of *rd*, if omitted in the assembly language instruction, is 31.

Register specifiers *rs* and *rd* may not be equal, because such an instruction does not have the same effect when re-executed. However, an attempt to execute this instruction is *not* trapped, and the result of executing such an instruction is undefined.

Since instructions must be word-aligned, a **Jump and Link Register** instruction must specify a target register (*rs*) whose two low-order bits are zero. If these low-order bits are not zero, an address exception will occur when the jump target instruction is subsequently fetched.

Operation:

```
32, 64    T:      temp ← GPR [rs]
                  GPR[rd] ← PC + 8
          T+1:    PC ← temp
```

Exceptions:

None

JR Jump Register JR

31 26	25 21	20 6	5 0
SPECIAL 000000	rs	0 000 0000 0000 0000	JR 001000
6	5	15	6

Format:

JR rs

Description:

The program unconditionally jumps to the address contained in general register *rs*, with a delay of one instruction.

Since instructions must be word-aligned, a **Jump Register** instruction must specify a target register (*rs*) whose two low-order bits are zero. If these low-order bits are not zero, an address exception will occur when the jump target instruction is subsequently fetched.

Operation:

32, 64	T:	temp ← GPR[rs]
	T+1:	PC ← temp

Exceptions:

None

LB — Load Byte — LB

31–26	25–21	20–16	15–0
LB 100000	base	rt	offset
6	5	5	16

Format:

LB rt, offset(base)

Description:

The 16-bit *offset* is sign-extended and added to the contents of general register *base* to form a virtual address. The contents of the byte at the memory location specified by the effective address are sign-extended and loaded into general register *rt*.

Operation:

32	T:	$vAddr \leftarrow ((offset_{15})^{16} \,\|\|\, offset_{15...0}) + GPR[base]$ $(pAddr, uncached) \leftarrow AddressTranslation\ (vAddr, DATA)$ $pAddr \leftarrow pAddr_{PSIZE-1...2} \,\|\|\, (pAddr_{1...0}\ xor\ ReverseEndian^2)$ $mem \leftarrow LoadMemory\ (uncached, BYTE, pAddr, vAddr, DATA)$ $byte \leftarrow vAddr_{1...0}\ xor\ BigEndianCPU^2$ $GPR[rt] \leftarrow (mem_{7+8*byte})^{24} \,\|\|\, mem_{7+8*byte...8*byte}$
64	T:	$vAddr \leftarrow ((offset_{15})^{48} \,\|\|\, offset_{15...0}) + GPR[base]$ $(pAddr, uncached) \leftarrow AddressTranslation\ (vAddr, DATA)$ $pAddr \leftarrow pAddr_{PSIZE-1...3} \,\|\|\, (pAddr_{2...0}\ xor\ ReverseEndian^3)$ $mem \leftarrow LoadMemory\ (uncached, BYTE, pAddr, vAddr, DATA)$ $byte \leftarrow vAddr_{2...0}\ xor\ BigEndianCPU^3$ $GPR[rt] \leftarrow (mem_{7+8*byte})^{56} \,\|\|\, mem_{7+8*byte...8*byte}$

Exceptions:

TLB refill exception
TLB invalid exception
Bus error exception
Address error exception

LBU — Load Byte Unsigned — LBU

31–26	25–21	20–16	15–0
LBU 100100	base	rt	offset
6	5	5	16

Format:

LBU rt, offset(base)

Description:

The 16-bit *offset* is sign-extended and added to the contents of general register *base* to form a virtual address. The contents of the byte at the memory location specified by the effective address are zero-extended and loaded into general register *rt*.

Operation:

32 T: $vAddr \leftarrow ((offset_{15})^{16} \| offset_{15...0}) + GPR[base]$
$(pAddr, uncached) \leftarrow AddressTranslation\ (vAddr, DATA)$
$pAddr \leftarrow pAddr_{PSIZE-1...2} \| (pAddr_{1...0}\ xor\ ReverseEndian^2)$
$mem \leftarrow LoadMemory\ (uncached, BYTE, pAddr, vAddr, DATA)$
$byte \leftarrow vAddr_{1...0}\ xor\ BigEndianCPU^2$
$GPR[rt] \leftarrow 0^{24} \| mem_{7+8*byte...8*byte}$

64 T: $vAddr \leftarrow ((offset_{15})^{48} \| offset_{15...0}) + GPR[base]$
$(pAddr, uncached) \leftarrow AddressTranslation\ (vAddr, DATA)$
$pAddr \leftarrow pAddr_{PSIZE-1...3} \| (pAddr_{2...0}\ xor\ ReverseEndian^3)$
$mem \leftarrow LoadMemory\ (uncached, BYTE, pAddr, vAddr, DATA)$
$byte \leftarrow vAddr_{2...0}\ xor\ BigEndianCPU^3$
$GPR[rt] \leftarrow 0^{56} \| mem_{7+8*byte...8*byte}$

Exceptions:

TLB refill exception
TLB invalid exception
Bus error exception
Address error exception

LD Load Doubleword 

31 ... 26	25 ... 21	20 ... 16	15 ... 0
LD 1 1 0 1 1 1	base	rt	offset
6	5	5	16

Format:

LD rt, offset(base)

Description:

The 16-bit *offset* is sign-extended and added to the contents of general register *base* to form a virtual address. The contents of the 64-bit doubleword at the memory location specified by the effective address are loaded into general register *rt*.

If any of the three least-significant bits of the effective address are non-zero, an address error exception occurs.

This operation is only defined for the R4000 operating in 64-bit mode. Execution of this instruction in 32-bit mode causes a reserved instruction exception.

Operation:

```
64   T:  vAddr ← ((offset15)^48 || offset15...0) + GPR[base]
         (pAddr, uncached) ← AddressTranslation (vAddr, DATA)
         mem ← LoadMemory (uncached, DOUBLEWORD, pAddr, vAddr, DATA)
         GPR[rt] ← mem
```

Exceptions:

TLB refill exception
TLB invalid exception
Bus error exception
Address error exception
Reserved instruction exception (R4000 in 32-bit user mode
R4000 in 32-bit supervisor mode)

LDCz Load Doubleword To Coprocessor LDCz

31 — 26	25 — 21	20 — 16	15 — 0
LDCz 1 1 0 1 x x*	base	rt	offset
6	5	5	16

Format:

LDCz rt, offset(base)

Description:

The 16-bit *offset* is sign-extended and added to the contents of general register *base* to form a virtual address. The processor reads a doubleword from the addressed memory location and makes the data available to coprocessor unit z. The manner in which each coprocessor uses the data is defined by the individual coprocessor specifications.

If any of the three least-significant bits of the effective address are non-zero, an address error exception takes place.

This instruction is not valid for use with CP0.

This instruction is undefined when the least-significant bit of the *rt* field is non-zero.

Execution of the instruction referencing coprocessor 3 causes a reserved instruction exception, not a coprocessor unusable exception.

*See the table "Opcode Bit Encoding" on next page, or "CPU Instruction Opcode Bit Encoding" at the end of Appendix A.

LDCz Load Doubleword To Coprocessor (continued) LDCz

Operation:

32	T:	vAddr ← ((offset$_{15}$)^{16} || offset$_{15...0}$) + GPR[base] (pAddr, uncached) ← AddressTranslation (vAddr, DATA) mem ← LoadMemory (uncached, DOUBLEWORD, pAddr, vAddr, DATA) COPzLD (rt, mem)
64	T:	vAddr ← ((offset$_{15}$)^{48} || offset$_{15...0}$) + GPR[base] (pAddr, uncached) ← AddressTranslation (vAddr, DATA) mem ← LoadMemory (uncached, DOUBLEWORD, pAddr, vAddr, DATA) COPzLD (rt, mem)

Exceptions:

TLB refill exception
TLB invalid exception
Bus error exception
Address error exception
Coprocessor unusable exception
Reserved instruction exception (coprocessor 3)

Opcode Bit Encoding:

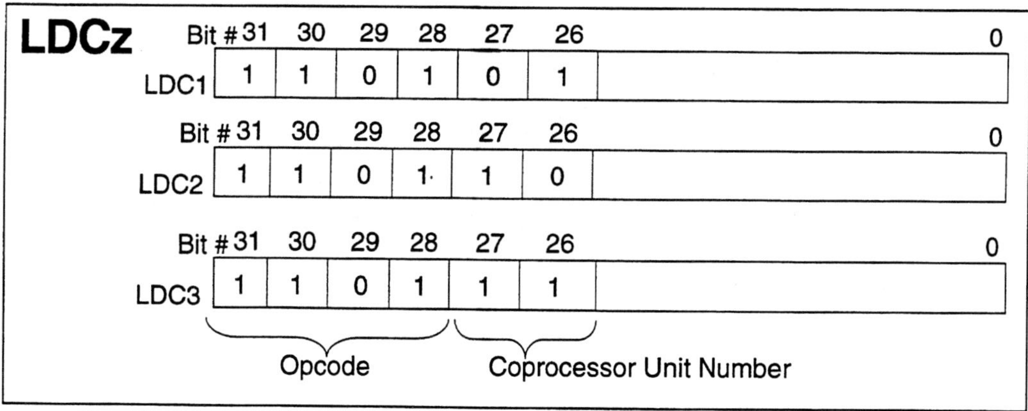

LDL　Load Doubleword Left　LDL

31　　26	25　　21	20　　16	15　　0
LDL 0 1 1 0 1 0	base	rt	offset
6	5	5	16

Format:

LDL rt, offset(base)

Description:

This instruction can be used in combination with the LDR instruction to load a register with eight consecutive bytes from memory, when the bytes cross a doubleword boundary. LDL loads the left portion of the register with the appropriate part of the high-order doubleword; LDR loads the right portion of the register with the appropriate part of the low-order doubleword.

The LDL instruction adds its sign-extended 16-bit *offset* to the contents of general register *base* to form a virtual address which can specify an arbitrary byte. It reads bytes only from the doubleword in memory which contains the specified starting byte. From one to eight bytes will be loaded, depending on the starting byte specified.

Conceptually, it starts at the specified byte in memory and loads that byte into the high-order (left-most) byte of the register; then it loads bytes from memory into the register until it reaches the low-order byte of the doubleword in memory. The least-significant (right-most) byte(s) of the register will not be changed.

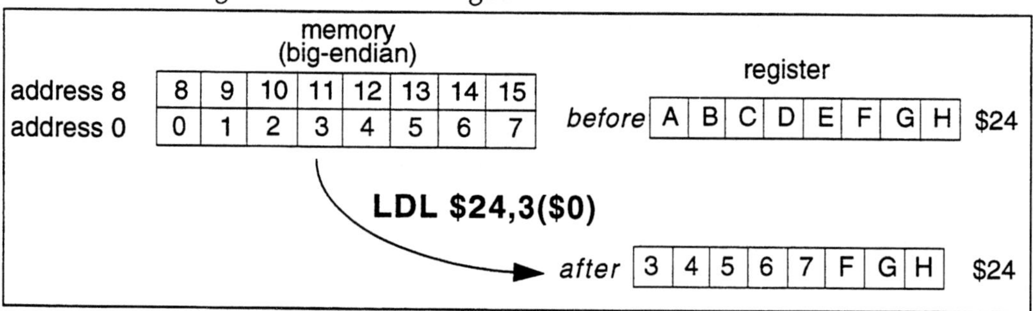

LDL — Load Doubleword Left (continued)

The contents of general register *rt* are internally bypassed within the processor so that no NOP is needed between an immediately preceding load instruction which specifies register *rt* and a following LDL (or LDR) instruction which also specifies register *rt*.

No address exceptions due to alignment are possible.

This operation is only defined for the R4000 operating in 64-bit mode. Execution of this instruction in 32-bit mode causes a reserved instruction exception.

Operation:

64 T: $\text{vAddr} \leftarrow ((\text{offset}_{15})^{48} \,||\, \text{offset}_{15...0}) + \text{GPR[base]}$

$(\text{pAddr, uncached}) \leftarrow \text{AddressTranslation (vAddr, DATA)}$

$\text{pAddr} \leftarrow \text{pAddr}_{\text{PSIZE}-1...3} \,||\, (\text{pAddr}_{2...0} \text{ xor ReverseEndian}^{3})$

if BigEndianMem = 0 then

  $\text{pAddr} \leftarrow \text{pAddr}_{\text{PSIZE}-1...3} \,||\, 0^{3}$

endif

$\text{byte} \leftarrow \text{vAddr}_{2...0} \text{ xor BigEndianCPU}^{3}$

$\text{mem} \leftarrow \text{LoadMemory (uncached, byte, pAddr, vAddr, DATA)}$

$\text{GPR[rt]} \leftarrow \text{mem}_{7+8*\text{byte}...0} \,||\, \text{GPR[rt]}_{55-8*\text{byte}...0}$

LDL Load Doubleword Left (continued) LDL

Given a doubleword in a register and a doubleword in memory, the operation of LDL is as follows:

LDL

Register	A	B	C	D	E	F	G	H
Memory	I	J	K	L	M	N	O	P

$vAddr_{2..0}$	BigEndianCPU = 0				BigEndianCPU = 1			
	destination	type	offset LEM	offset BEM	destination	type	offset LEM	offset BEM
0	P B C D E F G H	0	0	7	I J K L M N O P	7	0	0
1	O P C D E F G H	1	0	6	J K L M N O P H	6	0	1
2	N O P D E F G H	2	0	5	K L M N O P G H	5	0	2
3	M N O P E F G P	3	0	4	L M N O P F G H	4	0	3
4	L M N O P F G H	4	0	3	M N O P E F G H	3	0	4
5	K L M N O P G H	5	0	2	N O P D E F G H	2	0	5
6	J K L M N O P H	6	0	1	O P C D E F G H	1	0	6
7	I J K L M N O P	7	0	0	P B C D E F G H	0	0	7

LEM	Little-endian memory (BigEndianMem = 0)
BEM	BigEndianMem = 1
Type	AccessType (see Table 2-1) sent to memory
Offset	$pAddr_{2...0}$ sent to memory

Exceptions:

TLB refill exception
TLB invalid exception
Bus error exception
Address error exception
Reserved instruction exception (R4000 in 32-bit mode)

LDR Load Doubleword Right LDR

31 — 26	25 — 21	20 — 16	15 — 0
LDR 011011	base	rt	offset
6	5	5	16

Format:

LDR rt, offset(base)

Description:

This instruction can be used in combination with the LDL instruction to load a register with eight consecutive bytes from memory, when the bytes cross a doubleword boundary. LDR loads the right portion of the register with the appropriate part of the low-order doubleword; LDL loads the left portion of the register with the appropriate part of the high-order doubleword.

The LDR instruction adds its sign-extended 16-bit *offset* to the contents of general register *base* to form a virtual address which can specify an arbitrary byte. It reads bytes only from the doubleword in memory which contains the specified starting byte. From one to eight bytes will be loaded, depending on the starting byte specified.

Conceptually, it starts at the specified byte in memory and loads that byte into the low-order (right-most) byte of the register; then it loads bytes from memory into the register until it reaches the high-order byte of the doubleword in memory. The most significant (left-most) byte(s) of the register will not be changed.

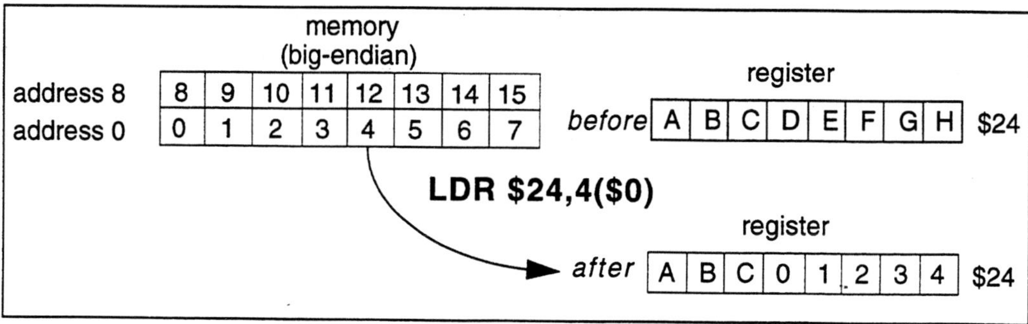

LDR Load Doubleword Right (continued) 

The contents of general register *rt* are internally bypassed within the processor so that no NOP is needed between an immediately preceding load instruction which specifies register *rt* and a following LDR (or LDL) instruction which also specifies register *rt*.

No address exceptions due to alignment are possible.

This operation is only defined for the R4000 operating in 64-bit mode. Execution of this instruction in 32-bit mode causes a reserved instruction exception.

Operation:

64	T:	$vAddr \leftarrow ((offset_{15})^{48} \| offset_{15...0}) + GPR[base]$
		$(pAddr, uncached) \leftarrow AddressTranslation (vAddr, DATA)$
		$pAddr \leftarrow pAddr_{PSIZE-1...3} \| (pAddr_{2...0}$ xor $ReverseEndian^3)$
		if BigEndianMem = 1 then
		$pAddr \leftarrow pAddr_{31...3} \| 0^3$
		endif
		$byte \leftarrow vAddr_{2...0}$ xor $BigEndianCPU^3$
		$mem \leftarrow LoadMemory (uncached, byte, pAddr, vAddr, DATA)$
		$GPR[rt] \leftarrow GPR[rt]_{63...64-8*byte} \| mem_{63...8*byte}$

LDR — Load Doubleword Right (continued)

Given a doubleword in a register and a doubleword in memory, the operation of LDR is as follows:

LDR

Register	A	B	C	D	E	F	G	H
Memory	I	J	K	L	M	N	O	P

vAddr$_{2..0}$	BigEndianCPU = 0				BigEndianCPU = 1			
	destination	type	offset		destination	type	offset	
			LEM	BEM			LEM	BEM
0	I J K L M N O P	7	0	0	A B C D E F G I	0	7	0
1	A I J K L M N O	6	1	0	A B C D E F I J	1	6	0
2	A B I J K L M N	5	2	0	A B C D E I J K	2	5	0
3	A B C I J K L M	4	3	0	A B C D I J K L	3	4	0
4	A B C D I J K L	3	4	0	A B C I J K L M	4	3	0
5	A B C D E I J K	2	5	0	A B I J K L M N	5	2	0
6	A B C D E F I J	1	6	0	A I J K L M N O	6	1	0
7	A B C D E F G I	0	7	0	I J K L M N O P	7	0	0

LEM	Little-endian memory (BigEndianMem = 0)
BEM	BigEndianMem = 1
Type	AccessType (see Table 2-1) sent to memory
Offset	pAddr$_{2...0}$ sent to memory

Exceptions:

TLB refill exception
TLB invalid exception
Bus error exception
Address error exception
Reserved instruction exception (R4000 in 32-bit mode)

LH — Load Halfword — LH

31–26	25–21	20–16	15–0
LH 100001	base	rt	offset
6	5	5	16

Format:

LH rt, offset(base)

Description:

The 16-bit *offset* is sign-extended and added to the contents of general register *base* to form a virtual address. The contents of the halfword at the memory location specified by the effective address are sign-extended and loaded into general register *rt*.

If the least-significant bit of the effective address is non-zero, an address error exception occurs.

Operation:

32	T:	$vAddr \leftarrow ((offset_{15})^{16} \parallel offset_{15...0}) + GPR[base]$ $(pAddr, uncached) \leftarrow AddressTranslation\ (vAddr, DATA)$ $pAddr \leftarrow pAddr_{PSIZE-1...2} \parallel (pAddr_{1...0}\ xor\ (ReverseEndian \parallel 0))$ $mem \leftarrow LoadMemory\ (uncached, HALFWORD, pAddr, vAddr, DATA)$ $byte \leftarrow vAddr_{1...0}\ xor\ (BigEndianCPU \parallel 0)$ $GPR[rt] \leftarrow (mem_{15+8*byte})^{16} \parallel mem_{15+8*byte...8*byte}$
64	T:	$vAddr \leftarrow ((offset_{15})^{48} \parallel offset_{15...0}) + GPR[base]$ $(pAddr, uncached) \leftarrow AddressTranslation\ (vAddr, DATA)$ $pAddr \leftarrow pAddr_{PSIZE-1...3} \parallel (pAddr_{2...0}\ xor\ (ReverseEndian \parallel 0))$ $mem \leftarrow LoadMemory\ (uncached, HALFWORD, pAddr, vAddr, DATA)$ $byte \leftarrow vAddr_{2...0}\ xor\ (BigEndianCPU^2 \parallel 0)$ $GPR[rt] \leftarrow (mem_{15+8*byte})^{16} \parallel mem_{15+8*byte...8*byte}$

Exceptions:

TLB refill exception
TLB invalid exception
Bus error exception
Address error exception

LHU Load Halfword Unsigned LHU

31 26	25 21	20 16	15 0
LHU 100101	base	rt	offset
6	5	5	16

Format:

LHU rt, offset(base)

Description:

The 16-bit *offset* is sign-extended and added to the contents of general register *base* to form a virtual address. The contents of the halfword at the memory location specified by the effective address are zero-extended and loaded into general register *rt*.

If the least-significant bit of the effective address is non-zero, an address error exception occurs.

Operation:

32	T:	$vAddr \leftarrow ((offset_{15})^{16} \,\|\|\, offset_{15...0}) + GPR[base]$ $(pAddr, uncached) \leftarrow AddressTranslation\ (vAddr, DATA)$ $pAddr \leftarrow pAddr_{PSIZE-1...2} \,\|\|\, (pAddr_{1...0}\ xor\ (ReverseEndian \,\|\|\, 0))$ $mem \leftarrow LoadMemory\ (uncached, HALFWORD, pAddr, vAddr, DATA)$ $byte \leftarrow vAddr_{1...0}\ xor\ (BigEndianCPU \,\|\|\, 0)$ $GPR[rt] \leftarrow 0^{16} \,\|\|\, mem_{15+8*byte...8*byte}$
64	T:	$vAddr \leftarrow ((offset_{15})^{48} \,\|\|\, offset_{15...0}) + GPR[base]$ $(pAddr, uncached) \leftarrow AddressTranslation\ (vAddr, DATA)$ $pAddr \leftarrow pAddr_{PSIZE-1...3} \,\|\|\, (pAddr_{2...0}\ xor\ (ReverseEndian^2 \,\|\|\, 0))$ $mem \leftarrow LoadMemory\ (uncached, HALFWORD, pAddr, vAddr, DATA)$ $byte \leftarrow vAddr_{2...0}\ xor\ (BigEndianCPU^2 \,\|\|\, 0)$ $GPR[rt] \leftarrow 0^{48} \,\|\|\, mem_{15+8*byte...8*byte}$

Exceptions:

TLB refill exception
TLB invalid exception
Bus Error exception
Address error exception

LL Load Linked LL

31–26	25–21	20–16	15–0
LL 110000	base	rt	offset
6	5	5	16

Format:

LL rt, offset(base)

Description:

The 16-bit *offset* is sign-extended and added to the contents of general register *base* to form a virtual address. The contents of the word at the memory location specified by the effective address are loaded into general register *rt*. In 64-bit mode, the loaded word is sign-extended.

This instruction implicitly performs a SYNC operation; all loads and stores to shared memory fetched prior to the LL must access memory before the LL, and loads and stores to shared memory fetched subsequent to the LL must access memory after the LL. The processor begins checking the accessed word for modification by other processors and devices.

Load Linked and Store Conditional can be used to atomically update memory locations as shown:

```
L1:
    LL      T1, (T0)
    ADD     T2, T1, 1
    SC      T2, (T0)
    BEQ     T2, 0, L1
    NOP
```

This atomically increments the word addressed by T0. Changing the ADD to an OR changes this to an atomic bit set.

This instruction is available in User mode, and it is not necessary for CP0 to be enabled.

LL Load Linked (continued) 

The operation of LL is undefined if the addressed location is uncached and, for synchronization between multiple processors, the operation of LL is undefined if the addressed location is noncoherent. A cache miss that occurs between LL and SC may cause SC to fail, so no load or store operation should occur between LL and SC, otherwise the SC may never be successful. Exceptions also cause SC to fail, so persistent exceptions must be avoided.

If either of the two least-significant bits of the effective address are non-zero, an address error exception takes place.

Operation:

32	T:	vAddr ← $((\text{offset}_{15})^{16} \parallel \text{offset}_{15...0})$ + GPR[base]
		(pAddr, uncached) ← AddressTranslation (vAddr, DATA)
		mem ← LoadMemory (uncached, WORD, pAddr, vAddr, DATA)
		GPR[rt] ← mem
		LLbit ← 1
		SyncOperation()
64	T:	vAddr ← $((\text{offset}_{15})^{48} \parallel \text{offset}_{15...0})$ + GPR[base]
		(pAddr, uncached) ← AddressTranslation (vAddr, DATA)
		pAddr ← $\text{pAddr}_{\text{PSIZE-1...3}} \parallel (\text{pAddr}_{2...0}$ xor (ReverseEndian $\parallel 0^2$))
		mem ← LoadMemory (uncached, WORD, pAddr, vAddr, DATA)
		byte ← $\text{vAddr}_{2...0}$ xor (BigEndianCPU $\parallel 0^2$)
		GPR[rt] ← $(\text{mem}_{31+8*\text{byte}})^{32} \parallel \text{mem}_{31+8*\text{byte}...8*\text{byte}}$
		LLbit ← 1
		SyncOperation()

Exceptions:

TLB refill exception
TLB invalid exception
Bus error exception
Address error exception

LLD Load Linked Doubleword

31 — 26	25 — 21	20 — 16	15 — 0
LLD 110100	base	rt	offset
6	5	5	16

Format:

LLD rt, offset(base)

Description:

The 16-bit *offset* is sign-extended and added to the contents of general register *base* to form a virtual address. The contents of the doubleword at the memory location specified by the effective address are loaded into general register *rt*.

This instruction implicitly performs a SYNC operation; all loads and stores to shared memory fetched prior to the LLD must access memory before the LLD, and loads and stores to shared memory fetched subsequent to the LLD must access memory after the LLD. The processor begins checking the accessed doubleword for modification by other processors and devices.

Load Linked Doubleword and Store Conditional Doubleword can be used to atomically update memory locations:

```
L1:
    LLD     T1, (T0)
    ADD     T2, T1, 1
    SCD     T2, (T0)
    BEQ     T2, 0, L1
    NOP
```

This atomically increments the word addressed by T0. Changing the ADD to an OR changes this to an atomic bit set.

LLD Load Linked Doubleword (continued) 

The operation of LLD is undefined if the addressed location is uncached and, for synchronization between multiple processors, the operation of LLD is undefined if the addressed location is noncoherent. A cache miss that occurs between LLD and SCD may cause SCD to fail, so no load or store operation should occur between LLD and SCD, otherwise the SCD may never be successful. Exceptions also cause SCD to fail, so persistent exceptions must be avoided.

This instruction is available in User mode, and it is not necessary for CP0 to be enabled.

If any of the three least-significant bits of the effective address are non-zero, an address error exception takes place.

This operation is only defined for the R4000 operating in 64-bit mode. Execution of this instruction in 32-bit mode causes a reserved instruction exception.

Operation:

```
64    T:   vAddr ← ((offset_15)^48 || offset_15...0) + GPR[base]
                (pAddr, uncached) ← AddressTranslation (vAddr, DATA)
           mem ← LoadMemory (uncached, DOUBLEWORD, pAddr, vAddr, DATA)
           GPR[rt] ← mem
           LLbit ← 1
           SyncOperation()
```

Exceptions:

TLB refill exception
TLB invalid exception
Bus error exception
Address error exception
Reserved instruction exception (R4000 in 32-bit mode)

LUI Load Upper Immediate LUI

31 — 26	25 — 21	20 — 16	15 — 0
LUI 0 0 1 1 1 1	0 0 0 0 0 0	rt	immediate
6	5	5	16

Format:

LUI rt, immediate

Description:

The 16-bit *immediate* is shifted left 16 bits and concatenated to 16 bits of zeros. The result is placed into general register *rt*. In 64-bit mode, the loaded word is sign-extended.

Operation:

32	T:	$GPR[rt] \leftarrow immediate \parallel 0^{16}$
64	T:	$GPR[rt] \leftarrow (immediate_{15})^{32} \parallel immediate \parallel 0^{16}$

Exceptions:

None

LW — Load Word — LW

31 26	25 21	20 16	15 0
LW 100011	base	rt	offset
6	5	5	16

Format:

LW rt, offset(base)

Description:

The 16-bit *offset* is sign-extended and added to the contents of general register *base* to form a virtual address. The contents of the word at the memory location specified by the effective address are loaded into general register *rt*. In 64-bit mode, the loaded word is sign-extended.

If either of the two least-significant bits of the effective address is non-zero, an address error exception occurs.

Operation:

32 T: $vAddr \leftarrow ((offset_{15})^{16} \,||\, offset_{15...0}) + GPR[base]$
$(pAddr, uncached) \leftarrow AddressTranslation\ (vAddr, DATA)$
$mem \leftarrow LoadMemory\ (uncached, WORD, pAddr, vAddr, DATA)$
$GPR[rt] \leftarrow mem$

64 T: $vAddr \leftarrow ((offset_{15})^{48} \,||\, offset_{15...0}) + GPR[base]$
$(pAddr, uncached) \leftarrow AddressTranslation\ (vAddr, DATA)$
$pAddr \leftarrow pAddr_{PSIZE-1...3} \,||\, (pAddr_{2...0}\ xor\ (ReverseEndian \,||\, 0^2))$
$mem \leftarrow LoadMemory\ (uncached, WORD, pAddr, vAddr, DATA)$
$byte \leftarrow vAddr_{2...0}.xor\ (BigEndianCPU \,||\, 0^2)$
$GPR[rt] \leftarrow (mem_{31+8*byte})^{32} \,||\, mem_{31+8*byte...8*byte}$

Exceptions:

TLB refill exception
TLB invalid exception
Bus error exception
Address error exception

LWCz Load Word To Coprocessor LWCz

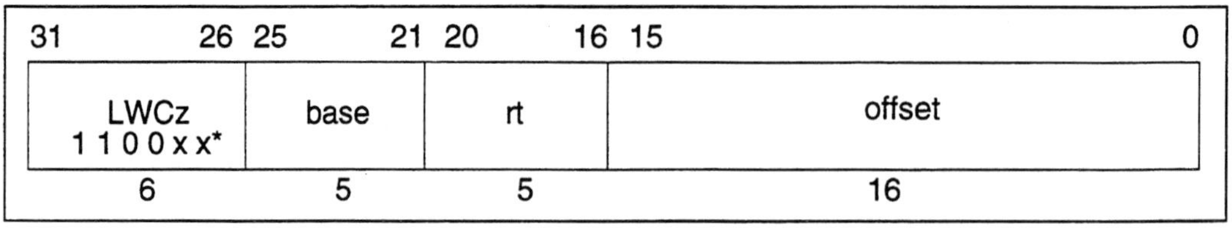

31 26	25 21	20 16	15 0
LWCz 1 1 0 0 x x*	base	rt	offset
6	5	5	16

Format:

LWCz rt, offset(base)

Description:

The 16-bit *offset* is sign-extended and added to the contents of general register *base* to form a virtual address. The processor reads a word from the addressed memory location, and makes the data available to coprocessor unit z.

The manner in which each coprocessor uses the data is defined by the individual coprocessor specifications.

If either of the two least-significant bits of the effective address is non-zero, an address error exception occurs.

This instruction is not valid for use with CP0.

*See the table "Opcode Bit Encoding" on next page, or "CPU Instruction Opcode Bit Encoding" at the end of Appendix A.

LWCz — Load Word To Coprocessor (continued) — LWCz

Operation:

32 T: $vAddr \leftarrow ((offset_{15})^{16} \,||\, offset_{15...0}) + GPR[base]$
$(pAddr, uncached) \leftarrow AddressTranslation\ (vAddr, DATA)$
$byte \leftarrow vAddr_{1...0}$
$mem \leftarrow LoadMemory\ (uncached, DOUBLEWORD, pAddr, vAddr, DATA)$
COPzLW (rt, mem)

64 T: $vAddr \leftarrow ((offset_{15})^{48} \,||\, offset_{15...0}) + GPR[base\}$
$(pAddr, uncached) \leftarrow AddressTranslation\ (vAddr, DATA)$
$pAddr \leftarrow pAddr_{PSIZE-1...3} \,||\, (pAddr_{2...0}\ xor\ (ReverseEndian \,||\, 0^2))$
$mem \leftarrow LoadMemory\ (uncached, DOUBLEWORD, pAddr, vAddr, DATA)$
$byte \leftarrow vAddr_{2...0}\ xor\ (BigEndianCPU \,||\, 0^2)$
COPzLW (byte, rt, mem)

Exceptions:

TLB refill exception
TLB invalid exception
Bus error exception
Address error exception
Coprocessor unusable exception

Opcode Bit Encoding:

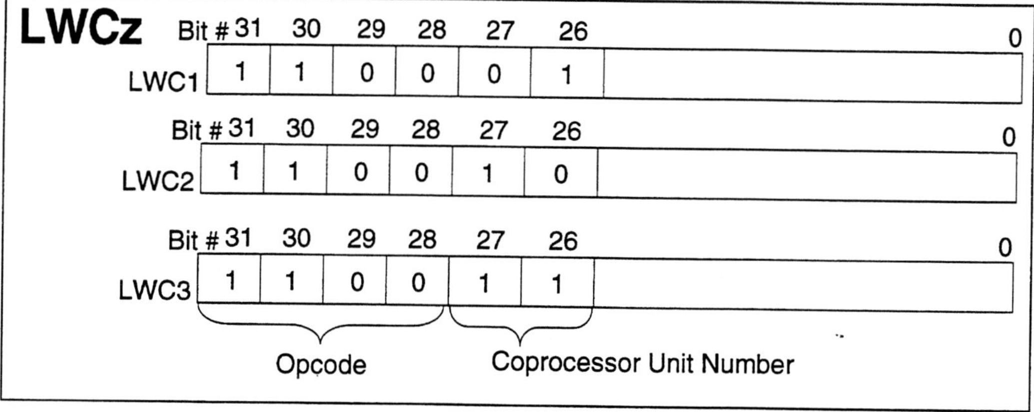

LWL — Load Word Left — LWL

31–26	25–21	20–16	15–0
LWL 100010	base	rt	offset
6	5	5	16

Format:

LWL rt, offset(base)

Description:

This instruction can be used in combination with the LWR instruction to load a register with four consecutive bytes from memory, when the bytes cross a word boundary. LWL loads the left portion of the register with the appropriate part of the high-order word; LWR loads the right portion of the register with the appropriate part of the low-order word.

The LWL instruction adds its sign-extended 16-bit *offset* to the contents of general register *base* to form a virtual address which can specify an arbitrary byte. It reads bytes only from the word in memory which contains the specified starting byte. From one to four bytes will be loaded, depending on the starting byte specified. In 64-bit mode, the loaded word is sign-extended.

Conceptually, it starts at the specified byte in memory and loads that byte into the high-order (left-most) byte of the register; then it loads bytes from memory into the register until it reaches the low-order byte of the word in memory. The least-significant (right-most) byte(s) of the register will not be changed.

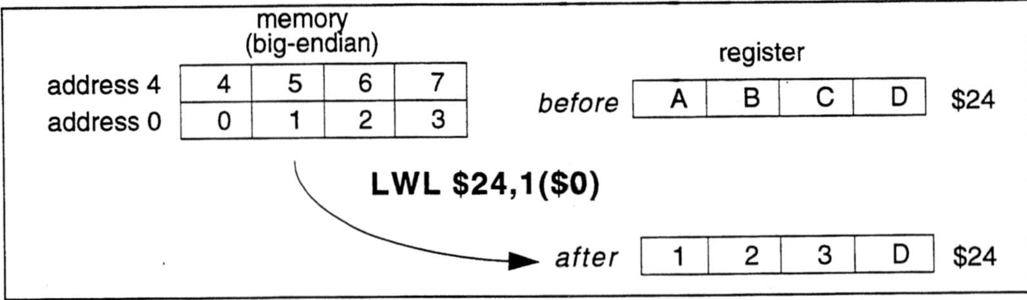

LWL **Load Word Left (continued)**

The contents of general register *rt* are internally bypassed within the processor so that no NOP is needed between an immediately preceding load instruction which specifies register *rt* and a following LWL (or LWR) instruction which also specifies register *rt*.

No address exceptions due to alignment are possible.

Operation:

```
32   T:   vAddr ← ((offset_15)^16 || offset_15...0) + GPR[base]
          (pAddr, uncached) ← AddressTranslation (vAddr, DATA)
          pAddr ← pAddr_PSIZE–1...2 || (pAddr_1...0 xor ReverseEndian^2)
          if BigEndianMem = 0 then
                pAddr ← pAddr_PSIZE–31...2 || 0^2
          endif
          byte ← vAddr_1...0 xor BigEndianCPU^2
          mem ← LoadMemory (uncached, byte, pAddr, vAddr, DATA)
          GPR[rt] ← mem_7+8*byte...0 || GPR[rt]_23–8*byte...0

64   T:   vAddr ← ((offset_15)^48 || offset_15...0) + GPR[base]
          (pAddr, uncached) ← AddressTranslation (vAddr, DATA)
          pAddr ← pAddr_PSIZE–1...3 || (pAddr_2...0 xor ReverseEndian^3)
          if BigEndianMem = 0 then
                pAddr ← pAddr_PSIZE–1...3 || 0^3
          endif
          byte ← vAddr_1...0 xor BigEndianCPU^2
          word ← vAddr_2 xor BigEndianCPU
          mem ← LoadMemory (uncached, 0 || byte, pAddr, vAddr, DATA)
          temp ← mem_31+32*word-8*byte...32*word || GPR[rt]_23-8*byte...0
          GPR[rt] ← (temp_31)^32 || temp
```

LWL Load Word Left (continued) LWL

Given a doubleword in a register and a doubleword in memory, the operation of LWL is as follows:

LWL								
Register	A	B	C	D	E	F	G	H
Memory	I	J	K	L	M	N	O	P

$vAddr_{2..0}$	BigEndianCPU = 0				BigEndianCPU = 1			
	destination	type	offset		destination	type	offset	
			LEM	BEM			LEM	BEM
0	S S S S P F G H	0	0	7	S S S S I J K L	3	4	0
1	S S S S O P G H	1	0	6	S S S S J K L H	2	4	1
2	S S S S N O P H	2	0	5	S S S S K L G H	1	4	2
3	S S S S M N O P	3	0	4	S S S S L F G H	0	4	3
4	S S S S L F G H	0	4	3	S S S S M N O P	3	0	4
5	S S S S K L G H	1	4	2	S S S S N O P H	2	0	5
6	S S S S J K L H	2	4	1	S S S S O P G H	1	0	6
7	S S S S I J K L	3	4	0	S S S S P F G H	0	0	7

LEM Little-endian memory (BigEndianMem = 0)
BEM BigEndianMem = 1
Type AccessType (see Table 2-1) sent to memory
Offset $pAddr_{2...0}$ sent to memory
S sign-extend of $destination_{31}$

Exceptions:

TLB refill exception
TLB invalid exception
Bus error exception
Address error exception

LWR Load Word Right LWR

31 26	25 21	20 16	15 0
LWR 100110	base	rt	offset
6	5	5	16

Format:

LWR rt, offset(base)

Description:

This instruction can be used in combination with the LWL instruction to load a register with four consecutive bytes from memory, when the bytes cross a word boundary. LWR loads the right portion of the register with the appropriate part of the low-order word; LWL loads the left portion of the register with the appropriate part of the high-order word.

The LWR instruction adds its sign-extended 16-bit *offset* to the contents of general register *base* to form a virtual address which can specify an arbitrary byte. It reads bytes only from the word in memory which contains the specified starting byte. From one to four bytes will be loaded, depending on the starting byte specified. In 64-bit mode, the loaded word is sign-extended.

Conceptually, it starts at the specified byte in memory and loads that byte into the low-order (right-most) byte of the register; then it loads bytes from memory into the register until it reaches the high-order byte of the word in memory. The most significant (left-most) byte(s) of the register will not be changed.

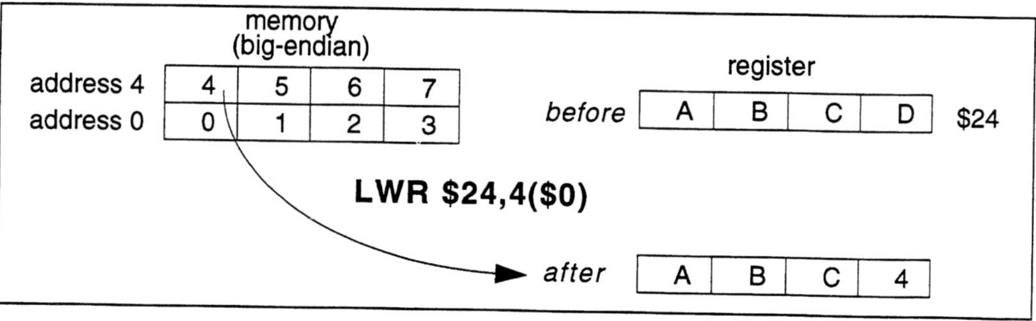

LWR — Load Word Right (continued) — LWR

The contents of general register *rt* are internally bypassed within the processor so that no NOP is needed between an immediately preceding load instruction which specifies register *rt* and a following LWR (or LWL) instruction which also specifies register *rt*.

No address exceptions due to alignment are possible.

Operation:

```
32   T:  vAddr ← ((offset15)^16 || offset15...0) + GPR[base]
         (pAddr, uncached) ← AddressTranslation (vAddr, DATA)
         pAddr ← pAddrPSIZE-1...2 || (pAddr1...0 xor ReverseEndian^2)
         if BigEndianMem = 0 then
                pAddr ← pAddrPSIZE-31...2 || 0^2
         endif
         byte ← vAddr1...0 xor BigEndianCPU^2
         mem ← LoadMemory (uncached, byte, pAddr, vAddr, DATA)
         GPR[rt] ← mem31...32-8*byte...0 || GPR[rt]31-8*byte...0

64   T:  vAddr ← ((offset15)^48 || offset15...0) + GPR[base]
         (pAddr, uncached) ← AddressTranslation (vAddr, DATA)
         pAddr ← pAddrPSIZE-1...3 || (pAddr2...0 xor ReverseEndian^3)
         if BigEndianMem = 1 then
                pAddr ← pAddrPSIZE-31...3 || 0^3
         endif
         byte ← vAddr1...0 xor BigEndianCPU^2
         word ← vAddr2 xor BigEndianCPU
         mem ← LoadMemory (uncached, 0 || byte, pAddr, vAddr, DATA)
         temp ← GPR[rt]31...32-8*byte...0 || mem31+32*word-32*word+8*byte
         GPR[rt] ← (temp31)^32 || temp
```

LWR Load Word Right (continued)

Given a word in a register and a word in memory, the operation of LWR is as follows:

LWR

Register	A	B	C	D	E	F	G	H
Memory	I	J	K	L	M	N	O	P

vAddr$_{2..0}$	BigEndianCPU = 0				BigEndianCPU = 1			
	destination	type	offset		destination	type	offset	
			LEM	BEM			LEM	BEM
0	S S S S M N O P	0	0	4	S S S S E F G I	0	7	0
1	S S S S E M N O	1	1	4	S S S S E F I J	1	6	0
2	S S S S E F M N	2	2	4	S S S S E I J K	2	5	0
3	S S S S E F G M	3	3	4	S S S S I J K L	3	4	0
4	S S S S I J K L	0	4	0	S S S S E F G M	0	3	4
5	S S S S E I J K	1	5	0	S S S S E F M N	1	2	4
6	S S S S E F I J	2	6	0	S S S S E M N O	2	1	4
7	S S S S E F G I	3	7	0	S S S S M N O P	3	0	4

LEM Little-endian memory (BigEndianMem = 0)
BEM BigEndianMem = 1
Type AccessType (see Table 2-1) sent to memory
Offset pAddr$_{2...0}$ sent to memory
S sign-extend of destination$_{31}$

Exceptions:

TLB refill exception
TLB invalid exception
Bus error exception
Address error exception

LWU Load Word Unsigned LWU

31 ... 26	25 ... 21	20 ... 16	15 ... 0
LWU 101111	base	rt	offset
6	5	5	16

Format:

LWU rt, offset(base)

Description:

The 16-bit *offset* is sign-extended and added to the contents of general register *base* to form a virtual address. The contents of the word at the memory location specified by the effective address are loaded into general register *rt*. The loaded word is zero-extended.

If either of the two least-significant bits of the effective address is non-zero, an address error exception occurs.

This operation is only defined for the R4000 operating in 64-bit mode. Execution of this instruction in 32-bit mode causes a reserved instruction exception.

Operation:

64	T:	$vAddr \leftarrow ((offset_{15})^{48} \,\|\, offset_{15...0}) + GPR[base]$ $(pAddr, uncached) \leftarrow AddressTranslation\ (vAddr, DATA)$ $pAddr \leftarrow pAddr_{PSIZE-1...3} \,\|\, (pAddr_{2...0}\ xor\ (ReverseEndian \,\|\, 0^2))$ $mem \leftarrow LoadMemory\ (uncached, WORD, pAddr, vAddr, DATA)$ $byte \leftarrow vAddr_{2...0}\ xor\ (BigEndianCPU \,\|\, 0^2)$ $GPR[rt] \leftarrow 0^{32} \,\|\, mem_{31+8*byte...8*byte}$

Exceptions:

TLB refill exception
TLB invalid exception
Bus error exception
Address error exception
Reserved instruction exception (R4000 in 32-bit mode)

MFC0 — Move From System Control Coprocessor — MFC0

31–26	25–21	20–16	15–11	10–0
COP0 010000	MF 00000	rt	rd	0 000 0000 0000
6	5	5	5	11

Format:

MFC0 rt, rd

Description:

The contents of coprocessor register *rd* of the CP0 are loaded into general register *rt*.

Operation:

32	T:	data ← CPR[0,rd]
	T+1:	GPR[rt] ← data
64	T:	data ← CPR[0,rd]
	T+1:	GPR[rt] ← $(data_{31})^{32}$ || $data_{31...0}$

Exceptions:

Coprocessor unusable exception

MFCz Move From Coprocessor MFCz

31 26	25 21	20 16	15 11	10 0
COPz 0 1 0 0 x x*	MF 0 0 0 0 0	rt	rd	0 000 0000 0000
6	5	5	5	11

Format:

MFCz rt, rd

Description:

The contents of coprocessor register *rd* of coprocessor *z* are loaded into general register *rt*.

Execution of the instruction referencing coprocessor 3 causes a reserved instruction exception, not a coprocessor unusable exception.

Operation:

```
32      T:      data ← CPR[z,rd]
        T+1:    GPR[rt] ← data
64      T:      if rd_0 = 0 then
                data ← CPR[z,rd_4...1 || 0]_31...0
                else
                data ← CPR[z,rd_4...1 || 0]_63...32
                endif
        T+1:    GPR[rt] ← (data_31)^32 || data
```

Exceptions:

Coprocessor unusable exception
Reserved instruction exception (coprocessor 3)

*See the table "Opcode Bit Encoding" on next page, or "CPU Instruction Opcode Bit Encoding" at the end of Appendix A.

MFCz Move From Coprocessor (continued) MFCz

Opcode Bit Encoding:

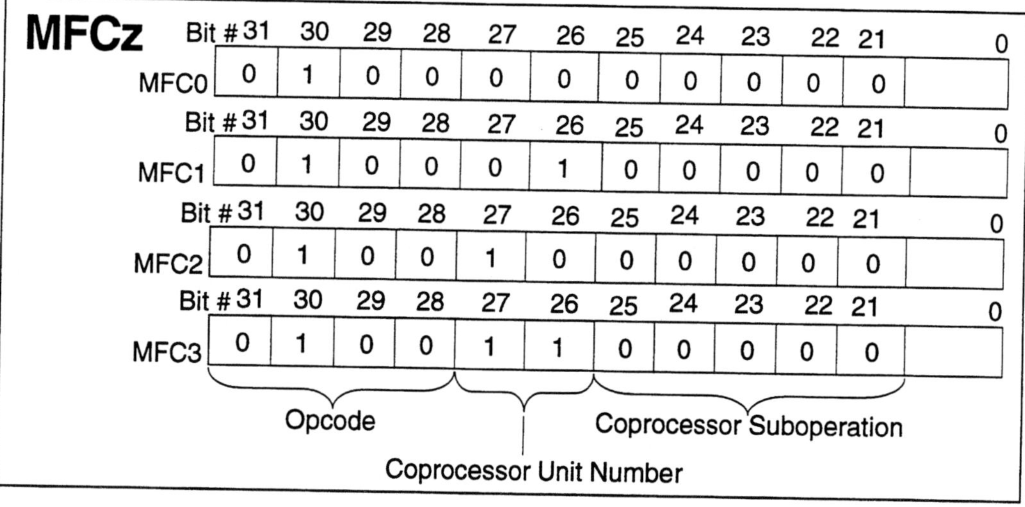

MFHI — Move From HI — MFHI

31–26	25–16	15–11	10–6	5–0
SPECIAL 000000	0 00 0000 0000	rd	0 00000	MFHI 010000
6	10	5	5	6

Format:

MFHI rd

Description:

The contents of special register *HI* are loaded into general register *rd*.

To ensure proper operation in the event of interruptions, the two instructions which follow a MFHI instruction may not be any of the instructions which modify the *HI* register: MULT, MULTU, DIV, DIVU, MTHI, DMULT, DMULTU, DDIV, DDIVU.

Operation:

32, 64	T:	GPR[rd] ← HI

Exceptions:

None

MFLO Move From Lo MFLO

31–26	25–16	15–11	10–6	5–0
SPECIAL 000000	0 00 0000 0000	rd	0 00000	MFLO 010010
6	10	5	5	6

Format:

MFLO rd

Description:

The contents of special register *LO* are loaded into general register *rd*.

To ensure proper operation in the event of interruptions, the two instructions which follow a MFLO instruction may not be any of the instructions which modify the *LO* register: MULT, MULTU, DIV, DIVU, MTLO, DMULT, DMULTU, DDIV, DDIVU.

Operation:

32, 64	T:	GPR[rd] ← LO

Exceptions:

None

MTC0 — Move To System Control Coprocessor — MTC0

31 26	25 21	20 16	15 11	10 0
COP0 010000	MT 00100	rt	rd	0 000 0000 0000
6	5	5	5	11

Format:

MTC0 rt, rd

Description:

The contents of general register *rt* are loaded into coprocessor register *rd* of CP0.

Because the state of the virtual address translation system may be altered by this instruction, the operation of load instructions, store instructions, and TLB operations immediately prior to and after this instruction are undefined.

Operation:

```
32, 64   T:      data ← GPR[rt]
         T+1:    CPR[0,rd] ← data
```

Exceptions:

Coprocessor unusable exception

MTCz Move To Coprocessor MTCz

31–26	25–21	20–16	15–11	10–0
COPz 0 1 0 0 x x*	MT 0 0 1 0 0	rt	rd	0 000 0000 0000
6	5	5	5	11

Format:

MTCz rt, rd

Description:

The contents of general register *rt* are loaded into coprocessor register *rd* of coprocessor z. Execution of the instruction referencing coprocessor 3 causes a reserved instruction exception, not a coprocessor unusable exception.

Operation:

```
32   T:    data ← GPR[rt]
     T+1:  CPR[z,rd] ← data

64   T:    data ← GPR[rt]31...0
     T+1:  if rd0 = 0
                CPR[z,rd4...1 || 0] ← CPR[z, rd4...1 || 0]63...32 || data
           else
                CPR[z,rd4...1 || 0] ← data || CPR[z,rd4...1 || 0]31...0
           endif
```

Exceptions:

Coprocessor unusable exception
Reserved instruction exception (coprocessor 3)

***Opcode Bit Encoding:**

MTCz	31	30	29	28	27	26	25	24	23	22	21	20–0
COP0	0	1	0	0	0	0	0	0	1	0	0	
COP1	0	1	0	0	0	1	0	0	1	0	0	
COP2	0	1	0	0	1	0	0	0	1	0	0	
COP3	0	1	0	0	1	1	0	0	1	0	0	

Bits 31–28: Opcode; Bits 27–26: Coprocessor Unit Number; Bits 25–21: Coprocessor Suboperation

MTHI — Move To HI — MTHI

31 … 26	25 … 21	20 … 6	5 … 0
SPECIAL 000000	rs	0 000 000000000000	MTHI 010001
6	5	15	6

Format:

MTHI rs

Description:

The contents of general register *rs* are loaded into special register *HI*.

If a MTHI operation is executed following a MULT, MULTU, DIV, or DIVU instruction, but before any MFLO, MFHI, MTLO, or MTHI instructions, the contents of special register *LO* are undefined.

Operation:

32,64	T–2:	HI ← undefined
	T–1:	HI ← undefined
	T:	HI ← GPR[rs]

Exceptions:

None

MTLO — Move To LO — MTLO

31–26	25–21	20–6	5–0
SPECIAL 000000	rs	0 000000000000000	MTLO 010011
6	5	15	6

Format:

MTLO rs

Description:

The contents of general register *rs* are loaded into special register *LO*.

If a MTLO operation is executed following a MULT, MULTU, DIV, or DIVU instruction, but before any MFLO, MFHI, MTLO, or MTHI instructions, the contents of special register *HI* are undefined.

Operation:

32,64	T–2:	LO ← undefined
	T–1:	LO ← undefined
	T:	LO ← GPR[rs]

Exceptions:

None

MULT Multiply MULT

31 26	25 21	20 16	15 6	5 0
SPECIAL 000000	rs	rt	0 00 0000 0000	MULT 011000
6	5	5	10	6

Format:

MULT rs, rt

Description:

The contents of general registers *rs* and *rt* are multiplied, treating both operands as 32-bit 2's complement values. No integer overflow exception occurs under any circumstances. In 64-bit mode, the operands must be valid 32-bit, sign-extended values.

When the operation completes, the low-order word of the double result is loaded into special register *LO*, and the high-order word of the double result is loaded into special register *HI*.

If either of the two preceding instructions is MFHI or MFLO, the results of these instructions are undefined. Correct operation requires separating reads of *HI* or *LO* from writes by a minimum of two other instructions.

MULT

Multiply (continued)

Operation:

32	T–2:	LO	$\leftarrow$ undefined
		HI	$\leftarrow$ undefined
	T–1:	LO	$\leftarrow$ undefined
		HI	$\leftarrow$ undefined
	T:	t	$\leftarrow$ GPR[rs] * GPR[rt]
		LO	$\leftarrow t_{31...0}$
		HI	$\leftarrow t_{63...32}$
64	T–2:	LO	$\leftarrow$ undefined
		HI	$\leftarrow$ undefined
	T–1:	LO	$\leftarrow$ undefined
		HI	$\leftarrow$ undefined
	T:	t	$\leftarrow \text{GPR[rs]}_{31...0} * \text{GPR[rt]}_{31...0}$
		LO	$\leftarrow (t_{31})^{32} \,\|\, t_{31...0}$
		HI	$\leftarrow (t_{63})^{32} \,\|\, t_{63...32}$

Exceptions:

None

MULTU Multiply Unsigned MULTU

31–26	25–21	20–16	15–6	5–0
SPECIAL 000000	rs	rt	0 00 0000 0000	MULTU 011001
6	5	5	10	6

Format:

MULTU rs, rt

Description:

The contents of general register *rs* and the contents of general register *rt* are multiplied, treating both operands as unsigned values. No overflow exception occurs under any circumstances. In 64-bit mode, the operands must be valid 32-bit, sign-extended values.

When the operation completes, the low-order word of the double result is loaded into special register *LO*, and the high-order word of the double result is loaded into special register *HI*.

If either of the two preceding instructions is MFHI or MFLO, the results of these instructions are undefined. Correct operation requires separating reads of *HI* or *LO* from writes by a minimum of two instructions.

MULTU — Multiply Unsigned (continued) — MULTU

Operation:

32	T–2:	LO	← undefined
		HI	← undefined
	T–1:	LO	← undefined
		HI	← undefined
	T:	t	← (0 || GPR[rs]) * (0 || GPR[rt])
		LO	← $t_{31...0}$
		HI	← $t_{63...32}$
64	T–2:	LO	← undefined
		HI	← undefined
	T–1:	LO	← undefined
		HI	← undefined
	T:	t	← (0 || $GPR[rs]_{31...0}$) * (0 || $GPR[rt]_{31...0}$)
		LO	← $(t_{31})^{32}$ || $t_{31...0}$
		HI	← $(t_{63})^{32}$ || $t_{63...32}$

Exceptions:

None

NOR Nor NOR

31 26	25 21	20 16	15 11	10 6	5 0
SPECIAL 000000	rs	rt	rd	0 00000	NOR 100111
6	5	5	5	5	6

Format:

NOR rd, rs, rt

Description:

The contents of general register *rs* are combined with the contents of general register *rt* in a bit-wise logical NOR operation. The result is placed into general register *rd*.

Operation:

32, 64	T:	GPR[rd] ← GPR[rs] nor GPR[rt]

Exceptions:

None

OR Or OR

31–26	25–21	20–16	15–11	10–6	5–0
SPECIAL 000000	rs	rt	rd	0 00000	OR 100101
6	5	5	5	5	6

Format:

OR rd, rs, rt

Description:

The contents of general register *rs* are combined with the contents of general register *rt* in a bit-wise logical OR operation. The result is placed into general register *rd*.

Operation:

32, 64	T:	GPR[rd] ← GPR[rs] or GPR[rt]

Exceptions:

None

ORI — Or Immediate — ORI

31–26	25–21	20–16	15–0
ORI 001101	rs	rt	immediate
6	5	5	16

Format:

ORI rt, rs, immediate

Description:

The 16-bit *immediate* is zero-extended and combined with the contents of general register *rs* in a bit-wise logical OR operation. The result is placed into general register *rt*.

Operation:

32	T:	$GPR[rt] \leftarrow GPR[rs]_{31...16} \parallel (immediate\ or\ GPR[rs]_{15...0})$
64	T:	$GPR[rt] \leftarrow GPR[rs]_{63...16} \parallel (immediate\ or\ GPR[rs]_{15...0})$

Exceptions:

None

SB Store Byte SB

31 … 26	25 … 21	20 … 16	15 … 0
SB 101000	base	rt	offset
6	5	5	16

Format:

SB rt, offset(base)

Description:

The 16-bit *offset* is sign-extended and added to the contents of general register *base* to form a virtual address. The least-significant byte of register *rt* is stored at the effective address.

Operation:

32	T:	$vAddr \leftarrow ((offset_{15})^{16} \parallel offset_{15...0}) + GPR[base]$ $(pAddr, uncached) \leftarrow AddressTranslation (vAddr, DATA)$ $pAddr \leftarrow pAddr_{PSIZE-1...2} \parallel (pAddr_{1...0} \text{ xor } ReverseEndian^2)$ $byte \leftarrow vAddr_{1...0} \text{ xor } BigEndianCPU^2$ $data \leftarrow GPR[rt]_{31-8*byte...0} \parallel 0^{8*byte}$ StoreMemory (uncached, BYTE, data, pAddr, vAddr, DATA)
64	T:	$vAddr \leftarrow ((offset_{15})^{48} \parallel offset_{15...0}) + GPR[base]$ $(pAddr, uncached) \leftarrow AddressTranslation (vAddr, DATA)$ $pAddr \leftarrow pAddr_{PSIZE-1...3} \parallel (pAddr_{2...0} \text{ xor } ReverseEndian^3)$ $byte \leftarrow vAddr_{2...0} \text{ xor } BigEndianCPU^3$ $data \leftarrow GPR[rt]_{63-8*byte...0} \parallel 0^{8*byte}$ StoreMemory (uncached, BYTE, data, pAddr, vAddr, DATA)

Exceptions:

TLB refill exception
TLB invalid exception
TLB modification exception
Bus error exception
Address error exception

SC — Store Conditional — SC

31–26	25–21	20–16	15–0
SC 111000	base	rt	offset
6	5	5	16

Format:

SC rt, offset(base)

Description:

The 16-bit offset is sign-extended and added to the contents of general register *base* to form a virtual address. The contents of general register *rt* are conditionally stored at the memory location specified by the effective address.

This instruction implicitly performs a SYNC operation; loads and stores to shared memory fetched prior to the SC must access memory before the SC; loads and stores to shared memory fetched subsequent to the SC must access memory after the SC.

If any other processor or device has modified the physical address since the time of the previous Load Linked instruction, or if an ERET instruction occurs between the Load Linked instruction and this store instruction, the store fails and is inhibited from taking place.

The success or failure of the store operation (as defined above) is indicated by the contents of general register *rt* after execution of the instruction. A successful store sets the contents of general register *rt* to 1; an unsuccessful store sets it to 0.

The operation of Store Conditional is undefined when the address is different from the address used in the last Load Linked.

This instruction is available in User mode; it is not necessary for CP0 to be enabled.

If either of the two least-significant bits of the effective address is non-zero, an address error exception takes place.

If this instruction should both fail and take an exception, the exception takes precedence.

SC — Store Conditional (continued) — SC

Operation:

```
32   T:  vAddr ← ((offset15)^16 || offset15...0) + GPR[base]
         (pAddr, uncached) ← AddressTranslation (vAddr, DATA)
         data ← GPR[rt]
         if LLbit then
             StoreMemory (uncached, WORD, data, pAddr, vAddr, DATA)
         endif
         GPR[rt] ← 0^31 || LLbit
         SyncOperation()

64   T:  vAddr ← ((offset15)^48 || offset15...0) + GPR[base]
         (pAddr, uncached) ← AddressTranslation (vAddr, DATA)
         pAddr ← pAddrPSIZE-1...3 || (pAddr2...0 xor (ReverseEndian || 0^2))
         data ← GPR[rt]63-8*byte...0 || 0^8*byte
         if LLbit then
             StoreMemory (uncached, WORD, data, pAddr, vAddr, DATA)
         endif
         GPR[rt] ← 0^63 || LLbit
         SyncOperation()
```

Exceptions:

TLB refill exception
TLB invalid exception
TLB modification exception
Bus error exception
Address error exception

SCD Store Conditional Doubleword SCD

31 26	25 21	20 16	15 0
SCD 111100	base	rt	offset
6	5	5	16

Format:

SCD rt, offset(base)

Description:

The 16-bit offset is sign-extended and added to the contents of general register *base* to form a virtual address. The contents of general register *rt* are conditionally stored at the memory location specified by the effective address.

This instruction implicitly performs a SYNC operation; loads and stores to shared memory fetched prior to the SCD must access memory before the SCD; loads and stores to shared memory fetched subsequent to the SCD must access memory after the SCD.

If any other processor or device has modified the physical address since the time of the previous Load Linked Doubleword instruction, or if an ERET instruction occurs between the Load Linked Doubleword instruction and this store instruction, the store fails and is inhibited from taking place.

The success or failure of the store operation (as defined above) is indicated by the contents of general register *rt* after execution of the instruction. A successful store sets the contents of general register *rt* to 1; an unsuccessful store sets it to 0.

The operation of Store Conditional Doubleword is undefined when the address is different from the address used in the last Load Linked Doubleword.

This instruction is available in User mode; it is not necessary for CP0 to be enabled.

If either of the three least-significant bits of the effective address is non-zero, an address error exception takes place.

SCD Store Conditional Doubleword (continued)

If this instruction should both fail and take an exception, the exception takes precedence.

This operation is only defined for the R4000 operating in 64-bit mode. Execution of this instruction in 32-bit mode causes a reserved instruction exception.

Operation:

```
64    T:   vAddr ← ((offset_15)^48 || offset_15...0) + GPR[base]
           (pAddr, uncached) ← AddressTranslation (vAddr, DATA)
           data ← GPR[rt]
           if LLbit then
               StoreMemory (uncached, DOUBLEWORD, data, pAddr, vAddr, DATA)
           endif
           GPR[rt] ← 0^63 || LLbit
           SyncOperation()
```

Exceptions:

TLB refill exception
TLB invalid exception
TLB modification exception
Bus error exception
Address error exception
Reserved instruction exception (R4000 in 32-bit mode)

SD Store Doubleword SD

31 — 26	25 — 21	20 — 16	15 — 0
SD 111111	base	rt	offset
6	5	5	16

Format:

SD rt, offset(base)

Description:

The 16-bit *offset* is sign-extended and added to the contents of general register *base* to form a virtual address. The contents of general register *rt* are stored at the memory location specified by the effective address.

If either of the three least-significant bits of the effective address are non-zero, an address error exception occurs.

This operation is only defined for the R4000 operating in 64-bit mode. Execution of this instruction in 32-bit mode causes a reserved instruction exception.

Operation:

64	T:	vAddr ← $((offset_{15})^{48} \| offset_{15...0}) + GPR[base]$ (pAddr, uncached) ← AddressTranslation (vAddr, DATA) data ← GPR[rt] StoreMemory (uncached, DOUBLEWORD, data, pAddr, vAddr, DATA)

Exceptions:

TLB refill exception
TLB invalid exception
TLB modification exception
Bus error exception
Address error exception
Reserved instruction exception (R4000 in 32-bit user mode
R4000 in 32-bit supervisor mode)

SDCz — Store Doubleword From Coprocessor — SDCz

31–26	25–21	20–16	15–0
SDCz 1 1 1 1 x x*	base	rt	offset
6	5	5	16

Format:

SDCz rt, offset(base)

Description:

The 16-bit *offset* is sign-extended and added to the contents of general register *base* to form a virtual address. Coprocessor unit *z* sources a doubleword, which the processor writes to the addressed memory location. The data to be stored is defined by individual coprocessor specifications.

If any of the three least-significant bits of the effective address are non-zero, an address error exception takes place.

This instruction is not valid for use with CP0.

This instruction is undefined when the least-significant bit of the *rt* field is non-zero.

Operation:

```
32   T:  vAddr ← ((offset_15)^16 || offset_15...0) + GPR[base]
         (pAddr, uncached) ← AddressTranslation (vAddr, DATA)
         data ← COPzSD(rt),
         StoreMemory (uncached, DOUBLEWORD, data, pAddr, vAddr, DATA)

64   T:  vAddr ← ((offset_15)^48 || offset_15...0) + GPR[base]
         (pAddr, uncached) ← AddressTranslation (vAddr, DATA)
         data ← COPzSD(rt),
         StoreMemory (uncached, DOUBLEWORD, data, pAddr, vAddr, DATA)
```

*See the table, "Opcode Bit Encoding" on next page, or "CPU Instruction Opcode Bit Encoding" at the end of Appendix A.

SDCz — Store Doubleword From Coprocessor (continued) — SDCz

Exceptions:

TLB refill exception
TLB invalid exception
TLB modification exception
Bus error exception
Address error exception
Coprocessor unusable exception

Opcode Bit Encoding:

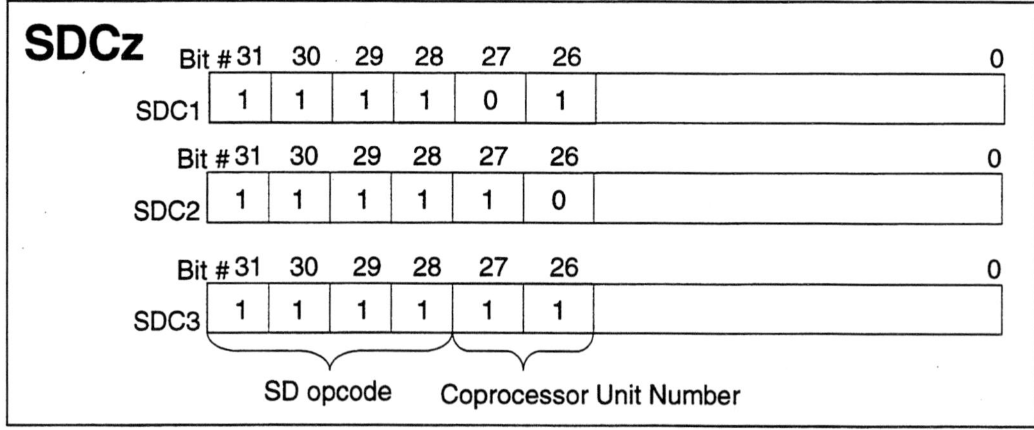

SDL Store Doubleword Left SDL

31 26	25 21	20 16	15 0
SDL 101100	base	rt	offset
6	5	5	16

Format:

SDL rt, offset(base)

Description:

This instruction can be used with the SDR instruction to store the contents of a register into eight consecutive bytes of memory, when the bytes cross a doubleword boundary. SDL stores the left portion of the register into the appropriate part of the high-order doubleword of memory; SDR stores the right portion of the register into the appropriate part of the low-order doubleword.

The SDL instruction adds its sign-extended 16-bit *offset* to the contents of general register *base* to form a virtual address which may specify an arbitrary byte. It alters only the word in memory which contains that byte. From one to four bytes will be stored, depending on the starting byte specified.

Conceptually, it starts at the most-significant byte of the register and copies it to the specified byte in memory; then it copies bytes from register to memory until it reaches the low-order byte of the word in memory.

No address exceptions due to alignment are possible.

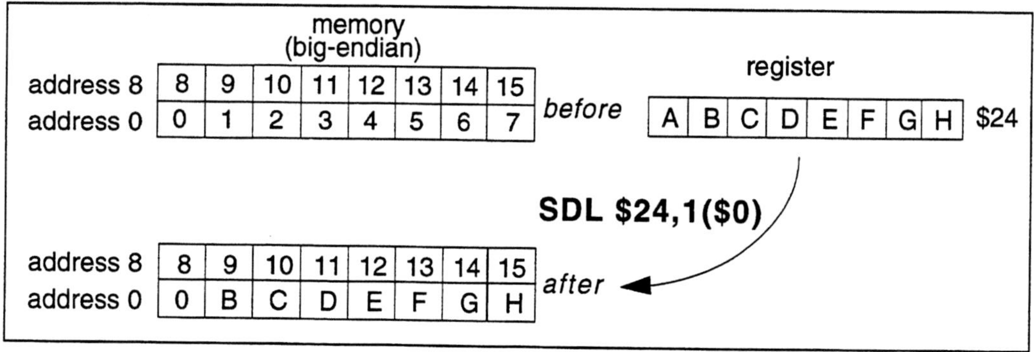

SDL Store Doubleword Left (continued) SDL

This operation is only defined for the R4000 operating in 64-bit mode. Execution of this instruction in 32-bit mode causes a reserved instruction exception.

Operation:

64	T:	$vAddr \leftarrow ((offset_{15})^{48} \parallel offset_{15...0}) + GPR[base]$
		$(pAddr, uncached) \leftarrow AddressTranslation (vAddr, DATA)$
		$pAddr \leftarrow pAddr_{PSIZE-1...3} \parallel (pAddr_{2...0}\ xor\ ReverseEndian^3)$
		If BigEndianMem = 0 then
		    $pAddr \leftarrow pAddr_{31...3} \parallel 0^3$
		endif
		$byte \leftarrow vAddr_{2...0}\ xor\ BigEndianCPU^3$
		$data \leftarrow 0^{56-8*byte} \parallel GPR[rt]_{63...56-8*byte}$
		Storememory (uncached, byte, data, pAddr, vAddr, DATA)

SDL Store Doubleword Left (continued) SDL

Given a doubleword in a register and a doubleword in memory, the operation of SDL is as follows:

SDL

Register	A	B	C	D	E	F	G	H
Memory	I	J	K	L	M	N	O	P

$vAddr_{2..0}$	BigEndianCPU = 0				BigEndianCPU = 1			
	destination	type	offset		destination	type	offset	
			LEM	BEM			LEM	BEM
0	I J K L M N O A	0	0	7	A B C D E F G H	7	0	0
1	I J K L M N A B	1	0	6	I A B C D E F G	6	0	1
2	I J K L M A B C	2	0	5	I J A B C D E F	5	0	2
3	I J K L A B C D	3	0	4	I J K A B C D E	4	0	3
4	I J K A B C D E	4	0	3	I J K L A B C D	3	0	4
5	I J A B C D E F	5	0	2	I J K L M A B C	2	0	5
6	I A B C D E F G	6	0	1	I J K L M N A B	1	0	6
7	A B C D E F G H	7	0	0	I J K L M N O A	0	0	7

LEM Little-endian memory (BigEndianMem = 0)
BEM BigEndianMem = 1
Type AccessType (see Table 2-1) sent to memory
Offset $pAddr_{2...0}$ sent to memory

Exceptions:

TLB refill exception
TLB invalid exception
TLB modification exception
Bus error exception
Address error exception
Reserved instruction exception (R4000 in 32-bit mode)

SDR — Store Doubleword Right — SDR

31–26	25–21	20–16	15–0
SDR 101101	base	rt	offset
6	5	5	16

Format:

SDR rt, offset(base)

Description:

This instruction can be used with the SDL instruction to store the contents of a register into eight consecutive bytes of memory, when the bytes cross a boundary between two doublewords. SDR stores the right portion of the register into the appropriate part of the low-order doubleword; SDL stores the left portion of the register into the appropriate part of the low-order doubleword of memory.

The SDR instruction adds its sign-extended 16-bit *offset* to the contents of general register *base* to form a virtual address which may specify an arbitrary byte. It alters only the word in memory which contains that byte. From one to eight bytes will be stored, depending on the starting byte specified.

Conceptually, it starts at the least-significant (rightmost) byte of the register and copies it to the specified byte in memory; then it copies bytes from register to memory until it reaches the high-order byte of the word in memory. No address exceptions due to alignment are possible.

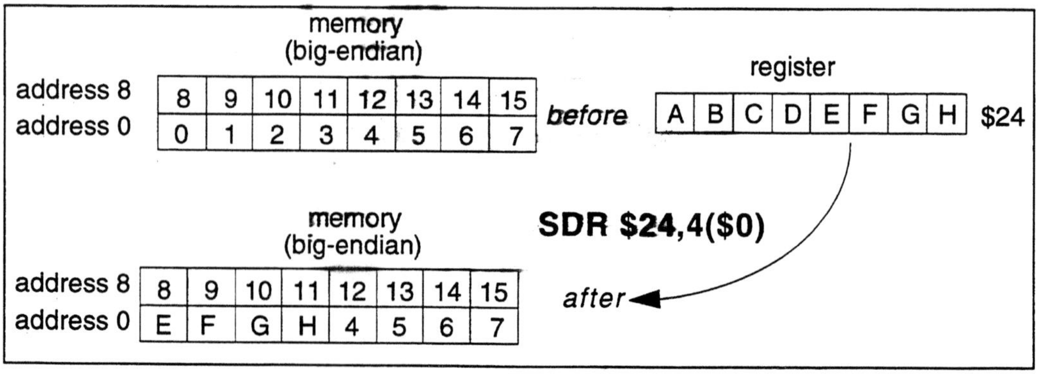

memory (big-endian) — before

address 8	8	9	10	11	12	13	14	15
address 0	0	1	2	3	4	5	6	7

register $24: A B C D E F G H

SDR $24,4($0)

memory (big-endian) — after

address 8	8	9	10	11	12	13	14	15
address 0	E	F	G	H	4	5	6	7

SDR — Store Doubleword Right (continued) — SDR

This operation is only defined for the R4000 operating in 64-bit mode. Execution of this instruction in 32-bit mode causes a reserved instruction exception.

Operation:

```
64    T: vAddr ← ((offset15)^48 || offset 15...0) + GPR[base]
         (pAddr, uncached) ← AddressTranslation (vAddr, DATA)
         pAddr ← pAddrPSIZE – 1...3 || (pAddr2...0 xor ReverseEndian^3)
         If BigEndianMem = 0 then
              pAddr ← pAddrPSIZE – 31...3 || 0^3
         endif
         byte ← vAddr1...0 xor BigEndianCPU^3
         data ← GPR[rt]63–8*byte || 0^(8*byte)
         StoreMemory (uncached, DOUBLEWORD-byte, data, pAddr, vAddr, DATA)
```

SDR — Store Doubleword Right (continued) — SDR

Given a doubleword in a register and a doubleword in memory, the operation of SDR is as follows:

SDR

Register	A	B	C	D	E	F	G	H
Memory	I	J	K	L	M	N	O	P

$vAddr_{2..0}$	BigEndianCPU = 0				BigEndianCPU = 1			
	destination	type	offset		destination	type	offset	
			LEM	BEM			LEM	BEM
0	A B C D E F G H	7	0	0	H J K L M N O P	0	7	0
1	B C D E F G H P	6	1	0	G H K L M N O P	1	6	0
2	C D E F G H O P	5	2	0	F G H L M N O P	2	5	0
3	D E F G H N O P	4	3	0	E F G H M N O P	3	4	0
4	E F G H M N O P	3	4	0	D E F G H N O P	4	3	0
5	F G H L M N O P	2	5	0	C D E F G H O P	5	2	0
6	G H K L M N O P	1	6	0	B C D E F G H P	6	1	0
7	H J K L M N O P	0	7	0	A B C D E F G H	7	0	0

LEM Little-endian memory (BigEndianMem = 0)
BEM BigEndianMem = 1
Type AccessType (see Table 2-1) sent to memory
Offset $pAddr_{2...0}$ sent to memory

Exceptions:

TLB refill exception
TLB invalid exception
TLB modification exception
Bus error exception
Address error exception
Reserved instruction exception (R4000 in 32-bit mode)

SH — Store Halfword — SH

31–26	25–21	20–16	15–0
SH 101001	base	rt	offset
6	5	5	16

Format:

SH rt, offset(base)

Description:

The 16-bit *offset* is sign-extended and added to the contents of general register *base* to form an unsigned effective address. The least-significant halfword of register *rt* is stored at the effective address. If the least-significant bit of the effective address is non-zero, an address error exception occurs.

Operation:

32	T:	$vAddr \leftarrow ((offset_{15})^{16} \,\|\, offset_{15...0}) + GPR[base]$
		$(pAddr, uncached) \leftarrow AddressTranslation\ (vAddr, DATA)$
		$pAddr \leftarrow pAddr_{PSIZE-1...2} \,\|\, (pAddr_{1...0}\ xor\ (ReverseEndian \,\|\, 0))$
		$byte \leftarrow vAddr_{1...0}\ xor\ (BigEndianCPU \,\|\, 0)$
		$data \leftarrow GPR[rt]_{31-8*byte...0} \,\|\, 0^{8*byte}$
		StoreMemory (uncached, HALFWORD, data, pAddr, vAddr, DATA)
64	T:	$vAddr \leftarrow ((offset_{15})^{48} \,\|\, offset_{15...0}) + GPR[base]$
		$(pAddr, uncached) \leftarrow AddressTranslation\ (vAddr, DATA)$
		$pAddr \leftarrow pAddr_{PSIZE-1...3} \,\|\, (pAddr_{2...0}\ xor\ (ReverseEndian^2 \,\|\, 0))$
		$byte \leftarrow vAddr_{2...0}\ xor\ (BigEndianCPU^2 \,\|\, 0)$
		$data \leftarrow GPR[rt]_{63-8*byte...0} \,\|\, 0^{8*byte}$
		StoreMemory (uncached, HALFWORD, data, pAddr, vAddr, DATA)

Exceptions:

TLB refill exception
TLB invalid exception
TLB modification exception
Bus error exception
Address error exception

SLL Shift Left Logical SLL

31 26	25 21	20 16	15 11	10 6	5 0
SPECIAL 000000	rs	rt	rd	sa	SLL 000000
6	5	5	5	5	6

Format:

SLL rd, rt, sa

Description:

The contents of general register *rt* are shifted left by *sa* bits, inserting zeros into the low-order bits.

The result is placed in register *rd.*

In 64-bit mode, the operand must be a valid sign-extended, 32-bit value.

Operation:

32	T:	$GPR[rd] \leftarrow GPR[rt]_{31-sa...0} \parallel 0^{sa}$
64	T:	$s \leftarrow 0 \parallel sa$ $temp \leftarrow GPR[rt]_{31-s...0} \parallel 0^{s}$ $GPR[rd] \leftarrow (temp_{31})^{32} \parallel temp$

Exceptions:

None

SLLV — Shift Left Logical Variable — SLLV

31–26	25–21	20–16	15–11	10–6	5–0
SPECIAL 000000	0 00000	rt	rd	0 00000	SLLV 000100
6	5	5	5	5	6

Format:

SLLV rd, rt, rs

Description:

The contents of general register *rt* are shifted left the number of bits specified by the low-order five bits contained in general register *rs*, inserting zeros into the low-order bits.

The result is placed in register *rd*.

In 64-bit mode, the operand must be a valid sign-extended, 32-bit value.

Operation:

32	T:	$s \leftarrow GP[rs]_{4...0}$
		$GPR[rd] \leftarrow GPR[rt]_{(31-s)...0} \,\|\|\, 0^s$
64	T:	$s \leftarrow 0 \,\|\|\, GP[rs]_{4...0}$
		$temp \leftarrow GPR[rt]_{(31-s)...0} \,\|\|\, 0^s$
		$GPR[rd] \leftarrow (temp_{31})^{32} \,\|\|\, temp$

Exceptions:

None

SLT — Set On Less Than — SLT

31–26	25–21	20–16	15–11	10–6	5–0
SPECIAL 000000	rs	rt	rd	0 00000	SLT 101010
6	5	5	5	5	6

Format:

SLT rd, rs, rt

Description:

The contents of general register *rt* are subtracted from the contents of general register *rs*. Considering both quantities as signed integers, if the contents of general register *rs* are less than the contents of general register *rt*, the result is set to one; otherwise the result is set to zero.

The result is placed into general register *rd*.

No integer overflow exception occurs under any circumstances. The comparison is valid even if the subtraction used during the comparison overflows.

Operation:

```
32   T:   if GPR[rs] < GPR[rt] then
                    GPR[rd] ← 0^31 || 1
          else
                    GPR[rd] ← 0^32
          endif
64   T:   if GPR[rs] < GPR[rt] then
                    GPR[rd] ← 0^63 || 1
          else
                    GPR[rd] ← 0^64
          endif
```

Exceptions:

None

SLTI Set On Less Than Immediate SLTI

31 — 26	25 — 21	20 — 16	15 — 0
SLTI 001010	rs	rt	immediate
6	5	5	16

Format:

SLTI rt, rs, immediate

Description:

The 16-bit *immediate* is sign-extended and subtracted from the contents of general register *rs*. Considering both quantities as signed integers, if *rs* is less than the sign-extended immediate, the result is set to one; otherwise the result is set to zero.

The result is placed into general register *rt*.

No integer overflow exception occurs under any circumstances. The comparison is valid even if the subtraction used during the comparison overflows.

Operation:

32	T:	if GPR[rs] < $(\text{immediate}_{15})^{16}$ || $\text{immediate}_{15...0}$ then
		GPR[rd] ← 0^{31} || 1
		else
		GPR[rd] ← 0^{32}
		endif
64	T:	if GPR[rs] < $(\text{immediate}_{15})^{48}$ || $\text{immediate}_{15...0}$ then
		GPR[rd] ← 0^{63} || 1
		else
		GPR[rd] ← 0^{64}
		endif

Exceptions:

None

SLTIU — Set On Less Than Immediate Unsigned — SLTIU

31 — 26	25 — 21	20 — 16	15 — 0
SLTIU 001011	rs	rt	immediate
6	5	5	16

Format:

SLTIU rt, rs, immediate

Description:

The 16-bit *immediate* is sign-extended and subtracted from the contents of general register *rs*. Considering both quantities as unsigned integers, if *rs* is less than the sign-extended immediate, the result is set to one; otherwise the result is set to zero.

The result is placed into general register *rt*.

No integer overflow exception occurs under any circumstances. The comparison is valid even if the subtraction used during the comparison overflows.

Operation:

```
32   T:   if (0 || GPR[rs]) < (immediate15)^16 || immediate15...0 then
                    GPR[rd] ← 0^31 || 1
          else
                    GPR[rd] ← 0^32
          endif
64   T:   if (0 || GPR[rs]) < (immediate15)^48 || immediate15...0 then
                    GPR[rd] ← 0^63 || 1
          else
                    GPR[rd] ← 0^64
          endif
```

Exceptions:

None

SLTU Set On Less Than Unsigned SLTU

31–26	25–21	20–16	15–11	10–6	5–0
SPECIAL 000000	rs	rt	rd	0 00000	SLTU 101011
6	5	5	5	5	6

Format:

SLTU rd, rs, rt

Description:

The contents of general register *rt* are subtracted from the contents of general register *rs*. Considering both quantities as unsigned integers, if the contents of general register *rs* are less than the contents of general register *rt*, the result is set to one; otherwise the result is set to zero.

The result is placed into general register *rd*.

No integer overflow exception occurs under any circumstances. The comparison is valid even if the subtraction used during the comparison overflows.

Operation:

```
32   T:   if (0 || GPR[rs]) < 0 || GPR[rt] then
                    GPR[rd] ← 0^31 || 1
          else
                    GPR[rd] ← 0^32
          endif
64   T:   if (0 || GPR[rs]) < 0 || GPR[rt] then
                    GPR[rd] ← 0^63 || 1
          else
                    GPR[rd] ← 0^64
          endif
```

Exceptions:

None

SRA Shift Right Arithmetic SRA

31 26	25 21	20 16	15 11	10 6	5 0
SPECIAL 000000	0 00000	rt	rd	sa	SRA 000011
6	5	5	5	5	6

Format:

SRA rd, rt, sa

Description:

The contents of general register *rt* are shifted right by *sa* bits, sign-extending the high-order bits.

The result is placed in register *rd*.

In 64-bit mode, the operand must be a valid sign-extended, 32-bit value.

Operation:

32	T:	$GPR[rd] \leftarrow (GPR[rt]_{31})^{sa} \parallel GPR[rt]_{31...sa}$
64	T:	$s \leftarrow 0 \parallel sa$
		$temp \leftarrow (GPR[rt]_{31})^{s} \parallel GPR[rt]_{31...s}$
		$GPR[rd] \leftarrow (temp_{31})^{32} \parallel temp$

Exceptions:

None

SRAV Shift Right Arithmetic Variable SRAV

31 26	25 21	20 16	15 11	10 6	5 0
SPECIAL 000000	rs	rt	rd	0 00000	SRAV 000111
6	5	5	5	5	6

Format:

SRAV rd, rt, rs

Description:

The contents of general register *rt* are shifted right by the number of bits specified by the low-order five bits of general register *rs*, sign-extending the high-order bits.

The result is placed in register *rd*.

In 64-bit mode, the operand must be a valid sign-extended, 32-bit value.

Operation:

32	T:	$s \leftarrow GPR[rs]_{4...0}$
		$GPR[rd] \leftarrow (GPR[rt]_{31})^{s} \parallel GPR[rt]_{31...s}$
64	T:	$s \leftarrow GPR[rs]_{4...0}$
		$temp \leftarrow (GPR[rt]_{31})^{s} \parallel GPR[rt]_{31...s}$
		$GPR[rd] \leftarrow (temp_{31})^{32} \parallel temp$

Exceptions:

None

SRL Shift Right Logical SRL

31–26	25–21	20–16	15–11	10–6	5–0
SPECIAL 000000	0 00000	rt	rd	sa	SRL 000010
6	5	5	5	5	6

Format:

SRL rd, rt, sa

Description:

The contents of general register *rt* are shifted right by *sa* bits, inserting zeros into the high-order bits.

The result is placed in register *rd*.

In 64-bit mode, the operand must be a valid sign-extended, 32-bit value.

Operation:

32	T:	$GPR[rd] \leftarrow 0^{sa} \mathbin{\|} GPR[rt]_{31...sa}$
64	T:	$s \leftarrow 0 \mathbin{\|} sa$
		$temp \leftarrow 0^{s} \mathbin{\|} GPR[rt]_{31...s}$
		$GPR[rd] \leftarrow (temp_{31})^{32} \mathbin{\|} temp$

Exceptions:

None

SRLV Shift Right Logical Variable SRLV

31–26	25–21	20–16	15–11	10–6	5–0
SPECIAL 000000	rs	rt	rd	0 00000	SRLV 000110
6	5	5	5	5	6

Format:

SRLV rd, rt, rs

Description:

The contents of general register *rt* are shifted right by the number of bits specified by the low-order five bits of general register *rs,* inserting zeros into the high-order bits.

The result is placed in register *rd.*

In 64-bit mode, the operand must be a valid sign-extended, 32-bit value.

Operation:

32	T:	$s \leftarrow GPR[rs]_{4...0}$
		$GPR[rd] \leftarrow 0^s \parallel GPR[rt]_{31...s}$
64	T:	$s \leftarrow GPR[rs]_{4...0}$
		$temp \leftarrow 0^s \parallel GPR[rt]_{31...s}$
		$GPR[rd] \leftarrow (temp_{31})^{32} \parallel temp$

Exceptions:

None

SUB　　Subtract　　SUB

31　　26	25　　21	20　　16	15　　11	10　　6	5　　0
SPECIAL 000000	rs	rt	rd	0 00000	SUB 100010
6	5	5	5	5	6

Format:

SUB rd, rs, rt

Description:

The contents of general register *rt* are subtracted from the contents of general register *rs* to form a result. The result is placed into general register *rd*. In 64-bit mode, the operands must be valid sign-extended, 32-bit values.

The only difference between this instruction and the SUBU instruction is that SUBU never traps on overflow.

An integer overflow exception takes place if the carries out of bits 30 and 31 differ (2's complement overflow). The destination register *rd* is not modified when an integer overflow exception occurs.

Operation:

32	T:	GPR[rd] ← GPR[rs] – GPR[rt]
64	T:	temp ← GPR[rs] - GPR[rt]
		GPR[rd] ← $(temp_{31})^{32}$ ‖ $temp_{31...0}$

Exceptions:

Integer overflow exception

SUBU Subtract Unsigned SUBU

31 26	25 21	20 16	15 11	10 6	5 0
SPECIAL 000000	rs	rt	rd	0 00000	SUBU 100011
6	5	5	5	5	6

Format:

SUBU rd, rs, rt

Description:

The contents of general register *rt* are subtracted from the contents of general register *rs* to form a result.

The result is placed into general register *rd*.

In 64-bit mode, the operands must be valid sign-extended, 32-bit values.

The only difference between this instruction and the SUB instruction is that SUBU never traps on overflow. No integer overflow exception occurs under any circumstances.

Operation:

32	T:	GPR[rd] ← GPR[rs] – GPR[rt]
64	T:	temp ← GPR[rs] - GPR[rt]
		GPR[rd] ← $(temp_{31})^{32}$ || $temp_{31...0}$

Exceptions:

None

SW — Store Word — SW

31–26	25–21	20–16	15–0
SW 101011	base	rt	offset
6	5	5	16

Format:

SW rt, offset(base)

Description:

The 16-bit *offset* is sign-extended and added to the contents of general register *base* to form a virtual address. The contents of general register *rt* are stored at the memory location specified by the effective address.

If either of the two least-significant bits of the effective address are non-zero, an address error exception occurs.

Operation:

```
32   T:  vAddr ← ((offset15)^16 || offset15...0) + GPR[base]
         (pAddr, uncached) ← AddressTranslation (vAddr, DATA)
         data ← GPR[rt]
         StoreMemory (uncached, WORD, data, pAddr, vAddr, DATA)
64   T:  vAddr ← ((offset15)^48 || offset15...0) + GPR[base]
         (pAddr, uncached) ← AddressTranslation (vAddr, DATA)
         pAddr ← pAddrPSIZE-1...3 || (pAddr2...0 xor (ReverseEndian || 0^2))
         byte ← vAddr2...0 xor (BigEndianCPU || 0^2)
         data ← GPR[rt]63-8*byte || 0^8*byte
         StoreMemory (uncached, WORD, data, pAddr, vAddr, DATA)
```

Exceptions:

TLB refill exception
TLB invalid exception
TLB modification exception
Bus error exception
Address error exception

SWCz Store Word From Coprocessor SWCz

31 ... 26	25 ... 21	20 ... 16	15 ... 0
SWCz 1 1 1 0 x x*	base	rt	offset
6	5	5	16

Format:

SWCz rt, offset(base)

Description:

The 16-bit *offset* is sign-extended and added to the contents of general register *base* to form a virtual address. Coprocessor unit *z* sources a word, which the processor writes to the addressed memory location.

The data to be stored is defined by individual coprocessor specifications.

This instruction is not valid for use with CP0.

If either of the two least-significant bits of the effective address is non-zero, an address error exception occurs.

Execution of the instruction referencing coprocessor 3 causes a reserved instruction exception, not a coprocessor unusable exception.

Operation:

32 T: $vAddr \leftarrow ((offset_{15})^{16} \| offset_{15...0}) + GPR[base]$
$(pAddr, uncached) \leftarrow AddressTranslation\ (vAddr, DATA)$
$byte \leftarrow vAddr_{1...0}$
$data \leftarrow COPzSW\ (byte, rt)$
StoreMemory (uncached, WORD, data, pAddr, vAddr, DATA)

64 T: $vAddr \leftarrow ((offset_{15})^{48} \| offset_{15...0}) + GPR[base]$
$(pAddr, uncached) \leftarrow AddressTranslation\ (vAddr, DATA)$
$pAddr \leftarrow pAddr_{PSIZE-1...3} \| (pAddr_{2...0}\ xor\ (ReverseEndian \| 0^2)$
$byte \leftarrow vAddr_{2...0}\ xor\ (BigEndianCPU \| 0^2)$
$data \leftarrow COPzSW\ (byte,rt)$
StoreMemory (uncached, WORD, data, pAddr, vAddr DATA)

*See the table "Opcode Bit Encoding" on next page, or "CPU Instruction Opcode Bit Encoding" at the end of Appendix A.

SWCz Store Word From Coprocessor (Continued) SWCz

Exceptions:

TLB refill exception
TLB invalid exception
TLB modification exception
Bus error exception
Address error exception
Coprocessor unusable exception
Reserved instruction exception (coprocessor 3)

Opcode Bit Encoding:

SWCz

	Bit # 31	30	29	28	27	26	0
SWC1	1	1	1	0	0	1	
SWC2	1	1	1	0	1	0	
SWC3	1	1	1	0	1	1	

Bits 31–28: SW opcode; bits 27–26: Coprocessor Unit Number

SWL — Store Word Left — SWL

31–26	25–21	20–16	15–0
SWL 101010	base	rt	offset
6	5	5	16

Format:

SWL rt, offset(base)

Description:

This instruction can be used with the SWR instruction to store the contents of a register into four consecutive bytes of memory, when the bytes cross a word boundary. SWL stores the left portion of the register into the appropriate part of the high-order word of memory; SWR stores the right portion of the register into the appropriate part of the low-order word.

The SWL instruction adds its sign-extended 16-bit *offset* to the contents of general register *base* to form a virtual address which may specify an arbitrary byte. It alters only the word in memory which contains that byte. From one to four bytes will be stored, depending on the starting byte specified.

Conceptually, it starts at the most-significant byte of the register and copies it to the specified byte in memory; then it copies bytes from register to memory until it reaches the low-order byte of the word in memory.

No address exceptions due to alignment are possible.

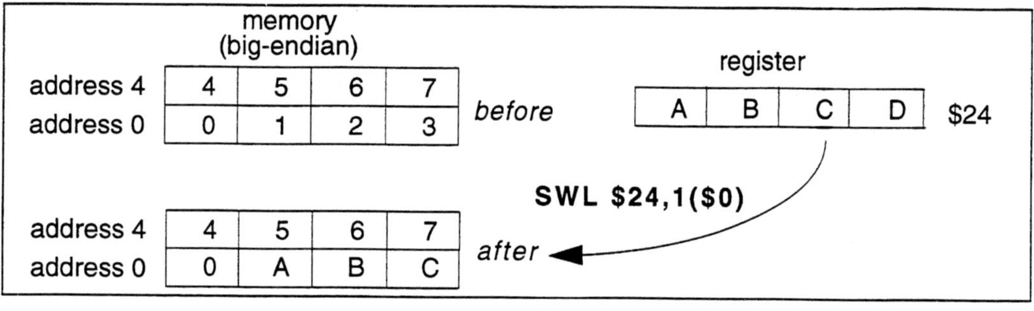

SWL Store Word Left (Continued) SWL

Operation:

```
32    T: vAddr ← ((offset15)^16 || offset 15...0) + GPR[base]
         (pAddr, uncached) ← AddressTranslation (vAddr, DATA)
         pAddr ← pAddrPSIZE –1...2 || (pAddr1...0 xor ReverseEndian^2)
         If BigEndianMem = 0 then
              pAddr ← pAddrPSIZE – 1...2 || 0^2
         endif
         byte ← vAddr1...0 xor BigEndianCPU^2
         data ← 0^(24–8*byte) || GPR[rt]31...24–8*byte
         Storememory (uncached, byte, data, pAddr, vAddr, DATA)
64    T: vAddr ← ((offset15)^48 || offset 15...0) + GPR[base]
         (pAddr, uncached) ← AddressTranslation (vAddr, DATA)
         pAddr ← pAddrPSIZE – 1...3 || (pAddr2...0 xor ReverseEndian^3)
         If BigEndianMem = 0 then
              pAddr ← pAddr31...2 || 0^2
         endif
         byte ← vAddr1...0 xor BigEndianCPU^2
         if (vAddr2 xor BigEndianCPU) = 0 then
              data ← 0^32 || 0^(24-8*byte) || GPR[rt]31...24-8*byte
         else
              data ← 0^(24-8*byte) || GPR[rt]31...24-8*byte || 0^32
         endif
         StoreMemory(uncached, byte, data, pAddr, vAddr, DATA)
```

SWL — Store Word Left (Continued) — SWL

Given a doubleword in a register and a doubleword in memory, the operation of SWL is as follows:

SWL

Register	A	B	C	D	E	F	G	H
Memory	I	J	K	L	M	N	O	P

$vAddr_{2..0}$	BigEndianCPU = 0				BigEndianCPU = 1			
	destination	type	offset		destination	type	offset	
			LEM	BEM			LEM	BEM
0	I J K L M N O E	0	0	7	E F G H M N O P	3	4	0
1	I J K L M N E F	1	0	6	I E F G M N O P	2	4	1
2	I J K L M E F G	2	0	5	I J E F M N O P	1	4	2
3	I J K L E F G H	3	0	4	I J K E M N O P	0	4	3
4	I J K E M N O P	0	4	3	I J K L E F G H	3	0	4
5	I J E F M N O P	1	4	2	I J K L M E F G	2	0	5
6	I E F G M N O P	2	4	1	I J K L M N E F	1	0	6
7	E F G H M N O P	3	4	0	I J K L M N O E	0	0	7

LEM	Little-endian memory (BigEndianMem = 0)
BEM	BigEndianMem = 1
Type	AccessType (see Table 2-1) sent to memory
Offset	$pAddr_{2...0}$ sent to memory

Exceptions:

TLB refill exception
TLB invalid exception
TLB modification exception
Bus error exception
Address error exception

SWR Store Word Right SWR

31 26	25 21	20 16	15 0
SWR 101110	base	rt	offset
6	5	5	16

Format:

SWR rt, offset(base)

Description:

This instruction can be used with the SWL instruction to store the contents of a register into four consecutive bytes of memory, when the bytes cross a boundary between two words. SWR stores the right portion of the register into the appropriate part of the low-order word; SWL stores the left portion of the register into the appropriate part of the low-order word of memory.

The SWR instruction adds its sign-extended 16-bit *offset* to the contents of general register *base* to form a virtual address which may specify an arbitrary byte. It alters only the word in memory which contains that byte. From one to four bytes will be stored, depending on the starting byte specified.

Conceptually, it starts at the least-significant (rightmost) byte of the register and copies it to the specified byte in memory; then copies bytes from register to memory until it reaches the high-order byte of the word in memory.

No address exceptions due to alignment are possible.

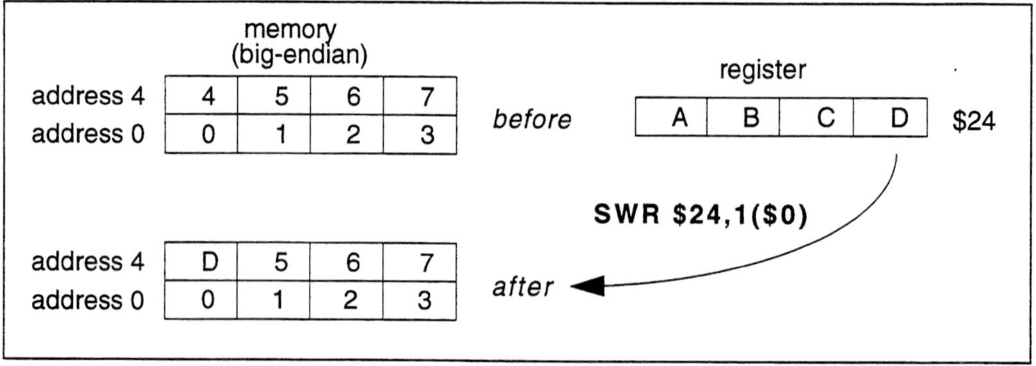

SWR Store Word Right (Continued) SWR

Operation:

```
32    T:  vAddr ← ((offset15)^16 || offset 15...0) + GPR[base]
          (pAddr, uncached) ← AddressTranslation (vAddr, DATA)
          pAddr ← pAddrPSIZE – 1...2 || (pAddr1...0 xor ReverseEndian^2)
          BigEndianMem = 0 then
              pAddr ← pAddrPSIZE – 31...2 || 0^2
          endif
          byte ← vAddr1...0 xor BigEndianCPU^2
          data ← GPR[rt]31–8*byte || 0^8*byte
          Storememory (uncached, WORD-byte, data, pAddr, vAddr, DATA)
64    T:  vAddr ← ((offset15)^48 || offset 15...0) + GPR[base]
          (pAddr, uncached) ← AddressTranslation (vAddr, DATA)
          pAddr ← pAddrPSIZE – 1...3 || (pAddr2...0 xor ReverseEndian^3)
          If BigEndianMem = 0 then
              pAddr ← pAddr31...2 || 0^2
          endif
          byte ← vAddr1...0 xor BigEndianCPU^2
          if (vAddr2 xor BigEndianCPU) = 0 then
              data ← 0^32 || GPR[rt]31-8*byte...0 || 0^8*byte
          else
              data ← GPR[rt]31-8*byte...0 || 0^8*byte || 0^32
          endif
          StoreMemory(uncached, WORD-byte, data, pAddr, vAddr, DATA)
```

SWR — Store Word Right (Continued) — SWR

Given a doubleword in a register and a doubleword in memory, the operation of SWR is as follows:

SWR

Register	A	B	C	D	E	F	G	H
Memory	I	J	K	L	M	N	O	P

$vAddr_{2..0}$	BigEndianCPU = 0				BigEndianCPU = 1			
	destination	type	offset		destination	type	offset	
			LEM	BEM			LEM	BEM
0	I J K L E F G H	3	0	4	H J K L M N O P	0	7	0
1	I J K L F G H P	2	1	4	G H K L M N O P	1	6	0
2	I J K L G H O P	1	2	4	F G H L M N O P	2	5	0
3	I J K L H N O P	0	3	4	E F G H M N O P	3	4	0
4	E F G H M N O P	3	4	0	I J K L H N O P	0	3	4
5	F G H L M N O P	2	5	0	I J K L G H O P	1	2	4
6	G H K L M N O P	1	6	0	I J K L F G H P	2	1	4
7	H J K L M N O P	0	7	0	I J K L E F G H	3	0	4

LEM	Little-endian memory (BigEndianMem = 0)
BEM	BigEndianMem = 1
Type	AccessType (see Table 2-1) sent to memory
Offset	$pAddr_{2...0}$ sent to memory

Exceptions:

TLB refill exception
TLB invalid exception
TLB modification exception
Bus error exception
Address error exception

SYNC Synchronize SYNC

31 — 26	25 — 6	5 — 0
SPECIAL 000000	0 0000 0000 0000 0000 0000	SYNC 001111
6	20	6

Format:

SYNC

Description:

The SYNC instruction ensures that any loads and stores fetched *prior to* the present instruction are completed before any loads or stores *after* this instruction are allowed to start. Use of the SYNC instruction to serialize certain memory references may be required in a multiprocessor environment for proper synchronization. For example:

Processor A		Processor B		
SW	R1, DATA	1:	LW	R2, FLAG
LI	R2, 1		BEQ	R2, R0, 1B
SYNC			NOP	
SW	R2, FLAG		SYNC	
			LW	R1, DATA

The SYNC in processor A prevents DATA being written after FLAG, which could cause processor B to read stale data. The SYNC in processor B prevents DATA from being read before FLAG, which could likewise result in reading stale data. For processors which only execute loads and stores in order, with respect to shared memory, this instruction is a NOP.

LL and SC instructions implicitly perform a SYNC.

This instruction is allowed in User mode.

Operation:

```
32, 64      T:     SyncOperation()
```

Exceptions:

None

SYSCALL System Call SYSCALL

31 — 26	25 — 6	5 — 0
SPECIAL 000000	Code	SYSCALL 001100
6	20	6

Format:

SYSCALL

Description:

A system call exception occurs, immediately and unconditionally transferring control to the exception handler.

The code field is available for use as software parameters, but is retrieved by the exception handler only by loading the contents of the memory word containing the instruction.

Operation:

```
32, 64  T:    SystemCallException
```

Exceptions:

System Call exception

TEQ — Trap If Equal — TEQ

31–26	25–21	20–16	15–6	5–0
SPECIAL 000000	rs	rt	code	TEQ 110100
6	5	5	10	6

Format:

TEQ rs, rt

Description:

The contents of general register *rt* are compared to general register *rs*. If the contents of general register *rs* are equal to the contents of general register *rt*, a trap exception occurs.

The code field is available for use as software parameters, but is retrieved by the exception handler only by loading the contents of the memory word containing the instruction.

Operation:

```
32, 64      T:   if GPR[rs] = GPR[rt] then
                      TrapException
                 endif
```

Exceptions:

Trap exception

TEQI Trap If Equal Immediate TEQI

31–26	25–21	20–16	15–0
REGIMM 000001	rs	TEQI 01100	immediate
6	5	5	16

Format:

TEQI rs, immediate

Description:

The 16-bit *immediate* is sign-extended and compared to the contents of general register *rs*. If the contents of general register *rs* are equal to the sign-extended *immediate,* a trap exception occurs.

Operation:

32	T:	if GPR[rs] = $(\text{immediate}_{15})^{16}$ || $\text{immediate}_{15...0}$ then
		TrapException
		endif

64	T:	if GPR[rs] = $(\text{immediate}_{15})^{48}$ || $\text{immediate}_{15...0}$ then
		TrapException
		endif

Exceptions:

Trap exception

TGE Trap If Greater Than Or Equal TGE

31–26	25–21	20–16	15–6	5–0
SPECIAL 000000	rs	rt	code	TGE 110000
6	5	5	10	6

Format:

TGE rs, rt

Description:

The contents of general register *rt* are compared to the contents of general register *rs*. Considering both quantities as signed integers, if the contents of general register *rs* are greater than or equal to the contents of general register *rt*, a trap exception occurs.

The code field is available for use as software parameters, but is retrieved by the exception handler only by loading the contents of the memory word containing the instruction.

Operation:

```
32, 64  T:  if GPR[rs] ≥ GPR[rt] then
                TrapException
            endif
```

Exceptions:

Trap exception

TGEI Trap If Greater Than Or Equal Immediate TGEI

31 26	25 21	20 16	15 0
REGIMM 000001	rs	TGEI 01000	immediate
6	5	5	16

Format:

TGEI rs, immediate

Description:

The 16-bit *immediate* is sign-extended and compared to the contents of general register *rs*. Considering both quantities as signed integers, if the contents of general register *rs* are greater than or equal to the sign-extended *immediate*, a trap exception occurs.

Operation:

32	T: if GPR[rs] ≥ $(\text{immediate}_{15})^{16} \,\|\, \text{immediate}_{15...0}$ then TrapException endif
64	T: if GPR[rs] ≥ $(\text{immediate}_{15})^{48} \,\|\, \text{immediate}_{15...0}$ then TrapException endif

Exceptions:

Trap exception

TGEIU — Trap If Greater Than Or Equal Immediate Unsigned — TGEIU

31–26	25–21	20–16	15–0
REGIMM 000001	rs	TGEIU 01001	immediate
6	5	5	16

Format:

TGEIU rs, immediate

Description:

The 16-bit *immediate* is sign-extended and compared to the contents of general register *rs*. Considering both quantities as unsigned integers, if the contents of general register *rs* are greater than or equal to the sign-extended *immediate*, a trap exception occurs.

Operation:

32	T:	if $(0 \mathbin{\|} GPR[rs]) \geq (0 \mathbin{\|} (immediate_{15})^{16} \mathbin{\|} immediate_{15...0})$ then
		    TrapException
		endif

64	T:	if $(0 \mathbin{\|} GPR[rs]) \geq (0 \mathbin{\|} (immediate_{15})^{48} \mathbin{\|} immediate_{15...0})$ then
		    TrapException
		endif

Exceptions:

Trap exception

TGEU Trap If Greater Than Or Equal Unsigned TGEU

31–26	25–21	20–16	15–6	5–0
SPECIAL 000000	rs	rt	code	TGEU 110001
6	5	5	10	6

Format:

TGEU rs, rt

Description:

The contents of general register *rt* are compared to the contents of general register *rs*. Considering both quantities as unsigned integers, if the contents of general register *rs* are greater than or equal to the contents of general register *rt*, a trap exception occurs.

The code field is available for use as software parameters, but is retrieved by the exception handler only by loading the contents of the memory word containing the instruction.

Operation:

```
T:     if (0 || GPR[rs]) ≥ (0 || GPR[rt]) then
            TrapException
       endif
```

Exceptions:

Trap exception

TLBP Probe TLB For Matching Entry TLBP

31–26	25	24–6	5–0
COP0 010000	CO 1	0 000 0000 0000 0000 0000	TLBP 001000
6	1	19	6

Format:

TLBP

Description:

The *Index* register is loaded with the address of the TLB entry whose contents match the contents of the *EntryHi* register. If no TLB entry matches, the high-order bit of the *Index* register is set.

The architecture does not specify the operation of memory references associated with the instruction immediately after a TLBP instruction, nor is the operation specified if more than one TLB entry matches.

Operation:

```
32   T:   Index← 1 || 0^25 || 1^6
          for i in 0...TLBEntries–1
               if (TLB[i]_95...77 = EntryHi_31...12) and  (TLB[i]_76 or
               (TLB[i]_71...64 = EntryHi_7...0)) then
                    Index ← 0^26 || i_5...0
               endif
          endfor
64   T:   Index← 1 || 0^31
          for i in 0...TLBEntries–1
               if (TLB[i]_167...141 and not (0^15 || TLB[i]_216...205))
                = EntryHi_39...13) and not (0^15 || TLB[i]_216...205)) and
               (TLB[i]_140 or (TLB[i]_135...128 = EntryHi_7...0)) then
                    Index ← 0^26 || i_5...0
               endif
          endfor
```

Exceptions:

Coprocessor unusable exception

TLBR Read Indexed TLB Entry TLBR

31 26	25	24 6	5 0
COP0 0 1 0 0 0 0	CO 1	0 000 0000 0000 0000 0000	TLBR 0 0 0 0 0 1
6	1	19	6

Format:

TLBR

Description:

The *G* bit (which controls ASID matching) read from the TLB is written into both of the *EntryLo0* and *EntryLo1* registers.

The *EntryHi* and *EntryLo* registers are loaded with the contents of the TLB entry pointed at by the contents of the TLB *Index* register. The operation is invalid (and the results are unspecified) if the contents of the TLB *Index* register are greater than the number of TLB entries in the processor.

Operation:

32	T:	PageMask ← $TLB[Index_{5...0}]_{127...96}$ EntryHi ← $TLB[Index_{5...0}]_{95...64}$ and not $TLB[Index_{5...0}]_{127...96}$ EntryLo1 ← $TLB[Index_{5...0}]_{63...32}$ EntryLo0 ← $TLB[Index_{5...0}]_{31...0}$
64	T:	PageMask ← $TLB[Index_{5...0}]_{255...192}$ EntryHi ← $TLB[Index_{5...0}]_{191...128}$ and not $TLB[Index_{5...0}]_{255...192}$ EntryLo1 ← $TLB[Index_{5...0}]_{127...65}$ || $TLB[Index_{5...0}]_{140}$ EntryLo0 ← $TLB[Index_{5...0}]_{63...1}$ || $TLB[Index_{5...0}]_{140}$

Exceptions:

Coprocessor unusable exception

TLBWI Write Indexed TLB Entry TLBWI

31 — 26	25	24 — 6	5 — 0
COP0 010000	CO 1	0 000 0000 0000 0000 0000	TLBWI 000010
6	1	19	6

Format:

TLBWI

Description:

The *G* bit of the TLB is written with the logical AND of the *G* bits in the *EntryLo0* and *EntryLo1* registers.

The TLB entry pointed at by the contents of the TLB *Index* register is loaded with the contents of the *EntryHi* and *EntryLo* registers.

The operation is invalid (and the results are unspecified) if the contents of the TLB *Index* register are greater than the number of TLB entries in the processor.

Operation:

32, 64T:	TLB[$\text{Index}_{5...0}$] ← PageMask || (EntryHi and not PageMask) || EntryLo1 || EntryLo0

Exceptions:

Coprocessor unusable exception

TLBWR Write Random TLB Entry TLBWR

31–26	25	24–6	5–0
COP0 010000	CO 1	0 000 0000 0000 0000 0000	TLBWR 000110
6	1	19	6

Format:

TLBWR

Description:

The *G* bit of the TLB is written with the logical AND of the *G* bits in the *EntryLo0* and *EntryLo1* registers.

The TLB entry pointed at by the contents of the TLB *Random* register is loaded with the contents of the *EntryHi* and *EntryLo* registers.

Operation:

32, 64T:	TLB[$\text{Random}_{5...0}$] ← PageMask || (EntryHi and not PageMask) || EntryLo1 || EntryLo0

Exceptions:

Coprocessor unusable exception

TLT — Trap If Less Than — TLT

31–26	25–21	20–16	15–6	5–0
SPECIAL 000000	rs	rt	code	TLT 110010
6	5	5	10	6

Format:

TLT rs, rt

Description:

The contents of general register *rt* are compared to general register *rs*. Considering both quantities as signed integers, if the contents of general register *rs* are less than the contents of general register *rt*, a trap exception occurs.

The code field is available for use as software parameters, but is retrieved by the exception handler only by loading the contents of the memory word containing the instruction.

Operation:

```
32, 64  T:  if GPR[rs] < GPR[rt] then
                TrapException
            endif
```

Exceptions:

Trap exception

TLTI Trap If Less Than Immediate TLTI

31 26	25 21	20 16	15 0
REGIMM 000001	rs	TLTI 01010	immediate
6	5	5	16

Format:

TLTI rs, immediate

Description:

The 16-bit *immediate* is sign-extended and compared to the contents of general register *rs*. Considering both quantities as signed integers, if the contents of general register *rs* are less than the sign-extended *immediate*, a trap exception occurs.

Operation:

32	T:	if GPR[rs] < $(\text{immediate}_{15})^{16}$ || $\text{immediate}_{15...0}$ then
		    TrapException
		endif

64	T:	if GPR[rs] < $(\text{immediate}_{15})^{48}$ || $\text{immediate}_{15...0}$ then
		    TrapException
		endif

Exceptions:

Trap exception

TLTIU Trap If Less Than Immediate Unsigned TLTIU

31–26	25–21	20–16	15–0
REGIMM 000001	rs	TLTIU 01011	immediate
6	5	5	16

Format:

TLTIU rs, immediate

Description:

The 16-bit *immediate* is sign-extended and compared to the contents of general register *rs*. Considering both quantities as signed integers, if the contents of general register *rs* are less than the sign-extended *immediate*, a trap exception occurs.

Operation:

```
32    T:  if (0 || GPR[rs]) < (0 || (immediate_15)^16 || immediate_15...0) then
              TrapException
          endif

64    T:  if (0 || GPR[rs]) < (0 || (immediate_15)^48 || immediate_15...0) then
              TrapException
          endif
```

Exceptions:

Trap exception

TLTU Trap If Less Than Unsigned TLTU

31 ... 26	25 ... 21	20 ... 16	15 ... 6	5 ... 0
SPECIAL 000000	rs	rt	code	TLTU 110011
6	5	5	10	6

Format:

TLTU rs, rt

Description:

The contents of general register *rt* are compared to general register *rs*. Considering both quantities as unsigned integers, if the contents of general register *rs* are less than the contents of general register *rt*, a trap exception occurs.

The code field is available for use as software parameters, but is retrieved by the exception handler only by loading the contents of the memory word containing the instruction.

Operation:

```
32, 64T:    if (0 || GPR[rs]) < (0 || GPR[rt]) then
                TrapException
            endif
```

Exceptions:

Trap exception

TNE — Trap If Not Equal — TNE

31–26	25–21	20–16	15–6	5–0
SPECIAL 000000	rs	rt	code	TNE 110110
6	5	5	10	6

Format:

TNE rs, rt

Description:

The contents of general register *rt* are compared to general register *rs*. If the contents of general register *rs* are not equal to the contents of general register *rt*, a trap exception occurs.

The code field is available for use as software parameters, but is retrieved by the exception handler only by loading the contents of the memory word containing the instruction.

Operation:

```
32, 64T:   if GPR[rs] ≠ GPR[rt] then
                TrapException
           endif
```

Exceptions:

Trap exception

TNEI Trap If Not Equal Immediate TNEI

31 — 26	25 — 21	20 — 16	15 — 0
REGIMM 000001	rs	TNEI 01110	immediate
6	5	5	16

Format:

TNEI rs, immediate

Description:

The 16-bit *immediate* is sign-extended and compared to the contents of general register *rs*. If the contents of general register *rs* are not equal to the sign-extended *immediate*, a trap exception occurs.

Operation:

```
32    T:  if GPR[rs] ≠ (immediate15)^16 || immediate15...0 then
              TrapException
          endif
64    T:  if GPR[rs] ≠ (immediate15)^48 || immediate15...0 then
              TrapException
          endif
```

Exceptions:

Trap exception

XOR Exclusive Or

31 26	25 21	20 16	15 11	10 6	5 0
SPECIAL 000000	rs	rt	rd	0 00000	XOR 100110
6	5	5	5	5	6

Format:

XOR rd, rs, rt

Description:

The contents of general register *rs* are combined with the contents of general register *rt* in a bit-wise logical exclusive OR operation.

The result is placed into general register *rd*.

Operation:

32, 64	T:	GPR[rd] ← GPR[rs] xor GPR[rt]

Exceptions:

None

XORI Exclusive OR Immediate XORI

31 26	25 21	20 16	15 0
XORI 0 0 1 1 1 0	rs	rt	immediate
6	5	5	16

Format:

XORI rt, rs, immediate

Description:

The 16-bit *immediate* is zero-extended and combined with the contents of general register *rs* in a bit-wise logical exclusive OR operation.

The result is placed into general register *rt.*

Operation:

32	T:	GPR[rt] ← GPR[rs] xor (0^{16} || immediate)
64	T:	GPR[rt] ← GPR[rs] xor (0^{48} || immediate)

Exceptions:

None

CPU Instruction Opcode Bit Encoding

The remainder of this Appendix presents the opcode bit encoding for the CPU instruction set (ISA and extensions), as implemented by the R4000. Figure A-2 lists the R4000 Opcode Bit Encoding.

Opcode

31...29 \ 28...26	0	1	2	3	4	5	6	7
0	SPECIAL	REGIMM	J	JAL	BEQ	BNE	BLEZ	BGTZ
1	ADDI	ADDIU	SLTI	SLTIU	ANDI	ORI	XORI	LUI
2	COP0	COP1	COP2	*	BEQL	BNEL	BLEZL	BGTZL
3	DADDIε	DADDIUε	LDLε	LDRε	*	*	*	*
4	LB	LH	LWL	LW	LBU	LHU	LWR	LWUε
5	SB	SH	SWL	SW	SDLε	SDRε	SWR	CACHE δ
6	LL	LWC1	LWC2	*	LLDε	LDC1	LDC2	LDC3
7	SC	SWC1	SWC2	*	SCDε	SDC1	SDC2	SDC3

SPECIAL function

5...3 \ 2...0	0	1	2	3	4	5	6	7
0	SLL	*	SRL	SRA	SLLV	*	SRLV	SRAV
1	JR	JALR	*	*	SYSCALL	BREAK	*	SYNC
2	MFHI	MTHI	MFLO	MTLO	DSLLVε	*	DSRLVε	DSRAVε
3	MULT	MULTU	DIV	DIVU	DMULTε	DMULTUε	DDIVε	DDIVUε
4	ADD	ADDU	SUB	SUBU	AND	OR	XOR	NOR
5	*	*	SLT	SLTU	DADDε	DADDUε	DSUBε	DSUBUε
6	TGE	TGEU	TLT	TLTU	TEQ	*	TNE	*
7	DSLLε	*	DSRLε	DSRAε	DSLL32ε	*	DSRL32ε	DSRA32ε

REGIMM rt

20...19 \ 18...16	0	1	2	3	4	5	6	7
0	BLTZ	BGEZ	BLTZL	BGEZL	*	*	*	*
1	TGEI	TGEIU	TLTI	TLTIU	TEQI	*	TNEI	*
2	BLTZAL	BGEZAL	BLTZALL	BGEZALL	*	*	*	*
3	*	*	*	*	*	*	*	*

COPz rs

25, 24 \ 23...21	0	1	2	3	4	5	6	7
0	MF	DMFε	CF	γ	MT	DMTε	CT	γ
1	BC	γ	γ	γ	γ	γ	γ	γ
2	CO							
3								

Figure A-2 R4000 Opcode Bit Encoding

COPz rt

20...19 \ 18...16	0	1	2	3	4	5	6	7
0	BCF	BCT	BCFL	BCTL	γ	γ	γ	γ
1	γ	γ	γ	γ	γ	γ	γ	γ
2	γ	γ	γ	γ	γ	γ	γ	γ
3	γ	γ	γ	γ	γ	γ	γ	γ

CP0 Function

5 ... 3 \ 2 ... 0	0	1	2	3	4	5	6	7
0	ϕ	TLBR	TLBWI	ϕ	ϕ	ϕ	TLBWR	ϕ
1	TLBP	ϕ	ϕ	ϕ	ϕ	ϕ	ϕ	ϕ
2	ξ	ϕ	ϕ	ϕ	ϕ	ϕ	ϕ	ϕ
3	ERET χ	ϕ	ϕ	ϕ	ϕ	ϕ	ϕ	ϕ
0	ϕ	ϕ	ϕ	ϕ	ϕ	ϕ	ϕ	ϕ
1	ϕ	ϕ	ϕ	ϕ	ϕ	ϕ	ϕ	ϕ
2	ϕ	ϕ	ϕ	ϕ	ϕ	ϕ	ϕ	ϕ
3	ϕ	ϕ	ϕ	ϕ	ϕ	ϕ	ϕ	ϕ

Figure A-2 (cont.) R4000 Opcode Bit Encoding

Key:

- * Operation codes marked with an asterisk cause reserved instruction exceptions in all current implementations and are reserved for future versions of the architecture.
- γ Operation codes marked with a gamma cause a reserved instruction exception. They are reserved for future versions of the architecture.
- δ Operation codes marked with a delta are valid only for R4000 processors with CP0 enabled, and cause a reserved instruction exception on other processors.
- ϕ Operation codes marked with a phi are invalid but do not cause reserved instruction exceptions in R4000 implementations.
- ξ Operation codes marked with a xi cause a reserved instruction exception on R4000 processors.
- χ Operation codes marked with a chi are valid only on R4000.
- ε Operation codes marked with epsilon are valid when the processor operating as a 64-bit processor. These instructions will cause a reserved instruction exception if 64-bit operation is not enabled.

FPU Instruction Set Details

B

This appendix provides a detailed description of each floating-point unit (FPU) instruction (refer to Appendix A for a detailed description of the CPU instructions). The instructions are listed alphabetically, and any exceptions that may occur due to the execution of each instruction are listed after the description of each instruction. Descriptions of the immediate causes and the manner of handling exceptions are omitted from the instruction descriptions in this appendix (refer to Chapter 7 for detailed descriptions of floating-point exceptions and handling).

Figure B-3 at the end of this appendix lists the entire bit encoding for the constant fields of the floating-point instruction set; the bit encoding for each instruction is included with that individual instruction.

B.1 Instruction Formats

There are three basic instruction format types:

- I-Type, or Immediate instructions, which include load and store operations
- M-Type, or Move instructions
- R-Type, or Register instructions, which include the two- and three-register floating-point operations.

The instruction description subsections that follow show how these three basic instruction formats are used by:

- Load and store instructions
- Move instructions
- Floating-Point computational instructions
- Floating-Point branch instructions

Floating-point instructions are mapped onto the MIPS coprocessor instructions, defining coprocessor unit number one (CP1) as the floating-point unit.

Each operation is valid only for certain formats. Implementations may support some of these formats and operations through emulation, but they only need to support combinations that are valid (marked *V* in Table B-1). Combinations marked *R* in Table B-1 are not currently specified by this architecture, and cause an unimplemented instruction trap. They will be available for future extensions to the architecture.

Table B-1 Valid FPU Instruction Formats

Operation	Source Format			
	Single	**Double**	**Word**	**Longword**
ADD	V	V	R	R
SUB	V	V	R	R
MUL	V	V	R	R
DIV	V	V	R	R
SQRT	V	V	R	R
ABS	V	V	R	R
MOV	V	V		
NEG	V	V	R	R
TRUNC.L	V	V		
ROUND.L	V	V		
CEIL.L	V	V		
FLOOR.L	V	V		
TRUNC.W	V	V		
ROUND.W	V	V		
CEIL.W	V	V		
FLOOR.W	V	V		
CVT.S		V	V	V
CVT.D	V		V	V
CVT.W	V	V		
CVT.L	V	V		
C	V	V	R	R

The coprocessor branch on condition true/false instructions can be used to logically negate any predicate. Thus, the 32 possible conditions require only 16 distinct comparisons, as shown in Table B-2 below.

Table B-2 Logical Negation of Predicates by Condition True/False

Condition			Relations				Invalid Operation Exception If Unordered
Mnemonic		Code	Greater Than	Less Than	Equal	Unordered	
True	False						
F	T	0	F	F	F	F	No
UN	OR	1	F	F	F	T	No
EQ	NEQ	2	F	F	T	F	No
UEQ	OGL	3	F	F	T	T	No
OLT	UGE	4	F	T	F	F	No
ULT	OGE	5	F	T	F	T	No
OLE	UGT	6	F	T	T	F	No
ULE	OGT	7	F	T	T	T	No
SF	ST	8	F	F	F	F	Yes
NGLE	GLE	9	F	F	F	T	Yes
SEQ	SNE	10	F	F	T	F	Yes
NGL	GL	11	F	F	T	T	Yes
LT	NLT	12	F	T	F	F	Yes
NGE	GE	13	F	T	F	T	Yes
LE	NLE	14	F	T	T	F	Yes
NGT	GT	15	F	T	T	T	Yes

Floating-Point Loads, Stores, and Moves

All movement of data between the floating-point coprocessor and memory is accomplished by coprocessor load and store operations, which reference the floating-point coprocessor *General Purpose* registers. These operations are unformatted; no format conversions are performed and, therefore, no floating-point exceptions can occur due to these operations.

Data may also be directly moved between the floating-point coprocessor and the processor by *move to coprocessor* and *move from coprocessor* instructions. Like the floating-point load and store operations, move to/from operations perform no format conversions and never cause floating-point exceptions.

An additional pair of coprocessor registers are available, called *Floating-Point Control* registers for which the only data movement operations supported are moves to and from processor *General Purpose* registers.

Floating-Point Operations

The floating-point unit operation set includes:

- floating-point add
- floating-point subtract
- floating-point multiply
- floating-point divide
- floating-point square root
- convert between fixed-point and floating-point formats
- convert between floating-point formats
- floating-point compare

These operations satisfy the requirements of IEEE Standard 754 requirements for accuracy. Specifically, these operations obtain a result which is identical to an infinite-precision result rounded to the specified format, using the current rounding mode.

Instructions must specify the format of their operands. Except for conversion functions, mixed-format operations are not provided.

B.2 Instruction Notation Conventions

In this appendix, all variable subfields in an instruction format (such as *fs*, *ft*, *immediate*, and so on) are shown in lower-case. The instruction name (such as ADD, SUB, and so on) is shown in upper-case.

For the sake of clarity, we sometimes use an alias for a variable subfield in the formats of specific instructions. For example, we use *rs* = *base* in the format for load and store instructions. Such an alias is always lower case, since it refers to a variable subfield.

In some instructions, the instruction subfields *op* and *function* can have constant 6-bit values. When reference is made to these instructions, upper-case mnemonics are used. For instance, in the floating-point ADD instruction we use *op* = COP1 and *function* = FADD. In other cases, a single field has both fixed and variable subfields, so the name contains both upper and lower case characters. Bit encodings for mnemonics are shown in Figure B-3 at the end of this appendix, and are also included with each individual instruction.

In the instruction description examples that follow, the *Operation* section describes the operation performed by each instruction using a high-level language notation.

Instruction Notation Examples

The following examples illustrate the application of some of the instruction notation conventions:

Example #1:

$$\text{GPR[rt]} \leftarrow \text{immediate} \,||\, 0^{16}$$

Sixteen zero bits are concatenated with an immediate value (typically 16 bits), and the 32-bit string (with the lower 16 bits set to zero) is assigned to General Purpose Register *rt*.

Example #2:

$$(\text{immediate}_{15})^{16} \,||\, \text{immediate}_{15..0}$$

Bit 15 (the sign bit) of an immediate value is extended for 16 bit positions, and the result is concatenated with bits 15 through 0 of the immediate value to form a 32-bit sign extended value.

B.3 Load and Store Instructions

In the R4000 implementation, the instruction immediately following a load may use the contents of the register being loaded. In such cases, the hardware *interlocks*, requiring additional real cycles, so scheduling load delay slots is still desirable, although not required for functional code.

The behavior of the load store instructions is dependent on the width of the *FGR*s.

- When the *FR* bit in the *Status* register equals zero, the *Floating-Point General* registers (*FGR*s) are 32-bits wide.
- When the *FR* bit in the *Status* register equals one, the *Floating-Point General* registers (*FGR*s) are 64-bits wide.

In the load and store operation descriptions, the functions listed in Table B-3 are used to summarize the handling of virtual addresses and physical memory.

Table B-3 Load and Store Common Functions

Function	Meaning
AddressTranslation	Uses the TLB to find the physical address given the virtual address. The function fails and an exception is taken if the required translation is not present in the TLB.
LoadMemory	Uses the cache and main memory to find the contents of the word containing the specified physical address. The low-order two bits of the address and the *Access Type* field indicates which of each of the four bytes within the data word need to be returned. If the cache is enabled for this access, the entire word is returned and loaded into the cache.
StoreMemory	Uses the cache, write buffer, and main memory to store the word or part of word specified as data in the word containing the specified physical address. The low-order two bits of the address and the *Access Type* field indicates which of each of the four bytes within the data word should be stored.

Figure B-1 shows the I-Type instruction format used by load and store operations.

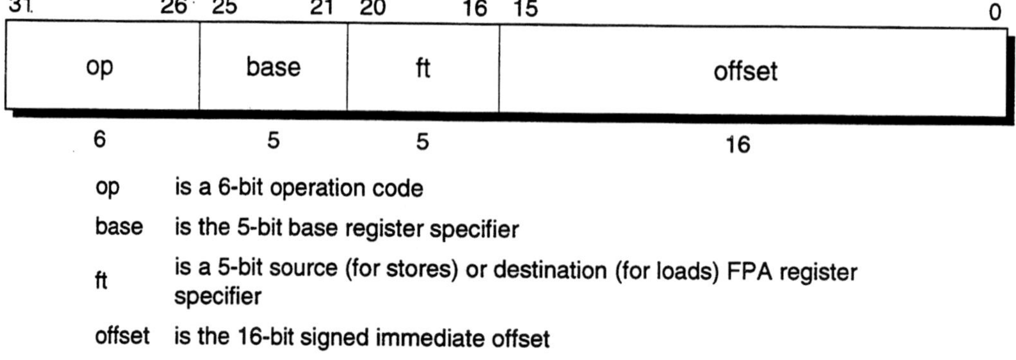

op is a 6-bit operation code

base is the 5-bit base register specifier

ft is a 5-bit source (for stores) or destination (for loads) FPA register specifier

offset is the 16-bit signed immediate offset

Figure B-1 Load and Store Instruction Format

All coprocessor loads and stores reference aligned-word data items. Thus, for word loads and stores, the access type field is always WORD, and the low-order two bits of the address must always be zero.

For doubleword loads and stores, the access type field is always DOUBLEWORD, and the low-order three bits of the address must always be zero.

Regardless of byte-numbering order (endianness), the address specifies that byte which has the smallest byte-address in the addressed field. For a big-endian machine, this is the leftmost byte; for a little-endian machine, this is the rightmost byte.

B.4 Computational Instructions

Computational instructions include all of the arithmetic floating-point operations performed by the FPU.

Figure B-2 shows the R-Type instruction format used for computational operations.

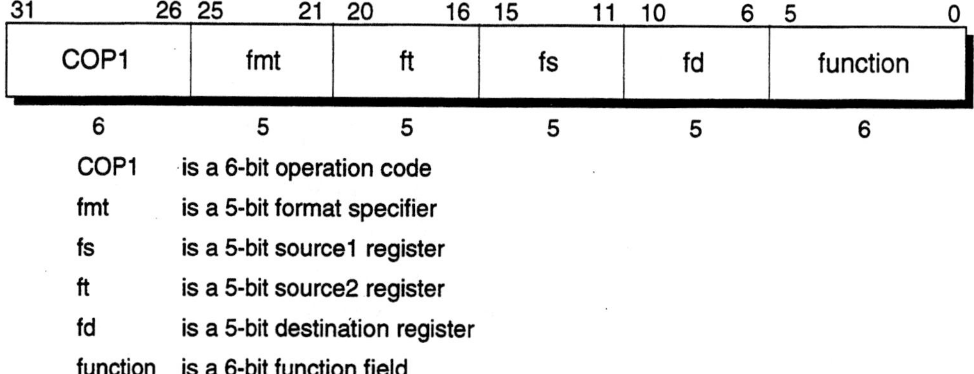

Figure B-2 Computational Instruction Format

The *function* field indicates the floating-point operation to be performed.

Each floating-point instruction can be applied to a number of operand *formats*. The operand format for an instruction is specified by the 5-bit *format* field; decoding for this field is shown in Table B-4.

Table B-4 Format Field Decoding

Code	Mnemonic	Size	Format
16	S	single	Binary floating-point
17	D	double	Binary floating-point
18	Reserved		
19	Reserved		
20	W	single	32-bit binary fixed-point
21	L	longword	64-bit binary fixed-point
22–31	Reserved		

Table B-5 lists all floating-point instructions.

Table B-5 Floating-Point Instructions and Operations

Code (5: 0)	Mnemonic	Operation
0	ADD	Add
1	SUB	Subtract
2	MUL	Multiply
3	DIV	Divide
4	SQRT	Square root
5	ABS	Absolute value
6	MOV	Move
7	NEG	Negate
8	ROUND.L	Convert to single fixed-point, rounded to nearest/even
9	TRUNC.L	Convert to single fixed-point, rounded toward zero
10	CEIL.L	Convert to single fixed-point, rounded to $+\infty$
11	FLOOR.L	Convert to single fixed-point, rounded to $-\infty$
12	ROUND.W	Convert to single fixed-point, rounded to nearest/even
13	TRUNC.W	Convert to single fixed-point, rounded toward zero
14	CEIL.W	Convert to single fixed-point, rounded to $+\infty$
15	FLOOR.W	Convert to single fixed-point, rounded to $-\infty$
16–31	–	Reserved
32	CVT.S	Convert to single floating-point
33	CVT.D	Convert to double floating-point
34	–	Reserved
35	–	Reserved
36	CVT.W	Convert to 32-bit binary fixed-point
37	CVT.L	Convert to 64-bit binary fixed-point
38–47	–	Reserved
48–63	C	Floating-point compare

In the following pages, the notation *FGR* refers to the 32 *General Purpose* registers *FGR0* through *FGR31* of the FPU, and *FPR* refers to the floating-point registers of the FPU.

- When the *FR* bit in the *Status* register (SR(26)) equals zero, only the even floating-point registers are valid and the 32 *General Purpose* registers of the FPU are 32-bits wide.
- When the *FR* bit in the *Status* register (SR(26)) equals one, both odd and even floating-point registers may be used and the 32 *General Purpose* registers of the FPU are 64-bits wide.

The following routines are used in the description of the floating-point operations to retrieve the value of an FPR or to change the value of an FGR:

32 Bit Mode

```
value <-- ValueFPR(fpr, fmt)
    /* undefined for odd fpr */
    case fmt of
        S, W:
            value <-- FGR[fpr+0]
        D:
            /* undefined for fpr not even */
            value <-- FGR[fpr+1] || FGR[fpr+0]
    end

StoreFPR(fpr, fmt, value):
    /* undefined for odd fpr */
    case fmt of
        S, W:
            FGR[fpr+1] <-- undefined
            FGR[fpr+0] <-- value
        D:
            FGR[fpr+1] <-- value63...32
            FGR[fpr+0] <-- value31...0
    end
```

64 Bit Mode

```
value <-- ValueFPR(fpr, fmt)
    case fmt of
        S:
            value <-- FGR[fpr]31...0
        D, L:
            value <-- FGR[fpr]
        W:
            value <-- FGR[fpr]
    end

StoreFPR(fpr, fmt, value):
    case fmt of
        S, W:
            FGR[fpr] <-- undefined32 || value
        D, L:
            FGR[fpr] <-- value
    end
```

ABS.fmt Floating-Point Absolute Value ABS.fmt

31–26	25–21	20–16	15–11	10–6	5–0
COP1 010001	fmt	0 00000	fs	fd	ABS 000101
6	5	5	5	5	6

Format:

ABS.fmt fd, fs

Description:

The contents of the FPU register specified by *fs* are interpreted in the specified format and the arithmetic absolute value is taken. The result is placed in the floating-point register specified by *fd*.

The absolute value operation is arithmetic; a NaN operand signals invalid operation.

This instruction is valid only for single- and double-precision floating-point formats. The operation is not defined if bit 0 of any register specification is set and the *FR* bit in the *Status* register equals zero, since the register numbers specify an even-odd pair of adjacent coprocessor general registers. When the *FR* bit in the *Status* register equals one, both even and odd register numbers are valid.

Operation:

```
T:    StoreFPR(fd, fmt, AbsoluteValue(ValueFPR(fs, fmt)))
```

Exceptions:

Coprocessor unusable exception
Coprocessor exception trap

Coprocessor Exceptions:

Unimplemented operation exception
Invalid operation exception

ADD.fmt Floating-Point Add ADD.fmt

31 26	25 21	20 16	15 11	10 6	5 0
COP1 010001	fmt	ft	fs	fd	ADD 000000
6	5	5	5	5	6

Format:

ADD.fmt fd, fs, ft

Description:

The contents of the FPU registers specified by *fs* and *ft* are interpreted in the specified format and arithmetically added. The result is rounded as if calculated to infinite precision and then rounded to the specified format (*fmt*), according to the current rounding mode. The result is placed in the floating-point register (*FPR*) specified by *fd*.

This instruction is valid only for single- and double-precision floating-point formats. The operation is not defined if bit 0 of any register specification is set and the *FR* bit in the *Status* register equals zero, since the register numbers specify an even-odd pair of adjacent coprocessor general registers. When the *FR* bit in the *Status* register equals one, both even and odd register numbers are valid.

Operation:

```
T:     StoreFPR (fd, fmt, ValueFPR(fs, fmt) + ValueFPR(ft, fmt))
```

Exceptions:

Coprocessor unusable exception
Floating-Point exception

Coprocessor Exceptions:

Unimplemented operation exception
Invalid operation exception
Inexact exception
Overflow exception
Underflow exception

BC1F — Branch On FPA False (Coprocessor 1) — BC1F

31–26	25–21	20–16	15–0
COP1 010001	BC 01000	BCF 00000	offset
6	5	5	16

Format:

BC1F offset

Description:

A branch target address is computed from the sum of the address of the instruction in the delay slot and the 16-bit *offset*, shifted left two bits and sign-extended. If the result of the last floating-point compare is false, the program branches to the target address, with a delay of one instruction.

Operation:

32	T–1:	condition ← not COC[1]
	T:	target ← $(\text{offset}_{15})^{14}$ ‖ offset ‖ 0^2
	T+1:	if condition then
		PC ← PC + target
		endif
64	T–1:	condition ← not COC[1]
	T:	target ← $(\text{offset}_{15})^{46}$ ‖ offset ‖ 0^2
	T+1:	if condition then
		PC ← PC + target
		endif

Exceptions:

Coprocessor unusable exception

BC1FL Branch On FPU False Likely (Coprocessor 1) BC1FL

31–26	25–21	20–16	15–0
COP1 0 1 0 0 0 1	BC 0 1 0 0 0	BCFL 0 0 0 1 0	offset
6	5	5	16

Format:

BC1FL offset

Description:

A branch target address is computed from the sum of the address of the instruction in the delay slot and the 16-bit *offset*, shifted left two bits and sign-extended.

If the result of the last floating-point compare is false, the program branches to the target address, with a delay of one instruction. If the conditional branch is not taken, the instruction in the branch delay slot is nullified.

Operation:

```
32    T–1:  condition ← not COC[1]
      T:    target ← (offset_15)^14 || offset || 0^2
      T+1:  if condition then
                PC ← PC + target
            else
                NullifyCurrentInstruction
            endif
64    T–1:  condition ← not COC[1]
      T:    target ← (offset_15)^46 || offset || 0^2
      T+1:  if condition then
                PC ← PC + target
            else
                NullifyCurrentInstruction
            endif
```

Exceptions:

Coprocessor unusable exception

BC1T — Branch On FPU True (Coprocessor 1) — BC1T

31–26	25–21	20–16	15–0
COP1 010001	BC 01000	BCT 00001	offset
6	5	5	16

Format:

BC1T offset

Description:

A branch target address is computed from the sum of the address of the instruction in the delay slot and the 16-bit *offset,* shifted left two bits and sign-extended. If the result of the last floating-point compare is true, the program branches to the target address, with a delay of one instruction.

Operation:

32	T–1:	condition ← COC[1]
	T:	target ← $(offset_{15})^{14}$ || offset || 0^2

	T+1:	if condition then
		  PC ← PC + target
		endif

64	T–1:	condition ← COC[1]
	T:	target ← $(offset_{15})^{46}$ || offset || 0^2

	T+1:	if condition then
		  PC ← PC + target
		endif

Exceptions:

Coprocessor unusable exception

BC1TL Branch On FPU True Likely (Coprocessor 1) BC1TL

31–26	25–21	20–16	15–0
COP1 010001	BC 01000	BCTL 00011	offset
6	5	5	16

Format:

BC1TL offset

Description:

A branch target address is computed from the sum of the address of the instruction in the delay slot and the 16-bit *offset*, shifted left two bits and sign-extended.

If the result of the last floating-point compare is true, the program branches to the target address, with a delay of one instruction. If the conditional branch is not taken, the instruction in the branch delay slot is nullified.

Operation:

```
32    T–1:   condition ← COC[1]
      T:     target ← (offset_15)^14 || offset || 0^2
      T+1:   if condition then
                 PC ← PC + target
             else
                 NullifyCurrentInstruction
             endif
64    T–1:   condition ← COC[1]
      T:     target ← (offset_15)^46 || offset || 0^2
      T+1:   if condition then
                 PC ← PC + target
             else
                 NullifyCurrentInstruction
             endif
```

Exceptions:

Coprocessor unusable exception

C.cond.fmt — Floating-Point Compare — C.cond.fmt

31–26	25–21	20–16	15–11	10–6	5–4	3–0
COP1 010001	fmt	ft	fs	0 00000	FC*	cond*
6	5	5	5	5	2	4

Format:

C.cond.fmt fs, ft

Description:

The contents of the floating-point registers specified by *fs* and *ft* are interpreted in the specified *format* and arithmetically compared.

A result is determined based on the comparison and the conditions specified in the instruction. If one of the values is a Not a Number (NaN), and the high-order bit of the *condition* field is set, an invalid operation exception is taken. After a one-instruction delay, the condition is available for testing with branch on floating-point coprocessor condition instructions.

Comparisons are exact and can neither overflow nor underflow. Four mutually-exclusive relations are possible as results: less than, equal, greater than, and unordered. The last case arises when one or both of the operands are NaN; every NaN compares unordered with everything, including itself.

Comparisons ignore the sign of zero, so +0 = –0.

This instruction is valid only for single- and double-precision floating-point formats. The operation is not defined if bit 0 of any register specification is set and the *FR* bit in the *Status* register equals zero, since the register numbers specify an even-odd pair of adjacent coprocessor general registers. When the *FR* bit in the *Status* register equals one, both even and odd register numbers are valid.

*See "FPU Instruction Opcode Bit Encoding" at the end of Appendix B.

C.cond.fmt — Floating-Point Compare (continued) — C.cond.fmt

Operation:

```
T:     if NaN(ValueFPR(fs, fmt)) or NaN(ValueFPR(ft, fmt)) then
                less ← false
                equal ← false
                unordered ← true
                if cond3 then
                     signal InvalidOperationException
                endif
       else
                less ← ValueFPR(fs, fmt) < ValueFPR(ft, fmt)
                equal ← ValueFPR(fs, fmt) = ValueFPR(ft, fmt)
                unordered ← false
       endif
       condition ← (cond2 and less) or (cond1 and equal) or
                         (cond0 and unordered)
       FCR[31]23 ← condition
       COC[1] ← condition
```

Exceptions:

Coprocessor unusable
Floating-Point exception

Coprocessor Exceptions:

Unimplemented operation exception
Invalid operation exception

CEIL.L.fmt — Floating-Point Ceiling to Long Fixed-Point Format — CEIL.L.fmt

31–26	25–21	20–16	15–11	10–6	5–0
COP1 010001	fmt	0 00000	fs	fd	CEIL.L 001010
6	5	5	5	5	6

Format:

CEIL.L.fmt fd, fs

Description:

The contents of the floating-point register specified by *fs* are interpreted in the specified source format, *fmt*, and arithmetically converted to the single fixed-point format. The result is placed in the floating-point register specified by *fd*.

Regardless of the setting of the current rounding mode, the conversion is rounded as if the current rounding mode is round to +∞ (2).

This instruction is valid only for conversion from single- or double-precision floating-point formats. When the *FR* bit in the *Status* register equals one, both even and odd register numbers are valid.

When the source operand is an Infinity, NaN, or the correctly rounded integer result is outside of -2^{63} to $2^{63}-1$, the Invalid operation exception is raised. If the Invalid operation is not enabled then no exception is taken and $2^{63}-1$ is returned.

CEIL.L.fmt — Floating-Point Ceiling to Long Fixed-Point Format (continued) — CEIL.L.fmt

Operation:

```
T:      StoreFPR(fd, L, ConvertFmt(ValueFPR(fs, fmt), fmt, L))
```

Exceptions:

Coprocessor unusable exception
Floating-Point exception

Coprocessor Exceptions:

Invalid operation exception
Unimplemented operation exception
Inexact exception
Overflow exception

CEIL.W.fmt — Floating-Point Ceiling to Single Fixed-Point Format — CEIL.W.fmt

31–26	25–21	20–16	15–11	10–6	5–0
COP1 010001	fmt	0 00000	fs	fd	CEIL.W 001110
6	5	5	5	5	6

Format:

CEIL.W.fmt fd, fs

Description:

The contents of the floating-point register specified by *fs* are interpreted in the specified source format, *fmt*, and arithmetically converted to the single fixed-point format. The result is placed in the floating-point register specified by *fd*.

Regardless of the setting of the current rounding mode, the conversion is rounded as if the current rounding mode is round to +∞ (2).

This instruction is valid only for conversion from a single- or double-precision floating-point formats. The operation is not defined if bit 0 of any register specification is set and the *FR* bit in the *Status* register equals zero, since the register numbers specify an even-odd pair of adjacent coprocessor general registers. When the *FR* bit in the *Status* register equals one, both even and odd register numbers are valid.

When the source operand is an Infinity or NaN, or the correctly rounded integer result is outside of -2^{31} to $2^{31}-1$, the Invalid operation exception is raised. If the Invalid operation is not enabled then no exception is taken and $2^{31}-1$ is returned.

CEIL.W.fmt — Floating-Point Ceiling to Single Fixed-Point Format (continued) — CEIL.W.fmt

Operation:

```
T:    StoreFPR(fd, W, ConvertFmt(ValueFPR(fs, fmt), fmt, W))
```

Exceptions:

Coprocessor unusable exception
Floating-Point exception

Coprocessor Exceptions:

Invalid operation exception
Unimplemented operation exception
Inexact exception
Overflow exception

CFC1 Move Control Word From FPU (Coprocessor 1) CFC1

31–26	25–21	20–16	15–11	10–0
COP1 0 1 0 0 0 1	CF 0 0 0 1 0	rt	fs	0 0 0 0 0 0 0 0 0 0 0 0
6	5	5	5	11

Format:

CFC1 rt, fs

Description:

The contents of the FPU control register *fs* are loaded into general register *rt*.

This operation is only defined when *fs* equals 0 or 31.

The contents of general register *rt* are undefined for time *T* of the instruction immediately following this load instruction.

Operation:

32	T:	temp ← FCR[fs]
	T+1:	GPR[rt] ← temp
64	T:	temp ← FCR[fs]
	T+1:	GPR[rt] ← $(temp_{31})^{32}$ || temp

Exceptions:

Coprocessor unusable exception

CTC1 — Move Control Word To FPU (Coprocessor 1) — CTC1

31–26	25–21	20–16	15–11	10–0
COP1 010001	CT 00110	rt	fs	0 000 0000 0000
6	5	5	5	11

Format:

CTC1 rt, fs

Description:

The contents of general register *rt* are loaded into FPU control register *fs*. This operation is only defined when *fs* equals 0 or 31.

Writing to *Control Register 31*, the floating-point *Control/Status* register, causes an interrupt or exception if any cause bit and its corresponding enable bit are both set. The register will be written before the exception occurs. The contents of floating-point control register *fs* are undefined for time *T* of the instruction immediately following this load instruction.

Operation:

32	T:	temp ← GPR[rt]
	T+1:	FCR[fs] ← temp
		COC[1] ← $FCR[31]_{23}$
64	T:	temp ← $GPR[rt]_{31...0}$
	T+1:	FCR[fs] ← temp
		COC[1] ← $FCR[31]_{23}$

Exceptions:

Coprocessor unusable exception
Floating-Point exception

Coprocessor Exceptions:

Unimplemented operation exception
Invalid operation exception
Division by zero exception
Inexact exception
Overflow exception
Underflow exception

CVT.D.fmt — Floating-Point Convert to Double Floating-Point Format — CVT.D.fmt

31–26	25–21	20–16	15–11	10–6	5–0
COP1 010001	fmt	0 00000	fs	fd	CVT.D 100001
6	5	5	5	5	6

Format:

CVT.D.fmt fd, fs

Description:

The contents of the floating-point register specified by *fs* is interpreted in the specified source format, *fmt*, and arithmetically converted to the double binary floating-point format. The result is placed in the floating-point register specified by *fd*.

This instruction is valid only for conversions from single floating-point format, 32-bit or 64-bit fixed-point format.

If the single floating-point or single fixed-point format is specified, the operation is exact. The operation is not defined if bit 0 of any register specification is set and the *FR* bit in the *Status* register equals zero, since the register numbers specify an even-odd pair of adjacent coprocessor general registers. When the *FR* bit in the *Status* register equals one, both even and odd register numbers are valid.

Operation:

```
T:    StoreFPR (fd, D, ConvertFmt(ValueFPR(fs, fmt), fmt, D))
```

Exceptions:

Coprocessor unusable exception
Floating-Point exception

Coprocessor Exceptions:

Invalid operation exception
Unimplemented operation exception
Inexact exception
Overflow exception
Underflow exception

CVT.L.fmt — Floating-Point Convert to Long Fixed-Point Format — CVT.L.fmt

31–26	25–21	20–16	15–11	10–6	5–0
COP1 010001	fmt	0 00000	fs	fd	CVT.L 100101
6	5	5	5	5	6

Format:

CVT.L.fmt fd, fs

Description:

The contents of the floating-point register specified by *fs* are interpreted in the specified source format, *fmt*, and arithmetically converted to the long fixed-point format. The result is placed in the floating-point register specified by *fd*.

This instruction is valid only for conversions from single- or double-precision floating-point formats.

When the source operand is an Infinity, NaN, or the correctly rounded integer result is outside of -2^{63} to $2^{63}-1$, the Invalid operation exception is raised. If the Invalid operation is not enabled then no exception is taken and $2^{63}-1$ is returned.

Operation:

```
T:    StoreFPR (fd, L, ConvertFmt(ValueFPR(fs, fmt), fmt, L))
```

Exceptions:

Coprocessor unusable exception
Floating-Point exception

Coprocessor Exceptions:

Invalid operation exception
Unimplemented operation exception
Inexact exception
Overflow exception

CVT.S.fmt — Floating-Point Convert to Single Floating-Point Format — CVT.S.fmt

31–26	25–21	20–16	15–11	10–6	5–0
COP1 010001	fmt	0 00000	fs	fd	CVT.S 100000
6	5	5	5	5	6

Format:

CVT.S.fmt fd, fs

Description:

The contents of the floating-point register specified by *fs* are interpreted in the specified source format, *fmt*, and arithmetically converted to the single binary floating-point format. The result is placed in the floating-point register specified by *fd*. Rounding occurs according to the currently specified rounding mode.

This instruction is valid only for conversions from double floating-point format, or from 32-bit or 64-bit fixed-point format. The operation is not defined if bit 0 of any register specification is set and the *FR* bit in the *Status* register equals zero, since the register numbers specify an even-odd pair of adjacent coprocessor general registers. When the *FR* bit in the *Status* register equals one, both even and odd register numbers are valid.

Operation:

```
T:    StoreFPR(fd, S, ConvertFmt(ValueFPR(fs, fmt), fmt, S))
```

Exceptions:

Coprocessor unusable exception
Floating-Point exception

Coprocessor Exceptions:

Invalid operation exception
Unimplemented operation exception
Inexact exception
Overflow exception
Underflow exception

CVT.W.fmt Floating-Point Convert to Fixed-Point Format CVT.W.fmt

31 26	25 21	20 16	15 11	10 6	5 0
COP1 010001	fmt	0 00000	fs	fd	CVT.W 100100
6	5	5	5	5	6

Format:

CVT.W.fmt fd, fs

Description:

The contents of the floating-point register specified by *fs* are interpreted in the specified source format, *fmt*, and arithmetically converted to the single fixed-point format. The result is placed in the floating-point register specified by *fd*. This instruction is valid only for conversion from a single- or double-precision floating-point formats. The operation is not defined if bit 0 of any register specification is set and the *FR* bit in the *Status* register equals zero, since the register numbers specify an even-odd pair of adjacent coprocessor general registers. When the *FR* bit in the *Status* register equals one, both even and odd register numbers are valid.

When the source operand is an Infinity or NaN, or the correctly rounded integer result is outside of -2^{31} to $2^{31}-1$, an Invalid operation exception is raised. If Invalid operation is not enabled, then no exception is taken and $2^{31}-1$ is returned.

Operation:

```
T:    StoreFPR(fd, W, ConvertFmt(ValueFPR(fs, fmt), fmt, W))
```

Exceptions:

Coprocessor unusable exception
Floating-Point exception

Coprocessor Exceptions:

Invalid operation exception
Unimplemented operation exception
Inexact exception
Overflow exception

DIV.fmt Floating-Point Divide DIV.fmt

31 26	25 21	20 16	15 11	10 6	5 0
COP1 010001	fmt	ft	fs	fd	DIV 000011
6	5	5	5	5	6

Format:

DIV.fmt fd, fs, ft

Description:

The contents of the floating-point registers specified by *fs* and *ft* are interpreted in the specified *format* and arithmetically divided. The result is rounded as if calculated to infinite precision and then rounded to the specified format, according to the current rounding mode. The result is placed in the floating-point register specified by *fd*.

This instruction is valid for only single or double precision floating-point formats.

The operation is not defined if bit 0 of any register specification is set and the *FR* bit in the *Status* register equals zero, since the register numbers specify an even-odd pair of adjacent coprocessor general registers. When the *FR* bit in the *Status* register equals one, both even and odd register numbers are valid.

Operation:

```
T:      StoreFPR (fd, fmt, ValueFPR(fs, fmt)/ValueFPR(ft, fmt))
```

Exceptions:

Coprocessor unusable exception
Floating-Point exception

Coprocessor Exceptions:

Unimplemented operation exception
Division-by-zero exception
Overflow exception
Invalid operation exception
Inexact exception
Underflow exception

DMFC1 Doubleword Move From Floating-Point Coprocessor DMFC1

31 … 26	25 … 21	20 … 16	15 … 11	10 … 0
COP1 0 1 0 0 0 1	DMF 0 0 0 0 1	rt	fs	0 0 0 0 0 0 0 0 0 0 0 0
6	5	5	5	11

Format:

DMFC1 rt, fs

Description:

The contents of register *fs* from the floating-point coprocessor is stored into processor register *rt*.

The contents of general register *rt* are undefined for time *T* of the instruction immediately following this load instruction.

The *FR* bit in the *Status* register specifies whether all 32 registers of the R4000 are addressable. When *FR* equals zero, this instruction is not defined when the least significant bit of *fs* is non-zero. When *FR* is set, *fs* may specify either odd or even registers.

Operation:

```
64    T:      if SR26 = 1 then
                  data ← CPR[1,fs]
              else
                  data ← CPR[1,fs4...1 || 0]
              endif

      T+1:    GPR[rt] ← data
```

Exceptions:

Coprocessor unusable exception

DMTC1 Doubleword Move To Floating-Point Coprocessor DMTC1

31–26	25–21	20–16	15–11	10–0
COP1 010001	DMT 00101	rt	fs	0 000 0000 0000
6	5	5	5	11

Format:

DMTC1 rt, fs

Description:

The contents of general register *rt* are loaded into coprocessor register *fs* of the CP1.

The contents of floating-point register *fs* are undefined for time *T* of the instruction immediately following this load instruction.

The *FR* bit in the *Status* register specifies whether all 32 registers of the R4000 are addressable. When *FR* equals zero, this instruction is not defined when the least significant bit of *fs* is non-zero. When *FR* equals one, *fs* may specify either odd or even registers.

Operation:

```
64    T:      data ← GPR[rt]
      T+1:    if SR26 = 1 then
                  CPR[1, fs] ← data
              else
                  CPR[1, fs4...1 || 0] ← data
              endif
```

Exceptions:

Coprocessor unusable exception

FLOOR.L.fmt — Floating-Point Floor to Long Fixed-Point Format — FLOOR.L.fmt

31–26	25–21	20–16	15–11	10–6	5–0
COP1 010001	fmt	0 00000	fs	fd	FLOOR.L 001011
6	5	5	5	5	6

Format:

FLOOR.L.fmt fd, fs

Description:

The contents of the floating-point register specified by *fs* are interpreted in the specified source format, *fmt*, and arithmetically converted to the single fixed-point format. The result is placed in the floating-point register specified by *fd*.

Regardless of the setting of the current rounding mode, the conversion is rounded as if the current rounding mode is round to $-\infty$ (3).

This instruction is valid only for conversion from single- or double-precision floating-point formats.

When the source operand is an Infinity, NaN, or the correctly rounded integer result is outside of -2^{63} to $2^{63}-1$, the Invalid operation exception is raised. If the Invalid operation is not enabled then no exception is taken and $2^{63}-1$ is returned.

FLOOR.L.fmt Floating-Point Floor to Long Fixed-Point Format (continued) FLOOR.L.fmt

Operation:

```
T:    StoreFPR(fd, L, ConvertFmt(ValueFPR(fs, fmt), fmt, L))
```

Exceptions:

Coprocessor unusable exception
Floating-Point exception

Coprocessor Exceptions:

Invalid operation exception
Unimplemented operation exception
Inexact exception
Overflow exception

FLOOR.W.fmt Floating-Point Floor to Single Fixed-Point Format FLOOR.W.fmt

31–26	25–21	20–16	15–11	10–6	5–0
COP1 010001	fmt	0 00000	fs	fd	FLOOR.W 001111
6	5	5	5	5	6

Format:

FLOOR.W.fmt fd, fs

Description:

The contents of the floating-point register specified by *fs* are interpreted in the specified source format, *fmt*, and arithmetically converted to the single fixed-point format. The result is placed in the floating-point register specified by *fd*.

Regardless of the setting of the current rounding mode, the conversion is rounded as if the current rounding mode is round to $-\infty$ (RM = 3).

This instruction is valid only for conversion from a single- or double-precision floating-point formats. The operation is not defined if bit 0 of any register specification is set and the *FR* bit in the *Status* register equals zero, since the register numbers specify an even-odd pair of adjacent coprocessor general registers. When the *FR* bit in the *Status* register equals one, both even and odd register numbers are valid.

When the source operand is an Infinity or NaN, or the correctly rounded integer result is outside of -2^{31} to $2^{31}-1$, an Invalid operation exception is raised. If Invalid operation is not enabled, then no exception is taken and $2^{31}-1$ is returned.

FLOOR.W.fmt Floating-Point Floor to Single Fixed-Point Format (continued) FLOOR.W.fmt

Operation:

```
T:    StoreFPR(fd, W, ConvertFmt(ValueFPR(fs, fmt), fmt, W))
```

Exceptions:

Coprocessor unusable exception
Floating-Point exception

Coprocessor Exceptions:

Invalid operation exception
Unimplemented operation exception
Inexact exception
Overflow exception

LDC1 Load Doubleword to FPU (Coprocessor 1) LDC1

31 — 26	25 — 21	20 — 16	15 — 0
LDC1 1 1 0 1 0 1	base	ft	offset
6	5	5	16

Format:

LDC1 ft, offset(base)

Description:

The 16-bit *offset* is sign-extended and added to the contents of general register *base* to form an unsigned effective address.

In 32-bit mode, the contents of the doubleword at the memory location specified by the effective address is loaded into registers *ft* and *ft+1* of the floating-point coprocessor. This instruction is not valid, and is undefined, when the least significant bit of *ft* is non-zero.

In 64-bit mode, the contents of the doubleword at the memory location specified by the effective address are loaded into the 64-bit register *ft* of the floating point coprocessor.

The *FR* bit of the *Status* register (SR_{26}) specifies whether all 32 registers of the R4000 are addressable. If *FR* equals zero, this instruction is not defined when the least significant bit of *ft* is non-zero. If *FR* equals one, *ft* may specify either odd or even registers.

If any of the three least-significant bits of the effective address are non-zero, an address error exception takes place.

LDC1 — Load Doubleword to FPU (Coprocessor 1) (continued) — LDC1

Operation:

```
32   T:   vAddr ← ((offset15)^16 || offset15...0) + GPR[base]
          (pAddr, uncached) ← AddressTranslation (vAddr, DATA)
          if BigEndianCPU = 1 then
              CPR[1, ft+1] ← LoadMemory (uncached, WORD,
                  pAddr+0, vAddr+0, DATA)
              CPR[1, ft+0] ← LoadMemory (uncached, WORD,
                  pAddr+4, vAddr+4, DATA)
          else
              CPR[1, ft+0] ← LoadMemory (uncached, WORD,
                  pAddr+0, vAddr+0, DATA)
              CPR[1, ft+1] ← LoadMemory (uncached, WORD,
                  pAddr+4, vAddr+4, DATA)
          endif
64   T:   vAddr ← ((offset15)^48 || offset15...0) + GPR[base]
          (pAddr, uncached) ← AddressTranslation (vAddr, DATA)
          data ← LoadMemory(uncached, DOUBLEWORD, pAddr, vAddr, DATA)
          if SR26 = 1 then
              CPR[1, ft] ← data
          else
              CPR[1, ft4...1 || 0] ← data
          endif
```

Exceptions:

Coprocessor unusable
TLB refill exception
TLB invalid exception
Bus error exception
Address error exception

LWC1 Load Word to FPU (Coprocessor 1) LWC1

31 26	25 21	20 16	15 0
LWC1 1 1 0 0 0 1	base	ft	offset
6	5	5	16

Format:

LWC1 ft, offset(base)

Description:

The 16-bit *offset* is sign-extended and added to the contents of general register *base* to form an unsigned effective address. The contents of the word at the memory location specified by the effective address is loaded into register *ft* of the floating-point coprocessor.

The *FR* bit of the *Status* register specifies whether all 64-bit *Floating-Point* registers are addressable. If *FR* equals zero, LWC1 loads either the high or low half of the 16 even *Floating-Point* registers. If *FR* equals one, LWC1 loads the low 32-bits of both even and odd *Floating-Point* registers.

If either of the two least-significant bits of the effective address is non-zero, an address error exception occurs.

LWC1 Load Word to FPU (Coprocessor 1) (continued) LWC1

Operation:

```
32    T:    vAddr ← ((offset_15)^16 || offset_15...0) + GPR[base]
            (pAddr, uncached) ← AddressTranslation (vAddr, DATA)
            CPR[1, ft] ← LoadMemory (uncached, WORD,
                      pAddr, vAddr, DATA)

64    T:    vAddr ← ((offset_15)^48 || offset_15...0) + GPR[base]
            (pAddr, uncached) ← AddressTranslation (vAddr, DATA)
            pAddr ← pAddr_PSIZE-1...3 || (pAddr_2...0 xor (ReverseEndian || 0^2))
            mem ← LoadMemory(uncached, WORD, pAddr, vAddr, DATA)
            byte ← vAddr_2...0 xor (BigEndianCPU || 0^2)
            if SR_26 = 1 then
                CPR[1, ft] ← undefined^32 || mem_31+8*byte...8*byte
            else if ft_0=0 then
                CPR[1, ft_4...1 || 0] ← CPR[1, ft_4...1 || 0]_64...32 || mem_31+8*byte...8*byte
            else
                CPR[1, ft_4...1 || 0] ← mem_31+8*byte...8*byte || CPR[1, ft_4...1 || 0]_31...0
            endif
```

Exceptions:

Coprocessor unusable
TLB refill exception
TLB invalid exception
Bus error exception
Address error exception

MFC1 — Move From FPU (Coprocessor 1) — MFC1

31–26	25–21	20–16	15–11	10–0
COP1 0 1 0 0 0 1	MF 0 0 0 0 0	rt	fs	0 000 0000 0000
6	5	5	5	11

Format:

MFC1 rt, fs

Description:

The contents of register *fs* from the floating-point coprocessor are stored into processor register *rt*.

The contents of register *rt* are undefined for time *T* of the instruction immediately following this load instruction.

The *FR* bit of the *Status* register specifies whether all 32 registers of the R4000 are addressable. If *FR* equals zero, MFC1 stores either the high or low half of the 16 even *Floating-Point* registers. If *FR* equals one, MFC1 stores the low 32-bits of both even and odd *Floating-Point* registers.

Operation:

```
32    T:      data ← CPR[1, fs];
      T+1:    GPR[rt] ← data

64    T:      if fs_0 = 0 then
                  data ← CPR[1, fs_4...1 || 0]_31...0
              else
                  data ← CPR[1, fs_4...1 || 0]_63...32
              endif
      T+1:    GPR[rt] ← (data_31)^32 || data
```

Exceptions:

Coprocessor unusable exception

MOV.fmt Floating-Point Move MOV.fmt

31–26	25–21	20–16	15–11	10–6	5–0
COP1 010001	fmt	0 00000	fs	fd	MOV 000110
6	5	5	5	5	6

Format:

MOV.fmt fd, fs

Description:

The contents of the FPU register specified by *fs* are interpreted in the specified *format* and are copied into the FPU register specified by *fd*.

The move operation is non-arithmetic; no IEEE 754 exceptions occur as a result of the instruction.

This instruction is valid only for single- or double-precision floating-point formats.

The operation is not defined if bit 0 of any register specification is set and the *FR* bit in the *Status* register equals zero, since the register numbers specify an even-odd pair of adjacent coprocessor general registers. When the *FR* bit in the *Status* register equals one, both even and odd register numbers are valid.

Operation:

```
T:    StoreFPR(fd, fmt, ValueFPR(fs, fmt))
```

Exceptions:

Coprocessor unusable exception
Floating-Point exception

Coprocessor Exceptions:

Unimplemented operation exception

MTC1 — Move To FPU (Coprocessor 1) — MTC1

31 26	25 21	20 16	15 11	10 0
COP1 0 1 0 0 0 1	MT 0 0 1 0 0	rt	fs	0 000 0000 0000
6	5	5	5	11

Format:

MTC1 rt, fs

Description:

The contents of register *rt* are loaded into the FPU general register at location *fs*.

The contents of floating-point register *fs* is undefined for time *T* of the instruction immediately following this load instruction.

The *FR* bit of the *Status* register specifies whether all 32 registers of the R4000 are addressable. If *FR* equals zero, MTC1 loads either the high or low half of the 16 even *Floating-Point* registers. If *FR* equals one, MTC1 loads the low 32-bits of both even and odd *Floating-Point* registers.

Operation:

```
32   T:      data ← GPR[rt]
     T+1:    CPR[1, fs] ← data

64   T:      data ← GPR[rt]31...0
     T+1:    if SR26 = 1 then
                  CPR[1, fs] ← undefined^32 || data
             else if fs0=0 then
                  CPR[1, fs4...1 || 0] ← CPR[1, fs4...1 || 0]63...32 || data
             else
                  CPR[1, fs4...1 || 0] ← data || CPR[1, fs4...1 || 0]31...0
             endif
```

Exceptions:

Coprocessor unusable exception

MUL.fmt Floating-Point Multiply MUL.fmt

31–26	25–21	20–16	15–11	10–6	5–0
COP1 010001	fmt	ft	fs	fd	MUL 000010
6	5	5	5	5	6

Format:

MUL.fmt fd, fs, ft

Description:

The contents of the floating-point registers specified by *fs* and *ft* are interpreted in the specified *format* and arithmetically multiplied. The result is rounded as if calculated to infinite precision and then rounded to the specified *format*, according to the current rounding mode. The result is placed in the floating-point register specified by *fd*.

This instruction is valid only for single- or double-precision floating-point formats.

The operation is not defined if bit 0 of any register specification is set and the *FR* bit in the *Status* register equals zero, since the register numbers specify an even-odd pair of adjacent coprocessor general registers. When the *FR* bit in the *Status* register equals one, both even and odd register numbers are valid.

Operation:

```
T:      StoreFPR (fd, fmt, ValueFPR(fs, fmt) * ValueFPR(ft, fmt))
```

Exceptions:

Coprocessor unusable exception
Floating-Point exception

Coprocessor Exceptions:

Unimplemented operation exception
Invalid operation exception
Inexact exception
Overflow exception
Underflow exception

NEG.fmt Floating-Point Negate NEG.fmt

31–26	25–21	20–16	15–11	10–6	5–0
COP1 010001	fmt	0 00000	fs	fd	NEG 000111
6	5	5	5	5	6

Format:

NEG.fmt fd, fs

Description:

The contents of the FPU register specified by *fs* are interpreted in the specified *format* and the arithmetic negation is taken (polarity of the sign-bit is changed). The result is placed in the FPU register specified by *fd*.

The negate operation is arithmetic; an NaN operand signals invalid operation.

This instruction is valid only for single- or double-precision floating-point formats. The operation is not defined if bit 0 of any register specification is set and the *FR* bit in the *Status* register equals zero, since the register numbers specify an even-odd pair of adjacent coprocessor general registers. When the *FR* bit in the *Status* register equals one, both even and odd register numbers are valid.

Operation:

```
T:    StoreFPR(fd, fmt, Negate(ValueFPR(fs, fmt)))
```

Exceptions:

Coprocessor unusable exception
Floating-Point exception

Coprocessor Exceptions:

Unimplemented operation exception
Invalid operation exception

ROUND.L.fmt Floating-Point Round to Long Fixed-Point Format ROUND.L.fmt

31–26	25–21	20–16	15–11	10–6	5–0
COP1 010001	fmt	0 00000	fs	fd	ROUND.L 001000
6	5	5	5	5	6

Format:

ROUND.L.fmt fd, fs

Description:

The contents of the floating-point register specified by *fs* are interpreted in the specified source format, *fmt,* and arithmetically converted to the long fixed-point format. The result is placed in the floating-point register specified by *fd*.

Regardless of the setting of the current rounding mode, the conversion is rounded as if the current rounding mode is round to nearest/even (0).

This instruction is valid only for conversion from single- or double-precision floating-point formats.

When the source operand is an Infinity, NaN, or the correctly rounded integer result is outside of -2^{63} to $2^{63}-1$, the Invalid operation exception is raised. If the Invalid operation is not enabled then no exception is taken and $2^{63}-1$ is returned.

ROUND.L.fmt — Floating-Point Round to Long Fixed-Point Format (continued) — ROUND.L.fmt

Operation:

```
T:      StoreFPR(fd, L, ConvertFmt(ValueFPR(fs, fmt), fmt, L))
```

Exceptions:

Coprocessor unusable exception
Floating-Point exception

Coprocessor Exceptions:

Invalid operation exception
Unimplemented operation exception
Inexact exception
Overflow exception

ROUND.W.fmt Floating-Point Round to Single Fixed-Point Format ROUND.W.fmt

31–26	25–21	20–16	15–11	10–6	5–0
COP1 010001	fmt	0 00000	fs	fd	ROUND.W 001100
6	5	5	5	5	6

Format:

ROUND.W.fmt fd, fs

Description:

The contents of the floating-point register specified by *fs* are interpreted in the specified source format, *fmt*, and arithmetically converted to the single fixed-point format. The result is placed in the floating-point register specified by *fd*.

Regardless of the setting of the current rounding mode, the conversion is rounded as if the current rounding mode is round to the nearest/even (RM = 0).

This instruction is valid only for conversion from a single- or double-precision floating-point formats. The operation is not defined if bit 0 of any register specification is set and the *FR* bit in the *Status* register equals zero, since the register numbers specify an even-odd pair of adjacent coprocessor general registers. When the *FR* bit in the *Status* register equals one, both even and odd register numbers are valid.

When the source operand is an Infinity or NaN, or the correctly rounded integer result is outside of -2^{31} to $2^{31}-1$, an Invalid operation exception is raised. If Invalid operation is not enabled, then no exception is taken and $2^{31}-1$ is returned.

ROUND.W.fmt Floating-Point Round to Single Fixed-Point Format (continued) ROUND.W.fmt

Operation:

```
T:    StoreFPR(fd, W, ConvertFmt(ValueFPR(fs, fmt), fmt, W))
```

Exceptions:

Coprocessor unusable exception
Floating-Point exception

Coprocessor Exceptions:

Invalid operation exception
Unimplemented operation exception
Inexact exception
Overflow exception

SDC1 Store Doubleword from FPU (Coprocessor 1) SDC1

31–26	25–21	20–16	15–0
SDC1 111101	base	ft	offset
6	5	5	16

Format:

SDC1 ft, offset(base)

Description:

The 16-bit *offset* is sign-extended and added to the contents of general register *base* to form an unsigned effective address.

In 32-bit mode, the contents of registers *ft* and *ft+1* from the floating-point coprocessor are stored at the memory location specified by the effective address. This instruction is not valid, and is undefined, when the least significant bit of *ft* is non-zero.

In 64-bit mode, the 64-bit register *ft* is stored to the contents of the doubleword at the memory location specified by the effective address. The *FR* bit of the *Status* register (SR_{26}) specifies whether all 32 registers of the R4000 are addressable. When FR equals zero, this instruction is not defined if the least significant bit of *ft* is non-zero. If FR equals one, *ft* may specify either odd or even registers.

If any of the three least-significant bits of the effective address are non-zero, an address error exception takes place.

SDC1 Store Doubleword from FPU (Coprocessor 1) (continued) SDC1

Operation:

```
32   T:   vAddr ← (offset15)^16 || offset15...0) + GPR[base]
          (pAddr, uncached) ← AddressTranslation (vAddr, DATA)
          if BigEndianCPU = 1 then
              StoreMemory (uncached, WORD, CPR[1, ft+1],
                  pAddr+0, vAddr+0, DATA)
              StoreMemory (uncached, WORD, CPR[1, ft+0],
                  pAddr+4, vAddr+4, DATA)
          else
              StoreMemory (uncached, WORD, CPR[1, ft+0],
                  pAddr+0, vAddr+0, DATA)
              StoreMemory (uncached, WORD, CPR[1, ft+1],
                  pAddr+4, vAddr+4, DATA)
          endif
64   T:   vAddr ← (offset15)^16 || offset15...0) + GPR[base]
          (pAddr, uncached) ← AddressTranslation (vAddr, DATA)
          if SR26 = 1
              data ← CPR[1, ft]
          else
              data ← CPR[1, ft4...1 || 0)
          endif
          StoreMemory(uncached, DOUBLEWORD, data, pAddr, vAddr, DATA)
```

Exceptions:

Coprocessor unusable
TLB refill exception
TLB invalid exception
TLB modification exception
Bus error exception
Address error exception

SQRT.fmt — Floating-Point Square Root — SQRT.fmt

31–26	25–21	20–16	15–11	10–6	5–0
COP1 010001	fmt	0 00000	fs	fd	SQRT 000100
6	5	5	5	5	6

Format:

SQRT.fmt fd, fs

Description:

The contents of the floating-point register specified by *fs* are interpreted in the specified *format* and the positive arithmetic square root is taken. The result is rounded as if calculated to infinite precision and then rounded to the specified *format*, according to the current rounding mode. If the value of *fs* corresponds to –0, the result will be –0. The result is placed in the floating-point register specified by *fd*.

This instruction is valid only for single- or double-precision floating-point formats.

The operation is not defined if bit 0 of any register specification is set and the *FR* bit in the *Status* register equals zero, since the register numbers specify an even-odd pair of adjacent coprocessor general registers. When the *FR* bit in the *Status* register equals one, both even and odd register numbers are valid.

Operation:

```
T:    StoreFPR(fd, fmt, SquareRoot(ValueFPR(fs, fmt)))
```

Exceptions:

Coprocessor unusable exception
Floating-Point exception

Coprocessor Exceptions:

Unimplemented operation exception
Invalid operation exception
Inexact exception

SUB.fmt Floating-Point Subtract SUB.fmt

31 26	25 21	20 16	15 11	10 6	5 0
COP1 010001	fmt	ft	fs	fd	SUB 000001
6	5	5	5	5	6

Format:

SUB.fmt fd, fs, ft

Description:

The contents of the floating-point registers specified by *fs* and *ft* are interpreted in the specified *format* and arithmetically subtracted. The result is rounded as if calculated to infinite precision and then rounded to the specified *format*, according to the current rounding mode. The result is placed in the floating-point register specified by *fd*.

This instruction is valid only for single- or double-precision floating-point formats.

The operation is not defined if bit 0 of any register specification is set and the *FR* bit in the *Status* register equals zero, since the register numbers specify an even-odd pair of adjacent coprocessor general registers. When the *FR* bit in the *Status* register equals one, both even and odd register numbers are valid.

Operation:

```
T:   StoreFPR (fd, fmt, ValueFPR(fs, fmt) – ValueFPR(ft, fmt))
```

Exceptions:

Coprocessor unusable exception
Floating-Point exception

Coprocessor Exceptions:

Unimplemented operation exception
Invalid operation exception
Inexact exception
Overflow exception
Underflow exception

SWC1 Store Word from FPU (Coprocessor 1) SWC1

31 … 26	25 … 21	20 … 16	15 … 0
SWC1 111001	base	ft	offset
6	5	5	16

Format:

SWC1 ft, offset(base)

Description:

The 16-bit *offset* is sign-extended and added to the contents of general register *base* to form an unsigned effective address. The contents of register *ft* from the floating-point coprocessor are stored at the memory location specified by the effective address.

The *FR* bit of the *Status* register specifies whether all 64-bit floating-point registers are addressable.

If *FR* equals zero, SWC1 stores either the high or low half of the 16 even floating-point registers.

If *FR* equals one, SWC1 stores the low 32-bits of both even and odd floating-point registers.

If either of the two least-significant bits of the effective address are non-zero, an address error exception occurs.

SWC1 Store Word from FPU (Coprocessor 1) (continued) SWC1

Operation:

```
32   T:   vAddr ← ((offset15)^16 || offset15...0) + GPR[base]
          (pAddr, uncached) ← AddressTranslation (vAddr, DATA)
          data ← CPR[1, ft]
          StoreMemory (uncached, WORD, data, pAddr, vAddr, DATA)

64   T:   vAddr ← ((offset15)^48 || offset15...0) + GPR[base]
          (pAddr, uncached) ← AddressTranslation (vAddr, DATA)
          pAddr ← pAddrPSIZE-1...3 || (pAddr2...0 xor (ReverseEndian || 0^2))
          byte ← vAddr2...0 xor (BigEndianCPU || 0^2)
          if SR26 = 1 then
              data ← CPR[1, ft]63-8*byte...0 || 0^8*byte
          else if ft0=0 then
              data  ← CPR[1, ft4...1 || 0]63-8*byte...0 || 0^8*byte
          else
              data ← 0^32-8*byte || CPR[1, ft4...1 || 0] 63...32-8*byte
          endif
          StoreMemory (uncached, WORD, data, pAddr, vAddr, DATA)
```

Exceptions:

Coprocessor unusable
TLB refill exception
TLB invalid exception
TLB modification exception
Bus error exception
Address error exception

TRUNC.L.fmt Floating-Point Truncate to Long Fixed-Point Format TRUNC.L.fmt

31 — 26	25 — 21	20 — 16	15 — 11	10 — 6	5 — 0
COP1 010001	fmt	0 00000	fs	fd	TRUNC.L 001001
6	5	5	5	5	6

Format:

TRUNC.L.fmt fd, fs

Description:

The contents of the floating-point register specified by *fs* are interpreted in the specified source format, *fmt*, and arithmetically converted to the single fixed-point format. The result is placed in the floating-point register specified by *fd*.

Regardless of the setting of the current rounding mode, the conversion is rounded as if the current rounding mode is round toward zero (1).

This instruction is valid only for conversion from single- or double-precision floating-point formats.

When the source operand is an Infinity, NaN, or the correctly rounded integer result is outside of -2^{63} to $2^{63}-1$, the Invalid operation exception is raised. If the Invalid operation is not enabled then no exception is taken and $2^{63}-1$ is returned.

TRUNC.L.fmt Floating-Point Truncate to Long Fixed-Point Format (continued) TRUNC.L.fmt

Operation:

```
T:    StoreFPR(fd, L, ConvertFmt(ValueFPR(fs, fmt), fmt, L))
```

Exceptions:

Coprocessor unusable exception
Floating-Point exception

Coprocessor Exceptions:

Invalid operation exception
Unimplemented operation exception
Inexact exception
Overflow exception

TRUNC.W.fmt Floating-Point Truncate to Single Fixed-Point Format TRUNC.W.fmt

31–26	25–21	20–16	15–11	10–6	5–0
COP1 010001	fmt	0 00000	fs	fd	TRUNC.W 001101
6	5	5	5	5	6

Format:

TRUNC.W.fmt fd, fs

Description:

The contents of the FPU register specified by *fs* are interpreted in the specified source format *fmt* and arithmetically converted to the single fixed-point format. The result is placed in the FPU register specified by *fd*.

Regardless of the setting of the current rounding mode, the conversion is rounded as if the current rounding mode is round toward zero (RM = 1).

This instruction is valid only for conversion from a single- or double-precision floating-point formats. The operation is not defined if bit 0 of any register specification is set and the *FR* bit in the *Status* register equals zero, since the register numbers specify an even-odd pair of adjacent coprocessor general registers. When the *FR* bit in the *Status* register equals one, both even and odd register numbers are valid.

When the source operand is an Infinity or NaN, or the correctly rounded integer result is outside of -2^{31} to 2^{31-1}, an Invalid operation exception is raised. If Invalid operation is not enabled, then no exception is taken and -2^{31} is returned.

TRUNC.W.fmt Floating-Point Truncate to Single Fixed-Point Format (continued) TRUNC.W.fmt

Operation:

T:	StoreFPR(fd, W, ConvertFmt(ValueFPR(fs, fmt), fmt, W))

Exceptions:

Coprocessor unusable exception
Floating-Point exception

Coprocessor Exceptions:

Invalid operation exception
Unimplemented operation exception
Inexact exception
Overflow exception

B.5 FPU Instruction Opcode Bit Encoding

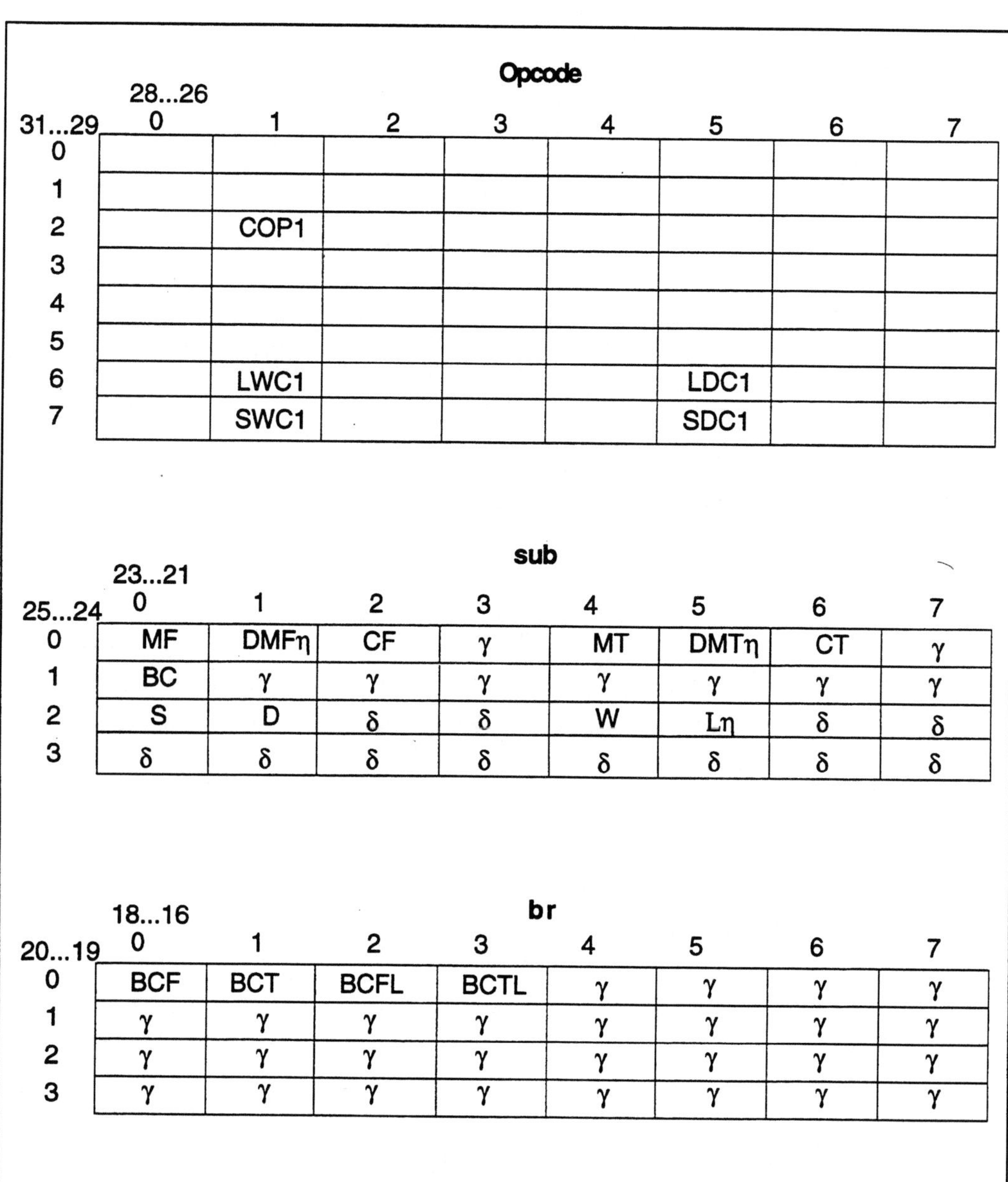

Opcode

31...29 \ 28...26	0	1	2	3	4	5	6	7
0								
1								
2		COP1						
3								
4								
5								
6		LWC1				LDC1		
7		SWC1				SDC1		

sub

25...24 \ 23...21	0	1	2	3	4	5	6	7
0	MF	DMFη	CF	γ	MT	DMTη	CT	γ
1	BC	γ	γ	γ	γ	γ	γ	γ
2	S	D	δ	δ	W	Lη	δ	δ
3	δ	δ	δ	δ	δ	δ	δ	δ

br

20...19 \ 18...16	0	1	2	3	4	5	6	7
0	BCF	BCT	BCFL	BCTL	γ	γ	γ	γ
1	γ	γ	γ	γ	γ	γ	γ	γ
2	γ	γ	γ	γ	γ	γ	γ	γ
3	γ	γ	γ	γ	γ	γ	γ	γ

Figure B-3 Bit Encoding for FPU Instructions

5...3 \ 2...0	0	1	2	3	4	5	6	7
0	ADD	SUB	MUL	DIV	SQRT	ABS	MOV	NEG
1	ROUND.Lη	TRUNC.Lη	CEIL.Lη	FLOOR.Lη	ROUND.W	TRUNC.W	CEIL.W	FLOOR.W
2	δ	δ	δ	δ	δ	δ	δ	δ
3	δ	δ	δ	δ	δ	δ	δ	δ
4	CVT.S	CVT.D	δ	δ	CVT.W	CVT.Lη	δ	δ
5	δ	δ	δ	δ	δ	δ	δ	δ
6	C.F	C.UN	C.EQ	C.UEQ	C.OLT	C.ULT	C.OLE	C.ULE
7	C.SF	C.NGLE	C.SEQ	C.NGL	C.LT	C.NGE	C.LE	C.NGT

(Column group heading: **function**)

Figure B-3 (cont.) Bit Encoding for FPU Instructions

Key:

γ Operation codes marked with a gamma cause a reserved instruction exception. They are reserved for future versions of the architecture.

δ Operation codes marked with a delta cause unimplemented operation exceptions in all current implementations and are reserved for future versions of the architecture.

η Valid for 64-bit mode only.

Subblock Ordering

C

A block of data elements (whether bytes, halfwords, words, or doublewords) can be retrieved from storage in two ways: in sequential order, or using a subblock order. This chapter describes these retrieval methods, with an emphasis on subblock ordering.

C.1 Sequential Ordering

Sequential ordering retrieves the data elements of a block in serial, or sequential, order.

Figure C-1 shows a sequential order in which byte 0 is taken first and byte 7 is taken last.

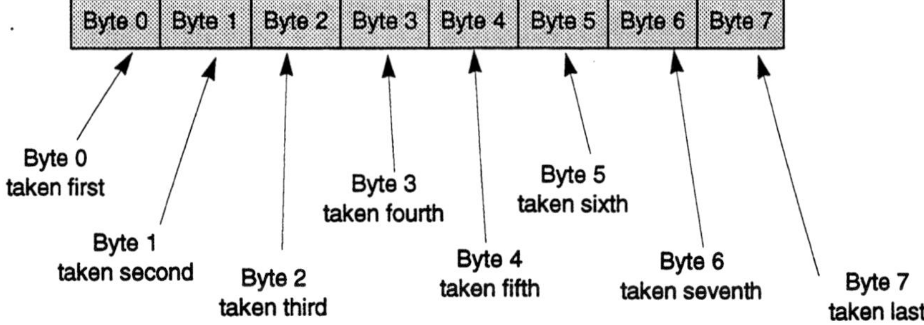

Figure C-1 Retrieving a Data Block in Sequential Order

C.2 Subblock Ordering

Subblock ordering allows the system to define the order in which the data elements are retrieved. The smallest data element of a block transfer for the R400 is a doubleword, and Figure C-2 shows the retrieval of a block of data that consists of 8 doublewords, in which DW2 is taken first.

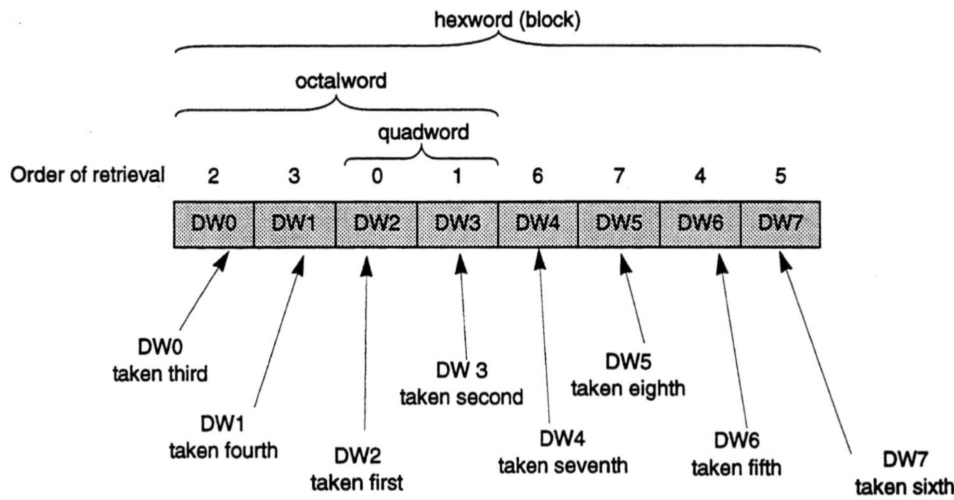

Figure C-2 Retrieving Data in a Subblock Order

Using the subblock ordering shown in Figure C-2, the doubleword at the target address is retrieved first (DW2), followed by the remaining doubleword (DW3) in this quadword.

Next, the quadword that fills out the octalword are retrieved in the same order as the prior quadword (in this case DW0 is followed by DW 1). This is followed by the remaining octalword (DW8, DW7, DW4, DW5), that fills out the hexword.

It may be easier way to understand subblock ordering by taking a look at the method used for generating the address of each doubleword as it is retrieved. The subblock ordering logic generates this address by executing a bit-wise exclusive-OR (XOR) of the starting block address with the output of a binary counter that increments with each doubleword, starting at doubleword zero (000_2).

Using this scheme, Tables C-1 through Table C-3 list the subblock ordering of doublewords for a 32-word block, based on three different starting-block addresses: 0010_2, 1011_2, and 0101_2. The subblock ordering is generated by an XOR of the subblock address (either 0010_2, 1011_2, and 0101_2) with the binary count of the doubleword (0000_2 through 1111_2). Thus, the eighth doubleword retrieved from a block of data with a starting address of 0010_2 is found by taking the XOR of address 0010_2 with the binary count of DW8, 0111_2. The result is 0101_2, or DW5 (shown in Table C-1).

The remaining tables illustrate this method of subblock ordering, using various address permutations.

Table C-1 Sequence of Doublewords Transferred Using Subblock Ordering: Address 0010_2

Cycle	Starting Block Address	Binary Count	Double Word Retrieved
1	0010	0000	0010
2	0010	0001	0011
3	0010	0010	0000
4	0010	0011	0001
5	0010	0100	0110
6	0010	0101	0111
7	0010	0110	0100
8	0010	0111	0101
9	0010	1000	1010
10	0010	1001	1011
11	0010	1010	1000
12	0010	1011	1001
13	0010	1100	1110
14	0010	1101	1111
15	0010	1110	1100
16	0010	1111	1101

Table C-2 Sequence of Doublewords Transferred Using Subblock Ordering: Address 1011_2

Cycle	Starting Block Address	Binary Count	Double Word Retrieved
1	1011	0000	1011
2	1011	0001	1010
3	1011	0010	1001
4	1011	0011	1000
5	1011	0100	1111
6	1011	0101	1110
7	1011	0110	1101
8	1011	0111	1100
9	1011	1000	0011
10	1011	1001	0010
11	1011	1010	0001
12	1011	1011	0000
13	1011	1100	0111
14	1011	1101	0110
15	1011	1110	0101
16	1011	1111	0100

Table C-3 Sequence of Doublewords Transferred Using Subblock Ordering: Address 0101_2

Cycle	Starting Block Address	Binary Count	Double Word Retrieved
1	0101	0000	0101
2	0101	0001	0100
3	0101	0010	0111
4	0101	0011	0110
5	0101	0100	0001
6	0101	0101	0000
7	0101	0110	0011
8	0101	0111	0010
9	0101	1000	1101
10	0101	1001	1100
11	0101	1010	1111
12	0101	1011	1110
13	0101	1100	1001
14	0101	1101	1000
15	0101	1110	1011
16	0101	1111	1010

Output Buffer $\Delta i/\Delta t$ Control Mechanism

D

The speed of the R4000 output drivers is controlled by a negative feedback loop that insures the drive-off times are only as fast as necessary to meet the system requirement for single cycle transfers. This guarantees the minimum ground bounce from $L^*(\Delta i/\Delta t)$ of the switching buffers, consistent with the system timing requirements.

D.1 Mode Bits

Four bits are used to control the pull-up and pull-down delays. These bits are initially set to the values in the mode bits **InitN<3:0>** for pull-up and **InitP<3:0>** for pull-down.

Under normal conditions, the Δi/Δt control mechanism is enabled to compensate the output buffer delay for any changes in the temperature or power supply voltage. The **EnblDPLL** mode bit is set for this mode of operation.

For situations where the jitter associated with the operation of the Δi/Δt control mechanism cannot be tolerated and where the variation in temperature and supply voltage after **ColdReset*** is expected to be small, the Δi/Δt control mechanism can be instructed to lock during **ColdReset*** and thereafter retain its control values. The **EnblDPLLR** mode bit is set and **EnblDPLL** is cleared for this mode of operation.

In addition, if both the **EnblDPLL** and **EnblDPLLR** mode bits are cleared, the speed of the output buffers are set by the **InitP<3:0>** and **InitN<3:0>** mode bits.

D.2 Delay Times

Currently, delays of 0.5T, 0.75T, and T are supported, corresponding to the **Drv0_50, Drv0_75,** and **Drv1_00** mode bits, where T is the **MasterClock** period. For example, in **Drv0_75** mode, the entire signal transmission path including the clock-to-Q, output buffer drive time, board flight time, input buffer delay, and setup time will be traversed in 0.75 * the **MasterClock** period, plus or minus the jitter due to the Δi/Δt control mechanism.

All output drivers on the R4000, with the exception of the clock drivers, are controlled by the Δi/Δt control mechanism. The delay due to the output buffer drive time component of the **SCAddr<17:0>, SCOEB, SCWRB, SCDCSB,** and **SCTCSB** pins is approximately 66% of the delay of drivers of the other pins.

By measuring the transmission line delay of the trace that connects the R4000 **IO_Out** and **IO_In** pins, the R4000 determines the worst case propagation delay from an R4000 output driver to a receiving device. This representative trace must have one and a half times the length and approximately the same capacitive loading as the worst case trace on any R4000 output.

The designer determines the trace characteristics by:

- measuring the longest path from an R4000 output driver to a receiving device, *L*
- calculating the maximum capacitive loading on any signal pin, *C*
- connecting an incident-wave trace of length *L* with a capacitive loading of *C* between the **IO_In** and **IO_Out** pins of the R4000
- connecting a reflected wave trace of length *L*/2 to the **IO_In** pin of the R4000.

An R4000 with appropriate traces connected to the **IO_In** and **IO_Out** pins is illustrated in Figure D-1.

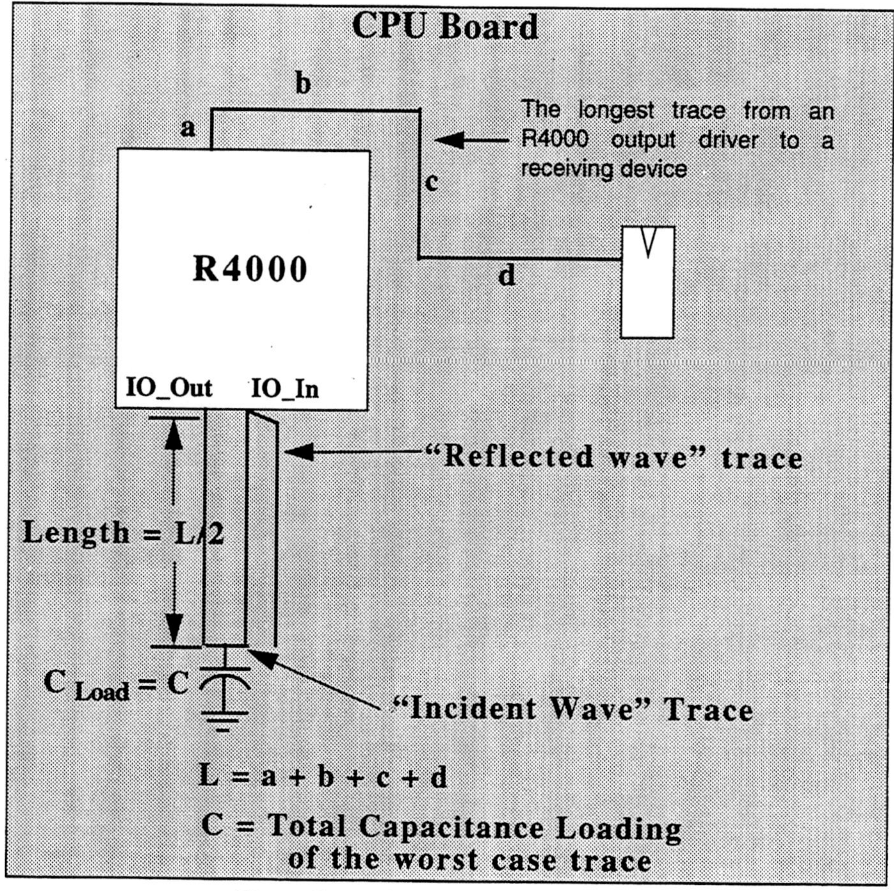

Figure D-1 O_In/IO_Out Board Trace

PLL Passive Components

E

The Phase Locked Loop circuit requires several passive components for proper operation, which are connected to **PLLCap0**, **PLLCap1**, **VccP**, and **VssP**, as illustrated in Figure E-1.

In addition, the capacitors for **PLLCap0** **(Cp)** and **PLLCap1** **(Cp)** can be connected to either **VssP** (as shown), **VccP**, or one to **VssP** and one to **VccP**. Note that **C2** and the **Cp** capacitors are incorporated into both the 179PGA and 447PGA package designs as surface-mounted chip capacitors.

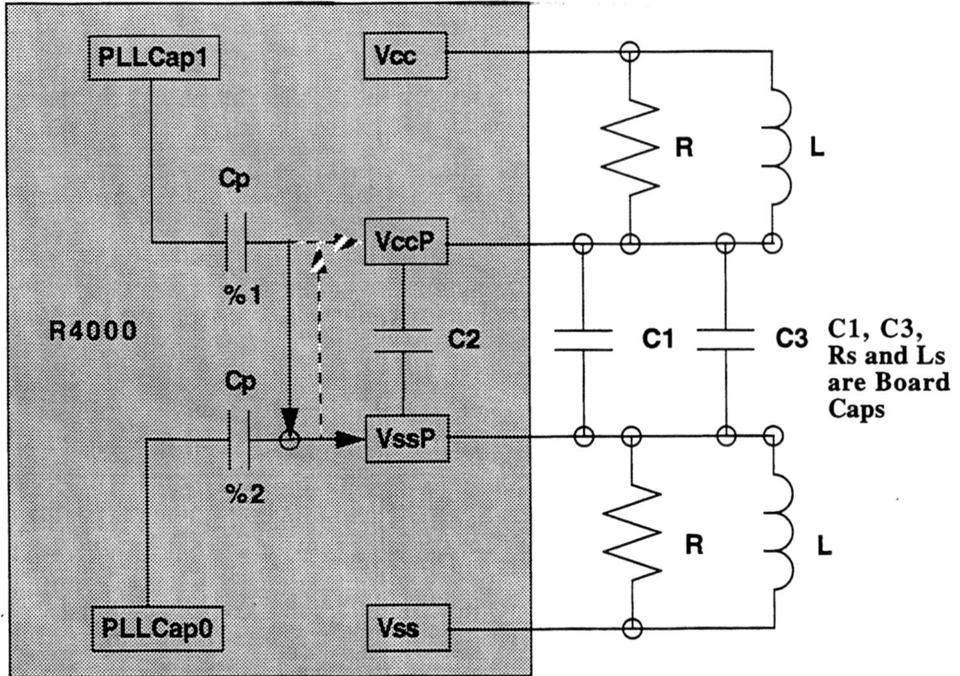

Figure E-1 PLL Passive Components

Figure E-2 shows a top view of the 179-pin package with capacitors.

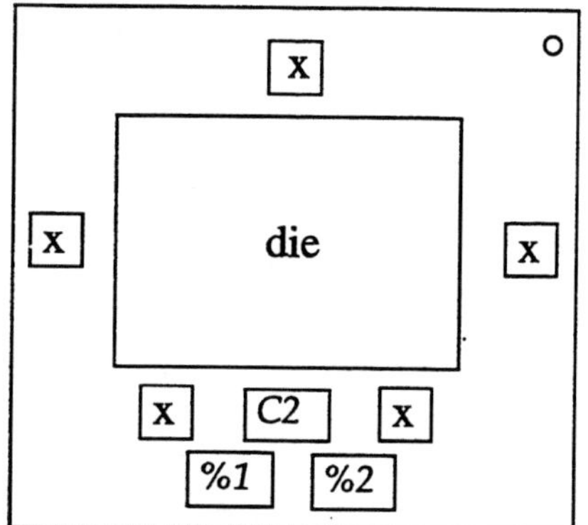

x: Vss-Vcc Bypass Caps
C2: VssP-VccP Bypass Caps
%1, %2: PLL Caps

Figure E-2 179-Pin Package

Figure E-3 shows a top view of the 447-pin package with chip capacitors.

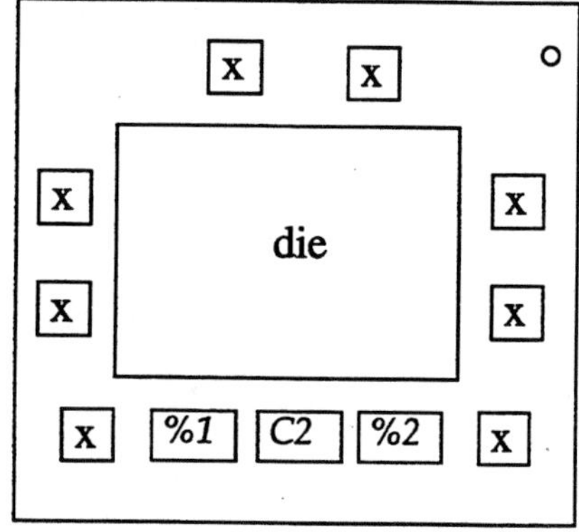

x: Vss-Vcc Bypass Caps
C2: VssP-VccP Bypass Caps
%1, %2: PLL Caps

Figure E-3 447-Pin Package

It is essential to isolate the analog power and ground for the PLL circuit (**VccP/VssP**) from the regular power and ground (**Vcc/Vss**). Initial evaluations have yielded good results with the following values:

```
R  = 5 ohms        C1 = 1 nF    C2 = 82 nF

C3 = 10 µF         Cp = 470 pF
```

Since the optimum values for the filter components depend upon the application and the system noise environment, these values should be considered as starting points for further experimentation within your specific application. In addition, the chokes (inductors: *L*) can be considered for use as an alternative to the resistors (*R*) for use in filtering the power supply.

R4000 Coprocessor 0 Hazards

F

Table F-1 lists the R4000 Coprocessor 0 hazards.

In this table, the number of instructions required between instruction A (which places a value in a CP0 register) and instruction B (which uses the same register as a source) is computed by the following formula:

```
(Destination stage of A) - [(Source stage of B) -1]
```

Table F-1 R4000 Coprocessor 0 Hazards

Operation	Source		Destination	
	Name	Stage	Name	Stage
MTC0	gpr rt	3	cpr rd	7
MFC0	cpr rd	4	gpr rt	7
TLBR	Index, TLB	5-7	PageMask, EntryHi, EntryLo0, EntryLo1	8
TLBWI TLBWR	Index or Random PageMask, EntryHi, EntryLo0, EntryLo1	5-8	TLB	8
TLBP	PageMask, EntryHi	3-6	Index	7
ERET	EPC or ErrorEPC, Status, TLB	4γ	Status.EXL, Status.ERL	4-8α
			LLbit	7
CACHE Index Load Tag			TagLo, TagHi, ECC	8β
CACHE Index Store Tag	TagLo, TagHi, ECC	7		
CACHE Hit ops			Status.CH	8
Instruction fetch	EntryHi.ASID Status.KSU, Status.EXL, Status.ERL, Status.RE, Config.K0C, Config.IB	0		
	Config.SB	3		
	TLB	2		
Instruction fetch exception			EPC, Status	8
			Cause, BadVAddr, Context	3
Coprocessor usable test	Status.CU, Status.KSU Status.EXL, Status.ERL	2		
Interrupt	Cause.IP, Status.IM Status.IE, Status.EXL Status.ERL	3		
Load/Store	EntryHi.ASID Status.KSU, Status.EXL, Status.ERL, Status.RE, Config.K0C, Config.DB TLB	4		
	Config.SB	7		
	WatchHi, WatchLo	4-5		

Table F-1 (cont.) R4000 Coprocessor 0 Hazards

Operation	Source		Destination	
	Name	Stage	Name	Stage
Load/Store exception			EPC, Status, Cause	8
			BadVAddr, Context	
TLB shutdown			Status.TS	7

The following notes apply to the table.

α Status.EXL and Status.ERL are permanently cleared in stage 8, but the effect of clearing them is visible to an instruction fetch starting in stage 4.

β Only one instruction needs to separate Index Load Tag and MFC0 Tag, even though α above would imply three instructions.

- The instruction following a MTC0 must not be a MFC0.
- The five instructions following a MTC0 to Status that changes KSU and sets EXL or ERL may be executed in the new mode, and not kernel mode. This can be avoided by setting EXL first, leaving KSU set to kernel, and later changing KSU.
- There must be two non-load, non-CACHE instructions between a store and a CACHE instruction directed to the same primary cache line as the store.

γ An ERET following an MTC0 instruction that sets the ERL bit in the *Status* register (Status.ERL) must be separated from the MTC0 by three instructions.

Index

D

E

F

J

K

L

M

N

O

P

R

V

W

X

Y